ENCYCLOPEDIA OF WORLD WRITERS
14TH THROUGH 18TH CENTURIES

Dr. Thierry Boucquey

GENERAL EDITOR
Department of French
Scripps College
Claremont University Consortium

Dr. Gary Johnson

ADVISER
Department of English
University of Findlay

Dr. Nina Chordas

ADVISER
Academic Programs
University of Alaska Southwest

☑®

Facts On File, Inc.

Encyclopedia of World Writers, 14th through 18th Centuries

Written and developed by BOOK BUILDERS LLC
Copyright © 2005 by BOOK BUILDERS LLC

Facts On File, Inc.
132 West 31st Street
New York NY 10001

Library of Congress Cataloging-in-Publication Data

Encyclopedia of world writers, beginnings to the twentieth century / Thierry Boucquey, general editor ; Gary Johnson, advisor ; Nina Chordas advisor ; [written and developed by Book Builders LLC].
    p. cm.
    General editor for v. 3: Marie Josephine Diamond; advisors, Maria DiBattista and Julian Wolfreys.
    Vol. 3 previously published as: Encyclopedia of 19th- and 20th-century world writers / Marie Josephine Diamond, general editor.
    Includes bibliographical references and index.
    ISBN 0-8160-6143-2 (set : alk. paper) — ISBN 0-8160-5190-9 (v. 1 : alk. paper) — ISBN 0-8160-5191-7 (v. 2 : alk. paper) — ISBN 0-8160-4675-1 (v. 3 : alk. paper) 1. Authors—Biography—Dictionaries. 2. Literature—Bio-bibliography—Dictionaries. I. Boucquey, Thierry. II. Diamond, Marie Josephine. III. Book Builders LLC. IV. Encyclopedia of 19th- and 20th-century world writers.
    PN451.E55 2005
    809'.003--dc22
                                  2004020551

Text design by Rachel L. Berlin
Cover illustration by Smart Graphics

Printed in the United States of America

VB FOF 10 9 8 7 6 5 4 3 2 1

This book is printed on acid-free paper.

CONTENTS

Preface   iv

Introduction   v

Timeline of Authors and Works   viii

Writers, Genres, and Works
    Covered, by Geographical Area   xiii

Entries A to Z   1

Selected Bibliography   315

Index   351

PREFACE

Increasingly, both in the United States and abroad, secondary and university curricula are becoming more comprehensive. As a result, students of literature and culture are surveying the vast contributions of authors from around the world.

Encyclopedia of World Writers, 14th through 18th Centuries presents the most important writers and anonymous works, predominantly outside of the English-language realm and covering the half-millennium between 1300 and 1800. Entries include discussions of poetry, fiction, religious writings, drama, epic, history, oral tradition, political science, maxims, biography, philosophy, nonfiction, and literary terminology. For authors, entries include a brief biography as well as a description or analysis of one or more of their works. Each entry is followed by the suggestion of a translation in English of the original work, whenever available, and recent scholarship on the subject.

We wish the readers a pleasant and exciting voyage into the realm of the world's masters and their literature. It is our hope that this volume will stimulate readers to further explore the work of these writers for the essence and exquisiteness that can only be suggested in this book.

Lastly, I wish to thank my daughters, Noëlle and Veronique, and my dear friends Jin and Joanne for all their love and support.

Thierry Boucquey
General Editor

INTRODUCTION

Encyclopedia of World Writers, 14th through 18th Centuries offers a comprehensive yet accessible overview of literature from around the world, covering the period from the beginning of the 14th century to about the year 1800. The survey spans the globe and, to guarantee the broadest possible coverage for entry selection purposes, represents 11 geographic domains: Africa, the Americas, Britain-Ireland, East Asia, Francophone Europe, Germany-Netherlands-Scandinavia, the Middle East, the Iberian Peninsula, Italy, Oceania-Pacific, and Russia-Eastern Europe.

For practical purposes, authors whose works span two periods (*i.e.,* late 1200s to early 1300s, or late 1700s to early 1800s) were placed in this volume because they are considered to be representative of the time periods covered. Early American authors have been included here because they belong to the literature of the "Americas," which also includes pre-Columbian and Latin American literature.

This volume contains nearly 300 entries that naturally include some giants of the global literary canon, such as Molière, Shakespeare, Cervantes, Wu Cheng-en, and Zeami. Additionally, a particular effort has been made to include a fair number of entries representing language and literature domains that traditionally are less studied in Western institutions. The volume also includes a significant number of lesser-known but nonetheless notable authors and works—from all domains—that have influenced global literary traditions and generated renewed scholarly research.

Also incorporated into this volume are definitions of important literary movements, genres, and phenomena such as neoclassicism, farce, and Kabuki, as well as literary terminology such as haiku, sonnet, and typology.

Aimed at both high school and college-level students, this encyclopedia endeavors to encourage and motivate the aspiring scholar to explore the literary wealth of world writers and their masterpieces. Tools at the students' disposal include biographical information, analyses of major works, appropriate cross-references, and the inclusion of titles of translated editions as well as suitable critical texts.

World literature is as varied as it is extensive. During the half-millennium spanning the years 1300 to 1800, many authors, movements, schools, and literatures have shaped national and supranational literary landscapes on all continents. A succinct overview of some of these developments is presented here to help orient the reader.

AFRICA

In addition to the eventual recording of Africa's rich and ancient oral tradition, Olaudah Equiano's gripping autobiographical slave narrative, as well as several Arabic poets such as Muyaka and Sayyid Abdallah (Ali bin Nasir), highlight the continent's literary contribution before 1800.

THE AMERICAS

The literature of the Americas as defined here falls into three categories: pre-Columbian writing, Latin American colonial texts, and early North American literature. The first includes the famous *Popol Vuh*, an epic that records the history of the ancient Quiche Maya from the creation to the 16th century. It miraculously survived and was copied from a Mayan hieroglyphic manuscript hidden from the iconoclast colonizers' view. Latin American colonial writing consists not only of eyewitness accounts of discovery and adventure by colonists such as Columbus or clergy such as De Motolinia but also of anticonqueror sentiment such as that of Gama or Cacamatzín. The literature of America comprises early accounts of the struggles and challenges of colony life, a series of powerful theological writings, and the prose writers of the 18th century. Among these, Benjamin Franklin's pragmatic yet philosophical prose, Thomas Jefferson's political writings, and Thomas Paine's political pamphlets occupy a prominent place.

BRITAIN AND IRELAND

As American readers are presumably more familiar with this literature, it will suffice to say here that only the most prominent or influential authors and works have been retained in this volume for the sake of reference and completeness.

EAST ASIA

Whereas in China the best poetry is to be found in the drama during this period (with notable exceptions such as Cao Xuequin or Wu Chengen's novels), Japan witnessed the beginning of new types of dramatic literature, such as Noh, Kabuki, and Bunraku. Authors such as Zeami inspired these genres, while Bashō was the leading force for bringing haiku to new heights. The highlight in Korean writing was King Se-jong's creation in 1438 of a new alphabet, considered by linguists to be the most efficient phonetic transcription to date, save the modern International Phonetic Alphabet.

FRANCOPHONE EUROPE

The late Middle Ages in France produced the outstanding lyric poet Villon, as well as growth of the drama, which includes cycle (mystery and morality) plays and the genre known as popular farce. The founders of the Pléiade movement, Ronsard and du Bellay, personify the spirit of the Renaissance that slowly permeates French culture after 1500, while the vigorous and ingenious work of contemporaries Rabelais and Montaigne laid the foundations of the classical age. Descartes's rationalism imbues the 17th century or *grand siècle,* which becomes the golden age of theater. In Racine's tragedies French verse reaches its height, while Molière's brilliant, satirical, social commentary sets the standard for much of subsequent comedy through the ages. The large volumes of the *Encyclopédie* dominate the Enlightenment or age of the philosophers, among whom Diderot, Rousseau, and especially Voltaire occupy prominent positions.

GERMANY-NETHERLANDS-SCANDINAVIA

Erasmus of Rotterdam personifies the pan-European humanist ideal but has no clear answer to the ideas of the Reformation. Emanating from Germany in the 16th century is Luther, whose translation of the Bible is probably the era's greatest literary achievement. One century apart, two influential philosophers, Leibniz and Kant, set the stage for the age of Aufklärung or Enlightenment and herald the coming of Germany's classical literary giants Schiller and Goethe. In the Netherlands, the mystic religious writing of Ruusbroec is especially noteworthy.

THE IBERIAN PENINSULA

The fame and scope of Cervantes's *Don Quixote* with its wonderful interpretation of the peasant mentality and satire of chivalry needs little comment. Creating some 2,000 plays, Lope de Vega founds the national Spanish drama, while Tirso de Molina invents the figure of Don Juan. In Portugal, de Camões achieves with *Os Lusiadas* the supreme Renaissance epic.

ITALY

The poet Petrarch is the first one to reconcile the Latin tradition and the new writing in the vernacular with an original style earmarked by refinement and simplicity. His friend and fellow humanist Boccaccio vividly portrays the rich drama of everyday human life in compelling comic tales that continue the medieval storytelling tradition. Machiavelli's famous *Prince* puts forward the idea that in politics one's goal justifies any means. Among nonprofessional writers, the elegant, crystal-clear prose of Galileo, the original poems and vivid letters of Michelangelo, and Leonardo da Vinci's incredible scientific speculations penned in priceless notebooks, stand out.

MIDDLE EAST

Muhammad Háfiz, who expresses a penetrating vision of life in a subtle satirical vein, is probably the finest lyrical poet Persia has ever produced, while in the 14th Century the historian and philosopher Ibn Khaldūn develops a methodology and ontology of history that rivals modern historiography.

OCEANIA AND PACIFIC

Australia, New Zealand, and the island nations of the South Pacific produced only sparse literature before the 19th century, although a few authors such as Banks or Wentworth merit mention.

RUSSIA AND EASTERN EUROPE

In Russia, Cantemir and Lomonosov are the first to write exclusively in "spoken" Russian. The poetry of Derzhavin paves the way to the golden age of Russian literature. In 1542, Polish astronomer Copernicus establishes the heliocentric theory of the universe.

In conclusion, this volume is a work of reference. As such, it provides a wealth of organized information on authors, works, and literary terms and periods, and responds to the demand for quick and readily accessible information. It is our sincere hope that this volume, in presenting the lives and work of some 300 creative individuals who have contributed to the rich patrimony of humankind's accomplishments, will persuade readers to undertake a journey of their own. We encourage them to discover the inexhaustible treasure of the world's literary legacy and to find solace in the beauty, recreation, and inspiration of a story told.

Thierry Boucquey
Huntington Beach, California

TIMELINE OF AUTHORS AND WORKS

Dates	Author	Dates	Author
n.d.–1558	Quetzalcoatl, myth of	ca. 1325–1408	Gower, John
n.d.–1700s	*Chilam Balam, The Books of*	1326–1390	Hāfiz
		1330–1386?	Langland, William
n.d.–1782	*Book of Chilam Balam of Chumayel, The*	ca. 1330–1400	Luo Guanzhong (Luo Kuan-chung)
n.d.–present	Mesoamerican mythology	1332–1406	Ibn Khaldūn
n.d.–present	*Komam Q'Anil, Epic of*	1337–1392	Jung Mong Joo
n.d.–present	Maya epics and fables	1337?–1404?	Froissart, Jean
n.d.–present	epics	ca. 1342–1400	Chaucer, Geoffrey
200s B.C.–A.D. 1800s	pastoral	1342–ca. 1416	Julian of Norwich
700s	*Rabinal Achi*	1363–1443	Zeami
800s?–1400s?	*Book of Dede Korkut, The*	ca. 1364–ca. 1431	Pisan, Christine de
1293–1381	Ruusbroec, Jan van	1370–1415	Hus, Jan
1300s?	*Cloud of Unknowing, The*	ca. 1370–1450	Lydgate, John
1300s	*Pearl* poet	1373–1438	Kempe, Margery
1300s	fabliaux	1380–1442	Nguyen Trai
late 1300s	*Sir Gawain and the Green Knight*	1380–1471	Kempis, Thomas á
		1394–1465	Orléans, Charles d'
late 1300s	*De-Ka-Nah-Wi-Da* and *Hiawatha*	ca.1397–1450	Se-jong
		ca.1397–1459	March, Ausiàs
1300s–1500s	Renaissance	1400s	Scottish poets of the 15th century
1300s–1600	humanism		
1300s–present	Kyogen	fl.? 1400s	Shi Naian (Shih Nai-an)
1300s–present	Noh	1400s–1600s	cycle, miracle, mystery, and morality plays
1304–1374	Petrarch		
1313–1375	Boccaccio, Giovanni	1400s–1800s	Ashanti tales
1313–1375	Ibn al-Khatīb	1400s–present	farce
1324–1387	Wycliffe, John	early 1400s–1472	Nikitin, Afanasij

Dates	Author
ca. 1402–ca. 1473	Nezahualcoyotl
1404–1472	Alberti, Leon Battista
1410?–1471	Malory, Thomas
1424?–1506?	Henryson, Robert
1431–after 1463	Villon, François
1432–1484	Pulci, Luigi
ca. 1435–unknown	Moquihuitzín
1435–1493	Kim Shi-sup
1449?–1481	Axayacatl of Tenochtitlán
1449–1492	Medici, Lorenzo de'
1450–1524	Marulić, Marko
1450–1600	classicism
1451–1506	Columbus, Christopher
ca. 1451–1512	Vespucci, Amerigo
1452–1519	Leonardo da Vinci
1454–1494	Poliziano, Angelo Ambrogini
1457?–1521	Brandt, Sebastian
ca. 1460–1529	Skelton, John
1463–1494	Pico della Mirandola, Count Giovanni
1464–1515	Nezahualpilli
1469–1527	Machiavelli, Niccolò
ca. 1469–1536	Erasmus, Desiderius
1470–ca. 1521	Waldseemüller, Martin
1470–1547	Bembo, Pietro
1473–1543	Copernicus, Nicolaus
1474–1533	Ariosto, Ludovico
1474–1566	Las Casas, Bartolomé de
1475–1564	Michelangelo Buonarroti
1478–1529	Castiglione, Baldessare
1478–1535	More, Sir Thomas
1483–1540	Guicciardini, Francesco
1483–1546	Luther, Martin
1485–1547	Cortés, Hernán
1490?–1559?	Cabeza de Vaca, Álvar Núñez
1491–1556	Ignatius of Loyola
1492–1549	Marguerite de Navarre
1492–1556	Aretino, Pietro
1494–1520	Cacamatzín of Texcoco
ca. 1494–1553	Rabelais, François
1494–1576	Sachs, Hans

Dates	Author
ca. 1495–ca. 1569	Motolinía, Toribio de
ca. 1495–1579	Jiménez de Quesada, Gonzalo
ca. 1496–1544	Marot, Clément
1496–1584	Díaz del Castillo, Bernal
1497–1540	Melanchthon, Philip
1500s	La Llorona
1500s	Popul Vuh
ca. 1500	Everyman
ca. 1500	Marieke van Nimwegen
late 1500s	Jin Ping Mei
ca. 1500–ca. 1582	Wu Chengen (Wu Ch'eng-en)
1503–1556	Della Casa, Giovanni
1505–1569	Rej, Mikkolaj
1509–1564	Calvin, John
ca. 1512–ca. 1572	López de Gómara, Francisco
1514–1564	Vesalius, Andreas
1515–1582	Teresa of Avila, St.
1519	Till Eulenspiegel
1520–ca. 1565	Staden, Hans
ca. 1520–1566	Labé, Louise
ca. 1522–1560	Bellay, Joachim du
1522–1607	Castellanos, Juan de
1524?–1580	Camões, Luíz Vaz de
1524–1585	Ronsard, Pierre de
ca. 1528–1569	Ferreira, António
1530–1584	Kochanowski, Jan
1533–1592	Montaigne, Michel de
1534–1597	Anchieta, José de
1534–1613	Léry, Jean de
1536–1584	Lee Yul Kok
1539–1600	Acosta, José de
1539–1616	Garcilaso de la Vega
1542–1591	John of the Cross, St.
1544–1595	Tasso, Torquato
1546–1615	Huh Joon
1547–1616	Cervantes, Saavedra Miguel de
1548–1600	Bruno, Giordano
1549–1589	Pléiade
1550–1616	Tang Xianzu (T'ang Hsíen-tsu)

Dates	Author	Dates	Author
1552–1630	Aubigné, Agrippa d'	1612?–1672	Bradstreet, Anne Dudley
1554–1586	Sidney, Sir Philip	1613–1680	La Rochefoucauld,
1559–1613	Argensola, Lupercio		François, duc de
	Leonardo de	1618–1677	Riebeeck, Jan van
1560–1621	Hariot, Thomas	1619–1655	Bergerac, Cyrano de
1561–1626	Bacon, Francis	ca. 1621–1682	Avvakum
1561–1627	Góngora y Argote, Luis de	1621–1695	La Fontaine, Jean de
1562–1631	Argensola, Bartolomé	1622–1673	Molière
	Leonardo de	1623–1662	Pascal, Blaise
1562–1635	Lope de Vega Carpio, Félix	1626–1696	Sévigné, Madame de
1564–1593	Marlowe, Christopher		(Marie de Rabutin-
1564–1616	Shakespeare, William		Chantel, marquise de
1564–1642	Galilei, Galileo		Sévigné)
1568–1610	Yuan Hungdao (Yüan	1627–1704	Bossuet, Jacques-Bénigne
	Hung-tao)	1628–1703	Perrault, Charles
1568–1627	Balbuena, Bernardo de	1631–1705	Wigglesworth, Michael
1568–1639	Campanella, Tommaso	1632–1677	Spinoza, Benedictus de
ca. 1570–after 1615	Prado, Diego de	1632–1791	*Jesuit Relations*
1572–1631	Donne, John	1633–1703	Pepys, Samuel
1572–1637	Jonson, Ben	1634–1693	Lafayette, Madame de
1580–1631	Smith, John		(Marie-Madeleine-Pioche
1580–1639	Ruiz de Alarcón, Juan		de la Vergne, comtesse de
1580–1645	Quevedo, Francisco de		Lafayette)
ca. 1580–1648	Tirso de Molina	ca. 1635–ca. 1711	Rowlandson, Mary
1585–1618	Bredero, Gerbrand	1635–present	Académie française
1587–1679	Vondel, Joost van den	1636–1711	Boileau-Despréaux,
1588–1649	Winthrop, John		Nicolas
1590–1657	Bradford, William	1639–1699	Racine, Jean
1592–1670	Comenius, Johann Amos	1639–1723	Mather, Increase
1596–1650	Descartes, René	1642–1729	Taylor, Edward
1600s–1700s	comedy of manners	1644–1694	Bashō
ca. 1600s–present	haiku	1645–1696	La Bruyère, Jean de
1600s–present	Kabuki	1646–1716	Leibniz, Gottfried Wilhelm
1600–1681	Calderón de la Barca,	1648–1695	Cruz, Sor Juana Inés de la
	Pedro	1648–1718	Kong Shangren (Kung
1601–1677	Rosales, Diego de		Shung-jen)
1603–1683	Williams, Roger	after 1650	*Sonsan of Kaarta, Epic of*
1604–1690	Eliot, John	1651–1715	Fénelon, François de
1607–1701	Scudéry, Madeleine de	1653–1725	Chikamatsu Monzaemon
1608–1674	Milton, John	1660–1731	Defoe, Daniel
1608–1684	Corneille, Pierre	1663–1728	Mather, Cotton
1611–ca. 1680	Li Yu	1664–1743	Peralta Barnuevo, Pedro de
1611–1682	Çelebi, Evliya	1666–1727	Knight, Sarah Kemble

Dates	Author	Dates	Author
1667–1745	Swift, Jonathan	1720–1772	Woolman, John
1668–1744	Vico, Giambattista	ca. 1720–1820	Abdallah, Sayyid
ca. 1672–1732	Cook, Ebenezer	1723–1792	Occom, Samson
1672–1750	Muratori, Ludovico Antonio	1724–1803	Klopstock, Friedrich Gottlieb
1673–1722	Beverly, Robert	1724–1804	Kant, Immanuel
1673–1723	Cantemir, Dimitrie	1728–1814	Warren, Mercy Otis
1675–1768	Olivares, Miguel de	1729–1781	Lessing, Gotthold
1681–1736	Prokopovitch, Feofan	1729–1796	Catherine the Great
1688–1744	Pope, Alexander	1729–1799	Parini, Giuseppe
1688–1763	Marivaux, Pierre Carlet de Chamblain de	1732–1799	Beaumarchais, Pierre-Augustin-Caron de
1688–1772	Swedenborg, Emanual	1732–1808	Dickinson, John
1689–1755	Montesquieu, Charles-Louis de Secondat, baron de	1735–1813	Crèvecoeur, J. Hector St. John de
1689–1761	Richardson, Samuel	ca. 1737–1783	Munford, Robert
1691–1756	Takeda Izumo	1737–1809	Paine, Thomas
1694–1778	Voltaire	1739–1823	Bartram, William
1695–1758	Graffigny, Madame Françoise de	1740–1795	Boswell, James
		1740–1795	Gama, José Basílio da
1697–1763	Prévost, Antoine-François	1740–1814	Sade, marquis de (Donatien-Alphonse-François)
1698–1782	Metastasio, Pietro		
1700s	Bunraku		
1700s	Enlightenment, Age of	1740–1829	Moore, Milcah Martha
1700s	novel, epistolary	1741–1803	Laclos, Pierre Choderlos de
1700s	Choon Hyang Jun		
1700s–1800s	Bamana Segu, Epic of	1743–1816	Derzhavin, Gavriil Romanovich
1701–1754	Wu Jingzi (Wu Ching-tzu)		
1703–1758	Edwards, Jonathan	1743–1820	Banks, Joseph
1706–1790	Franklin, Benjamin	1743–1826	Jefferson, Thomas
1707–1793	Goldoni, Carlo	1744–1803	Herder, Johann Gottfried
1710–1780	Carver, Jonathan	1745–1797	Equiano, Olaudah
1711–1765	Lomonosov, Mikhail	ca. 1747–1795	Santa Cruz y Espejo, Francisco Javier Eugenio de
1711–ca. 1806	Hammon, Jupiter		
1712–1778	Rousseau, Jean-Jacques		
1713–1784	Diderot, Denis	1749–1802	Radishchev, Alexander Nikolayevich
1715–1764	Cao Xuequin (Ts'ao Hsüeh-ch'in)		
ca. 1715–after 1778	Carrío de la Vandera, Alonso	1749–1803	Alfieri, Vittorio
		1749–1832	Goethe, Johann Wolfgang von
1717–1783	Alembert, Jean Le Rond d'	1751–1772	Encyclopedia
1718–1777	Sumarokov, Alexander Petrovich	1751–1820	Murray, Judith Sargent
		1752–1817	Dwight, Timothy

Dates	Author	Dates	Author
1752–1832	Freneau, Philip Morin	1767–1829	Golenishchev-Kutuzov, Pavel Ivanovich
ca. 1753–1784	Wheatley, Phillis		
1758–1815	Nikolev, Nikolai Petrovich	1768–1844	Krylov, Ivan
1758–1831	Ryokan	1769–1816	Ozerov, Vladislav Aleksandrovich
ca. 1758–1833	Tench, Watkin		
1759–1805	Schiller, Friedrich von	1771–1810	Brown, Charles Brockden
1760–1837	Dmitriev, Ivan Ivanovich	1772–1801	Novalis
1762–ca. 1815	Watling, Thomas	1772–1829	Schlegel, Friedrich
1762–1824	Rowson, Susanna	1774–1829	Bunina, Anna
1762–1836	Jung Yak Yong	1776–1827	Fernández de Lizardi, José
1763–after 1809	Shen Fu	1777–1811	Kleist, Heinrich von
1763–1827	Kobayashi Issa	1779–1831	Izmailov, Aleksandr
1763–1838	Andrada e Silva, José Bonifácio de	1780–1847	Olmedo, José Joaquin
		1786–1856	Kim Jung Hee
1765–1831	Jippensha Ikku	d. 1786	Olivares, Míguel de, Padre
1766–1830	Pushkin, Vasilii L'vovich	1788–1860	Schopenhauer, Arthur

WRITERS, GENRES, AND WORKS COVERED, BY GEOGRAPHICAL AREA

AFRICA

Abdallah, Sayyid (Ali Bin Nasir)
Ashanti tales
Bamana Segu, Epic of
Equiano, Olaudah (Gustavus Vassa)
Muyaka (Haji al-Ghassaniy)
Riebeeck, Jan van
Sonsan of Kaarta, Epic of

THE AMERICAS

Acosta, José de
Anchieta, José de
Andrada e Silva, José Bonifácio de
Axayacatl of Tenochtitlán
Balbuena, Bernardo de
Bartram, William
Beverly, Robert
Book of Chilam Balam of Chumayel, The
Bradford, William
Bradstreet, Anne
Brown, Charles Brockden
Cabeza de Vaca, Álvar Núñez
Cacamatzín of Texcoco
Carrío de la Vandera, Alonso
Carver, Jonathan
Castellanos, Juan de
Chilam Balam, The Books of

Columbus, Christopher
Cook, Ebenezer
Cortés, Hernán
Crèvecoeur, J. Hector St. John de
Cruz, Sor Juana Inés de la
De-Ka-Nah-Wi-Da and *Hiawatha*
Díaz del Castillo, Bernal
Dickinson, John
Dwight, Timothy
Edwards, Jonathan
Eliot, John
Fernández de Lizardi, José
Franklin, Benjamin
Freneau, Philip Morin
Gama, José Basílio da
Garcilaso de la Vega
Hammon, Jupiter
Hariot, Thomas
Jefferson, Thomas
Jesuit Relations
Jiménez de Quesada, Gonzalo
Knight, Sarah Kemble
Komam Q'Anil, Epic of
Las Casas, Bartolomé de
Léry, Jean de
Llorona, La
López de Gómara, Francisco
Mather, Cotton
Mather, Increase

Maya epics and fables
Mesoamerican mythology
Moore, Milcah Martha
Moquihuitzín
Motolinía, Toribio de
Munford, Robert
Murray, Judith Sargent
Nahuatl poetry
Nezahualcoyotl of Texcoco
Nezahualpilli
Occom, Samson
Olivares, Miguel de
Olmedo, José Joaquín
Paine, Thomas
Peralta Barnuevo, Pedro de
Popol Vuh
Quetzalcoatl, myth of
Rabinal Achi
Rosales, Diego de
Rowlandson, Mary
Rowson, Susanna
Ruiz de Alarcón, Juan
Santa Cruz y Espejo, Francisco
Smith, John
Staden, Hans
Taylor, Edward
Vespucci, Amerigo
Warren, Mercy Otis
Wheatley, Phillis
Wigglesworth, Michael
Williams, Roger
Winthrop, John
Woolman, John

ASIA

China
Cao Xuequin (Ts'ao Hsüeh-ch'in)
Jin Ping Mei (Chin P'ing Mei)
Kong Shangren (Kung Shang-jen)
Li Yu
Luo Guanzhong (Luo Kuan-chung)
Shen Fu
Shi Naian (Shih Nai-an)
Tang Xianzu (T'ang Hsien-tsu)
Wu Chengen

Wu Jingzi (Wu Ching-tzu)
Yuan Hungdao (Yüan Hung-tao)

Japan
Bashō
Bunraku
Chikamatsu Monzaemon
haiku
Jippensha Ikku
Kabuki
Kobayashi Issa
Kyogen
Noh
Ryokan
Takeda Izumo
Zeami

Korea
Choon Hyang Jun
Huh Joon
Jung Mong Joo
Jung Yak Yong
Kim Jung Hee
Kim Shi-sup
Lee Yul Kok
Se-jong

Vietnam
Nguyen Trai

EUROPE

allegory
classicism
comedy of manners
cycle, miracle, mystery, and morality plays
fabliaux
farce
humanism
neoclassicism
novel, epistolary
pastoral
rationalism
romance
sonnet
tragedy

Britain/Ireland

Bacon, Francis
Boswell, James
Chaucer, Geoffrey
Cloud of Unknowing, The
Defoe, Daniel
Donne, John
English ballad
Gower, John
Henryson, Robert
Jonson, Ben
Julian of Norwich
Kempe, Margery
Langland, William (*Piers Plowman*)
Lydgate, John
Malory, Thomas
Marlowe, Christopher
Milton, John
More, Sir Thomas
Pearl poet
Pepys, Samuel
Pope, Alexander
Richardson, Samuel
Shakespeare, William
Sidney, Sir Philip
Sir Gawain and the Green Knight
Skelton, John
Swift, Jonathan
Wycliffe, John

French-Speaking Europe

Alembert, Jean Le Rond d'
Aubigné, Agrippa d'
Beaumarchais (Pierre-Auqustin-Caron de)
Bellay, Joachim du
Bergerac, Cyrano de
Boileau-Despréaux, Nicolas
Bossuet, Jacques-Benigne
Calvin, John
Corneille, Pierre
Descartes, René
Diderot, Denis
Encyclopedia
Fénélon, François de Salignac de la Mothe
Froissart, Jean
Graffigny, Madame Françoise de
Labé, Louise

La Bruyère, Jean de
Laclos, Pierre Choderlos de
Lafayette, Madame de
Lafontaine, Jean de
La Rochefoucauld, François, duc de
Marguerite de Navarre
Marivaux, Pierre Carlet de Chamblain de
Marot Clément
Molière (Jean-Baptiste Poquelin)
Montaigne, Michel de
Montesquieu, Charles-Louis de Secondat, baron de
Orléans, Charles d'
Pascal, Blaise
Perrault, Charles
Pisan, Christine de
Pléiade
Prévost, Antoine-François
Rabelais, François
Racine, Jean
Ronsard, Pierre de
Rousseau, Jean-Jacques
Sade, marquis de
Scudéry, Madeleine
Sévigné, Madame de
Villon, François
Voltaire (François-Marie Arouet)

German-Speaking Europe, Scandinavia, and the Netherlands

Brandt, Sebastian
Bredero, Gerbrand
Erasmus, Desiderius
Everyman (Elckerlijk)
Goethe, Johann Wolfgang von
Herder, Johann Gottfried
Kant, Immanuel
Kempis, Thomas á
Kleist, Heinrich von
Klopstock, Friedrich Gottlieb
Leibniz, Gottfried Wilhelm
Lessing, Gotthold
Luther, Martin
Marieke van Nimwegen
Melanchthon, Philip
Novalis (Frederick Leopold, baron von Hardenberg)
Ruusbroec, Jan van
Sachs, Hans

Schiller, Friedrich von
Schlegel, Friedrich
Schopenhauer, Arthur
Spinoza, Benedictus de
Swedenborg, Emanual
Till Eulenspiegel
Vesalius, Andreas
Vondel, Joost van den
Waldseemüller, Martin (inc. *Mundus Novus*)

Italy

Alberti, Leon Battista
Alfieri, Vittorio
Aretino Pietro
Ariosto, Ludovico
Bembo Pietro
Boccaccio, Giovanni
Bruno, Giordano
Campanella, Tommaso
Castiglione, Baldessare
commedia dell'arte
Della Casa, Giovanni
Galilei, Galileo
Goldoni, Carlo
Guicciardini, Francesco
Leonardo da Vinci
Machiavelli, Niccolò
Medici, Lorenzo de'
Metastasio, Pietro
Michelangelo Buonarroti
Pico della Mirandola
Muratori, Ludovico Antonio
Parini, Giuseppe
Petrarch
Poliziano, Angelo Ambrogini (Politian)
Pulci, Luigi
Tasso, Torquato
Vico, Giambattista

Russia and Eastern Europe

Avvakum
Bunina, Anna
Cantemir, Dimitrie
Catherine the Great
Comenius, Johann Amos
Copernicus, Nicolaus
Derzhavin, Gavriil Romanovich

Dmitriev, Ivan Ivanovich
Golenishchev-Kutuzov, Pavel Ivanovich
Hus, Jan
Izmailov, Aleksandr
Kochanowski, Jan
Krylov, Ivan
Lomonosov, Mikhail
Marulić, Marko
Nikitin, Afanasij
Nikolev, Nikolai Petrovich
Ozerov, Vladislav Aleksandrovich
Prokopovitch, Feofan
Pushkin, Vasilii L'vovich
Radishchev, Alexander Nikolayevich
Rej, Mikkolaj
Sumarokov, Alexander Petrovich

Spain and Portugal

Argensola, Lupercio Leonardo de &
   Bartolomé Leonardo de
Calderón de la Barca, Pedro
Camões, Luíz Vaz de
Cervantes Saavedra, Miguel de
Ferreira, António
Góngora y Argote, Luis de
John of the Cross, St.
Ignatius of Loyola
Lope de Vega Carpio, Félix
March, Ausiàs
Tirso de Molina
Quevedo Francisco de
Teresa of Ávila, St.

MIDDLE EAST

Book of Dede Korkut, The
Çelebi, Evliya
Hāfiz
Ibn al-Khatīb
Ibn Khaldūn

OCEANIA & PACIFIC

Banks, Joseph
Prado, Diego de
Tench, Watkin
Watling, Thomas

Abdallah, Sayyid (Ali bin Nasir)
(ca. 1720–1820) *poet*

Little is known of the life of Sayyid Abdallah bin Ali bin Nasir, a poet and Muslim theologian of East African descent who wrote in Swahili. He is the author of two seminal poems of Swahili classical literature, *Al-Inkishafi,* or *The Soul's Awakening,* and the *Takhmisa,* or *Songs of Liongo.* Though these two are his only known poems, it is likely that he wrote several other Swahili poems, as yet not attributed to him.

The Soul's Awakening is a religious song that describes the horrors of hell for those who forsake the counsel of Islam. According to Professor Cora Agatucci, the song tells the story of the fall of Pate, a city-state in Africa, as an example of the "vanity of earthly life" (African Timeline). Nasir wrote the song after 1749, which makes it one of the earliest examples of written Swahili poetry. It remains unfinished but is an excellent early example of Swahili ritual songs by a pioneer in the language.

A Work by Sayyid Abdallah

Al-Inkishafi: The Soul's Awakening. Translated by William Hichens. Nairobi: Oxford University Press, 1972.

Académie française (1635–present)
movement/school

The Académie française was founded in 1635 by Cardinal Richelieu, chief minister of King Louis XIII, as a means of regulating the French language and influencing the direction of French literature. The Académie française has acted ever since as France's supreme court of letters, passing judgment on questions of language and literature.

France was experiencing a surge in cultural activity in 1633, when Richelieu learned of a group of men with literary interests who were meeting informally in Paris and who were interested in the purity of the French language. He granted them his protection, and they became the charter members of the Académie française. According to its statutes, its purpose was "to work with possible care and diligence to give certain rules to our language and to render it pure, eloquent and capable of treating the arts and sciences." The members were given the task of compiling grammatical rules and creating an official dictionary of the French language.

The parliament of Paris initially refused to recognize the Académie's role in cultural and literary matters. Richelieu saw his opportunity to prove the Académie's usefulness in 1637, when controversy broke out over Pierre CORNEILLE's immensely popular play *Le Cid*, which several prominent critics condemned for immorality and ignoring the rules of classical drama. Richelieu ordered Corneille to submit his play to the Académie for judgment, and the members agreed with Corneille's critics. Because of its important role in settling the controversy, the Académie was accepted and its authority assured.

The 40 members of the Académie were known as the Forty Immortals. Men were elected to vacant posts by the members with the king's approval. Seventeenth-century members included Jean RACINE, Nicolas BOILEAU-DESPRÉAUX, and Jean de LA FONTAINE, among others. One famous exception was MOLIÈRE, who was not admitted because he was also an actor, which then was regarded as a disreputable profession.

In 1672 Louis XIV took the Académie under his protection, moved it to the Louvre, and gave the members their own library. In addition to publishing the first edition of the French dictionary (1694), the Académie held public readings of new literary works and awarded prizes for prose speeches and poetry.

Members tended to be conservative in questions of language and literature, looking to classical Greece and Rome for models of proper writing. But not all members agreed. In 1687, Perrault read to the Académie his poem, "The Century of Louis the Great," which praised authors of his own day as equals or superiors of classical authors. This gave rise to a dispute among the members, known as the Quarrel of the Ancients and Moderns.

Secret balloting on new members was instituted in 1671, but many members owed their election to court influence or favoritism by women of the literary salons. As a result, many members of the 18th century had little literary expertise. One of the most prominent ENLIGHTENMENT thinkers, VOLTAIRE, ridiculed the Académie. While he was elected as a member in 1746, his efforts to interest other members in new literary projects failed.

The election of another free-thinker, Jean d'ALEMBERT, led to the formation of a strong group of radical Enlightenment thinkers within the Académie. They urged the consideration of works on more modern subjects in literary competitions, but they, too, had little influence on traditionalist members.

The Académie was abolished along with other royal academies in 1793, during the French Revolution. It became part of the Institut National in 1795. It regained its former name and statutes in 1816, however, and its current members are still responsible for editing the official French dictionary.

The Académie française remains largely conservative, but it provides a forum for literary ideas, stands as a cultural tradition, and influences standard French spelling.

Works about the Académie Française

Levi, Anthony. *Richelieu and the Making of France.* New York: Carroll and Graf, 2000.

Racevskis, Karlis. *Voltaire and the French Academy.* Chapel Hill: University of North Carolina Department of Romance Languages, 1975.

Acosta, José de (1539–1600) *theologian, philosopher, naturalist*

José de Acosta was born in Medina del Campo and entered the Society of Jesus when he was 12. Spain sent him as a Jesuit missionary to Peru and Mexico, where he lived from 1570 to 1587. Although he authored various minor works, three notable titles brought him fame.

In 1589 Acosta published *De natura novi orbis,* a valuable historical and scientific sourcebook that is considered to be his most important work. It joins the author's missionary concerns with his scientific interests by placing Mexico and Peru in harmony with the popular scientific view of reality of the time. Acosta translated *De natura* into Spanish and published it along with *Historia natural y moral de las Indias* into a single work. In *Historia natural* he studies the problems he found in Mexico and Peru and speculates on their origins. He presents a view of the New World as part of the natural order assigned by God to nature and the course of history.

Another of Acosta's important works is *De procuranda indorum salute,* also published in 1588. In this work, he examines the fundamental problems of evangelization in America in the 16th century. Significantly, the work is the first systematic and complete presentation of early missionary problems with the balancing of rights, obligations, and parochial functions in the New World.

Acosta's works are important because they represent the ideological culmination of the religious, philosophical, and scientific conquest of the New World in terms of the historical and ontological process of incorporating the New World into existing culture.

English Versions of Works by José de Acosta

Natural and Moral History of the East and West Indies. Whitefish, Mont.: Kessinger Publishing, 2003.
Natural and Moral History of the Indies. Translated by Frances M. Lopez-Morillas. Raleigh, N.C.: Duke University Press, 2002.

Works about José de Acosta

Burgaleta, Claudio M. *José De Acosta, S.J. (1540–1600): His Life and Thought.* Chicago: Loyola Press, 1999.
Shepherd, Gregory J. *An Exposition of José De Acosta's "Historia Y Moral de Las Indias," 1590.* New York: Edwin Mellen Press, 2002.

Alberti, Leon Battista (1404–1472)
architect, writer

During the 15th and 16th centuries, Europe experienced an explosive growth of culture, philosophy, and science, which has come to be known as the RENAISSANCE. Although the Renaissance affected many countries, it had the greatest impact in Italy, where brilliant artists, writers, and thinkers lived and worked. Among these people was Leon Battista Alberti.

Alberti was born in the Italian port city of Genoa, the illegitimate son of Lorenzo Alberti, a merchant from Florence who had been exiled from his native city. Lorenzo conducted a prosperous business that had interests throughout the Mediterranean world, and he ensured that Leon received an excellent education in the Latin classics and the law.

After his father's death, Alberti took a position with the administration of the Vatican, while at the same time he began to explore writing. He became fascinated with language, history, music, art, and architecture, and his writings on these subjects began to attract an increasingly large number of readers. He wrote in both Latin and the vernacular Italian, so that both the well-educated and the layman could read his works. Soon, many powerful figures in various Italian city-states sought out Alberti for advice on artistic and literary subjects. He also began designing architectural projects of his own, though he had never received an education in architecture and was entirely self-taught in the field.

For the remainder of his life, Alberti continued writing, working on his architecture, and assisting the powerful men of Italy. He moved constantly from court to court and eventually died in Rome.

Alberti was a good architect, although his work would be surpassed by other Renaissance masters. He is better known for his literary work than for his architecture, and his writings had a tremendous influence on art and architecture long after his death.

Alberti's writings are brilliant descriptions of the artistic and cultural world in which he lived, and they provide valuable insight into Renaissance Italy. He composed love poetry, biographies, Ciceronian dialogues, a satirical comedy about court life and philosophy titled *Momus* (ca. 1450), fables, and a 10-book survey of architecture. He also produced writings on family customs in Florence. One such work is his *Della famiglia,* a prose dialogue in four books in which he reveals discussions among three generations of his family regarding their social values and business ethics. Alberti wrote the piece to defend his family against its critics. His discussions of children's education and marriage in books one and two of *Della famiglia* clearly show that Alberti was influenced by Aristotle and Xenophon. Book three concerns the Alberti family's responsibility to earn, save, invest, and spend money, while book four concerns friendship.

Another classical influence on Alberti was Lucian, whose penchant for satire Alberti adopts in a collection of short dialogues titled *Intercenales*. This work is noteworthy for its having introduced a playful tone into serious Renaissance literature in Italy.

One of Alberti's most crucial works was *On Painting* (1430s), in which he analyzes and explains the technical aspects of painting, paying particular attention to an artist's perspective in creating realistic, three-dimensional images.

The most famous of Alberti's treatises is *On the Art of Building* (1440s), in which he presents his thoughts and ideas concerning architecture. Alberti discusses everything from the architecture of ancient Rome to techniques for contemporary urban planning. Centuries after it was written, *On the Art of Building* remained the single most important reference work in the field of architecture.

Alberti had a tremendous influence on the artists and architects who came after him, including his friend Filippo Brunelleschi, perhaps the most influential architect of the Renaissance, and LEONARDO da Vinci, who apparently studied Alberti's works. His exploration of so many different interests and subjects marked him as a true Renaissance man.

English Versions of Works by Leon Battista Alberti

Momus. Translated by Sarah Knight and edited by Virginia Brown. Cambridge, Mass.: Harvard University Press, 2003.

On the Art of Building in Ten Books. Translated by Joseph Rykwert, Neil Leach, and Robert Tavenor. Cambridge, Mass.: MIT Press, 1991.

The Family in Renaissance Florence. Translated by Renee N. Watkins. Long Grove, Ill.: Waveland Press, 1994.

Works about Leon Battista Alberti

Grafton, Anthony. *Leon Battista Alberti: Master Builder of the Italian Renaissance.* New York: Hill and Wang, 2000.

Tavernor, Robert. *On Alberti and the Art of Building.* New Haven, Conn.: Yale University Press, 1999.

Alembert, Jean Le Rond d' (1717–1783)
mathematician, philosopher

Jean d'Alembert was one of the leading minds of the French ENLIGHTENMENT, along with such thinkers as MONTESQUIEU, ROUSSEAU, and VOLTAIRE, and he contributed to the monumental ENCYCLOPEDIA, a 28-volume work masterminded by Denis DIDEROT. The illegitimate son of the famed hostess Madame de Tencin, d'Alembert was abandoned as a baby on the steps of the church of St. Jean-Le-Rond and remained loyal to his adopted mother throughout his life. A diligent student of mathematics and physics, d'Alembert became a member of the Academy of Sciences at age 24. After making the acquaintance of Denis Diderot and other French philosophers, d'Alembert found himself agreeing to contribute to the *Encyclopedia.* D'Alembert wrote the memorable preface, the *Preliminary Discourse,* in which he proposes a theory of knowledge based on John Locke's ideas. D'Alembert also authored several tracts on his mathematical discoveries, the arts, and sciences. Both Russia and Prussia tried to lure him into their service, but d'Alembert chose to remain in Paris, where he died at age 66.

In 1743 d'Alembert published his new interpretation of Newton's Third Law, in which he maintains that forces that resist acceleration must be equal and opposite to the forces that produce the acceleration. This came to be known as "d'Alembert's principle." Until 1754 he continued publishing his work on algebra, calculus, and also physical astronomy, in which he solved the precession of the equinoxes.

Biographers characterize d'Alembert as a man who had little use for wealth or sycophants and instead adored truth and reason. His preface to the *Encyclopedia,* first published in 1751, is the best example of his practical if unpolished style and his adherence to the egalitarian ideals and the spirit of scientific inquiry that characterized the Enlightenment. D'Alembert and the encyclopedists, clinging to their beliefs despite pressure from the conservatives, contributed to the dissolution of the ancient social and political institutions of France, which crumbled at the beginning of the Revolution.

An English Version of a Work by Jean Le Rond d'Alembert

Preliminary Discourse to the Encyclopedia of Diderot. Translated by Richard N. Schwab. Chicago: University of Chicago Press, 1995.

Works about Jean Le Rond d'Alembert

Crumey, Andrew. *D'Alembert's Principle.* New York: St. Martin's Press, 1998.
Diderot, Denis. *Rameau's Nephew and d'Alembert's Dream.* Translated by Leonard Tancock. New York: Penguin Classics, 1976.
Hankins, Thomas L. *Jean d'Alembert: Science and the Enlightenment.* Oxford: Clarendon Press, 1970.

Alfieri, Vittorio (1749–1803) *poet, dramatist*

Vittorio Alfieri was born in the northern Italian aristocracy of the early 18th century. While he studied at the Military Academy of Turin, one of the best colleges in Europe, the sheltered life of an aristocrat did not suit him. He was eager to see the world, instead, and embarked on a romantic and extensive series of travels across Europe (1776–1777), going as far as Russia and Sweden, some of which he details in his *Vita (Life).*

Alfieri had a strong sense of Italian nationalism and rebelled against French classical culture, which was so prominent among his class and age. As a result, he attempted to create plays that would rival French drama.

Alfieri's experiences in Paris during the French Revolution would color much of what he wrote. In his *Ode to America's Independence,* for example, he presents his views on both the French and the American revolutions, which reveals a decided favoritism for the Americans' desire for independence.

Alfieri wrote a total of 19 tragedies, many of them published in the 1780s, as well as political treatises such as *Of Tyranny* (1777), political poems, and an autobiography. Although he was influenced by classicism, much of his work is considered characteristic of the pre-Romantic period of Italian literature. His works are remembered for the national conscience they restored to Italian culture.

English Versions of Works by Vittorio Alfieri

Of Tyranny. Translated and edited by Julius A. Molinaro and Beatrice Corrigan. Toronto: University of Toronto Press, 1961.
The Tragedies of Vittorio Alfieri. Edited by Edgar Alfred Bowrin. Westport, Conn.: Greenwood Press, 1970.

Works about Vittorio Alfieri

Betti, Franco. *Vittorio Alfieri.* Boston: Twayne, 1984.
Caso, Adolph. *Alfieri's Ode to America's Independence.* Boston: Branden Press, 1976.

allegory

An allegory is a story in which characters represent abstract qualities, and the literal story line is less important than the symbolic truth that the story both conceals and dramatizes. An allegory is similar to both a parable, the kind of story used in the Christian Gospels to illustrate moral truths, and a fable, in which a story dramatizes a practical insight about life. An allegory, however, is more elaborate than either a parable or a fable and is developed in more detail. More complicated allegories reveal a multiplicity of meanings.

In classical literature there are many famous examples of allegory, including the allegory of the cave in Plato's *Republic,* where Plato likens human life to the existence of cave-dwellers who can see reality only in the form of shadows cast on a wall. In addition, several of the stories in Ovid's *Metamorphoses* invite allegorical interpretation.

The allegory received its fullest expression in medieval and RENAISSANCE Europe. Early Christian writers such as Augustine, and medieval religious writers who followed him, extended the parable form to help convey spiritual concepts. As medieval romances grew in popularity, writers defused charges of frivolity leveled against their preoccupation with secular passions by including religious meanings. In *The Divine Comedy,* for example, Dante achieved a complete fusion between romance and religious poetry, and every event and conversation can be understood on several levels.

In some allegories, such as William LANGLAND's *Piers Plowman,* characters bear the names of abstract qualities (Piers meets and talks with deadly sins such as Gluttony and Sloth, and virtues such as Truth and Peace). In other allegories, the characters seem to be real people with whom the reader can identify while at the same time symbolizing moral dilemmas. For example, in the 14th-century English romance SIR GAWAIN AND THE GREEN KNIGHT, Sir Gawain, although a good knight and a hero, is also an ordinary, flawed human being; but the Green Knight who challenges him, the host who entertains him, and the host's lady who tempts him all have a symbolic function that is not fully explained and that challenges the reader to search for the best interpretation.

Renaissance examples of allegory include Torquato TASSO's *Gerusalemme Liberata,* Ludovico ARIOSTO's *Orlando Furioso,* and Edmund Spenser's *The Faerie Queene* (1590, 1596). Jonathan SWIFT used allegorical techniques in his *A Tale of a Tub,* and writers and filmmakers to this day use allegory to engage at once the reader's emotions and intellect.

Other Works Featuring Allegory

Bunyan, John. *The Pilgrim's Progress.* Mineola, N.Y.: Dover, 2003.
Dryden, John. "Absalom and Achitophel," in *Selected Poetry and Prose of John Dryden.* Edited by Earl Miner. Los Angeles: Random House, 1969.

Works about Allegory

Lewis, C. S. *The Allegory of Love: A Study in Medieval Tradition.* New York: Oxford University Press, 1990.
Fletcher, Argus. *Allegory: The Theory of a Symbolic Mode.* Ithaca, N.Y.: Cornell University Press, 1982.

Anchieta, José de (1534–1597) *missionary, teacher, linguist*

Dubbed the "Apostle of Brazil," José de Anchieta is influential for his contributions as a writer to the foundations of Brazilian culture. He is also noted for his concern for the welfare of the Brazilian Indians demonstrated through his efforts to protect the Indians from exploitation under Portuguese colonization. Anchieta helped to establish several Jesuit schools, including colleges at Rio, Bahia, and Pernambuco. He was instrumental in helping to found the cities of São Paulo and Rio de Janeiro.

Anchieta mastered several Indian languages and helped make the Tupi tongue the main language of communication among the Indians. Noted for his linguistic studies, he wrote a grammar of the Tupi language (*Arte de grammatica da lingoa . . . do Brasil*), which was widely used by missionaries. He also compiled a Tupi-Portuguese dictionary. He translated prayers, hymns, and the catechism into Indian languages. To teach religious faith, he wrote catechetical texts, canticles, dialogues, and religious plays in Tupi and in Portuguese.

Anchieta's numerous letters and reports, spanning the years from 1554 to 1594, provide an important historical record of Brazil's development in the 16th century. He wrote poetry, composing verses in Portuguese, Spanish, Latin, and Tupi (*De beata virgine dei matre Maria; Primeiras letras*). He is also noted for writing didactic religious plays and is credited with authoring the first, short religious plays acted in Bahia.

Works about José de Anchieta

Baker, Mona, ed. *Routledge Encyclopedia of Translation Studies.* New York: Routledge, 2001.

Dominian, Helen G. *Apostle of Brazil: The Biography of Padre José de Anchieta.* New York: Exposition Press, 1958.

Andrada e Silva, José Bonifácio de

(1763–1838) *poet, scientist, political figure*

Known as the "Patriarch of Independence," José Bonifácio de Andrada e Silva was one of the most influential figures in Brazilian history. Extremely well educated, Andrada e Silva received degrees in law and philosophy in 1787 and 1788, respectively, from the University of Coimbra. He also studied other topics, such as mathematics, geology, and astronomy. After graduating, Andrada e Silva joined the Science Academy of Lisbon, where he gained international recognition for his achievements in the sciences. His contributions in this area are many, including his discovery of four previously unknown minerals and eight unknown species.

After a long absence from home while conducting scientific research abroad, Andrada e Silva returned to Brazil in 1819 and immediately became politically active. In October of 1821, he wrote "Lembranas e Apontamentos do Governo Provisorio de São Paulo," said to be the most important document in Brazilian history, for laying the foundation of modern-day Brazil. Andrada e Silva is given credit for the unification of Brazil in 1822, an act that many proudly state contained little bloodshed. Without his efforts, Brazil would have separated into smaller divisions during the disintegration of Portuguese control in the early 1800s. He was named the first minister under the new constitution he had helped establish, but his intense insistence on a liberal constitution led to his banishment from Brazil in 1823–29. He later returned to Brazil and tutored Emperor Pedro II's sons.

As a writer, Andrada e Silva's work was fueled by his political vehemence. In "Poesias Avulsas," he explored a "natural pantheism that expressed his intellectual character and scientific curiosity," a curiosity that sparked the same in others of his time (Rupert). The work was published under a pseudonym and has been republished in numerous volumes since its original publication in 1825.

Works about José Bonifácio de Andrada e Silva

Amaral, Ricardo C. *José Bonifácio de Andrada e Silva.* Brazil: Brazilian Communications Group, 1999.

Burns, E. Bradford. *A History of Brazil,* 3rd ed. New York: Columbia University Press, 1993.

Aretino, Pietro (1492–1556) *poet, playwright*

Known for his scathing satire, Italian author Pietro Aretino was one of the most notorious writers of his time. His daring ridicule of powerful figures earned him fame throughout Europe.

Born in Arezzo on April 20, Aretino rejected the family name of his father ("Aretino" means "from Arezzo") and moved first to Perugia and then to Rome in 1517, where he became an enthusiastic participant in, and critic of, aristocratic society. He was shrewd and ruthless, often resorting to blackmail and claims of public influence with popes and nobles. Indeed, he would gain during his lifetime the favor of Pope Leo X and the patronage of Giulio de' Medici, who became Pope Clement VII. Aretino drew most of his wealth from gifts from nobles, and many of his works are, at their core, satirical weapons Aretino used in his political maneuvers.

Six volumes of Aretino's letters express a great deal of his satire and cynicism concerning the powerful. Rome and its citizens were frequent targets of his wit, as expressed in his works *Ragionamenti* and *I diloghi*. His 1524 collection of sonnets, *Sonetti lussuriosi* (Lewd sonnets), precipitated his exile (perhaps the source of his animosity) from Rome.

Aretino wrote a number of comedies that are less malicious and add portraits of the lower class. His first and perhaps best-known comedy, *Cortigiana* (*The Courtesan*, 1525), explores the lives of the lower class in papal Rome. Using the plot line of a practical joke played by the duke of Mantua, *Il Marescalo* (1526–27) presents a comedic reprimand of courtly life and is known for its frank exploration of sexuality. Aretino also wrote the tragedy *Orazia* (The horatii, 1546), a verse play based on Livy's account of Horatii and Curiatii. It provides a fine example of Aretino's versatility as a dramatist and poet.

Reacting to Pietro BEMBO'S carefully refined writings, Aretino wrote eloquent prose, verse, and letters, using common, everyday speech and focusing on a greater variety of subjects. He is remembered for leading the way to a more provocative style of writing in 16th-century Italy.

English Versions of Works by Pietro Aretino

Aretino's Dialogues. Translated by Raymond Rosenthal and edited by Margaret Rosenthal. New York: Marsilio, 1999.

The Marescalco. Translated and edited by Leonard G. Sbrocchi and J. Douglas Campbell. New York: Italica, 2003.

Works about Pietro Aretino

Cleugh, James. *The Divine Aretino.* New York: Stein and Day, 1966.

Waddington, Raymond B. *Aretino's Satyr: Sexuality, Satire, and Self-Projection in Sixteenth-Century Literature and Art.* Toronto: University of Toronto Press, 2003.

Argensola, Bartolomé Leonardo de
(1562–1631) *poet, historian* and
Argensola, Lupercio Leonardo de
(1559–1613) *poet, playwright, historian*

The brothers Argensola came from an aristocratic family and followed very similar literary paths. They were educated at Huesca and Zaragoza, with Bartolomé also studying at Salamanca. Both joined the Academia Imitatoria (Academy of Imitators), a prestigious literary society that promoted the use of classical writers such as Horace as models. In fact, the brothers were known as the "Spanish Horaces," both excelling at moral and satirical verse.

As leaders of the Aragonese School, they reacted against the complex baroque style of GÓNGORA Y ARGOTE, then in vogue. By contrast, their writing is restrained and intellectual. In their time, however, they epitomized good literary taste with emphasis on balance and formal perfection.

In 1599 Lupercio became chief historian of Aragon. But in 1608, at the invitation of the conde de Lemos, viceroy of Naples, both brothers moved to Naples. There Lupercio served as secretary of state, while both continued their literary activities: Lupercio founded his own literary society, Academia de los Ociosos (Academy of Idlers), and Bartolomé became literary adviser and court poet.

Toward the end of his life, Lupercio assessed his own work rather harshly and had his poems burned. His version of Horace's *Beatus ille* is, however, considered to be among the finest in Spanish. Luckily, his son Gabriel had made copies of most of his poems.

There were, however, some notable differences between the two. Lupercio, who disliked popular theater, wrote three tragedies in the style of the Roman dramatist Seneca: *Filis,* now lost, and *Alejandra* and *Isabella,* both gloomy and violent.

Bartolomé, who also wrote under the name "Luis de Escatrón," was regarded as the more accomplished stylist for his sonnets and didactic verse. Unlike Lupercio, he was ordained into the priesthood, serving as rector of Villahermosa and later canon of the cathedral at Zaragoza. When Lupercio died in Naples, Bartolomé returned to Spain, where he took Lupercio's old job as chief historian of Aragon. In this role, both brothers produced important official historical records.

Contemporary writers such as FÉLIX LOPE DE VEGA and Miguel de CERVANTES held the Argensola brothers in high esteem. Their poems were collected by

Lupercio's son and published posthumously in a single collection called *Rimas*. English versions of works by the Argensola brothers are not in print.

Ariosto, Ludovico (1474–1533) *poet, playwright*

Ludovico Ariosto was born at Reggio, Italy, and was the first of 10 children. When his father died in 1500, Ariosto became the head of the household. In 1503 he entered the service of Cardinal Hippolytus, who employed him as a diplomat and ambassador as well as poet; however, when Ariosto declined to move to Hungary with the cardinal, he was dismissed. He then took service with Duke Alfonso d'Este and, except for a three-year term as governor of one of the outlying provinces, he was allowed to remain in Ferrara to compose, perform, and publish his work. In 1526 he married his lifelong love, Alessandra Benucci.

Though today he is remembered for his EPIC poem *Orlando Furioso*, Ariosto also wrote a variety of plays, lyric verse, and satires. His dramatic pieces show the influence of Plautus and Terence; his earliest play, *The Chest of Gold* (1508), was the first of its kind to use modern stage settings. For the *Supposes* (1509), set in Ferrara, Raphael painted the cityscape that served as the backdrop, and *The Necromancer* (1520) introduced a new stock character in the form of the villain Iachelino, a magician and sage. Ariosto wrote *Lena* for a wedding in 1528, and later began *The Students*, which he never finished.

Ariosto's *Satires* are written in three-line rhymed stanzas and contain a great deal of autobiographical material. Like Horace, he treated the satire as a mirror of daily life.

Ariosto's lyric and occasional poems were not published as a collection until 1546. Many of them had been written while he was a student, or in the service of Hippolytus. A number of the sonnets, addressed to Alessandra and composed in the form perfected by PETRARCH, show his style maturing as the artist perfected the tools he would use to craft his masterwork, *Orlando Furioso*.

Ariosto lived during the peak of the Italian RENAISSANCE, and *Orlando Furioso*, which he spent half his life writing and revising, is completely a product of the Renaissance at its height. The character of Orlando evolved from the historical Roland, who served in the army of Charlemagne. In turn, Ariosto's character evolved as the product of previous works about Roland, including *The Song of Roland* (11th century), PULCI's *The Greater Morgante* (1482), and Boiardo's *Orlando Innamorato* (Orlando in love, 1494), which he never finished.

In 1506 Ariosto took up where Boiardo left off. The first edition of *Orlando Furioso* (Orlando the mad) appeared in 1516, the second in 1521, and the third, expanded and revised edition in 1532. The work preserves the grand vision and sprawling scope of the legends in three main storylines that hold the work together. The first is an account of Charlemagne's perpetual war with the Saracens; the second concerns Orlando's passion for Angelica; and the final story involves the love affair of Ruggiero and Rinaldo's sister Bradamante.

Ariosto composed *Orlando* in highly polished eight-line stanzas, or octaves, and he frequently intervenes to comment on the larger themes of love, war, and the fragility of the human mind and soul. He understood the nature of the quest, and all of his characters search for different things: love, glory, victory, paradise, and peace. In addition, he combines classical, medieval, and contemporary material to create a work that blends tragedy, comedy, and epic in an enormously varied and vital style.

The *Five Cantos*, which appeared after Ariosto's death, were thought to be additions to the *Furioso*. John Harington first translated the *Furioso* into English in 1591. Edmund Spenser began *The Faerie Queene* with the intention of surpassing Ariosto's achievement, and Walter Scott learned Italian simply so he could read *Orlando* in the original.

Though critics from the beginning have debated over the quality of Ariosto's style, they can agree to what biographer Griffin calls "the stupendous impact of the *Furioso* on European literature." A work as much about limits as it is about extremes, as much about human failure as it is about human achievement, the themes of *Orlando Furioso* continue to hold compelling relevance to the writing and study of literature.

English Versions of Works by Ludovico Ariosto

Orlando Furioso. Translated by Guido Waldman. New York: Oxford University Press, 1998.

Orlando Furioso: Part One. Translated by Barbara Reynolds. New York: Viking Press, 1975.

Works about Ludovico Ariosto

Finucci, Valeria. *Renaissance Transactions: Ariosto and Tasso*. Durham, N.C.: Duke University Press, 1999.

Griffin, Robert. *Ludovico Ariosto*. New York: Twayne, 1974.

Ashanti tales (1400s–1800s) *folklore*

The Ashanti (or Asante) built an empire in the region of present-day Ghana that flourished for several centuries and reached its peak of influence in the 18th century. The Ashanti kingdom, one of the most powerful in West Africa, interacted with the increasing number of Europeans, and was famous for its wealth in gold, its well-armed military, and its efficient administration. Ashanti royalty had court poets to compose songs commemorating their ancestors and accomplishments, while the folktales circulating at all levels of society provided a method of social cohesion by formulating and communicating cultural values, mores, and customs.

The Ashanti folktales often tell a moral lesson, describe a myth, or answer a question about the natural world. In the tradition of fables from those of Aesop to the *Panchatantra,* most of the Ashanti tales use animal characters to represent human qualities such as jealousy, honesty, greed, and bravery. Ananse, the spider, is a trickster figure who appears in many of the Ashanti tales. As in the Coyote Tales of the Hopi, the stories portray Ananse as clever, successful, funny, lazy, or deceived, and almost end with a moral. One tale that describes how wisdom entered the world begins with the image of Ananse the spider putting all the wisdom into a large pot and trying to carry it up a tall tree to hide it. Frustrated by failure, he throws the pot to the ground and it breaks, thus freeing the wisdom for use by all peoples.

A recent retelling of an Ashanti story by Tololwa Mollel, illustrated by Andrew Glass, portrays the greedy side of Ananse's nature. Ananse, who had hoarded his food before a large drought, refuses to share with any of the other animals, even when Akye the Turtle comes to visit. Akye gives the gluttonous Ananse a taste of his own medicine by inviting him to a feast where Ananse is unable to eat a bite. In an adaptation by Verna Aardema, with pictures by Bryna Waldman, Anansi, as a human figure, gets tricked at his own game when he goes out looking for a fool. The stories turn on the function of shame and friendship in Ashanti culture and convey the moral that hard work merits reward, while dishonesty creates consequences.

Many Ashanti tales celebrate the cleverness of the small, as does Jessica Souhami's rendering of the traditional tale of Osebo the leopard, who disobeys Nyame the Sky-God by refusing to give him his drum. The small tortoise Achi-cheri, laughed at by the other animals, manages to trick Osebo and deliver the drum to Nyame, who rewards her by giving her a hard outer shell to protect her from the jealousy of others. The theme of social harmony appears frequently in Ashanti tales, reflecting the cultural belief that animals, objects, and even places preserve a life and a spirit of their own. Society in the world of the folktales is ruled by a chief whose office is indicated by his stool, but while chiefs resolve disputes and give judgments, the tales reveal the importance of respect, honesty, and joint action at all levels of the Ashanti community.

Ashanti folktales still circulate as part of the oral literature of present-day Ghana, and the staging of stories provides a means of bringing together people of all ages and social strata. Storytelling is associated with wisdom and knowledge in Ghanaian culture, so the best storytellers are usually older men and women. The audience gathers in a circle around the narrator, participates in a call-and-response style, and shows appreciation by singing or applauding. A skilled storyteller draws on the audience's body language, facial expressions, and comments for inspiration.

The Ashanti tales have proved popular in English and are often adapted into picture books for young readers, preserving the vital culture, artistic achievements, and imaginative myths of a powerful and influential people.

English Versions of Ashanti Tales

Appiah, Peggy. *The Pineapple Child and Other Tales from Ashanti*. London: Carlton Books, 1995.

Chocolate, Deborah M. Newton. *Talk, Talk: An Ashanti Legend*. Mahwah, N.J.: Troll Associates, 1993.

Courlander, Harold. *A Treasury of African Folklore*. New York: Marlowe & Company, 2002.

Rattray, Robert. *Akan-Ashanti Folk Tales*. New York: AMS Press, 1983.

Works about Ashanti Tales

Larungu, Rute. *Myths and Legends from Ghana for African-American Cultures*. Akron, Ohio: Telcraft Books, 1992.

McCaskie, T. C. *State and Society in Pre-Colonial Asante*. Cambridge: Cambridge University Press, 1995.

Musgrove, Margaret W. *Ashanti to Zulu: African Traditions*. New York: Puffin, 1992.

Thompson, Carol. *The Asante Kingdom*. New York: Franklin Watts, 1999.

Aubigné, Agrippa d' (1552–1630) *poet, nonfiction writer*

Agrippa d'Aubigné lived during one of the most turbulent times in French history—the years of the Wars of Religion (1562–98) between the Catholics and the Protestants. He participated in the Protestant cause throughout the wars and served as equerry and diplomat under Henri di Navarre (later Henry IV).

He was born near Pons, and after his mother's death his father, Jean d'Aubigné, sent him to be raised by his cousin, Michelle Joly. In his autobiography (*Sa vie à ses enfants*), he claims to have been able to read and translate Latin, Greek, and Hebrew by age 10. In 1565 d'Aubigné studied in Geneva but eventually returned to France, where he completed his education. He wrote many of his early poems from 1571 to 1573, inspired by his love for Diane Salviati, which were published in 1874 under the title *Printemps*. Mostly a collection of sonnets, the poems in *Printemps* were written in the Petrarchan style.

In 1572 he narrowly escaped the St. Bartholomew's Day massacre in Paris, and this tragedy strengthened his Protestant resolve. He joined the court of Henri de Navarre, which he satirized in later writings. D'Aubigné continued to fight for the Protestant cause until 1593, when Henri converted to Catholicism. Starting in 1579, d'Aubigné began work on *Les Tragiques* (1616), a long poetic "denunciation of the evils he sees about him and of the enemies of the Reformation" (Harvey and Heseltine, 35).

At the same time d'Aubigné was writing *Les Tragiques*, he also completed *L'Histoire universelle*, published from 1618 to 1620. This historical narrative focuses on the years from 1550 to 1601. In 1617 he published *Aventures du baron de Fæneste*, a satirical novel about the Catholic faith. In 1620 his *L'Histoire universelle* was condemned to be burned, and d'Aubigné was to stand trial. Instead he fled to Geneva, where he remained until his death. Before that, in 1626, he wrote his autobiography, which was published posthumously. D'Aubigné's strong beliefs and great learning are reflected in his body of work.

An English Version of a Work by Agrippa d'Aubigné

His Life, to His Children. Edited and translated by John Nothnagle. Lincoln: University of Nebraska Press, 1989.

Works about Agrippa d'Aubigné

Cameron, Keith. *Agrippa d'Aubigné*. Boston: Twayne, 1977.

Regosin, Richard L. *The Poetry of Inspiration: Agrippa d'Aubigné's Les tragiques.* Chapel Hill: University of North Carolina Press, 1970.

Avvakum (Avvakum Petrovich)
(ca. 1621–1682) *nonfiction writer*

Avvakum was born into a peasant family in the Nizhnii Novgorod region of Muscovy. Raised by a devout mother, Avvakum married and entered the church at a young age, and by age 30, he was an archpriest.

Beginning in 1653, Avvakum spent nine years in exile in Siberia because he opposed recent changes to Russian Orthodox church books and services. Upon his return to Moscow, he continued to agitate against the reforms. A 1667 church council condemned opponents of the reforms as heretics, and Avvakum found himself and his family exiled to the far north. There he wrote his autobiography, polemical works attacking the reforms, and letters to followers. These followers deemed him a martyr when he was burned at the stake for his religious views.

Avvakum is best known for his autobiography *Zhitie* (*Life;* publication date unknown). It is a multifaceted work that combines simple, vernacular prose with formal religious language. Drawing inspiration from hagiographies (written stories of saint's lives), Avvakum depicts himself as a pious man who suffers for his defense of the true faith.

N. K. Gudzy notes the "boldness" inherent in Avvakum's writing, his "extremely high opinion of himself and his consciousness of enormous spiritual superiority over ordinary people." Unlike most hagiographies, however, *Life* makes its protagonist seem human. At one point, for example, Avvakum is "lying on the stove, naked, under a covering made from birch bark," and he has to retrieve his priestly clothing from "mess and dirt."

Avvakum is remembered for having written one of Russia's earliest autobiographies, and his simple yet graphic portrayal of his life's events, beliefs, and emotions has given him a place in world literature.

English Versions of a Work by Avvakum

The Life of Archpriest Avvakum by Himself. In *Medieval Russia's Epics, Chronicles, and Tales,* rev. ed. Edited by Serge A. Zenkovsky. New York: E.P. Dutton 1974.
The Life of Archpriest Avvakum by Himself. Translated by Kenneth N. Brostrom. Ann Arbor: Michigan Slavic Publications, University of Michigan, 1979.

Works about Avvakum

Gudzy, N. K. "Archpriest Avvakum and His Works." Translated by Susan Wilbur Jones. In *History of Early Russian Literature.* New York: Octagon Books, 1970.
Michels, Georg Michels. *At War with the Church: Religious Dissent in Seventeenth-Century Russia.* Stanford, Calif.: Stanford University Press, 1999.

Axayacatl of Tenochtitlán (1449?–1481)
poet, ruler

Axayacatl of Tenochtitlán was the son of Prince Tezozomoctzin and Huitzilxochitzin, a woman from Tlacopan. While his father did not rule in Tenochtitlán (present-day Mexico City), Axayacatl and two of his brothers became *huey tlatoanai* (supreme ruler) of the Aztec Empire. Axayacatl was elected ruler in 1468 at the insistence of Tlacaelel, a powerful Mexican counselor, despite being only 19 years old.

Axayacatl showed great bravery in combat as the ruler of Tenochtitlán. He led three great battles against the Tlatexica nation, the Matlatzinca of Toluca, and the Purépecha of Michoacán, though the last of these was a severe defeat for Axayacatl and his men. During this time, Axayacatl also supervised the carving of the Sun Stone, which combined Aztec mythology, religion, and the science of the calendar. Shortly after the unveiling of the Sun Stone, Axayacatl fell ill and never recovered.

The battle with the Purépecha served as the inspiration for one of the two great poems attributed to Axayacatl, "Huehueh Cuicatl," or "Song of the Elders." The poem expresses the weariness felt by the poet after the defeat, and honors the soldiers who died in battle. Axayacatl's other poem, "Ycuic Axayacatzin, Mexico Tlatohuani," or "Song of Axayacatl, Lord of Mexico," recalls his famous ancestors and the glories of the Aztec Empire. Unfortunately, one of Axayacatl's own sons, Montezuma II, would see the end of Aztec glory in 1520. Though Axayacatl's reign lasted only 13 years and his poetic output was limited, he is remembered as one of the great poets and rulers of the Aztec Empire.

See also NAHUATL POETRY.

English Versions of Works by Axayacatl of Tenochtitlán
Flower and Song: Poems of the Aztec Peoples. Translated by Edward Kissam and Michael Schmidt. Ypsilanti, Mich.: Bilingual Press, 1983.

Leon-Portilla, Miguel. *Fifteen Poets of the Aztec World.* Norman: University of Oklahoma Press, 1992.

Works about Axayacatl of Tenochtitlán
Leon-Portilla, Miguel. *Aztec Thought and Culture: A Study of the Ancient Nahuatl Mind.* Translated by Jack Emory Davis. Norman: University of Oklahoma Press, 1990.

Meyer, Michael C., and William H. Beezley, eds. *The Oxford History of Mexico.* Oxford: Oxford University Press, 2000.

Bacon, Francis (1561–1626) *nonfiction writer*

Francis Bacon was born in London, the youngest son of Sir Nicholas and Lady Ann Bacon, and educated at Cambridge University. He spent three years as a youth in France as an assistant to the English ambassador but was recalled to England in 1579 by his father's sudden death.

For employment, Bacon turned to the law, qualifying for the bar in 1582. He also became a member of Parliament in 1583, earning a reputation as an eloquent orator, and served every year thereafter until 1621.

Even during his early years in Parliament Bacon was at work on a project inspired by his disillusionment with the dry and derivative education he had received at Cambridge. His *Great Instauration,* or renewal, of learning was a plan, in his words, "to set philosophy into a more fertile path." The project came to include models of "new learning," plans for universities, and methods of experimentation and observation.

Education and the law, however, were not Bacon's only interests. He published one of his greatest works, *Essays,* in 1597. To *essay* is to weigh something to determine its value, and an essay is an informal exploration of a topic; the form had been pioneered by Michel de MONTAIGNE in France, but Bacon was the first to attempt it in English. In each essay in his collection, he treats topics such as friendship, truth, and wealth by alluding to classical and biblical stories, using extended metaphors, and using biting aphorisms (pithy sayings). Bacon added to the work over the years, and the published version (1625) contains 58 essays.

The ascension to the throne of King James I brought good times for Bacon. The new monarch knighted him and appointed him king's counsel, and in 1606 solicitor general. Bacon dedicated his 1605 work *The Advancement of Learning*—the first part of the *Great Instauration*—to James I in the hope that the king would support his educational reforms. In this Bacon was disappointed, but his career continued to flourish.

He became the nation's attorney general in 1613, a member of the king's Privy Council in 1616, and lord chancellor—the highest position for a judge—in 1618. In quiet moments he continued to work on the *Great Instauration.* In the second part of this work, the famous *Novum Organum* (*New Tool,* 1620), he explains his theory of scientific method, particularly the need for subjecting hypotheses to empirical tests.

In 1621 came disgrace: Bacon was charged with having accepted a bribe, and he admitted his guilt. He served a short jail sentence and was stripped of public office. This sudden fall from power could have crushed Bacon's spirit, but it did not. He seized the opportunity to devote the last years of his life to his studies. By this time, the *Novum Organum* was known in learned communities throughout Europe, and Bacon corresponded with admiring foreign scholars. In addition, he continued to record his observations of natural phenomena, which can be found in the third part of the *Great Instauration,* titled *Sylva Sylvarum (The Wood of the Woods).* This collection of observations and records of scientific experiments was published the year after Bacon's death. It includes *The New Atlantis,* a utopian fable about a land called Bensalem, where people work together in service of "the knowledge of causes and secret motions of things; and the enlarging of the bounds of human empire, to the effecting of all things possible." Here, science is not the mental plaything of scholars but the useful tool of practical people who wish to improve the human condition.

Although the last two parts of the *The Great Instauration* were never written, Bacon achieved lasting recognition for his achievements in the philosophy of science. He describes himself in these words:

> Being gifted by nature with desire to seek, patience to doubt, fondness to meditate, slowness to assert, readiness to consider, carefulness to dispose and set in order.

It was this combination of gifts that made Bacon, according to his biographer Rosalind Davies, "a major figure in the intellectual tradition of Europe."

Works by Francis Bacon

Francis Bacon: The Major Works. Edited by Brian Vickers. New York: Oxford University Press, 2002.
The Advancement of Learning. Edited by Michael Kiernan. New York: Oxford University Press, 2000.

Works about Francis Bacon

Gaukroger, Stephen. *Francis Bacon and the Transformation of Early-Modern Philosophy.* New York: Cambridge University Press, 2001.

Jardin, Lisa, and Alan Stewart. *Hostage to Fortune: The Troubled Life of Francis Bacon, 1561–1626.* New York: Hill and Wang, 1999.

Balbuena, Bernardo de (1568–1627)
poet

According to Menéndez y Pelayo, the birth of Spanish-American poetry can be linked to Bernardo de Balbuena. Celebrating both Mexico and Spain in his poems, Balbuena draws on nature to display his overwhelming love for both countries. His greatest poem "El Bernardo" (1624) displays his feelings of the influence of poet Ludovico ARIOSTO and other Latin EPIC poets. Not an autobiography, "El Bernardo" focuses on the adventures of the famous Spanish hero Bernardo del Carpio. The poem also explores the constructions and oppositions that exist between the ideologies of the superior figure and that of the inferior figure (Nicolopulos).

Born in Val de Peñas, Spain, Balbuena moved at an early age with his parents to La Mancha, Mexico, where he spent his childhood and gained an education. As an adult, he served as the chaplain to the Audiencia of New Galicia for six years (until 1592) and, in 1620, was named the bishop of Puerto Rico. He died in Puerto Rico.

He composed most of his writings in the 1590s on frontier lands in the west of Mexico (Nicolopulos), but his "La grandeza mejicana" (1604) is thought by some scholars to mark the beginning of Spanish-American poetry. Another well-known and well-received poem, "Siglo de oro en las selvas de Eriphile" (1608), is "a very learned pastoral romance abounding in beautiful poetic passages" (Knight). All of Balbuena's works reveal the influence of the places he lived, his knowledge of classical poetry, and the inner visions of a master poet.

An English Version of Works by Bernardo de Balbuena

The Heroic Poem of the Spanish Golden Age. Edited by Frank Pierce. New York: Oxford University Press, 1947.

A Work about Bernardo de Balbuena

Van Horne, John. *El Bernardo of Bernardo de Balbuena: A Study of the Poem.* Urbana: University of Illinois, 1927.

Bamana Segu, Epic of (1700s–1800s)
African epic

The Bamana empire flourished around the upper Niger River, from the 17th century to the 19th century. Its capital was Segu, near Bamako, the present capital of Mali on northwest Africa. Segu saw the reigns of 19 kings before it was conquered in 1861–62 by the Muslim Tukulor army. The *Epic of Bamana Segu* tells the troubled story of the most memorable of these 19 kings: Mamani Biton Kulubaly (ca. 1712–55), Ngolo Jara (ca. 1766–87), Monzon Jara (ca. 1787–1808), and Faama Da Jara (1808–27). Of these, Kulubaly was the founder of the Segu empire, and most versions of the epic begin with his story and end with the ascension of the Jara dynasty and its demise. The epic is therefore a complex history of dynastic successions, wars, and family stories.

Also called the Segu cycle, the *Epic of Bamana Segu* is viewed by many scholars as a foil for the famous *Epic of Sundiata*. While *Sundiata* is about legitimate authority, the *Epic of Bamana Segu* is just the opposite and shows the darker side of power struggles. It is valued for the glimpse it provides into the history and oral literature of the Bamana empire.

See also EPIC; EPIC OF SONSAN OF KAARTA.

An English Version of the *Epic of Bamana Segu*

Johnson, John-William, et al., eds. *Oral Epics from Africa.* Bloomington: Indiana University Press, 1997.

Works about the *Epic of Bamana Segu*

Banbera, Tayiru. *A State of Intrigue, The Epic of Bamana Segu.* David C. Conrad, ed. London: Oxford University Press, 1990.

Belcher, Stephen. *Epic Traditions of Africa.* Bloomington: Indiana University Press, 1999.

Courlander, Harold, and Ousmane Sako. *The Heart of the Ngoni, Heroes of the African Kingdom of Segu.* New York: Crown, 1982.

Djata, Sundiata A. *The Bamana Empire by the Niger.* Princeton, N.J.: Markus Wiener Publishers, 1997.

Banks, Joseph (1743–1820) *nonfiction writer*

Joseph Banks was born in 1743 in London, the son of William Banks, a wealthy landowner, and Sarah Banks. He was educated at Harrow and Eton, and in 1760 entered Christ Church, Oxford. The classical curriculum, however, was not to his liking. His true passion lay in the study of botany, so he hired Israel Lyons, a botany instructor, to come to Oxford to educate him in the field. Banks became not only a botanist but also a patron of science.

At age 23, he traveled to Newfoundland and Labrador to collect plants, animals, and rocks. The same year he was elected to the Royal Society of London. His voyages allowed him to engage in what he loved most—discovering and collecting new botanical specimens. Such pursuits led to the start of the Banks Herbarium.

He embarked on his most famous voyage to Tahiti in 1768, aboard the *Endeavour* with the legendary Captain James Cook. Banks and his team collected more than 800 new specimens. He also immersed himself in Tahitian culture, learning the language and even getting a small tattoo. This voyage—and tales of his exploits—earned him much fame back in England.

His next and last voyage was to Iceland in 1772, and in 1778 he was elected president of the Royal Society, an office he held until his death in 1820. He also helped fund the journey of the infamous and mutinous *Bounty*.

Banks is known more for his scientific contributions and discoveries than for his writing, but he kept an extensive journal of his voyage with Cook, which was not published until 1962, when an edited version appeared. In addition to the journals,

Banks kept voluminous notes on his discoveries and pursuits, and engaged in large amounts of correspondence. His correspondents included Lord Nelson and Benjamin FRANKLIN, and his letters shed light on the age in which he lived, "an age in which geographical and scientific discoveries surpassed anything previously dreamt of" (Alexander, 41).

A Work by Joseph Banks
The Letters of Joseph Banks: A Selection, 1768–1820. Edited by Neil Chambers. London: Imperial College Press, 2000.

Works about Joseph Banks
Gascoine, John. *Science in the Service of Empire: Joseph Banks, the British State, and the Uses of Science in the Age of Revolution.* New York: Cambridge University Press, 1998.

O'Brian, Patrick. *Joseph Banks: A Life.* Chicago: University of Chicago Press, 1997.

Bartram, William (1739–1823) *naturalist, explorer, historian, illustrator*
Son of the noted botanist John Bartram, William Bartram is best known for his published account of his botanical expedition (1773–78) in the southeastern United States. Published in 1791, *Travels Through North and South Carolina, Georgia, East and West Florida, the Cherokee Country, the Extensive Territories of the Muscogulges, or Creek Confederacy and the County of the Chactaws,* is considered an American classic of language and science. Composed in elaborate prose, it contains comprehensive and entertaining descriptions of the flora and fauna, the geologic formations, and the Native American tribes of the southeastern United States. Many of the subjects illustrated represent the first record of an American plant or animal.

As a trained natural scientist, Bartram traveled through the South, nothing in detailed descriptions and illustrations the characteristics of almost everything he encountered. He portrays nature through personal experience as well as scientific observation. In addition to natural history subjects, he provides an account of southeastern Native Americans that is considered one of the best of the period.

Other significant writings attributed to Bartram include a manuscript titled *Pharmacopedia.* Three articles appearing in other publications include, "Anecdote of an American Crow," "Description of an American Species of Certhia, or Creeper," and "Account of the Species, Hybrids, and other Varieties of the Vine of North America."

In terms of literary influence, *Travels* is noted as a source for Samuel Taylor Coleridge's *Kubla Khan* and *The Ancient Mariner.* William Wordsworth, Thomas Carlyle, Ralph Waldo Emerson, and François-Auguste-René de Chateaubriand also considered the work with high regard. The book was an immediate success in Europe and was published in many editions and translations throughout the world. It is still considered a valuable record of discoveries in natural history.

A Work by William Bartram
William Bartram: Travels and Other Writings. New York: Library of America, 1996.

Works about William Bartram
Cashier, Edward J. *William Bartram and the American Revolution on the Southern Frontier.* Columbia: University of South Carolina Press, 2000.

Ewan, Joseph. *William Bartram: Botanical and Zoological Drawings, 1756–1788. Reproduced from the Fothergill Album in the British Museum (Natural History).* Philadelphia: American Philosophical Society, 1958.

Bashō (Matsuo Bashō, Matsuo Kinsakin, Matsuo Munefusa) (1644–1694) *poet*
Matsuo Kinsakin was born near Ueno, Japan, southeast of Kyoto. After changing names periodically during his childhood and young adulthood, as was customary at that time, Kinsakin took the name Bashō.

Bashō's father was a low-ranking samurai in the service of Tōdō Yoshikiyo, the ruling lord of Ueno. Bashō's mother's parents migrated to Iga province from Iyo province. As a boy, Bashō became a page at Ueno Castle and a study companion to young Yoshitada, the Tōdō family heir. Bashō and Yoshitada shared an interest in the Japanese poetry form HAIKU, and together they studied and published poetry. In 1666, Yoshitada died suddenly, leading Bashō to abandon his post at Ueno Castle to wander for several years. It is believed he went either to Kyoto to study literature, philosophy, and calligraphy or to a Kyoto monastery to become a Buddhist monk and study Zen. To support himself, he worked as a poet's scribe and took a number of other odd jobs. He later moved to Edo (now Tokyo) and continued to study, write, and publish haiku. This period of wandering was the first of many journeys and expeditions that he detailed in his writings.

By the time he was in his 30s, Bashō had established himself as an independent master and haiku. He spent the last 10 years of his life on pilgrimage, visiting famous places and meeting with other poets and disciples. He died of a stomach ailment at age 50, by which time he had taught poetry to nearly 2,000 students.

Bashō's haiku is known for its simple, unpretentious style and its honest, sincere treatment of his subject matter. Influenced strongly by Zen Buddhism, Bashō developed haiku from a form that relied largely on puns, slang, parody, and vulgar subjects to one that explored authentic human experience and perception through subtle but familiar images from nature. He is credited with establishing the 5–7–5 syllable pattern used in haiku to this day.

Although Bashō wrote many impersonal and sad haiku, he did not abandon the playful, light-hearted approach of his predecessors that made earlier varieties of haiku popular among the accessible to all classes of Japanese people in the 16th and 17th centuries. Through his command of language, experimentation, and talent, Bashō refined haiku and realized the form's potential. Since his

lifetime, haiku has remained an important form of poetry, and Bashō, a major poet.

Written when he was 42, Bashō's most famous poem exemplifies his mature style and typifies haiku in general:

> *The old pond;*
> *A frog jumps in—*
> *The sound of the water.*

In 1689, approximately three years after he wrote "The Old Pond," Bashō embarked on a two-year, 1,500-mile journey around Japan, traveling with friends, disciples, and fellow poets from Edo to Ogaki. His masterpiece, *The Narrow Road to the Deep North* (1977), is based on his experiences during this journey and combines both haiku and haiku-like prose. He opens the travel diary by professing his very personal vision of travel:

> The sun and the moon are eternal voyagers; the years that come and go are travelers too. For those whose lives float away on boats, for those who greet old age with hands clasping the lead ropes of horses, travel is life, travel is home. And many are the men of old who have perished as they journeyed.

He continues in the same poetic vein throughout *The Narrow Road,* using words to create soulful images of what lay in his heart. In the following lines, for example, a combination of Bashō's thoughts of ancient battles fought in Japan and his view of the landscape upon which those battles took place causes him to remark:

> Sitting on my sedge hat . . . , I wept for a long time.

> *A dream of warriors,*
> *and after dreaming is done,*
> *the summer grasses.*

During the three decades that he wrote poetry, Bashō elevated haiku from a game and pastime to a serious literary genre. His influence on writers from Charles-Pierre Baudelaire and Stéphane Mallarmé to Jack Kerouac and Amy Lowell demonstrates his strength as a writer and his universal and lasting impact and appeal.

English Versions of Works by Bashō

The Complete Basho Poems. Edited by Keith Harrison. Minneapolis, Minn.: Black Willow Press, 2002.

A Haiku Journey: Bashō's "Narrow Road to a Far Province." Translated by Dorothy Britton. New York: Kodansha America, 2002.

Narrow Road to the Interior, and Other Writings. Translated by Sam Humill. Boston: Shambhala Publications, 2000.

The Narrow Road to Oku. Translated by Donald Keene. New York: Kodansha America, 1997.

Works about Bashō

Downer, Lesley. *On the Narrow Road: Journey into a Lost Japan.* New York: Summit Books, 1989.

Ueda, Makoto. *Bashō and His Interpreters.* Palo Alto, Calif.: Stanford University Press, 1995.

———. *Matsuo Bashō.* New York: Kodansha International, 1983.

Beaumarchais, Pierre-Augustin Caron de (1732–1799) *dramatist*

Born in Paris, the young Pierre was brought up in his father's trade of watchmaking. At age 21, he became watchmaker to the king and, following his marriage to the widow of a court official, he took the name Beaumarchais from one of her properties. He led various careers as a musician, pamphleteer, businessman, and arms dealer to the colonies during the American Revolution. Throughout his life he was in and out of court, jail, and briefly, after the French Revolution, exile. Upon his return to Paris, he found both his fortunes and his health in decline, and died suddenly of a stroke at age 67.

Today Beaumarchais's reputation as a flamboyant character overshadows his reputation as a playwright. His first two plays, *Eugénie* (1767) and *The Two Friends* (1769), showed promise but were only modestly successful. In 1775 his new play *The Barber of Seville* opened to disappointing response and discouraging reviews. A few quick revisions led to a new version of the play running the next night, to a much warmer reception; audiences were delighted with the witty, inventive, scheming Figaro, who in fact somewhat resembled his creator. Difficulties with censors kept the sequel, *The Marriage of Figaro,* from appearing until 1784, but its success reinvigorated French drama and Beaumarchais's fortune. Following difficulties in his personal and professional life, however, his reputation began to suffer. *The Tartar* (1787) was a success, but *The Guilty Mother* (1792), the third in the Figaro series, was not considered up to the original's standards. The *Memoirs* Beaumarchais published of his early escapades exhibit brilliant writing, but after his troubles with the new republican government and later Napoleon, the French public did not find his second set of *Memoirs* as inspiring as the first.

After his death, Beaumarchais's fame was eclipsed when his two most original and intricate plays were turned into stunning operas: Rossini rewrote *The Barber of Seville,* and Mozart adapted *The Marriage of Figaro.* Nonetheless, biographer William Howarth calls Beaumarchais "the supreme all-rounder of his age: a man of action and ideas, of vision and achievement, of ambition and energy on a heroic scale."

An English Version of Works by Pierre-Augustin Caron de Beaumarchais

The Figaro Trilogy. Translated by David Coward. New York: Oxford University Press, 2003.

A Work about Pierre-Augustin Caron de Beaumarchais

Grendel, Frederic. *Beaumarchais: The Man Who Was Figaro.* New York: HarperCollins, 1977.

Bellay, Joachim du (ca. 1522–1560) *poet, scholar*

Joachim du Bellay was born in Anjou, the son of a gentleman farmer. His parents died when he was nine or 10 years old, and his brother René took care of him. From what he tells us in his poems, he seems to have been an unhappy child, and he was often ill.

As an adult, Bellay had a close friendship with Pierre de RONSARD. They studied together in Paris at the famous College de Coqueret, whose principal, Jean Dorat, inspired in them an enthusiasm for the literature of antiquity.

In 1549 Bellay published two works: *The Defense and Illustration of the French Language*, in which he states the principles of HUMANISM and calls for a renewal of French poetry, arguing that French should be treated as an equal to Latin and other languages; and a collection of poems titled *The Olive*, which presents a series of Petrarchan SONNETS.

In 1553 Bellay journeyed to Rome with his second cousin, Cardinal Jean du Bellay. During his time in Rome, Bellay became disenchanted, both with the cardinal and with Rome itself, which he found shockingly immoral. After returning to Paris in 1558, he began to pour his feelings into his poetry and created some of his best work, including *The Regrets* and *The Antiquities of Rome*. The poems in these collections reveal Bellay's leanings toward the elegiac and the satirical, as well as the influences of Ovid and Horace. His subjects include political machinations, moral and papal decadence, spiritual barrenness, and the hypocrisy of the French court.

Du Bellay is remembered for the high quality of his verse: his perfection of the sonnet form, imagery, rhythm, musical resonance, and his skillful use and knowledge of the power of language.

English Versions of Works by Joachim du Bellay

Lyrics of the French Renaissance: Marot, Du Bellay, Ronsard. Edited by Norman R. Shapiro. New Haven, Conn.: Yale University Press, 2002.
The Regrets. Translated by David R. Slavitt. Boston: Northwestern University Press, 2003.

Works about Joachim du Bellay

Hartley, David. *Patriotism in the Work of Joachim du Bellay: Study of the Relationship Between the Poet and France.* Lewiston, N.Y.: Edwin Mellen Press, 1993.
Keating, Clark L. *Joachim du Bellay.* New York: Twayne, 1971.
Tucker, Georges Hugo. *The Poet's Odyssey: Joachim Du Bellay and Les Antiquitez de Rome.* Oxford: Oxford University Press, 1991.

Bembo, Pietro (1470–1547) *poet*

Italian humanist and scholar Pietro Bembo is celebrated for his contribution to the development and standardization of the Italian language and for his dedication to pursuing the classical ideal. His education was provided primarily by his father Bernardo Bembo, an important political figure in Venice. Like his father, Bembo enjoyed much social, political, and religious notoriety. He was well favored by Lucrezia Borgia and respected by the powerful Medici family and the church. In 1513 he became secretary to Pope Leo X in Rome; in 1529 he was appointed historiographer of Venice; and in 1539 he was named a cardinal by Pope Paul III and so returned to Rome, where he later died.

Bembo was a master stylist of both Latin and Italian and revised his works several times. He modeled his Latin writings on Cicero and wrote the treatise on Italian grammar, *Prose della Volgar Lingua* (Prose in the vernacular, 1525). This treatise contributed to the regularization of the Italian language to that of the Tuscan dialect used by PETRARCH and BOCCACCIO.

Another Italian prose work for which Bembo is celebrated is *Gli Asolani* (1505), a story featuring a wedding feast at Asola, during which a revealing dialogue discussing Platonic love occurs. Bembo also wrote much poetry and edited the poems of Dante and Petrarch, to whom his poems are often compared.

Pietro Bembo's scholarship and his enthusiasm for the Italian language and his country (which was still developing a sense of nationality) significantly influenced many great writers and thinkers, including Ludovico ARIOSTO, Baldessare CASTIGLIONE, and Torquato TASSO.

English Versions of Works by Pietro Bembo

Gli Asolani. Translated by Rudolf B. Gottfried. Bloomington: Indiana University Press, 1954.

The Prettiest Love Letters in the World: Letters between Lucrezia Borgia and Pietro Bembo. Translated by Hugh Shankland. London: Collins Harvill, 1987.

Works about Pietro Bembo

Murphy, James J., and Izora Scott. *Controversies over the Imitation of Cicero in the Renaissance: With Translations of Letters between Pietro Bembo and Gianfrancesco Pico.* Mahwah, N.J.: Lawrence Erlbaum Associates, 1995.

Raffini, Christine. *Marsillo Ficino, Pietro Bembo, Baldassare Castiglione: Philosophical, Aesthetic, and Political Approaches in Renaissance Platonism.* New York: Peter Lang, 1998.

Bergerac, Cyrano de (1619–1655) *poet, dramatist*

Behind the character of the swashbuckling Cyrano de Bergerac of legend is a real-life, 17th-century Frenchman who was famous in his own time for his unusual nose, literary flair, contrary ideas, and reputation as a brilliant swordsman. Born in Paris as Savinien de Cyrano, the fourth son of Abel de Cyrano and Esperance Bellanger, he was first schooled under a private tutor and later at college in Paris. After joining a company of guards, Cyrano's misfortune in being severely wounded twice within 14 months persuaded him to take up the intellectual life. He returned to Paris and adopted the name de Bergerac after another family estate, which was later sold. He associated with a group of lively intellectuals, including MOLIÈRE, and developed a reputation for being brilliant and scandalous, having fought more than 100 duels. Although his premature death at age 35 was likely due to disease, legend has it that he suffered an accident with a falling wooden beam.

Later scholars accuse de Bergerac of plagiarizing much of his work, but it was the habit of intellectuals at the time to freely borrow from one another. He was thought even during his own lifetime to be somewhat mad; one anonymous contemporary said of his popular *States and Empires of the Sun and Moon,* "I think he had one quarter of the moon in his head." He was known for being a free-thinker, and his opinions often provoked controversy. Upon publication, many of his works were heavily censored, including various letters, his comedy *The Pedant Outwitted* (1645, a satire of teachers and their methods from which Molière later borrowed), and his TRAGEDY *The Death of Agrippina* (1653), which earned him literary acclaim. His tales of voyages to the sun and moon (*Moon* was written in 1648, and *Sun* begun in 1650, but never finished) are satires on existing social problems and contain some of his most clear and vigorous prose. A collection of his works titled *Different Works* was published in 1657, two years after de Bergerac's death, and does not include *The Other World* (written in 1650), perhaps because of his typical, yet original, satirical treatment of social ills. De Bergerac's friend Lebret published his own revision of *The Other World* in 1657, titling it *Comic History.*

While de Bergerac's works sank into obscurity in the 18th century, his legend remained, and it is the legend that Edmond Rostand (1868–1918) recovered in his memorable play *Cyrano de Bergerac* (1897).

An English Version of Works by Cyrano de Bergerac

Other Worlds: The Comical History of the States and Empires of the Moon and Sun. Translated by Geoffrey Strachan. London: New English Library, 1976.

Works about Cyrano de Bergerac

Chweh, Crystal R. *Readings on Cyrano de Bergerac.* San Diego, Calif.: Greenhaven Press, 2001.

Rostand, Edmond. *Cyrano de Bergerac.* Translated by Christopher Fry. New York: Oxford University Press, 1998.

Beverly, Robert (1673–1722) *historian*

Robert Beverly is remembered for his history of the state of Virginia, *The History and Present State of Virginia . . . by a Native of the Place,* first published in 1705. In contrast to the common patronizing tone in reference to the colonies that characterized British writings of the time, the work is distinguished from other early American books by an original style that does not attempt to duplicate an Oxford literary manner. The 1705 edition of *The History* is noted for its humor and acerbic sarcasm, particularly in its criticism of royal governors and lack of enterprise among Virginia planters. The book continues to be important because of Beverly's originality, shrewd observations, and humorous commentaries.

Although the historical material for the early years of the colony largely derives from the earlier published accounts of Captain John Smith and other chroniclers, the sections dealing with the Indians are considered to be of particular importance to history. Beverly links the freedom of the New World with the original Native American inhabitants.

In 1722 Beverly published a second edition of *The History,* considered to be less colorful and critical than the first edition. Along with the second edition, Beverly published *The Abridgement of the Public Laws of Virginia,* a work that he had compiled for his own use as a working magistrate.

The History is considered to be one of the major achievements of early American prose. Popular in its time, the book was translated into French and printed four times by 1718. Beverly's keen insight into contemporary political and social matters provides a valuable contribution to the study of American history.

A Work about Robert Beverly

Literary History of the United States: History, vol. 1, 3rd ed., rev. Edited by Robert E. Spiller, et al. New York: Macmillan, 1963.

Boccaccio, Giovanni (1313–1375) *poet*

Boccaccio was born to Boccaccino de Chelino, a Florentine banker, and an unidentified mother. Boccaccio himself spread the fiction that she was a well-born Parisian woman, but more likely she was from Certaldo. His father trained Boccaccio in the family business, and they moved to Naples in 1322, opening an exciting chapter in Boccaccio's life. At the time, Naples was a center of culture as well as business, and his place in his father's bank gave Boccaccio access to aristocratic circles, as well as to the royal library. He enrolled at the University of Naples to study canon law, beginning his training in Latin. In 1341 a change in the family fortunes obliged Boccaccio to return to Florence. The move was initially an unhappy one; Florence at the time was a middle-class city of bankers and as yet had no university, but Boccaccio's association with people from all walks of life gave him a supplementary education, which became as important to his poetry and prose as his formal studies.

In 1350, Boccaccio met PETRARCH, who had an enormous impact on Boccaccio's personal and intellectual life, and with whom Boccaccio shared an enduring friendship. In the late 1350s he took minor orders in the church. Having no patron to support his art, Boccaccio's fortunes were never secure, and he received occasional commissions from the Commune of Florence, which sometimes required him to travel as a city ambassador. Later in life he settled in Certaldo. With Boccaccio died the last of the "three crowns" of Italy—Dante and Petrarch being the others—who had given shape to Italian literature and launched a new humanism that would inform the RENAISSANCE.

As a reader, Boccaccio devoured books, making no distinctions between the classic and the middle-brow. His social interactions brought him into contact with a variety of cultures, from the French romance to the heritage of the Byzantines, through the Greek world with which Naples was in close contact. As a writer, he tried his hand at every genre, in Latin as well as in his native Italian. In the vernacular, his great inspiration was Dante; his first work in Italian, *Diana's Hunt* (1334), responds to a challenge in Dante's *New Life* and uses the terza rima form that Dante invented for the *Divine Comedy.* His other vernacular works include the *Filostrato* (1335), which means "one overcome by love" in Greek, and is an epic treatment of the love affair between Troilus and Cressida set within the Trojan War; *Filocolo* (1336), which means "weariness of love," and is a Byzantine romance describing the love affair of Florio and Biancifiore; and *Teseida* (1339), the story of the love of Palemone and Arcita for the beautiful Amazon Emilia. Boccaccio began *Teseida* as a martial EPIC, but the story becomes a romantic fiction as the two knights battle for Emilia's love. He also wrote *Comedy of the Florentine Nuns* (1341–42), an amusing, gossipy pastoral ALLEGORY, and *Love Vision* (1342–43), which uses some of the same characters and deals with love as an ennobling, transforming force.

Love was a popular theme that Boccaccio returned to repeatedly. In *Elegy of the Lady Fiammetta* (1343–44), he tells the story of the woman he called the great love of his life. He writes that he first saw Fiammetta in church on Easter Sunday. Historians, who have not been able to identify a real-life Fiammetta, suspect that Boccaccio modeled this experience on Petrarch's sighting of Laura. Other works inspired by Petrarch include *Fate of Illustrious Men* (written between 1355 and 1360) and *Famous Women* (1361).

The Nymphs of Fiesole (1344–46) is a pastoral fable that imaginatively describes the origins of the city of Fiesole, and *Corbaccio* (*Old Crow*, 1354) is a satirical dream vision. Boccaccio also continuously composed poetry between 1340 and 1375, collected in *Rime* (*Rhymes*).

He completed the encyclopedic *Genealogies of the Pagan Gods* and *The Life of Dante* in 1363. Over a span of years he wrote a series of *Eclogues* inspired by Virgil and Petrarch, which he finished in 1372.

The Middle Ages, in which Boccaccio lived, faced many crises within political, commercial, and ecclesiastic institutions. New cultural movements challenged existing thought; new social classes challenged the well-established hierarchies. Part of this environmental upheaval led to a lifelong feeling of insecurity on the part of the artist about his own fame and impact, but at the same time, it contributed an enormous energy to his work. Boccaccio's artistic gift was his ability to observe and render the detail that is life, and that in turn lends his stories a shimmering vitality.

Critical Analysis

The Decameron (1351) is Boccaccio's greatest work, and its influence spread quickly throughout Italy and across Europe. The story is a portrait of the age, disguised as a lesson in storytelling, disguised as a series of amusing tales. The book, whose title means "ten days" in Greek, collects the stories of 10 young aristocrats who set out on a journey from Florence to a country villa to avoid the Black Death, which infected Italy in 1348. The seven women and three men fill their time by singing songs and telling stories.

Boccaccio dedicates the book to those who are unhappy in love, but the stories' subjects range widely. The tales of the first day have no particular topic, which leads the group to adopt themes. The stories of the second and third day discuss whether humans are victims of fate or can occasionally control their destinies. The fourth and fifth days deal first with love as a destructive force, then as a constructive pursuit. The sixth day addresses the nature of storytelling and the power of language, while days seven and eight witness lively arguments on the subject of relations between men and women, leaving the ninth day open to different, related topics. The 10th day takes up the subject of liberality, rounding out the novel with 100 complete novellas.

One of the most remarkable things about *The Decameron* is the freedom of expression Boccaccio gives to the female characters. Literature previous to Boccaccio traditionally portrayed women as untouchable, practically inhuman models of virtue—witches or mischievous vixens who caused misery and sorrow. Some of Boccaccio's women represent these stereotypes, but most are independent, intelligent women who think and speak for themselves, as does Lady Filippa in story VI. 7, who challenges the law:

> . . . as I am sure you know, the laws should be equal for all and should be passed with the consent of the people they affect. In this case these conditions were not fulfilled . . . furthermore, when this law was put into effect, not a single woman gave her consent, nor was any one of them ever consulted about it; therefore, it may quite rightly be called a bad law.

This is a very forward-thinking argument, considering that Western women would not be given the right to vote until almost 500 years later. Though Boccaccio wrote about clever women in his work, he was known to discourage the women of his household from reading *The Decameron* so they would not be influenced to behave as freely as the female characters in the work.

Humor abounds throughout the book, perhaps as the only recourse for those left in the wake of a plague that destroyed a third of the population. For its variety of character, thrilling narrative style, and the vastness of its fictional world contained within stories of manageable size, scholar Thomas Bergin calls *The Decameron* "the most readable of all recognized masterpieces." Other scholars have criticized the book because it does not take up any debate about transcendent values, nor does it seek to teach a lesson about anything. But Boccaccio poignantly illustrates the fragility, fallibility, and basic decency of humanity in a world in which changing values brought morals into question and in which destiny was not preordained. Though occasionally accused of being rowdy in nature, *The Decameron* ultimately suggests that wisdom comes through humor and peaceful relations through tolerance.

It would be hard to overestimate the impact of Boccaccio's creative spirit. Translator Daniel Donno says, "Boccaccio reveals himself as the psychologist of the human heart." The sheer unbounded energy in his work, the tragedy and comedy portrayed side by side, make Boccaccio a monument in the history of literature.

English Versions of Works by Giovanni Boccaccio

Famous Women. Translated and edited by Virginia Brown. Cambridge, Mass.: Harvard University Press, 2001.

Life of Dante. Translated by F. G. Nichols. London: Hesperus Press, 2002.

Nymphs of Fiesole. Translated by Joseph Tusiani. Madison, N.J.: Fairleigh Dickinson University Press, 1971.

The Decameron. Translated by G. H. McWilliam. New York: Penguin, 2003.

The Elegy of Lady Fiammetta. Translated and edited by Mariangela Cause-Steindler and Thomas Mauch. Chicago: University of Chicago Press, 1990.

Works about Giovanni Boccaccio

Addington, John. *Giovanni Boccaccio as Man and Author.* New York: AMS Press, 1968.

Branca, Vittore. *Boccaccio: The Man and His Works.* Translated by Richard Monges. New York: New York University Press, 1976.

Hollander, Robert. *Boccaccio's Dante and the Shaping Force of Satire.* Ann Arbor: University of Michigan Press, 1997.

Kirkham, Victoria. *Fabulous Vernacular: Boccaccio's Filocolo and the Art of Medieval Fiction.* Ann Arbor: University of Michigan Press, 2001.

Boileau-Despréaux, Nicolas

(1636–1711) *poet, satirist, critic*

Nicolas Boileau-Despréaux was born into a family of well-off professionals in Paris. He studied at the college of Beauvais, originally for the priesthood, but then began to study law and was admitted to the bar in 1656. He never practiced, however, because his father died, leaving him a small inheritance that allowed him to devote himself full-time to writing poetry. In 1677, along with Jean RACINE, he was appointed historiographer to Louis XIV, and in 1684 was received as a member of the ACADÉMIE FRANÇAISE.

Boileau's first poems were popular satires on contemporary poets and writers. His tight, elegant style and belief that poetry should be both moral and instructive made him a friend of Pierre CORNEILLE and a proponent of NEOCLASSICISM.

Boileau's fame and critical influence increased when he published *The Art of Poetry* in 1674. This poem, written in four cantos, basically re-states viewpoints held by classical writers such as Aristotle and Horace. Boileau offers prospective poets pithy advice about choosing subjects for poetry, using language appropriate for the subject, and creating a heightened but true mirror of nature that readers will recognize and respond to emotionally. Boileau also used his poems to mock contemporaries whom he felt ignored the rules of decorum and style; he criticized Madeleine de SCUDÉRY for "making Cato a gallant and Brutus a beau." Boileau admired writers who emulated the ancient EPIC poets and dramatists in their observation of universal human nature and the UNITIES of time, place, and action.

Boileau's *Art of Poetry* was translated into several languages and influenced many European writers of the 17th and 18th centuries. The veneration of classical authors and models, the emphasis on sense and order, the straightforward yet elegant language that we associate with the ENLIGHTENMENT came about in part because of Boileau.

An English Version of Works by Nicolas Boileau-Despréaux

Nicholas Boileau-Despréaux: Selected Criticism. Translated by Ernest Dilworth. New York: Bobbs-Merrill, 1965.

Works about Nicolas Boileau-Despréaux

Colton, Robert E. *Juvenal and Boileau: A Study of Literary Influence.* Port Jervis, N.Y.: Lubrecht and Cramer, 1987.

———. *Studies of Classical Influence on Boileau and la Fontaine.* Hildesheim, Germany: Georg Olms, 1996.

Corum, Robert T. *Reading Boileau: An Integrative Study of the Early Satires, vol. 15.* West Lafayette, Ind.: Purdue University Press, 1997.

Book of Chilam Balam of Chumayel, The

THE BOOKS OF CHILAM BALAM consist of 14 books, of which portions of only eight remain, that record more than 1,000 years of Maya history and culture. *Chilam* means "prophet" or "interpreter of the Gods." *Balam,* meaning "jaguar," is the name of the *chilam* credited with cowriting *The Book of Chilam Balam of Chumayel,* one of the books included in *The Books of Chilam Balam.* Each book was written by more than one *chilam,* as the purpose of the books was not only to record events, but also to link past ages and events with the present. The stories in the books, therefore, manifested differently as time passed, changing as the storytellers changed, similar to the way in which fables, legends, and myths changed in the oral tradition.

Many towns in the Yucatán kept a record of the histories and prophecies of Balam. Chumayel was one of those towns. *The Book of Chilam Balam of Chumayel* was written in the Maya language, and its existing form was compiled by Don Juan Josef Hoil of Chumayel in 1782. The book records countless events of Maya history, including the Spanish conquest of the Yucatán in the 16th century; Maya mythology and religion; poetry; prophecies of Maya seers; and compositions on astrology and the Maya calendar.

The eight remaining *Books of Chilam Balam* are the most important original records of Maya culture available today for the historical and cultural information they provide.

English Versions of *The Book of Chilam Balam of Chumayel*

Heaven Born Merida and Its Destiny, The Book of Chilam Balam of Chumayel. Translated by Munro

Edmonson. Austin: University of Texas Press, 1986.

The Book of Chilam Balam of Chumayel. Translated by Ralph L. Roys. Norman: University of Oklahoma Press, 1967.

A Work about *The Book of Chilam Balam of Chumayel*

Leon-Portilla, Miguel, and Earl Shorris, et al. *In the Language of Kings: An Anthology of Mesoamerican Literature-Pre-Columbian to the Present.* New York: W.W. Norton, 2001.

Book of Dede Korkut, The   (800s?–1400s?)

The Book of Dede Korkut is a collection of stories that, together, form an epic story of the nomadic Oghuz people who lived in Central Asia before settling in what is now Turkey. *The Book of Dede Korkut* is composed of a prologue and 12 independent stories sharing characters and imagery. Generally the stories show Oghuz life and events in Central Asia in the ninth and 10th centuries, though some stories reference earlier events. These stories were handed down through the oral tradition by minstrels performing for chiefs, or khans, and the book as it exists today was most likely compiled during the mid-1400s.

The narration of the work is mainly in prose, but the passages of dialogue, which occupy about one-third of the text, are in intricately rhymed verse. The narrator is an unnamed minstrel who frequently addresses his audience as "my khan." In the prologue he introduces the audience to the sage Dede Korkut (Grandfather Korkut) and his wise sayings.

Korkut is presented as both an eyewitness to the events described and the author of many of the poetic passages. For example, after the dramatic action of the second story, "The Sack of the House of Salur Kazan," in which Salur Kazan and his allies avenge themselves on the infidels who captured Kazan's wife and other members of his household, it is Dede Korkut who praises the bittersweet victory:

> *Where now are the noble heroes who*
> *thought that the world was theirs? . . .*
> *To whom did the mortal world remain—*
> *The world where men come and go,*
> *The world which is rounded off by death?*

Since 1815 *The Book of Dede Korkut* has been translated into numerous languages. In his article "Whither Dede Korkut?" writer Alireza Asgharzadeh calls the *Dede Korkut* "an invaluable collection of epos and stories, bearing witness to the language, the way of life, religions, traditions and social norms of the peoples inhabiting different portions of Central Asia, Caucasia and the Middle-East centuries before the emergence of Islam."

English Versions of *The Book of Dede Korkut*

The Book of the Dede Korkut. Translated by Geoffrey L. Lewis. New York: Penguin, 1998.

The Book of Dede Korkut: A Turkish Epic. Translated and edited by Faruk Sümer, Ahmet E. Uysal, and Warren S. Walker. Austin: University of Texas Press, 1991.

A Work about *The Book of Dede Korkut*

Nerimanoglu, Kamil Veli. *The Poetics of "The Book of Dede Korkut."* Ankara, Turkey: Ataturk Culture Center Publications, 1999.

Bossuet, Jacques-Bénigne   (1627–1704)
orator, historian, clergyman

Jacques-Bénigne Bossuet was born in Dijon, in a family that had occupied judicial functions for centuries. His father was a judge in the *parlement* of Dijon. Educated by the Jesuits in his youth, Bossuet went to Paris in 1642 to study at the Collège de Navarre. He was ordained a priest and received a doctorate in divinity in 1652.

That same year he was appointed archdeacon of Metz in northern France. Metz had a large Protestant population, and Bossuet engaged in many polemics with Protestant leaders over religious matters. He also gained a reputation as an outstanding speaker. His sermons were well known throughout the area, and he often delivered sermons to powerful church and state figures in Paris as well.

Bossuet became the bishop of Condom in southwest France in 1669. He continued to have close ties with the French monarchy and Catholic Church leadership. Because of his oratorical abilities, Bossuet was asked to deliver funeral orations for important Catholic figures, such as Henrietta Maria, the widow of Charles I of England.

In 1670 Bossuet was hired by King Louis XIV to tutor his son, the Dauphin. Bossuet wrote books and manuals of politics, philosophy, and history with which to instruct his new pupil.

Bossuet felt that monarchy was the best form of government to advance the views of the church. He wrote several treatises to this end, including *Statecraft Drawn from the Very Words of the Holy Scriptures,* which uses scripture to provide proof of the divine right of kings.

Bossuet is celebrated for his eloquence and the poetic quality of his sermons and orations. His debates with Protestants and his crusading work to try to reintegrate Protestants into the Catholic Church are also key parts of his legacy. He is remembered as a staunch defender of the infallibility of the Catholic Church and the French monarchy, though many of his views are now seen as old-fashioned in light of reforms within the Catholic Church.

See also FÉNÉLON.

English Versions of Works by Jacques-Bénigne Bossuet

Discourse on Universal History. Translated by Elborg Forster and edited by Orest Ranum. Chicago: University of Chicago Press, 1976.
Politics Drawn from the Very Words of Holy Scripture. Translated by Patrick Riley. New York: Cambridge University Press, 1999.

Works about Jacques-Bénigne Bossuet

Chadwick, Owen. *From Bossuet to Newman.* New York: Cambridge University Press, 1987.

Reynolds, Ernest Edwin. *Bossuet.* Garden City, N.Y.: Doubleday, 1963.

Boswell, James (1740–1795) *biographer, journal writer, travel writer*

James Boswell was born in Edinburgh. His father, Alexander Boswell, was an important judge and laird (owner of a landed castle) and his mother, Euphemia Boswell, was descended from a branch of Scottish royalty. His father expected him to enter the legal profession; conflict with his father's expectations exacerbated the psychological depression that Boswell suffered from throughout his life. He died in London of progressive kidney failure on May 19.

Boswell studied at the University of Edinburgh from 1753 to 1759. In 1759 he took up the study of law at Glasgow, but soon ran away to London, where he acquired a lasting taste for both the literary life of the English capital and for its sensual delights.

After returning to Scotland in 1762, Boswell passed his exams in civil law. Rather than beginning his legal practice, he persuaded his father to allow him to return to London to seek a military appointment. It was during this visit that Boswell met Samuel Johnson. He records their meeting in his *Life of Johnson:*

> Johnson unexpectedly came into the shop; and Mr. Davies [the book store's owner] having perceived him through the glass-door in the room in which we were sitting, advancing towards us,—he announced his aweful approach to me, somewhat in the manner of an actor in the part of Horatio, when he addresses Hamlet on the appearance of his father's ghost, "Look, my Lord, it comes."

The allusion to Hamlet's ghost aptly captures the spirit of the relationship between the two men: Johnson would become a father-figure to Boswell, giving him advice and emotional support. In turn, Boswell became a disciple of Johnson, dedicating the last years of his life to composing his *Life of Johnson.*

During this same visit Boswell began keeping a personal journal, an activity he continued until his death. Had he written nothing else, he would figure importantly in British literary history for composing this rich and full account of 18th-century life. Boswell recorded all of his foibles and flaws, details of his irrepressible vanity, and his sexual appetite, offering an almost unparalleled access into the labyrinthine complexities of the human personality.

Beginning in 1764, Boswell traveled throughout Europe, striking up friendships with many well-known figures, including ROUSSEAU and VOLTAIRE. After returning from his travels, Boswell published his first important book, *An Account of Corsica* (1768). Johnson wrote of it: "I know not whether I could name any narrative by which curiosity is better excited, or better gratified."

Boswell established a legal practice in Scotland, residing at his ancestral estate at Auchinleck, although he made annual visits to London. In 1773 he and Johnson undertook a tour of the Scottish Highlands and later published very different accounts of the trip. Johnson's *A Journey to the Western Isles* (1775) objectively describes the life and manners of the Scottish country and people, while Boswell's *Journal of a Tour to the Hebrides* (1785) is a highly personal account. Its emphasis on conversation previewed the approach that Boswell would later take in his *Life of Johnson.*

Boswell's later years were clouded by his failure to establish a successful legal practice in England and by his increasing difficulties with alcoholism. After Johnson's death in 1784, Boswell began the massive undertaking of composing his friend's biography, closely assisted and encouraged by Shakespearean scholar Edmond Malone. The first edition of the book was published in 1791, to great acclaim, and was a heroic and successful attempt to preserve Johnson for posterity. Boswell records hundreds of pages of Johnson's conversation, thus offering the reader immediate access to Johnson's personality and living presence. In part, Boswell was simply fulfilling Johnson's own theory of biography, as set forth in *Rambler #60,* which advocates an impartial "display [of] the minute details of daily life." Nevertheless, in its historical context, Boswell's *Life* was daring and controversial for its frank revelation of Johnson's personal life. Though critics argue the accuracy of many details in the work, its proportionality, and its psychological development (or lack thereof), few contest Boswell's overall accomplishment. As Marshall Waingrow states, "No matter how many new facts are brought to light, Samuel Johnson will always be somebody's hypothesis, . . . [and no other hypothesis] has pleased so many, or is likely to please so long, as Boswell's."

Works by James Boswell

Journal of a Tour to Corsica and Memoirs of Pascal Paoli. New York: Turtle Point Press, 2002.
Life of Johnson. IndyPublish.com, 2002.

Works about James Boswell

Martin, Peter. *A Life of James Boswell.* New Haven, Conn.: Yale University Press, 2000.
Sisman, Adam. *Boswell's Presumptuous Task: The Making of the Life of Dr. Johnson.* New York: Farrar, Straus and Giroux, 2000.
Vance, John, ed. *Boswell's Life of Johnson: New Questions, New Answers.* Athens: University of Georgia Press, 1985.

Bradford, William (1590–1657) *colonial and religious leader*

William Bradford was born in Yorkshire, England. He joined a Separatist church in Scrooby at age 16, and three years later moved to Holland to avoid religious persecution from the Church of England. In Holland, he became a leader of the Scrooby Separatists and encouraged the church to establish a settlement in the Virginia colonies. In 1620 Bradford was among the 102 pilgrims who sailed for the

New World on the *Mayflower*. The ship landed on the shores of New England at Plymouth Rock on December 20, 1620.

Bradford was among the Pilgrims who drafted the Mayflower Compact (1620), a brief document that set out the Pilgrims' rights and duties under God and law, and helped to establish what is considered to be the first democracy in the American Colonies. After the death of the Plymouth colony's first governor, John Carver, in the spring of 1621, Bradford took over the leadership of the colony and remained at the center of government until his death. During this period, he was reelected as governor 30 times.

Though Bradford was essentially a colonial and church leader, not a writer, he produced one of the most important historical works of 17th-century America, *Of Plymouth Plantation*. This history, which he began in 1630 and eventually extended to two volumes, is a detailed account of the voyage of the *Mayflower,* the landing at Plymouth Rock, and the many hardships the Pilgrims faced while trying to establish their colony, including losing more than half of their inhabitants to sickness during the first winter. In its pages, Bradford also describes how the Pilgrims met Squanto, a Pawtuxet Native American interpreter who spoke English. Squanto helped them form an essential alliance with the local Wampanoag people, which played a crucial role in the colony's survival during its first brutal winter in the New World. Because the history was written as a record to be passed on to future inhabitants of the Plymouth Colony and not for wider publication, Bradford wrote in a simple manner, devoid of any unnecessary stylistic flourishes. His account is straightforward, personal, and readable. *Of Plymouth Plantation* remains the most important firsthand account of the early settlement of the American colonies available today.

A Work by William Bradford

Of Plymouth Plantation. Introduction by Samuel Eliot Morison. New York: Knopf, 2001.

Works about William Bradford

Anderson, Douglas. *William Bradford's Books: Of Plimmoth Plantation and the Printed Word*. Baltimore, Md.: Johns Hopkins University Press, 2003.

Westbrook, Perry D. *William Bradford*. Boston: Twayne, 1978.

Bradstreet, Anne Dudley (1612?–1672)
poet

The place of Anne Dudley's birth is unknown, but she grew up in Lincolnshire, England. Her father, Thomas, was steward to the earl of Lincoln. Dudley received an excellent education for a woman of the era; she had private tutors and was allowed to use the earl's large library. In 1628 she married Simon Bradstreet. Two years later, Anne and her husband and parents sailed for New England so they could openly practice their Puritan faith. When Bradstreet first saw New England, she was frightened by its wildness, but she came to believe that God had chosen this life for her.

Bradstreet and her husband had eight children. They moved around to various settlements in Massachusetts, finally settling in North Andover. Simon Bradstreet served twice as royal governor of Massachusetts.

Bradstreet wrote poetry for her own enjoyment and that of her family. She never intended her work to be published, but her brother-in-law, without her permission, published a volume of her poems in England in 1650, under the title *The Tenth Muse Lately Sprung up in America*. Bradstreet's early poems are conventional and give little indication that the author lived in the untamed wilderness of America. She is read today for her later work, which was published after her death. Her later poetry, more deeply felt and less conventional, focuses on Bradstreet's daily life as a settler; her emotions as she faces life's hardships, including the loss of the family home to fire and the dangers of childbirth; her religious beliefs; and nature. Addressing her husband during a pregnancy, Bradstreet writes:

How soon, my dear, death may my steps attend.
How soon't may be thy lot to lose thy friend.

Bradstreet was influenced by a number of poets, including Raleigh, Spenser, SIDNEY, and DONNE. Her most famous work is a poem titled "Contemplations" (1678) in which she ponders time's ability to destroy mortal things but not spiritual ones. In this poem, as in most of her later works—both verse and prose—Bradstreet reveals her wisdom, simplicity, and generosity.

Works by Anne Dudley Bradstreet

The Works of Anne Bradstreet. Edited by Jeannie Hensley. Cambridge, Mass.: Harvard University Press, 1981.

Works about Anne Dudley Bradstreet

Martin, Wendy. *An American Triptych: Anne Bradstreet, Emily Dickinson, Adrienne Rich.* Chapel Hill: University of North Carolina Press, 1984.

Rosenmeier, Rosamund. *Anne Bradstreet Revisited.* Boston: Twayne, 1981.

Brandt, Sebastian (1457?–1521) *poet*

Sebastian Brandt was born in Strasbourg on the cusp of the early German humanist movement. He called himself by the Latin name Titio, meaning "firebrand." He graduated in 1477 from the University of Basel, then an important center of humanist studies. In 1484 he received his license to teach and practice law, and in 1485 married Elisabeth Burg. In 1489 he earned his doctoral degree and in 1490 published his first books, a series of law texts. In 1501 Brandt moved back to Strasbourg. He served in various administrative positions in the city and as sometime-adviser to Emperor Maximilian. In 1514 he met the influential humanist scholar ERASMUS.

In his lifetime, largely during the period spent at Basel, Brandt wrote several Latin tracts and a collection of poems published as *Various Songs.* He translated many Latin classics into German, thus elevating the respect for literature in the vernacular. Brandt's most famous work, *The Ship of Fools* (1494), shows the moral and religious conviction of its author as well as his conservative point of view. The pure, unadorned style reflects Brandt's learning in both the Greek and Latin tradition and provides a cutting social commentary on human sins and foibles. Each chapter addresses a type of fool, united with the theme of the ship. The moral teachings of the work borrow largely from biblical and classical authorities, but the unique satire and biting humor make for entertaining reading. No one escapes the author's keen eye, including himself. In chapter 111, the "Apology of the Poet," he confesses: "Of folly I was never free, / I've joined the fool's fraternity." But, he adds, he hopes "That I'll improve in time through wit, / If God will grant such benefit."

Woodcuts illustrating each type of fool accompanied the text, which perhaps helped account for its popularity. Translator Edwin Zeydel calls *The Ship of Fools* "the most famous book of its time." Six editions came out in Brandt's lifetime, and the work was translated into Latin, French, English, Flemish, and Dutch. With this book, Zeydel says, "German literature entered for the first time into the stream of European letters."

An English Version of a Work by Sebastian Brandt

The Ship of Fools. Translated by Edwin H. Zeydel. New York: Dover, 1988.

A Work about Sebastian Brandt

Van Cleve, John. *Sebastian Brant's* The Ship of Fools *in Critical Perspective, 1800–1991.* New York: Camden House, 1993.

Bredero, Gerbrand (1585–1618) *poet*

Gerbrand Adriaensz Bredero was born in Amsterdam to a middle-class family. His father, Adriaen Cornelisz, was a shoemaker; his mother, Mary Gerbrand, supervised his education in English, French, and the classics. When he was very young his family lived next door to the meeting place of the Eglantine, the most prominent literary guild of the city, which attracted him to poetry. Poetry, however, was not a trade on which a Dutchman could subsist in the Netherlands; even Joost van den VONDEL had to support himself with a mercantile business. Bredero trained and worked as a painter. In 1611 he was invited to join the Eglantine but in 1617 left to join the Dutch Academy founded by his friend Simon Coster. Bredero died at age 33.

His first play *Rodderick and Alphonsus* appeared in 1611; *Griane* followed in 1612. His series of FARCES *The Farce of the Miller* (1612), *The Farce of the Cow* (1612), and *The Farce of Simon without Sweetness* (1612–13) show his key strengths, his ability for social satire, his eye for local color, and his ear for dialect. *Lucelle* (1613) was a romance with a traditionally imperiled heroine. His masterpieces were *The Little Moor* (1615) and *The Spanish Brabanter* (1617).

Translator H. David Brumble says *The Spanish Brabanter*, "if not the greatest play ever written in the Netherlands, is perhaps the most beloved." Brabant, now the northern part of Belgium, was a cultural center of the Dutch-speaking world. The play concerns the escapades of two rascals: Jerolimo, an ambitious but poverty-stricken Brabanter, and his servant Robbeknol. What the play lacks in narrative force it makes up for in character; its people vividly render the color and speech of daily life in early Amsterdam. Aside from its entertaining characters, the quick, lilting style of the writing preserves at least four Dutch dialects, conveying a true appreciation of the cultural diversity of the Amsterdam of Bredero's time.

An English Version of a Work by Gerbrand Bredero

The Spanish Brabanter. Translated by David H. Brumble III. Binghamton, N.Y.: Medieval and Renaissance Texts and Studies, 1982.

A Work about Gerbrand Bredero

Schama, Simon. *The Embarrassment of Riches: An Interpretation of Dutch Culture in the Golden Age.* New York: Vintage, 1997.

Brown, Charles Brockden (1771–1810)
novelist

The writer known as the father of American literature was born in Philadelphia to Elijah Brown, a merchant, and Mary Armitt. Brown's parents sent their son to the Friends Latin School, where he gained a basic knowledge of Latin and Greek. Although he was being groomed to become a lawyer, Brown found himself captivated by the writings of Jean-Jacques ROUSSEAU and Samuel RICHARDSON and decided to pursue a literary career.

Brown was one of the first American authors to make a living by writing. After *Alcuin: A Dialogue* (1798) became a success, he composed the Gothic novels *Edgar Huntly* (1799), the two-volume *Arthur Mervyn* (1799–1800), and *Ormond* (1799). He also edited a series of periodicals and pamphlets and planned a work of geography, never completed.

Wieland; or, The Transformation: An American Tale (1798), Brown's most popular novel, tells the disturbing tale of how the lives of Theodore and Clara Wieland are altered when Carwin, a ventriloquist, appears in their small town. Having been raised to believe in the existence of a divine ruler, Theodore and Clara mistake Carwin's voices for the voice of God, and Theodore eventually imagines he has been ordered to destroy his entire family.

Brown's intentions for his novels are just as important as the plots he devised. While some critics dismissed the novel as a genre potboiler about love and seduction, Cathy N. Davidson observes that Brown wanted to demonstrate the "intellectual benefits of novel reading." In *Wieland*, according to Clark, he dramatizes the "evil effects" that "credulity and superstition" have on the mind and raises but does not resolve basic questions. Michael T. Gilmore notes that we are left wondering, "How do we know something?" and "What constitutes trustworthy evidence?" In addition to offering cutting comments on social ills that provoke outrage and call for reform, the troubling questions of Brown's works anticipate the psychological realism that developed in American literature in the following century.

Works by Charles Brockden Brown

Three Gothic Novels. New York: Library of America, 1998.

Works about Charles Brockden Brown

Clark, David Lee. *Charles Brockden Brown: Pioneer Voice of America.* New York: AMS Press, 1966.
Davidson, Cathy N. *Revolution and the Word: The Rise of the Novel in America.* New York: Oxford University Press, 1986.

Bruno, Giordano (Filippo Bruno, Giordano Nolano) (1548–1600)
philosopher

The son of a soldier, Giovanni Bruno, and Fraulissa Savolino, Bruno was christened Filippo in the town of Nola, Italy. He took the monastic name Giordano in 1565, when he entered the monastery of San Domenico in Naples. There his brilliance and his progressive thought brought him to the attention of the Inquisition, and he was expelled from the monastery. In 1576 Bruno fled Italy, and over the next 16 years he lived in France, England, and Germany, where he wrote, taught, and gave lectures. He returned to Italy in 1591 and was arrested the following year. Two years later, he was convicted of heresy and was later burned at the stake.

Bruno produced a voluminous body of work in both Italian and Latin. The most influential of these are philosophical dialogues written in Italian between 1583 and 1585, while he was living in England: *The Expulsion of the Triumphant Beast; The Heroic Frenzies; Cause, Principle, and the One; The Infinite Universe and Worlds; The Ash Wednesday Supper;* and *The Cabal of the Horse Pegasus.*

Bruno's style is infused with his personality and reveals why he was so often forced to escape apparent safe havens. He had absolutely no patience for people with whom he disagreed. Many passages ridiculing his adversaries are sprinkled throughout his prose. In *The Ash Wednesday Supper* (1584), for instance, he refers to Andreas Osiander (who wrote the preface to the first edition of Nicolaus COPERNICUS's famous scientific tract) as "That idiot, who so mightily feared that one could be driven mad by the teaching of Copernicus!" In contrast, Bruno elevates himself in the preface to *The Ash Wednesday Supper* when he claims his readers "will be astonished that such great things will be completely explained so succinctly." Despite his quarrelsome and arrogant personality, Bruno's philosophical thought was profound and his beliefs revolutionary. His insistence that freedom of thought is necessary to advance human knowledge, his acceptance of the Copernican theory, and his proposal that the universe is infinite were controversial beliefs in his time, and his writings about them eventually led to his death.

Bruno's cosmology or theories of how the universe works were based on the work of Copernicus, but greatly expanded upon them. Bruno was a theoretical philosopher rather than a scientist, and many of his beliefs rest on his ideas about God rather than on an understanding of the physical universe. Bruno's most famous and most dangerous theory was his belief in an infinite universe. It would be blasphemous, Bruno reasoned, to think God, an infinite being, could be confined to a finite universe. His reasoning opened a door to many questions about other traditional foundations and beliefs. The speakers of Bruno's dialogues advocate free-thinking and an ethical standard based on scientific principles, rather than on what Bruno considered as outdated morality. The senses, Bruno taught, were not the limit but rather the starting point of knowledge, and reason must be used to learn things the senses could not comprehend. In accord with this, human virtue rested within human intellect and not as some external state of perfection. In addition, Bruno believed that ethical standards must be based on a process of critical thought, not on fear of punishment by a monitoring, measuring God.

Bruno's beliefs upset church authorities because traditional theology rested on the idea that humans were the center of the universe. In medieval cosmology, the world was a hierarchy, with God as the judge and benefactor of all. Bruno's theories shattered the long-held distinction between celestial and terrestrial, threatening the basis of ethical rules and the very nature of human identity in a way the Inquisition could not condone. Bruno's execution for heresy led many later thinkers to treat his beliefs with skepticism, and only in the last century has a truer understanding of Bruno's philosophy evolved. He was the first staunch defender of Copernicus and the first to depart significantly from the teachings of Ptolemy and Aristotle, important authorities during the Middle Ages and the RENAISSANCE. His cosmology led the way for the work of Galileo and his philosophical beliefs and anticipated the work of SPINOZA and René DESCARTES.

English Versions of Works by Giordano Bruno

Cause, Principle and Unity and Essays on Magic. Translated by Robert D. Lucca and Richard J. Blackwell. New York: Cambridge University Press, 1998.

The Expulsion of the Triumphant Beast. Translated by Arthur D. Imerti. Lincoln: University of Nebraska Press, 1992.

Works about Giordano Bruno

Gatti, Hilary. *The Renaissance Drama of Knowledge: Giordano Bruno in England.* New York: Routledge, 1989.

White, Michael. *The Pope and the Heretic: The True Story of Giordano Bruno, the Man Who Dared to Defy the Roman Inquisition.* New York: Harper-Collins, 2003.

Bunina, Anna (1774–1829) *poet*

Anna Bunina's childhood and adult life were not carefree. She was the last of six children. Her mother died giving birth to her, and Bunina was sent to live with her mother's sister. For many years afterward, she alternated living with her older sisters and aunts.

No matter the elegance of the home in which she lived, Bunina's education was ignored. When her father died, she remedied her neglected edu-

cation by using her small inheritance to move to St. Petersburg and hire tutors. She describes her first attempts at writing as similar to "imitating the bees in the garden": ". . . I seem this very moment / To see those little bees! / The beauty flies! She seems all gold" (Rosslyn 17).

Bunina's writing is extremely important for its relation to the position and struggles of women and to historical developments involving women's roles in Russia. Her poetry offers "rare insight into the generally-ignored female experience of her culture" before the affects of romanticism had occurred in Russia (Rosslyn xiii).

What is perhaps the greatest surprise about Bunina is that she was one of the first writers (male or female) to financially survive by writing. She was not wealthy, and she often struggled to make ends meet, but she succeeded because she "wrote with originality, put translation and imitation to her own purpose, [and] presented a specifically feminine and individual image of the creative writer" (Rosslyn xiii).

Though unaccepted by literary authorities of the time and little studied until the late 20th century, it is undeniable that Bunina had literary talent. She also perceived the social plight of women long before it became a social debate. Bunina "introduced her biography into her poems. Not all are autobiographical or introspective, but many are presented as the poet's subjective, even confessional, writing" (Rosslyn xiv).

Works about Anna Bunina

Rosslyn, Wendy. *Anna Bunina (1774–1829) and the Origins of Women's Poetry in Russia.* Studies in Slavic Language & Literature, vol. 10. New York: Edwin Mellen Press, 1997.

Tomei, Christine D., ed. *Russian Women Writers,* vols. 1–3. New York: Garland Publishing, 1999.

Bunraku (1700s)

Bunraku is a traditional form of Japanese puppet theater. The earliest appearance of puppet theater in Japan occurs in the 12th century, when wandering performers put on one-person puppet shows. Later puppet theater appeared at Shinto shrines and may have been used for religious purposes. In the 16th century, at a shrine in Nishinomiya, puppeteers performed plays depicting legends of the god Ebisu, and these became so well renowned the puppeteers were invited to the palace to perform for the emperor. Also around the same time, the performances of *jōruri*, traveling troubadour-like narrators who played the *biwa* (Japanese lute), became prevalent. The term *jōruri* comes from a 15th-century legend about a princess of the same name.

In 1684 the chanter Takemoto Gidayu opened a puppet theater in Osaka and became a patron of CHIKAMATSU MONZAEMON, who is known as the greatest *jōruri* playwright. Chikamatsu's influence on *jōruri* marks a shift from performances of historical legends and myth to portrayals closer to the everyday life of his audience. After Chikamatsu's death in 1725 and until about 1780, *jōruri* enjoyed a period of unsurpassed popularity, which waned sharply toward the end of the 18th century. Puppet theater, however, underwent a revival at this time. The term *bunraku* is a product of this revival and was named for Uemura Bunrakuken, a puppeteer from Awaji who began producing puppet plays in Osaka.

At the peak of its popularity, Bunraku puppet plays offered a freshness and creativity that rivaled KABUKI theater. Chikamatsu Hanji, a playwright and narrator writing in the 1770s, was known for his storylines featuring complicated relationships and wildly improbable happy endings. Several bunraku plays endure as classics and are still performed in Japanese theaters today. In addition, bunraku theater greatly influenced the productions of renowned director Julie Taymor, who directed the Broadway play *The Lion King*.

English Versions of Bunraku

Four Major Plays of Chikamatsu. Translated by Donald Keene. New York: Columbia University Press, 1961.

Gerstle, Andrew C., Kiyoshi Inobe, and William Malm. *Theater as Music: The Bunraku Play "Mt. Imo and Mt. Se."* Ann Arbor: University of Michigan, 1990.

Works about Bunraku

Adachi, Barbara C. *Backstage at Bunraku: A Behind-the-Scenes Look at Traditional Japanese Theater.* New York: Weatherhill, 1985.

Hironaga, Shuzaburo. *Bunraku Handbook: A Comprehensive Guide to Japan's Unique Puppet Theater, with Synopses of All Popular Plays.* Tokyo: Maison des Arts, 1976.

Cabeza de Vaca, Álvar Núñez
(ca. 1490?–1559?) *explorer*

Cabeza de Vaca was born in Jérez de la Frontera in Spain. Almost nothing is known of his childhood or early adult life. Around age 37, he sailed with Pánfilo de Narváez to Florida, to become one of only four men who survived the expedition. He wandered throughout Florida and Mexico for nine years, from 1527 to 1536, during which time he was taken captive by the Indians. His written account of his experiences is considered to be one of the best accounts of early American exploration. *Naufragios y relación de la jornada que hizo a la Florida con el adelantado Pánfilo de Narváez* was first published in Spain in 1542. Modern translations include C. Covey's 1962 edition, *Adventures in the unknown interior of America,* and the 2003 National Geographic Adventure printing of *The Narrative of Cabeza de Vaca.*

La relación is remarkable for its descriptions of the geography and the indigenous peoples of North America. The descriptions are related through the eyes of a Spaniard who survived by acculturation to the native societies. The work is also important because in it Cabeza de Vaca defends the natives against abuse by Spanish conquistadors, which he witnessed on the northern frontiers of New Spain. As a narrative of suffering and privation, Cabeza de Vaca's account has no equal in the annals of North American exploration.

Cabeza de Vaca later became governor of Paraguay (1540–45). His experience in Paraguay was filled with conflict due to resentment from enemies who objected to his generous attitude toward the Indians. After he was sent back to Spain in chains in 1545, he wrote a bitter account of the experience, *Los commentarios,* with the help of his secretary Pedro Hernández in 1554. *Los commentarios* was published together with an edited version of *La relación* in Valladolid in 1555.

English Versions of a Work by Álvar Núñez Cabeza de Vaca
Narrative of Cabeza de Vaca. Translated and edited by Rolena Adorno and Patrick C. Pautz. Lincoln: University of Nebraska Press, 2003.
The Journey and Ordeal of Cabeza de Vaca: His Account of the Disastrous First European Exploration of the American Southwest. Translated by Cyclone Covey. Mineola, N.Y.: Dover, 2004.

Works about Álvar Núñez Cabeza de Vaca
Menard, Valerie. *Alvar Núñez Cabeza de Vaca.* Hockessin, Del.: Mitchell Lane Publishers, 2002.

Rodriguez, Alfred. *Plus Ultra: Life and Times of Alvar Núñez Cabeza de Vaca.* Lincoln, Neb.: iUniverse, 2001.

Cacamatzín of Texcoco (1494–1520)
poet, ruler

Cacamatzín was born into the most famous family in Texcoco (in present-day Mexico). His father, Nezahualpilli, served as a ruler of Texcoco and was also a skilled poet, architect, and observer of stars. Cacamatzín's uncle was Montezuma, the powerful ruler of Tenochtitlán, the center of the Aztec Empire. Cacamatzín attended the *calmecac,* or priestly school, in Texcoco. He was also instructed in the arts of war by his father and other military leaders.

After Nezahualpilli's death in 1515 and after Montezuma intervened on his behalf, Cacamatzín was chosen as the ruler of Texcoco over his half brother, Ixtlilxochitl. This decision caused a split in Texcoco politics. Ixtlilxochitl left the kingdom and gathered an army with which to challenge Cacamatzín's sovereignty. Montezuma again stepped in with his army to help Cacamatzín retain power in Texcoco.

The arrival of the Spanish explorer Hernán CORTÉS in Mexico added to the intrigue that plagued Cacamatzín's brief life as ruler. When Cortés and his men entered Tenochtitlán in late 1519, Cacamatzín was imprisoned with Montezuma and others. His plight worsened when Cortés left and Pedro de Alvarado, a particularly brutal Spanish leader, assumed command of Tenochtitlán. Cacamatzín was bound and tortured with burning coals. He later witnessed the Spanish massacre of nobles, priests, and unarmed warriors at the traditional indigenous feast of Toxcatl. Cacamatzín gave voice to these horrors in his poetry, when he wrote "A mist wraps round the song of the shields, / over the earth falls a rain of darts." The few poems of Cacamatzín that remain in existence were written during the last days of his life. He was either hanged or fatally stabbed when the Spanish left Tenochtitlán in 1520. His poems, "Cacamatzín Icuic," or "Songs by Cacamatzín," are a record of his brief life as a ruler and poet at the end of the Aztec era.

A Work about Cacamatzín of Texcoco
León-Portilla, Miguel. *Fifteen Poets of the Aztec World.* Norman: University of Oklahoma Press, 1992.

Calderón de la Barca, Pedro
(1600–1681) *playwright, poet*

Calderón de la Barca was born in Madrid, the third of six children, to a noble family of modest fortune. Destined by his father to become a priest, he attended the prestigious Imperial Jesuit College in Valladolid, where he began studying literature and theology. He completed his studies at the University of Salamanca, but after the death of his parents abandoned his ecclesiastical career and began writing.

Calderón de la Barca began writing plays in 1623, which were performed at the royal court in Madrid. Over the next few years, he wrote numerous other theatrical works, including comedies, tragedies, and religious pieces. Calderón de la Barca quickly developed notoriety if not fame in the Spanish capital not only for his writing, but also for his nonliterary activities. He inspired, for example, the animosity of the illustrious playwright LOPE DE VEGA CARPIO by breaking into the convent where the latter's sister resided in pursuit of a comic actor who had wounded Calderón de la Barca's brother. Moreover, his parodies of clergymen in his plays resulted in the condemnation of his work by prominent religious figures.

Controversies aside, the decade between 1630 and 1640 was the most productive for Calderón de la Barca and probably the most crucial in terms of his development as a playwright. During this time, he produced his best and most representative works, including his masterpiece *La vida es sueño* (*Life Is a Dream,* 1636). The play recounts the story of Segismundo who, after being shut away in a tower by his father, King Basilio, breaks out of his prison and rises to power. In this play many of the themes essential to Calderón de la Barca's work and the drama of the Spanish Golden Age in general find their most moving expression, including the nature of reality and fantasy, the damaging effects of human pride and honor, and humankind's struggle for freedom against the forces of nature and destiny.

After participating and being wounded in military campaigns, Calderón de la Barca began writing again after 1640 and resumed his religious career. He continued these religious and literary activities until his death four decades later, composing a prolific number of dramas.

For his mastery of various verse forms, moving depiction of human struggles, and original exploration of existential themes, Calderón de la Barca remains one of the most important figures of Spanish literature. His influence has spread beyond the confines of his native country, and he has both directly and indirectly helped shape Western drama and literature over the past four centuries.

An English Version of Works by Pedro Calderón de la Barca

Six Plays. Translated by Edwin Honig. New York: Iasta, 1995.

A Work about Pedro Calderón de la Barca

Hesse, Everett Wesley. *Calderón de la Barca.* New York: Twayne, 1967.

Calvin, John (1509–1564) *theologian, religious leader, reformer*

Born in Noyon, France, Jean Cauvin (John Calvin is the anglicized form of his name) was the son of a middle-class Catholic lay administrator. Calvin was educated at the University of Paris with the intent to become a priest. However, after his father had a break with church authorities, Calvin was sent to study law in Orléans from 1528 to 1531. He remained very interested in theological study and, after his return to Paris in 1531, he became part of a radical student movement that called for reform in the Church. Calvin began to study Greek, Hebrew, and Latin in order to make a seri-

ous analysis of the scriptures and classical texts. In 1532, he published his first work, *Commentary on Lucius Anneas Seneca's Two Books on Clemency.*

Calvin gradually began to move toward Protestantism as a result of his association with Nicolas Cop and other reformers at the University of Paris. However, because of his involvement with the reform movement, Calvin was forced to leave Paris. He made his way to Basel, Switzerland, a Protestant city, where he began to systematically study theology. In Basel, he began to write his most influential work, *Institutio Christianae Religionis,* or *Institutes of the Christian Religion.* This work was a commentary on the Bible and a response to critics of Protestantism. The work outlined what would become the fundamentals of Calvinism: the doctrine of predestination, which proposed that people can be saved only by God's grace, not by good works, and that God grants salvation only to the chosen, or elect; the literal truth of the Bible; and the idea of a church community where God is at the head and all other members are equal. Calvin revised and expanded the *Institutes* many times throughout his life. The first edition was published in 1536; Calvin's final edition was published in 1560.

The publication of the *Institutes* gained Calvin fame among Protestant reformers and led to his settlement in Geneva to help establish Protestantism. Calvin quickly became a Protestant leader but was forced into exile in 1638 by Geneva's town council with whom he had clashed over the right of excommunication.

After three years in the city of Strasbourg, Calvin was invited back to Geneva, where the town council had become more amenable to his brand of Protestantism. His religious reforms, known as the *Ecclesiastical Ordinances* (1641), were quickly instituted. These ordinances included compulsory religious education and his ideal of a church community founded on the equality of all members. The city enforced Calvinist morality, which included bans on gambling, dancing, and swearing. The religious zeal of Calvinist Geneva reached a peak in 1553, when the Spanish theologian

Michael Servetus was burned at the stake for preaching unorthodox beliefs.

During this time, Calvin authored extensive commentaries on books of the Bible. He first published a commentary on Romans in 1539, followed by the other letters of St. Paul and the remaining New Testament books, excluding Revelation and most of the Old Testament books. Other works include *The Harmony of the Three (Synoptic) Gospels* (1563) and *Sermons on Job.*

Calvin's legacy remains undiminished to this day. He is generally considered to be the most important Protestant reformer other than Martin LUTHER. His writings on church organization and his commentaries on the books of the Bible are still important theological works that have influenced Protestant churches throughout the world.

English Versions of Works by John Calvin

Calvin's Commentary on Seneca's De Clementia. Translated by Ford Lewis Battles and Andre Malan Hugo. Leiden: E.J. Brill, 1969.
Institutes of the Christian Religion, 2 vols. Translated by John Allen. Philadelphia: Presbyterian Board of Christian Education, 1928.
On the Christian Faith: Selections from the Institutes, Commentaries and Tracts. Edited by John T. McNeill. Indianapolis, Ind.: Liberal Arts Press, 1957.

Works about John Calvin

Bouwsma, William J. *John Calvin: A Sixteenth-Century Portrait.* New York: Oxford University Press, 1989.
Breen, Quirinus. *John Calvin: A Study in French Humanism,* 2nd ed. Hamden, Conn.: Archon Books, 1968.
Walker, Williston. *John Calvin: The Organizer of Reformed Protestantism.* Eugene, Ore.: Wipf and Stock, 2004.

Camões, Luíz Vaz de (Camoëns)
(1524?–1580) *poet, playwright*

The details of Camões's life are not fully clear, though it is known that he was born in Portugal to a family from Galicia. After studying at Coimbra University, he moved to Lisbon in 1543. He fought abroad as a soldier for some time, losing an eye in Morocco, and eventually enlisted for service in India. He lived in Asia, from India to the China Seas, for 17 years, a number of which were spent at the Indian seaport of Goa.

When he returned to Portugal in 1570, he brought with him the manuscript for *Os Lusíadas* (published 1572), an EPIC poem dedicated to the young king Sebastian of Portugal. The poem, which celebrates the nation of Portugal, earned him royal accolades and a pension too small to support him. He lived his remaining years in poverty and died heartbroken on June 10, when Philip II of Spain invaded Camões's beloved homeland.

Camões's poetry, including odes, satires, SONNETS, epigrams, and elegies, was not substantially published under his name until 1595 in the collection *Rimas.* He was also the author of multiple comedies, including *Amphitriões* (in which he adapts works by Plautus) and *Filodemo,* but his goal was to write a national epic, and to this end the hero of his epic poem is not a man, but a nation. *Os Lusíadas,* written in ottava rima, describes the story of Vasco da Gama's voyage throughout the world, relating many of the adventures he encountered and serving as a record of many main events in Portuguese history. Da Gama, however, is not the hero of the poem but represents the country of Portugal. His exploits are intended to emphasize different aspects of the glory of is homeland. Camões's true love for his country is obvious in the depth of feeling he brings to his writing.

The structure of *Os Lusíadas* is based on Homer's *Aeneid.* The epic is peopled by such characters as Fate, Venus, Mars, Bacchus, Mercury, Neptune, Hindu chiefs, and the Nereids. At the beginning of the story, the gods hold a meeting to discuss the fate of da Gama's voyage. The various godly personages weave in and out of da Gama's extensive journey, appearing throughout the world as he travels. In part two of the first book, Camões begins with a statement about the grand and sweeping nature of the narrative he is about to tell, writing that "My song shall sow through the world's every part."

Over the years, Camões's work has been very influential on poets of the English-speaking world. He was a major influence on MILTON, Poe, Melville, Wentworth, and Dickinson. VOLTAIRE was known to call him the "Portuguese Virgil." Camões's appeal was wide and deep, making his relative obscurity today somewhat surprising—many of his works have not been translated into English, and many translations are out of print. Nevertheless, Camões is remembered for having developed the Portuguese lyric to the highest levels of beauty and style and for his influence on the development of Portuguese drama.

English Versions of Works by Luíz Vaz de Camões

"Dear Gentle Soul." Translated by Roy Campbell in *World Poetry: An Anthology of Verse from Antiquity to Our Time.* Edited by Katharine Washburn and John S. Major. New York: Quality Paperback Book Club, 1998.

The Lusiads. Translated by Sir Richard Fanshawe. Carbondale: Southern Illinois University Press, 1963.

The Lusiads of Luíz de Camões. Translated by Leonard Bacon. New York: Hispanic Society of America, 1950.

Works about Luíz Vaz de Camões

George, Monteiro. *The Presence of Camões: Influences on the Literature of England, America and Southern Africa.* Lexington: University of Kentucky Press, 1996.

Thorlby, Anthony, ed. *The Penguin Companion to Literature 2, European.* Middlesex, England: Penguin Books, 1969.

Campanella, Tommaso (1568–1639)
philosopher, theologian

Tommaso Campanella is one of the main intellectuals of the Italian RENAISSANCE. Born in the region of Naples, his real name was Giovan Domenico, and his father was an illiterate cobbler. Campanella entered the Dominican order in 1582, where he adopted the name "Tommaso."

Campanella was very interested in medicine and philosophy, avidly reading Plato, Galen, and Hippocrates. Among his other major influences are Averroës and St. Thomas Aquinas. The intellectual atmosphere in Naples at the time allowed him to come in contact with a diverse range of topics, such as astrology, magic, and mysticism.

His opposition to Aristotle is at the center of Campanella's philosophy. In his masterpiece, *The City of the Sun* (1602), he bases his reasoning on Plato and criticizes Aristotle. The poem, published in 1623, takes the form of a dialogue in which Campanella juxtaposes the justice of a utopian city with communist ideals.

In 1599, Campanella led a peasant revolt in Calabria, for which he was arrested and incarcerated. He spent 27 years in prison, during which time he was tortured and after which he was exiled and went to Paris, where he died.

Campanella wrote most of his works while in prison. While his works are complex and often ambiguous, Campanella is remembered for his metaphysical lyrical poetry and his numerous treatises on astronomy, theology, and rhetoric.

See also Giordano BRUNO; Galileo GALILEI.

English Versions of Works by Tommaso Campanella

The City of the Sun: A Poetical Dialogue. Translated by Daniel John Donno. Berkeley: University of California Press, 1982.

The Defense of Galileo. Translated and edited by Grant McColley. New York: Arno Press, 1975.

Works about Tommaso Campanella

Bonansea, Bernardino M. *Tommaso Campanella: Renaissance Pioneer of Modern Thought.* Washington, D.C.: Catholic University of America Press, 1969.

Headley, John. *Tommaso Campanella and the Transformation of the World.* Princeton, N.J.: Princeton University Press, 1997.

Cantemir, Dimitrie (Dmitri Kantemir, Kantemiroglu) (1673–1723) *historian, philosopher*

Dimitrie Cantemir was born in Moldavia at a time when it was under Ottoman control. As a Moldavian noble, he received an excellent education. He lived in Constantinople from 1688 to 1710, initially as a hostage to ensure his family's loyalty to the Ottomans. During this time he married Casandra Cantacuzino. Their son Antiokh Kantemir (1708–44) would later become famous in Russia for his satirical poetry.

In 1710 Dimitrie became prince (or "hospodar") of Moldavia and, as ruler, secretly allied himself with Emperor Peter I of Russia. When the Ottomans defeated Peter's army in 1711, Cantemir fled Moldavia with his family and numerous subjects, but Peter I rewarded him with an estate and an annual pension. In 1722 Cantemir traveled with Peter as a key adviser in another campaign against the Ottomans. Cantemir fell ill during the journey, however, and returned to his Ukrainian estate, where he died in August of the following year.

Cantemir's *The Divan or The Wise Man's Parley with the World or The Judgement of the Soul with the Body* (1698) was the first published book written in the Romanian language. His other works, most written in Latin, include *Hieroglyphic History* (1703–05), a satiric fable about Romanian politics; *An Examination of the Nature of Monarchy* (1714), which praises monarchy in general and Peter I in particular; *Concerning the System of the Mohammedan Religion* (1722); and descriptions of Middle Eastern music that musicologists still consider valuable.

Cantemir is most famous for his histories, whose readers included VOLTAIRE and possibly Jonathan SWIFT. *Description of Moldavia* (1716) and *Chronicle of the Romanians, Moldavians, and Vlachs* (begun in 1717) cover the history and culture of his native land. In *The History of the Growth and Decay of the Ottoman Empire* (1716), he turns his attention to the Ottomans' gain of control over outlying territories. He writes that the Ottoman Turks prefer not brute force but more subtle political devices, which he calls "treacherous mechanica." He argues that the Ottomans have been in decline since 1672 and that Peter I should attack them.

Orest Subtelny has described Cantemir as "an industrious and self-disciplined individual who had firsthand experience in the areas about which he wrote." According to Subtelny, Cantemir's works "marked not only a high point in Romanian cultural history but were also major events in European scholarship" and are valued for "providing precious data and rare insights."

See also ENLIGHTENMENT.

An English Version of a Work by Dimitrie Cantemir

Dimitrie Cantemir. Historian of South East European and Oriental Civilizations. Extracts from The History of The Ottoman Empire. Edited by Alexandru Dutu and Paul Cernovodeanu. Bucharest: Association internationale d'études du sud-est européen, 1973.

Works about Dimitrie Cantemir

Kellogg, Frederick. *A History of Romanian Historical Writing.* Bakersfield, Calif.: Charles Schlacks, 1990.

Subtelny, Orest. *Domination of Eastern Europe: Native Nobilities and Foreign Absolutism, 1500–1715.* Kingston and Montreal: McGill-Queen's University Press, 1986.

Cao Xuequin (Ts'ao Hsüeh-ch'in) (1715–1764) *poet, novelist*

Cao Xuequin was of Chinese descent but he was born in the Manchu Banner system. A bannerman was a person who owed hereditary military service to the Manchu, who were rulers of China from the 17th to the early 20th centuries. Very little is known about Cao's life except that he was either the grandson or grandnephew of the well-known scholar-gentry Cao Yin (1658–1712), who rose to prominence during the reign of Emperor Kangxi (Kang-hsi). Cao Yin had apparently been Kangxi's companion and playmate in the latter's youth, and his loyalty to the emperor reaped rewards in the form of a promotion to the post of superintendent of the Imperial Textile Factories at Nanking. Though most facts about the novelist Cao remain undetermined, it is commonly believed that a few years after Cao was born, the Cao family fell upon hard times.

The family enjoyed a brief reprieve from hardship during the reign of Qian Long (Ch'ien-lung); however, they were to suffer greater misfortunes later, including a disastrous fire that destroyed most of their property. The only source of information regarding Cao's life after the fire is a number of poems addressed to him and written by his friends. One poem describes Cao as living in greatly reduced circumstances in the western suburb of Beijing (Peking), while another suggests that Cao's family survived mostly on gruel. Cao died an embittered, heartbroken, and impoverished man in 1764, grieving over his son's untimely death. Cao himself was apparently suffering from a terminal illness.

Cao's main work is the novel *The Dream of the Red Chamber* (also known as *The Story of the Stone* or *Dream of Red Mansions*), of which only 80 chapters exist. It is somewhat of an autobiographical novel reflective of Cao's own life experiences. Scholars believe that several events narrated in the novel, including the fire, are actual incidents that occurred during the novelist's short life. The variant copies and versions of the novel, bearing different dates, may be accounted for by the fact that Cao's 80 chapters were left in more or less unfinished form. The discrepancies and controversies surrounding these variant versions do not reduce the value of *The Dream of the Red Chamber* and its significance in the field of Chinese and world literature. As Chi-Chen Wang states in his introduction to his translation of the work:

It is the first and only autobiographical novel in traditional Chinese literature, the first to give a true picture of the complexities of life in a large family, the first to show that love can be painful and end in tragedy. It reflects a dis-

tinctly personal point of view and has a unity of plot beyond that of mere chronology. Its characters are drawn with subtlety and truth, as its dialogue is faithful to the colloquial idiom.

Cao's work should be examined not only in the temporal context of its composition, but also in terms of the history of Chinese literature and its development. As novels rose from the rank of folk traditions, they were never considered part of the scholarly literary genre. It was not until well into the latter part of the Ming and early Qing (Ch'ing) dynasties that the genre of Chinese novel became more established in Chinese literature. *The Dream of the Red Chamber* also became one of four great Chinese novels, the other three being *The Journey to the West* by WU CHENGEN; *Golden Lotus* from the JIN PING MEI by Xiao Xiaosheng (Hsiao-hsiao-sheng); and *The Scholars* by WU JINGZI (Wu Ching-tzu). Cao's work shares many similarities with earlier works influenced by Confucian ideas and ethics, not only in terms of content, but also in the extensive use of formalized literary language intermixed with more colloquial forms of expression, to describe characters.

Critical Analysis

The Dream of the Red Chamber is ultimately a realistic portrayal of family life and relationships, although it is commonly viewed as a love story. The subject of the novel is the Jia family and the tragic tale of their downfall from a position of affluence and power. The word *jia (chia)* is a homonym of the Chinese character or word for family; thus, the Jia family represents a generic upper-class family susceptible to the ravages of time.

The book opens with an explanation of how the story came to be and why it is important:

Four thousand six hundred and twenty-three years ago the heavens were out of repair. So the Goddess of Works set to work and prepared 36,501 blocks of precious jade. . . . [She] cast aside the single remaining block upon one of the celestial peaks. . . .

One day a Buddhist and a Taoist priest, who happened to be passing that way . . . noticed the disconsolate stone. . . .

"Indeed, my friend, you are not wanting in spirituality," said the Buddhist priest to the stone. . . . "But we cannot be certain that you will ever prove to be of any real use; and, moreover, you lack an inscription, without which your destiny must necessarily remain unfulfilled."

Thereupon he put the stone in his sleeve and rose to proceed on his journey.

"And what, if I may ask," inquired his companion, "do you intend to do with the stone . . . ?"

"I mean," replied the other, "to send it down to earth, to play its allotted part in the fortunes of a certain family now anxiously expecting its arrival. You see, when the Goddess of Works rejected this stone, it used to fill up its time by roaming about the heavens, until chance brought it alongside of a lovely crimson flower. Being struck with the great beauty of this flower, the stone remained there for some time, tending its protégée with the most loving care, and daily moistening its roots with the choicest nectar of the sky, until at length, yielding to the influence of disinterested love, the flower changed its form and became a most beautiful girl.

"'Dear stone,' cried the girl, in her newfound ecstasy of life, 'the moisture you have bestowed upon me here I will repay you in our future state with my tears!'"

Ages afterwards, another priest, in search of light, saw this self-same stone lying in its old place . . . and saw that it bore a plain unvarnished tale of Beauty and anguish walking hand in hand—"The downward slope to death," telling how a woman's artless love had developed into deep, destroying passion; and how from the thrall of a lost love one soul had been raised to a sublimer, if not a purer conception of man's mission upon earth. He therefore copied it out from beginning to end.

Thus, *The Dream of the Red Chamber* begins. Using a variety of characters with personality traits ranging from conniving to sensible and weak, Cao was able to weave together a tale of disappointment, intrigue, love, and melancholy. His intricate and detailed descriptions of the moods and mentality of his characters allow readers to simultaneously criticize and empathize with them.

The form of the novel is episodic and may be divided into three parts. The first section comprises episodes representing the Jia family at the height of prosperity. Cao describes ordinary daily actions and events in the Jia mansion, which include illustrations of family quarrels, illnesses, and the expectations and fears of some of the main characters. The story contains a long list of characters, which is a common trait of Chinese novels. The main plot revolves around the key figures Baoyu (Pao-yu), Taiyu (Tai-yu), Baozhai (Pao-chai), and the matriarch of the Jia family. The triangular love story involving the three young people parallels the tragic unfolding of misfortunes, which leads eventually to the Jias' downfall. The main theme of the first section focuses on the idea of hubris, or overweening pride that comes before a fall. The predominant image is that of an apparently stable household perching precariously on shaky foundations.

The second part of the novel describes the development of recurring incidents that contribute to the downfall of the Jia family. In the last section of the novel, exemplified in the last chapter of the novel, the main theme is the idea of rebuilding the family, which is now in a shambles. The incidents experienced by the Jia family parallel that of Cao's family.

The structure of *The Dream of the Red Chamber* is representative of the typical Chinese convention whereby chapters are linked to others via the use of repetition. At the end of each chapter in the book, there is always a phrase informing what will happen in the next chapter.

Besides the key themes of stability, instability, and hubris, there are several other important influences that can be discerned in Cao's writing. One main influence is the importance of supernaturalism, as can be seen in the beginning, as well as throughout the tale. A typical device used in Chinese novels is the use of dreams to foretell or to inform the main characters of their impending misfortune or experience. Dreams can sometimes be utilized to guide the actors' behavior. In the book, dream sequences such as Baoyu's desire for marital consummation not only mark the thin line that separates the supernatural and mundane worlds, but also influence the characters' actions. For example, Baoyu's desire to consummate his union with his cousin, Taiyu, which is foreshadowed in his dream, leads him to hastily seek a substitute in his personal maid.

Another important theme is the influence of three elements of Chinese society: Buddhism, Confucianism, and Daoism (Taoism). The Confucian elements of the novel are exemplified in the characters' rigid attitudes and behavior. Daoist elements are represented both metaphorically and philosophically through the Daoist priest who reappears throughout the story and through the illuminating discussion about origins of the magic stone. Finally Buddhist ideas are encapsulated in the way Baoyo perceives life after he loses his favorite jade, Taiyu dies, and his marriage with Baozhai fails.

As Liu Wuchi points out in the foreword to Knoerle's critical study of *The Dream of the Red Chamber*:

> The study of *The Dream of the Red Chamber (Hung-loumeng)*, which continues to attract critical attention today in China and abroad, has acquired a designation of its own: *Hunghsueh*, or "Red-ology." No other Chinese novel at any period of China's long literary history has aroused such an immense interest in scholarly communities as this mid-eighteenth century novel by Ts'ao Hsüeh-ch'in, the impoverished scion of a once wealthy official family.

English Versions of a Work by Cao Xuequin

The Dream of the Red Chamber. Translated by Chi-Chen Wang. New York: Twayne, 1958.

The Dream of the Red Chamber. Translated by Florence and Isabel McHugh. New York: Pantheon Books, 1958.

Works about Cao Xuequin

Hsia, C. T. "Love and Compassion in 'Dream of the Red Chamber.'" *Criticism* 5 (Summer 1963): 261–271.

Knoerle, Jeanne. *The Dream of the Red Chamber: A Critical Study*. Bloomington: Indiana University Press, 1972.

Wu Shi-Chang. *On the Red Chamber Dream*. Oxford: Clarendon Press, 1961.

Carrío de la Vandera, Alonso (ca. 1715–after 1778) *explorer, travel writer*

Little is known of Alonso Carrío de la Vandera's early life, other than that he was born in Gijón. As an adult, he moved to Mexico in 1735, but later moved to Lima, where he spent the majority of his life. He held government positions from 1746 until his death. His writings have been said to encompass 300 years of history, and "by subverting colonial order," to open the door to "new forms of expression" that arose after Peruvian independence (Cevallos-Candau).

His most well known work is *El lazarillo de ciegos caminantes (El Lazarillo: A Guide for Inexperienced Travelers)*, which served as a guidebook for travelers using the road from Buenos Aires to Lima. He attributed the work to his partner, Calixto Bustamante Carlos Inca, who was known by the nickname of Concolorcorvo, or "crow with color." It was also under this pseudonym that Vandera wrote, creating obvious identity confusion.

El lazarillo was written in 1775, and is now considered by many as the precursor to the Spanish-American novel. Vandera was traveling during a time of insurgent exploration, whether by mule, boat, or foot. "Concolorcorvo inscribed himself within a tradition that goes back to classical times and at the close of the eighteenth century enjoyed enormous prestige and popularity" (Stolley 250). *El lazarillo* is not only a tour of the 1771 South American postal system, but also a social and political commentary. It is riddled with satirical humor and observations of the native peoples he encountered in his travels, and while Vandera was writing in the genre of the TRAVEL NARRATIVE, his work also contains novel elements such as stories and descriptions of people and settings. For this reason, *El lazarillo* is somewhat of a "hybrid text," which has made it difficult for scholars to categorize the work on numerous levels. Of course, it is Vandera's subversion of form and practice that opened the door to "new forms of expression" (Cevallos-Candau). This element of his work, as well as the historical and cultural information Vandera provides make *El lazarillo* worth remembering.

An English Version of a Work by Alonso Carrío de la Vandera

El Lazarillo: A Guide for Inexperienced Travelers Between Buenos Aires and Lima, 1773. Translated by Walter D. Kline. Bloomington: Indiana University Press, 1965.

A Work about Alonso Carrío de la Vandera

Franco, Jean. *An Introduction to Spanish-American Literature.* Cambridge: Cambridge University Press, 1995.

Carver, Jonathan (1710–1780) *explorer, travel writer*

Jonathan Carver was one of the most famous travelers and travel writers of the 18th century. Between the years of 1766 and 1768, Carver explored the territory beyond the Mississippi, hoping to find a northwest passage between the Atlantic and Pacific Oceans. Starting in Boston, his journey westward took him to what is present-day Minnesota. He followed the Mississippi River nearly to the site of Minneapolis on the Minnesota River. In a second journey, he reached Lake Superior.

The account of his travels, *Travels through the Interior Parts of North America in the Years 1766, 1767, 1768,* is the first description in English of the areas that he explored. A noteworthy feature of the book is a detailed map of the western Great Lakes and upper Mississippi Valley area. Published in 1778, *Travels through the Interior Parts of North America* became one of the most popular early travel accounts in America. It was translated into foreign languages and printed in 30 editions, 16 of which appeared by 1798. Wordsworth, Coleridge, Chateaubriand, and SCHILLER admired it.

Despite the book's popular success, Carver received little financial reward or acclaim as an author during his lifetime. Unsuccessful in his attempts to recover payment for the expenses of his expedition, he traveled to England to make a case for payment of his services. He worked in England as a cartographer and secured a publisher for his travel journals. The publisher, however, added material from other writers without attribution, damaging Carver's literary reputation and financial security. Only after the British Museum acquired the original travel journals and publication drafts in the early 20th century was Carver's reputation as an explorer and author restored.

During 1778 and 1779, Carver authored two additional works, *The New Universal Georgraphy* and *Treatise on the Culture of the Tobacco Plant.* He died destitute in 1780. Today historians and scholars recognize Carver's contributions to 18th-century travel literature and historical records. However, few of his works remain in print.

Works by Jonathan Carver

A Treatise on the Culture of the Tobacco Plant. London: Printed by the author, 1779.

The Journals of Jonathan Carver and related documents, 1766–1770. Edited by John Parker. St. Paul: Minnesota Historical Society Press, 1976.

Travels through the Interior Parts of North America in the Years 1766, 1767, and 1768. London: Printed by J. Walter, 1778.

Castellanos, Juan de (1522–1607) *poet, historian*

Juan de Castellanos is best known for his rhymed chronicle, *Elegías de varones ilustres de Indias (Elegies of Illustrious Men of the Indies)*, which describes the discovery and conquest of America. At 150,000 lines, it is the longest poem written in the Spanish language and is one of the longest written poems in world literature.

Written in the tradition of EPIC poetry, *Elegies* is divided into four sections, the first of which deals with the discovery of America and includes material on the conquest of Mexico and Venezuela. The second part continues the history of Venezuela, Cabo de la Vela, and Santa Marta. The third section covers the history of the governorships of Cartagena, Popayán, Atioquia, and Chocó; the fourth part concludes with a history of the new kingdom of Granada.

Since he arrived in America as a youth and spent many years in the New World, Castellanos considered himself an American Spaniard. Starting in America as a soldier and later becoming a priest, Castellanos lived a life rich in experience. He wrote about the highlights of his experiences as an acolyte, a pearl fisherman, a soldier, adventurer, and parish priest living in areas of the New World, ranging from Puerto Rico to Colombia.

His writings appealed to RENAISSANCE preferences for narrative literature. Stylistically his narratives are described as sincere, passionate, and facetious in the use of irony. He also shows close attention to detail in the careful descriptions of the flora and fauna of the American world.

Elegies has been recognized as one of the most remarkable works in world literature. It is a rich source of information for the periods of discovery and conquest, placing Castellanos among the most authoritative of early historians of the New World.

An English Version of a Work by Juan de Castellanos

The Narrative of the expedition of Sir Francis Drake to the Indies and the taking by him of Carthagena.

Translated by Walter Owen. Buenos Aires: [s.n.], 1952.

Castiglione, Baldessare (1478–1529) *nonfiction writer*

Castiglione was the quintessential courtier. He served as a military commander, diplomat, adviser, and papal nuncio. His experience and his connections at court provided the raw material for his only known work, *The Courtier* (1528). He spent much of his life revising the work, which he originally began in 1516. When it was finally published, it was a huge success both in Italy and abroad.

The Courtier seeks to describe proper aristocratic behavior and is a dialogue among Castiglione's closest friends. To pass the time, they discuss the characteristics of the ideal courtier. Because the speakers differ, there is disagreement over many issues. However, what emerges is a general image of the ideal RENAISSANCE man: a well-educated, skilled soldier and equestrian. Castiglione describes the perfect courtier's aspect as *sprezzatura*, loosely meaning "nonchalance"; the courtier should "practice in all things a certain sprezzatura . . . and make whatever is done or said appear to be without effort [or] thought. . . ." In addition to describing a courtier's skills and education, Castiglione also describes how court ladies should behave, how courtiers should advise a prince, and the ideals of platonic love.

The Courtier was translated by Thomas Hoby in 1561. It was extremely influential in determining proper courtly behavior; writers such as William SHAKESPEARE and Edmund Spenser drew on it to describe aspects of court life in their own works. *The Courtier* also provides an essential bridge between the chivalric code of the Middle Ages and the more politically charged era of the Renaissance, adapting many concepts of chivalry into modes of conduct appropriate to a Renaissance court. As critics Robert Hanning and David Rosand explain, Castiglione's work serves as "a gauge for so many aspects of Renaissance culture—from language and literature to art and music, courtiership and politics to humor and feminism, Neoplatonic idealism to the most cynical realism." Castiglione, they say, "stands as the truest . . . reflection of the . . . High Renaissance."

An English Version of a Work by Baldessare Castiglione

The Book of the Courtier. Translated by Leonard Eckstein Opdycke. Mineola, N.Y.: Dover, 2003.

Works about Baldessare Castiglione

Falvo, Joseph D. *The Economy of Human Relations: Castiglione's Libro del Cortegiano.* New York: P. Lang, 1992.

Hanning, Robert W. *Castiglione: The Ideal and the Real in Renaissance Culture.* New Haven, Conn.: Yale University Press, 1983.

Catherine the Great (Empress Catherine II of Russia) (1729–1796) *political philosopher, memoirist, literary dilettante*

Catherine was born in Pomerania as Sophia Augusta Fredericka, princess of Anhalt-Zerbst. She traveled to Russia in 1744, converted to Orthodoxy, took the name Ekaterina (Catherine), and married Peter, who became Peter III in 1761. Less than six months later, Catherine's supporters staged a coup d'etat that left Peter dead and Catherine on the throne.

During Catherine's reign, the Russian empire expanded its power and territories through annexations and war. The government also implemented legal, educational, and administrative reforms, and arts and literature flourished. Catherine issued charters granting rights to nobles and townspeople (excluding peasants and serfs), and she weathered a major crisis, the Pugachev Revolt (1773–74). In the last decade of her reign, the French Revolution frightened her into imposing stricter censorship and other controls. Her son Paul succeeded her after she died of a stroke at age 67.

Catherine read Beccaria, MONTESQUIEU, Tacitus, and Plutarch; she also corresponded with VOLTAIRE and DIDEROT. As empress, she planned to put EN-LIGHTENMENT thought into practice. In *The Antidote* (1770), she alludes to her "enlightened" role in Russia's legislative reform: "The sovereign, carefully gathering from all sides the principles which most enable men to be happy, herself makes a code of them and says to her subjects: here are the principles which in my opinion can make you happy!"

Besides state documents, Catherine composed letters, memoirs, journal articles, short stories, and plays. While her fiction is mediocre, her memoirs and letters are down-to-earth and engaging. As G. A. Gukovskii notes, her works "present a picture of the literary, and even the ideological, battles of the period."

See also Gavriil DERZHAVIN; Alexander RADISHCHEV.

English Versions of Works by Catherine the Great

Documents of Catherine the Great; The Correspondence with Voltaire and the Instruction of 1767 in the English Text of 1768. Edited by W. F. Reddaway. New York: Russell and Russell, 1971.

Memoirs of Catherine the Great. Translated and edited by Lowell Bair. New York: Bantam, 1957.

Two Comedies by Catherine the Great. Edited and translated by Lurana Donnels O'Malley. Amsterdam: Harwood Academic Publishers, 1998.

Works about Catherine the Great

Alexander, John T. *Catherine the Great: Life and Legend.* Oxford: Oxford University Press, 1989.

de Madariaga, Isabel. *Catherine the Great: A Short History.* New Haven, Conn. and London: Yale University Press, 2002.

Raeff, Marc, ed. *Catherine the Great: A Profile.* New York: Hill and Wang, 1972.

Çelebi, Evliya (Evliya Efendi, "Siyyah") (1611–1682) *adventurer, historian*

Evliya was born in Constantinople, the capital of the Ottoman Empire. He attended that city's college of Hamid Efendi, and while there began to dream of "traveling over the whole earth . . ." His only major work is a history and travelogue known simply as *The Book of Travels*, which he began near the end of his life but never finished. The four completed volumes present a partial history of the Ottoman Empire and its peoples.

Travels begins with a historical sketch of the Ottoman Empire, including the area's pre-Ottoman history. This is followed by a history of Evliya's own family and childhood. The work includes a vision of the prophet Mohammed that Evliya vividly imagines taking place in the mosque of Akhí-Çelebi. Evliya intends to ask the prophet for his *shifáat* (help) but accidentally utters *siyáhat* (the gift of traveling), which becomes his calling. The mosque in the dream lends Evliya the surname Çelebi, but he likes to call himself "Siyyah," or "The Traveler."

Çelebi moves on to describe his early life as a soldier and the many battles he participated in against the Ottoman Empire's enemies. He also comments on Ottoman administrative structure and the people, languages, and customs of the provinces he visits. He provides lists of notable persons and economic statistics gathered from tax rolls and other records, all of which has been invaluable to modern historians.

Çelebi's style depends on the subject at hand. Writing of sultans, folk customs, or ancient history, he displays wit and poetic talent; for administrative and economic details he uses a brief, matter-of-fact style of reporting; and his descriptions of battles are in lively but mostly unadorned prose.

Çelebi continued to serve the sultan well into old age, venturing throughout the Mediterranean, Western Europe, North Africa, and Central Asia. Although Çelebi often describes himself as "the humble writer," his *Book of Travels* has few equals in terms of style and detail.

English Versions of Works by Evliya Çelebi

Evliya Çelebi in Diyarbekir: The Relevant Section of the Seyahatname. Translated and edited by Martin van Bruinessen and Hendrik Boeschoten. Leiden and New York: E.J. Brill, 1988.
Evliya Çelebi in Albania and Adjacent Regions: Kosovo, Montenegro, Ohrid. Translated and edited by

Robert Dankoff and Robert Elsie. Boston: Brill, 2000.

Cervantes Saavedra, Miguel de
(1547–1616) *novelist, poet, playwright*
Miguel de Cervantes Saavedra was born in Alcalá, Spain, the fourth child of Rodrigo de Cervantes and Leonor de Cortinas. Little is known for certain about the early life and adolescence of the author of *Don Quixote*, and frequent gaps in his biography have led many later scholars and admirers to attribute the adventures of the book's eponymous hero to his author and creator. Many parallels exist, not the least of them being that the book's hero is a gentleman of La Mancha. Likewise the character Saavedra tells a story in Part I of *Don Quixote* about being held prisoner in a Turkish bagnio in Algiers, an experience shared by the author, who later took the family name Saavedra as his own.

Cervantes's upbringing was marked by the struggles of his father, a surgeon, to keep the family from poverty. After a series of removes to elude creditors, Rodrigo settled his family in Madrid in 1567, and Miguel attempted to catch up on his education. He received attention for a collection of occasional poems he wrote for the family of the Spanish king, Philip II, but shortly thereafter was forced to leave Madrid after wounding a young man in a duel, a deed punishable by 10 years of exile and the loss of his right hand. Cervantes traveled to Italy and entered the service of Cardinal Acquaviva.

The Catholic Spain of Philip II suffered from two chief pressures: the Protestant threat of Reformation thought as advocated by ERASMUS, LUTHER, and adherents of HUMANISM, and the Islamic threat of the Turks of the Ottoman Empire. Answering the second of these, Miguel joined the military in 1570 and was promptly sent into battle. He was wounded at Lepanto in 1571 and lost the use of his left hand. He returned to active duty a few months later and fought in several more battles, distinguishing himself for heroism. He then spent the winter in Naples, Italy, an experience that left a rich imprint on his later writing.

In 1575 en route from Naples to Barcelona with his brother Rodrigo, Miguel's ship was captured by Barbary pirates and all the passengers were captured and taken to Algiers. Highly glowing letters of recommendation, which Miguel carried with him in hope of finding a government post upon his return to Madrid, led his captors to believe him a member of the high nobility and therefore a very valuable captive. Rodrigo gained his freedom relatively early, but Miguel languished in prison for five years, failing at a series of escape attempts. Finally, in 1580, his family paid the enormous ransom, and Cervantes returned to Spain broke, in debt, and permanently injured.

He hoped to make his fortune in the New World, but his requests for a colonial position were not granted. Instead, he was given a job as a tax collector, which required extensive travel and provided more trials. He was briefly jailed twice due to disagreements about his handling of state finances, and after fathering children with two different women, he married young Catalina de Palacios, with whom he had no children. In the next year he published a PASTORAL romance, *Galatea* (1685), a story of shepherds and fair maidens.

For the next 20 years, Cervantes wrote frequently but produced nothing notable. Two plays, *Life in Algiers* and *The Baths of Algiers,* use his own experience to dramatic effect, but Spanish theater was entirely monopolized by the polished and gifted LOPE DE VEGA. Cervantes continued to read extensively in all forms and genres; he knew the lyrics of PETRARCH and the writings of GARCILASO DE LA VEGA, the EPIC romances of Boiardo, ARIOSTO, and TASSO, BOCCACCIO's *Decameron,* and the *Eclogues* of Virgil. He also continued to write poetry, which was considered the literature of the upper classes, but Cervantes was not a particularly remarkable poet. During one of his stays in prison he conceived the idea of writing a novel about a valiant but delusional *hidalgo*, or gentleman, and the character of Don Quixote was born.

Part I of *The History of the Ingenious Gentleman Don Quixote of La Mancha* appeared in 1605, and was an instant success. Readers were delighted and entertained by the fantastic antics of the idealistic and indiscriminate knight-errant. Yet the work, for all its popularity, was largely considered a boisterous FARCE; "true" literature was either poetry or drama, and *Don Quixote*, with its self-conscious literary techniques, was of a new type altogether.

Cervantes later experimented with other forms, publishing a poetic mock-epic *Voyage to Parnassus* in 1614 and *Eight Comedies and Eight New Interludes* in 1615. His 12 short stories, collected under the title *Exemplary Novels* and published in 1613, are equal to *Don Quixote* in style and execution, but less often read. Critics often divide these short stories into two types, realistic or romantic. In the prologue to the tales, Cervantes represented them as model tales, wholesomely educational, but the bawdy nature of certain stories made some readers and critics doubt the moral value of the fictions.

Don Quixote remained the sole reason for his fame, and when a spurious and anonymous sequel came out in 1614, an outraged Cervantes hurried to publish his own authentic Part II in 1615. He did not have long to enjoy the acclaim or to finish his latest and, in his eyes, greatest ROMANCE, *The Trials of Persiles and Segismunda* (1617). He died in 1616, the same year as the English poet and playwright SHAKESPEARE.

Like Shakespeare, Cervantes stands as a monument in his country's literature. According to biographer Jean Canavaggio, Cervantes is considered not only "the incarnation and epitome of the Golden Age of Spain," but also the inventor of the modern novel.

Critical Analysis

New readers often approach *Don Quixote* knowing only that it is a parody of what Cervantes himself called "impossible fictions" and what French essayist Michel de MONTAIGNE called "wit-besotting trash"—the medieval romances with their themes of chivalry and courtly love. The book's modest and humble hero—who bears many similarities to Cervantes—has a peculiar affliction: He has read so many of these stories that they have addled his wits. Cervantes writes:

Don Quixote so buried himself in his books that he read all night from sundown to dawn, and all day from sunup to dusk, until with virtually no sleep and so much reading he dried out his brain and lost his sanity. . . . Indeed, his mind was so tattered and torn that, finally, it produced the strangest notion any madman ever conceived . . . he decided to turn himself into a knight errant, traveling all over the world with his horse and his weapons.

Calling himself Don Quixote, the gentleman-turned-knight recruits a neighboring peasant, Sancho Panza, to be his "squire," and they set off. To Don Quixote, rambling over the countryside in search of fame and glory, every inn he encounters is a castle and every person he meets becomes part of his self-imagined romance. In the course of his hero's adventures, Cervantes exposes, with crushing irony, how unfit an idealistic and half-mad dreamer is in the "real" world. Many of his exploits—such as chopping up a puppet play because he thinks the puppets are powered by a sorcerer, or the famous moment where he jousts with windmills, thinking them giants, and is ignobly thrown from his horse—make Don Quixote look ridiculous, foolish, even dangerous. Yet Cervantes tells his tale in a mild, confidential voice that endears his hero to the reader and somehow laments the passing of the chivalric ideal.

This narrative style, whereby the author overtly involves the reader in the story and calls upon the audience to make moral judgments about the characters and their decisions, is part of the novel's innovation. The author is self-consciously aware that he is crafting a story, and characters in the story read the works of a certain Miguel de Cervantes, including Don Quixote. Adding to the fun, the hero becomes angry to hear that his exploits are misrepresented in the falsely authored Part II of his book. In addition, songs, SONNETS, and letters stretch the limits of genre and form, and embedded tales elaborate the action, digress from the main story, and often provide sparkling narratives that could stand alone.

Some of the stories narrated in Don Quixote are obviously drawn from Cervantes's own life. In a substantial episode known as the "Captive's Tale," where a former captive of a Algerian bagnio recounts his imprisonment, he refers to a man named Saavedra whom he knew there, and who was a favorite of the Algerian ruler. Yet the categories of parody or loose autobiography barely begin to describe this lengthy and complex work.

Part of the book's success is due to its obvious sympathies for the lives of everyday people and its wickedly cutting observations on the false and limiting practice of certain Spanish attitudes and customs. Cervantes questions the very nature of art and reality and examines the ways in which humans relate to one another in their projects of shaping identities and following dreams, falling in love and enduring failures, always mistaking, correcting, learning, and teaching one another.

Ultimately, Don Quixote is a book about books. The hero's bibliomania has led to his unique madness, and large swaths of the narrative are devoted to discussions of and literary criticism about other works of fiction. Throughout the work, the narrator assumes the humble stance of a poorly educated, confused author overwhelmed by his material. In his Prologue he pokes sly fun at the pompous literature of his day, scattered with footnotes and obscure allusions. He invents a "friend" who gives him the prosaic advice to make up his own references:

And as for those missing marginal references, the names of all the books and writers where you went hunting for the wit and wisdom quoted in your history, all you have to do is scribble in any bits and pieces of Latin you happen to remember. . . . And with a pinch of Latin here, and a pinch of Latin there, they might even think you're a scholar, which isn't a bad reputation, these days.

The impact of Don Quixote on Western literature can scarcely be underrated. Not only is it felt by many to be the first and greatest of novels, but also the consciousness of its hero has entered the language; "quixotic" is used to describe someone romantic and idealistic to an impractical degree. Novelist Mark Twain used *Don Quixote* as his model when he wrote the American picaresque *Adventures of Huckleberry Finn,* and William Faulkner read Cervantes more often than he read the Bible. The 400 years of the novel in Western literature owe themselves to the moment when Miguel de Cervantes, idle and in jail, began his own epic quest to cast down the ideology of chivalric fiction and find a new way of looking at life—essentially, in the words of novelist Milan Kundera, "to comprehend the world as a question."

English Versions of Works by Miguel de Cervantes Saavedra

Don Quixote. Translated by Tobias Smollett. New York: Modern Library, 2004.

Don Quixote: The Ingenious Hidalgo de la Mancha. Translated by John Rutherford. New York: Penguin Books, 2003.

Exemplary Stories. Edited by Lesley Lipson. Oxford: Oxford University Press, 1998.

The Portable Cervantes. Translated by Samuel Putnam. New York: Viking Press, 1976.

Works about Miguel de Cervantes Saavedra

Busoni, Rafaello. *The Man Who Was Don Quixote: The Story of Miguel Cervantes.* New York: Prentice Hall, 1982.

Marlowe, Stephen. *The Death and Life of Miguel de Cervantes.* New York: Arcade Books, 1997.

Saffar, Ruth El., ed. *Critical Essays on Cervantes.* Boston: G.K. Hall, 1986.

Weiger, John G. *The Substance of Cervantes.* Cambridge: Cambridge University Press, 1985.

Chaucer, Geoffrey (ca. 1342–1400) *poet*

Though more is known about the life of Geoffrey Chaucer than many other English poets of his time, including William LANGLAND and the author of the poems *Pearl* and *SIR GAWAIN AND THE GREEN KNIGHT,* the precise year of his birth remains a mystery. His parents, John and Agnes, were part of a well-to-do merchant family who lived in Ipswich, near London. Though "Chaucer" in the French of the time meant "shoe-maker," the family trade was wine making. In 1359 Chaucer traveled to France with the army of King Edward III and was captured but quickly ransomed. In 1366 he married Philippa, daughter of Sir Gilles of Hainault, and in 1367 he joined the king's household as an esquire or general servant, and possibly studied law at the Inns of the Court.

In his lifetime Chaucer made several trips to France on business for various kings, and between the years 1370 and 1372 he traveled to Italy. The French chronicler FROISSART reports that Chaucer returned to France in 1377. After the Peasant's Revolt of 1381, Chaucer gradually removed from London to Kent, where he served on the peace commission and later took a post as warden of the king's forest. When Richard was deposed in 1399, Chaucer passed smoothly from the service of one king to the other, but did not live long enough to enjoy the favor of Henry IV. Chaucer died one year later and was buried in Westminster Abbey. The monument of his death suggests what his life's work achieved: He was the first to occupy what became the Poet's Corner, which now serves as the final resting place for such luminaries as SHAKESPEARE and John DONNE, symbolizing Chaucer's place as the fountainhead of modern English poetry.

As his work suggests, young Geoffrey received a thorough education in the classics of Latin literature, including Virgil, Claudius, Lucan, Statius, and Ovid. He knew French and could read as well as compose French poetry, and the French poet Eustace Deschamps wrote a ballade praising Chaucer for his English translation of the medieval classic *Romance of the Rose.* Chaucer's trip to Italy had a profound effect on him; he likely met PETRARCH and BOCCACCIO and discovered the works of Dante. His English contemporaries Thomas Usk and John GOWER spoke highly of him, and in his own time Chaucer as a poet was well respected, if not always well paid.

He wrote the first of his major works in 1368 as an elegy for Blanche, the wife of John of Gaunt.

The Book of the Duchess contains many of the elements of the courtly love poems made popular by the French poets Guillaume de Machaut and Jean de Meun; it includes a lovelorn narrator, a dream vision that takes place in May, and a dialogue with a mysterious Black Knight. Chaucer most likely wrote or began his other major poems, *The Parliament of Fowls, The House of Fame,* and *Troilus and Criseyde,* as well as his translation of *The Consolations of Philosophy* by Boethius, while he was serving as a controller in the customhouse between 1374 and 1386. The Trojan War as told in Homer was a popular subject for medieval tales, and the story of the fatal love of Troilus, a prince of Troy, for the modest widow Criseyde had been the subject of works by many skilled poets, from Boccaccio to Benoît de Saint-Maure. Chaucer's *The Legend of Good Women,* which he never finished, contains a list of the poet's works, some of which have descended to posterity and some of which are lost. In the centuries after his death many poems written by contemporaries or imitators were erroneously attributed to Chaucer, but peculiarities of language and style have helped scholars identify the spurious works. One of Chaucer's greatest achievements was that by writing in English, instead of the Latin or French then used in government and clerical documents, he helped make the native, vernacular language more accepted in higher circles.

Critical Analysis

Although Chaucer was famous in his own time, he is best known today for his unfinished masterpiece *The Canterbury Tales.* For this work, Chaucer drew upon all his careers as soldier, esquire in the king's household, diplomat, customs controller, justice of the peace, member of Parliament, clerk of the king's works, and forest official. He used his experiences and his encounters with people from all stations to create a work of unparalleled variety. He probably began writing the *Tales* piecemeal in 1387; evidence suggests he began some of the stories before deciding to use the narrative framework of a pilgrimage to Canterbury. The technique of using a frame story to pull together very different narratives had been used before, by the composer of *The Thousand and One Nights* and by Gower in his *Confession of Amant.* Chaucer added a new twist by drawing his characters from all walks of life. The pilgrims include a knight and a squire, a landowner and a lawyer, a miller and a reeve, a clerk and a merchant, and several religious figures including nuns and priests, as well as a parson, pardoner, summoner, and friar—all of whom tell individual tales.

In the Prologue to *The Canterbury Tales,* the pilgrims assemble at an inn kept by Harry Bailly, the high-spirited host who decides to go with them. Their destination is the shrine where Thomas à Becket was murdered in 1170, a popular destination for those interested in religious sites. Bailly proposes a storytelling contest: Each of the pilgrims will tell two stories on the way to the shrine and two on the way back, and the pilgrim who tells the best story will win a dinner paid for by all the others. The descriptions of the pilgrims in the Prologue show Chaucer's eye for authentic detail and his ear for dialogue. His portraits are often deeply ironic, and behind the narrator's naïve voice the reader can see sharp critiques of the vices, social problems, and injustices of Chaucer's day.

One of the most popular pilgrims with modern readers is the Wife of Bath, who is described as gap-toothed and a bit deaf. Vain about her clothing and a famous scold, she is full of abundant energy; she has had five husbands, often goes on pilgrimages, and is an early feminist in her defense of women. The Wife's deafness is the consequence of a fistfight with her most recent husband over the issue of wifely obedience. He liked to read to her from a book about wicked wives, which made her so angry she finally tore up the book and threw it into the fire. The Wife's tale begins a debate about the basis of marriage, which other pilgrims take up and elaborate. She tells a story set in the time of King Arthur, when the queen gives an erring knight the task of discovering the one thing that women most want. The knight meets a hideous old woman who promises to tell him the answer to the riddle if he marries her. Chastened and desperate, the knight agrees, and reports to the queen:

> *"My liege lady, generally," said he,*
> *'Women desire to have sovereignty*
> *As well over their husbands as over their love,*
> *And to be in mastery of him above;*
> *This is your great desire, though you have*
> * me killed;*
> *Do as you wish, I am here at your will."*

The knight's life is spared because he gives the correct answer, and his joy increases when, after their marriage, he discovers that the loathsome old woman was really a beautiful young maiden under a spell.

Aside from the tale-telling framework, the *Tales* are held together by interwoven themes of love, justice, religious devotion, and the relations between men and women. These connected meanings give the individual tales a sense of coherence, despite the fact that the manuscript exists in 10 fragments.

Scholars often wonder if Chaucer ever intended to finish all the stories, for he wrote a conclusion in the form of a Retraction, in which he apologizes for the works he had written. Given that this type of apology was a medieval convention and that Chaucer was known for his subtle yet effective humor, some doubt that he really regretted writing the work. In any case, *The Canterbury Tales* has become a landmark in the history of English and world literature. G. K. Chesterton calls Chaucer "not only the father of all our poets, but the grandfather of all our novelists." Even now, translator Louis Untermeyer says that Chaucer "comes among us with unbounded vitality, gross, delicate, lavishly inclusive. . . . No poet has ever done more."

Works by Geoffrey Chaucer

Chaucer's Dream Poetry. Edited by Helen Phillips and Nick Havely. Longman Annotated Text Series. Upper Saddle River, N.J.: Pearson Education, 1997.
The Canterbury Tales. Translated by Nevill Coghill. New York: Penguin Books, 2003.
The Complete Poetry and Prose of Geoffrey Chaucer. Edited by John H. Fisher. Boston: Heinle and Heinle, 1990.

Works about Geoffrey Chaucer

Bisson, Lillian M. *Chaucer and the Late Medieval World.* New York: Palgrave Macmillan, 2000.
Bloom, Harold. *Geoffrey Chaucer.* Bloom's Modern Critical Views Series. Langhorne, Pa.: Chelsea House, 2003.
Halliday, F. E. *Chaucer and His World.* North Yorkshire, U.K.: House of Stratus, 2001.
Ward, Adolphus William. *Geoffrey Chaucer.* La Vergne, Tenn.: International Law and Taxation Publishers, 2003.

Chikamatsu Monzaemon (1653–1725)
dramatist

The great Japanese playwright Chikamatsu Monzaemon was born Sugimori Nobumori in Echizen, on Japan's main island of Honshu. His father, a minor samurai, abandoned his feudal holdings around 1665 to become a *ronin,* or wandering samurai. He moved with his family to the imperial capital of Kyoto, where Chikamatsu found service with the court aristocracy as a teenager. Scholars do not know how he first became involved in the theater, but some have speculated that a nobleman he served was a patron of the BUNRAKU, the popular and prestigious puppet theater for which Chikamatsu was to compose most of his major works.

He wrote his first bunraku play, *The Soga Heir,* in 1683, which received some acclaim. In the following year, he wrote his first play for KABUKI, and in 1686 he achieved his first genuine renown with *Kagekiyo Victorious,* which was widely hailed for its originality and deviation from the stagnant formulas of the puppet play. For a 10-year period beginning in 1693, Chikamatsu wrote primarily for Kabuki, a form of traditional Japanese theater known for its exaggerated acting and brightly-colored sets and costumes. By 1703, however, he was again writing exclusively for the puppet theater, probably because Bunraku treated the playwright's original text with greater reverence than the more free-spirited Kabuki. In *Naniwa Miyage* by Hozumi Ikan, a friend of Chikamatsu relates the playwright's views of how puppet theater differs from live acting:

> *Jōruri* differs from other forms of fiction in that, since it is primarily concerned with puppets, the words must all be living and full of action. Because *jōruri* is performed in theaters that operate in close competition with those of the *kabuki*, which is the art of living actors, the author must impart to lifeless wooden puppets a variety of emotions, and attempt in this way to capture the interest of the audience. . . . Even descriptive passages like the *michiyuki* [the journey], to say nothing of the narrative phrases and dialogue, must be charged with feeling or they will be greeted with scant applause.

In 1705 he moved to Osaka, the Bunraku capital of Japan, and until his death worked primarily for the famous bunraku chanter Takemoto Gidayu. Takemoto's lavish puppet theater Takemotoza staged the premieres of most of Chikamatsu's later works, which would eventually number around 150 plays.

Chikamatsu's works fall into two broad categories: historical romances and domestic tragedies. Although the former were tremendously popular in the 18th century, the latter are more highly esteemed for their accurate and vivid portraits of Japanese society. Peopled by samurai, farmers, merchants, housewives, thieves, and prostitutes, they feature believable characters that speak colloquial dialogue in realistic (and often rather sordid) settings such as streets, shops, brothels, and teahouses. They are also noteworthy for a remarkably modern, naturalistic conception of drama in which the protagonists gain tragic stature when the pressures of society drive them to extreme acts. The stories' realism was centuries ahead of its time. Most of the domestic tragedies are based on actual incidents, and Chikamatsu rarely spent more than a few weeks on any given work so it would be as

topical as possible when presented; for instance, he finished *The Love-Suicides at Sonezaki* (1703) within two weeks of the celebrated double suicide by an assistant in the Osaka firm of Hirano and a prostitute named Ohatsu, upon which it was based. The assistant and Ohatsu committed suicide in the Sonezaki Shrine, from which the play takes its name. This play and the similarly themed *Double Suicide at Amijima* (1720) proved so popular that they touched off a widespread vogue for lovers' suicides both on stage and in real life.

Few of Chikamatsu's historical ROMANCES survive, one of which is the spectacular *Battles of Coxinga*, a lavish swashbuckling melodrama based loosely on the life of a 17th-century Chinese pirate who unsuccessfully attempted to restore the Ming dynasty to his country's throne. Written in 1715, it was the playwright's most popular work during his lifetime and for many years after his death.

Critical Analysis

The Love-Suicides at Sonezaki is perhaps Chikamatsu's most famous and characteristic play. Written in 1703, its plot bears a marked similarity to that of Alexandre Dumas's *Lady of the Camellias*, written some 150 years later. It is the story of Tokubei, a bankrupt merchant who rejects a lucrative arranged marriage for the love of the indentured prostitute Ohatsu. The lovers are unable to escape the respective fates that threaten to separate them forever and commit suicide together. As they prepare to die, Tokubei says to Ohatsu: "You make me feel so confident in our love that I am not worried even by the thought of death. . . . Let us become an unparalleled example of a beautiful way of dying."

The final act the lovers perform together is prefaced by "one of the loveliest passages in Japanese literature," according to Donald Keene. It is spoken by Ohatsu, in the final lines of a 100-line lyric, one of the only stretches of verse in a predominantly prose drama:

> *It's strange, this is your unlucky year*
> *Of twenty-five, and mine of nineteen.*

It's surely proof how deep are our ties
That we who love each other are cursed alike.
All the prayers I have made for this world
To the gods and to the Buddha, I here and now
Direct to the future: in the world to come
May we be reborn on the same lotus!

Ohatsu's final line is a reference to an ancient Buddhist belief that after a double-suicide, the lovers would spend eternity on the same lotus leaf.

For the quality of his prose, Chikamatsu is often called "the Japanese Shakespeare." In the words of translator Donald Keene, "we can only marvel that he could produce such astonishing textures of language," especially given the truncated schedule under which he generally worked. Scholars also view him as just as quintessential a playwright of the Japanese Tokugawa period as Shakespeare was of the English Elizabethan. Unfortunately, the modern Japanese theater rarely performs Chikamatsu's plays, due to a sharp decline in Bunraku's popularity since the late 18th century. Most contemporary Japanese audiences know him primarily through Kabuki and film adaptations of his works, many of which diverge significantly from the source material.

Works by Chikamatsu Monzaemon

Five Late Plays. Translated by C. Andrew Gerstle. New York: Columbia University Press, 2001.
Major Plays of Chikamatsu. Translated by Donald Keene. New York: Columbia University Press, 1990.

Works about Chikamatsu Monzaemon

Gerstle, C. Andrew. *Circles of Fantasy: Convention in the Plays of Chikamatsu.* Cambridge, Mass.: Harvard University Press, 1986.
Gerstle, C. Andrew. "Heroic Honor: Chikamatsu and the Samurai Ideal," *Harvard Journal of Asiatic Studies* (December 1997): 307–382.
Heine, Stephen. "Tragedy and Salvation in the Floating World: Chikamatsu's Double Suicide Drama as Millenarian Discourse," *Journal of Asian Studies* (May 1994): 367–394.

Chilam Balam, The Books of (n.d.–1700s)

Like THE BOOK OF CHILAM BALAM OF CHUMAYEL, *The Book of the Chilam Balam of Tizimin* and *The Book of the Chilam Balam of Mani* are parts of *The Books of Chilam Balam,* a record of Mayan history and culture based on stories firmly rooted in Mayan oral literature. The *Tizimin* book, while it contains prophecy, is more historical in nature and tone than the *Mani* book, which is more prophetic. In terms of dating the manuscripts, it is important to remember that Maya literature contains no linear, or chronological, history. As authors Leon-Portilla and Earl Shorris point out, "The Maya priests who wrote the books of the Chilam Balams were expected to predict the future based on the past, then to record what happened during the predicted period."

The Book of Chilam Balam of Tizimin covers, roughly, Maya history from the seventh to the 19th centuries and focuses on the Itza and Xiu peoples and their interaction with the ultimate conquering by the Spanish. It includes, among other stories and predictions, "The Last Flight of the Quetzal Prince," a story about Tecum; "The Death of Cuauhtemoc," a description of the Mexican prince's death; and "Crónica de Chac-Xulub-Chen," a story of the tragic enslavement of the Maya people.

The Book of the Chilam Balam of Mani roughly covers the same time period as the *Tizimin* book, but it is written in the future tense, giving it a prophetic tone and nature. Its focus is on the Spanish conquest of the Maya, and its stories include "The Prophecy and Advice of the Priest Xupan Nauat," "The Prophetic Words of the Great Prophets, The Principal Goods of the Underworld, and the Great Priests," and "The Prophecy of Oxlahun-Ti-Ku-for Katun 13 Ahau: Recital of the Priest of Chilam Balam," among others.

The Books of Chilam Balam represent not only a desperate attempt to cement dying wisdom, but also a mourning of the fate of the people it represents. "Should we not lament," the book asks defiantly, "in our suffering, grieving for the loss of our maize and the destruction of our teachings concerning the universe of the earth and the universe of the heavens?" As one of the Great Priests states in "The Prophetic Words of the Great Prophets,"

> I wrote this not to speak of our poverty but to make known the events that happened in the life of our ancestors.

In this, the contributors to *The Books of Chilam Balam* succeeded, and their efforts represent today a rare historical, cultural, and literary record of the Maya people.

English Versions of *The Books of Chilam Balam*

The Ancient Future of the Itza: The Book of Chilam Balam of Tizimin. Translated by Munro S. Edmonson. Austin: University of Texas Press, 1982.

The Book of the Jaguar Priest: A Translation of the Book of Chilam Balam of Tizimin. Translated by Maud Worcester Makemson. New York: Henry Schuman, 1951.

A Work about *The Books of Chilam Balam*

Leon-Portilla, Miguel, Earl Shorris, et al. *In the Language of Kings: An Anthology of Mesoamerican Literature—Pre-Columbian to the Present.* New York: W.W. Norton, 2001.

Choon Hyang Jun (1700s) *novel*

Choon Hyang Jun is a novel that was published anonymously in Korea during the 18th century. It tells of the love between Choon Hyang, the beloved only daughter of a *kisaeng*—a professional entertainer, or courtesan—and Yi Toryong (or, in some versions, Yi Mongyong), the aristocratic son of a provincial governor in Namwon, southwestern Korea. Because of the social disparity between them, and because Yi Toryong is still dependent on his parents, they keep their attachment secret. The lovers are separated when Yi Toryong's father is transferred to a position in the capital. Choon Hyang is defenseless when the new governor begins to pursue her, but she will not consider being unfaithful to Yi Toryong. Furious at the impudence of her refusal, the governor has her publicly whipped and then imprisoned. She is near death from grief and humiliation when Yi Toryong, who has passed the examination for public office and has become a high-ranking official, returns to rescue her and to have the lecherous governor fired for abusing his office.

Although it has a fairy tale-like happy ending, the story contains elements of realism and biting social commentary in its depiction of the corrupt official and the underlings who are too timid to resist his injustices. There are also poignant passages about the unfair situation of the *kisaeng* entertainers who are scorned for taking up a profession that was the only one available in Korea at the time for women who had to earn their own living.

Choon Hyang is one of the most beloved characters in Korean literature. Her story is the basis for the most popular of the *pansori* Korean operas and for several Korean films, including the very first sound movie made in Korea, the classic *Chun Hyang* of 1935. A 1992 Japanese anime film, *The Legend of Chun Hyang*, transforms the heroine into a warrior princess.

English Versions of *Choon Hyang Jun*

A Classical Novel: Ch'un-hyang. Translated by Chin In-sook. Seoul, Korea: Korean International Centre, 1970.

The Love of Choon Hyang. Retold by Chi Sun Rhee. Chapel Hill, N.C.: Professional Press, 2000.

Virtuous Women: Three Classic Korean Novels. Translated by Richard Rutt and Kim Chong-un. Korea: Kwang Myong, 1974.

classicism (1450–1600)

Classicism broadly refers to a number of movements in art, literature, architecture, and music that took place at various times. To call something "classic" typically means the object is the best representative of its kind. Classicism as a literary movement generally refers to a renewed interest in and imitation of the art of ancient Greece and Rome, since the period in which these civilizations flourished is frequently referred to as the Classical Age in the history of Western Europe. This interest is usually marked by aesthetic standards reflecting the classical ideals of balance, clarity, concise expression, and concern for form.

More precisely, classicism refers to a movement during the RENAISSANCE when a rediscovery of the works of Greek and Roman rhetoricians and philosophers, such as Plato and Cicero, contributed to a new set of literary ideals. Part of the broader HUMANISM movement, these new standards of harmony, restraint, and idealism can be seen in the works of Italian writers PETRARCH, Dante, and BOCCACCIO. Likewise, artists in the circle of Cosimo de Medici, including MICHELANGELO Buonarroti, and other European authors followed the Italian precedents, as can be seen in the writings of Englishmen Francis BACON and Ben JONSON. Later on, French classicism, also known as NEO-CLASSICISM, particularly valued reason, intellect, simplicity, and symmetry, as shown in the works of PASCAL, DESCARTES, LA ROUCHEFOUCAULD, RACINE, and CORNEILLE.

In the 18th century, archaeological discoveries of the ruins of Herculaneum and Pompeii further revived interest in classical art. The classical period of German literature, 1750–1820, resulted in the dramas of SCHILLER and GOETHE and the music of Haydn, Mozart, and Beethoven. A Victorian classicism in England in the 19th century made "classical" synonymous with conservatism and the valuing of traditional forms over individual expression. Likewise, the 20th century witnessed its own revival of the models of classical Greece and Rome, reflecting the belief that the works of these periods reached a standard of beauty never rivaled in Western art.

Works about Classicism

Bennett, Benjamin. *Modern Drama and German Classicism: Renaissance from Lessing to Brecht.* Ithaca, N.Y.: Cornell University Press, 1986.

Honour, Hugh. *Neo-Classicism.* New York: Penguin Books, 1996.

Lange, Victor. *The Classical Age and German Literature, 1740–1815.* New York: Holmes and Meier, 1982.

Turner, Frederick. *Natural Classicism: Essays on Literature and Science.* New York: Paragon House, 1985.

Zerner, Henri. *Renaissance Art in France: The Invention of Classicim.* Paris: Flammarion, 2004.

Cloud of Unknowing, The   (1300s?)

The Cloud of Unknowing was written by an anonymous 14th-century mystic for individuals dedicated to serving Christ and to knowing God through practicing a contemplative, mystical life. Over the past several hundred years, however, the work's readership has grown to a much larger audience. The 17 surviving manuscripts of the work attest to its popularity during the Middle Ages, and *The Cloud* is now often studied alongside Eastern religious works, such as the Upanishads, in addition to other works by religious writers of the age, including JULIAN OF NORWICH's *Revelations of Divine Love.*

The author of *The Cloud of Unknowing* also is believed to have written the following letters, treatises, and short tracts: *The Epistle of Prayer, The Epistle of Discretion in the Stirrings of the Soul, The Epistle of Privy Counsel,* and *The Treatise of Discerning of Spirits.* All of these works show a remarkable similarity in the obvious influence of Dionysius and Richard of St. Victor, but *The Cloud of Unknowing* is superior to the other works in its clarity of thought, contemplation of the divine, and lively prose style.

The author, who was probably a monk, challenges readers to practice rigorous discipline while contemplating God by abandoning all attachment to forms and objects. In this sense, then, the mystic asks his readers to engage in metaphysical meditation, that which is "beyond the physical." Some scholars interpret the cloud of the work's title as a metaphorical cloud that becomes present when one abandons reasoned analysis and enters an intangible place of unknowing. Other scholars interpret the cloud as a metaphor for the "darkness" that blinds humans to God's love. *The Cloud of Unknowing*'s message, however, seems to be that by abandoning typical modes of understanding the world and faith and by embracing love, one will experience "a loving impulse and a dark gazing into the simple being of God himself."

See also Margery KEMPE.

An English Version of *The Cloud of Unknowing*

Underhill, Evelyn, ed. *The Cloud of Unknowing: The Classic of Medieval Mysticism.* Mineola, N.Y.: Dover, 2003.

A Work about *The Cloud of Unknowing*

Johnston, William. *The Mysticism of the Cloud of Unknowing.* New York: Fordham University Press, 2000.

Columbus, Christopher (Cristóbal Colón, Cristoforo Colombo)
(1451–1506) *explorer*

One of the most famous figures in Western history, Columbus fundamentally changed the course of history with his discovery of the Americas in the late 1400s. By focusing European attention on the unexplored continents of North and South America, Columbus set the stage for the eventual Western domination of the world, which would last for centuries. His discovery also marked the beginning of the destruction of Native American civilization, for which he and the Spanish have been severely criticized.

Columbus was Italian, born in the city of Genoa. At that time, Genoa was a powerful city-state, and Italy was experiencing the political and cultural transformation of the RENAISSANCE. Relatively little is known about Columbus's early life.

His father was a weaver of wool and could not afford an extensive education for his children.

Columbus apparently became a sailor in his teens, although the exact date is unknown. He served on merchant vessels, traveling throughout the Mediterranean. He also ventured into those parts of the Atlantic that were well known to Europeans, voyaging to England and even as far north as Iceland.

He eventually made his permanent home in Portugal, which was then in the midst of an era of extensive sea exploration, begun earlier in the century by Prince Henry the Navigator. The goal of the Portuguese was to send vessels all the way around Africa to find a trade route to the East Indies, where access to expensive spices would make Portugal a fabulously wealthy nation.

Columbus intensely studied the question of how to reach the Indies. He eventually decided that, rather than sail east around Africa, it was better to sail west across the Atlantic Ocean. Contrary to popular belief, educated people in the 15th century knew the world was a sphere, but the idea of a voyage across the unexplored Atlantic was still regarded as foolhardy.

Finding no support in Portugal for his navigational plan, Columbus journeyed to Spain, where he won the support of Queen Isabella and King Ferdinand. Their support proved to be one of the most important decisions in history.

In the summer of 1492, Columbus set sail in three vessels. As was customary for sea captains, Columbus kept a daily journal throughout the voyage. It would eventually be called the *Book of the First Navigation and Discovery of the Indies,* often referred to as the *Journal of the First Voyage.* Although the voyage was comparatively quiet, the weeks that passed without sight of land began to wear on the crewmen's morale. Finally, on October 12, the tiny fleet sighted land. Historians have disputed where Columbus actually landed in the New World, although most evidence suggests that it was the island of San Salvador in the Bahamas.

Columbus explored the surrounding territory for several weeks, believing that he had discovered islands off the coast of China. He was unaware that the land he had found was, in fact, part of an entirely new and unknown continent. His lack of understanding continued until his death.

After returning from his voyage, Columbus secured additional funding and, over the course of the next few years, made three additional voyages of discovery to the New World. Each would chart new territories and promote further exploration. Columbus also worked at establishing Spanish colonies in the new lands, which resulted in the annihilation and enslavement of native populations.

Toward the end of his life, Columbus fell out of favor with Spain's rulers. He died on May 20, but his discoveries radically changed the course of history. Until the late 15th century, Europe had been focused on the Mediterranean and the struggles against the Muslim powers to the East. After Columbus, however, Europe increasingly turned its attention to the Americas. The empires created by various nations there would bring wealth and power to Western civilization and would result in the creation of new nations, including the United States of America.

In addition to being an able sea captain, Columbus was a skilled writer. The *Book of the First Navigation and Discovery of the Indies* was far more than a stilted, dull logbook. His account of the voyage contains exact descriptions of the people and places encountered during the voyage, as well as musings on the future of Spanish policy. It also contains a lively sense of adventure, which inspired numerous explorers who came after Columbus.

English Versions of a Work by Christopher Columbus

Across the Ocean Sea: A Journal of Columbus's Voyage. Edited by George Sanderlin. New York: Harper and Row, 1966.

The Four Voyages. Translated by J. M. Cohen. New York: Penguin Classics, 1992.

Works about Christopher Columbus

Hale, Edward Everett. *Life of Christopher Columbus from His Own Letters and Journals.* IndyPublish, 2002.

Kneib, Martha. *Christopher Columbus: Master Italian Navigator in the Court of Spain.* New York: Rosen Publishing, 2003.

Morison, Samuel Eliot. *Admiral of the Ocean Sea: A Life of Christopher Columbus.* New York: MJF Books, 1942.

comedy of manners   (1600s–1700s)

The comedy of manners is a genre of drama that was most popular in 17th- and 18th-century Europe and focused on human society and behavior. Comedies of manners concentrate on how characters conduct themselves in social situations. The plays are usually satirical, because they show a society or social group's foibles and vices in order to demonstrate how foolish the behavior is. The hallmarks of a comedy of manners are stock social stereotypes, such as the imperious matron; the witty, high-spirited heroine; and the self-important fool. The plots usually revolve around mistaken identities, thwarted young lovers in conflict with status-conscious parents or guardians, and convoluted plans to get money and/or position. Finally, while a comedy of manners can have enough physical humor in it to border on FARCE, it primarily relies on witty repartee for most of its humor.

While one can argue that the plots and basic characters were laid out in the early Roman comedies of Menander and Plautus, the genre is usually associated with 17th-century France and England. MOLIÈRE's comedies poked fun at such social phenomena as pretentious women in *Les Précieuses Ridicules* (*The Affected Young Ladies,* 1659) and possessive husbands in *L'École des Femmes* (*The School for Wives,* 1662).

Molière's plays were translated into English by William Wycherley in the 1670s and, combined with the English tradition of social comedy of Ben JONSON, created the stylish, artificial Restoration sex comedies of the second half of the 17th century. Plays such as Sir George Etherege's *The Man of Mode* (1676), Wycherley's own *The Country Wife* (1675), and William Congreve's *The Way of the World* (1700) were high points in an age that valued cynical observations served in high style. A century later, English playwrights such as Oliver Goldsmith, with *She Stoops to Conquer* (1773), and Richard Brinsley Sheridan, with *The School for Scandal* (1777), would revive the style with gentler satire and more pointed morals. Comedies of manners survived into the 19th century with the witty comedies of Oscar Wilde, and many of their conventions can be seen in Hollywood screwball comedies of the 1930s and 1940s, as well as in contemporary situation comedies.

Works about the Comedy of Manners

Knutson, Harold C. *The Triumph of Wit: Molière and Restoration Comedy.* Columbus: Ohio State University Press, 1968.

Palmer, John. *The Comedy of Manners.* New York: Russell and Russell, 1962.

Sharma, Ram Chandra. *Themes and Conventions in The Comedy of Manners.* Folcroft, Pa.: Folcroft Library Editions, 1977.

Comenius, Johann Amos (Jan Ámos Komenský) (1592–1670) *theologian, educator*

Johann Amos Comenius was born in Nivnice, Moravia, in what is now the Czech Republic. His parents died when he was 12 years old. Four years later, he was sent to the Brethren's school at Prerov, Moravia, and encouraged to pursue a career in the Protestant ministry. In 1613 he attended the University of Heidelberg, where he was influenced by the works of Francis BACON and the Protestant millennialists, who worked to achieve salvation on Earth through science and good works.

The beginning of the Thirty Years' War forced Comenius, who was by this time a Protestant minister, to go into hiding. While in hiding, his wife and two children died of the plague. This tragedy, along with the religious intolerance of the Austrian rulers, led him to write the classic religious ALLEGORY, *The Labyrinth of the World and the Paradise of the Heart* (1618), in which he voices his worldly despair and spiritual consolation.

Six years later, Comenius moved to Leszno, Poland, where he published his two famous educational texts, *The Gates of Languages Unlocked* (1631) and *The Great Didactic* (1637). The first is a Latin instructional text written in both Czech and Latin. The idea of learning Latin through a comparison with the vernacular became very popular, and Comenius's book was translated into most European and Asian languages. The *Great Didactic* is a text on educational theory in which Comenius advocates full-time schooling for all children and the teaching of native and European cultures.

In 1641 Comenius was invited to England to establish a school of social reform, but his plans were interrupted by the outbreak of the English Civil War. He then moved to Sweden, where he developed a series of textbooks modeled on his educational theory. When the Thirty Years' War ended in 1648, Comenius returned to Poland and was named a bishop of the Brethren's Unity Church in Leszno.

In 1652 he moved to Amsterdam, where he spent the rest of his life writing and refining his educational treatises. He is recognized for his internationalism and educational reforms that shaped much of the modern system of education in Germany.

English Versions of Works by Johann Amos Comenius

Selections. Translated by Iris Urwin, with Introduction by Jean Piaget. Paris: UNESCO, 1957.

The Great Didactic of John Amos Comenius. Translated by M. W. Keatinge. London: A. and C. Black, 1921.

Works about Johann Amos Comenius

Murphy, Daniel. *Comenius: A Critical Reassessment of His Life and Work.* Dublin: Irish Academic Press, 1995.

Sadler, John Edward. *J. A. Comenius and the Concept of Universal Education.* London: Allen and Unwin, 1966.

Spinka, Matthew. *John Amos Comenius: That Incomparable Moravian.* Chicago: University of Chicago Press, 1943.

commedia dell'arte

Commedia dell'arte, the improvisational comic theater featuring beloved characters like Harlequin and Columbine, originated in Italy in the 1500s. It takes its name from the Italian for "skilled comedy," because it was performed by professional troupes, in contrast to the learned and scripted *commedia erudita*, performed by amateurs in learned academies.

Commedia dell'arte performances were based on a *scenario*, or outline, of the plot, which was placed backstage for the actors to consult. Few scenarios remain, however, because they were only blueprints for the performance, though Flaminio Scala, an actor with the Duke of Mantua's troupe, published a collection in 1611.

The characters, each of whom had a distinctive mask or costume, included the foolish father Pantalone; the pedantic Dottore (Doctor) Graziano; the thwarted young lovers Isabella and Lelio; the bragging but cowardly soldier Captain Spavento; the comical servants, both crafty (Brighella) and dimwitted (Arlecchino or Harlequin); and the saucy servant girl Columbine. The actors filled out the scenario with their own improvised lines and *lazzi*, or physical gags, which often developed into long comic routines, and they had to be quick-witted to adapt to what their fellow actors were doing.

The origins of commedia dell'arte may lie in the plays of Plautus and Terence, ancient Roman FARCES, and the comedy of medieval minstrels and jesters. The first troupes to perform commedia dell'arte formed around 1550 and found patronage at the courts of Venice and Mantua. They soon began performing at royal courts in Germany, England, and France.

Commedia dell'arte greatly influenced French playwrights. MOLIÈRE and MARIVAUX, for example, based many of the characters and plots in their comedies on Italian originals, and SHAKESPEARE refers to the popularity of the Italian theater in England in *As You Like It.*

Although commedia dell'arte declined after the middle of the 18th century, its spirit lives on in many classics of world literature and even in modern comedic performances, such as those by Charlie Chaplin and the Marx Brothers.

Works of Commedia dell'Arte

Scala, Flamminio. *Scenarios of the Commedia dell'arte: Flamminio Scala's Teatro delle favole rappresentive.* Translated by Henry F. Salerno. New York: New York University Press, 1967.

Jonson, Ben. *Valpone.* Edited by Robert Watson. New York: W.W. Norton, 2003.

Works about Commedia dell'Arte

Heck, Thomas F. *Commedia Dell' Arte: A Guide to the Primary and Secondary Literature.* Lincoln, Neb.: iUniverse, 2000.

Richards, Kenneth, and Laura Richards. *The Commedia dell'Arte: A Documentary History.* Cambridge, Mass.: Blackwell for the Shakespeare Head Press, 1990.

Cook, Ebenezer (ca. 1672–1732) *poet, satirist*

Ebenezer Cook is best known for his 1708 political satire, *The Sot-weed Factor: or a Voyage to Maryland.* A sot-weed factor is a tobacco agent, or trader. The 26-page poem is a satirical treatment of English views on colonial America through the eyes of a downtrodden tobacco agent who has come to America to make his fortune. The poem depicts the early colonies as an unrelenting place, where frauds and unsavory characters prey upon the naïve. At the end of the poem, the tobacco agent leaves America wishing never to see "this Cruel, this inhospitable Shoar" again. The form and style of the poem are modeled on Samuel Butler's *Hudibras,* a celebrated 17th-century satire. The work has received renewed attention in contemporary times, serving as the inspiration for the protagonist in John Barth's comic picaresque novel, *The Sot-Weed Factor* (1960), in which Cook plays the main character.

Cook is believed to have authored works published under the names E. Cooke and E. C. Gent. Several elegies are attributed to him, including an elegy to Thomas Bradley (1727), an elegy on the death of Nicholas Lowe (1728), and two elegies honoring Governor Benedict Leonard Calvert and Justice William Lock (1732).

Other significant works include the 1730 publication of *Sotweed Redivivus; or, The Planters Looking Glass* by E. C. Gent. *The Maryland Muse,* his longest work, was published in 1731 and is a satire of Nathaniel Bacon's rebellion.

Cook's works serve as a window into the life of early America and the difficulties of new settlers hoping to make their fortunes in commerce. Though his work is satirical and certainly a caricature at times, Cook's insights remain of historical significance to this day.

Works by Ebenezer Cook

Early Maryland Poetry: The Works of Ebenezer Cook. Edited by Bernard C. Steiner. Baltimore, Md.: Printed by John Murphy Company, 1900.

The Sot-weed Factor. London: Printed and sold by D. Bragg, 1708; reprinted, New York, 1865.

Works about Ebenezer Cook

Coers, Donald Vernon. *A Review of the Scholarship on Ebenezer Cook and a Critical Assessment of His Works.* College Station: Texas A&M University, University Microfilms, 1974.

Edward H. Cohen, *Ebenezer Cooke: The Sot-Weed Canon.* Athens: University of Georgia Press, 1975.

Copernicus, Nicolaus (1473–1543)
scientist

After the collapse of the classical civilizations of Greece and Rome, virtually no scientific work was done in Europe for nearly 1,000 years. It wasn't until the 16th century, with the beginning of the

Scientific Revolution, that science once again became a major force in Europe. One of the earliest and most important figures of this period was Nicolaus Copernicus, the Latinized form of his name (Mikotaj Kopernik).

Copernicus was born on February 19, in the Polish town of Torun. He was the youngest of four children. His father, Mikolaj Koppernigk, was a wealthy merchant whose peasant ancestors had come from the Silesian village of Koperniki. His mother, Barbara Watzenrode, came from a prominent family. Her brother Lucas Watzenrode adopted the Copernicus children after their father's death, which occurred when Nicolaus was 10 years old.

Copernicus enrolled at the University of Krakow in 1491. Following the ideas of HUMANISM, the university offered a variety of courses in the arts and sciences. Copernicus's studies included law, Latin, philosophy, and geography. The young scholar bought a copy of Euclid's work on geometry. He also began to use the name Copernicus, a Latinized version of Koppernigk. In 1496 he traveled to Italy to continue his studies. The next few years saw him studying law and medicine at universities in Bologna, Padua, and Ferrara. He read the works of Avicenna, Hippocrates, Galen, and Aristotle. He also spent a year teaching mathematics in Rome.

Copernicus was a true RENAISSANCE man, displaying a wide range of interests and abilities not only in his studies but also in his later occupations. After 1506, when he returned from abroad, he spent six years as a medical attendant and adviser to Lucas Watzenrode. He took part in diplomatic missions, practiced medicine, wrote treatises on monetary reform, and performed the duties of a church canon. He also translated into Latin the *Moral, Pastoral, and Amorous Letters* of Theophylactus Simocatta, a seventh-century Byzantine writer. The translation, dedicated to Copernicus's uncle, appeared in print in 1509.

During all this time, Copernicus also developed an intense interest in mathematics and astronomy. By the beginning of the 16th century, astronomy had not advanced beyond what was known to the ancient Greeks, and Copernicus read the astronomical works of such ancient thinkers as Aristotle and Ptolemy. Their view of the universe held that the Earth was the center and that everything, including the Sun, planets, and stars, rotated around the Earth. This view was adopted as religious dogma by the Roman Catholic Church.

During many years of personal study, combining direct astronomical observation with intense mathematical calculation, it gradually dawned on Copernicus that the ancient view of the universe was incorrect. As early as 1507, and in his handwritten *Little Commentary* of 1514, he hypothesized that the Earth rotated around the Sun, rather than the other way around. This cosmological idea had first been proposed by a Greek scientist, Aristarchus of Samos, but had been rejected by his fellow Greeks. Copernicus was the first modern thinker to come to this conclusion, which became known as the Copernican Theory.

In 1515 Copernicus began to write his greatest work, *De Revolutionibus Orbium Coelestium (On the Revolutions of the Heavenly Spheres)*, in support of his heliocentric theory. Being a very modest and serene man, however, he was not particularly eager to publish his findings. He was encouraged to do so by his friend Georg Joachim Rheticus, who shared his interests in mathematics and astronomy. *On the Revolutions* was finally published in 1543, a year that also saw the publication of VESALIUS'S seminal work on anatomy. Copernicus, old and ill, suffered a stroke that year. According to legend, he died a few hours after seeing an advance copy of his book. *On the Revolutions* summarizes Copernicus's entire life work. It begins with general arguments in favor of the idea that the Earth moves around the Sun. It then explains how the heliocentric solar system looks and uses this model to explain why the year has four seasons. Subsequent sections discuss in more detail the motions of the known planets—Earth, Mercury, Venus, Mars, Jupiter, and Saturn. Copernicus's hypotheses involved fewer complicated rules and celestial motions than previous astro-

nomical systems. More important, he based his ideas not on abstract reasoning but on observations of the physical world around him.

Copernicus clearly knew that his theories would be controversial. To make them seem less radical and more authoritative, he supported them not only with data drawn from his own observations, but also with quotations from classical authors such as Cicero and Plutarch. Copernicus notes passages in which these authors raised the possibility that the Earth moved. "Taking occasion thence," he writes:

> I too began to reflect upon the earth's capacity for motion. And though the idea appeared absurd, yet I knew that others before me had been allowed freedom to imagine what circles they pleased in order to represent the phenomena of the heavenly bodies. I therefore deemed that it would be readily granted to me also.

In addition, Copernicus mentions that he has received encouragement from two churchmen, and he dedicates his work to Pope Paul III.

Large portions of European society did in fact resist heliocentrism. Catholics as well as Protestants like Martin LUTHER claimed that Copernicus's theories contradicted the Bible. The Catholic Church persecuted a number of scholars, including Giordano BRUNO and Galileo GALILEI, for writing that the Earth moved around the Sun. *On the Revolutions* remained on the Catholic Church's Index of Prohibited Books from 1616 until 1820.

In his book *Copernicus: The Founder of Modern Astronomy,* Angus Armitage notes that Copernicus's

> great contribution to astronomy lay not in his originality but in his development of those ideas into a systematic planetary theory . . . which was to make possible the triumphs of Kepler and Newton in the following century.

Johann Wolfgang von GOETHE emphasizes the astronomer's significance more forcefully: "Of all the discoveries and opinions proclaimed," he writes, "nothing surely has made such a deep impression on the human mind as the science of Copernicus."

English Versions of Works by Nicolaus Copernicus

Complete Works, 4 vols. Edited by Pawel Czartoryski. London: Palgrave Macmillan, 1972–92.

On the Revolutions: Nicholas Copernicus' Complete Works. Translated by Edward Rosen and edited by Jerzy Dobrzycki. Baltimore, Md.: Johns Hopkins University Press, 1992.

Three Copernican Treatises. Translated by Edward Rosen. Mineola, N.Y.: Dover, 2004.

Works about Nicolaus Copernicus

Armitage, Angus. *Copernicus: The Founder of Modern Astronomy.* New York and London: Thomas Yoseloff, 1957.

Crowe, Ivan. *Copernicus.* Gloucestershire, U.K.: Tempus Publishing, 2004.

Gingerich, Owen. *The Book Nobody Read: Chasing the Revolutions of Nicolaus Copernicus.* New York: Walker, 2004.

Kuhn, Thomas S. *The Copernican Revolution: Planetary Astronomy in the Development of Western Thought.* Cambridge, Mass.: Harvard University Press, 1957.

Corneille, Pierre (1608–1684) *dramatist*

Pierre Corneille was born in Rouen, France, and educated at the excellent Jesuit school there. Although he won prizes for poetry during his school years, he followed his father into the law, and maintained his legal practice in Rouen for most of his life. At the same time, he wrote the plays that established his reputation as one of the three great dramatists (with RACINE and MOLIÈRE) of France's classical century.

In 1629 a traveling theatrical troupe led by the actor Montdory passed through Rouen. Corneille showed Montdory a play he had written, the comedy *Mélite.* Montdory took it on, and when the company performed it in Paris, it was a great success. Corneille produced a succession of comedies and tragicomedies (plays that deal with serious themes but usually end happily) in the next few years, most of them with Montdory and his company in mind.

Corneille's talent came to the attention of Cardinal Richelieu (1585–1642), the powerful prime minister to France's King Louis XIII (1601–43; r. 1610–43). Richelieu invited Corneille to join a group that became known as the "Five Authors," through whose efforts Richelieu hoped to establish a great dramatic tradition in France, based on the classical aesthetics of Aristotle. Richelieu would propose outlines of plays, and the Five Authors would collaborate to realize them. Corneille was involved in several joint projects with the Five Authors during the years from 1635 to 1638, but he withdrew from the group, perhaps because he chafed at the lack of artistic freedom it offered.

A project of his own, the tragicomedy *Le Cid* (1637), was Corneille's most spectacular success up to that time. It is based on legends about an 11th-century Spanish hero, Rodrigo Díaz de Vivar (ca. 1040–1099). In battles against the Arabs, who held much of Spain at the time, Rodrigo earned the Arab epithet of "Cid," or lord. In the play, Rodrigue and Chimène, two young nobles at the Spanish court in Seville, are in love, but their hopes to marry are dashed by a quarrel between their fathers in which Chimène's father, the count of Gormas, slaps Rodrigue's father. Honor demands that Rodrigue challenge the count to a duel, and when Rodrigue kills the older man, honor demands that Chimène seek the death penalty for Rodrigue. Rodrigue responds by offering Chimène his sword so that she can take her revenge on him herself, but love restrains her. An attack by a Moorish army provides an opportunity for Rodrigue to show himself an indispensable hero. The king pardons Rodrigue for the count's death, and after a few more twists in the plot Chimène is at last able to give in to her love.

Audiences in Paris flocked to see *Le Cid.* Some of Corneille's rival playwrights were jealous of his success and eager to find fault. A battle of pamphlets, known as "the quarrel of *Le Cid*," ensued. The pamphlets issued on both sides became so vicious that Richelieu ordered a halt, but he did allow the ACADÉMIE FRANÇAISE to have the last word with a document that tore the play apart on both ethical and aesthetic grounds. The quarrel was the first full discussion of the rules on which French classical theater was based. Although audiences continued to vindicate Corneille's choices in *The Cid*, in subsequent plays Corneille, like other playwrights of the period, observed Aristotle's UNITIES of dramatic action more closely and made clearer genre distinctions. He wrote no more tragicomedies.

Corneille continued to place his protagonists in positions of emotional conflict in the three great tragedies (see TRAGEDY) that followed. Two of them, *Horace* (1640) and *Cinna* (1641), are set in ancient Rome and involve conflicts between love, family duty, and patriotism. In *Polyeucte* (1642) the hero, an Armenian prince in the days of the Roman Empire, is torn between his love of his wife and the new Christian faith he has embraced. These plays are the center of Corneille's reputation today.

One of his most successful works is not a play but a verse translation (1651–56) of *The Imitation of Christ* by THOMAS À KEMPIS. By the 1670s, Molière and Racine, and even younger brother Thomas Corneille (1625–1709), whose career as a dramatist Corneille had helped substantially, had eclipsed the older writer in the attention of the public and of the royal patrons who allowed the drama to flourish. As the scholar Vincent Cheng remarks, "the age that idealized and understood the larger-than-life Cornelian hero with noble passions and pride of self was no more."

An English Version of Works by Pierre Corneille

The Cid/Cinna/The Theatrical Illusion. Translated and with an introduction by John Cairncross. New York: Penguin, 1975.

Works about Pierre Corneille

Carlin, Claire L. *Pierre Corneille Revisited.* Boston: Twayne, 1999.

Goodkin, Richard E. *Birth Marks: The Tragedy of Primogeniture in Pierre Corneille, Thomas Corneille, and Jean Racine.* Philadelphia: University of Pennsylvania Press, 2000.

Cortés, Hernán (1485–1547) *chronicler, explorer, conquistador*

Hernán Cortés was the Spanish explorer and conquistador who conquered Montezuma's Aztec Empire and was responsible, in large part, for the Spanish conquest of Mexico. He was born in Medellín, Spain, and studied law at the University of Salamanca. Eager for adventure, he abandoned his law studies for trips abroad, and in 1504 undertook the first of several voyages to the New World. In 1519 he became captain-general of his own armada and set sail for the Yucatán.

Between 1519 and 1526, Cortés wrote his *Cartas de relación (Letters of Report),* five long reports addressed to Charles V in which he describes Spanish operations in Mexico. The first letter, now lost, has been replaced in editions of *Cartas de relación* by report addressed to Holy Roman Emperor Charles V (King Charles I of Spain) in July of 1519 by the regent of Villa Rica de la Vera Cruz, relating Cortés's arrival in Mexico. The second letter, dated October 30, 1520, describes the entry of Cortés and his men into the Mexican hinterland. *Carta III* dates to May 15, 1522, and covers experiences in Tlaxcalan territory. *La quarta relación* (October 15, 1524) deals with Cortés's Spanish rival, Diego Velázquez, while the fifth letter, dispatched on September 3, 1526, relates the Honduras expedition.

Cortés's reports are considered models of their kind, demonstrating a lucid, elegant prose and a clear, concise, direct writing style. Though they glorify his ruthless conquest, the letters exhibit Cortés's grasp of the complex issues surrounding the Spanish invasion, as well as an appreciation for detail in describing the splendor of Mexican civilization. While Cortés expresses admiration for the culture of the Mexican Indians, it is evident in his writings that he understood their future only in terms of political and cultural assimilation to the European way of life. Nevertheless, Spanish chronicles like the letters of Cortés and the history of Bernal DÍAZ DEL CASTILLO remain valuable sources of information about the way of life of the peoples of Mexico before the Conquest.

An English Version of Works by Hernán Cortés

Letters From Mexico. Translated by Anthony Pagden. New Haven, Conn.: Yale University Press, 2001.

Works about Hernán Cortés

Collis, Maurice. *Cortés and Montezuma.* New York: New Directions, 1999.

Gordon, Helen Heightsman. *Voice of the Vanquished: The Story of the Slave Marina and Hernán Cortés.* New York: University Editions, 1995.

Ramen, Fred. *Hernán Cortés: The Conquest of Mexico and the Aztec Empire.* New York: Rosen Publishing Group, 2003.

Crèvecoeur, J. Hector St. John de (Michel-Guillaume-Jean de Crèvecoeur) (1735–1813) *essayist*

J. Hector St. John de Crèvecoeur was raised by his parents, Marie-Anne-Therese and Guillaume Jean de Crèvecoeur, in Normandy, France. The rigorous Jesuit school he attended required pupils to learn Latin, French, mathematics, catechism, and ethics. After graduating, he traveled to England, Canada, and New York, supporting himself by working as a surveyor and cartographer.

In 1769 he settled on a farm in New York with his wife, Mehetable, and began to compose essays about America and his experience as a farmer. His desire to remain neutral in the debates about Great Britain's control of the colonies made life difficult for him. He was imprisoned on suspicion of serving as an American spy. Upon release, he went to England, sold his essays, which he titled

Letters from an American Farmer (1782), and then journeyed back to France. In 1783 he returned to America and learned that his wife was dead and his farm destroyed. Seven years later, he moved back to France, where he continued living until his death.

Letters from an American Farmer secured for Crèvecoeur a place in literary history. The 12 letters are composed by James, a fictional narrator, and are directed to a European friend. In the third and most frequently cited letter, Crèvecoeur's narrator asks, "What . . . is the American, this new man?" The American, he answers, is a man who reaps the "rewards" of his own industry and is "at liberty . . . to follow the dictates" of his conscience without governmental interference. Other letters, especially those addressing issues relating to slavery and the American Revolution, are not so optimistic. Norman S. Grabo observes that *Letters* "brilliantly bespoke a new and arresting voice in American letters," and they "depicted both the American dream and its brutal subversive nightmare."

Works by Crèvecoeur

Letters from an American Farmer. Edited by Susan Manning. Oxford: Oxford University Press, 1998.

More Letters from an American Farmer: An Edition of the Essays in English Left Unpublished by Crèvecoeur. Edited by Dennis D. Moore. Athens: University of Georgia Press, 1995.

Works about Crèvecoeur

Allen, Gay Wilson, and Roger Asselineau. *American Farmer: The Life of St. John de Crèvecoeur.* New York: Penguin, 1990.

Philbrick, Thomas. *St. John de Crèvecoeur.* Farmington Hills, Mich.: Gale Group, 1970.

Cruz, Sor Juana Inés de la (Juana Ramírez de Asbaje) (1648–1695) *poet, playwright*

Sor Juana Inés de la Cruz was born in the town of San Miguel de Nepantla to a Creole mother and a

Spanish father. An extraordinarily gifted child, she was able to read by age three, was composing verse by age seven, and moved to Mexico City to be educated in the court of Mancera at age eight.

Less for religious inclinations than for a desire for peace, reflection, and the opportunity to write, Sor Juana opted for a religious life, entering first a Carmelite convent (1667) and later that of the order of Saint Jerome. It was at this time that she assumed the name Juana Inés de la Cruz.

She published her first book of poems in Madrid in 1689. With this and other publications, Sor Juana became famous throughout the Spanish-speaking world, and prominent writers and public personalities praised her work. Nevertheless, her prodigious talents as well as her outspoken opinions regarding the rights and roles of women also won her the animosity of many peers and superiors. After a long and difficult illness, she died alone in her convent, a victim of the plague.

Besides occasional verse and *villancicos*, a traditional folk verse form, Sor Juana wrote philosophical reflections and satires. In addition, her love poems are to this day among the best in the Spanish language. Her single greatest work may be "Primer sueño" (ca. 1680), a long poem with elements of ALLEGORY and rich symbolism that owes part of its inspiration to the Spanish writer Francisco de QUEVEDO's poem of the same name.

Though Sor Juana's plays and prose are also of a very high quality, it is primarily for her poetry that she is remembered. Her work shows not only a remarkable mastery of verse forms, but also incredible variety and energy. After being neglected during the 19th and early 20th centuries, Sor Juana is now seen as one of the great poets of Mexico and the Spanish language.

An English Version of Works by Sor Juana Inés de la Cruz

Sor Juana's Love Poems. Translated by Joan Larkin and Jaime Manrique. New York: Painted Leaf Press, 1997.

A Work about Sor Juana Inés de la Cruz

Flynn, Gerard. *Sor Juana Inés de la Cruz.* New York: Twayne 1971.

cycle, miracle, mystery, and morality plays (1400s–1600s)

Four types of drama that emerged from the 14th century to the 17th century were the cycle, miracle, mystery, and morality plays. While these plays were all founded on religious and secular thought, they vary slightly in purpose, subject matter, theme, and form of presentation.

Cycle plays, dramatized biblical stories of the Old and New Testaments, were one of the most important and popular forms of drama during the late Middle Ages and into the RENAISSANCE. The most well-known cycles are the Chester, York, Wakefield (Townley), and N-Town plays. The plays were performed sequentially, beginning with the *Fall of Lucifer* or the *Creation of Adam and Eve,* and closing with *The Last Judgment.* Written by clerics and performed by trade guilds, such as the tanners, tailors, and cooks and innkeepers guilds, the plays involved participation by both church clergy and laypersons. Such collaboration promoted the spread of biblical stories to a wide, mostly secular audience. Performances occurred out-of-doors on pageant-wagons, and audiences traveled from wagon to wagon to see a particular living story, or wagons moved to meet the crowd.

The plays were linked thematically and typologically. Recurring themes unite the individual stories, such as the theme of obedience in *Fall of Lucifer* and *Abraham and Isaac,* and Old Testament stories anticipated New Testament stories. The play of *Abraham and Isaac,* for example, with its emphasis on sacrifice, anticipates the later story of Christ's sacrifice for humankind.

Many of the cycle plays were written by well-educated people, as can be seen in the plays attributed to the "Wakefield Master," and they are valued for their representation of early popular (as opposed to court) drama.

Historically, cycle plays were an outgrowth of the annual holy day of Corpus Christi (Body of Christ), wherein the Eucharist was paraded through the church and then shown to onlookers congregating outside. Through close association with the Corpus Christi processional, cycle plays are also called Corpus Christi plays. These dramas are sometimes also referred to as miracle plays, but the cycle plays are less religious in tone and dogma.

Miracle plays differ from cycle plays in that they focus on the lives of, and miracles performed by, saints. For this reason, they are also known as "saints' plays" and "conversion plays." Miracle plays may also present miraculous stories of objects becoming sacred, such as the transformation of bread into the holy Eucharist. Although many scholars consider the term "miracle play" to include the genre of mystery play, others distinguish miracle plays from mystery plays by way of their source material. Whereas mystery plays are based upon scripture, miracle plays are not. However, the fact that no extant miracle play exists in the English language that has not been revised to modern tastes makes this definition of "miracle" difficult. The drama *Mary Magdalene* relies upon scriptural accounts as does *The Conversion of St. Paul,* for example. Moreover, as scholar Alfred W. Pollard suggests, what also confuses the distinction between the miracle and the mystery play is that the word *miracle* was used to describe both miracle and morality plays as far back as the 12th century.

Examples of plays recognized as miracle plays—since they resemble miracles more than any other dramatic form—are *The Conversion of St. Paul, Mary Magdalene,* and *The Play of the Sacrament.*

Another similar genre was the morality play, which was a staple of medieval drama that evolved side-by-side with mystery and miracle plays. Mystery plays mainly dramatized events in biblical history to highlight themes of salvation. The morality play, evolving from the medieval sermon, conveyed a moral truth or lesson using allegorical terms. In these plays, qualities or concepts were represented as people, and the characters' names indicated in obvious ways the quality they personified. The early plays dealt with fundamental issues such as the conflict between good and evil, the fall of man, and redemption. The purpose of the morality play was didactic; its object was to instruct the audience on the application of Christian doctrine to everyday life and the cultivation of character. Some of the most well-known morality plays in English are *The Castle of Perseverance* (ca. 1405), *Mankind,* and *EVERYMAN* (early 1500s).

The morality plays were not grim tragedies; rather, many contained comic scenes, which at times descended into venial or boisterous humor. Modern scholars frequently dismiss the morality plays as dull reading, primarily because of their allegorical nature and attention to abstract constructs. For medieval audiences, however, the plays had real ethical and moral significance and thus were popular even into the Renaissance. Near the end of the 15th century, the morality play evolved into the moral interlude, which still focused on an ethical teaching but was likely to be shorter, with a limited number of characters. After 1500, the increasing tendency to personify devils, include mischief makers, and improvise ribald jokes to amuse the audience became indications of secularization of which the Catholic Church did not approve. Later, the appearance of Reformation thought caused a complete separation between the morality play and the church. With their focus on the struggle between good and evil within the individual, some of the later morality plays show a complex sophistication of theme, layers of meaning, and a depth of characterization that point the way to the evolution of Elizabethan drama.

Cycle, Miracle, Mystery, and Morality Plays

Cawley, A. C. ed. *Everyman and Medieval Miracle Plays.* London: J.M. Dent, 1974.

Happe, Peter. *Four Morality Plays.* New York: Viking Press, 1988.

Lesker, G. A. *Three Late Medieval Morality Plays.* New York: W.W. Norton, 1984.

Lumiansky, R. M., and D. Mills, eds. *The Chester Mystery Cycle,* vol. 1. Rochester, N.Y.: Boydell and Brewer, 1974.

Rose, Martial, ed. *The Wakefield Mystery Plays: The Complete Cycle of Thirty-Two Plays.* New York: W.W. Norton, 1994.

Works about Cycle, Miracle, Mystery, and Morality Plays

Harty, Kevin J. *Chester Mystery Cycle: A Casebook.* London: Taylor and Francis, 1992.

Kolve, V. A. *The Play Called Corpus Christi.* Palo Alto, Calif.: Stanford University Press, 1966.

Mills, David. *Recycling the Cycle: The City of Chester and Its Whitsun Plays,* vol. 4. Toronto, Ontario: University of Toronto Press, 1998.

Pollard, Alfred W., ed. *English Miracle Plays, Moralities and Interludes: Specimens of the Pre-Elizabethan Drama.* Oxford: Oxford University Press, 1978.

D

Defoe, Daniel (1660–1731) *novelist, poet, journalist, nonfiction writer*

Daniel Defoe was born in London to James Foe, a merchant, and his wife, Alice. He was raised with a strongly Puritanical leaning and sent to Dissenting schools. In 1684 he married Mary Tuffley and established himself as a merchant in London. Defoe retained his early religious principles and in 1685 joined the duke of Monmouth's unsuccessful rebellion against the Catholic king, James II. In 1692 he declared bankruptcy after having been previously imprisoned for debt.

Sometime in the 1680s, Defoe began writing political pamphlets, which critics continue to attempt to identify, as he published hundreds of works anonymously. One of the earlier works is *An Essay on Projects* (1697), about social improvement. Defoe achieved a major success with the poem *The True-Born Englishman* (1701), a satire of narrow-minded national pride.

Defoe increasingly became interested in creating narrative personae. *The Shortest Way with Dissenters* (1702) demonstrated the dangers of irony. The pamphlet ironically presents the voice of a religious zealot advocating extreme treatment of dissenters: "Now, let us *Crucifie the Thieves*. Let her Foundations be establish'd upon the Destruction of her Enemies: The Doors of Mercy being always open to the returning Part of the deluded People: let the Obstinate be rul'd with the Rod of Iron." His plan backfired, however; the pamphlet was declared libelous, and Defoe was jailed once again.

While in prison, Defoe struck a bargain with an important member of Parliament, Robert Harley, agreeing to write political propaganda for his freedom. He received £200 a year to work as a government agent, producing a journal, *The Review*, from 1704 to 1713. He changed his name from "Foe" to "Defoe" in 1703, and in 1713 was jailed yet again for a satirical pamphlet.

The turning point in Defoe's career came in 1719, when he published *Robinson Crusoe*. With this work, Defoe transformed himself from a prolific hack writer into one of the earliest and most important English novelists. Over the next five years, he wrote a rapid succession of novels modeled on this successful formula: first-person, realistic, episodic narratives of remarkable individuals. *Robinson Crusoe* tells the story of a man stranded on an island, *Moll Flanders* (1722) was a thief, and *Roxana* (1724) a prostitute. Other works purported to be first-person accounts of major historical events, such as *Memoirs of a Cavalier* (1720), set during the English Civil War, and *Journal of the*

Plague Year (1722), a remarkable reconstruction of life in London during an outbreak of the plague.

One of Defoe's last important works was *Tour thro' the Whole Island of Great Britain* (1724–27), an economic survey of England and Scotland. Although he wrote in a wide range of genres, Defoe is best remembered as a novelist.

Critics have argued whether Defoe was the first English novelist, but they tend to agree that his works were important in developing the standard of realism in the novel. In *The Rise of the Novel,* Ian Watt praises *Moll Flanders* for its "formal realism" while noting its literary defects: "Defoe's prose is not in the ordinary sense well-written, but it is remarkably effective in keeping us close to the consciousness of Moll Flanders as she struggles to make her recollection clear. . . ."

Critics also have noted the exploration of themes of identity and subjectivity in many of Defoe's works. *Colonel Jack* (1722), for example, tells a story of the rise of a street urchin from thief to gentleman. J. R. Hammond calls it "remarkable for its insight into the mind of a child." Critic Hans Turley praises *Captain Singleton* (1720) as "the most important of [Defoe's] pirate works and particularly significant in a history of the novel that emphasizes psychological realism and domestic subjectivity."

Recently, critics have begun to value *Roxana,* Defoe's last novel, as perhaps his masterpiece. The book was intended to be a "woman's novel," imitative of the popular courtship novels of Eliza Haywood and Penelope Aubin.

Defoe's first reputation, however, rests on *Robinson Crusoe,* in which critics have found fertile ground for exploring issues of race and colonialism in the early 18th century.

Other Works by Daniel Defoe

A General History of Pyrates. Edited by Manuel Schonhorn. New York: Dover, 1999.
Memoirs of an English Officer and Two Other Short Novels. London: Victor Gollancz, 1970.
The Shortest Way With the Dissenters and Other Pamphlets. Oxford: Basil Blackwell, 1927.
The Travel and Historical Writings of Daniel Defoe. Edited by W. R. Owens and P. N. Furbank. London: Pickering and Chatto, 2002.

Works about Daniel Defoe

Lund, Roger, ed. *Critical Essays on Daniel Defoe.* New York: G.K. Hall, 1997.
Novak, Maximilian E. *Daniel Defoe: Master of Fictions: His Life and Ideas.* Oxford: Oxford University Press, 2001.
West, Richard. *Daniel Defoe: The Life and Strange, Surprising Adventures.* New York: Carroll and Graf, 1998.

De-Ka-Nah-Wi-Da and *Hiawatha*
(late 1300s)

Current knowledge of this traditional story of the Iroquois is based on writings made in the 19th century. In *De-Ka-Nah-Wi-Da* and *Hiawatha,* as told by Glen Welker, a young mother learns in a dream that she will give birth to a son who will bring peace. This child, De-Ka-Nah-Wi-Da, grows to manhood and helps Chief Hiawatha bring peace to warring tribes.

In some stories, Hiawatha was originally known as Ta-ren-ya-wa-gon, the Great Upholder of the Heavens, a spirit or god who chose to become a mortal. In other stories, he was the chief of his people, a man who De-Ka-Nah-Wi-Da met as he was attempting to spread peace among all the peoples of the land. According to legend, De-Ka-Nah-Wi-Da gave this chief the name Hiawatha, as well as the task of teaching peace and balance.

For many years, the Iroquois and other tribes prospered under Hiawatha's influence. This prosperity was threatened, however, when new, fierce, uncivilized tribes invaded the lands. When the Onondaga, Mohawk, Oneida, Cayuga, and Seneca turned to Hiawatha for counsel, Hiawatha told them:

You five tribes must be like the five fingers of a warrior's hand joined in gripping the war club. Unite as one, and then your enemies will recoil before you back into the northern wastes from whence they came.

When the tribes united, Hiawatha gave them a common name—Ako-no-shu-ne, the Iroquois. Based on Iroquois oral tradition, the story of De-Ka-Nah-Wi-Da and Hiawatha has been told and retold and continues to the present day, garnering widespread interest in the history, customs, and stories of the Iroquois people.

An English Version of *Hiawatha*

Huffstetler, Edward W. *Myths of the World: Tales of Native America.* New York: MetroBooks, 1996.

Della Casa, Giovanni (1503–1556) *poet, scholar, cleric*

Giovanni Della Casa took his name from his birthplace, La Casa, in the Italian region of Tuscany. He grew up in Mugello and, while studying at various universities, composed a number of light lyric poems, some rather licentious. He became a priest in 1537 and was named archbishop of Benevento in 1544. Though he hoped to become a cardinal like his mentor Pietro BEMBO, Della Casa was instead sent to Venice as the papal nuncio.

Between 1547 and 1549 Della Casa wrote a series of weighty orations or *Political Discourses,* in which he lamented the dangers facing Italy. Despite the triumphs of art and learning that characterized Italy during the High RENAISSANCE, Della Casa and his peers felt threatened by the ideals of the Protestant Reformation. As part of the Counter-Reformation to preserve the Catholic Church, Della Casa introduced Venice to the Inquisition, a board of clerics committed to suppressing what they viewed as heretical ideals. Though an author himself, Della Casa helped found the papal index of forbidden books.

When his patron, Pope Paul III, died in 1549, Della Casa removed to the Venetian countryside and began composing *Galateo,* a treatise on man-

ners. Written in the style of Baldessare CASTIGLIONE's *Courtier,* but borrowing the witty flair of BOCCACCIO, *Galateo* prescribed proper behavior for all levels of society. The work was enormously popular and widely read from the moment it appeared in print in 1558, along with Della Casa's *Poems.*

The *Poems,* written in Latin, showed Della Casa's reworking of the classic style established by PETRARCH. He followed the style of Horace, Catullus, Virgil, and Propertius to tell his stories of exile and redemption. Though important in their own right, the authoritative majesty of Della Casa's *Poems* and the passionate playfulness of his lyrical songs or *canzoniere* were far overshadowed in popularity by *Galateo,* for whose witty advice and clever insights Della Casa is best remembered.

English Versions of Works by Giovanni Della Casa

Galateo. Translated by Konrad Eisenbichler and Kenneth R. Bartlett. Toronto: Centre for Reformation and Renaissance Studies, 1986.
Giovanni della Casa's Poem Book. Edited by John Van Sickle. Binghamton, N.Y.: Medieval and Renaissance Texts and Studies, 1999.

Works about Giovanni Della Casa

Berger, Harry. *The Absence of Grace: Sprezzatura and Suspicion in Two Renaissance Courtesy Books.* Stanford, Calif.: Stanford University Press, 2000.
Santosuosso, Antonio. *Bibliography of Giovanni Della Casa: Books, Readers, and Critics.* Florence: L.S. Olschki, 1979.

Derzhavin, Gavriil Romanovich (1743–1816) *poet*

Gavriil Romanovich Derzhavin was born into a poor noble family and spent his early years in Kazan. He learned to read and write Russian and German and in 1762 he began military duty in St. Petersburg, witnessing the palace coup that brought CATHERINE THE GREAT to the throne. The influence of Russian poets Mikhail LOMONOSOV and Alexander SUMAROKOV showed in Derzhavin's early works, but gradually his poems developed a more lyrical and distinct style.

Derzhavin participated in the military suppression of the Pugachev revolt (1773–75) and wrote "Ode on the Death of Bibikov" (1774) in memory of one of his commanders. In 1776 he published *Odes Translated and Composed Near Chitalagai Mountain*, largely dealing with natural imagery.

In 1777 Derzhavin transferred to the civil service and during these years wrote his most highly-regarded poems. "The Bride" (1778) celebrates his marriage to Ekaterina Bastidion. "Ode to Felitsa" praises Catherine II's virtues and humorously contrasts them with the vices of her advisers and of the poet himself. "God," combines an exaltation of the divine with a celebration of humanity and the individual. In "The Waterfall," commemorating the death of statesman Grigorii Potemkin, Derzhavin uses the image of a waterfall to review Potemkin's life and achievements.

After his retirement in 1803, Derzhavin published *Anacreontic Songs* (1804), a collection of 109 lyric poems, assembled a four-volume edition of his writings in 1808, composed his memoirs (1811–12), and helped found the Society of Lovers of the Russian Word, a group that opposed the literary innovations of Nikolai Karamzin. In his final years, the patriotic Derzhavin wrote poems mourning Russia's losses during the Napoleonic Wars and rejoicing over France's defeat.

As a poet, Derzhavin drew inspiration from current events and writers, as well as from ancient authors Horace and Anacreon. His odes, satires, and lyric poems display his gift for visual imagery. They also reflect Derzhavin's love of nature, appreciation for the pleasures of life, and concern with the inevitability of death. Many scholars consider Derzhavin the most important Russian poet of his time.

An English Version of Works by Gavriil Romanovich Derzhavin

Poetic Works. Translated by Alexander Levitsky and Martha T. Kitchen. Providence, R.I.: Brown University, 2001.

Works about Gavriil Romanovich Derzhavin

Crone, Anna Lisa. *Daring of Dershavin: The Moral and Aesthetic Independence of the Poet in Russia.* Columbus, Ohio: Slavica Publishers, 2001.

Hart, Pierre R. *G. R. Derzhavin: A Poet's Progress.* Columbus, Ohio: Slavica Publishers, 1979.

Descartes, René (1596–1650) *nonfiction writer, philosopher, scholar*

René Descartes was born in La Haye, France, to Joachim Descartes, a counselor in the French parliament. In 1606 he entered the Jesuit school of La Flèche in Anjou, where he studied classics, logic, philosophy, and mathematics. He received a law degree and a *bacalaureat* (B.A.) in 1616 from the University of Poitiers. He enlisted at a military school in Breda, Holland, where he studied mathematics with the Dutch scientist Isaac Beeckman (1588–1637). After serving briefly in the Bavarian army (1619), he embarked on eight years of travel, spending time in Bohemia, Hungary, Italy, Holland, and France. He ultimately settled in Holland, where he lived from 1628 to 1648, maintaining correspondence across Europe with many of the most important mathematicians and philosophers of his day.

In 1648 Descartes was persuaded by Queen Christina of Sweden to accept a position at her court. The queen was so eager to study mathematics with Descartes that she demanded his presence at five o'clock every morning. Breaking his lifelong habit of getting up at 11 A.M., and suffering in the northern climate, Descartes caught pneumonia, which ultimately killed him.

Critical Analysis

When Descartes moved to Holland, he began work on a scientific work, *The World, or Treatise on*

Light. He had nearly finished it when he learned that the Italian scientist Galileo GALILEI was being tried for defying church teaching by publishing his findings about the Earth's movement around the Sun. In the circumstances, Descartes decided not to publish his work on light or anything about the world as it actually is; instead he confined his publishing to speculative works about how the world could be.

Descartes' first two published works, and the ones for which he is best known, are *Discourse on Method* (1637) and *Meditations on First Philosophy* (1641). At the beginning of *Meditations* he writes, "I should withhold from assent no less carefully from opinions that are not completely certain and indubitable than I would from those that are patently false."

With this statement Descartes sets out his underlying purpose: to establish a methodology that is based on skepticism, eventually labeled "Cartesian doubt." His experiments with light had brought the phenomenon of optical illusions to his attention. Since one's senses can deceive one, Descartes supposes "that everything I see is false. . . . I have no senses whatever." From this piece of reasoning he concludes that the only thing of which he can be certain is that he thinks. As he explains in *Discourse on Method:*

> I resolved to assume that everything whatever entered into my mind was no more true than the illusions of my dreams. But immediately afterwards I noticed that whilst I thus wished to think all things false, it was absolutely essential that the "I" who thought this should be somewhat, and remarking that this truth *"I think, therefore I am"* was so certain and so assured that all the most extravagant suppositions brought forward by the skeptics were incapable of shaking it, I came to the conclusion that I could receive it without scruple as the first principle of the Philosophy for which I was seeking.

There is a split in Cartesian thought between the evidence of the senses, which must remain uncertain, and pure thought. The philosopher, according to Descartes, is required to progress from a simple idea, one that can be known without any prior knowledge, to ideas that can be known only because of one's knowledge of the chain of ideas that proceeds from the first one. Hence, as the scholar Emily Grosholz points out, "the argument of the *Meditations* [the basis of all Descartes thought] critically limits the extent of human knowledge to ideas proportional to the 'I think' with which it begins." This limitation requires the Cartesian philosopher to ignore other possibilities, excluding, for example, considerations of the body.

Descartes' thought has remained extremely important and influential. Cartesian philosophy took hold in France almost immediately. In England, however, his influence was less immediate. The Cartesian distrust of the evidence of the senses ran directly contrary to British empiricism, a philosophy built upon direct sensory evidence and typified by the work of Francis BACON and John Locke. Later skeptical philosophers such as David Hume renewed interest in Descartes in the 18th century. "Over the centuries and with currently renewed intensity," as Grosholz observes, Descartes' *Meditations* "has never failed to inspire serious discussion among philosophers."

English Versions of Works by René Descartes

Discourse on Method and Meditations on First Philosophy, 4th ed. Translated by Donald Cress. Indianapolis, Ind.: Hackett Publishing, 1999.

Discourse on Method and The Meditations. Translated by F. E. Sutcliffe. New York: Penguin Books, 1998.

Philosophical Essays and Correspondence. Edited by Roger Ariew. Indianapolis, Ind.: Hackett Publishing, 2000.

The Philosophical Writings of Descartes, vol. one. Edited by John Cottingham, et al. New York: Cambridge University Press, 1985.

Treatise of Man. Translated by Thomas Steele Hall. New York: Prometheus Books, 2003.

Works about René Descartes

Ariew, Roger, and Marjorie Grene, eds. *Descartes and His Contemporaries: Meditations, Objections, and Replies.* Chicago: University of Chicago Press, 1995.

Cottingham, John, ed. *The Cambridge Companion to Descartes.* New York: Cambridge University Press, 1992.

Grosholz, Emily. *Cartesian Method and the Problem of Reduction.* New York: Oxford University Press, 1991.

Sorell, Tom. *Descartes: A Very Short Introduction.* New York: Oxford University Press, 2000.

Díaz del Castillo, Bernal (1496–1584)
explorer, nonfiction writer

Bernal Díaz del Castillo was born in Medina del Campo. He began a career of expeditions to the New World when he was 18 and served as a soldier in several expeditions, but he is best known for his service under Hernán CORTÉS in the Yucatán. The Cortés expedition inspired Díaz del Castillo's chronicle, *Historia verdadera de la conquista de la Nueva España* (*The True History of the Conquest of New Spain*, 1632). He was in his 60s when he began writing and died in Santiago de los Caballeros in Guatemala at age 88.

The True History of the Conquest of New Spain is a soldier's eyewitness account, told from Díaz del Castillo's perspective, of the campaigns of Cortés. By his own account, Díaz del Castillo was eager to leave a record of his dramatic experiences in the New World for his children and grandchildren. Unlike other famous conquistadors, Díaz del Castillo does not distinguish himself through military deeds; his fame rests solely on his comprehensive historical chronicle.

The True History of the Conquest of New Spain is largely autobiographical and has the value of authenticity. The narration encompasses the years from 1517 to 1524, the period of Cortés's disastrous expedition to Las Hibueras (Honduras). Later additions and corrections provide information up to the year 1568. Throughout, Díaz del Castillo demonstrates a remarkable memory for details, including names of persons, places, and horses. In a straightforward and conversational style, he describes the men's hopes, fears, and personalities. He also analyzes Cortés's psychology, vividly portrays the Spanish conqueror in action, and provides a wealth of information on the Aztec empire and civilization, including a memorable description of Tenochtitlán.

Modern critics consider Díaz del Castillo's work a valuable source for the study of Mexico's history and one of the greatest Spanish-American historical narratives. The chronicle is noted for its drama, detail, and recording of the extremes of human experience.

English Versions of a Work by Bernal Díaz del Castillo

Conquest of New Spain. Translated by J. M. Cohen. New York: Viking Press, 1963.

The Discovery and Conquest of Mexico: 1517–1521. Translated by A. P. Maudslay and edited by Genaro Garcia. New York: Da Capo Press, 2004.

Works about Bernal Díaz del Castillo

Cerwin, Herbert. *Bernal Díaz, Historian of the Conquest.* Norman: University of Oklahoma Press, 1963.

Grauer, Ben. *How Bernal Díaz's "True History" Was Reborn.* New York: B. Grauer, 1955.

Dickinson, John (1732–1808) *politician*

The American Revolution was far more than simply a military conflict. It also was an era when ideas of political philosophy were fundamentally reconsidered. Questions were debated and discussed regarding the nature of government, the relations between citizens and the state, and how to create societies that have a proper balance of freedom and order. The American revolutionaries were forced to ask themselves whether they should break their ties with Great Britain, and if so, what kind of independent nation they would create. Among the brilliant men involved in these critical debates was John Dickinson.

Dickinson was born in Maryland to an ordinary Quaker family. They moved to Delaware when Dickinson was still very young, and throughout his adult life he was involved with the affairs of both Delaware and Pennsylvania. He began studying law in Philadelphia and spent three years in London completing his studies. Upon his return to America, he established a successful legal practice.

By the mid-1760s, relations between Great Britain and the American colonies were breaking down, beginning with the issue of the Stamp Act in 1765, when Britain attempted to tax the colonists without their consent. Elected to the legislative assembly of Pennsylvania, Dickinson began speaking out against British policies, which he felt were oppressive. He also began writing political tracts upholding his views. Soon his reputation spread throughout America and he became one of the most popular men in the colonies.

In late 1767 Dickinson began writing a series of articles titled *Farmer's Letters,* in which he assumed the guise of an educated common man, a commonly used method for writing political tracts at the time. In these articles, he attacked the British legal and political positions with both logic and passion, laying out the arguments of the Americans in a clear and profound style. The *Farmer's Letters* had an immense impact in both America and Britain, where they were reprinted with the help of Benjamin FRANKLIN. By 1774 Dickinson was one of the most popular men in America.

With the outbreak of military hostilities in 1775, Dickinson became a member of the Continental Congress, which struggled to fight a war while also endeavoring to solve the overall issues. Dickinson strongly opposed the movement to issue a declaration of independence, believing that some sort of compromise with Great Britain was still possible and that America could never survive on its own. He wrote an eloquent petition to King George III, which was rejected. His opposition to

independence caused him to lose his popularity, and his final defeat was confirmed by the Declaration of Independence in July 1776.

Dickinson remained a patriot, serving in the American army during the war. Though he had opposed breaking away from Britain, once America was committed to independence, Dickinson fought hard for it. After his army service, he served in a variety of political offices in both Delaware and Pennsylvania.

After the war, Dickinson wrote in support of the U.S. Constitution but effectively retired from public life. He died in his home in Delaware on February 14.

Dickinson is remembered as an honest statesman who defended his beliefs even when they were not popular with the people. At the same time, he defended his nation with energy and determination, even when he believed it was moving in the wrong direction. His clear and sharp political writings stand as a model for not only the ideas they contained but also the manner in which they were written.

Works by John Dickinson

Letters from a Farmer in Pennsylvania to the Inhabitants of the British Colonies. Murrieta, Calif.: Classic Textbooks, 2003.
The Political Writings of John Dickinson. Edited by Paul Leicester Ford. New York: Da Capo Press, 1970.

Works about John Dickinson

Bradford, M. E. *A Better Guide than Reason: Federalists and Anti-Federalists.* Introduction by Russell Kirk. Somerset, N.J.: Transaction Publishers, 1994.
Flower, Milton E. *John Dickinson: Conservative Revolutionary.* Charlottesville: University Press of Virginia, 1983.

Diderot, Denis (1713–1784) *philosopher, encyclopedist*

Denis Diderot ranks with MONTESQUIEU, VOLTAIRE, and ROUSSEAU as a leader in the French ENLIGHTEN-

MENT. Within this intellectual circle he was known by the nickname "Pantophile" because his thought encompassed all subjects.

Like Rousseau, who was first a friend and later a bitter critic, Diderot came from an artisan family—his father was a master cutler—and gave voice to the discontents and aspirations of middle-class groups. But the content of his thought extended far beyond any narrow bounds that might have been imposed by his socioeconomic origins. Diderot was an intellectual rebel, thoroughly committed to atheism and to a revolution in aesthetics and political theory.

As a youth in Langres, Diderot received a secondary education from the Jesuits and took preliminary steps toward entering that order by receiving his tonsure. At age 16 he moved to Paris, where he matriculated at the University of Paris, receiving a master of arts degree in 1732. He abandoned his plan to enter the clergy and also declined to take degrees in law or medicine, actions that angered his family. During the years from 1728 until 1740, Diderot may have worked briefly as a law clerk, and he most certainly continued his independent studies in a wide range of fields. He supported himself by tutoring and translating books from English into French. But not much more is known of his life until 1740, when his literary career began to blossom.

In the eyes of his family, Diderot was behaving irresponsibly. His father cut off all financial support and also refused to assent to his son's request in 1743 for permission to marry Anne-Toinette Champion. In an effort to show his displeasure and to enforce his will on his son, the elder Diderot resorted to a standard practice of the time: He had his son incarcerated for a short period in a monastery near Troyes. Upon his release, young Diderot returned to Paris, where he and Mademoiselle Champion were secretly married.

During the early 1740s, Diderot was circulating in various cafés and coffeehouses, making contacts with philosophes such as Rousseau and Condillac. His English translations began to appear in 1742, but the year 1745 marked the solid establishment

of his career. In that year, he published a translation of the *Essay on Merit and Virtue* by Anthony Ashley Cooper, third earl of Shaftesbury.

The Shaftesbury translation helped to secure Diderot a position with the publisher André Le Breton as a translator of the Chambers *Cyclopedia.* Although never completed, the Chambers project gave birth to the great ENCYCLOPEDIA, one of the major publications of the Enlightenment.

Critical Analysis

The process of creating the *Encyclopedia* took nearly three decades, and it would eventually contain 17 volumes of text and 11 additional volumes of engravings and illustrations. It was one of the most astonishing literary achievements of all time.

Many of the most famous and important thinkers and writers of the Enlightenment contributed to the *Encyclopedia,* including Voltaire, Rousseau, Montesquieu, and numerous other prominent men of letters. Diderot became its general editor in 1747, with assistance from Jean Le Rond d'ALEMBERT in the realms of mathematics and science, and he also contributed a large number of articles.

The *Encyclopedia* was originally intended as simply an amassing of human knowledge, but it gradually developed into an extensive social commentary as well. It criticized organized religion in general and the Catholic Church in particular. It also seemed to disparage monarchial forms of government.

During his years of working on the *Encyclopedia,* Diderot also wrote and published many other works. In 1749 he published *Lettre sur les aveugles,* or *Letter on the Blind,* which questioned the existence of God. He followed this with *Lettre sur les sourds et muets,* or *Letter on the Deaf and Dumb,* which was a wide-ranging work dealing with various linguistic subjects and demonstrating Diderot's broad intellect.

Diderot also wrote a number of novels and plays, perhaps the most famous being his play *Père de famille,* or *Father of a Family.* It was produced in 1758, and became a standard of dramatic pieces based on middle-class characters, rather than aristocratic ones. His novels include *La Religieuse (The Nun)*, in which he subtly criticizes the entire notion of nunneries; *Le Neveu de Rameau (Rameau's Nephew)*, a continuing dialogue with the composer Rameau's nephew, which Diderot wrote and rewrote for 20 years; and *Jacques le fataliste et son maître (Jacques the Fatalist and His Master)*, in which Diderot includes elements of his philosophy.

Diderot's unorthodox views on religion and government got him into serious trouble with the authorities. The *Encyclopedia* was placed on the Catholic Church's list of forbidden books and was publicly burned. In 1749 Diderot was imprisoned for his anti-Christian beliefs.

In 1773 he traveled to Russia, having been invited there by CATHERINE THE GREAT. The empress had corresponded with Diderot and was very fond of him. She continued to support him financially until his death.

Although Diderot is not as well remembered as other figures of the Enlightenment, particularly Voltaire and Rousseau, he was one of the most important writers and thinkers of the time. His quest to continue publishing his ideas, despite the authorities' persecution and threats, represented a courageous resistance to censorship. By collecting the ideas of Enlightenment thinkers and publishing them in the *Encyclopedia*, as well as by making crucial contributions of his own, Diderot greatly influenced Western intellectual thought.

English Versions of Works by Denis Diderot

Jacques the Fatalist and His Master. Translated by David Coward. Oxford: Oxford University Press, 1999.

Denis Diderot's The Encyclopedia; Selections. Edited and translated by Stephen J. Gendzier. New York: Harper and Row, 1967.

Rameau's Nephew and Other Works. Translated by Jacques Barzun and Ralph H. Bowen. Indianapolis, Ind.: Hackett, 2001.

Selected Philosophical Writings. Cambridge: Cambridge University Press, 1953.

Works about Denis Diderot

Fellows, Otis. *Diderot*. Boston: Twayne, 1989.

Wilson, Arthur M. *Diderot*. New York: Oxford University Press, 1972.

Dmitriev, Ivan Ivanovich (1760–1837)
fable writer, poet

Ivan Ivanovich Dmitriev was born on his family's estate. His father was a wealthy Russian nobleman, and Dmitriev received a good education and, as was customary for Russian nobles at the time, joined the military in 1775. Dmitriev had a brilliant career: he became a senator, a member of the state council, and the minister of justice (1810). Throughout his career, he remained devoted to literature and used his satirical talents to highlight weaknesses in official measures.

Dmitriev's early literary taste was influenced by French, Greek, and Roman classics. The decisive influence in Dmitriev's life, however, was Karamzin, in whose house Dmitriev met all the important figures of the Russian literary world.

In 1791 a collection of Dmitriev's works appeared in the *Moscow Journal*, published by Karamzin. The critics received his debut warmly, praising his fairy tale *Fashionable Wife* and his song "Little Dove." The latter was immediately set to music and became highly popular. Dmitriev later published other works in the literary journals *Aglaia* and *Aonid*. In 1795 he released his first collection of poems under the title *And My Little Things*, followed by a popular songbook, *Pocket Songbook, or a Collection of Best Secular and Folk Songs*. His *Fables, Fairy Tales*, and *Apologues* went through numerous editions during and after his life, and both his poetry and prose brought a romantic spirit to Russian literature.

Dmitriev's fairy tales and fables are favored for their light and elegant language and the musical flow of verse. While Dmitriev borrowed most of his themes from French literature, his use of satire makes his works unique. He aimed his well-known satire, *Alien Talk*, at the current fashion of writing pseudo-classical odes, which were often stiff in language and devoid of meaning. Because *Alien Talk* helped exterminate outdated literary forms and introduced a new approach to poetry, Dmitriev is counted among the great reformists of Russian literature.

English Versions of Works by Ivan Ivanovich Dmitriev

Bowring, John, ed. *Specimens of the Russian Poets,* 2 vols. Boston: Cummings and Hilliard, 1822.

Pushkin, Alexander. *The Bakchesarian Fountain.* Translated by W. D. Lewis. New York: Ardis Publishers, 1987.

Works about Ivan Ivanovich Dmitriev

Lincoln, W. Bruce. *Sunlight at Midnight: St. Petersburg and the Rise of Modern Russia.* New York: Basic Books, 2002.

Volkov, Solomon. *Conversations with Joseph Brodsky: A Poet's Journey through the Twentieth Century.* New York: Free Press, 2002.

Donne, John (1572–1631) *poet, preacher*

John Donne was born in London into a family with strong Catholic roots. His mother was related to Thomas MORE, famously beheaded by Henry VIII. Donne's uncle was executed in 1594 for performing Masses, and his brother died while in prison for harboring a priest. Donne studied at both Cambridge and Oxford, and later acquired a promising post as secretary to Lord Keeper Sir Thomas Edgerton. Then, in 1601, he abruptly ruined his career by eloping with Edgerton's niece, Anne More. He spent much of his life away from London, helping raise his 12 children. During this period he read voluminously; wrote but did not publish a treatise on suicide, *Biathanatos;* and published two anti-Catholic tracts, *Pseudo-martyr* (1610) and *Ignatius His Conclave* (1611). In 1611 and 1612 he commemorated the death of Anne Drury, his patron's 14-year-old daughter, with *Anniversaries,* two lengthy and enigmatic poems about the decay of the world and the progress of the soul.

Pseudo-martyr earned the admiration of King James, who urged Donne to enter the ministry. Donne took orders in 1615 and began a very successful ecclesiastical career. In the last decade of his life, as dean of St. Paul's in London, he was the most famous preacher of his age.

In 1624 he published *Devotions,* a series of 24 prayerful meditations upon his near-fatal illness. Death was a frequent subject in his later meditations. He was said to have preached his own funeral sermon in *Death's Duel* (1630), and near the very end he posed for his monument in his funeral sheets. Soon after his death, the poems on which much of his later fame rests were published as a book, accompanied by elegies penned by such poets as Ben JONSON and Thomas Carew. Donne's elegies are rhymed erotic poems that address a lover, describe an amorous situation, or develop a philosophy of love. In "To His Mistress Going to Bed," the speaker of the poem urges his beloved to undress, describes the process in ingenious images, and compares caressing her to the excitement of global exploration. Contemplating exploration in conjunction with caressing a woman's body provokes thoughts of conquest and rule, sexual dominance, ideas of New World treasure, and finally expectations of honor.

Donne's art is one of radical compression. In one of his great religious SONNETS, he summarizes all the possible modes of death in two lines:

> *All whom war, dearth, age, agues, tyrannies,*
> *Despair, law, chance, hath slain. . . .*

His logic, reaching out to extremely diverse areas of experience, asks the reader to pay attention, hold possibilities in suspension, and finally draw conclusions without explicit statement.

If Donne's concise, compressed lyric poems are like miniature dramas so self-involved as to suggest someone acting in front of a mirror, then the sermons are lengthy performances that offer instruction and spiritual solace. For instance, trying to conceive of the angelic wisdom that the saved shall experience on Judgment Day, Donne argues. "There our curiosity shall have this noble satisfaction." He then reviews at some length the human ways of knowing (school, books, experience) and uses a metaphor in which the world is a library. Despite the greatness of this library, however, it is nothing compared to the knowledge of God's glory.

Despite a revival of interest in Donne's work, spearheaded by the critic T. S. Eliot in the early part of the 20th century, Donne's popularity has waned in the last few decades. One reason is the loss of interest in the lyric form of poetry in the current age. Another is Donne's mode of masculine self-assertion, which some may equate with misogyny. Nevertheless, Donne remains a striking artist who left a work charged with intellectual energy. Through self-dramatization, he fashioned a persona, earthly and spiritual, that came alive through his works.

Other Works by John Donne

John Donne: The Complete English Poems. New York: Penguin, 1971.
John Donne's Sermons on the Psalms and Gospels: With a Selection of Prayers and Meditations. Edited by Evelyn M. Simpson. Berkeley: University of California Press, 2003.
The Sermons of John Donne. Edited by George R. Potter and Evelyn Simpson. Berkeley: University of California Press, 1984.

Works about John Donne

Corthell, Ronald. *Ideology and Desire in Renaissance Poetry: The Subject of Donne.* Detroit, Mich.: Wayne State University Press, 1997.
Edwards, David L. *John Donne: Man of Flesh and Spirit.* Grand Rapids, Mich.: William B. Eerdmans, 2002.
Papazia, Mary Arshagouni, and Ronald Corthell, eds. *John Donne and the Protestant Reformation: New Perspectives.* Detroit, Mich.: Wayne State University Press, 2003.

Dwight, Timothy (1752–1817) *clergyman, poet, teacher*

Timothy Dwight, grandson of the famous theologian Jonathan EDWARDS, displayed an early inclination for learning. He entered Yale College at age 13 and graduated with highest honors at age 17. Dwight worked as principal of a grammar school before returning to Yale to teach as a tutor and to complete a master's degree. In 1777 he entered military service as chaplain of the Connecticut Continental Brigade, during which time he wrote patriotic songs, the most memorable of which is "Columbia, Columbia, to Glory Arise." After leaving the army, he became active in politics, farming, education, and church life in Massachusetts.

In 1783 he was ordained as a pastor in the parish of Greenfield Hill, Connecticut. His experiences inspired one of his most important works, *Greenfield Hill.* Two years later he published *The Conquest of Canaan,* considered the first EPIC poem produced in America.

In 1795 Dwight was elected president of Yale College, a position he held for more than 21 years. As a moralist and professor of theology, he greatly influenced the students, who wrote about him in their notebooks.

While Dwight was accepted during his time as one of the principal men of letters, modern interpretations view his poetry as dated and characterized by an artificial elevation of style, common to other poetry of the time. Nevertheless, his works are important for their insight into 18th-century America and for the place they hold in that country's literary tradition.

Works by Timothy Dwight

America; or, A Poem on the Settlement of the British Colonies. New Haven: T. and S. Green, 1780.
Greenfield Hill. New York, Conn.: AMS Press, 1970.
The Conquest of Canaan; A Poem in Eleven Books. Westport, Conn.: Greenwood Press, 1970.

Works about Timothy Dwight

Cunningham, Charles E. *Timothy Dwight.* New York: Macmillan, 1942.
Silverman, Kenneth. *Timothy Dwight.* New York: Twayne, 1969.

Edwards, Jonathan (1703–1758)
theologian, philosopher

Jonathan Edwards was born in East Windsor, Connecticut, to Reverend Timothy Edwards and Esther Stoddard, the daughter of Reverend Solomon Stoddard, who was one of the most influential ministers in 18th-century New England.

From an early age, Edwards possessed a remarkable curiosity about the relationship between the natural world and God. His keen attention to the details of nature can be discerned in his legendary "Of Insects" (1715); an essay that contains firsthand descriptions of the way spiders move and spin their webs and that concludes with observations about how these "flying insects" provided him with the perfect occasion to "behold and admire the wisdom" of God.

Edwards's interest in nature continued throughout his life. From 1727 until a few years before his death, the theologian-philosopher kept a notebook in which he recorded how "natural things" like the "waves and billows of the sea in a storm" and the "blue sky, the green fields and trees, and pleasant flowers" were "ordered for types of spiritual things." The private notebook, eventually entitled *Images of Divine Things* (1948), was not published until almost 200 years after Edwards's death.

At age 18, Edwards entered Yale College, where he studied Latin and Greek grammar, Hebrew, logic, ethics, religion, arithmetic, and natural philosophy. After receiving his B.A., he spent two years immersed in theological studies at Yale. In 1726 he became the colleague of his esteemed grandfather in Northampton, Massachusetts, and when, in 1729, Stoddard died, he assumed full spiritual leadership of the congregation. Edwards led a highly disciplined life in Northampton, rising in the early hours of the dawn and spending, on average, 13 hours each day in his study. Nevertheless, he lived more than the life of the mind. In 1727 he married Sarah Pierrepont; their union was affectionate and resulted in the birth of 11 children.

In order to appreciate the masterly artistry of his many sermons, it is essential to understand that the relationship between the intellect and emotions preoccupied Edwards. In "A Divine and Supernatural Light" (1734), he introduced his congregation to his notion of the "sense of the heart." Those who experience this "sense" simultaneously have "light in the understanding as well as an affected heart." Edwards insisted that the true "sense of the heart" was imparted to humans by God and could not be attained through mere human effort. A minister could, however, do his best to foster within unconverted individuals a longing for God's grace, and this is precisely what Edwards did in his most well known sermon, "Sinners in the Hands of an Angry God" (1741).

Edwards delivered this sermon during the height of the Great Awakening (a time when preachers were making a concerted effort to revive interest in religion), and it focuses on the inevitable damnation of sinners despite their present complacency. There is, Edwards announces, nothing that "keeps wicked men at any one moment out of hell, but the mere pleasure of God." Edwards, who was greatly influenced by John Locke's thesis that knowledge is acquired through experience, created a rhetorical environment that forced his listeners to experience—both mentally and emotionally—the precariousness of their spiritual condition. His sermon was incredibly effective. One person in attendance described how people were "crowding up to the pulpit, crying for mercy." He gave his listeners a sensible understanding of the argument he was presenting, and therein lies his artistic genius. He was, as Perry Miller points out in *Jonathan Edwards,* an "artist who happened to work with ideas instead of poems or novels."

Despite Edwards's many successes, his congregation dismissed him in 1750, due to his desire to impose stricter qualifications for church membership. In 1751 he settled in Stockbridge, Massachusetts, as local pastor and missionary to a group of Native Americans. Then, in 1758, he was elected president of the College of New Jersey (now Princeton) and died of smallpox shortly thereafter.

Works by Jonathan Edwards

A Jonathan Edwards Reader. Edited by Harry S. Stout and Kenneth P. Minkema. New Haven, Conn.: Yale University Press, 1995.

The Sermons of Jonathan Edwards: A Reader. Edited by Wilson H. Kimnach, Kenneth P. Minkema, and Douglas A. Sweeney. New Haven, Conn.: Yale University Press, 1999.

Works about Jonathan Edwards

Gallagher, Edward J. "'Sinners in the Hands of an Angry God': Some Unfinished Business," *New England Quarterly: A Historical Review of New England Life and Letters* 73:2 (June 2000): 202–221.

Miller, Perry. *Jonathan Edwards.* New York: Meridian Books, 1959.

———. *Errand into the Wilderness.* Cambridge, Mass.: Harvard University, 1956.

Eliot, John (1604–1690) *teacher, missionary, linguist*

John Eliot was born in Hertfordshire, England, and studied for the ministry at Jesus College, Cambridge University. He received a bachelor of arts degree in 1622 and taught in a grammar school in Essex, where he became associated with the Puritan Separatist Thomas Hooker. When Hooker escaped to the Netherlands, Eliot decided to immigrate to New England.

Eliot arrived in Boston in 1631 and served as a pastor for a short time in Boston before he was assigned as a teacher at Roxbury Church in Massachusetts. Eliot served as a teacher until 1641 and helped found the Roxbury Latin School. He then assumed a position as sole pastor of the church in Roxbury and held the position for the remainder of his life.

Eliot developed a strong interest in converting the Native Americans to Christianity. Realizing that language differences created a barrier to the delivery of Christian sermons and teachings, Eliot began a study of the local Algonquian language in 1643. He took a Native American boy who knew English into his home and learned the Algonquian language through the boy's pronunciations. In 1647 Eliot delivered his first sermon to the natives in their own language. To further advance Christian teachings, Eliot began translating the Bible into the Algonquian language in 1653. The New Testament was published in 1661 followed by the Old Testament in 1663. The completed work has the distinction of being the first complete Bible to be printed on the American continent.

In addition, Eliot helped Native Americans set up independent schools, seminaries, and communities. By 1674 there were 14 established communities for the "Praying Indian"; the best known of these was located at Natick. The outbreak of King Philip's War (1675–76) destroyed all of the communities, and the natives who survived were exiled to Deer Island. Eliot's final publication, *Dying Speeches & Counsels of such Indians as dyed in the Lord,* contains the dying speeches of eight Indians. It reveals Eliot's loss of spirit from both the events and results of the war and the undoing of his life's work. After Eliot's death, four of the communities were rebuilt but gradually faded away.

Not only was Eliot a pastor and missionary to the native populations but he was also a prolific writer. In addition to his translation of the Bible, he wrote a number of books in Native American languages as well as in English. In 1640 a collaborative work, *The Whole Booke of Psalmes Faithfully Translated into English Metre,* was published as a literal translation of Psalms designed to fit metrically with tunes familiar to Puritan congregations. It was an attempt to improve upon the Sternhold-Hopkins psalter that was popular among the Puritans while they were in England. Commonly known as *The Bay Psalm Book,* the coauthors of this work included John Cutter, Richard Mather, Thomas Welde, and John Wilson.

Eliot founded the first genuine Native American missions in the American colonies. His work with the Algonquians and his use of native language set the standard that missionaries followed for the next two centuries.

Works by John Eliot

John Eliot's Indian Dialogues. Edited by Henry W. Bowden and James P. Ronda. Westport, Conn.: Greenwood Press, 1980.

The Bay Psalm Book, a facsimile reprint of the first edition of 1640. Chicago: University of Chicago Press, 1956.

The Eliot Tracts. Edited by Michael P. Clark. Westport, Conn.: Praeger Publishers, 2003.

Works about John Eliot

Bross, Kristina. "Dying Saints, Vanishing Savages: 'Dying Indian Speeches' in Colonial New England Literature," *Early American Literature* 36:3 (2001): 325–352.

Winslow, Ola Elizabeth. *John Eliot, "Apostle to the Indians."* Boston: Houghton Mifflin, 1968.

Encyclopedia (*Encyclopédie ou dictionnaire raisonné des sciences, des arts et des métiers*) (1751–1772)

During the 18th century, Europe went through an intellectual transformation, with new ideas on the rise and old ideas on the decline. This period was known as the ENLIGHTENMENT. The general theme of the Enlightenment was the need to subject all ideas to rigorous criticism and examination. Concepts of religion, politics, art, literature, and social organization were now being methodically analyzed on a wide scale. Although the Enlightenment took place all over Europe, it had its greatest impact in France, where it was heavily opposed by the church and by social and political conservatives.

Many brilliant and towering intellectual figures won their fame during the Enlightenment, perhaps the most famous being VOLTAIRE and Jean-Jacques ROUSSEAU. There were literally dozens of great scholars during this era, and they left their mark on the intellectual history of the Western world.

Aside from the works of Voltaire and Rousseau, the greatest literary achievement of the Enlightenment was the *Encyclopedia,* which came into being when many leading thinkers embarked on the ambitious project of collecting the sum total of human knowledge. Their purpose was to make the information accessible to the educated public.

The men who compiled the *Encyclopedia* included Denis DIDEROT, Jean Le Rond d'ALEMBERT, Voltaire, and Rousseau. Diderot, however, dominated the writing, editing, and publication of the work, with d'Alembert as the next greatest contributor. Voltaire wrote several articles for the project and was always willing to help with advice on various matters. Rousseau wrote a few pieces on music theory but eventually became disgusted with the undertaking and withdrew. Other intellectuals who participated in creating the *Encyclopedia* included political philosopher Charles MONTESQUIEU, economist Anne-Robert-Jacques Turgot, and mathematician Antoine-Nicolas de Condorcet.

The first volume was published in 1751, and publication continued for more than 20 years. The *Encyclopedia* would eventually amount to 28 volumes, the final one being printed in 1772. Addendums would continue to be published until 1780.

While the amount of information and material contained within the *Encyclopedia* was immense, it was far from impartial, for the creators of the work held very strong opinions on the subjects about which they wrote. In terms of metaphysics, Diderot and his allies were strongly committed to the beliefs of the English philosopher John LOCKE, dismissing the ideas of those who disagreed with him. Similarly, the scientific articles held to the theories of Isaac Newton, rejecting the notions of opposing scientists. Many articles in the *Encyclopedia* were biased toward democratic and constitutional forms of government, and clearly hostile to religion, but the work as a whole revealed a philosophical tolerance unusual in its day.

From the beginning, the *Encyclopedia* encountered fierce opposition from religious and political authorities, who attempted to suppress the entire work. Most European states had well-funded government departments whose job it was to prevent works considered harmful or dangerous from reaching the public. This was particularly true in France, where the *Encyclopedia* was published.

Religious authorities despised the creators of the *Encyclopedia* because of their critical evaluation of religious ideas, unflinching defense of the scientific method, and questioning of the church's role in social and political spheres. Political authorities opposed the *Encyclopedia* because it questioned the validity of absolute monarchy and called for a less cruel and severe legal system. In short, the authorities disliked and distrusted the *Encyclopedia* because it challenged the status quo and tried to tell the people that the way things were was not the way they had to be.

The first official reaction came in 1752, after the publication of the first two volumes. The censors decreed that the volumes be banned; nevertheless, publication continued. In 1759 the French authorities decreed that the *Encyclopedia* as a whole was banned, and all sale and publication of it were forbidden. Despite this, Diderot and his allies bravely carried on with the work in secret. They continued to write the articles and print the volumes, working clandestinely and trying to hide their activities from the censors. The efforts of the French government to repress the work only added to its popularity.

The *Encyclopedia* was one of the great achievements of the 18th century. Diderot and his collaborators had created a masterly work, immense in its scope and radical in its implications. They did so in the face of difficult and dangerous obstacles, giving the people of Europe a great gift of knowledge. In summary, the work of the encyclopedists was a monument to the Enlightenment itself.

English Versions of Works from the *Encyclopedia*

Alembert, Jean le Rond d'. *Preliminary Discourse to the Encyclopedia of Diderot.* Translated by Richard N. Schwab. Indianapolis, Ind.: Bobbs-Merrill, 1963.

Diderot, Denis. *A Diderot Pictorial Encyclopedia of Trades and Industry.* Edited by Charles C. Gillispie. Mineola, N.Y.: Dover, 1994.

Russell, Terence M., and Ann-Marie Thornton, eds. *Gardens and Landscapes in the Encyclopédie of Diderot and d'Alembert: The Letterpress Articles and Selected Engravings.* Aldershot, Hampshire, U.K.: Ashgate Publishing, 1999.

Works about the *Encyclopedia*

Darnton, Robert. *The Business of Enlightenment: A Publishing History of the Encyclopedia, 1775–1800.* Cambridge, Mass.: Harvard University Press, 1979.

Lough, John. *Essays on the Encyclopedie of Diderot and D'Alembert.* London: Oxford University Press, 1968.

Werner, Stephen. *Blueprint: A Study of Diderot and the "Encyclopédie" Plates.* Birmingham, Ala.: Summa Publications, 1993.

English ballad

The ballad is a narrative song composed and recited by individuals and sung to a melodic accompaniment that follows the pattern of the verses. In England, the first ballads were folk ballads, meaning that they were products of an oral tradition. Folk ballads were sung before such narratives, or stories, were written down.

English folk ballads share several characteristics with ballads from other countries, and many are based upon songs from other nations. They usually tell stories of common folk rather than the aristocracy, and they focus upon a central event, situation, or character; feature a strong, dramatic element; and display what scholar Gordon Hall Gerould calls an "impersonal quality." Although the events described in the ballad may be terrible or horrendous (such as the loss of a child or a murder), the action receives little commentary. Other aspects of ballads include an element of the supernatural, displays of physical courage, an emphasis on domestic life, and a motif of love.

Although English folk ballads follow multiple forms, a traditional form prevails. The standard ballad stanza is composed of four-line stanzas that rhyme *abcb*. The first and third lines of the stanzas contain four accented syllables, and lines two and three carry three accented syllables. The amount of unstressed syllables varies, and the rhyme is not always perfect. Most ballads contain a refrain, and many folk ballads use assonance (similar vowel sounds with differing consonant sounds) rather than rhyme.

The ballad "The Three Ravens" tells of a dead knight who is carried away by a deer before three ravens successfully consume his decaying body. "Lord Rendal" is a song about a lover who has been betrayed by his beloved and lies sick and dying. Not all ballads, however, focus upon death. Other popular ballads celebrate successes, such as those recounting stories of Robin Hood and his adventures. In "Robin Hood and Allen-a-Dale," Robin Hood helps Allen, a soon-to-be loyal servant, by saving Allen's beloved from marriage to an old knight.

Ballads were a major form of literature and entertainment in the Middle Ages. While they remained popular with the advent of printing and the spread of new forms of literature, by the 18th century they came to be taken seriously as historical artifacts. During this time, English ballads were collected by scholars such as Thomas Percy and Sir Walter Scott. These collections played a significant role in the genesis of English Romantic poetry and inspired writers such as William Wordsworth, Samuel Taylor Coleridge, and John Keats.

Works of Ballads

Child, Francis James. *English and Scottish Popular Ballads.* New York: Dover, 1965.

Works about Ballads

Gerould, Gordon Hall. *The Ballad of Tradition.* Oxford: Clarendon Press, 1932.

Percy, Thomas. *Reliques of Ancient English Poetry,* 3 vols. London: Routledge, 1996.

Enlightenment, Age of (1700s)

During the 18th century, a dramatic intellectual movement swept over Europe, particularly the nation of France. The movement set off an explosion of scholarly and literary achievement equal to any period of Western history. Generally, the Enlightenment is thought to have lasted from the early years of the 18th century to sometime before the outbreak of the French Revolution in 1789. During the Enlightenment, dozens of brilliant thinkers and writers questioned some of the most basic assumptions of Western society. Political, religious, and social ideas that had been accepted for centuries were critically examined, and the consequences had a tremendous impact on Western society.

At the heart of the Enlightenment was a belief in the power of RATIONALISM, the ability to arrive at answers to difficult and complicated questions through the power of human reason and experience. Enlightenment thinkers believed that all questions must be answered rationally, without recourse to authority or intuition. Furthermore, Enlightenment thinkers believed that every element of human society should be open to rigorous questioning, no matter how sacred others considered it. These beliefs stemmed from some of the scientific discoveries occurring at the time, such as those by Sir Isaac Newton. As a result, some of the most controversial elements of the Age of Enlightenment involved religion.

The thinkers and writers of the Enlightenment were known as philosophes. They were not philosophers in the traditional sense, but rather individuals who sought to spread the ideas of philosophy to the general public. The philosophes achieved this through the use of nearly every genre of literature; Enlightenment ideas were expressed in poetry, novels, dramas, pamphlets, and various reference works.

By far the most famous and influential of the philosophes was VOLTAIRE. From the 1720s until his death in 1778, Voltaire produced a constant stream of literature in various genres, including plays, short stories, novels, essays, and pamphlets. Through his writing, he attacked censorship of the press, religious intolerance, backward legal systems, and outdated political ideas. His hugely popular writings helped spread Enlightenment ideas throughout the literate populations of Europe and the United States. His most successful work, *Candide,* is one of the two great literary works of the Enlightenment period.

Voltaire was not alone; the Enlightenment produced a very large number of influential literary figures. Denis DIDEROT wrote a series of works, both fiction and nonfiction, expressing Enlightenment ideas. Jean Le Rond d'ALEMBERT did fundamental

new work in mathematics while pursuing philosophical studies, and Baron de MONTESQUIEU wrote the highly influential *Spirit of Laws,* which greatly affected 18th-century political thought.

However, not all thinkers and writers of the Age of Enlightenment were devoted to rationalism. Many people, including members of the clergy, distrusted the philosophes, because their ideas seemed to threaten the status of religion in Western society. Jean-Jacques ROUSSEAU, for instance, taught that the key to human understanding of the world was not the power of human reason, but rather involved emotion and intuition. This point of view resulted in an intense dispute between Rousseau and Voltaire, which lasted throughout their lives.

Perhaps the greatest literary production of the Age of Enlightenment was the ENCYCLOPEDIA. Jointly edited by Diderot and d'Alembert, and featuring contributions from Voltaire and other philosophes, the *Encyclopedia* sought to systematize human knowledge after examining it with a thoroughly rational point of view. Government authorities sought to censor the work and prevent its publication, as well as harassing and imprisoning those who worked on it.

Despite such resistance, Enlightenment ideals spread far and wide. The intellectual flowering that took place in Scotland during the latter half of the 18th century owed a great deal to the scholarship and literature of the Enlightenment. During the American Revolution, the political ideas that motivated the American radicals were largely borrowed from the French philosophes. Finally, when the French Revolution began in 1789, the revolutionaries looked to the ideas of the Enlightenment for inspiration as they sought to topple the French monarchy and create a republic in its place.

In a larger sense, the Age of Enlightenment fundamentally altered the intellectual environment of the Western world. The modern, rational insistence on solid evidence when answering difficult questions, which is at the heart of both the modern scientific method and the Western legal system, is a legacy of Enlightenment thought. So, too, are the

Western traditions of freedom of thought and expression, which are enshrined in the political systems of nearly all Western nations.

Works of the Age of Enlightenment

Beccaria, Cesare. *On Crimes and Punishments.* Translated by David Young. Indianapolis, Ind.: Hackett, 1997.

Buffon, Georges-Louis Leclerc. *Natural History, General and Particular.* Translated by William Smellie. Bristol, U.K.: Thoemmes Press, 2001.

Helvetius, Claude-Adrien. *Claude-Adrien Helvetius: Philosophical Works.* Bristol, U.K.: Thoemmes Press, 2000.

Holbach, Paul Henri Thiery. *System of Nature,* vol. 1. Translated by H. D. Robinson and edited by Denis Diderot. Manchester, U.K.: Clinamen Press, 2000.

Hume, David. *Essays: Moral, Political, and Literary.* Edited by Eugene F. Miller. Indianapolis, Ind.: Liberty Fund, 1991.

Works about the Age of Enlightenment

Gay, Peter. *The Enlightenment: The Science of Freedom.* New York: W.W. Norton, 1996.

Jacob, Margaret C. *Living the Enlightenment: Freemasonry and Politics in Eighteenth-Century Europe.* Oxford: Oxford University Press, 1994.

Porter, Roy. *The Enlightenment.* New York: Palgrave Macmillan, 2001.

epic   (n.d.–present)

The term *epic* generally refers to long, episodic narrative poems featuring larger-than-life characters who engage in actions requiring great courage and strength. Epic heroes hold national or international importance and are celebrated as symbols of national values and embodiments of the heroic ideal. Such greatness is underscored by the epic's elevated, formal style, an objective point of view, and a vast, expansive setting.

Historically, epics were recited to audiences as songs by bards. As writing increased in popularity, however, these long story-songs were written down and circulated in book form.

Epics typically begin with an invocation (a prayer) to a muse, whom the narrator asks for inspiration to tell a valuable and memorable story. The epic then begins in the middle of a central action or key event, a technique known as *in medias res* (Latin for "in the middle of things"). Thus, the epic's narrative opens in the middle of a serious and significant moment, such as a battle. In Homer's *Iliad,* for instance, the drama opens after the war between the Greek forces and the inhabitants of Troy has been raging for 10 years.

After opening *in medias res,* the epic's story unfolds, and the history of the dramatic action is revealed intermittently. The narrator frequently digresses from the action's central plot to tell the history of a particular character or some other story, a digression that adds meaning to the main action and to the epic's main themes. In Virgil's *Aeneid,* for instance, the narrator departs from the main story to discuss a highly valuable and symbolic shield that was forged by Vulcan and given to Aeneas by his mother.

Another common characteristic shared by epics is an element of supernaturalism. Gods, spirits, and angels interject themselves in human affairs and act as supernatural forces influencing the epic's characters and actions. In some epics, in fact, the hero is part divine, as in the *Aeneid,* where Venus, the goddess of love, is Aeneas's mother.

Other key characteristics of epics include extensive cataloging of things and characters (resembling lists in the Old Testament), elaborate. comparisons known as epic similes, and long formal speeches.

Epics generally fall into two categories, the folk epic and the art epic. Folk epics are works of unknown authorship and are composed by several individuals. Art epics, on the other hand, are those thought to be written by a single author. The art epic is generally more moral in its purpose and more critical about the events and characters portrayed. Additionally, the events of these epics typically take place further in the past.

Important folk epics include Homer's *Iliad* and *Odyssey,* the Old English *Beowulf,* the German *Nibelungenlied,* and the East Indian *Mahabharata.*

The *Aeneid*, by P. Vergilius Maro (Virgil), the *Divine Comedy* by Dante Alighieri, and *Paradise Lost* by John MILTON are examples of the art epic.

Works about Epics
Merchant, Paul. *The Epic.* London: Methuen, 1971.
Newman, John Kevin. *The Classical Epic Tradition.* Madison: University of Wisconsin Press, 1986.

Equiano, Olaudah (Gustavus Vassa) (1745–1797) *autobiographer*
Olaudah Equiano was born in the Benin region of what is now Nigeria. His name means "one favoured, and having a loud voice and well spoken." His father was a distinguished man in in Essaka, a village along the Niger River. When Equiano was 11, he was kidnapped and sold into slavery. Eventually, he was sent to Virginia, where he was bought and put to work on a plantation. He was then sold to Michael Henry Pascal, a lieutenant in the Royal Navy. After years of sailing around the world with Pascal, Equiano was able to buy his freedom in 1766.

Equiano settled in London, where he became an active member of the movement to abolish slavery in Britain. At age 44, he published the work that was to make him famous, his autobiography *The Interesting Narrative of the Life of Olaudah Equiano, Or Gustavus Vassa* (1789). This immensely popular work influenced many African-American writers who followed him, including Frederick Douglass, Ralph Ellison, Toni Morrison, and Malcolm X.

The Interesting Narrative tells the story of Equiano's life, but its real purpose is to demonstrate the essential humanity of people of color and, to some extent, to question the perception of whites as "civilized" and Africans as "uncivilized." In the first chapter, Equiano describes the life and customs of his native village in terms that suggest that the simplicity of Benin life was quite superior to life in the great cities to which he had traveled. From this simple life, Equiano is plunged into hell. In the hold of the slave ship that transports him to Barbados, the stench is "absolutely pestilential" and "the shrieks of the women, and the groans of

the dying, [render] the whole scene of horror almost inconceivable."

The structure and style of *The Interesting Narrative* show the influence of 18th-century writers such as DEFOE, ROWLANDSON, and FRANKLIN. Equiano traces his progress from slavery to escape to freedom, and while he uses a conventional form, the details of his story are unique to his own experiences.

One important theme of the narrative is the question of identity, symbolized in the various names Equiano is given and must accept. In Virginia he is given two names, Michael and Jacob, while on board ship, he is called Gustavus Vassa. Equiano's struggle with his identity prefigures the struggles of generations of enslaved peoples and their descendants. Critic Robert J. Allison writes that "Equiano's book . . . reminds us of the lives of millions who did not live to tell their stories."

An English Version of a Work by Olaudah Equiano
The Interesting Narrative of the Life of Olaudah Equiano, or Gustavus Vassa, the African. New York: Random House, 2004.

A Work about Olaudah Equiano
Cameron, Ann. *The Kidnapped Prince: The Life of Olaudah Equiano.* New York: Random House, 2000.

Erasmus, Desiderius (ca. 1469–1536) *theologian, philosopher*
During the late 15th and early 16th centuries, the artistic and literary influences of the RENAISSANCE, which were first felt in Italy, spread across Europe. The rediscovery of the knowledge and literature of ancient Greece and Rome allowed scholars to promote learning. HUMANISM, a new, secular way of viewing the world, gradually began to replace the static, religiously obsessed thought that had dominated the intellectual climate of the Middle Ages. Humanism was largely devoted to the study of human beings as they exist in the world, rather than the study of religion and theology. One of the

foremost writers and thinkers of this time period, who became known as the "Prince of Humanists," was Desiderius Erasmus.

Erasmus was born in the Dutch city of Rotterdam. Because of his birthplace, he is often known simply as "Erasmus of Rotterdam." Little is known of his family or his early life, although it is known that he was the son of a priest. He received a solid education in monastic schools and, briefly, at the University of Paris. He took priestly orders in 1492, but never adopted the profession, preferring to devote his life to academic studies.

Over the course of his life, Erasmus wandered from one part of Europe to another, never settling down in one place for very long. At various times, he lived in France, Switzerland, Italy, and England. He told his friends that he considered his library, which he took with him in his travels, to be his home. He lived a celibate and meticulous life, never paying much attention to money or possessions. He intensely disliked personal disputes and tried to stay on good terms with everyone. Although he held very strong views about the shortcomings of the Roman Catholic Church, he always expressed them with a strong sense of irony, almost as if to disguise what he really believed.

Because of his assuaging personality, he was held in extremely high regard throughout Europe and was on friendly terms with some of the most famous rulers, statesmen, and intellectual figures of the day. Although he remained loyal to the Catholic Church throughout his life, Erasmus also corresponded with Martin LUTHER, the chief figure of the Protestant Reformation. He made a strong effort to stay neutral in the great religious and intellectual debates that erupted throughout Europe during the 16th century. However, in the intensely belligerent atmosphere of the Protestant Reformation, even Erasmus would be unable to stay entirely removed from the conflict.

In 1499 Erasmus visited England, where he met and befriended the great humanist scholar, Sir Thomas MORE, with whom he shared a devoted and intellectually-vibrant friendship for the rest of his life. One year later, he published *Adages*, which is essentially a collection of sayings and proverbs from ancient Greek and Roman literature. It reflects the author's knowledge of classical texts, as well as his preoccupation with the purity of the Greek and Latin languages.

A few years after the publication of *Adages*, Erasmus published his second major work, *The Enchiridion*. This book, which would later have a huge impact on the English and American Puritan communities, describes the author's belief that piety should be a simple matter of the heart and rely less on the formal ritual of the church. He viewed religious life as pure and simple, something that could be created from the heart, but he never rejected the church's authority, as Luther would later do.

Critical Analysis

In 1509, while living in England at the invitation of King Henry VIII, Erasmus wrote his most celebrated work, *In Praise of Folly*. With brilliant use of irony and symbolism, he cleverly describes much of what he dislikes about contemporary European culture, particularly in terms of the religious establishment. *In Praise of Folly* was printed in 1511 and became very popular, going through several editions within the author's lifetime. The church, however, disapproved of the work and began to look upon Erasmus with suspicion.

The book was written in polished Latin and was dedicated to Thomas More. Erasmus intended the audience of the book to be a small number of fellow humanists. He was taken by surprise when the book became very popular with many people from different levels of society and differing educational backgrounds.

Erasmus uses the character of Folly, whom he describes as a foolish woman, to speak his mind regarding various aspects of European society. He ironically declares that folly and stupidity allow people to live the kinds of lives they live; if it weren't for folly, people simply would not put up with things as they are. He ridicules various conventions concerning romance and marriage. In addition, in his discussions of intellectuals and authors, he declares them also to be victims of folly.

The most important aspects of *In Praise of Folly* are the criticisms Erasmus leveled against the religious institutions of the Catholic Church. He ridicules theologians whose debates he considers to be nonsensical wastes of time. He also attacks monks as illiterate hypocrites. In general, Erasmus criticizes all those elements of contemporary religion that he considered to detract from pure, heartfelt religious devotion.

In Praise of Folly was very popular but was also widely criticized. Because of his skillful use of irony and wit, Erasmus was shielded from official censure by the church. Although he always remained loyal to the Catholic Church, *In Praise of Folly* contributed to the Protestant Reformation by creating an image of the church as vulnerable to censure and by exposing many of the church's flaws.

In 1516 Erasmus published a Greek translation of the New Testament, which he had prepared and edited. It was an enormous feat of intellectual skill, and it increased readership of the Bible. However, like *In Praise of Folly,* it was regarded with distrust by many Catholic leaders and scholars.

A few years after the publication of his Greek version of the New Testament, the Protestant Reformation began. Very quickly, European theologians and intellectuals were being pressured to choose sides, supporting either Martin Luther and the Protestants or the Roman Catholic Church. Erasmus tried desperately to remain neutral. He wrote Luther, calling on him to restrain his anti-Catholic fervor, and he asked all sides of the dispute to resolve their arguments through logical compromise. In this effort to keep the peace, Erasmus was doomed to fail. He was trying to be a reasonable man in an unreasonable age. By trying to please both sides, he pleased neither; Luther denounced Erasmus for not joining the Reformation, while the Catholic Church later declared him a heretic for refusing to condemn Luther.

The Protestant Reformation dominated the remainder of Erasmus's life. In the mid-1520s, at More's urging and in response to Luther's bitter attack on his character, Erasmus wrote *Hyperaspistes,* also known as *A Weighty Consideration.* In this work, he criticizes Luther for his hatred of all who disagree with him and, in effect, asks Luther for an apology. While the work reflects Erasmus's compromising attitude, it had little impact on the bitter and violent disputes raging throughout Europe.

Elderly and in failing health, Erasmus moved from place to place, accused by Catholics of being a secret Protestant and charged by Protestants of being a Catholic reactionary. He finally found refuge among fellow humanists in Basel, Switzerland, where he later died in the home of a friend.

Erasmus's fame is based on his enormous influence on the literary culture of his age, which raised the study of classical languages to a respected and even revered profession. By doing so, he powerfully advanced intellectual activities of all kinds.

English Versions of Works by Desiderius Erasmus

Adages of Erasmus. Translated by Margaret Mann Phillips. Cambridge: Cambridge University Press, 1964.

Erasmus on Women. Edited by Erika Rummel. Ontario: University of Toronto Press, 1996.

In Praise of Folly. Translated by Clarence Miller. New Haven, Conn.: Yale University Press, 1979.

Selections from Erasmus. IndyPublish, 2004.

Works about Desiderius Erasmus

Augustijn, Cornelis. *Erasmus: His Life, Works and Influence.* Translated by J. C. Grayson. Toronto: University of Toronto Press, 1991.

Crompton, Samuel Willard. *Desiderius Erasmus.* Langhorne, Pa.: Chelsea House Publishers, 2004.

Faulkner, John Alfred. *Erasmus: The Scholar.* Miami, Fla.: International Law and Taxation, 2003.

Huizinga, Johan. *Erasmus and the Age of Reformation.* London: Phoenix Press, 2002.

Mee, Charles L. *Erasmus: The Eye of the Hurricane.* New York: Coward, McCann & Geoghegan, 1973.

Everyman (ca. 1500) *medieval drama*

Though the author of the English play *Everyman* is unknown, he was probably an Englishman who translated it from a copy of a Dutch play of the same name at the beginning of the 16th century. *Everyman* is an example of a morality play, a type of medieval drama that addressed the questions of how to live a good Christian life and how best to prepare for death.

Everyman conveys the message that preparation for death requires giving up worldly possessions, repenting of sins, asking God for mercy, and submitting oneself to be judged on the merit of works, or good deeds. Everyman (who, as his name suggests, represents the average person) is summoned by Death and finds he is not ready to be called to God for his "reckoning," for he has spent his life pursuing wealth. One by one, the friends Everyman calls upon for help desert him, and in his increasing isolation and despair he learns finally that only knowledge and good deeds will benefit him in the final judgment. The play teaches that knowledge includes both self-knowledge, arrived at by using the five wits or senses, and knowledge of God, made possible only through humility.

The story-type of the false friends first appears in an oriental collection of fables called *Barlaam and Josaphat,* which was a popular sourcebook for medieval sermons. *Everyman* is often praised for its natural language, which is not elevated or obscure. The play makes the moral points that death is the end of all things, and wrongdoing, while it may be enjoyable at the moment, always carries penalties in the end. Scholar A. C. Cawley calls *Everyman* "one of the finest, if not one of the most typical, of medieval Catholic moral plays."

See also William LANGLAND.

Editions of *Everyman*

Cawley, A. C., ed. *Everyman and Medieval Miracle Plays.* New York: Everyman's Library, 1965.

Coldewey, John C., ed. *Early English Drama: An Anthology.* New York: Garland Publishing, 1993.

Conley, John, et al., eds. *The Mirror of Everyman's Salvation.* Amsterdam: Rodopi Editions, 1985.

Works about *Everyman*

Beadle, Richard, ed. *The Cambridge Companion to Medieval English Theatre.* Cambridge: Cambridge University Press, 1994.

Gilman, Donald, ed. *Everyman & Company.* New York: AMS Press, 1989.

Wickham, Glynne. *The Medieval Theatre.* Cambridge: Cambridge University Press, 1987.

fabliaux (1300s)

The fabliaux are short medieval bawdy tales, usually told in verse, that originated in France during the 12th century. The fabliaux usually take place in the present in middle- and lower-class settings. The plots are humorous, usually scatological or sexual. Marie de France included two fabliaux about amorous women in her *lais,* and many fabliaux originated from court writers and even clergymen. The fabliaux subvert conventional morality, celebrating trickery and sexual pleasure over honesty and chastity.

By 1300, the fabliaux had peaked as a fashionable literary genre in France, but Geoffrey CHAUCER would create some of the best examples of the form for his *Canterbury Tales,* including "The Miller's Tale," "The Reeve's Tale," and "The Summoner's Tale." Each centers on middle- and lower-class characters, possessive impotent husbands, and lusty young wives and their enterprising lovers. Each features some painful or embarrassing physical punishment. Finally, each punishes the self-righteous and socially conscious characters and rewards the cunning and carnal.

One variant of the fabliaux is the bestiary, or beast fable, which Chaucer used in "The Nun's Priest's Tale." This tale features Chanticleer the rooster and how he is almost fooled into becoming dinner for a fox. The beast fable's most popular cycle was that of Reynard the Fox, which featured animals taking on the social positions and attitudes of feudal society. The king was a lion, a wolf was Reynard's prosecutor, and Reynard was a trickster-courtier, intent on fooling others for his own ends. Like Aesop's fables, these fabliaux featured animals portraying human character types, but unlike those fables, these were longer narratives that did not teach a specific moral. Their satire targeted different social classes and the worst traits associated with them. Fabliaux were a welcome diversion from the idealistic allegorical romances and lofty courtly love literature of the Middle Ages.

English Versions of Fabliaux

Duval, John, trans. *Cuckolds, Clerics, & Countrymen: Medieval French Fabliaux.* Fayetteville: University of Arkansas Press, 1982.

Harrison, Robert L. *Gallic Salt: Eighteen Fabliaux translated from the Old French.* Berkeley: University of California Press, 1974.

Spiegel, Harriet. *Marie de France: Fables.* Toronto: University of Toronto Press, 1987.

Works about Fabliaux

Benson, Larry D., and Theodore M. Andersson. *The Literary Content of Chaucer's Fabliaux: Texts and Translations.* Indianapolis, Ind.: Bobbs-Merrill, 1971.

Bloch, Howard R. *The Scandal of the Fabliaux.* Chicago: University of Chicago Press, 1986.

Lacy, Norris J. *Reading Fabliaux.* Birmingham, Ala.: Summa Publications, 1999.

farce (1400s–present)

A farce is a theatrical genre that uses exaggerated comic situations and stereotypical characters. The genre developed in 15th-century France and has maintained its popularity to the present day. However, it is often considered to be a lower form of comedy because of its reliance on crude physical humor and improbable plots.

While elements of farce can be found in ancient Greek and Roman plays, especially the works of Aristophanes and Plautus, the term itself comes from the Old French word meaning "stuffing." The first French farces were brief pieces of clowning and gymnastics inserted into religious plays by the actors. Later, French playwrights wrote entirely farcical works, one famous example being *Maistre Pierre Pathelin* (ca. 1470).

Farces continued to be a popular theatrical genre throughout the 18th and 19th centuries. They also found a new form in films during the 20th century, especially in the work of Charlie Chaplin and the Marx Brothers.

See also Cyrano de BERGERAC; William SHAKE-SPEARE.

English Versions of Farces

A Dozen French Farces: Medieval to Modern. Translated and edited by Albert Bermel. New York: Limelight Editions, 1997.

Six Medieval French Farces: Translated by Thierry Boucquey. Lewiston, N.Y.: Edwin Mellen Press, 1999.

Works about Farce

Bermel, Albert. *Farce: A History from Aristophanes to Woody Allen.* New York: Simon & Schuster, 1982.

Milner Davis, Jessica. *Farce.* New Brunswick, N.J.: Transaction, 2003.

Fénelon, François de Salignac de la Mothe (1651–1715) *theologian, novelist*

François de Salignac de la Mothe Fénelon was born in Périgord, France, the second son of Pons de Salignac and his wife, Louise. He studied the humanities and philosophy at the University of Cahors, was ordained as a priest, and became a doctor of theology in 1677. In 1681 he became director of the Congregation of New Catholics, where he was in charge of instructing Protestant women who had converted. He fell under suspicion for his association with Madame Guyon and Quietism, her slightly unorthodox blend of mystical piety and "pure love," and was eventually exiled to his archbishopric, where his gentleness, humanity, and eloquence earned him the nickname "the Swan of Cambrai."

The letters Fénelon wrote throughout his life continue to impart wisdom to followers of the Christian faith. He also authored several treatises on points of religion and education. In 1689 he was made the tutor of the grandson of Louis XIV, for whom he wrote the *Fables* and *Dialogues of the Dead* (both in 1690) for reading practice and instruction. In 1695 he began *Telemachus* (completed in 1699), which is remembered as his masterpiece. He described it as "a fabulous narrative in the form of a heroic poem . . . into which I incorporated the major lessons suitable for a prince." A sequel to Homer's *Odyssey,* it tells the adventures of Ulysses's son Telemachus within the frame of a moral lesson on simplicity and strength in adversity. Since the narrative shows that the king is but a man and therefore fallible, the work was seen as a harsh criticism of the regime of Louis XIV. It was enormously popular for its literary quality, but it also ensured its author's disgrace. Despite this, future generations remembered Fénelon, and his biographer J. Lewis may says he is "the exemplar of all that is noblest and most gracious in the genius of France."

English Versions of Works by François de Salignac de la Mothe Fénelon

Fenelon: Meditations on the Heart of God. Edited by Hal M. Helms. Orleans, Mass.: Paraclete Press, 1997.

Fénelon: Telemachus. Edited by Patrick Riley. New York: Cambridge University Press, 1994.

Works about François de Salignac de la Mothe Fénelon

Davis, James Herbert, Jr. *Fénelon.* Boston: Twayne, 1979.

Little, Katharine Day. *Francois de Fenelon: Study of a Personality.* New York: Harper and Brothers, 1951.

St. Cyres, Viscount. *Francois de Fenelon.* New York: Kennikat, 1970.

Fernández de Lizardi, José Joaquín

(1776–1827) *novelist, journalist*

José Joaquín Fernández de Lizardi was born in Mexico City, and as a youth studied theology before becoming a clerk for an Acapulco magistrate. In 1810 Mexico launched its war for independence against Spain, and Fernández de Lizardi joined the revolutionaries two years later. For this he was briefly imprisoned, and upon his release founded a pro-revolutionary newspaper called *The Mexican Thinker.* In his newspaper and many pamphlets, Lizardi called for an end to Spanish rule, racial and social equality, and curbs in the church's power. For his continuing anti-clerical sentiments, the Roman Catholic Church excommunicated him.

In 1816 Fernández de Lizardi wrote his best-known work, the picaresque novel *The Itching Parrot (El periquillo sarniento).* A colorful satire of all aspects of Mexican society, *The Itching Parrot* takes its title from the nickname of its protagonist, who occupies numerous professions throughout the novel, including monk, gambler, and doctor. The work also shows the influence of many philosophers of the French ENLIGHTENMENT, particularly in its respect for science and logic and its disdain for superstition. In this passage, for example, an African character questions the morality of slavery:

How can I obey properly the precepts of that religion which obliges me to love my neighbor as myself . . . [yet approves my] buying for a pittance a poor black, making him a slave to serve . . . and treating him at times perhaps little better than a beast?

Fernández de Lizardi also wrote three other novels, *Miss Quixote and Her Cousin* (1819), *Sad Nights and Happy Days* (1823), and *Don Catrin de Fachenda* (1826). He died in Mexico City of tuberculosis. For his unyielding advocacy of his country's freedom, Mexicans regard Fernández de Lizardi as a national hero. Most scholars consider *The Itching Parrot* the first true Latin American novel, and it is highly prized for its detailed and vivid portrayal of early 19th-century Mexican society, and for its strikingly contemporary views on politics and morality.

English Versions of Works by José Joaquín Fernández de Lizardi

The Itching Parrot. Translated by Eugene Pressley and Katherine Anne Porter. Garden City, N.Y.: Doubleday, 1942.

The Mangy Parrot. Translated by David Frye. Indianapolis, Ind.: Hackett, 2004.

Works about José Joaquín Fernández de Lizardi

Benitez-Rojo, Antonio. "Jose Joaquin Fernandez de Lizardi and the Emergence of the Spanish American Novel as National Project," *Modern Language Quarterly* (June 1996): 325–340.

Vogeley, Nancy J. *Lizardi and the Birth of the Novel in Spanish America.* Gainesville: University Press of Florida, 2001.

Ferreira, António (ca. 1528–1569) *poet, playwright*

António Ferreira was born in Lisbon, Portugal, to a noble family with ties to the monarchy. As a child, Ferreira developed a deep love for his native city, and after spending 13 years at Coimbra University studying Latin, classical literature, poetry, plays, and law, he returned home as a judge of the appeals court.

Though Ferreira was a judge, he spent a great deal of time with a group of intellectual poets and cultivated his poetic talents. He disdained the masses, which he felt were ignorant, and fought for intellectual freedom from church domination. Ferreira was also very patriotic. He encouraged the use of Portuguese, instead of Spanish, in the writing of poetry. Ferreira wrote many different kinds of poems in the classical mode, from epigrams and eclogues to odes and Petrarchan SONNETS. He achieved some fame posthumously for his sonnets in honor of his wives, Maria Leite, and later, Maria Pimentel. His son published Ferreira's first edition of poetry, *Poemas Lusitanos,* 30 years after Ferreira's death.

Ferreira also wrote several pieces for the theater. His first two plays, *Bristo,* about friends who become romantic rivals, and *Cioso,* about a jealous husband, were comedies that did not arouse much interest either in Portugal or the world abroad. However, his third play, *Inês de Castro,* was the first original RENAISSANCE TRAGEDY written in Portuguese. The play develops a famous episode in the history of the Portuguese monarchy, the murder of Prince Peter's mistress by his father for political reasons. The play served as a model for many later playwrights, including CAMÕES, one of Portugal's greatest writers. Ferreira was one of the major voices in the establishment of a Portuguese literature.

English Versions of Works by António Ferreira

The Comedy of Bristo, or, The Pimp (Comédia do Fanchono ou de Bristo). Translated by John R. C. Martyn. Ottawa, Canada: Dovehouse Editions, 1990.

The Tragedy of Ines de Castro. Translated by John R. C. Martyn. Coimbra, Portugal: Universidad de Coimbra, 1987.

A Work about António Ferreira

Earle, T. F. *The Muse Reborn, The Poetry of António Ferreira.* New York: Oxford University Press, 1988.

Franklin, Benjamin (1706–1790) *nonfiction writer, journalist, publisher, scientist, political figure*

More than 200 years after his death, Benjamin Franklin remains one of the most famous and influential figures in American history. He is counted among the first of the great writers produced by the emerging American nation.

Franklin was born in Boston, the 10th son of Josiah Franklin, a candle-maker who had immigrated to Massachusetts from England. Although he received only a few years of schooling, Franklin was clearly a highly intelligent youth. When he was 12, he was apprenticed to his older brother, James, who had set up a print shop and begun publishing a newspaper titled *The New England Courant.* He also met and was influenced by the Puritan leader, Cotton MATHER.

While working for his brother, Franklin wrote a series of anonymous essays under the pseudonym "Silence Dogood." These essays presented brilliant and biting commentary on the social conditions of New England and caused something of a stir in Boston. The essays were Franklin's earliest important writings, and they were remarkably lucid and penetrating, considering that their author was only a teenager.

After being mistreated by his brother, Franklin ran away to Philadelphia, where he found work at a local print shop. He spent some time in London before settling permanently in Philadelphia. He soon established himself as an independent businessman, launching his own printing shop. His sound business sense and his willingness to work hard soon paid off, and his business became very profitable.

Franklin became an important part of the civic life of Philadelphia. With a number of friends, he established the Junto Club, a social group that discussed politics, science, and philosophy, and that worked to improve life in the city. Working with his friends, Franklin established the city's first lending library, a fire department, a police force, an academy, which later evolved into the University of

Pennsylvania, a hospital, and a public forum where clergy of any religion were allowed to preach. These institutions helped make Philadelphia America's premier city of the time.

In 1729 Franklin began printing his own newspaper, *The Pennsylvania Gazette.* It quickly became the leading newspaper of the colony. In addition to publishing and editing the paper, Franklin wrote much of the material himself, including articles on ordinary news and advertisements, as well as important political issues, science, and literature. Franklin saw his newspaper as both a source of personal profit and a means of improving everyday life in his community.

In 1732 he embarked on his most successful printing and writing project, *Poor Richard's Almanac.* In the 18th century, almanacs were extremely popular and useful as sources of information for farmers and tradesmen. They dealt with such subjects as when to plant and harvest crops, the dates on which specific holidays would fall, and weather conditions of different seasons. Franklin's almanac rapidly became a bestseller, not only in Pennsylvania, but also throughout the American colonies.

Poor Richard was much more than simply a way to dispense routine information. Like his newspaper, he used it as an educational tool to promote common sense, healthy skepticism, strong work ethics, and sound financial principles. Later in his life, Franklin would collect many of the sayings from *Poor Richard's Almanac* and publish them as a separate work, entitled *The Way to Wealth.*

The success of *The Pennsylvania Gazette* and *Poor Richard's Almanac,* made possible by his brilliant writing and his shrewd business practices, allowed Franklin to make a great deal of money. He invested his earnings in Philadelphia real estate and satellite printing operations in other colonies. By the time he had reached middle age, he was a wealthy man.

Franklin expanded his interests to include scientific work, and his research into the nature of electricity is one of his chief claims to fame. In 1752 he conducted a test using a brass key tied onto a kite, to determine whether lightning is a form of electricity. This may be the most famous scientific experiment in history. In addition to electricity, Franklin also conducted scientific research into meteorology, hydrodynamics, and numerous other scientific subjects. His writings on these subjects were published in many different languages, were widely read, and had substantial influence on later scientific developments.

From the mid-1750s to the end to his life, Franklin turned his attention to the political events of the American Revolution, and he made his most important mark on the world as a statesman and diplomat. In 1757 he traveled to Great Britain to serve as the representative of the colony of Pennsylvania. He became friends with some of the leading English and Scottish writers and thinkers of the day and received an honorary degree from Oxford University.

When the crisis between Great Britain and its colonies began, starting with the Stamp Act crisis in 1765, Franklin devoted himself to ending the quarrel and restoring good faith and harmony between the British and the Americans. For many years, he saw himself as a loyal citizen of the British Empire and was willing to do anything to save it from destruction. He wrote several articles calling for peace and reconciliation, which were published in both British and American newspapers.

In 1771, during a lull in the crisis, Franklin began writing *The Autobiography of Benjamin Franklin,* which would become his literary masterpiece. His work on the project was still incomplete when the American Revolution began.

Unsuccessful in his efforts to preserve peace, and having been humiliated and insulted by the British government, Franklin eventually sided with the colonists and was elected to the Continental Congress. He assisted Thomas JEFFERSON in writing the Declaration of Independence. Franklin was then selected by Congress as its representative to France, with the objective of gaining French support in the war against Britain.

Franklin arrived in France in late 1776 and immediately became the most popular person in the country. French citizens were enthralled by his charm and humor, and he became a favorite at aristocratic parties in Paris. He wrote numerous propaganda pieces to raise support for the American cause, which were printed in French newspapers. Franklin's influence helped persuade France to sign an alliance with the United States, which helped the colonies gain their independence. In 1784, while still in France, Franklin resumed writing the *Autobiography*.

With the war over, Franklin returned to his beloved Philadelphia. In 1787 he served as a delegate to the Constitutional Convention, although his age and ill health were beginning to take their toll. He continued to work on the *Autobiography*, but it was still incomplete when he died on April 17.

Franklin stands today as the personification of the American dream. Coming from very humble origins, he rose through hard work and determination to become one of the greatest men of his age. He achieved greatness in an incredible variety of fields, from journalism and literature to science and diplomacy. Through his witty yet thought-provoking writings, he left behind a testament to the potential of America.

Critical Analysis

Franklin's greatest literary achievement was unquestionably his *Autobiography*. It was the first true classic of American literature. In it, Franklin tells the story of his life, using it as a means to communicate to his readers his personal work ethic and sense of morality.

Franklin begins his life story by relating his family's history and his own upbringing in the city of Boston. He then tells, with a humorous and self-effacing sense of drama, the tale of his running away from Boston and arriving in Philadelphia. The image of a young Franklin, walking up the street from the city's docks, penniless and with a large loaf of bread stuffed under each arm, has become an American icon. Franklin continues the story of his life in Philadelphia and his involvement in scientific and public affairs, up to his departure for London in 1757.

In the *Autobiography*, Franklin provides a list of 13 virtues he tried to live up to throughout his life. These virtues were temperance, silence, order, resolution, frugality, industry, sincerity, justice, moderation, cleanliness, tranquility, chastity, and humility. He modestly points out, however, that he was not always successful in keeping these virtues.

Franklin's *Autobiography* was designed to inspire Americans to aspire to become better in all that they do. In writing his masterpiece, Franklin was telling his countrymen that they, too, could achieve greatness, if only they were virtuous, hardworking, and determined.

Works by Benjamin Franklin

Autobiography and Other Writings. Oxford: Oxford University Press, 1993.
A Benjamin Franklin Reader. Edited by Walter Isaacson. New York: Simon & Schuster, 2003.
Wit and Wisdom from Poor Richard's Almanack. Edited by Steve Martin, with Introduction by Dave Barry. New York: Random House, 2000.

Works about Benjamin Franklin

Brands, H. W. *The First American: The Life and Times of Benjamin Franklin.* New York: Doubleday, 2000.
Morgan, Edmund S. *Benjamin Franklin.* New Haven, Conn.: Yale University Press, 2002.

Freneau, Philip Morin (1752–1832) *poet, editor, journalist*

Philip Freneau was the oldest of five children born to Agnes Watson and Pierre Fresneau (old spelling), a wine merchant. He enjoyed a privileged upbringing in New York and New Jersey, though his father often struggled financially. At a boarding school in New York and a Latin school in New

Jersey, Philip received an education in Latin, geography, composition, and arithmetic. He also read Horace, Cicero, Lucian, and Xenophon. In the fall of 1768, Philip entered the College of New Jersey (now Princeton), where he discovered his ambition to become a writer.

The titles of a few of his many poems—"The Rising Glory of America" (1771), "America Independent" (1778), and "To the Memory of Brave Americans" (1781)—point to why Freneau became known as the poet of the American Revolution. He composed, with some input from a classmate, the first and most important of these poems during his senior year of college. Emory B. Elliott Jr. observes that "The Rising Glory of America" is a "patriotic poem of epic design," which speaks "of a time when a united nation should rule the vast continent from the Atlantic to the Pacific." For a time, Freneau served as editor of *The Freeman's Journal* (1781–84) and the *National Gazette* (1791–93), writing fervently in support of the Revolution. Although he was intensely committed to addressing the political matters of his day, he also, according to Elliott, experienced a longing to "escape social turmoil and war." He expressed his more romantic side in "The Wild Honeysuckle" (1786), a beautiful poem that, as Jacob Axelard points out, uses the "fragrant flowers that bloom for a little while and then wilt away" to symbolize the "sad immutable destinies" of humankind.

Other Works by Philip Morin Freneau

Poems, 1786 and Miscellaneous Works (1778) of Philip Freneau. Delmar, N.Y.: Scholars Facsimiles and Reprints, 1975.
The Last Poems of Philip Freneau. Temecula, Calif.: Reprint Services Corporation, 1993.

Works about Philip Morin Freneau

Austin, Mary. *Philip Freneau: The Poet of the Revolution.* Temecula, Calif.: Reprint Services Corporation, 1993.

Elliott, Emory B., Jr. "Philip Freneau," in *A Princeton Companion.* Edited by Alexander Leitch. Princeton, N.J.: Princeton University Press, 1978.

Froissart, Jean (1337?–1404?) *chronicler, poet*

Jean Froissart was born in Valenciennes, France, around the start of the Hundred Years War. He received clerical instruction in Latin and later joined the church. For several years he lived in England as the secretary to Queen Phillipa; after her death, he found patrons in Wenscelas, Duke of Brabant, and Guy of Blois. He traveled extensively, including to Scotland and Italy, and composed and compiled his major work, the *Chronicles,* from his time in England until his death. The four books of the *Chronicles* cover events all over western Europe and in later centuries were as widely read in England as they were in France.

Froissart also wrote poetry and the last French Arthurian ROMANCE, *Meliador* (composed in the 1380s). In 1395 he presented a volume of his poetry to Richard II of England, and four years later recorded that monarch's deposition as the closing event in the *Chronicles.*

In his love poetry Froissart was influenced by Guillaume de Machaut and Guillaume de Lorris, and his contributions to the genre in turn influenced his English contemporary, Geoffrey CHAUCER. It is possible that in his travels, which enlarged his worldview and are reflected in his historical writings, he met the poet PETRARCH while in Italy.

Froissart's contributions turned historiography in a new direction: instead of simply recording events as a parade of remarkable figures, he made the story of how he came to learn of these events part of the larger narrative, adding an original touch.

Though Froissart has been thought shallow by some historians for his sympathy for the aristocracy and his attachment to the knightly ideal, his *Chronicles* are a monument to French literature and his poetry demonstrates considerable range, leading critics like Donald Maddox to consider him "one of the great synthesizing minds of the fourteenth century and one of the most engaging writers of his age."

English Versions of Works by Jean Froissart

Chronicles. Translated by John Joliffe. New York: Penguin Books, 2001.

Jean Froissart: An Anthology of Narrative and Lyric Poetry. Edited by K. M. Figg and R. B. Palmer, New York: Routledge, 2001.

Works about Jean Froissart

Ainsworth, Peter. *Jean Froissart and the Fabric of History.* Oxford: Clarendon Press, 1997.

Maddox, Donald, and Sara Sturm-Maddox. *Froissart Across the Genres.* Gainesville: University Press of Florida, 1998.

Galilei, Galileo (1564–1642) *scientist, writer*
Galileo Galilei is often considered to be the father of modern science. He is most famous for perfecting the telescope and using it to make numerous astronomical discoveries, including the moons of Jupiter and the rings of Saturn. He also did groundbreaking work in physics and set the foundations for the modern scientific method.

Galileo is also well known for the persecution he suffered at the hands of the Catholic Church. He believed, correctly, in the Copernican Theory, the idea put forward by Nicolaus COPERNICUS that the Earth moves around the Sun. The official position of the church was that the Copernican Theory was false and that the Sun moved around the Earth. After using his writing abilities to try to persuade the public of the correctness of his views, the Church ordered Galileo not to speak of the subject again and, threatening torture, made him recant his ideas before the Inquisition.

In addition to his skill as a scientist, Galileo had considerable talent as a writer. He combined these two gifts in his efforts to popularize science, helping ordinary people to understand the scientific discoveries he was making, particularly in astronomy.

The first of his great literary works was titled *The Starry Messenger.* Galileo published this book in 1610, only months after he had discovered the moons of Jupiter with his new telescope. In this book, he discusses the moons of Jupiter, the surface features of Earth's Moon, and the fact that the Milky Way is made up of innumerable stars. One interesting aspect of *The Starry Messenger* is that it was written in Italian, rather than in Latin, as was customary for academic books at that time. Galileo wanted ordinary people to be able to read his book and understand its contents, so he wrote it in the everyday language of the country.

Galileo's next book, *Dialogue Concerning the Two Chief Systems of the World,* would become his most famous and the one that caused him the most trouble with authorities. The work represented his efforts to convince the public that the Copernican Theory was correct. When it was published in 1632, the Catholic Church tried to prevent its distribution.

The *Dialogue* was written in the style of Plato, taking the form of a long conversation among three different people. Salviati is an intelligent man who represents Galileo's own views in support of the Copernican Theory; Simplicio is a rather slow-witted character who represents those who oppose Galileo's views; and Sagredo is an open-minded man who hosts the discussion and tries to make up his mind as to which of his guests is correct.

It is clear that Galileo did not intend for an objective presentation of every viewpoint of the debate; he clearly presents Salviati's ideas as those that any intelligent person would believe, and he ridiculed Simplicio's ideas. One primary reason the *Dialogue* created such a problem for Galileo was that many viewed Simplicio's character as a caricature of Pope Urban VIII.

Galileo wrote his final great work, *Discourse on Two New Sciences* (1638), toward the end of his life, after he had been sentenced to lifelong house arrest by the church. Rather than a work of popular literature, this piece is a far more academic work of scientific writing in which Galileo put together a lifetime of thinking and experimentation on the physics of motion. This work would later have a strong influence on the great English scientist Isaac Newton, helping him develop his theory of gravitation.

Galileo was clearly one of the great scientists of history, and his gifts as a writer and his determination allowed him to spread his scientific ideas across Europe. Many of his discoveries and theories shaped the course of future science, astronomy, and math.

English Versions of Works by Galileo Galilei

Achievement of Galileo. Translated and edited by James D. Brophy and Henry Paolucci. Toronto, Ontario: Griffon House, 2003.

Dialogue Concerning the Two Chief Systems of the World. Translated by Stillman Drake. New York: Modern Library, 2001.

Discoveries and Opinions of Galileo. Translated by Drake Stillman. New York: Doubleday, 1989.

Works about Galileo Galilei

Biagioli, Mario. *Galileo Courtier: The Practice of Science in the Culture of Absolutism.* Chicago: University of Chicago Press, 1994.

Reston, James. *Galileo: A Life.* New York: Harper-Collins, 1994.

Sharratt, Michael. *Galileo: Decisive Innovator.* New York: Cambridge University Press, 1996.

Sobel, Dava. *Galileo's Daughter: A Historical Memoir of Science, Faith, and Love.* New York: Walker and Company, 1999.

Gama, José Basílio da (1740–1795) *poet, author*

José Basílio da Gama was an important Brazilian poet of the Colonial Period (1500–1822). He completed his Jesuit novitiate in 1759, the same year the order was expelled from Brazil. Leaving Brazil for Rome, he pursued education in Italy and Portugal, where he was influenced by Italian NEOCLASSICISM. When he returned to Brazil in 1767, he was sent by the Inquisition to Portugal to face possible deportation to Angola. He received a pardon by composing a wedding poem for the daughter of a local minister, the marquês de Pombal.

He is best known for his masterpiece epic poem, *O Uraguai,* an account of the Portuguese-Spanish war against the Jesuit-controlled reservation Indians of the Uruguay River basin. Through this narrative poem composed in blank verse, Gama expresses sentiment against the conquerors, a sentiment he also expressed earlier in a SONNET dedicated to the Peruvian Tupac Amaru. In *O Uraguai,* Gama also shows appreciation for the natural Brazilian environment and presents an idealistic view of Indian life and customs. The poem is a forerunner of the romantic nationalism that later developed in 19th-century Brazilian literature.

José Basílio da Gama belonged to a group of Brazilian writers known as the Arcadians. These writers also included Cláudio Manuel da Costa (1729–89) and Tomás Antônio Gonzaga (1744–1810), among others. The Arcadians are remembered for their lyric and epic poems and were highly involved in the "Minas Conspiracy" ("Conjuração Mineira"), a liberation movement to free Brazil from Portuguese rule.

Gama, along with several other Brazilian poets (including Gonzaga, who wrote the pastoral love poem *Marília de Dirceu,* and Friar José de Santa Ritta Durão, who wrote the EPIC *Caramurú,* or *Sea*

Dragon, celebrating the discovery of Bahia), also joined a writers' academy in the mining town of Minas Gerais in Brazil. This academy and its poets were responsible for introducing to Brazil many new ideas that had arisen in France, some of them revolutionary, and for influencing the work of future writers such as José Gonçalves de Magalhães (1811–82) and António Gonçalves Dias (1823–64).

An English Version of a Work by José Basílio da Gama

The Uruguay: A Historical Romance of South America. Berkeley: University of California Press, 1982.

Garcilaso de la Vega (El Inca)
(1539–1616) *historian*

El Inca Garcilaso de la Vega was a gifted writer and Peruvian historian. His father was the conquistador Sebastían Garcilaso de la Vega and his mother was the Inca princess Isabel Chimpu Ocllo. Garcilaso, fusing his diverse racial and cultural backgrounds, came to represent the traumatic process of conquest and cultural blending initiated by Spain in the New World.

El Inca Garcilaso's first literary achievement was a Castilian translation of the Italian Leo Hebreo's *Philosophy of Love* or *Dialogh: d'amore* (1590). His project in translating this major work of Neoplatonism anticipated his lifelong work of balancing and cultivating two very different cultures.

Garcilaso's second publication was *Florida del Inca,* or *The Florida of the Incas* (1605). Based on secondhand accounts of the Hernando de Soto expedition, this work provides most of the information that exists on the conquistador. Although well received in Garcilaso's time, due to its imaginative tone, *The Florida* is today considered more of a historical novel than a historical document.

Garcilaso's knowledge of Inca civilization through his mother uniquely positioned him to be the ideal chronicler of the Inca people. His most important work was *The General History of Peru,* a two-volume work. The first part appeared in 1606 as *Real Commentaries* and describes the history of the Inca until the arrival of the Spaniards. In describing the myths, poetry, traditions, and rituals of the Inca, Garcilaso gives them the character of a utopia in the manner of RENAISSANCE ideals. The second part of the *Commentaries* appeared as *The General History of Peru* in 1617. The early influence of Neoplatonist thought shows in Garcilaso's descriptions of the coming of the Spaniards and the events thereafter, vindicating both the earlier way of life and the fusion of the new culture with the old. This landmark work established Garcilaso de la Vega as an authority on Peruvian history.

English Versions of Works by Garcilaso de la Vega

Poems. Translated by Elias L. Rivers. London: Grant & Cutler, 1981.

Royal Commentaries of the Incas and General History of Peru. Austin: University of Texas Press, 1966.

Works about Garcilaso de la Vega

Castanien, Donald Gardner. *El Inca, Garcilaso de la Vega.* Boston: Twayne, 1970.

Varner, John Grier. *El Inca: The Life and Times of Garcilaso de la Vega.* Austin: University of Texas Press, 1968.

Goethe, Johann Wolfgang von
(1749–1832) *poet, novelist, playwright*

During the late 18th and early 19th centuries, Europe experienced an intellectual and literary movement known as Romanticism, which rejected pure reason in favor of human emotional experience. This was in reaction to the scientific RATIONALISM of the earlier ENLIGHTENMENT period. Romanticism found its most intense expression in Germany. Of all the outstanding writers and thinkers who emerged in Germany during this time, none had greater influence or more lasting fame than the brilliant and controversial Johann Wolfgang von Goethe. Indeed, many historians consider him the single greatest German writer who has ever lived.

Goethe was born into a moderately prominent family and, as a young man, received an excellent education. He became fluent in several languages and was fascinated with literature and art from a very early age. As a student at the University of Leipzig, Goethe rejected the neoclassical tradition of the Enlightenment in favor of the natural and emotional beliefs of the emerging Romantic movement.

While studying in the city of Strasbourg, Goethe came under the influence of Johann HERDER, one of the founders of the Sturm und Drang movement. Herder contributed to Goethe's drift away from NEOCLASSICISM and introduced him to the writings of William SHAKESPEARE, which would greatly influence him. During this time, Goethe wrote an essay about the Gothic cathedral in Strasbourg titled *Von deutscher Baukunst,* which means "On German Architecture," which Herder included in a collection of similar works he was editing.

Goethe settled down in the German city of Weimar in the mid-1700s, and he spent most of the rest of his life there and at the nearby University of Jena. His presence in Weimar helped make the city one of the great centers of European culture. At first, he intended to pursue a legal career and held a number of official positions in the local government. The powerful Duke Karl August, who ruled Weimar, proved to be an excellent patron, and it seemed as if Goethe would enjoy a prosperous legal and political career. However, after experiencing a personal awakening during a two-year visit to Italy in the late 1780s, Goethe returned to Weimar determined to pursue a career in literature rather than law.

Goethe had already written a great deal of poetry and dramatic pieces while pursuing his legal career. His earliest major work was *Die Leiden des jungen Werther (The Sorrows of Young Werther).* It is considered one of the most important works of the Sturm und Drang movement.

During his first years after returning from Italy, Goethe produced a great deal of poetry and other work. After accompanying Duke Karl August during the Prussian invasion of France in 1792 (during which he witnessed the famous French victory at the Battle of Valmy), Goethe wrote an account of

events titled *Campagne in Frankreich—1792 (The Campaign in France in 1792).* His writing was heavily influenced by his study of the literature of ancient Greece and Rome. He also pursued a number of scientific studies, publishing essays on optics and the nature of color.

During these years, Goethe began an extremely productive collaboration with Friedrich von SCHILLER. Although they often disagreed with each other, the thought-provoking critiques they exchanged had tremendous influence on the literary output of both. Furthermore, they shared the common goal of creating a unique literary and artistic culture within Germany, equal to the culture of ancient Greece.

Throughout the 1790s, Goethe labored on his masterpiece, *Faust,* which has become his most famous work and ranks as one of the most influential and important works produced in all of literature. He had, in fact, been working on pieces of it for many years, but the first part of *Faust* wasn't published until 1808. That same year, Goethe was summoned to meet no less a personage than Napoleon Bonaparte, who then ruled nearly all of Europe. Napoleon's desire to meet Goethe reflected the fame he had achieved as a writer.

Although universally respected as a writer, Goethe became increasingly unpopular with the German public. This was partly due to his admiration for Napoleon (hated by most Germans), his unorthodox religious views, and his seeming lack of interest in German political unification. Throughout the last few decades of his life, Goethe continued to produce enormous numbers of novels and plays and continued his studies of science, art, and history.

In the late 1820s, Goethe wrote the second half of *Faust,* which was published just before his death. Although the second half is somewhat different in style from the first, there is a clear continuity between the two, as they contain the same themes and ideas.

Perhaps more than any other writer, Goethe can be seen as the central figure of Romanticism, in the same way that VOLTAIRE can be seen as the central figure of the Enlightenment. Goethe's writings reflect the influence of Herder, Immanuel KANT, Shakespeare, and a number of classical Greek and Roman writers. But Goethe was a strikingly original writer who did perhaps more than anyone else to create a uniquely German literature. He oversaw the transformation of a European culture based on French rationalism to one based on German Romanticism, which would dominate European culture for generations to come.

Critical Analysis

Goethe's first major work, *The Sorrows of Young Werther*, delineates Werther's hopeless love for Lotte Buff, the wife of his close friend. Driven to self-alienation and psychological breakdown, no longer able to live without his beloved, Werther commits suicide. Werther expresses his misery in terms that resonated widely, especially with young readers: "My creative powers have been reduced to a senseless indolence. I cannot be idle, yet I cannot seem to do anything either. When we are robbed of ourselves, we are robbed of everything." Goethe explained his motivation for writing the novel in terms of his heightened spiritual and emotional awareness: "I tried to release myself from all alien emotions, to look kindly upon what was going on around me and let all living things, beginning with man himself, affect me as deeply as possible, each in its own way." The emotions and local color are placed in the foreground of his work.

In Goethe's second major novel, *Wilhelm Meister's Apprenticeship* (1795–96), Goethe continues to explore themes of love and alienation. However, the novel presents a more optimistic outlook on life. Like Werther, Wilhelm suffers a tragic blow after an unsuccessful courtship. Unlike Werther, however, Wilhelm begins to actively seek out other values in life. He dedicates himself to work and becomes a playwright and an actor. In the end, Wilhelm is spiritually satisfied with his newfound outlet for passion. The novel remains thematically consistent with the Romantic school; however, critics have noted the emergence of the conservative side of Goethe's thinking. Unlike many of his contemporaries, Goethe was not impressed by the uprising and violence of the French Revolution. He supported liberty and progress but also maintained that the aristocracy had an important role in society. Many younger readers began to criticize Goethe for what they saw as subservience to the upper classes.

The first part of Goethe's dramatic masterpiece, *Faust,* appeared in 1808. This drama became his passion, and he worked on it for more than 30 years. Based on the play by the English Renaissance dramatist Christopher MARLOWE, it tells a chilling story of a man who sells his soul for knowledge. Faust makes a contract with Mephistopheles to die as soon as his thirst for knowledge is satisfied. Faust is driven to despair when Margaret, an innocent woman, is condemned to death for giving birth to Faust's illegitimate child. He finally realizes that his lust for knowledge has led to tragic mistakes.

In the second part of *Faust*, which appeared in 1838, Faust marries the beautiful Helen of Troy and creates a happy community of scholars. The bliss of his good deeds brings satisfaction at old age, and Mephistopheles is about to demand satisfaction. But Faust's changed attitudes and good heart are rewarded, as angels descend from the sky in the final scene of the play and take Faust to heaven. The play brought Goethe international success and had a profound influence on modern drama.

During his illustrious career, Goethe produced in addition a number of important poetical works. He also provided literary guidance to his close friend Schiller and produced several of his plays. When Goethe died, he was buried next to Schiller in Weimar.

Although it is difficult to measure the influence of Johann Wolfgang von Goethe, he ranks among the giants of world literature. He is a dominant figure of German Romanticism, and his novels, poems, and plays are still widely read and studied.

English Versions of Works by Johann Wolfgang von Goethe

Erotic Poems. Edited by Hans R. Vaget and translated by David Luke. New York: Oxford University Press, 1999.

Faust. Edited by Cyrus Hamlin and translated by Walter W. Arndt. New York: W.W. Norton, 2000.

Italian Journey. Translated by Elizabeth Mayer. New York: Penguin, 1992.

The Sorrows of Young Werther and Selected Writings. Translated by Catherine Hutter. New American Library, 1987.

The Works of Johann Wolfgang Von Goethe, vol. 1. IndyPublish.com, 2004.

Works about Johann Wolfgang von Goethe

Blackie, John Stuart. *The Wisdom of Goethe.* Whitefish, Mont.: Kessinger Publishing, 2004.

Eckermann, Johann. *Conversations of Goethe.* Translated by John Oxenford. New York: Da Capo Press, 1998.

Sime, James. *Life of Johann Wolfgang Goethe.* La Vergne, Tenn.: University Press of the Pacific, 2003.

Wagner, Irmgard. *Goethe.* Boston: Twayne, 1999.

Williams, John. *The Life of Goethe: A Critical Biography.* Malden, Mass.: Blackwell Publishers, 2001.

Goldoni, Carlo (1707–1793) *dramatist*

Carlo Goldoni was born in Venice to Giulio Goldoni and his wife, Margherita. He studied grammar and rhetoric in Perugia and Rímini, but his interest in the theater continually drew him away from his studies and later practice in law. He traveled often and served in various political positions, earning frequent rejections and sometimes hostile displeasure for his satires and musical dramas. Despite his prodigious output and his fame—VOLTAIRE called him "Italy's MOLIÈRE"—Goldoni struggled throughout his life with hostile critics, poverty, and frequent removals in search of supportive patrons or escape from creditors. He reportedly died poor and blind, buried in an unknown grave.

In all, Goldoni wrote five tragedies (see TRAGEDY), 16 tragicomedies, and 137 comedies, in addition to 57 scenarios for actors of the COMMEDIA DELL'ARTE. The historical tragedy *Belisario* (1734) was his first success, followed by *A Man of the World* (1738), *A Lady of Charm* (1743), and *The Servant of Two Masters* (1744–45). *The Cunning Widow* (1748), *A Girl of Honor* (1749), and *The Good Wife* (1749) showed Goldoni's emerging talent and accomplished style, but his fearlessness continued to provoke audiences. In 1750 *The Gentleman and the Lady,* the first Italian comedy without masks, infuriated nobles who felt that Goldoni had exposed their secrets. He continued to write, producing dozens of plays a year and learning again and again that in drama of the 18th century, serious tragedy belonged to the French stage, while Italians were expected to write buffoonish comedies. Goldoni dwelled on this paradox in his memoirs, subtitled *For a Better Understanding of the History of His Life and Theater* (1787).

Goldoni also contributed to musical productions, writing, among many others pieces, libretti put to music by Piccinni, Haydn, Mozart, Vivaldi, and others. Goldoni's works infused new life into a stagnant art form and became an important voice for the concerns of the middle-class, ultimately reforming Italian and European drama.

English Versions of Works by Carlo Goldoni

Carlo Goldoni's Villeggiatura Trilogy. Translated by Robert Cornthwaite. Lyme, N.H.: Smith and Kraus, 1995.

The Comedies of Carlo Goldoni. Westport, Conn.: Hyperion Press, 1978.

The Servant of Two Masters. Adapted by Dorothy Louise. Chicago: Ivan R. Dee, 2003.

Works about Carlo Goldoni

Holme, Timothy. *A Servant of Many Masters: The Life and Times of Carlo Goldoni.* London: Jupiter Books, 1976.

Reidt, Heinz. *Carlo Goldoni.* Translated by Ursule Molinaro. New York: Ungar Publishing, 1980.

Golenishchev-Kutuzov, Pavel Ivanovich (1767–1829) *poet, translator*

Pavel Golenishchev-Kutuzov was born in St. Petersburg, in the family of the head of Marine

College, Admiral Ivan Golenishchev-Kutuzov. The family was related to the celebrated Russian prince and army commander, Mikhail Kutuzov. Pavel entered military service at age nine and later participated in the war with Sweden. At age 29, he left the military and began his brilliant political career. He became the czar's counselor, a senator, and one of the curators of the Moscow University.

Golenishchev-Kutuzov won a stable place in history as an avid enemy of KARAMZIN. The enmity was not exclusively literary, for Golenishchev-Kutuzov considered Karamzin a dangerous revolutionary. The battle took place not only on journal pages; Golenishchev-Kutuzov also wrote scathing denunciations of Karamzin and send them to the czar.

Golenishchev-Kutuzov's literary career began in 1791 with the publication of a series of his poems in a literary journal, *Russian Literature Lover's Interlocutor*. He wrote a number of solemn odes devoted to Catherine II and Pavel I. These odes became the subject of severe satire written by DIMITRIEV, who considered them outdated, stiff, and inappropriate for contemporary literature.

One of Golenishchev-Kutuzov's main projects was his literary journal *Companion to Education* (1802–06), in which he published a great number of poems and translations, including translations of such famous authors as Gray, Sappho, Pindar, and Geziod. In 1803–04, he also published three separate volumes of his poetry.

Although Golenishchev-Kutuzov's poetry was far from the ideal of perfection, he entered history as an important political figure, a prolific translator, and a poet.

A Work about Pavel Ivanovich Golenishchev-Kutuzov

Vroon, Ronald, and John E. Malmstad, ed. "Fet and the Poetic Tradition: Anapestic Tetrameter in the Work of Polonsky, Golenishchev-Kutuzov, and Lokhvitskaya," in *Readings in Russian Modernism*. To Honor Vladimir Fedorovich Markov. Moscow: Nauka, 1993.

Góngora y Argote, Luis de (1561–1627)
poet

Luis de Góngora was born to the judge Francisco de Argote and his wife, Leonor de Góngora, in the city of Cordova in southern Spain. At an early age his family determined that he would become a priest, and though the poet himself seemed to have no particular inclination for the religious life, he was ordained a clergyman at age 14. He went on to attend the University of Salamanca but, due to his dissipated lifestyle and interests in poetry, never received a degree.

By age 19, Góngora's poetry had already begun circulating in manuscript form and it received the praise of such well known writers as Miguel de CERVANTES, who paid tribute to the young writer in his *Canto a Caliope* (1585). Over the next three decades Góngora lived extravagantly, sinking himself in debt but establishing himself as a gifted poet and well-known figure in his native city. In 1617 he relocated to Madrid, where he was named the king's chaplain and where he spent the next 10 years fulfilling his religious duties and continuing to write poetry. He sold his house in 1625 and returned to Cordova, where he died two years later.

Góngora is considered almost exclusively as a lyric poet, and his work can be separated into two periods. While his early work tends to be straightforward and affirmative, his later poems are characterized by the density of their language and darkness. His first poems appeared in 1580, when he contributed to a collection of poetry dedicated to the duke of Olivares, the prime minister of Philip IV. Much of Góngora's early poetry shows him experimenting with simple styles and forms, such as the octosyallabic *romance* and the festive *letrilla*, a short verse form with a refrain that was frequently written for either amorous or satiric purposes. As early as 1585, however, in his SONNET "A Córdoba" ("To Córdoba"), Góngora shows the first traces of the ornate baroque style that would come to be his trademark.

In Spain, Góngora's talent for satire and his elegant style attracted attention. He directed several cutting poems at corrupt life in Valladolid, then the Spanish capital, and made a lifelong enemy of his fellow poet QUEVEDO. In 1603 Góngora was the largest contributor to *Flores de poetas ilustres (Flowers of Illustrious Poets)* and gained the patronage of the marqués de Ayamonte, to whom he dedicated several sonnets.

Subsequent travels around Galicia moved Góngora to more poetry, including *La oda a la toma de Larache (Ode on the Taking of Larache,* 1610), a work of extravagant allusion concerning the occupation by Spanish troops of the north African city of Larache. Thereafter Góngora expanded the scope of his projects, working on the *Fábula de Polifemo y Galatea (Fable of Polyphemus and Galatea,* 1612) at the same time as *Las soledades (Solitudes,* 1613). His *Polifemo* shows an innovative reworking of Ovid's myth, a theme also treated by his contemporary LOPE DE VEGA. *Las soledades* recounts the adventures of a shipwrecked youth among a group of shepherds. Góngora, however, never completed the long poem, and it was his dissatisfaction with it that led him to turn to the darker tone and more complicated style of his later works.

The *Fábula de Piramo y Tisbe (Fable of Pyramus and Thisbe,* 1618) is perhaps the finest example of Góngora's use of ancient myth, though blended with an ironic amount of skepticism. Góngora's later poems, such as *Panegyric to the Duke of Lerma* (1617), the prime minister at the time, reflect his need for patrons. Personal trials including debt, rivalry, disgrace, and the death of his patrons led to a self-imposed exile from Spain and the end of Góngora's poetic output.

Góngora was recognized by later generations of Spanish writers and critics, and in the 20th century in particular he began to be recognized as a major figure in the development of Spanish poetry. He is seen today as an enigmatic but crucial poet who helped initiate the modern period of Spanish verse and whose message and language remain relevant and moving.

English Versions of Works by Luis de Góngora y Argote

Las Soledades. Translated by Philip Polack. London: Bristol Classical Press, 1997.

Selected Shorter Poems. London: Anvil Press Poetry, 1995.

The Fable of Polythemus and Galatea. Translated by Miroslav John Hanak. New York: P. Lang, 1988.

The Sonnets of Luis de Gongora. Translated by R. P. Calcraft. Durham, N.C.: University of Durham, 1980.

Works about Luis de Góngora y Argote

Beverley, John. *Aspects of Gongora's "Soledades."* Amsterdam: Benjamins, 1980.

de Groot, Jack. *Intertextuality Through Obscurity: The Poetry of Federico Gárcia Lorca and Luis de Góngora.* New Orleans: University Press of the South, 2003.

Foster, David William. *Luis de Góngora.* New York: Twayne, 1973.

McCaw, R. John. *The Transforming Text: A Study of Luis de Góngora's Soledades.* Potomac, Md.: Scripta Humanistica, 2000.

Gower, John   (ca. 1325–1408) *poet*

Revered by Geoffrey CHAUCER as "Moral Gower," John Gower is one of the most important English poets of the 14th century. He is best recognized for three works: *Speculum Meditantis (Mirror of Man),* written in French; *Vox Clamantis (Voice of One Crying)* written in Latin; and *Confessio Amantis (Lover's Confession),* written in English.

Little is known about Gower's life, but evidence indicates he was a lawyer and a "purchasour," one who bought and sold lands. We also know that Chaucer and he were friends. That Chaucer granted Gower power of attorney while on leave to Italy, as well as dedicated his *Troilus and Criseyde* to Gower, attests to their camaraderie.

Gower's *Confessio Amantis* is his greatest work. A lively verse narrative of approximately 30,000 lines, *Confessio* presents a series of stories illustrating various aspects of the seven deadly sins. At times, the framework appears to clash with the nature of the tales, but *Confessio* seeks to both delight and instruct, and its strong moral purpose is clear.

The work features the character of a lover who begs Venus, the goddess of love, for relief from Cupid's fiery dart. His plea for her "pity and mercy" requires the lover to confess to Genius, a "worthy priest." In so doing, a dialogue between Genius and the lover begins, and stories including those of Nauplius and the Greeks (Benoit de Sainte-Maure's *Roman de Troie*) and Jason and Medea (from Ovid's *Metamorphoses*) are told. Following the lover's lengthy confession, Venus presents him with a rosary, declares him "a lover never more," and commends him to "go where moral virtues dwell." Released from her hold and forgiven for his sins, the lover returns home to devote himself to prayer.

In these well-told stories within *Confessio,* readers find examples of how and how not to live, and as Terence Tiller observes, details "of medieval life as it really was." For these and other merits found in Gower's *Confessio* and his other writings, Gower continues to be praised and recognized as one of the period's finest writers.

An English Version of a Work by John Gower

Tiller, Terence, trans. *Confessio Amantis: [The Lover's Shrift].* Baltimore, Md.: Penguin, 1963.

A Work about John Gower

Fisher, John H. *John Gower: Moral Philosopher and Friend of Chaucer.* New York: New York University Press, 1964.

Graffigny, Madame Françoise de (Françoise d'Issembourg d'Happoncourt Grafigny) (1695–1758) *novelist, playwright*

Françoise de Graffigny, who spent much of her early years in Lunéville and was a great-niece of the engraver Jacques Callot, entered the literary scene at age 43, when she moved to Paris. Before that, she spent nine weeks at VOLTAIRE's Chateau de Cirey in 1738 and 1739, apparently escaping ill treatment from her husband. While there, she wrote several letters each day to various friends, letters apparently filled with gossip and innuendo about the life of the famous writer and his wife. These letters gained her some notoriety and were later published in her *Vie privée de Voltaire et de Mme du Châtelet* in 1820.

In Paris Graffigny was a frequent guest in various literary circles. An early short story she wrote met with harsh criticism, so she decided to "learn her craft" before publishing again (Niklaus, 356). The result was her greatest and best-known work, *Lettres d'une péruvienne* (1747). The epistolary NOVEL is the sentimental tale of an Inca princess, Zilia, kidnapped and brought to France. In France she is protected by a nobleman named Déterville, who falls in love with her. The novel is composed of the letter she writes to her brother, Aza, who was also to have become her husband. It was one of the first French works to portray a foreigner's view of French society. The novel blended "romance, feminist protest, and social satire" (France, 354) and was a phenomenal and lasting success, going through at least 10 reprints in Graffigny's lifetime.

Graffigny also wrote a comedy, *Cénie* (1750), which was successful on the stage and admired by DIDEROT. Another play, *La Fille d'Aristide,* was not so well received. Still, her literary legacy rests mainly on the merits of her novel, which remains in print.

An English Version of a Work by Françoise de Graffigny

Letters from a Peruvian Woman. Translated by David Kornacker. New York: Modern Language Association of America, 1993.

Works about Françoise de Graffigny

Calder, Martin. *Encounters with the Other: A Journey to the Limits of Language through Works by Rousseau, Defoe, Prevost and Graffigny.* New York: Rodopi, 2003.

Showalter, English. *Madame de Graffigny and Rousseau: Between the Two Discours.* Oxford: Voltaire Foundation, 1978.

Guicciardini, Francesco (1483–1540)
historian, writer

Francesco Guicciardini was a member of an influential Florentine family, close to the Medicis. He studied law, developed a political career, and wrote numerous works of great historical value. His first political appointment was in Spain, as the ambassador of the Florentine Republic (1512–13). He later held numerous political posts, many of them fraught with danger, upheaval, and the struggle for power in Florence. When Guicciardini retired, he began working on his historical writings, which he had been composing throughout his political career.

In his *Considerations on the Discourses of Machiavelli* (ca. 1530), Guicciardini reveals his concept of history, which was centered on the idea that self-interest inspires action, which must be governed by law. This concept conflicts with the ideas set forth by MACHIAVELLI, who claimed that the conflict was what made ancient Rome great.

Guicciardini's earlier works include, among others, the *Florentine Histories* (1508–09), which covers the years 1378 to 1509; *Discourse on Ordering the Popular Government* (1512), in which he argues for gradual, rather than radical, change; and *Ricordi* (1528), his reflections on politics.

His main work, *The History of Italy*, analyzes Italy's history between 1494 and 1534. In *The History* (published between 1561 and 1564), Guicciardini attempts to explain the decline of Italy and the general failure of Italian statesmanship. It is an important work because it sets Italy within the larger framework of European history and because Guicciardini innovatively presents his characters, showing "how events were moulded by the chance interplay of different personalities" (Brand and Pertile, 196). *The History of Italy* found a large reading audience across Europe and was translated into numerous languages, including French, Latin, German, and English.

English Versions of Works by Francesco Guicciardini

The History of Italy. Edited by Sidney Alexander. Princeton, N.J.: Princeton University Press, 1984.

Sweetness of Power: Machiavelli's Discourses & Guicciardini's Considerations. Translated by James B. Atkinson and David Sices. DeKalb: Northern Illinois University Press, 2002.

Works about Francesco Guicciardini

Bondanella, Peter E. *Francesco Guicciardini.* Boston: G.K. Hall, 1976.

Brand, Peter, and Lino Pertile. *The Cambridge History of Italian Literature.* New York: Cambridge University Press, 1999.

Philipps, Mark. *Francesco Guicciardini: The Historian's Craft.* Toronto: University of Toronto Press, 1977.

Gustavas Vassa
See EQUIANO, OLAUDAH.

H

Hāfiz (Hāfez, Shams ud-Dīn Mohammad)
(1326–1390) *poet*

Shams ud-Dīn Mohammad grew up in the town of Shiraz, in Persia, the son of Bahā'ud-Dīn, a merchant. Shiraz was a thriving center of Islamic culture renowned for its wines and gardens, and it is where the poet later known as Hāfiz (also Hāfez) spent his life. Hāfiz acquired a thorough education in both the Persian and Arabic languages and traditions and earned the title Khajeh Hāfiz, an honor assigned to those who had memorized the Koran (Qur'an) and were thus qualified to teach it. Hāfiz worked for a time as a baker's apprentice and copyist but became known for his lectures and commentaries on religious texts.

During Hāfiz's life the politics of the region were quite unstable and violent. In an age when poets were dependent on patrons, Hāfiz relied on his wit to keep favor throughout the changes in leadership. One story explains how he gained favor with Timur Lang, who consolidated power in Central Asia and began his conquest of the old Il-Khānid empire around 1380. When Timur entered Shiraz, he scolded Hāfiz for the following verses: "If that Turk of Shiraz would take my heart in his hand, I would give for his Hindu [i.e., black] mole both Bukhárá and Samarqand." Timur was angry because he had worked hard to build both these

places and could not believe that anyone would trade them for the affections of a slave. Hāfiz is said to have replied, "Sir, it is because of such prodigality that I have fallen into poverty and hard times." Timur was charmed, and Hāfiz was rewarded instead of imprisoned.

Hāfiz is considered the finest and most popular lyric poet of the Persian language, variously referred to as Sun of the Faith, Tongue of the Hidden, and Interpreter of Secrets. His poetry has both deeply spiritual and sensual aspects. His *Diwan* (which simply means a collection of poems) was gathered after his death and has been widely translated and enormously influential. Aside from being admired for their technical ability and depth of expression, the poems of the *Diwan* have even been used to foretell the future.

The 500 poems of the *Diwan* are in the form of a *ghazal*, a series of between five and 12 couplets often unified by a single image or theme. *Ghazals* were often set to music. The complexity and rigidity of the *ghazal* defeated lesser poets, but the form helped Hāfiz create intensely beautiful poetry.

One of Hāfiz's trademarks is his use of descriptions of earthly love to explore the mystical meaning of divine love. Like his predecessor Rūmī, Hāfiz was a practitioner of Sufi, which has its roots in Indian mysticism and Islam. The highest goal of Sufi practice is union with the divine, which Hāfiz imagines as a sort of spiritual intoxication. Sufi wisdom teaches that the essence of God and indeed all things is love, and many of Hāfiz's verses address the beauty and freedom of true devotion. These lines translated by Elizabeth Gray, for example, use layered imagery to portray both the teaching of God and the love of God as nourishing water:

> O beggar at the cloister door, come to the
>   monastery of the Magi,
> for the water they give makes hearts rich.

Since the *ghazal* is not a narrative form, meaning it does not tell a story, Hāfiz's poems are instead deep contemplations on faith, love, and longing. A famously complex poet, Hāfiz uses contradicting metaphors that puzzle and fascinate readers, such as these lines from Gray's translation: "Since the kohl of our insight is the dust of your doorway, / Please tell us, where do we go from this threshold?"

As these lines suggest, Hāfiz also uses questions within his poems to engage the reader in his thoughts. His deeply personal meditations, his sensual descriptions of love and unity, and the optimism of his faith make reading his poetry a universally beautiful experience, which perhaps explains why Hāfiz has been one of the most famous and best-loved Persian poets, and still has devoted followers to this day.

English Versions of Works by Hāfiz

Drunk on the Wine of the Beloved: Poems of Hafiz. Translated by Thomas Rain Crowe. Halifax, Nova Scotia: Shambhala, 2001.
Hafiz of Shiraz: Thirty Poems. Translated by John Heath-Stubbs. Kincardine, Scotland: Handsel Books, 2003.
New Nightingale, New Rose. Translated by Richard le Gallienne. Oregon House, Calif.: Bardic Press, 2003.
The Gift: Poems by Hafiz, the Great Sufi Master. Translated by Daniel Ladinsky. New York: Penguin, 1999.

Works about Hāfiz

Cloutier, David. *Hafiz of Shiraz.* Translated by Muriel Rukeyser. Greensburg, Pa.: Unicorn Press, 1988.
Loloi, Parvin. *Hafiz, Master of Persian Poetry: A Critical Bibliography.* London: I.B. Tauris, 2004.
Pourafzal, Haleh, and Roger Montgomery. *The Spiritual Wisdom of Hafez: Teachings of the Philosopher of Love.* Rochester, Vt.: Inner Traditions International, 1998.

haiku

Haiku is a form of Japanese poetry that is structured in three lines of five, seven, and five syllables, respectively. Haiku is often used to express the poet's emotional or spiritual response to a natural object, such as a frog or a blossom. It became popular in Japan around the 17th century and is similar to the much older tanka form, though shorter in length.

Originally, haiku was meant to be part of longer verse, called linked poems, to which additional lines of poetry were added. Eventually, poets began to write the haiku as stand-alone poems.

The structure of haiku relies on imagery and requires concise expression. The focus is often on an impression of an instant, a moment captured in time, as in these two haiku:

> My hut, in spring:
>   true, there is nothing in it—
>   there is Everything!
>   (by Yamaguchi Sodō, 1642–1716)

> Eaten by the cat!
>   perhaps the cricket's widow
>   is bewailing that.
>   (by Enomoto Kikaku, 1661–1704)

Haiku is notoriously difficult to translate into English because its structure is built around syllables rather than rhyme schemes. Translators are challenged to keep the original structure and remain true to the original meaning of the poem.

One of the first practitioners of haiku was BASHŌ, who wrote the following poem:

> *Octopus in a trap*
> *Its dreams are fleeting under*
> *The Summer moon.*

The simplicity of Bashō's haiku made the form attractive to later Zen poets, who used it to express their meditations.

Another haiku master was KOBAYASHI ISSA, whose prolific writing produced some of the finest Japanese poetry of all time, including these lines:

> *In its eye*
> *the far-off hills are mirrored—*
> *dragonfly!*

Haiku is still written today by many poets, including children. One of the beauties of the form is its versatility of subject matter, which can range from the seasons to rice, or from stones in a stream to tears on a child's cheek. Few verse forms provide such classic imagery, inherent with meaning and mood, as haiku.

Works of Haiku

Bashō Matsuo. *The Complete Basho Poems.* Edited by Keith Harrison. Minneapolis, Minn.: Black Willow Press, 2002.

Cobb, David, ed. *Haiku: The Poetry of Nature.* Universe Books & Publishing, 2002.

Kobayashi Issa. *Spring of My Life.* Translated by Sam Hamill. Boston: Shambhala Publications, 1997.

Simmons, Fred. *Contemporary Urban Haiku.* Philadelphia: Xlibris, 2003.

Ueda, Makoto. *Far Beyond the Field: Haiku by Japanese Women.* New York: Columbia University Press, 2003.

Washington, Peter, ed. *Haiku.* Westminster, Md.: Alfred A. Knopf, 2003.

Works about Haiku

Aitken, Robert. *A Zen Wave: Basho's Haiku and Zen.* Washington, D.C.: Shoemaker and Hoard, 2003.

Yasuda, Kenneth. *Japanese Haiku: Its Essential Nature and History.* Princeton, N.J.: Princeton University Press, 2002.

Hammon, Jupiter (1711–ca. 1806) *poet, religious writer*

Jupiter Hammon was born a slave on October 17, on the estate of Henry Lloyd, near Oyster Bay, on Long Island, New York. His father was a slave whom the Lloyds called Opium, while his mother, possibly named Rose, was sold when Jupiter was quite young.

The Lloyds were relatively kind masters, and Hammon was educated alongside some of the Lloyd sons, who had private tutors. In 1733 he was swept up in the "Great Awakening" religious revival and bought his first Bible from Henry Lloyd (Johnson, 210). The poems and prose tracts that he wrote and later published are all heavily religious in nature and filled with biblical imagery.

On Christmas Day, 1760, Hammon published his first poem, *An Evening Thought, Salvation by Christ, with Penetential Cries.* The 22-stanza poem is written in the style of a Negro spiritual and focuses on salvation after death. Some of Hammon's other works include *A Winter Piece,* a sermon that compares black slaves with the Samaritans in Palestine, and an essay titled *An Address to the Negroes in the State of New-York* (1787), his most widely circulated work.

Although he was never directly outspoken in his opposition to slavery, Hammon found his own unique way of arguing for equality for all people. He wrote in *An Address:* "I should be glad if others, especially the young Negroes, were to be free." Many critics debate the artistic merit of Hammon's works, and some criticize him for using Christianity to justify his lot in life. But O'Neale argues that Hammon "couched his antislavery protests in biblical symbols because the Bible was the cultural reference of his times and because slave supporters contorted a few of its verses to justify the enslavement of blacks." Hammon's is an important voice—not only in the past and the slave society in which he lived, but also today in American and world literature.

Works by Jupiter Hammon

America's First Negro Poet: The Complete Works. Edited by Stanley Austin Ransom. New York: Associated Faculty Press, 1983.

Works about Jupiter Hammon

Clark, Margaret Goff. *Their Eyes on the Stars: Four Black Writers.* New York: Garland, 1973.
O'Neale, Sondra A. *Jupiter Hammon and the Biblical Beginnings of African-American Literature.* Metuchen, N.J.: Scarecrow, 1993.
Wegelin, Oscar. *Jupiter Hammon.* Miami, Fla.: Mnemosyne, 1969.

Hariot, Thomas (Thomas Harriot)
(1560–1621) *nonfiction writer*

Thomas Hariot was born in Oxford, where he later studied at St. Mary's Hall. Primarily known as a scientist and mathematician, he became the mathematics and science tutor in Sir Walter Raleigh's household. Not only did he build a telescope at the same time that Galileo GALILEI built his, he also discovered the law of refraction, sunspots, and Jovian satellites. In addition, he included inventions in his *Artis analyticae praxis ad aequationes algebraicas resolvendas* (1631) that established the modern form of algebra.

Hariot also wrote *A Briefe and True Report of the New Found Land of Virginia* (1588). This report was written during his expedition to America with Richard Grenville in 1585–86. Hariot helped Grenville with navigation, astronomy, study of the native people and lands, and the supervision of mapping. The report first appeared in 1588 and was reissued two years later in another edition with illustrations by John White. In addition, the report appeared with other chronicles of exploration in Richard Hakluyt's *Principal Navigations* (1589).

In *A Briefe and True Report*, Hariot pays careful attention to the land's economic possibilities. He lists resources as commodities with brief descriptions of them, mentioning how they are currently used and how they might be exploited further or exported for use by the English. For example, he discusses the healthful properties of tobacco, which became a profitable export for the British colonies:

> [T]hey use to take the fume or smoke thereof by sucking it through pipes made of claie into their stomacke and heade; from when it purgeth superfluous fleame and other grosse humors, openeth all the pores and passages of the body . . . wherby their bodies are notably preserved in health, and know not many greevious diseases wherewithall wee in England are oftentimes afflicted.

The report reads as factual and scientific but also borders, as this passage does, on promotion. Primarily, Raleigh and his associates, including Hariot, were interested in assuring their ventures in America would succeed. While none of Hariot's scientific work was published during his lifetime, his report is important for the unique glimpse it provides into merchant mentality and the exploration of early America.

Works by Thomas Hariot

A Briefe and True Report of the New Found Land of Virginia. Edited by Paul Hulton. Mineola, N.Y.: Dover, 1972.
The Greate Invention of Algebra: Thomas Harriot's Treatise on Equations. Edited by Jacqueline Stedall. New York: Oxford University Press, 2003.

Works about Thomas Hariot

Shirley, John William. *Thomas Harriot: A Biography.* Oxford: Clarendon Press, 1983.
Fox, Robert, ed. *Thomas Harriot: An Elizabethan Man of Science.* Burlington, Vt.: Ashgate, 2000.

Henryson, Robert (1424?–1506?) *poet*

Nothing beyond his poetry is known of Robert Henryson, who wrote in Middle Scots. One of Henryson's major works is *The Morall Fabillis of*

Esope the Phrygian (1568), a collection of 13 animal fables based on those of Aesop. One of the finest is Henryson's telling of the story of the country mouse and the city mouse. This tale, like all the others, ends with a moral:

> Great abundance and blind prosperity
> Often make an evil conclusion.
> The sweetest life, therefore, in this country
> Is security with few possessions.

Henryson wrote a third long poem, *Orpheus and Euridice,* based on the classical myth about two lovers, Orpheus, a musician, and his wife Euridice. When Euridice dies, Orpheus plays the lyre so beautifully the gods are moved to allow him to bring her back, but they stipulate that he must not look at her until they reach the upper world. Orpheus forgets the condition and looks at Euridice, thereby losing her again to death.

Henryson is best known for his poem *The Testament of Cresseid,* a 616-line sequel to Geoffrey CHAUCER's *Troilus and Criseyde* (ca. 1385). Set during the Trojan War of classical antiquity, *Troilus and Criseyde* tells of the love of the Trojan prince Troilus for Criseyde, who swears to be true, only to betray him after she has been captured by the Greek warrior Diomede. In his sequel Henryson follows Cresseid's fate after Diomede abandons her: She becomes a prostitute and eventually a victim of leprosy. Though the disease is presented as a fitting punishment for Cresseid's sins, Henryson is sympathetic as well as stern. Here is Cresseid's father's reaction to her disease:

> He looked on her ugly leprous face,
> Which before was as white as a lily; . . .
> he knew well that was no cure
> For her sickness, and that doubled his pain.
> Thus was their care enough between the
>   two of them.

Henryson's poem is a great work in its own right, as the poet parallels the physical degeneration of Cresseid with her spiritual redemption. The 20th-century poet and critic Tom Scott wrote that Henryson is Scotland's "supreme poet": "No other Scottish poet, before or since, has given us so comprehensive a view of life."

Works by Robert Henryson
Selected Poems of Robert Henryson and William Dunbar. Edited by Douglas Gray. New York: Penguin, 1998.

A Work about Robert Henryson
Kindrick, Robert L. *Robert Henryson.* Boston: Twayne, 1979.

Herder, Johann Gottfried (1744–1803)
philosopher

Among the great thinkers and writers who emerged from Germany during the late 18th and early 19th centuries was Johann Herder. He played an important role in the development of the German intellectual movement known as Romanticism, which emphasized human emotion (over pure reason) and nature. In addition, Herder contributed greatly to the rise of nationalism, the feeling of intense loyalty to one's nation or ethnic group, which would have a tremendous impact on the political events of later centuries.

Herder was born in the town of Mohrungen, in a part of Germany known as East Prussia. He spent most of his life as a preacher in the German city of Weimar, but it seems clear that his intellectual activities, rather than preaching, absorbed him throughout his life. He would develop an intense pride in being culturally German, and his reflections on national culture would be the basis of his most important ideas.

Herder is considered one of the founders of the movement known as Sturm und Drang (1771–78), which roughly translates as "storm and stress" and was derived from F. M. Klinger's play by the same name (1777). This movement stressed the power of German literary and artistic culture and gradually evolved into Romanticism. One of Herder's works from this period is his manifesto *Von deutscher Art und Kunst* (*On German Character and Art,* 1773), which celebrates the uniqueness of German literature, art, and architecture, and was influenced by ROUSSEAU.

In his *Materials for the Philosophy of the History of Mankind* (1784) Herder advocates the political ideal known as *Volk,* roughly translated as "people" or "nation." Herder used the term in reference to people united by shared linguistic and cultural ties. In *Materials,* he expresses his ideas about *Volk* in relation to his ideas of progress, presenting a cyclical view, rather than a linear view, of how civilizations are born, grow, and die.

Herder had enormous influence on German culture and literature. He influenced numerous writers, including GOETHE; contributed to the Sturm und Drang movement; and developed the concept of *Volk,* which contributed to the nationalism that dominated European politics for centuries.

An English Version of Works by Johann Gottfried Herder
Herder: Philosophical Writings. Translated and edited by Michael N. Forster. Cambridge: Cambridge University Press, 2002.

A Work about Johann Gottfried Herder
Koepe, Wulf. *Johann Gottfried Herder: Language, History and the Enlightenment.* Columbia, S.C.: Camden House, 1990.

Huh Joon (Ho Chun) (1546–1615)
medical scholar
Born into the Moogwan, or military class, in the middle of the Chosun dynasty, Huh Joon was destined to compile *Tongui pogam (Exemplar of Korean Medicine).* For its time, this encyclopedia was the most comprehensive medical work of its kind in all Asia. Today it is still highly regarded as a standard text of traditional medicine, although English translations are not in print.

Despite the later success of *Tongui pogam,* Huh Joon's early scholastic aspirations were thwarted because of his status as an illegitimate child; this automatically excluded him from sitting for the civil service exam generally reserved for the scholarly class. Instead, he was forced to study medicine, as doctors in Korea were then considered inferior to literati.

Huh Joon's reputation gradually spread, and in 1575 he became a physician in the royal court. Not long after, his extraordinary medical skills got him a promotion as personal physician to King Sun Jo himself.

It was also in this period that the king commissioned the compilation of a new medical text to bring up to date two previous encyclopedias that had been instigated by KING SE-JONG. This work had not long commenced when it was halted by a Japanese invasion in 1592. During this crisis, however, Huh Joon continued to see after the king's health. In 1597 the work of compiling the medical text was assigned to him, and he was duly given access to the royal archives. On the death of the chief court physician, Huh Joon replaced him.

In 1608 the work of compilation still incomplete, the king, Huh Joon's staunchest supporter, died. Thereafter jealous court officials had him wrongfully imprisoned. Fortunately, a prince whom Huh Joon had previously treated interceded on his behalf and obtained his release. He was then able to complete his medical research, which resulted in a 25-volume work of 3,137 pages.

Tongui pogam had taken 16 years to compile and was published in 1610. It is especially notable for stressing the medicinal value and dangers of alcohol. In addition to this work, Huh Joon also translated five important medical texts from Chinese into Korean.

In 1615 Huh Joon retired with the rank of Sungrokdaebu, second only to the highest. Given the rigid class structure of Chosun society, this was indeed singular recognition of his medical genius.

humanism (1300–1600)
Humanism describes a trend of thought taking place during the European RENAISSANCE that originated as a literary movement and developed into a

philosophy. Humanism was closely related to CLAS-SICISM, as much effort was directed toward recovering the works of writers of ancient Greece and Rome. Characterized by an interest in classical forms and subjects of poetry, spawning revolutionary ideas about education and scholarship, and aided by the diffusion of printing, humanism spread quickly from its origins in Italy to France, Spain, Portugal, Great Britain, Germany, and the Low Countries.

The writer most responsible for introducing humanistic ideals in Italy was PETRARCH, who self-consciously offered Greek and Roman works as models for poetry. In his treatise *On His Own Ignorance and That of Others* (1368), Petrarch summed up the works of his authorities, Aristotle, Cicero, and Seneca, while emulating their style. His recovery of the classical tradition, his appreciation of the individual, his quest for earthly fame and achievement, and his sense of a dawning new age became hallmarks of the new modes of thought that spread throughout Italy. In Florence, politician Coluccio Salutati recovered Quintilian and revolutionized the teaching of rhetoric; Vergerio wrote the first modern educational tract, *On Noble Customs and Liberal Studies of Adolescents* (1402–03); and Leonardo Bruni's translations made Plato, Plutarch, and Xenophon available to a broader reading public.

While Petrarch and others like him advocated a solitary life of contemplation as the scholarly ideal, second-generation humanists felt it their duty to actively contribute to civic life, resurrecting the classical age's republican ideals along with its literary sensibilities. At the same time, artists showed a new interest in realistic representations of the human body, as seen in the works of MICHELANGELO. Humanistic values spread rapidly among the elite, including women scholars like Alessandra Scala and Isotta Nogarola. Works like the histories of BOCCACCIO show the humanists' perceptions that their age was witnessing a revival of learning, rather than participating in the continual decline that had marked the philosophy of the Middle Ages.

Thinkers in Spain, inheriting from both the Italian innovations and the works of the Dutch philosopher ERASMUS, used and elaborated on the gifts of humanism, including the new poetics and a revised system for historical inquiry. Humanistic scholarship reached Germany and the Low Countries through the marriage of Maximilian and Mary of Burgundy in 1473, which brought Germany into the Hapsburg Empire. Though drawing on Italian sources, humanism in these countries took on a distinctly Christian character, revitalizing interest in the landmarks of Christian antiquity, like the works of Augustine. The educational philosophies developed in these circles showed a strong belief in the human potential for self-improvement, a belief shared by English educators John Cheke and Roger Ascham. Sir Thomas MORE is probably the best representative of British humanism, though his belief in freedom of thought and expression led to his beheading by Henry VIII. Also in England, Latin translations of Galen influenced medical thought as well as literary conceptions of personality.

In France, humanist thought reached its peak in the works of Jacques Lefèvre d'Étaples on religion and philosophy, ideas reflected in the literature of MAROT and RABELAIS. Other humanist figures in France include Budé, who is credited with the rise of legal humanism, bringing lawyers, magistrates, and public administrators under the influence of humanist thought; and MONTAIGNE, whose works perhaps mark the outer limit of the extension of humanism. In his *Essays* he admits to an appreciation for the classical past but encourages forward vision and new ideas rather than a return to old ideals.

Though in the Renaissance humanism was essentially a program of study rather than a formulated philosophy, it came to encompass not only teachings in grammar, rhetoric, and history, but also ideas about moral philosophy. In the present-day sense, humanism refers to any viewpoint that is human-centered. In its own time, the humanist interest in and regard for the individual set the stage for the early modern period in Europe.

English Versions of Works of Humanism

Erasmus, Desiderius. *The Praise of Folly and Other Writings*. Edited by Robert M. Adams. New York: W.W. Norton, 1989.

Ficino, Marsilio. *Three Books on Life*. Edited by Carol V. Kaske and John R. Clark. Binghamton, N.Y.: Medieval and Renaissance Texts and Studies, 1989.

More, Thomas. *Utopia*. London: Everyman's Library, 1992.

Petrarch. *Selections from the Canzoniere and Other Works*. Translated by Mark Musa. Oxford: Oxford University Press, 1999.

Works about Humanism

Fubini, Riccardo. *Humanism and Secularization: From Petrarch to Valla*. Translated by Martha King. Raleigh, N.C.: Duke University Press, 2003.

Kristeller, Paul Oskar. *Renaissance Thought and Its Sources*. Edited by Michael Mooney. New York: Columbia University Press, 1979.

Nauert, Charles G., Jr. *Humanism and the Culture of Renaissance Europe*. Cambridge: Cambridge University Press, 1995.

Hus, Jan (John Huss) (1370–1415)
theologian

Jan Hus was born in the village of Husinec in Bohemia (now in the Czech Republic), from which he took his name. Although the son of poor peasants, he graduated from the University of Prague in 1394. He became dean of philosophy there in 1401, one year after becoming a priest, and became renowned for giving his sermons in the Czech vernacular, rather than in Latin, for the benefit of the common people.

The writings of the English religious reformer John WYCLIFFE on the abuses of the Roman Catholic clergy greatly influenced Hus, who allied himself with a pro-reform and strongly-Czech nationalist faction at the university. The Bohemian Church was very wealthy and powerful, and the ideas of Hus and his allies met with much opposition. In 1409 he became rector of the university, following a mass exodus of the conservative German faculty. In 1412, however, the church excommunicated Hus for his criticism of its sale of papal indulgences, a corrupt practice that the reformers despised. He fled Prague and lived in the castles of several aristocratic supporters, writing many treatises in Latin and Czech, as well as a collection of sermons and many letters. Many of these documents were widely distributed in Prague. Two years later, Hus was treacherously taken prisoner at the Council of Constance in Switzerland and tried for heresy. He heroically refused to renounce his beliefs and was burned at the stake.

In his writings, most written during his two-year exile, Hus espoused the doctrines of predestination over indulgence and biblical over clerical supremacy, holding Christ to be the true head of the church rather than the pope. In these beliefs, he followed Wycliffe. His most famous work is the massive *De Ecclesia (The Church)*, which comprehensively outlines his religious beliefs. His treatises in Czech are considered masterpieces of that nation's literature and language, the most famous being *Exposition of the Faith, of the Ten Commandments and of the Lord's Prayer*. Today, Czechs remember Hus as one of their greatest national heroes. The world remembers him as a landmark religious thinker whose writings foreshadowed the Protestant Reformation.

English Versions of Works by Jan Hus

The Church. Translated by David S. Schaff. Westport, Conn.: Greenwood, 1974.

The Letters of Jan Hus. Translated by Matthew Spinka. Manchester, U.K.: Manchester University Press, 1972.

Works about Jan Hus

Didomizio, Daniel. "Jan Hus's De Ecclesia: Percursor of Vatican II?" *Theological Studies* (June 1999): 267–280.

Spinka, Matthew. *John Hus: A Biography*. Princeton, N.J.: Princeton University Press, 1968.

Ibn al-Khatīb (Abu 'Abdallah Muhammad, Lisan al-Din, Abenaljatib, Ben al-Hatib, al-Jatib) (1313–1375) historian, poet

Abu 'Abdallah Muhammad Ibn al-Khatīb was born at Loja, some 30 miles outside Granada, Spain. During his lifetime, Ibn al-Khatīb was the preeminent literary figure in Spain. He wrote more than 60 volumes of history, poetry, and medical and religious texts. Among these is his *Círculo*, a collection of biographical works about the men who were associated with Granada's history, religion, and politics. Ibn al-Khatīb also compiled a volume of Andalusian Arabic poetry, as well as a history of Granada and works on Sufism and philosophy.

Ibn al-Khatīb served at the royal court in Granada for many years and became a highly influential figure. However, political intrigues and his feud with another scholar and minister in Granada, Ibn Zamraq (1333–92), who had once been his pupil, forced al-Khatīb to flee Spain for North Africa in the late 1360s. Ibn al-Khatīb was eventually imprisoned in Fez, where he was put to death. Afterward, he was given the name Lisan al-Din, which means "Tongue of the Religion" and was bestowed in honor of his poetry.

An English Version of a Work by Ibn al-Khatīb

The Jaysh al-tawshih of Lisan al-Din Ibn al-Khatib. Edited by Alan Jones. Cambridge, U.K.: Trustees of the "E.J.W. Gibb Memorial," 1997.

A Work about Ibn al-Khatīb

Irwin, Robert. *Night and Horses and the Desert: An Anthology of Classical Arabic Literature.* New York: Anchor Books, 1999.

Ibn Khaldūn (Abu Zayd 'Abd al-Rahman ibn Muhammad) (1332–1406) historian, philosopher

Ibn Khaldūn was born in Tunis to an aristocratic Spanish Arab from Andalusia. After an intensive religious and literary education, he began a career of government service. He eventually filled top posts in many of the major Arab capitals of North Africa, Egypt, and Spain, but a tendency to make enemies kept him on the run.

In 1375 he took his family to seclusion in a castle in Algeria, where for the next four years he wrote his famous *Muqaddimah. Muqaddimah* is translated as *The Prolegomena*, which literally means "initial discussions" or "introductory essays." Ibn Khaldūn thus wrote this work as an introduction to history. He also used it as an introduction to a later work, titled *Kitab al-'Ibar,* a historical chronicle. In *Muqaddimah,* he takes a historical and philosophical approach to the progress of events in the past. He examines the methods needed to separate fact from fiction and develops what he calls a "science of culture," a theory that would explain the social transformations that take place across time.

Exploring the principles for understanding politics, economics, urban life, and education, he developed a concept of *'asabbiyah,* or social cohesion, the force that binds together tribes and clans. According to Ibn Khaldūn, this force, combined with a sense of religious mission, can impel new groups to seize power in a society. Various political and psychological factors then begin to eat away at the new power group. Thus, he explains the cyclical nature of history: One group conquers, becomes civilized and complacent, gains wealth and stature, and then becomes vulnerable to attack from a new group.

In other parts of *Muqaddimah,* Ibn Khaldūn discusses the arts and sciences. The information he provides specifically on the art of writing has been particularly useful to historians in tracking the development of Andalusian and North African literary developments. In *Night & Horses & The Desert,* Robert Irwin states that Ibn Khaldūn "hated the fancy flourishes which had become fashionable among the chancery officials of his day." Irwin supports this claim with a quote from Franz Rosenthal's translation from *Muqaddimah* in which Ibn Khaldūn states:

Recent authors employ the methods and ways of poetry in writing prose. [Their writing] contains a great deal of rhymed prose and obligatory rhymes as well as the use of the *nasih* before the authors say what they want to say. When one examines such prose, [one gets the impression that] it has actually become a kind of poetry. It differs from poetry only through the absence of metre. In recent times, secretaries took this up and employed it in government correspondence. They restricted all prose writing to this type, which they liked. They mixed up [all the different] methods in it. They avoided straight prose and affected to forget it, especially the people of the East.

Regarding poets themselves, Ibn Khaldūn praises IBN AL-KHATIB as one of the greatest Arabic poets in the history of Spain, stating in the *Muqaddimah* that "[Ibn al-Khatib] possessed an unequalled linguistic habit. His pupils followed in his footsteps" (Irwin).

In addition, Ibn Khaldūn comments on different forms of poetry, such as the *muwashshah,* a form of poetry that included five rhymed stanzas and appeared in classical Arabic literature during the ninth or 10th century. These poems were intended to be sung and were often accompanied by performance. Ibn Khaldūn tells us:

The *muwashshah* consists of branches and strings in great number and different metres. A certain number [of branches and strings] is called a single verse [stanza]. There must be the same number of rhymes in the branches [of each stanza] and the same metre [for the branches of the whole poem] throughout the whole poem. The largest number of stanzas employed is seven. Each stanza contains as many branches as is consistent with purpose and method. Like the *qasida,* the *muwashshah* is used for erotic and laudatory poetry (Irwin).

According to Irwin, Ibn Khaldūn also commented on such poems being "popular both with the court and with the populace at large because they were easy to understand."

For the rest of his life, Ibn Khaldūn worked on his massive universal history, the *Kitab al-'Ibar (The Book of Examples),* in which he discusses the Persians, Israelites, Arabs, and Romans, among others. In a clear, concise, and thoughtful narrative style, he provides invaluable information on the history of North Africa and Spain, which he intended to be instructional. It was his belief that those in the present and the future could learn from events and people in the past.

From age 50, he spent most of his life in Cairo, lecturing under the patronage of the Mamluk sultan, serving as a notoriously incorruptible judge, and continuing his writing. His fame was such that, when he was trapped in Damascus under a Mongol siege in 1400, the fierce chieftain Tamurlane (Timur) had him brought from the city. For seven weeks, Ibn Khaldūn enjoyed the conqueror's hospitality, lecturing and writing surveys on request. Such was his relationship with Timur that the two often engaged in friendly debates concerning political and social issues. Ibn Khaldūn used these debates as the basis of his work *Ta'rif,* a brief autobiography.

Ibn Khaldūn died in Cairo. His teachings and historical works stimulated a resurgence of historical writing in Egypt and Turkey during the 15th and 16th centuries. Since then, translations of his works into Spanish, English, French, and other languages have given him a worldwide reputation as one of the most original philosophers of Arabic history.

English Versions of Works by Ibn Khaldūn

An Arab Philosophy of History: Selections from the Prolegomena of Ibn Khaldun of Tunis (1332–1406). Translated by Charles Philip Issawi. Princeton, N.J.: Darwin Press, 1987.

The Muqaddemah: An Introduction to History. Translated by Franz Rosenthal. Princeton, N.J.: Princeton University Press, 1969.

Works about Ibn Khaldūn

Al-Azmeh, Aziz. *Ibn Khaldun: An Essay in Reinterpretation.* New York and Budapest: Central European University Press, 2003.

Baali, Fuad. *Social Institutions: Ibn Khaldun's Social Thought.* Lanham, Md.: University Press of America, 1992.

Brett, Michael. *Ibn Khaldun and the Medieval Maghrib.* Brookfield, Vt.: Ashgate Variorum, 1999.

Irwin, Robert. *Night and Horses and The Desert: An Anthology of Classical Arabic Literature.* New York: Anchor Books, 1999.

Ignatius of Loyola (1491–1556) *saint, religious writer*

Ignatius of Loyola's *Spiritual Exercises* is one of the most influential and widely used texts in Christian spiritual discipline. Born Inigo de Loyola in the Basque province of Guipuzcoa in northern Spain, the young Ignatius was bred for a life in RENAISSANCE Spain's aristocratic circles. He entered the military and in 1521 was seriously wounded during the siege of Pamplona. Loyola was taken prisoner by the French, but they were so impressed by his bravery that they treated him more as a wounded guest than a prisoner. Loyola's leg was so severely damaged by a cannonball that it had to be broken and reset twice; it never healed successfully, and he limped the rest of his life.

During his convalescence, Loyola underwent a spiritual transformation and embraced Christ as his model and savior. He recovered and went on a pilgrimage in 1522. After his return, he decided to study for the priesthood and attended the Universities of Alcalá, Salamanca, and Paris. During this period, he formulated what became the *Spiritual Exercises* and taught them to fellow students.

In 1538 Loyola and some of his companions went to Rome and offered their services to the pope, who set them to teaching scripture and preaching. In 1540 Pope Paul III formally approved Ignatius's group, the Society of Jesus, which dedicated itself to serving wherever the pope sent its members. Loyola was elected the first superior general of the order; within 20 years, new members and new missions of the society, also known as the Jesuits, appeared as far away as India. The Jesuits would become one of the most influential and controversial religious orders of the Roman Catholic

Church. Loyola died in 1556 and was granted sainthood in 1622.

The *Spiritual Exercises* is a four-week program that leads its disciples to contemplation of their sinfulness, God's greatness and love, and greater perfection in their soul in order to discern God's will for them. Loyola recommends visualization and emotional identification with Jesus' joy and suffering so that participants can truly understand God's love. The *Spiritual Exercises* has been translated in several major languages, and its systematic, emotionally engaging approach to prayer has influenced the spiritual lives of millions.

English Versions of a Work by Ignatius of Loyola

Ganss, George E. *Ignatius of Loyola: Spiritual Exercises and Selected Works*. Mahwah, N.J.: Paulist Press, 1991.

Mullan, Father Elder, S.J., trans. *The Spiritual Exercises of Saint Ignatius of Loyola*. New York: P.J. Kennedy and Sons, 1914.

A Work about Ignatius of Loyola

Idigoras, J. Ignacio Tellechea. *Ignatius of Loyola: The Pilgrim Saint*. Translated by Cornelius Michael Buckley. Chicago: Loyola Press, 1994.

Izmailov, Aleksandr (1779–1831) *fable writer, poet, novelist, journalist*

Aleksandr Izmailov was born in Vladimir, Russia, to a bankrupt nobleman. He was educated at a military school and worked almost his entire life in the Ministry of Finance in St. Petersburg. Toward the end of his life, he was appointed the vice-governor of Tver, near Moscow. However, he lost this prestigious position because of his bitter criticism of the customs and social system of the province.

Izmailov edited and published a number of literary journals and anthologies, and was a member of the Letters, Science, and Arts Lovers Free Society, established to advance the cause of Russian literature. Izmailov's admiration for the prose style of KARAMZIN shows in his novel *Eugene, or Fatal Consequences of a Poor Upbringing* (1799–1801). In effect, this novel created the genre of the *conte moral* or moral fable in Russian literature. Written in the same vein of moral education, handmade copies of Izmailov's poem "Instructions for My Wife, the Vice-Governor's First Lady" circulated throughout the Russian empire. Izmailov's gift for satire, however, is best seen in his numerous fables.

Based on daily scenes from the life of petty bureaucrats and merchants, Izmailov's fables are full of both good-natured humor and biting sarcasm. His tendency for unabridged realism and rough language account for Izmailov's fame as a "writer not for ladies." Some of his most famous fables are "Goldfinch-Astronomer," "Drunkard," and "Passion for Poem-Making." Critic Belinsky notes that Izmailov's fables "insult esthetic taste by their triviality, but some of them stand out due to their genuine giftedness and peasant-like originality."

An English Version of Works by Aleksandr Izmailov

Anthology of Russian Literature: From the Tenth Century to the Close of the Eighteenth Century. Edited by Leo Weiner. Honolulu: University Press of the Pacific, 2001.

A Work about Aleksandr Izmailov

Schonle, Andreas. *Authenticity and Fiction in the Russian Literary Journey, 1790–1840*. Cambridge, Mass.: Harvard University Press, 2000.

Jefferson, Thomas (1743–1826) *political writer*

Thomas Jefferson was born in Albermarle County, Virginia, to Jane and Peter Jefferson, a Virginia official, surveyor, and owner of vast tracts of land. The education of the country's future third president proceeded in a series of stages: At age five, he was sent to a local school to learn reading and writing; At nine, he boarded with a clergyman who guided him in a study of Latin, Greek, and French; and at 14, he received tutoring by a classical scholar to prepare for college. When he entered the College of William and Mary, he came into contact with intellectuals who introduced him to philosophy, law, and legal philosophy. During his lifetime, Jefferson also studied architecture, the arts, math, natural and applied sciences, politics, and religion. His personal library contained nearly 10,000 books and pamphlets and was purchased by Congress when it was establishing its own library. Later, in 1797, he was elected president of the American Philosophical Society, a position he held for 18 years.

As a writer, he composed eight works, as well as 60 volumes of other works that comprise his many treatises, letters, state papers, an autobiography (published posthumously), presidential addresses, and journal entries. In his works, which reflect his personal, philosophical, political, and social views,

he was influenced, among others, by Benjamin FRANKLIN, Harrington, MILTON, Locke, MONTESQUIEU, Helvetius, and VOLTAIRE.

Yet Jefferson was not simply an intellectual. With his childhood friends, he roamed the countryside, rode horses, and passed many hours hunting and fishing. When his father died, he inherited, at age 14, thousands of acres of land, which he strove to cultivate with the assistance of some 150 slaves. He corresponded with horticulturists and often asked for new seeds and plantings for his estates. For a number of decades, he kept diaries in which he recorded observations about the natural world and the type of work being done on his plantations. He also devoted a large portion of his time to putting to use his ever-increasing knowledge of architecture. When he was 26, he began building Monticello, an estate that he was constantly expanding and remodeling.

Not long after starting work on Monticello, Jefferson fell in love with Martha Wayles Skelton. They wed in 1772 and had six children, only two of whom survived to adulthood. Martha died after only 10 years of marriage, and Jefferson never remarried.

The year 1768 was a turning point for Jefferson; it was the year he was elected to the House of Burgesses, and it marks his formal entrance into the political sphere. Drawing on his knowledge of John Locke's theories regarding man's natural right to liberty, he composed *A Summary View of the Rights of British America* (1774), a series of resolutions that challenged Great Britain's authority over the colonies. A year later, he began serving as a delegate to the Continental Congress and drafted the Declaration of Independence in 1776.

In 1779 he was elected governor of Virginia. In 1785 he assumed a post as minister to France. That same year *Notes on the State of Virginia,* his only book, was published. He wrote it in response to questions that had been posed by the marquis de Barbé-Marbois, secretary of the French legation at Philadelphia. The work has been divided into 23 sections, each covering a different topic. The topics range from slavery to civil rights, education, religious freedom, natural resources, geography, and more. Jefferson's comments on slavery reveal that he is aware of the wrongness of slavery, and they are prophetic of the war that would later ensue:

> I tremble for my country when I reflect that God is just; that His justice cannot sleep forever; that . . . a revolution of the wheel of fortune, an exchange of situation, is among possible events; that it may become probable. . . . The spirit of the master [slaveholder] is abating, that of the slave rising from the dust, his condition mollifying, the way, I hope, preparing, under the auspices of heaven, for a total emancipation.

In 1789 Jefferson was named the first secretary of state. In 1797 he became vice president. In 1800 Jefferson was elected president of the United States.

In his first inaugural address, he states, "though the will of the majority is in all cases to prevail, that will, to be rightful, must be reasonable; that the minority possess their equal rights, which equal laws must protect, and to violate would be oppression."

Jefferson was reelected president in 1804, and after his second term retired to his beloved Monticello. He died on July 4, 1826—the 50th anniversary of the Declaration of Independence.

Critical Analysis

Without a doubt, the most important document that Jefferson composed was the Declaration of Independence. In 1776, shortly after Richard Henry Lee proposed that the colonies should be free and independent, Congress elected Jefferson and four others to draft a more formal and detailed declaration that would legitimate—both morally and legally—the colonists' desire to become autonomous. Although all the members of the committee offered ideas, Jefferson was the document's principal author. John Adams explained that when Jefferson entered Congress, he "brought with him" a "happy talent for composition"; his writings were "remarkable" for their "felicity of expression." Jefferson channeled his talents into creating a document that would, in Thomas Gustafson's words, "ring the alarm bell for the fight for independence in all thirteen colonies at the same time" and "unify in sentiment colonists who shared markedly different . . . ideas."

To achieve these ends, Jefferson infused the language of the Declaration with ENLIGHTENMENT principles. Two passages from the opening paragraphs are especially important to examine in this regard. The Declaration begins with the following statement: "When, in the Course of human Events, it becomes necessary for one People to dissolve the Political Bands which have connected them with another, and to assume among the Powers of the Earth, the separate and equal Station to which the Laws of Nature and of Nature's God entitle them, a decent Respect to the Opinions of Mankind requires that they should declare the causes which impel them to the Separation." Jefferson followed this finely phrased announcement with one that has come to embody the fundamental tenets of the American nation: "We hold these Truths to be self evident, that all Men are created equal, that they are endowed by their Creator with certain unalienable Rights, that among these are Life, Liberty, and the Pursuit of Happiness." These words reveal Jefferson's reliance on the ideas that John Locke expressed in *Treatises of Civil Government,* especially those related to natural rights to "life, liberty, and property." Jefferson, influenced by Francis Hutcheson, a Scottish philosopher, opted to substitute people's right to property with his right to pursue happiness. The natural rights philosophy espoused by Locke and Hutcheson was vague enough to appeal to the colonists, despite their many underlying differences, and it set up a framework for understanding the magnitude of crimes the British committed against the inhabitants of the colonies.

After establishing this framework of rights, Jefferson devotes the main portion of the Declaration to cataloging the "long Train of Abuses and Usurpations" perpetuated against the colonists by George III, the king of Great Britain. Some of the charges against the king include his having "refused his Assent to Laws, the most wholesome and necessary for the public Good," "refused to pass other Laws for the Accommodation of large Districts of People, unless those People would relinquish the Right of Representation in the Legislature," "called together Legislative Bodies at Places unusual, uncomfortable, and distant," "has dissolved Representative Houses . . . for opposing with manly Firmness his Invasions on the Rights of the People," and "endeavored to bring on the Inhabitants of our Frontiers, the merciless Indian Savages." In effect, Jefferson was demonstrating that the colonists were not absolving their "Allegiance to the British Crown" for "light" or "transient Causes," but were, instead, exercising their right to "alter or . . . abolish" a tyrannical government that consistently ignored or deliberately violated their basic rights.

Absent from the final draft of the Declaration are Jefferson's statements regarding slavery. In his draft, he described slavery as a "cruel war against human nature itself," one that desecrated the "sacred rights of life and liberty." Even though Jefferson argued that it was the British king who was "determined to keep open a market where MEN should be bought and sold," slaveholding delegates in the northern and southern colonies took offense at these remarks. To ensure that they would sign the Declaration, the passages on slavery were removed.

It should be noted that Jefferson's stance on race-related issues was a complicated one. Earlier, in *Notes on the State of Virginia,* he argued that

blacks were "inferior to the whites in body and mind." In addition, it was not until he was on his deathbed that Jefferson freed a handful of his most loyal slaves. Jefferson's attitudes on African Americans and the institution of slavery were, like many of his contemporaries, equivocal and prone to change. It was not until 1863, nearly 40 years after Jefferson's death, that the country, under the guidance of President Abraham Lincoln, made the official decision to put an end to slavery.

The Declaration of Independence did not achieve its goals through its originality. As Jefferson himself remarked in 1825, he had not aimed to "find out new principles, or new arguments never before thought of." Rather, he desired to "place before mankind the common sense of the subject, in terms so plain and firm as to command their assent," and he used his powerful mastery of language to craft a document that would be regarded as an "expression of the American mind."

Works by Thomas Jefferson

Light and Liberty: Reflections on the Pursuit of Happiness. Edited by Eric Petersen. New York: Random House, 2004.
State of the Union Addresses of Thomas Jefferson. IndyPublish.com, 2004.
The Life and Selected Writings of Thomas Jefferson. Edited by Adrienne Koch and William Peden. New York: Random House, 2004.

Works about Thomas Jefferson

Gustafson, *Thomas. Representative Words: Politics, Literature, and the American Language, 1776–1865.* New York: Cambridge University Press, 1992.
Pflueger, Lynda. *Thomas Jefferson: Creating a Nation.* Berkeley Heights, N.J.: Enslow Publishers, 2004.
Ramazani, Rouhollah K. *Future of Liberal Democracy: Thomas Jefferson and the Contemporary World.* New York: Palgrave Macmillan, 2004.

Jesuit Relations (1632–1791)

The *Jesuit Relations* are a series of reports sent from French Jesuit missionaries in North America to their superiors in Europe, which give a fascinating account of the missionaries' lives with the natives. Written largely in French and Latin, and intended to garner support for the missions at home in Europe, *Jesuit Relations* appeared annually in France between 1632 and 1673. The first English edition, by Reuben Gold Thwaites, originally published between 1896 and 1901, also included reports written by Jesuits after 1673 and up to 1791. One such report was written by Father Jacques Marquette and tells of his 1674 journey to the mouth of the Mississippi River.

In 1625 the first Jesuit missionaries went to the areas of Quebec, Montreal, and Three Rivers, which were occupied by French settlers and traders. The missionaries lived with the Huron and Algonquin, who were often threatened by the Iroquois. One of the most famous sections of *Jesuit Relations* tells how Isaac Jogues, Jean de Brebeuf, and other missionaries were captured and killed by the Iroquois and became known as martyrs for the faith.

The Jesuits, founded by IGNATIUS OF LOYOLA in 1634, were known for their learning. The Jesuits' reports combined scientific observations of Native American life with religious reflections and descriptions of native cultures and religious beliefs. In addition, Jean de Brébeuf wrote a detailed description of the Huron language.

The Jesuits were accurate observers, though their reports reflected an outsiders' view of native cultures. For instance, in *Jesuit Relations* they describe the gods and spirits of the natives as "demons" and their shamans or religious healers as "sorcerers." At the same time, they celebrate the natives' natural virtues, including patient endurance and lack of greed. Father Paul LeJeune wrote: "Those little fops that are seen elsewhere are only painted images of men, compared with our Indians." Later accounts of the natives by Europeans elevated this into the notion of the "noble savage."

Today, the reports known as *Jesuit Relations* are an important source for historians of French colonization in North America, as well as for ethnographers and anthropologists studying Native Americans of the 17th century.

English Versions of *Jesuit Relations*

The Jesuit Relations and Allied Documents: Travels and Explorations of the Jesuit Missionaries in North America (1610–1791). With an Introduction by Reuben Gold Thwaites. Selected and edited by Edna Kenton. Toronto: McLelland and Stewart, 1998.

Women in New France: Extracts from the Jesuit Relations. Edited by Claudio R. Salvucci. Bristol, Pa.: Arx Publishing, 2004.

Works about *Jesuit Relations*

Blackburn, Carole. *Harvest of Souls: The Jesuit Missions and Colonialism in North America, 1632–1650.* Montreal: McGill-Queen's University Press, 2004.

Greer, Allan, ed. *The Jesuit Relations: Natives and Missionaries in Seventeenth-Century North America.* Boston: Bedford/St. Martin's, 2000.

Jiménez de Quesada, Gonzalo
(ca. 1495–1579) *conquistador*

Gonzalo Jiménez de Quesada led a successful military campaign in South America that resulted in the conquest of the region now known as Colombia. His account of his adventures, known as *The Conquest of New Granada,* survives only in excerpts copied by others from the original.

Trained as a lawyer in his native Granada, Jiménez de Quesada was assigned as magistrate to the South American colony of Santa Marta in 1535. In the following year, he was commissioned to search for El Dorado. After eight months in the tropical forests where he and his party endured incredible hardships, Jiménez de Quesada reached the central plain of Colombia inhabited by the Chibcha tribe. In the wake of his arrival, Zipa the Chibcha ruler fled. Jiménez de Quesada then established Santa Fé de Bogotá as the capital of New Granada. He found wealth there, and a dispute with two rivals over the conquest soon followed. He returned to Spain to obtain official recognition of his claim but succeeded in gaining only an honorary title.

After a period in which he was ignored by the Spanish Crown and imprisoned by the governor of New Granada, he was released and appointed marshal of Granada (1550) and councilor of Bogotá for life. But Jiménez de Quesada's craving for riches eventually returned. In 1569 he resumed his pursuit of El Dorado, leading an expedition of 500 men up the Orinoco River. It proved a disaster, and he returned after three years with only 25 of the original company.

As an administrator, Jiménez de Quesada is credited with protecting the rights of the ordinary colonists against powerful landholders and officials. However, his treatment of the natives was inconsistent, varying from humane to brutal as it suited his purpose. This led to a native insurrection late in his career, which he quickly quelled.

Afflicted by leprosy, Jiménez de Quesada retired to his country house to write an account of his various campaigns and died without fulfilling his ambition of discovering El Dorado. His relentless thirst for riches and his failed quest for El Dorado, the mythical city of gold, excited the imaginations of other Spanish writers, including, critics have speculated, Miguel de CERVANTES.

A Work about Gonzalo Jiménez de Quesada

Arciniegas, German. *Knight of El Dorado: The Tale of Don Gonzalo Jiménez de Quesada and His Conquest of New Granada.* Translated by Mildred Adams. Oxford, U.K.: Greenwood, 1968.

Jin Ping Mei (Chin P'ing Mei) (late 1500s)
novel

Jin Ping Mei (*Chin P'ing Mei*; known in English as *The Plum in the Golden Vase* and *Golden Lotus*) is one of the first and most sophisticated Chinese novels of the modern age. It is one of the four greatest Chinese novels, along with *San Guo Zhi*

Tong Su Yan Yi (*San-kuo chih t'ung-su yen-I; Romance of the Three Kingdoms,* 1321–23; pub. 1522), by Luo Guanzhong (Lo Kuan-chung); *Shui Hu Zhuan* (*Shui-hu chuan; Outlaws of the Marsh,* ca. 1368) by SHI NAIAN (Shih Nai-an) and Luo Guanzhong (Lo Kuan-chung); and *Xiyouji* (*Hsi Yu Chi; The Journey to the West,* 1592) by WU CHENG-EN (Wu Cheng-en). However, though *Jin Ping Mei* is often grouped with and compared to these other works, it is considered by many to surpass them in terms of symbolic and structural complexity.

The novel comprises 100 chapters totaling 2,923 pages in the original wood-block printing of 1618. The plot details the rise and fall of a middle-class provincial household led by Ximen Qing (Hsi-men Ch'ing) between 1112 and 1127 during the Song (Sung) dynasty. While the story takes place in the provincial town of Qingho (Ch'ing-ho) and concerns a middle-class family, the setting is meant to reflect the anonymous author's critique of Peking and the later Ming dynasty. Critics have read the novel as a neo-Confucian critique of the immorality of the Ming ruling class and its inability to establish and maintain order according to Confucian precepts.

The novel achieved fame not only for its scathing critique of Ming rulers, but also for its graphic depiction of sex. *Jin Ping Mei* describes in detail the immorality of Ximen Qing and his wives and servants, who catered to his basest desires. Ximen Qing's gruesome death is brought about directly by his libido as he dies after taking too much of an aphrodisiac brought to him by a mysterious Indian monk.

Jin Ping Mei's important place in world literary history is well deserved. It was the first Chinese novel with a unitary plot structure. Critics have argued that only *The Tale of Genji* and *Don Quixote* equaled the novel's complexity at the time of its publication.

English Versions of *Jin Ping Mei*

The Golden Lotus, 4 vols. Translated by Clement Egerton. London: Routledge, 1939, 1972, 1995.
The Plum in the Golden Vase or, Chin P'ing Mei; Volume One: *The Gathering;* Volume Two: *The Rivals.*

Translated by David Tod Roy. Princeton, N.J.: Princeton University Press, 1993.

A Work about *Jin Ping Mei*

Carlitz, Katherine. *Rhetoric of Chin P'ing Mei*. Bloomington: Indiana University Press, 1986.

Jippensha Ikku (1765–1831) *novelist*

Tradition has it that Jippensha Ikku was born into a family of minor samurai, or warrior class. As a boy he served in a samurai household but left to spend his youth in Osaka's *chonin* society. At age 30, he traveled to Edo (in 1868 renamed Tokyo), the old capital of Japan, and lived by his writing while lodging at a bookshop.

In 1802 Jippensha began writing the work for which he is best known today—*Tokai dochu hizakurige* (*Shank's Pony along the Tokaido*; also known as *Shank's Mare*)—an extremely popular comic novel about Japan's *chonin*, or townsfolk. It is a picaresque novel, consisting of loose episodes that do not contribute to an overall plot. The only unifying device is the presence of the main characters in each episode. This serialized structure perfectly reflects the Japanese world view with its emphasis on the present and its appreciation of individual details. Ikku continued writing episodes for *Shank's Pony* until 1822.

Set along the main highways of Japan, *Shank's Pony* is a sharply realistic depiction of the behavior and speech of the Edo *chonin*. The episodes typically take place in brothels, inns, or teahouses, where the heroes Yajiro and Kitahachi encounter a colorful array of townspeople and travelers.

Noticeably absent from the novel, however, are upper-class samurai and peasants. True to *chonin* life in the smallest detail, Jippensha describes only the kinds of people with whom lower-class *chonin* would interact in daily life. Consequently, the novel conveys *chonin* disinterest in the lives of peasants.

The novel is also notable for its resemblance to KYOGEN, a form of Japanese comic theater, and for its inclusion of *kyoka*, short satirical verses, which Jippensha uses to deflate Japanese superstitions.

For example, the heroes meet a ghost that turns out to be an undershirt hung out to dry, while a monster is revealed to be smoke from a distant fire.

It is not known how Jippensha died, but his characteristic wit is memorialized by one popular tale. It tells how Jippensha requested fireworks to be placed in his coffin so that when he was cremated the spectacular display would both startle and amuse the funeral party.

An English Version of a Work by Jippensha Ikku

Shank's Mare or Hizakurige: Japan's Great Comic Novel. Translated by Thomas Satchell. Rutland, Vt.: Charles E. Tuttle, 1990.

John of the Cross, St. (Juan de Yepes) (1542–1591) *poet, mystic*

Juan de Yepes was born to Gonzalo de Yepes and Catalina Álvarez in the village of Fontiberos. He studied at the University of Salamanca, took vows as a Carmelite brother, and became known as John of the Cross.

In 1567 John joined TERESA OF AVILA in her cause of church reform, helping to found monasteries of the Barefoot Carmelites. In 1577 John's reform activities landed him in prison in Toledo, and there he began composing the short verses called the "Stanzas of the Soul." These light, mystical verses outline his views on the soul's progress toward what he considered the highest state of being, the union with God, which could be achieved only through rigid self-denial, the surrender of will, and a series of spiritual tests he called "nights." He describes the soul's final union with the divine in the rapturous terms of a lover encountering a beloved.

After his escape from prison, John developed and recorded his teachings in two treatises, *Ascent of Mount Carmel* and *Dark Night of the Soul*. The *Spiritual Canticle*, written down in 1584, evolved from the visionary "Stanzas," and describes in detail the upward flight of the soul and the 10 rungs on the "ladder of love" that reach to God. In 1586 he wrote

"The Living Flame of Love," a four-stanza poem accompanied by commentary in which he compares the knowledge of God to a consuming fire.

John's writings were not collected until his death and not officially published by the Carmelite Order until 1630. He was made a saint in 1726. He is remembered as one of the best Christian mystics and poets, as beloved as St. Francis of Assisi. The *Spiritual Canticle* remains the best example of the challenging ideals and beautiful language of this highly disciplined and inspiring man.

English Versions of Works by St. John of the Cross

The Collected Works of Saint John of the Cross. Translated by Kieran Kavanaugh and Otilio Rodriguez. Washington, D.C.: ICS Publications, 1991.
The Poems of St. John of the Cross. Translated by Roy Campbell. London: Harvill Press, 2000.

Works about St. John of the Cross

Burrows, Ruth. *Ascent to Love: The Spiritual Teaching of St. John of the Cross.* Starrucca, Pa.: Dimension Books, 2000.
Herrera, Robert A. *Silent Music: The Life, Work, and Thought of St. John of the Cross.* Grand Rapids, Mich.: William B. Eerdmans, 2004.

Jonson, Ben (1572–1637) *dramatist, poet, nonfiction writer*

Ben Jonson was born in London. His father, a clergyman, died before Jonson's birth. Although his mother then married a poor tradesman, Jonson received a high-quality education at the Westminster Grammar School. After stints as a bricklayer's apprentice and a military serviceman, he became an actor. He had his first success as a playwright with *Every Man in His Humor* (performed 1598, printed 1601), in which William SHAKESPEARE acted. Jonson's intent in this play and the ones that followed was to mock, or satirize, the folly of his audiences so they would be shamed into improving their behavior.

Shortly after *Every Man in His Humor* hit the stage, Jonson was imprisoned for killing a man in a duel. He admitted his guilt, but was released after forfeiting his goods and being branded on the thumb. The following year *Every Man Out of His Humor*, which illustrates the shortcomings of jealous, overambitious people, was performed. The play's memorable characters include the miser Macilente, the sarcastic clown Carlo Buffone, and Puntarvolo, an arrogant knight, all of whom came from the Italian tradition of the COMMEDIA DELL'ARTE. The onlookers Mitis and Cordatus comment on the ridiculousness of these characters. They are Jonson's moral compass, the holders of a perspective with whom we would like to identify, even if we see ourselves in the fools.

In 1605 Jonson again found himself in jail, briefly, for collaborating on *Eastward Ho!* (1605), a comedy with references to the Scots that offended the Scottish-born king James I. In spite of this disagreement with King James, Jonson's career flourished during James's reign and with the king's support.

By 1616 Jonson had written his greatest plays, including *Volpone, or the Fox* (1605), a satire about greed and the respect accorded to the wealthy rather than the morally superior. Next came *Epicoene, or the Silent Woman* (1609), a critique of the period's contradictory view of women, which represented the ideal woman as a silent one.

The Alchemist (1610), a satire about superstitions and how tricksters make use of them, was written in supple blank verse and is arguably Jonson's greatest achievement. The central character, Subtle, a fraudulent alchemist (someone who is supposedly able to turn ordinary metals into gold), embodies the vice of greed. The play follows Subtle's hilariously successful swindles until he is caught and punished through a marriage to the obnoxious Dame Pliant. Jonson's genius with plot is evident in his ability to catch up his villain-heroes in their own schemes.

Jonson also composed masques, dramatic entertainments with dances and music that were performed at court, often by the royal family and their friends. Jonson's best masques include *The Masque of Blackness* (1606), *The Masque of Beauty* (1608), and *The Masque of Queens* (1609). In addition to the masque proper, which celebrates the order produced by royal authority, these works include what Jonson called anti-masques, comic dramatizations of the forces of misrule.

Jonson's nondramatic poetry was held in such high regard that in 1616 King James began giving him a yearly salary for it. Jonson wrote in a wide range of poetic forms, including epigrams, lyrics, and tributes. His "Song: to Celia" is based on letters by the Greek writer Philostratus. The poem's opening lines are among the most famous in English literature:

> Drink to me only with thine eyes,
> And I will pledge with mine;
> Or leave a kiss but in the cup,
> And I'll not look for wine.

Jonson was also an important literary critic. His critical stance was that of a neoclassicist. In his own plays he observed classical ideals such as the dramatic UNITIES, derived from Aristotle's *Poetics*, which require that a play contain one action that takes place in a single day and in a single location. In the neoclassicist view, a play that does not observe the unities puts too much strain on the audience's belief. Thus, Jonson's famous observation about Shakespeare, that he "wanted art," means not that Shakespeare is a bad writer, but that his plays do not maintain the unities.

At the end of his life, Jonson was regarded by many as England's greatest living writer, and a number of young poets, styling themselves as the "Sons of Ben," gathered around him to enjoy his wit and learn their craft. After suffering a stroke in 1628, Jonson spent the remainder of his life bedridden. Upon his death, he was buried in Westminster Abbey, where he remains to this day beneath a tombstone reading "O rare Ben Jonson."

Works by Ben Jonson

The Alchemist and Other Plays. Edited by Gordon Campbell. New York: Oxford University Press, 1998.

The Complete Poems. Edited by George Parfitt. New York: Penguin, 1988.

Works about Ben Jonson

Loewenstein, Joseph. *Ben Jonson and Possessive Authorship.* New York: Cambridge University Press, 2002.

Mickel, Leslie. *Ben Jonson's Antimasques: A History of Growth and Decline.* Brookfield, Vt.: Ashgate Publishing, 1999.

Summers, Claude J., and Ted-Larry Pebworth. *Ben Jonson Revised.* New York: Twayne, 1999.

Julian of Norwich   (1342–ca. 1416)
religious writer

When Julian of Norwich was 30 years old, she experienced intense, spiritual visions that led her to live as a religious recluse in a room attached to St. Julian's Church in Norwich, England. The practice of living in seclusion was not uncommon during the period, and those who chose to live such a life were known as "anchorites." Little is known about Julian; even the name "Julian" refers not to her Christian name but to the church she occupied. We do know, however, the date of her life-changing visions—May 13, 1373—and we have four manuscripts of the narrative of her mystical encounters.

Julian's *Revelations of Divine Love* (also known as *A Book of Showings*) consists of a highly vivid account of the visions she encountered while severely ill. These revelations are examined through a theologically informed and spiritually sophisticated lens. What likely strikes present-day readers most is not Julian's facility with both Latin and English but the intense, graphic quality of her descriptions. She describes the blood that drips from Christ's crown of thorns as running down like heavy drops of rain falling from the eaves of a house in a rainstorm. The roundness of the drops, she adds, resembles the scales of herrings. Perhaps even more startling, however, is Julian's comparison of Jesus to a mother figure. "The mother," she writes, "can lay her child tenderly to her breast. But our tender Mother Jesus can lead us . . . into his blessed breast . . ., and shew us . . . the joys of heaven . . . [and] endless bliss." The feminization of Christ, while rather unusual today, was not uncommon during the period.

Revelations of Divine Love in some ways resembles works by other religious mystics, such as Margery KEMPE and the author of THE CLOUD OF UNKNOWING. Julian of Norwich's emphasis, however, is on Christ's love for humankind, and the excitement and inspiration she derived from her vision sets her work apart.

English Versions of Works by Julian of Norwich

A Lesson of Love: The Revelations of Julian of Norwich (Unabridged). Lincoln, Neb.: iUniverse, 2003.
The Revelations of Divine Love of Julian of Norwich. Translated by James Walsh. St. Meinrad, Ind.: Abbey Press, 1961.

Works about Julian of Norwich

Baker, Denise Nowakowski. *Julian of Norwich's Showings: From Vision to Book*. Princeton, N.J.: Princeton University Press, 1994.
McAvoy, Liz Herbert. *Authority and the Female Body in the Writings of Julian of Norwich and Margery Kempe*. London: Boydell and Brewer, 2004.

Jung Mong Joo (Chŏng Mong-ju, P'oun) (1337–1392) *scholar, poet, diplomat*

Born in the final years of the Koryo dynasty, Jung Mong Joo is often referred to as the father of Neo-Confucianism in Korea. While in his 20s, he became a member of the faculty of Songgyungwan University. With other noted Korean scholars, he established the Chinese classics as the core curriculum with emphasis on the interpretations of Zhu Xi (Chu Hsi).

Jung Mong Joo distinguished himself as a capable diplomat. In 1377 he was sent to Japan to establish ties with the Ashikaga military regime and to negotiate the return of Koreans captured by Japanese pirates. In 1386 he was ambassador to China at the court of the newly founded Ming dynasty at Nanjing (Wanking).

During this period, the Koryo dynasty was under threat from within and without. In 1388 when the Ming dynasty tried to annex northern Koryo territories, the Koryo king dispatched an army under General Yi Song-gye to deal with the crisis. Yi instead turned against Koryo and attempted to seize the government, while his son tried to persuade Jung Mong Joo to change sides. Jung Mong Joo, however, remained staunchly loyal to Koryo and responded to the taunts of Yi's son with the following poem, which he wrote in the traditional Korean form of *sijo*:

> Though this frame should die and die
> though I die a hundred times
> My bleached bones all turn to dust
> my very soul exist or not
> What can change the undivided heart
> that glows with faith toward my lord?

The poem has become famous as a classic expression of Korean fidelity. Not long after he wrote the poem, Jung Mong Joo was murdered by members of the Yi faction on the Sojukkyo Bridge at Kaesong for his refusal to switch sides. Thus, in death, he became a symbol of Confucian loyalty. In 1517 during the Chosun dynasty, Jung Mong Joo was posthumously inducted into the national academy to take his place alongside the other great Korean philosophers.

An English Version of Works by Jung Mong Joo

"Spring Mood" and "Untitled Poem." In *Anthology of Korean Literature from Early Times to the Nineteenth Century*. Compiled and edited by Peter H. Lee. Honolulu: University of Hawaii, 1981.

Jung Yak Yong (Jeong Yak-jong, Chong Yag-yong, Dasan, Tasan) (1762–1836) *philosopher, poet, reformer*

The founder of the Shirhak, or "Practical Learning" philosophy, Jung Yak Yong was one of Korea's leading philosophers. As a proponent of Shirhak, he went outside the conservative limits of philosophy, writing about a wide range of subjects, including history, education, law, mathematics, science, agriculture, and engineering. Born at Kwangju, he was brother-in-law of Yi Sunghun, the first Korean convert to Catholicism, and the uncle of Chong Hasang, the Catholic martyr. He himself converted to Catholicism in 1784. He was educated in the standard Korean and Chinese classics and acquired a taste for the religion and learning of the West.

Upon passing the civil service examination in 1780, Jung Yak Yong went on to hold several government positions. He was a lecturer at Songgyungwan University, assistant minister of defense, and personal secretary and close adviser to King Chongjo. In 1794 as secret royal inspector of Kyonggi, he submitted a report in verse on rural poverty. Soon after, he performed duties as magistrate in the Hwanghae province.

The king's death in 1801 coincided with the infamous Catholic persecutions of the time. Jung yak Yong was fortunate to be saved because of his royal connections, but his penchant for social reform resulted in his exile in 1802.

He spent the next 18 years at Kangjin in Cholla Province, where he developed the doctrine of Shirhak in opposition to the old Confucian values of the Yi dynasty. Shirhak advocated new utilitarian solutions to national problems. In his famous work *Kyongse yp'yo* (Design for good government), he articulated a new concept of government. In *Mongmin simso* (Handbook for tending the people), he proposed agrarian and economic reforms; and in *Humhum sinso* (New work on sentencing), a treatise on capital punishment, he demanded justice for the poor.

In 1818 he returned from exile to his native Kwangju. Refusing to reenter government service, Jung Yak Yong continued his philosophical project. His numerous prose and poetic writings not only analyze in depth the social problems and injustices of his era, but also propose solutions within the innovative framework of Shirhak. His writings are thus considered the theoretical basis of Korea's economic and political modernization.

A Work about Jung Yak Yong

Setton, Mark. *Chong Yagyong: Korea's Challenge to Orthodox Neo-Confucianism.* Albany: State University of New York Press, 1997.

Kabuki (1600s–present)

Kabuki, the Japanese popular theater, originated in the early 1600s. A female dancer and former temple attendant named Okuni assembled a troupe of female dancers and actors who gained wide popularity for their parodies of Buddhist ceremonies. Okuni's Kabuki (literally meaning "song-dance-skill") was the first theatrical entertainment in Japanese history for the common people, in contrast to the classical, aristocratic NOH and its predecessors. Okuni's erotic and arguably blasphemous performances (and pervasive rumors that her troupe doubled as a brothel) caused the government to ban women from performing on stage in 1629. Young boys took on female roles for some years, but this practice ended in 1652, when the state again intervened. At this point, mature men began playing all women's roles, a practice that continues to the present day. By the early 1700s, Kabuki had abandoned satire and salaciousness to present serious and moving contemporary dramas, often about commoners rather than samurai. In contrast to the ritualistic, solemn, and aristocratic Noh, however, kabuki delighted audiences of all classes with its spectacular stage effects, beautiful scenery, sympathetic characters, and exuberant performances. Its rise in popularity mirrored the ascent in social status of Japan's long-despised merchant class, and protagonists of Kabuki dramas often sprang from their ranks. Many Kabuki plays were based on actual events; *Chushingura (The 47 Ronin)* was inspired by the legendary ritual suicide of a group of samurai in 1703. Similarly, many of the Kabuki written by the great dramatist Chikamatsu MONZAEMON were inspired by actual lovers' suicides, as were his more numerous works for the BUNRAKU (puppet theater).

As the 18th century wore on, two distinct schools of Kabuki developed. "Soft" Kabuki, centered in the thriving commercial city of Osaka, produced plays that were realistic in style and often domestic in theme. "Hard" Kabuki, by contrast, originated in the samurai-dominated city of Edo (now Tokyo), capital of Japan's shogun, or military commander in chief. It was highly stylized and violent, and influenced by Noh to a greater extent than its Osaka counterpart.

Many common themes in Kabuki derive from Buddhist and Confucian thought and include vengeance, the transience of life, and, above all, the insoluble conflicts between society and the individual, between passion and morality, between conscience and duty. Notwithstanding these ambitious themes, most Kabuki plays are better performance vehicles than literary works, though some are unqualified masterpieces. One of these is *Sukeroku, Flower of Edo,* about a young samurai who plots revenge with his lover after an evil warlord murders his father. Written by Tsuchi Jihei in 1713, its ornate procession and crowd scenes, spectacular swordplay, and uproarious comedy have long made it a favorite of Japanese theater. Another, less-uplifting classic Kabuki drama is *Chronicle of the Battle of Ichinotani*. Loosely based on historical events, it revolves around a noble general's tragic attempts to reconcile conflicting duties to his emperor and his lord. Arguably the best Kabuki texts, from a literary point of view, are those of Chikamatsu's puppet plays that were adapted for Kabuki after his death; indeed, these works make up nearly half of the current Kabuki stage repertoire.

Kabuki today remains a highly popular art form, and is regularly performed at two large theaters in Tokyo: the commercially focused, star-driven Kabuki Theater, and the more historically oriented, textually faithful National Theater. Many younger actors and directors at these and other companies are attempting to update their discipline using Western stage techniques and special effects. Classic Kabuki plays have inspired numerous films, and after 400 years it remains Japan's most popular genre of traditional theater. Kabuki has also influenced Western dramatists ranging from Bertolt Brecht to Steven Sondheim, and since the mid-1980s has become increasingly popular in the United States.

An English Version of Kabuki

Kabuki: Five Classic Plays. Translated by James R. Brandon. Honolulu: University of Hawaii Press, 1992.

Works about Kabuki

Halford, Aubrey S. *The Kabuki Handbook.* Rutland, Vt.: C.E. Tuttle, 1956.

Leiter, Samuel L., ed. *The Kabuki Reader: History and Performance.* Armonk, N.Y.: M.E. Sharpe, 2002.

Yamaguchi, Masao. "Noh and Kabuki: The Beauty of Form," *UNESCO Courier* (April 1983): 15–18.

Kant, Immanuel (1724–1804) *philosopher*

Considered to be one of the most influential thinkers of modern times, Immanuel Kant represents a link between the ENLIGHTENMENT philosophy of the 18th century and the Romanticist thinking of later times. His writings on metaphysics and the nature of understanding had enormous influence throughout the Western world. His greatest work, *A Critique of Pure Reason,* is one of the most important works of philosophy ever written.

Kant was born in the German city of Königsberg, which is today the city of Kaliningrad. Throughout his life, he never traveled outside the vicinity of the city of his birth. After graduating from the University of Königsberg, he worked for a time as a private tutor before he became a professor at the university. He would continue to teach at the university until his death, simultaneously producing an impressive amount of intellectual writings. Kant never married or had a family, and it was said that his daily routine never changed throughout the whole of his life. He was very well liked and respected by the people of the city of Königsberg.

Although Kant's life was relatively uneventful, his philosophical influence was enormous. In fact, he was one of the most important philosophers of all time. His influence was most deeply felt in the field of epistemology. Epistemology concerns the nature of knowledge and asks questions about how human beings know what they know (or what they think they know). During Kant's time, fierce debate was raging in the field of epistemology. On one side were thinkers who believed that all knowledge came from direct experience or observation, an idea known as *empiricism*. On the other hand there were philosophers who maintained that some human knowledge was innate, or built into the human mind itself, and that people did not need to acquire it through experience or observation. This debate had serious implications for philosophy, religion, and the nature of knowledge itself.

Kant's works formed a bridge between these two points of view. In 1781 he published his masterpiece *A Critique of Pure Reason,* which went a long way toward resolving the philosophical dispute. In this work, Kant describes his own view of epistemology and explains how he believed human beings acquired knowledge.

Although Kant is best known for his epistemology, he also produced works on a wide variety of other subjects. He wrote about political philosophy in *A Critique of Practical Reason* (1788), in which he states his belief in the freedom of the individual and the right of every person to self-government. He quietly sympathized with both the American Revolution and the French Revolution.

In addition to epistemology and political philosophy, Kant had a substantial influence on ethics, which is the study of how people decide what is morally right and what is morally wrong. He laid out his ethical philosophy in *Metaphysics of Ethics*, which was published in 1797. For a long time, European thinkers had believed that human beings possessed an innate sense of morality, given to them by God. Kant, on the other hand, believed that human beings discover what is right and wrong simply through the use of reason.

Kant also believed that religious ideas should be based on human reason, rather than on biblical revelation. This unorthodox attitude toward religion caused the king of Prussia, Frederick William II, to forbid Kant to write or teach about religion.

In addition to philosophy, Kant also wrote about scientific subjects. In 1755 he published *General Natural History and Theory of the Heavens*, which was influenced by Isaac Newton. In this book, he theorizes that astronomical systems such as galaxies and solar systems might develop from a spinning, gaseous nebula. This idea, astonishing at the time, is now the accepted scientific theory for how such formations come to be. Kant also wrote about geography and mathematics.

The philosophical work of Kant drew much of its inspiration from earlier thinkers. Kant himself stated that he was greatly impressed with the writings of the Scottish philosopher David Hume, although he challenged many of Hume's ideas. Jean-Jacques ROUSSEAU also influenced Kant, although more in a political than philosophical sense.

Although Kant's political, ethical, religious, and scientific thought is important, he is best known for his work on epistemology, and it would be in this field that he had his greatest impact. Both during his own time and after his death, his ideas influenced a wide variety of thinkers and philosophers, such as Johann Wolfgang von GOETHE, other German writers of the Romantic period, and Georg Wilhelm Friedrich Hegel (who, in turn, had a tremendous impact on Karl Marx). Kant's political views were greatly influenced by Rousseau, who favored a government that was not dependent on a monarchy, which both Rousseau and Kant viewed as a "violation of human dignity." And, like Thomas JEFFERSON, he believed that humans deserved to act according to the will of the majority and to what was best for all, rather than being subjected to rules created by a wealthy and "noble" ruling class. Much of 19th- and 20th-century European philosophy is based on Kant's work.

Critical Analysis

Of all the many works that Kant produced over the course of his life, by far the most famous and influential is *A Critique of Pure Reason*, a detailed and exact description of his system of epistemology in which Kant explains how he believes human beings acquire their knowledge.

European intellectuals had been debating the nature of human knowledge for centuries before Kant. One point of view held that the basis of human knowledge was empiricism, the idea that all human knowledge comes from direct experience and observation. According to this idea, the human mind is a "blank slate" before it experiences or observes anything. No human can have any knowledge of something unless he or she directly experiences or observes it. One of the key thinkers of empiricism was the English philosopher John Locke.

The other point of view held that certain types of knowledge could be known to the human mind independently of experience or observation, because human beings possessed reason enough to figure things out. A clear example of this is human knowledge of mathematics. Humans can solve mathematical problems through the use of their reason alone, without observing or experiencing the problem beforehand. According to this school of thought, knowledge of mathematical logic was innate, which means that human beings possess it simply because they are gifted with human reason.

However, Kant perceived that some things exist beyond human knowledge and are generated by a phenomenon outside the scope of human understanding. This *Ding-an-sich* (thing-in-itself) can only be perceived through creative and intellectual faculties but not fully understood.

In *A Critique of Pure Reason,* Kant combines the two points of view to form a new system of epistemology. He declares that both types of knowledge exist and are equally important. Some knowledge is empirical and comes from direct experience and observation, while other knowledge is innate and simply is the gift of human reason.

An example of an empirical statement might be, "The horse is brown." This cannot be known through innate knowledge, because people must see the horse to know that it is brown. However, if people directly observe the horse and see that it is, indeed, a brown horse, they can be said to have empirical knowledge of the horse's color.

An example of an innate statement might be, "All brown horses are brown." This can be known innately, without having to bother with observing brown horses to make sure they are brown. The truth of the statement is contained within the statement itself and therefore cannot logically be false. Similarly, one could say, "All brown horses are horses" and know, independent of empirical evidence, that the statement is true.

Kant's genius was simply to point out that different types of human knowledge will apply in different circumstances. In some cases, empirical knowledge is called for, such as when a person is trying to determine the physical characteristics of a particular thing. In other cases, innate knowledge is called for, such as when a person is trying to solve a mathematical problem.

On morality, Kant granted that moral action is guided by duty. Duty, he perceived as the core of freedom; thus, according to Kant's philosophy, "freedom rests upon the submission of the will to the sublime moral law." He believed in God, who instilled in humans a moral consciousness, and it is this consciousness that spurs action, and the human soul that guides morality and ethical behavior.

The unification of the two types of knowledge allowed Kant to develop an entirely new way of viewing human knowledge. It bridged the gap between those who believed in empirical knowledge and those who believed in innate knowledge, and in almost all of his works, he saw a deep and abiding connection between knowledge and faith in God. His philosophy also advanced, if not made possible, much of the philosophical and scientific work that has taken place since Kant's time.

English Versions of Works by Immanuel Kant

A Critique of Judgment. New York: Barnes and Noble, 2004.

A Critique of Pure Reason. Translated and edited by Paul Guyer and Allen Wood. Cambridge: Cambridge University Press, 1998.

Groundwork for the Metaphysics of Morals. New Haven, Conn.: Yale University Press, 2002.

Kant: Metaphysical Foundations of Natural Science. Edited by Michael Friedman. New York: Cambridge University Press, 2004.

Observations on the Feeling of the Beautiful and Sublime. Translated by John T. Goldthwait. Berkeley: University of California Press, 2004.

On Education. Mineola, N.Y.: Dover, 2003.

Works about Immanuel Kant

Allison, Henry E. *Kant's Transcendental Idealism: An Interpretation and Defense.* New Haven, Conn.: Yale University Press, 2004.

Anderson-Gold, Sharon. *Unnecessary Evil: History and Moral Progress in the Philosophy of Immanuel Kant.* Albany: State University of New York Press, 2001.

Kuehn, Manfried. *Kant: A Biography.* New York: Cambridge University Press, 2001.

Melnick, Arthur. *Themes in Kant's Metaphysics and Ethics.* Washington, D.C.: Catholic University of America Press, 2004.

Pasternack, Lawrence R. *Immanuel Kant: Groundwork of the Metaphysics of Morals in Focus.* London: Taylor and Francis, 2002.

Kempe, Margery (1373–1438) *memoirist*

Margery Kempe was born in the English seaport of Bishop's Lynn to the prominent official John Brunham. Around age 20 she married John Kempe, with whom she had 14 children. Following difficulties in childbirth, failed business endeavors, and an increasing number of visions, in which she was visited by and held conversations with Christ and the Virgin Mary, Margery, at age 40, struck a bargain with her husband to end her duties as a wife so she might take up her calling as a pilgrim of faith. She occupied herself with visiting holy places and people all over England and as far away as Germany and Jersulem. One of Margery's most affecting visits was to JULIAN OF NORWICH, the anchorite famous for recording her own visions. With the help of two separate scribes, Margery dictated an account of her turbulent life in what is now called *The Book of Margery Kempe,* the first autobiography in English.

To the excitement of literary historians, Kempe's manuscript was "discovered" in 1934. It is valued for its descriptions of the experiences of a middle-class laywoman of the 15th century. For some modern readers, the *Book* can be inaccessible due to Kempe's highly emotional form of expression and her devout religious fervor. The strength of personality that endowed Kempe with the motivation to record her life also sparked many conflicts with her contemporaries. Some found her excessive and noisy weeping bothersome, and others accused her of preaching, which women were not allowed to do. Furthermore, Kempe was suspected of practicing heresy, or not conforming with the beliefs of the Christian Church. Though tried on successive occasions, Kempe defended herself and was always acquitted. For Kempe, the difficulties she encountered and the trials she endured served only to prove the rightness of the path she had undertaken. The following passage from the *Book* is typical of its tone and theme:

> And then this creature, seeing all these adversities coming on every side, thought they were the scourges of our Lord that would chastise her for her sin. Then she asked God for mercy, and forsook her pride, her covetousness, and the desire that she had for worldly dignity, and did great bodily penance, and began to enter the way of everlasting life as shall be told hereafter.

Kempe's faith was the most important thing in her life, and her concern with her own errors and atonement for them is constant. Throughout the work, her interactions with her visions and her active fantasies about participating in scenes of Christ's birth and death are described much more frequently, and in more vivid detail, than interactions with her fellow humans. The above passage demonstrates her belief that all her challenges are merely tests of faith meant to guide her back to God. Most curiously, she refers to herself throughout her autobiography in the third person, often using the term "this creature." This allowed her to distance herself from the narrative, which may have been a tactic to avoid further charges of heresy. Regardless, she proves her humility by portraying herself as no more than one of God's many creatures.

Kempe's determination to record her life is surprising and daring, especially since she, like most women of her class, was unable to read or write. Once considered, in the words of Lynn Staley, the account of a "possibly hysterial, certainly emotional, woman," Kempe's *Book* is valuable as a record of everyday life in England and as a depiction of one woman's struggles toward faith, identity, and self-preservation in a world largely controlled by men. Kempe believed she could personally and directly experience God's love and mercy, and she maintained that belief despite opposition. Modern readers must keep in mind that the Kempe we see is filtered through others, the scribes who wrote what Kempe dictated; it is, therefore, impossible to guess the extent to which these scribes modified the narrative as she told it. Still, the *Book* is a clear and honest account of human faith. B. A. Windeatt observes that "in the *Book* we hear recorded, however tidied, [we discover] much of the accent of an authentic voice, the voice of a medieval Englishwoman of unforgettable character, undeniable courage and unparalleled experience."

Works by Margery Kempe

The Book of Margery Kempe. Edited and translated by Lynn Staley. New York: W.W. Norton, 2001.

The Book of Margery Kempe. Translated by B. A. Windeatt. New York: Penguin Books, 1994.

Works about Margery Kempe

Gallyon, Margaret. *Margery Kempe of Lynne and Medieval England.* Norwich, U.K.: Canterbury Press, 1995.

McEntire, Sandra J., ed. *Margery Kempe: A Book of Essays.* New York: Garland Publishing, 1992.

Kim Jung Hee (Kim Chung-hui, Ch'usa, Yedang, Wandang) (1786–1856) *artist, calligrapher, scholar*

Representative of the flowering of the late Choson period, Kim Jung Hee is regarded as one of Korea's greatest calligraphers. He was born into an aristocratic family, and his talents manifested themselves at an early age. By six he was already a competent calligrapher; and at age 16 he was accepted as a pupil by the revered statesman Pak Che-ga.

Kim Jung Hee's teen years, however, were marred by personal tragedy. His mother died, followed in quick succession by several close relatives, including his wife. In spite of such adversity, Ch'usa nonetheless passed the civil service examination at age 23.

In 1809 he accompanied his father to China as part of a delegation to the Qing dynasty. While there, he was a student of the Chinese scholar Wang Fanggang, who introduced him to the intellectual and artistic circles of Beijing. Ch'usa thus returned to Korea with a significant advantage over his scholarly peers.

As leader of the Northern Group, he pioneered historical research on epigraphy in Korea, producing the first text on Korean inscriptions. His main achievement, however, was the creation of a unique style of calligraphy known as *ch'usach'e*. In this style the strong strokes of early Chinese epigraphy (*Ye*) complement the vibrancy of grass script (*ch'o*).

In paintings, Kim Jung Hee's work synthesizes the individual self-expression of the Wu school and the minimalist Son tradition with its sparing but disciplined brushwork. He also excelled at orchid paintings in which the simplicity of a single bloom harmonizes with inscriptions surrounding it.

Exiled to Cheju Island as a result of factional fighting, Kim Jung Hee made productive use of his time by perfecting the individuality of his style. He was recalled in 1848 by King Hongjong, only to be exiled again to Pukch'ong in 1851 as a result of another intrigue.

As a highly original artist and connoisseur of taste, Kim Jung Hee made a great impact on the visual arts of the 19th century. Because he shared his knowledge, he raised the level of art and made it accessible to many.

Kim Shi-sup (Kim Sisup) (1435–1493) *fiction writer*

As a child, Kim Shi-sup was very precocious. He lived in the early years of the Yi dynasty and as a young man held an administrative position at the Korean court during the reign of Tanjong. After Tanjong was overthrown by Se Jo, Kim Shi-sup shaved his head and became an itinerant Buddhist monk rather than serve the usurper.

At age 30, he settled at Kumo-san, near Kyongju, where he developed a reputation for eccentric behavior. His collection of stories *Kumo Sinhwa (New Stories from Golden Turtle Mountain)* is named after this location. Kim Shi-sup wrote the five stories in the collection in classical Chinese and used as his sources supernatural tales called *chuanqi (ch'uan-ch'i),* or "tales of wonder." These folk tales typically dealt with love affairs between mortals and other-worldly beings, as well as dream voyages to the dark underworld or exotic places, such as the Dragon Palace. Kim Shi-sup's story "Yisaeng kyujang chŏn" (Student Yi peers over the wall) contains many elements characteristic of the *ch'uan-ch'I,* such as a ghost wife, an exchange of poems, and a moral lesson at the end of the tale.

Kim Shi-sup's writing is, moreover, marked by allusions, or veiled references, to Chinese literature, especially a work by Qu You (Ch'ü Yu;

1341–1427) called *Jiandeng xinhua (Chien-teng hsin-hua;* New tales written while cutting the wick), from which he drew much inspiration.

Kim Shi-sup returned to Seoul after Se Jo died but did not take up a government position again. Like other educated men of this period, he also wrote verse, but it is for his stories that he is most remembered.

An English Version of a Work by Kim Shi-sup

"Student Yi Peers Over the Wall." In *Anthology of Korean Literature from Early Times to the Nineteenth Century.* Compiled and edited by Peter H. Lee. Honolulu: University of Hawaii Press, 1981.

Kleist, Heinrich von (1777–1811)
dramatist, novelist

Heinrich von Kleist, born in Frankfurt into a family of the minor Prussian nobility, led a life as troubled as the political fortunes his native country would experience under Napoleon. After entering the Prussian army in 1792, following his family's tradition of military service, Kleist found that his temperament did not suit a life of rigid discipline and unquestioning obedience. He resigned in 1799 to devote himself to study, but overtaxed himself at the University of Frankfurt and left in 1800 to seek a cure for his health. He settled in Switzerland, intending to take up the rustic life, but his fiancée, Wilhelmine von Zenge, declined to join him, and their engagement ended.

In the following years, he turned to writing plays and reading the works of the great philosophers; he identified with ROUSSEAU and LEIBNIZ, but reading KANT's theories about the absence of absolute truth shattered Kleist, who believed the search for truth was his chief goal in life. Lack of funds forced him to take a position as a civil servant in 1805, which he resigned the next year to take up the series of travels, failed enterprises, bursts of writing, and bouts of desperation that marked the remaining years of his life. In this time he spent six months in prison after being mistaken for a spy. Disillusioned by the cool reception given

his plays, disappointed by the failure of his literary enterprises, destitute, and feeling he had failed his family, Kleist ended his own life in an act of double suicide with his friend Henriette Vogel, who was dying of uterine cancer.

Throughout his life, Kleist wrote many letters. Those which he wrote to his elder half sister Ulrike, the one person he felt never abandoned him, show a sensitive nature torn between grandiose ambition and keen despair. His first play, *The Family Schroffenstien* (1803), was a gloomy tragedy that debated the adequacy of reason as a guide for human existence. He next began *Robert Guiscard*, a TRAGEDY based on the life of the historical Norman adventurer, but frustration with his progress led him to burn the manuscript in a fit of temper. Also in 1803 he began work on *The Broken Jug*, inspired by a competition among his friends. Completed in 1806, the play, a FARCE of justice taking place in a courtroom where the judge himself is the perpetrator of the crime, emerged as one of the best German comedies. *Amphitryon*, begun in 1803 as a translation of the play by MOLIÈRE, examines in detail the inner torment of its female character, Alcmene. In *Penthesilea* (1807), Kleist drew on his own anguish to create the violent, passionate tale of the doomed Amazon queen who loved and destroyed Achilles. In *Kate of Heilbronn* (1810), a medieval fairy tale with knights and maidens, he created a different sort of heroine, patterned on his ideal of the virtuous, self-sacrificing woman. His *Battle of the Teutoburger Wald* (begun in 1808) shows the stirrings of a nationalism that would culminate in the patriotic spirit of his last and best work, *Prince Friedrich of Homburg*, written in 1810. *Friedrich* was never staged during Kleist's life because his patrons did not approve of a Prussian soldier feeling such a desperate fear of death, but the play, subtle in its psychology, rather emphasizes the ideals of enlightened devotion and service to country.

Kleist also wrote a number of short stories, which survive, and a novel, which likely met the same fate as *Robert Guiscard*. Some critics hail Kleist as a forerunner of the age of modern drama, and had he been born a hundred years later, it is possible audiences would have appreciated him. The criticism of his contemporary GOETHE, who had a low opinion of the German Romantic spirit in general, did much to discourage Kleist. His writings return again and again to the impact of fate on human life, the causes and consequences of chaos, and the imperative to find some means of spiritual protection or understanding of the broader design. If Kleist failed in anything, it was in finding a way to reconcile his vivid interior world with the forces at work in the outer one. Though he never succeeded in surpassing the brilliance of Goethe or SCHILLER, his influence on later dramatists and thinkers grounds him firmly in the tradition of great German literature.

English Versions of Works by Heinrich von Kleist

The Marquise of O—and Other Stories. Translated by Martin Greenberg. New York: Ungar, 1973.

Heinrich von Kleist: Three Major Plays. Translated by Carl R. Mueller. Lyme, N.H.: Smith and Kraus, 2001.

Works about Heinrich von Kleist

Allan, Sian. *The Plays of Heinrich von Kleist: Ideals and Illusions.* New York: Cambridge University Press, 1996.

Brown, Hilda Meldrum. *Heinrich von Kleist: The Ambiguity of Art and the Necessity of Form.* Oxford: Oxford University Press, 1998.

Klopstock, Friedrich Gottlieb

(1724–1803) *poet, essayist, playwright*
Friedrich Klopstock was born in the city of Quedlinburg to the lawyer and government adviser Gottlieb Klopstock and his wife, Anna Maria. He attended high school in his hometown before going on to study theology at the universities of Jena and Leipzig.

In Leipzig, Klopstock published the first three cantos from his *Messiah*, a work that engaged him for the next 50 years and established his reputation as a poet of extraordinary talent. After stays in Switzerland and Denmark, Klopstock settled in Hamburg, where he produced the bulk of his literary work and spent the rest of his life.

A mild-mannered, religious man, Klopstock reveals his personality and disposition in many ways in his writing. *Messiah* is his best and most representative work, which he himself referred to as his "primary life's purpose." This long poem recounts the story of the death and resurrection of Jesus and his redemption of humankind. Written in hexameters, an unfamiliar verse form for German poetry at the time, the work stands out not only for the density and beauty of the language but also for its unique representation of Christ.

ENLIGHTENMENT thinkers portrayed Jesus as a kind of exemplary moralist, but Klopstock depicts him as an intermediary between God and man, a medium of God's eternal nature. Klopstock's intentions in writing the work were not only literary but also spiritual, as he sought to set down Christian revelatory experience in an enduring form that would speak to all human beings.

Though Klopstock also wrote literary essays and biblical dramas, it is chiefly for *Messiah*, as well as his lyric poetry, that he is now remembered. GOETHE, SCHILLER, Hölderlin, and the great German Romantic writers were among the admirers of Klopstock's work. His influence on German poetry has been and continues to be fundamental.

An English Version of Works by Friedrich Gottlieb Klopstock

Kohl, Karin M. *Rhetoric, the Bible, and the Origins of Free Verse: The Early Hymns of Friedrich Gottlieb Klopstock.* New York: W. de Gruyter, 1990.

Works about Friedrich Gottlieb Klopstock

Hilliard, Kevin. *Philosophy, Letters, and the Fine Arts in Klopstock's Thought.* London: Institute of Germanic Studies, 1987.

Lee, Meredith. *Displacing Authority: Goethe's Poetic Reception of Klopstock.* Heidelberg: Universitätsverlag C. Winter, 1999.

Knight, Sarah Kemble (1666–1727) *diarist*

Sarah Kemble Knight was the oldest daughter of Elizabeth and Thomas Kemble, a merchant. Sometime in the late 1680s, she married Richard Knight, an older man who, it is believed, worked as a ship-master and London agent for an American business. She gave birth to her only child in 1689, the same year that her father died. Upon his passing, she was rumored to have taken charge of the family business affairs. Over time, she developed expertise in legal matters, became adept at settling estates, worked as a shopkeeper, and taught school. Legend has it that Benjamin FRANKLIN was one of her pupils, but no official documentation exists to support this claim. Knight's active participation in the workforce reveals that not all Puritan women were consigned to the domestic world of hearth and home.

In 1704, two years before her husband's death, Knight embarked alone on a horseback journey from her home in Boston to Connecticut, reportedly to settle the estate of one of her cousins. *The Journal of Madam Knight* (1825), the chronicle of her courageous expedition, is filled with descriptions of the rocky and mountainous roads she traveled with her various guides; the difficulties she encountered when trying to cross rivers; her attempts at steeling her nerves as she made her way through dark, dangerous nights; the manner in which her hosts prepared meals; and the sometimes comical manners and customs of the people she met. Emory Elliott notes that Knight adopted "techniques of the mock-epic and elements of the picaresque," a genre that is autobiographical in nature and makes use of satire, especially when describing the social classes. The content of Knight's journal, which was published nearly a century after her death, points to its significance in the history of American literature. Her narrative provides us with a woman's perspective of 18th-century American life. The worldliness of her account stands in stark contrast to the more inward and spiritually-oriented journals kept by her Puritan predecessors and contemporaries.

A Work by Sarah Kemble Knight

The Journal of Madam Knight. Boston: D.R. Godine, 1972.

A Work about Sarah Kemble Knight

Bush, Sargent. "Introduction," in *Journeys in New Worlds: Early American Women's Narratives.*

Edited by William L. Andrews. Madison: University of Wisconsin Press, 1990.

Kobayashi Issa (Yatarô) (1763–1827) *poet*

Kobayashi Issa is one of the few acknowledged masters of the Japanese poetic art of HAIKU. Haiku is a form of unrhymed poetry consisting of 17 syllables in three lines of five, seven, and five syllables, respectively. Haiku often deal with the natural world, focusing on a single moment that is transformed by the poet's vision into an idea of enduring significance. Kobayashi's poetry is especially beloved by the Japanese because of its humor and simplicity.

Kobayashi Issa was born Kobayashi Yatarô on May 5, in Kashiwabara, Shinano province, Japan. Later in life, he adopted the pseudonym Issa, which means "cup of tea." Issa's father was a poor farmer who was widowed not long after his son was born. His remarriage a few years later created difficulties for Issa, who was mistreated by his stepmother.

At age 14, he was sent to Tokyo to study with the poet Nirokuan Chikua, who taught the boy haiku. After Chikua's death, Kobayashi traveled throughout the southwestern part of Japan, publishing his first collection of poetry *Tabishui (Travel Gleanings)* in 1795. This work was followed by many others, including *Chichi No Shuen Nikki (Diary of My Father's Last Days,* 1801), *Shichiban-Nikki (Seventh Diary,* 1810), and *Oraga Haru (The Year of My Life).*

During his lifetime, Kobayashi wrote more than 20,000 haiku. His sweet sense of humor is evident in this simple poem in which he finds affinity with a frog:

> *Frog and I*
> *eyeball*
> *To eyeball.*

And his love of nature and ability to observe acutely can be seen in this poem about the wind:

> *Cool breeze*
> *Tangled*
> *In a grass-blade.*

Kobayashi led a lonely life for many years, a fact reflected in many of his haiku. This one in particular evokes a sense of the lonely boy sent from home at an early age:

> Come with me
> and play
> Parentless sparrow.

After the death of Kobayashi's father in 1801, his stepmother tried to prevent him from inheriting the property his father had left him. It was not until 1813 that he finally was able to collect his inheritance. In the next year he married for the first time at age 52, but his married life was to be filled with sorrow. Four children died in infancy, and his wife, Kiku, died in childbirth. Of her death he wrote:

> My grumbling wife—
> if only she were here!
> This moon tonight . . .

His second marriage was a failure, ending in divorce after only a few months. He married a third time but died on June 1, before the birth of his fifth child, a daughter.

A poem titled "Kobayashi Issa" by Victor Hernandez Cruz beautifully sums up Kobayashi's genius and his ability to see so much in the tiniest aspects of existence:

> His eyes were binoculars
> small things
> Had the fury of the cosmos.
>
>   . . . .
>
> The horizon smiles with Issa. . . .

English Versions of Works by Kobayashi Issa

Spring of My Life. Translated by Sam Hamill. Boston: Shambhala Publications, 1997.

The Year of My Life. Translated by Nobuyuki Yuasa. Berkeley: University of California Press, 1972.

Works about Kobayashi Issa

Gollub, Matthew. Cool Melons—Turn to Frogs! The Life and Poems of Issa. New York: Lee and Low Books, 1998.

Ueda, Makoto, trans. Dew on the Grass: The Life and Poetry of Kobayashi Issa. The Netherlands: Brill Academic Publishers, 2004.

Kochanowski, Jan (1530–1584) poet

Jan Kochanowski was born in Sycyna in central Poland. Because his family was of the Polish gentry, he was able to receive an excellent education in the classics. He enrolled in the Krakow Academy in 1544, but left in 1547 after the death of his father. After leaving Krakow, he went to the University of Wittenberg in present-day Germany. In 1552 he studied in Italy after receiving funds from Prince Albrecht of Königsberg. Little is known about Kochanowski's studies there, because none of his letters or journals of that time exist or have been found.

When Kochanowski returned to Poland, he held appointments at the royal court of King Zygmunt August and wrote poetry in Latin and Polish. Some of his poetry was commissioned by various noblemen to commemorate special occasions or political events. His works include A Game of Chess (1562), Susanna (1562), Concord (1564), and The Satyr (1564). Kochanowski retired from court life in 1570 and lived at Czarnolas, a country estate, where he composed the bulk of his poetry, including his tragedy, Dismissal of the Grecian Envoys, between 1570 and his death in 1584.

His poetry was based on the classical traditions of Greek, Roman, and early Christian writings. He translated the Psalms into Polish between 1570 and 1578. His cycle of poems Laments was written in 1580, after the death of his daughter. These poems describe man's relation to God and are considered to be the greatest works written in the early Polish language. After Kochanowski's death in 1584, his collected Epigrams were published, as well as the first printing of his early Songs. While Kochanowski wrote his early works in Latin, he was among the first to use Polish to write poetry, for which he achieved lasting fame.

Works by Jan Kochanowski

Poems of Jan Kochanowski. Edited by George R. Noyes, et al. Berkeley: University of California Press, 1928.

Treny: The Laments of Kochanowski. Translated by Adam Czeriawski and edited by Piotr Wilczek. Oxford: Legenda, 2001.

A Work about Jan Kochanowski

Welsh, David. *Jan Kochanowski*. New York: Twayne, 1974.

Komam Q'Anil, Epic of (Xhuwan Q'Anil, El Q'Anil, El Kanil, Man of Lightning)

(n.d.–present) *Mayan epic*

The *Epic of Komam Q'Anil* tells the story of El Q'anil, the "Man of Lightning." Myths of El Q'anil are part of the oral tradition of the Jakaltek Maya people of Guatemala. In the EPIC, the narrator recounts the history of the Jakaltek Maya, explaining how their lands were given to them by the first father and how they learned the knowledge of hieroglyphics. Eventually, they were dispersed from their land by natural disasters and wandered in the wilderness until they came to Ajul, near the present-day village of Jacaltenango, which became their new land.

When the people heard news of a distant war and felt pains for those dying, they decided to join the fight. El Q'anil, the "Man of Lightning," is introduced in the form of a boy named Xhuwan, who is chosen to carry the Jakalteks' supplies to battle. He is forbidden, however, to return to his people after engaging in the war. Xhuwan summons lightning to save his people from destruction, undertakes a great adventure journey, and then leads the people to victory in the fight. Unable to return to Ajul, he retires to the southern volcano called El Q'Anil, from where he can watch over his people as an immortal.

The *Epic of Komam Q'Anil* is known today by the Jakaltek Maya and taught to all of their children to reinforce their people's identity. It is also an important symbolic image of endurance through adversity for an indigenous people whose very existence today is challenged by the modern world.

A Work about the *Epic of Komam Q'Anil*

Montejo, Victor. *El Q'Anil, Man of Lightning: A Legend of Jacaltenango*. Translated by Wallace Kaufman and Susan G. Rascon. Tucson: University of Arizona Press, 2001.

Kong Shangren (Kung Shang-jen)

(1648–1718) *scholar, playwright, poet*

Kong Shangren was one of the major playwrights of the K'ang-hsi era. A descendant of Confucius, Kong Shangren spent the early years of his life in the traditional studies of the literati. As a scholar, he was an exponent of Kaozhengxue (*Kao-cheng hsueh;* "Empirical studies").

In 1684 he served as a lecturer to the Kangxi (K'ang-hsi) emperor, who visited the writer's native province of Chufu. As a result of this meeting, Kong Shangren was appointed to a position in the Directorate of Education. From 1685 to 1689, he served on an irrigation project in Yangchow. In this capacity, he traveled to various historical landmarks and became acquainted with the remnants of the Ming dynasty. His poems and prose, reflective of this time, are collected in a volume called *Hu hai ji* (*Hu-hai chi; Poems from the Lakes and Seas*).

In 1694 Kong Shangren began composing dramas. His first, *Xiao hu lei* (*Hsiao-hu lei; The Little Thunderclap*), was based on a Tang dynasty instrument in his collection. Kong Shangren researched its historical origins and created a story of a love affair between a poet and a palace concubine. The play's exhaustive factual information was far in advance of other attempts at historical drama.

Taohuashan (*T'ao-hua shan; Peach Blossom Fan*) was Kong Shangren's next theatrical effort and shows even more exhaustive research, including bibliographical notes and a chronology of events of the reign of Chong-Zhen (Ch'ung-chen) in the southern Ming dynasty. In addition, the characters are all based on real people. The play was written to demonstrate Kong Shangren's idea that social obligations are more important than individual rights. The play includes the story of a group of honest intellectuals who wish to save their country from invasion and anarchy. They are opposed by a group of power-hungry politicians.

Soon after the play's premiere, Kong Shangren retired from his official position, but he continued writing, producing two more collections of poems before his death.

Peach Blossom Fan has become one of China's most famous historical dramas, for which critics have praised Kong Shangren for his skillful handling of a complex plot, innovative theatrical form, and tragic vision.

An English Version of a Work by Kong Shangren

Peach Blossom Fan. Translated by Chen Shih-Hsiang, Cyril Birch, and Harold Action. Boston: Cheng and Tsui, 2000.

A Work about Kong Shangren

Lu, Tina. *Persons, Roles and Minds: Identity in* Peony Pavilion *and* Peach Blossom Fan. Palo Alto, Calif.: Stanford University Press, 2001.

Krylov, Ivan (1768–1844) *fabulist, journalist, playwright*

Ivan Krylov was born in Moscow to a poor officer who, though informally educated, loved to read. Ivan was nine when his father died, leaving his wife and two sons with little legacy except for a chest full of books. Krylov began working as a copyist to support the family.

At age 14, Krylov moved to St. Petersburg. He worked as a government clerk, explored theatrical and literary circles, and tried his hand at literature. His first important work, the opera *Coffee Mill,* satirized the hypocrisy of seemingly progressive thinkers. The publisher to whom Krylov brought *Coffee Mill* praised the work and encouraged the young writer with a considerable sum of money, but refused to publish the opera.

After writing a sequence of scarcely successful tragedies and comedies, Krylov finished a harshly critical comedy called *Mischief-Makers.* In the main characters of the comedy, Krylov's contemporaries easily recognized influential figures of the theatrical and literary world, some of whom were Krylov's patrons or supporters. His benefactors were outraged and the opera was banned.

In 1789 Krylov began a monthly publication called *Supernatural Mail.* The journal caricatured Russian society in the form of a fantastic correspondence between gnomes and a wizard. Censors soon shut the journal down. In 1790 Krylov decided to devote himself to literary work and retired from his public service.

He then began another project, the *Spectator,* another journal that did not survive the censors. Its closure was not surprising considering the severely satirical nature of the work, which mercilessly criticized the tendencies of Russian society to imitate the West, to admire all things French, and to neglect the native language and culture. Some of Krylov's important works of the period include the articles "Speech Made by a Scapegrace in a Gathering of Fools," "Thoughts of a Fashionable Philosopher," and a play, *Praise to the Science of Killing Time,* all of which demonstrate his use of satire to expose social ills.

Krylov's real fame followed his discovery that his satirical talent could be best expressed in fables. This genre had enjoyed popularity across many cultures and all ages, as evidenced by the fables of Aesop, Phaedrus, the Indian *Panchatantra,* and the poetess Marie de France. Krylov began in 1805 by translating and publishing two fables by the French poet Jean de LA FONTAINE, which received the critics' highest praise. In 1809 Krylov published a separate edition of his own fables, which brought him enormous success. The *Fables* became a classic during his lifetime; the books were sold in huge numbers, and the czar personally asked Krylov to accept the title of Honorary Academician of the Russian Academy.

In his fables, Krylov combines a well-developed skill of observation with his trademark ironic skepticism. His satire did not reproach society for its sins but invited people to see their own shortcomings and laugh at them. The fable *Quartet,* for example, describes four animals attempting to play a brass quartet without knowing how to play or read music. Though the animals change places, the quality of their music does not improve. "However you seat yourselves, my friends, you are still not good musicians," the fable concludes. Similarly, *A Crow and a Fox* describes a vain crow, tricked by the shameless flattery of an artful fox into letting go of a piece of cheese. One of the most famous fables, *A Fox and Grapes,* tells a story of a fox who fails to get hold of grapes growing too high and mollifies herself by concluding that "the grapes must not be ripe, anyway."

Krylov was the first to step out of the tradition of using bookish words and poeticisms in the fables. By visiting fairs, markets, and public holidays, he acquired a thorough knowledge of colloquial or everyday language, which he then used in his writing. Sharp, proverbial phrases make his fables catchy and easy to remember. He often minimizes the traditional moral that concludes a fable, or else disposes of it completely. His fables are not dry moralizations but rather picturesque and engaging portrayals of real life. Over time, his fables have become an integral part of Russian literature, contributing through their popularity to conversational phrases in the Russian language and becoming a deeply embedded part of the country's folklore.

English Versions of Works by Ivan Krylov

15 Fables of Krylov. Translated by Guy Daniels. New York: Macmillan, 1965.

Krylov's Fables. Translated by Ivan Krylov. Westport, Conn.: Hyperion Press, 1977.

Russian Satiric Comedy: Six Plays. Edited and translated by Laurence Senelick. New York: Performing Arts Journal Publications, 1983.

Works about Ivan Krylov

Hamburger, Henri. *The Function of the Predicate in the Fables of Krylov.* Amsterdam: Rodopi, 1981.

Stepanov, Nikolay. *Ivan Krylov.* New York: Twayne, 1973.

Kyogen (1300s–present)

The Kyogen (pronounced *kee-OH-gen;* "crazy words") are Japanese folk plays that portray the simple emotions and everyday experiences of regular people. The plays, which developed into their modern form in the 14th century, are meant to encourage a quiet sort of comic joy at the follies of a common life.

The modern form of Kyogen theater developed out of a combination of the comic farcical productions of Sarugaku and the athletic dance performances called Dengaku. Kwanami Kiyotsugu and his son ZEAMI Motokiyo honed the art form, presenting a performance in front of Shogun Yoshimitsu in 1374. Kwanami named the performance style Kyogen, which means "mad words" to emphasize the subtle comic effect of the plays.

Kyogen were handed down orally, with only the general outline and a sketchy sense of the dialogue preserved from generation to generation. This gave the plays flexibility and encouraged continual innovation. Various schools developed over the years, including Okura, Sagi, Izumi and Nomura. In more recent centuries the works have been written down and presented in various volumes, few of which are still in print.

The productions of Kyogen plays are simple, performed on a plain stage with minimal props. Fans are frequently used, as are weapons such as spears, swords, and bows and arrows. The players often wear wooden masks that represent, most commonly, a rogue, a woman, an old man, a young man, a monkey, and a fox. The comic elements of the performances are physical in nature, a matter of situation rather than of character. Popular superstitions play an important role, and there is little or no love interest portrayed.

English Versions of Kyogen

Morley, Carolyn Anne. *Transformation, Miracles, and Mischief: The Mountain Priest Plays of Kyogen.* Ithaca, N.Y.: Cornell University East Asia Program, 1993.

Sakanishi, Shio. *Japanese Folk Plays: The Ink-smeared Lady and Other Kyogen.* Tokyo: C.E. Tuttle, 1960.

Works about Kyogen

Keene, Donald. *Seeds in the Heart: Japanese Literature from Earliest Times to the Late Sixteenth Century.* New York: Henry Holt, 1993.

Takeda, Sharon Sadako. *Miracles and Mischief: Noh and Kyogen Theater in Japan.* Los Angeles: Los Angeles County Museum of Art Agency for Cultural Affairs, 2002.

Labé, Louise (ca. 1520–1566) *poet*

Louise Labé was the daughter of a middle-class rope maker in Lyon, France, and as a child received education in languages, music, and riding. In 1543 she married another rope maker, Ennemond Perrin, her senior by almost three decades. Around 1556, she left the literary circles of Lyon to live in the countryside, where the plague brought a premature end to her life.

Labé began writing her first SONNETS in 1546. In these sonnets she employs not only the form but also many of the themes used by the Italian poet PETRARCH. In 1552 she began to write *The Debate Between Folly and Love*, an expressive work full of diverse structures and several voices. In the next year she began writing her *Elegies* and in 1555 published *The Complete Works of Louise Labé of Lyon*, which was reprinted several times within the next year. Some biographers attribute Labé's popularity to the increasing social prominence of women in the mid-16th century, when literature by and about women became fashionable. Certain critics accused Labé of being immodest and unwomanly, while others praised her lavishly, considering her an admirable writer and exemplary woman.

Labé's narrative voice is that of a woman who possesses intellectual and poetic power and is highly aware of herself. In her verse she combines the Italian forms with the traditions of the early Greek poet Sappho to write about female desire and to characterize women as being both intellectual and erotic, with mental as well as material abilities. Labé continually resisted prevailing cultural notions that limited women to roles as courtesans, companions, or domestic servants; instead, her poetry presents women as active, independent subjects who are capable of thought as well as feeling. In *The Debate Between Folly and Love*, Labé scatters her poetry with allusions to classical mythology that demonstrate her learning, and gives her characters sly observations about the way wisdom is underappreciated in society. For instance, the character of Mercury makes a point about how often folly prevails in the world, observing that "for every wise man who is talked about on earth, there will be ten thousand fools who will be popular with the common people."

Labé's shorter poems abound with themes and images that express passionate love and lofty heights of feeling, as can be seen in these lines from Sonnet 18 (translated by Edith Farrell):

> *Kiss me. Again. More kisses I desire.*
> *Give me one your sweetness to express.*

Give me the most passionate you possess.
Four I'll return, and hotter than the fire.

Labé's women are not crushed by disappointment or despair, however; when the narrator of the second elegy addresses a lover who has left her for another, she taunts him for not seeing her worth, declaring:

And know that elsewhere there's no one like
> *me.*
I don't say that she might have more
> *beauty,*
But never will a woman love you more
Nor bring more fame to lay it at your door.

Throughout her work, Labé demanded that women be recognized and acknowledged as capable of intelligent action as well as desire.

Labé's manuscripts and their circulation are proof that women had active roles as authors, readers, and patrons of the artistic RENAISSANCE taking place in France in the 16th century. Labé herself was known to entertain poets, writers, and other learned people in her private salon, and the writer Pernette du Guillet was a great friend of hers. In her writing Labé encouraged women to write and sell their own works and also to support each other in a female literary community. She firmly believed in self-improvement through education for women, and expressed this in the dedication of her *Works*. Addressing her friend Clemence de Bourges, she conveys her characteristic beliefs that writing is a form of self-knowledge and that intellectual pleasures are preferable to sensual ones. She encourages her female readers to exercise their minds, inspire one another, and devote themselves to the study of literature and the sciences to gain recognition from and equality with men. Like an earlier Frenchwoman, Christine de PISAN, Labé's work expresses the voice of an educated and feeling woman who was skilled enough to use and refuse convention where necessary, making a valuable contribution to the French Re-naissance as well as a call for the emancipation of women.

English Versions of Works by Louise Labé

Debate of Folly and Love: A New English Translation with the Original French Text. Translated by Anne-Marie Bourbon. New York: Peter Lang, 2000.
Louise Labé: Sonnets. Translated by Graham D. Martin. Austin: University of Texas Press, 1972.
Louise Labé's Complete Works. Edited and translated by Edith R. Farrell. Troy, N.Y.: Whitson Publishing, 1986.

Works about Louise Labé

Baker, Deborah Lesko. *The Subject of Desire: Petrarchan Poetics and the Female Voice in Louise Labé.* West Lafayette, Ind.: Purdue University Press, 1996.
Cameron, Keith. *Louise Labé: Renaissance Poet and Feminist.* Oxford, England: Berg Publishers, 1991.
Moore, Mary B. *Desiring Voices: Women Sonneteers and Petrarchism.* Carbondale: Southern Illinois University Press, 2000.

La Bruyère, Jean de (1645–1696)
moralist, nonfiction writer

Jean de la Bruyère was born in Paris to a comptroller general of municipal revenue. He studied law, was admitted to the bar, and practiced until 1673, when he purchased a position from the treasurer of finances of Caen. La Bruyère stayed in Paris until he became history tutor to the duc de Condé's son and moved to the duke's chateau in Chantilly. He became friends with the duke and eventually received a pension that allowed him to stay with the duke's household. He became a member of the ACADÉMIE FRANÇAISE in 1693 and died of apoplexy in 1696.

La Bruyère is principally remembered for a book he published anonymously in 1688, *Les Caractères de Théophraste, traduits du Grec, avec les caractères et les moeuers de ce siècle (The Characters of Theophrastes, translated from the Greek, with por-*

traits and mores of this century). While the first part is a translation of an ancient Greek work, the second half is a collection of character sketches and moral observations that have yielded plenty of meaningful quotations still used today. For example, "Life is a tragedy for those who feel and a comedy for those who think" comes from La Bruyère.

His aphorisms reveal an amused distance that allows him to make unflattering observations about human nature and society without sounding outraged or pompous. La Bruyère recognized that love sometimes fades, people follow their own interests, and God does not always reward the deserving with wealth and power, but his laconic phrasing does not betray anger or disgust.

La Bruyère's simple, well-balanced phrasing, appropriate diction, and keen observations make him admirable not only as a stylist but also as an observer of human nature whose truths can still surprise and inspire.

An English Version of a Work by Jean de La Bruyère

Van Laun, Henri, trans. *Characters*. London: Oxford University Press, 1963.

Works about Jean de La Bruyère

Knox, Edward C. *Jean de la Bruyère*. New York: Twayne, 1974.

Mourgues, Odette de. *Two French Moralists: La Rochefoucauld & La Bruyère*. New York: Cambridge University Press, 1978.

Laclos, Pierre Choderlos de (Pierre-Ambroise-François Choderlos de Laclos) (1741–1803) *novelist*

Pierre Choderlos de Laclos was born in Amiens, France. As an adult, he entered the French army and, in 1782, when he was an artillery captain, he wrote and published his only novel, *Les liaisons dangereuses (Dangerous Liaisons)*. It was a best-seller, albeit a scandalous one. After the Reign of Terror ended and Napoleon came to power, Napoleon promoted Laclos to general, and Laclos's first command was in Taranto, Italy, where he died of dysentery.

What makes *Dangerous Liaisons* such a significant novel is how it perfectly encapsulates 18th-century Western fiction while exploring universal human themes and psychology. Laclos admired the epistolary NOVELS of Samuel RICHARDSON and used the form to reveal his characters' social facades, as well as their real thoughts and motivations. His novel also operates as a response to the philosophy of Jean-Jacques ROUSSEAU, while touching on themes later explored by the Marquis de SADE.

On the one hand, Laclos seems to side with Rousseau's contempt for the vanity, hypocrisy, and unnaturalness of contemporary French society, but in his depiction of Madame de Tourvel, Laclos implicitly critiques Rousseau's idealism. Rousseau's belief in humanity's inherent goodness also seems to have influenced the character of Valmont. Valmont eventually reveals a capacity for intimacy and empathy when he falls in love with Madame de Tourvel, which reveals that his libertine behavior is learned rather than innate. His death, however, like Madame de Tourvel's, indicates that morally upright and emotionally vulnerable people cannot survive in a society that is dominated by people like the Marquise de Merteuil.

The marquise is an impressive portrait of complete egotism that looks forward to some of Sade's notorious libertine philosophers. She is a fascinating, multifaceted monster who thrives in a society where the appearance of sincerity and virtue matters more than those qualities themselves.

In 1987 Christoper Hampton adapted the novel for the stage, which Stephen Frears later filmed. Laclos's mastery of the epistolary form and his acute psychological portraits have made *Dangerous Liaisons* a widely read and well-regarded classic.

English Versions of a Work by Pierre Choderlos de Laclos

Parmée, Douglas, trans. *Les Liaisons Dangereuses*. New York: Oxford University Press, 1995.

Stone, P. W. K., trans. *Les Liaisons Dangereuses*. New York: Penguin Classics, 1961.

Works about Pierre Choderlos de Laclos

Byrne, P. W. "The Moral of Les Liaisons Dangereuses: A Review of the Arguments." *Essays in French Literature* 23 (1986): 1–18.

Rosbottom, Ron. *Choderlos de Laclos.* Boston: Twayne, 1978.

Thelander, Dorothy R. *Laclos and the Epistolary Novel.* Geneva: Librairie Droz, 1963.

Lafayette, Madame de (Marie-Madeleine Pioche de la Vergne, comtesse de Lafayette) (1634–1693)
novelist

Marie-Madeleine Pioche de la Vergne was born to parents of the minor nobility. Her father died when she was 15, and her mother promptly remarried de Sévigné, whose niece, the Marquise de SÉVIGNÉ, would become one of Madame de Lafayette's closest friends. Another girlhood friend, Henriette, the English princess exiled in France, provided Marie-Madeleine with access to the court of the Sun King, Louis XIV, and later employed her as a memoirist. In 1655, by marrying Comte Jean-François Motier, she became Madame de Lafayette. Later she set up permanent residency in Paris, where she presided over frequent gatherings of famous intellectuals, artisans, nobility, and political figures, and entertained occasional visits from her husband, who remained at their country estate.

Though she had a markedly ungrammatical writing style, as shown in both her letters and her manuscripts, Madame de Lafayette had a keen mind informed by her early education in languages and literature, provided in part by her friend Ménage. A cultivated intellect was an uncommon thing for women of her day, since popular opinion held that all knowledge necessary to success could be learned in polite company, and too much learning spoiled a woman by turning her into a "bluestocking." Madame de Lafayette was admired in her own day for her wit, her honesty, her fine qualities of mind, and what her friend Madame de Sévigné called her "divine reason." Though a prominent and influential figure, Madame de Lafayette kept quiet about her personal affairs, and in fact never claimed authorship of the books she published. For this reason several works were later attributed to her whose true authorship remains doubtful.

No doubt exists, however, that Madame de Lafayette authored *The Princess of Cleves,* the book that has established her place in literary history. She first proved her abilities for astute understanding and acute perception through her first literary effort, a written portrait of her friend the marquise. She then wrote a novel called *The Princess of Montpensier* and undertook a collaborative enterprise with her friends LA ROCHEFOUCAULD and Segrais to write *Zaïde,* a colorful pseudo-history. Reading historical sources for her novel *The Princess of Cleves* and associating with contemporary artists MONTAIGNE and LA FONTAINE broadened Madame's literary horizons, and her circulation among aristocratic company sharpened her perceptions of human nature while spoiling what had never been an optimistic attitude about romantic love. She recorded the intrigues of the court of Louis XIV in her *Memoirs on the Court of France 1688–1689* and *The Secret History of Henrietta of England.* Her last work, *The Countess of Tende,* appeared in print several years after her death.

The Princess of Cleves can be called the first historical novel, since it takes place in a French court of the 16th century. It is also the first psychological novel for, while telling the story of the princess's illicit love for the dashing duke of Nemours, the prose steers away from conventional depictions of romance in order to study the characters' desires and motivations for their actions. Published in 1678, the book provoked vivid response and sparked the first-ever reader survey in the *Mercure Galant,* which asked readers if they felt the princess was right or wrong to confess to her husband. The storm of public opinion proved that the novel was something out of the ordinary, embodying all the principles of classicism but departing from the traditions of the romance novel to set a new standard. More than history, more than romance, *The Princess of Cleves* is ultimately a tale about doomed passions and moral dilemmas.

Madame de Lafayette's outlook on love was never romantic and continued to sour as she aged, confirmed in part by the painful experiences she observed around her, including the excesses of her friend Henriette, who suffered a sudden and extremely painful death. She used her work to examine the views of her own time and to explore ethical issues with analytical precision. Translator J. M. Shelmerdine attributes her greatness to "a power to observe human nature, to create characters and tell a story, an ability to understand human difficulties and sympathize with human weaknesses."

English Versions of Works by Madame de Lafayette

Madame de Lafayette: The Princesse de Clèves. Translated by Terence Cave. New York: Oxford University Press, 1999.

The Secret History of Henrietta, Princess of England. Translated by J. M. Shelmerdine. New York: Howard Fertig, 1993.

Works about Madame de Lafayette

Haig, Stirling. *Madame de Lafayette.* New York: Twayne, 1970.

Raitt, Janet. *Madame de Lafayette and 'La Princesse de Clèves'.* London: George G. Harrap, 1971.

La Fontaine, Jean de (1621–1695) *poet, novelist*

Jean de La Fontaine was born in Château-Thierry to Charles, a government official, and Françoise Pidoux, the daughter of King Henry IV's physician. At age 20, after a classical secondary education, he began religious studies in Paris. Monastic life, however, did not agree with La Fontaine's temperament, and, after briefly dabbling in law studies, he returned to Château-Thierry, where he spent days of leisure reading the classics of Ovid, Virgil, and Horace, to whom he alludes in his poetry, as well as the works of French poets RABELAIS, Malherbe, and MAROT.

In 1647 the dreamy poet obliged his father by marrying 14-year-old Marie Héricart, with whom he had one son. But La Fontaine was neither a good husband nor a good father. He craved variety and excitement and was patently unable to remain loyal to one woman. His cheery sensuality, gracious manners, and simplicity endeared him to the many women he courted and lead to various shameful adventures. La Fontaine himself alludes reflectively to this character flaw in his poem "Papillon du Parnasse" ("Poetic Butterfly") as translated by Marie-Odile Sweetser in *La Fontaine:*

> I go from flower to flower, from one object
> of love to another.
> To many pleasures, I add a little reputation.
> I would go higher perhaps in the temple of
> Fame
> If in one genre only I had spent my life
> But after all I am flighty in verse as in love.

La Fontaine started writing near midlife and soon became the protégé of Louis XIV's minister of finances, Nicolas Fouquet, who built the opulent chateau of Vaux-le-Vicomte. La Fontaine frequented the salons of Paris, where he befriended such illustrious courtiers as Mademoiselle de SCUDÉRY, Madame de LAFAYETTE, Madame de SÉVIGNÉ, Charles PERRAULT, LA ROCHEFOUCAULD, and MOLIÈRE, among others.

After the duchess of Orléans became his patroness in 1665, La Fontaine gained wealth and fame with the publication of his first volume of *Contes et nouvelles en vers (Tales and Novels in Verse)*, a four-volume series of lively, salacious tales that was published between 1665 and 1674 and quickly gained notoriety. In *Cognitive Space and Patterns of Deceit in La Fontaine's Contes*, Catherine Grisé states, "The narratives he chose present typical trickster motifs in sexual contexts. La Fontaine's choice of this focus is one of the strong identifying characteristics of the *Contes*." Given the author's natural propensity for love and intrigue, the success of his provocative tales came as no surprise.

Critical Analysis

La Fontaine quickly reached the pinnacle of his career with the publication in 1668 of his world-renowned *Fables choisies, mises en vers (Selected Fables, Put into Verse)*. Inscribing himself in the lineage of the Greco-Roman fabulists Aesop and Phaedrus, he also drew on the Indian fables by Pilpay and the wildly popular emblem books of his generation. *Fables* has been translated into countless languages and illustrated by great artists, such as Oudry, Doré, Fragonard, and Chagall. La Fontaine's genius lies in the transformation of a merely didactic genre into an entirely new mold where witty, playful, and elegant styles turn each fable into a little masterpiece, regardless of the moral lesson it conveys. The fables' human comedy unfolds in a countryside setting where wild and domestic animals, men, women, gods, and fairies enact or personify human foibles. For example, in the brief fable "The Fox and the Grapes," as translated by James Michie in *La Fontaine: Selected Fables,* a fox cannot reach a bunch of mouth-watering grapes he craves for lunch. Instead of dwelling on his failure, the fox reassures himself that the grapes are not worth the picking:

> He would have dearly liked them for his
> lunch,
> But when he tried and failed to reach the
> bunch:
> "Ah, well, it's more than likely they're not
> sweet—
> Good only for fools to eat!"
> Wasn't he wise to say they were unripe
> Rather than whine and gripe?

Remarks David Rubin in *A Pact with Silence*, "the unique excellence of the *Fables* has inspired most critics and historians to sequester them, to see them as a miracle without precedent. . . ."

Over the course of 30 years, La Fontaine completed three volumes of fables, 12,000 verses in all. Even so, his election to the prestigious ACADÉMIE FRANÇAISE was fraught with difficulty before King Louis XIV finally ratified it in 1684.

Concludes Geoffrey Grigson in *La Fontaine: Selected Fables*, "Brevity, structure, matters of style, choice of language, insertion of old among new, quick movement . . . La Fontaine was expert in them all. . . . Sainte-Beuve once called Mozart, for grace, lightness and facility, 'the La Fontaine of music.'"

English Versions of Works by Jean de La Fontaine

Complete Tales in Verse. Translated by Guido Waldman. London: Routledge, 2001.
La Fontaine: Selected Fables. Translated by James Michie. New York: Viking Press, 1979.

Works about Jean de La Fontaine

Fumaroli, Marc, and Jean Marie Todd, trans. *The Poet and the King: Jean de la Fontaine and His Century.* Chicago: University of Notre Dame Press, 2002.
Rubin, David Lee. *A Pact with Silence: Art and Thought in The Fables of Jean de La Fontaine.* Columbus: Ohio State University Press, 1991.
Sweetser, Marie-Odile. *La Fontaine.* Boston: Twayne, 1987.

Langland, William (1330–1386?) *poet*

Little is known about the identity of the author of the poem known as *The Vision of Piers Plowman*. Certain notes on the surviving manuscripts lead scholars to believe that his name was William Langland, and he was most likely born in western England. He was educated to enter the church but, because he married, he was not allowed to enter the higher (and more wealthy) orders of the priesthood. Most scholars assume that the narrator of *Piers Plowman*, a poor itinerant clerk referred to as Will, reflects the author very closely.

The Vision of Piers Plowman is a complex creation. The text exists in three versions, which literary historians have named the A, B, and C texts. The A text, incomplete, is presumably the first draft; the B text, which is complete and was published during the author's lifetime, is considered the best example of Langland's poetry; and the C text reflects revisions the author continued to make throughout his life. Scholars use the language of the poem and references to outside historical events to determine when the poet was writing. Langland lived at the same time as Geoffrey CHAUCER and the poet who wrote *Pearl* and SIR GAWAIN AND THE GREEN KNIGHT.

The poem is structured as a dream vision, which was an extremely popular poetic technique in French and English literature from the 12th to the 14th centuries. The poem is an ALLEGORY, which means that its fictional characters and events are meant to parallel if not actual people, then at least actual situations. The language is in Middle English, which, because it strikes the modern eye as peculiar, can be off-putting for some readers. In lines 5–6 the poet sets his scene as follows:

> Ac on a May morwenynge on Malverne
> hilles
> Me bifel a ferly, of Fairye me thoughte.

In modern English, the poet is simply saying that on a May morning, while he was wandering in the Malvern hills, he met a creature whom he thought was a fairy. The straightforward voice, pleasant surroundings, and dreamy quality of the poetry as introduced here continue throughout the poem.

To understand the *Vision*'s deeper messages, one must understand that English culture at this time was completely fused with and governed by the institutions of the monarchy and the Christian Church, which were seen as the human and divine authorities for life. The journey Will undertakes to search for truth and to discover how to live well represents a real concern of the 14th-century English citizen. Facing a world that had been transformed by plague and living in the midst of transition, many readers would have shared Will's disgust over the hypocrisy, greed, and idleness he saw around him, and would have identified with his wish for a return to order and meaning.

The character of Piers Plowman—who appears only briefly in the poem but with such impact that he lends the whole work his name—was probably not invented by the author but was borrowed from folk legend. (Another example of a popular, enduring English folk legend is Robin Hood.) A record of the 1381 Peasant's Revolt lists Piers Plowman as one of the leaders. Though historically inaccurate, this reference suggests that Piers was a representative figure for the newly mobile working class, perhaps because his message was that every person had a valuable role to play in society, and every person, king or peasant, could expect an equal reward in heaven if he performed his role well. As a symbol of the farmer working his field, Piers represents the lowest estate or class of medieval society, but he is also an icon for useful industry and, most important, his work provided food for all.

Translator A. V. C. Schmidt calls *Piers Plowman* a "truthful picture of the life of the common people in the fourteenth century" and considers it "a masterpiece of medieval English literature, worthy to stand beside Chaucer's *Canterbury Tales* as representative of the culture of its age." The poem also contains a modern relevance, however, in its complaints about dishonesty and lack of charity, the sophisticated insights into the workings of human society and human nature, and the poem's message that love, kindness, and tolerance are the foundational values of human life. Beyond that, the lyric and intricate poetic styles are a sheer joy to read. Little could William Langland have guessed he was writing a work that would thrill audiences seven centuries later, just as it did his own.

An English Version of a Work by William Langland

William Langland: Piers Plowman. Translated and edited by A. V. C. Schmidt. New York: Oxford University Press, 1992.

Works about William Langland

Boulay, F. R. H. *The England of Piers Plowman: William Langland and His Vision of the Fourteenth*

Century. Rochester, N.Y.: Boydell and Brewer, 1991.

Hewett-Smith, Kathleen M. *William Langland's Piers Plowman: A Book of Essays.* New York: Routledge, 2001.

La Rochefoucauld, François, duc de
(1613–1680) *historian, moralist*

François de La Rochefoucauld was born into a noble family of ancient lineage. He came of age during the Fronde, or French civil wars, when the French monarchy fought to consolidate its power against the nobility. These wars eventually led to Louis XIV's decision to create an absolute monarchy in which the nobles were divested of real political power. La Rochefoucauld fought against the monarchy and its prime ministers and, in 1652, surrendered and went into self-imposed exile on his estates in Angoumois. He missed the social and intellectual stimulation of court life and later settled in Paris, where he attended salons, the literary gatherings of noblemen and women that welcomed philosophers, critics, and writers. La Rochefoucauld developed a very close friendship with the writer Madame de LAFAYETTE; some of her detractors even thought he wrote her novels. In reality, he probably served as a trusted sounding board for her ideas and drafts.

While La Rochefoucauld published memoirs that have been invaluable to scholars of 17th-century France, his literary fame rests on his collection of elegantly worded, worldly aphorisms, *Réflexions ou sentences et maxims morales* (*Reflections or moral sentences and maxims*, 1665). La Rochefoucauld's cynical and pessimistic attitude toward humans' self-absorption and vanity does not detract from the insight and elegance of his phrases: "Our virtues are most frequently but vices disguised" and "Hypocrisy is the homage vice pays to virtue" are examples of his well-balanced sentences and awareness of people's ability to delude themselves. To La Rochefoucauld, words such as *love, honor,* and *virtue* were meant to disguise people's baser emotions from themselves in order to maintain a favorable self-image or *amour propre.* At the dawn of the ENLIGHTENMENT, La Rochefoucauld knew that "the understanding is always the dupe of the heart."

English Versions of Works by François, duc de La Rochefoucauld

Moral Maxims. Edited by Irwin Primer. Newark: University of Delaware Press, 2002.

The Maxims of La Rochefoucauld. Translated by Louis Kronenberger. New York: Random House, 1959.

Works about François, duc de La Rochefoucauld

Bishop, Morris. *The Life and Adventures of La Rochefoucauld.* Ithaca, N.Y.: Cornell University Press, 1951.

Hodgson, Richard G. *Falsehood Disguised: Unmasking the Truth in La Rochefoucauld.* West Lafayette, Ind.: Purdue University Press, 1995.

Horowitz, Louise K. *Love and Language: A Study of the Classical French Moralist Writers.* Columbus: Ohio State University Press, 1977.

Mourgues, Odette de. *Two French Moralists: La Rochefoucauld & La Bruyère.* Cambridge: Cambridge University Press, 1978.

Las Casas, Bartolomé de   (1474–1566)
historian, activist

Bartolomé de Las Casas was the son of a Spanish merchant and served as a soldier in his youth. He studied Latin at the University of Seville and in 1502 traveled to Hispaniola, in the West Indies. After becoming a Dominican priest in 1524, Las Casas made valiant efforts to minister to the Indians and improve their treatment at the hands of the invaders. In his later years, Las Casas figured greatly at the Spanish court, and was also a prolific writer of treatises, petitions, histories, and correspondence.

His first work, *The Only Way* (1537), outlined his policies for evangelizing the Indians. In his *Brief Report of the Destruction of the Indians* (1542), he took a stance in defense of the Indian peoples and harshly criticized Spanish colonial policy for the cruelties inflicted on the native populations. Upon a return to America in 1545, Las Casas issued his famous *Confesionario,* or *Regulations for the Confessors of Spaniards,* in which he declared that absolution should be withheld from landowners who owned slaves. Forced by opposition to return to Spain, Las Casas began writing his *General History of the Indies* (1561), which describes events in the New World from 1492 to 1520. The work has special interest as a biography of Columbus and is considered to be the single best source of information on Columbus's discovery of America. In its entirety, the 417 chapters take up three books and suggest that God will punish Spain for its treatment of the Indians.

Though critics considered Las Casas an enemy of Spain, his admirers hailed him as one of the great spiritual leaders of the Spanish conquest of the New World. His large body of work made important contributions to political theory, history, and anthropology, and his idealization of the American Indian, whom he considered to be naturally rational and good, was an early version of the "noble savage" idea that influenced philosophy for hundreds of years.

English Versions of Works by Bartolomé de Las Casas

In Defense of the Indians. Translated by Stafford Poole. DeKalb: Northern Illinois University Press, 1992.

Short Account of the Destruction of the Indies. Translated by Nigel Griffin. New York: Penguin, 1999.

Works about Bartolomé de Las Casas

Hanke, Lewis. *All Mankind Is One: A Study.* DeKalb: Northern Illinois University Press, 1994.

Remesal, Antonion de. *Bartolome De Las Casas, 1474–1566.* Translated by Felix Jay. New York: Edwin Mellen Press, 2002.

Lee Yul Kok (Yi Yulgok, Yi Yi)
(1536–1584) *philosopher*

One of the most famous Neo-Confucian scholars of Korea, Yi Yi is more commonly known by his pen name Lee Yul Kok, which means "chestnut val-

ley." Born near Kangnung, he passed the literary examination and achieved the scholarly title of *Chinsa* by age 13. His widowed mother Sin Saimdang, a remarkably learned woman, was responsible for his education.

In his teens Lee Yul Kok absorbed Chinese classics, like *Laozi* and *Zhuangzi,* as well as Buddhist writings. At age 15, when his mother died, he retired to the Buddhist sanctuary at Kumgang Mountains for three years and studied *Chan* Buddhism.

On returning home in 1556, Lee Yul Kok rejected Buddhism for its otherworldliness and embraced Confucianism for its commitment to political and social life. At age 22, he spent two days at Tosan with the elder sage T'oegye; both men were impressed with each other.

After astonishing success in the civil service examinations, he entered public office in 1559. Though often in poor health, he quickly rose to the highest ranks of government. In 1572 he moved to Haeju. Falling ill there, he resigned his position to devote his time to scholarship. By then his own thinking had evolved, and he had come to disagree with the fundamental basis of T'oegye's philosophy. Lee Yul Kok emphasized practicality in contrast to T'oegye's introspection. He participated in the famous Four-Seven Debate ("Four Beginnings, Seven Emotions"), which attempted to resolve the most complex issues and tensions within Korean Neo-Confucianism. To this controversy, he introduced two new terms: *tosim* ("original goodness") and *insim* ("concupiscence").

In his later years, he resumed government service and proposed new policies in taxation, education, and defense. While serving as minister of defense, he proposed a standing army; while the proposal was rejected, subsequent invasions by Japan would prove the need for such an army.

Lee Yul Kok's productive life spanned a period of relative stability. He died at the peak of his career at age 48. His writings, seen as a reflection of not only his life but also the 16th-century world in which he lived, have been preserved in *Yulgok Chip.* They include his major work *Kyongmong Yogyol (A Key to Annihilating Ignorance)* and a *sijo,* or poem-cycle, called *Kosan Kugok (Nine Songs of Kosan)*.

An English Version of a Work by Lee Yul Kok

The Four-Seven Debate: An Annotated Translation of the Most Famous Controversy in Korean Neo-Confucian Thought. Translated by Michael C. Kalton, et al. Albany: State University of New York Press, 1994.

Works about Lee Yul Kok

Chung, Edward Y. *Korean Neo-Confucianism of Yi T'oegye and Yi Yulgok: A Reappraisal of the "Four-Seven Thesis" and Its Practical Implications for Self-Cultivation.* Albany: State University of New York Press, 1995.

Ro, Young-chan. *Korean Neo-Confucianism of Yi Yulgok.* Albany: State University of New York Press, 1988.

Leibniz, Gottfried Wilhelm (1646–1716)
philosopher, mathematician, nonfiction writer

During the age of the Scientific Revolution and the first stirring of the ENLIGHTENMENT, European thinkers were exploring a variety of new fields of thought in both science and philosophy. One of the most influential of these intellectuals was Gottfried Wilhelm Leibniz, who made key contributions to philosophy, theology, mathematics, and political theory.

Leibniz was born in the German city of Leipzig, to Friedrich Leibniz, a professor of moral philosophy at the University of Leipzig, and his wife, Catharina, the daughter of a lawyer. Although his father died not long after Leibniz was born, the young man grew up in the scholarly atmosphere of a university town and spent a great deal of time studying in his father's library. He eventually became a student at the University of Leipzig, where he studied philosophy and law.

Leibniz entered the diplomatic service of the elector of Mainz and, in 1672, was sent as an ambassador to Paris, then the center of European art and culture, and home to Leibniz for the next four years. During his time there, Leibniz would meet and befriend some of the greatest minds at work in Europe, including the Dutch astronomer Christian Huygens and the French philosopher Nicolas de Malebranche. Leibniz also traveled to London during this time and met several leading English scientists. After demonstrating a calculating machine he had invented, Leibniz was elected to the prestigious Royal Society.

Leibniz showed his mathematical genius during his years in Paris. He invented the mathematical system now known as differential calculus, unaware that the great English scientist Isaac Newton had already done so many years before. Leibniz published his findings in a book titled *Nova Methodus Pro Maximus et Minimus,* which means "New Method for the Greatest and the Least." The publication of Leibniz's work before Newton's gave rise to a furious dispute between the two men, each accusing the other of claiming credit for the discovery. In truth, both men independently discovered the same thing.

In 1676 Leibniz left Paris and settled in Hanover, his home for the rest of his life when he was not traveling. He undertook a variety of administrative tasks for the duke of Hanover but devoted most of his time and energy to his own intellectual pursuits.

In the late 1680s, Leibniz wrote *Discourse on Metaphysics,* which presented his concept of metaphysics and the nature of existence. Leibniz was one of the most influential Western thinkers in the field of metaphysics, and the philosophical system he conceived is one of the most complex philosophical works in all of Western thought.

Essentially, Leibniz saw all of reality as being composed of immaterial particles, including human thought, which he called *monads.* According to Leibniz, monads are not matter, but matter is somehow composed of monads. By this system of metaphysics, Leibniz sought to reconcile empiricists (those who believed all existence was purely physical) with dualists (those who saw reality as being made up of both physical and nonphysical qualities). Toward the end of his life,

Leibniz elaborated and expanded on this idea in his work *Monadology.*

Leibniz was also very influential in the field of theology. Some philosophers had stated that if God were all-powerful and all-good, evil would not exist. Therefore, according to these thinkers, God either was not good and all-powerful or simply did not exist. In *Théodicée,* Leibniz claims evil itself does not exist, that everything that happens is for the best, and that the best possible world for people must include free will. VOLTAIRE later ridiculed this idea in his famous novel *Candide,* which includes a bumbling character named Dr. Pangloss, who many scholars believe is a caricature of Leibniz.

Throughout his career, Leibniz energetically worked to create scientific and philosophical societies throughout Europe to allow intellectuals from many countries to exchange scholarly information. In 1700 the Berlin Society for the Sciences was established, with Leibniz as its first president. He met Peter the Great, czar of Russia, and urged him to adopt radical educational and social reforms throughout Russia.

In mathematics and philosophy, Leibniz earned a place as one of the foremost thinkers of Western civilization. His writings would later influence Immanuel KANT, and his mathematical work would greatly contribute to the efforts of future mathematicians.

English Versions of Works by Gottfried Wilhelm Leibniz

Correspondence. Edited by Samuel Clarke and Roger Ariew. Indianapolis, Ind.: Hackett Publishing, 2000.
Monadology and Other Philosophical Essays. Translated by Paul Schrecker and Anne Martin Schrecker. Indianapolis, Ind.: Bobbs-Merrill, 1965.
Philosophical Texts. Edited by R. S. Woolhouse and Richard Francks. Oxford: Oxford University Press, 1998.

Works about Gottfried Wilhelm Leibniz

Kynell, Kurt von S. *Mind of Leibniz: A Study in Genius.* Lewiston, N.Y.: Edwin Mellen Press, 2003.
Lefevre, Wolfgang. *Between Leibniz, Newton, and Kant: Philosophy and Science in the Eighteenth Century.* Hingham, Mass.: Kluwer Academic Publishers, 2001.
Rescher, Nicholas. *On Leibniz.* Pittsburgh, Pa.: University of Pittsburgh Press, 2003.

Leonardo da Vinci (1452–1519) *painter, architect, sculptor, engineer, scientist*

In the 15th century, Italy was experiencing a period of cultural and intellectual vitality known as the RENAISSANCE. It was a time of brilliance in literature, science, and the arts. Among the great geniuses of this time was Leonardo da Vinci. He is remembered today not only as the creator of some of the greatest works of art in human history but also as a man whose interests and passions encompassed an incredibly wide variety of fields, including painting, sculpture, architecture, engineering, music, geology, anatomy, biology, astronomy, and cartography.

Leonardo was born on April 15 in the town of Vinci, just outside Florence. He was the illegitimate son of a lawyer and lived out his childhood with his grandparents. When he was an adolescent, his father brought him to Florence to learn a trade. Because his illegitimate birth prevented Leonardo from joining the legal profession, his father set him up as an apprentice artist in the studio of Andrea del Verrocchio, a respected artist and craftsman. Leonardo spent several years in Verrocchio's workshop, gradually mastering the arts of painting, sculpture, and architecture.

In his youth, Leonardo developed an overriding and passionate curiosity about the natural world. He had a strong affinity for animals, particularly birds and horses, and became a vegetarian. He was fascinated by flora and other plants, as well as scenes of natural beauty, such as mountains or waterfalls. He expressed this curiosity about the natural world in his sketchbooks. Leonardo customarily carried a notebook with him wherever he went and filled them with drawings of anything that caught his attention. Many of these sketchbooks survive to this day, filled with Leonardo's observations and brilliant drawings.

By the late 1470s, Leonardo had left Verrocchio's workshop and had set himself up as an independent artist. He was commissioned by the monks of San Donato to create a painting for their main altar. Although the *Adoration of the Magi* is considered by many art historians to have been Leonardo's first great masterpiece, he never finished it. Indeed, a tragic element of his life was his seeming inability to complete many of his most important works.

In the early 1480s, Leonardo left Florence and moved to the city-state of Milan, then ruled by Duke Ludovico Sforza. Leonardo spent nearly two decades in Milan, and it was during this period that his genius reached its height. He became a trusted adviser to Duke Ludovico Sforza on matters of art and culture, as well as military engineering.

Leonardo's scientific work soon became an important part of his life. His notebooks from this period are filled with sketches and jotted notes concerning his scientific theories. Although his scientific work was unknown to the general public, it can now be seen that his understanding of physics and many other fields of science far surpassed that of anyone else in his time.

It was also during his years in Milan that Leonardo attempted to fulfill one of his great dreams: building a machine that would allow him to fly. He had long been fascinated by the flight of birds and studied the subject intensely, hoping for knowledge that would allow him to build a flying machine. His notebooks are filled with sketches of proposed designs, including one for a helicopter-type machine and others of various gliders and machines with flapping wings. It is not known if he actually built prototypes of any of these machines or if he attempted to fly any of them.

Through all this time, Leonardo continued to work on his art. Indeed, in the late 1490s, he created one of the most famous pieces of art in the world, *The Last Supper,* in which he depicts the famous scene from the Bible in which Jesus announces to his apostles that one of them will betray him. Leonardo created the painting for the monastery of Santa Maria delle Grazie, where it still exists today.

Leonardo's other great artistic project during this period was the creation of a giant bronze statue of a horse and rider, which was to memorialize the father of Duke Ludovico. The artist spent many years on this project, which was to be of unprecedented size. His notebooks are filled with preparatory sketches, and he created a full-scale clay statue as a model. Unfortunately, just as Leonardo was to begin casting the bronze, Milan was attacked by its enemies and the bronze had to be used for cannon. Later, the highly regarded clay model was destroyed by soldiers using it for target practice.

In 1499, fleeing a French invasion of northern Italy, Leonardo left Milan and spent the next few years wandering through Italy. He advised the leaders of Venice in how to defend their city from the Turks and spent a few months working as a military engineer for Cesare Borgia, a warlord famous for both his brilliance and his cruelty. During this period, Leonardo met and befriended the political philosopher Niccolò MACHIAVELLI.

During the next few years, Leonardo moved among Florence, Milan, and Rome. He painted some of his greatest works, including the portrait known as the *Mona Lisa,* one of the most famous paintings in history, and continued his scientific investigations into nature, filling his notebooks with his thoughts.

Toward the end of his life, Leonardo left Italy and took up residence in France, living as a guest of the French king. He died in the town of Cloux on May 2.

The life of Leonardo da Vinci has come to symbolize the great potential of the human mind. Leonardo himself has become the idealization of the "Renaissance Man," one who does not concern himself with only one particular activity, but whose skills and talents embrace a wide variety of different fields and interests.

Critical Analysis

Although he is best known as a painter, Leonardo's notebooks, taken collectively, constitute a great literary masterpiece. Throughout his life, he would record his observations about people or nature in these notebooks, and he eventually amassed an incredible amount of information.

Leonardo does not seem to have organized his notebooks in any particular manner. Each of them seems to be filled randomly, so that a single page might have preparatory sketches of horses, observations concerning the flow of a river, or even shopping lists. Nor do the individual notebooks concern any individual themes. In addition, for reasons which are not clear, the notebooks were written backward and in reverse, from right to left. One can read the notebooks clearly only by holding a mirror up to the page.

Apart from a story of seeing a kite as a boy and a possibly fictitious story about exploring a dark cave, there are remarkably few details about Leonardo's personal life. This may be because he did not wish information about his private life to become known, or it may simply be that he did not consider such matters to be of particular importance.

Leonardo's notebooks are famous largely for the incredible scientific speculations they contain. Sketches of cannon firing projectiles demonstrate his knowledge of ballistics, while his numerous sketches of flowing rivers betray a highly advanced knowledge of hydrodynamics. He also recorded numerous astronomical observations, as well as astonishing designs for new inventions, including flying machines, proposals for submarines, tanks, bicycles, parachutes, gear shifts, and water pumps.

Leonardo's notebooks reveal a mind of the highest order and knowledge that was far in advance of his time. However, because his notebooks were not published until many centuries after his death, his discoveries did not make any significant impact on Western civilization. Had his scientific breakthroughs and inventions become widely known among his contemporaries, the course of history would likely have been very different.

Works by Leonardo da Vinci

Leonardo on Art and the Artist. Mineola, N.Y.: Dover, 2002.

The Notebooks of Leonardo da Vinci. IndyPublish.com, 2003.
The Wisdom of Leonardo da Vinci. Translated by Wade Baskins. New York: Barnes and Noble, 2004.

Works about Leonardo da Vinci

Atalay, Bulent. *Math and the Mona Lisa: The Art and Science of Leonardo da Vinci.* Washington, D.C.: Smithsonian Institution Press, 2004.
Baskins, Wade, trans. *The Wisdom of Leonardo da Vinci.* New York: Barnes and Noble, 2004.
Bramly, Serge. *Leonardo: The Artist and the Man.* Translated by Sian Reynolds. New York: Penguin Books, 1994.
Nicholl, Charles. *Leonardo da Vinci: Flights of the Mind.* New York: Viking, 2004.
White, Michael. *Leonardo: The First Scientist.* New York: St. Martin's Griffin, 2000.

Léry, Jean de (1534–1613) *historian, clergyman*

A French Protestant during an age of violent religious conflict, Jean de Léry wrote his now famous work, *History of a Voyage to the Land of Brazil (Histoire d'un voyage faict en la terre de Brésil),* when, at age 23, he was invited to join a mission to establish a refuge for persecuted Protestants on a French-controlled island off the coast of Brazil. In this history, Jean de Léry tells of his 10-month stay among a Brazilian tribe allied to the French. His strategy consists in foregrounding his cultural biases, while critically observing the customs of the Brazilians as well as the French, and in rendering each relative to the other. For instance, the intertribal cannibalism practiced by their Brazilian hosts horrifies the Europeans, but when his fellows kill the tribe's egg-laying hens for meat, he conveys the Brazilians' dismay at the Europeans' uncivilized behavior.

Jean de Léry published his celebrated history in 1578, 20 years after his return to France. During the intervening years, religious civil wars had raged throughout Europe. Trapped for seven months during the siege of Sancerre, a city in central

France, de Léry wrote another history, *Histoire memorable de la ville de Sancerre* (*A Memorable History of the City of Sancerre*, 1574), in which he recounts the hardship, famine, and cannibalism he witnessed during that siege. De Léry's vivid descriptions and close attention to behavior have placed him among the forebears of modern ethnography.

An English Version of a Work by Jean de Léry

Whatley, Janet, trans. *History of a Voyage to the Land of Brazil*. Berkeley: University of California Press, 1990.

A Work about Jean de Léry

Lestringant, Frank. "The Philosopher's Breviary: Jean de Léry in the Enlightenment," in *New World Encounters*. Edited by Stephen Greenblatt. Berkeley: University of California Press, 1993.

Lessing, Gotthold (1729–1781) *critic, dramatist*

Gotthold Lessing is considered the first modern German intellectual, an innovator in the fields of drama, literary criticism, and religious theory. Born in Saxony to a pastor and his wife, Lessing was sent to an elite school where he learned Hebrew, Greek, Latin, and French. He attended the University of Leipzig, where he studied theology, then medicine, and found himself drawn to the theater. He received his master of arts in 1752 and moved to Berlin, aspiring to be the German MOLIÈRE. After joining the Prussian army in 1760, he served five years as a secretary and then returned to Berlin. Never financially secure, he joined the National Theater, which closed; he then attempted to establish a publishing house, which failed. Finally he accepted a post as librarian to the duke of Braunschweig. In 1776 he married Eva Koenig, who died a year later in childbirth.

Though notoriously unexpressive about his private life, Lessing was known for being argumentative and having an opinion on virtually every topic, none of which he feared to express in print.

His first literary efforts were as a reviewer and critic, and he wholeheartedly aspired to establish a German literary tradition and nurture good taste in the reading public. Though unafraid of risk, Lessing was eminently rational. His greatest influences were Aristotle, SHAKESPEARE, and most of all Denis DIDEROT, whose essays and plays he translated into German in 1760. In 1754 he wrote *The Rehabilitations of Horace* and began to translate Sophocles, though he left that project unfinished. In 1759 he published a collection of fables, and in 1766 he released *Laocoon*, a critique on painting and poetry. This series of essays shows Lessing as a developed, efficient judge and critic at the height of his style.

At a young age Lessing composed *Damon* and *The Young Scholar* (1747), both strongly influenced by the French tradition. He followed this with *The Freethinker* (1748), *The Old Maid* (1749), and *The Jews* (1749), which reflect his concern with religion. *The Treatise* and *Women Will Be Women* (1750) show the influence of Plautus, while *The Misogynist* (1755) depicts a classic love-triangle. In *Miss Sara Sampson* (1755) Lessing turned to the English countryside, borrowing the theme of the sentimental tragedy and the domestic atmosphere from English novels by RICHARDSON and Fielding. *Philotas* (1759) looks at kings and princes at war, exploring themes of patriotism, honor, love of glory, and filial devotion. Though very Greek in its plot, development, and execution, the artistry of *Philotas* is marred by long monologues that weaken the action. The playwright at this point was interested in ideas, not character.

Minna von Barnhelm (1767) is a comedy of manners, perhaps the most frequently performed German comedy, full of scheming characters and a playful, ironic tone. *Emilia Galotti* (1722), a tragedy set in an Italian court, contains all the standard elements of a plotting minister, a desirous prince, and a doomed maiden. Though quite carefully constructed, the play was perhaps too political to please audiences. The jewel of Lessing's dramatic output is *Nathan the Wise* (1779), a sophisticated comedy disguised as a fairy tale, which is essentially a dialogue between the three main religions of the West. *Nathan* was hailed by critics as a new kind of play, a modern morality play whose characters have a symbolic value far beyond their temporal existence.

Lessing's humanitarian goals and his concern with ethics rather than orthodoxy emerge in his treatises. After joining the Freemasons, he published *Conversation for the Freemasons* (1780), which portrays his disillusionment with the aristocratic elite. *Proof of the Spirit and of Power* (1777), *The Testament of John* (1777), *The Religion of Christ* (1780), and *The Education of the Human Race* (1780) reflect his efforts to separate the truth of the Christian religion from its historical foundation. Lessing appreciated the ethical significance of Christian thought but remained skeptical about certain historical proofs.

Above all, Lessing maintained a position as an independent thinker, loyal to moral feeling but not to institutions. As a humanist, Lessing believed freedom was the ultimate ideal, and friendship the means through which true humanity proves itself. Lessing's beliefs transcended the rationalist approach of the ENLIGHTENMENT, which held reason as the highest pursuit; for Lessing, compassion, not reason, guided spiritual development. His commitment to free-thinking, fraternity, and to building a native tradition have led Lessing to be identified as the founder of German literature.

English Versions of Works by Gotthold Lessing

Laocoon: An Essay on the Limits of Painting and Poetry. Translated by Edward A. McCormick. Baltimore, Md.: Johns Hopkins University Press, 1990.

Lessing's Theological Writings: Selections in Translation. Translated by Henry Chadwick. Palo Alto, Calif.: Standford University Press, 1994.

Nathan the Wise, Minna von Barnhelm, and Other Plays and Writings. Edited by Peter Demetz. New York: Continuum, 1991.

Works about Gotthold Lessing

Brown, F. Andrew. *Gotthold Ephraim Lessing.* New York: Twayne, 1971.

Yasukata, Toshimasa. *Lessing's Philosophy of Religion and the German Enlightenment.* Oxford: Oxford University Press, 2002.

Li Yu (Li Yü) (1611–ca. 1680) *playwright, critic, novelist, essayist*

Born into a family of literati, Li Yu was acknowledged in his lifetime as a literary genius. However, because he failed the civil service examination, he was forced to earn a living by his writing.

Being a resourceful man, Li Yu organized a successful theater company and soon was able to lead a life of luxury and move in high circles. His epicurean lifestyle is reflected in his prose work *Xian-qing ou-ji (Hsien ch'ing ou-chi; Random Ventures in Idleness).* The philosophy of this book is summarized by a Chinese phrase that means "enjoy oneself," for Li Yu rejected Confucian pedantry and moral strictures, as well as the Daoist notion of the simple life, the practice of foot-binding, and education for women. In his day, the ideas Li Yu put forth in *Random Ventures in Idleness* were quite radical. Not all of the work was seen as such, however; he includes a rather tame section, in comparison, that is devoted to architecture and landscape, which influenced Japanese aesthetic taste.

For the theater, Li Yu wrote 10 romantic comedies, which are characterized by risqué elements and often deal with controversial topics. Not content to be a mere playwright, however, Li Yu also wrote a treatise on stagecraft. In this work, he criticizes works of extreme length and proposes the idea of "one principal character, one plot." He used this theory in his own works, especially his short stories in which, conversely, the influence of the theater can also be seen.

Li Yu's first collection of short stories, *Wu-sheng xi (Wu-sheng hsi; Silent Operas,* 1654), features an intrusive narrator and achieves ironic effects by pitting appearance versus reality. His next collection, *Shi-er Lou (Shih-erh lou; Twelve Towers),* is a series of 12 tales linked by the word for "tower" in each title and written in the Chinese vernacular.

In addition, Li Yu also wrote an erotic novel, *Jou pu tuan (The Carnal Prayer Mat),* which tells the story of Scholar Vesperus, an orphan who turns from his amoral life to Zen Buddhism and a life of enlightenment. To avoid censorship, Li Yu disguised the book under different titles.

Li Yu's works were banned a century later in the reign of Qianlung (Ch'ien-lung). Since the May Fourth Movement, however, his works have resurfaced, and Li Yu's contribution to the development of Chinese fiction has been recognized.

English Versions of Works by Li Yu
Carnal Prayer Mat. Translated by Patrick Hanan. Honolulu: University of Hawaii Press, 1996.
Chinese Amusement: The Lively Plays of Li Yu. Translated by Eric P. Henry. North Haven, Conn.: Shoe String Press, 1980.
Tower for the Summer Heat. Translated by Patrick Hanan. New York: Columbia University Press, 1998.

Works about Li Yu
Chun-shu Chang, and Shelley H. Chang. *Crisis and Transformation in Seventeenth-Century China.* Ann Arbor: University of Michigan Press, 1998.
Hanan, Patrick. *Invention of Li Yu.* Cambridge, Mass.: Harvard University Press, 1988.

Llorona, La (1500s) *Aztec legend*
The legend of La Llorona (The Weeping Woman) evolved from stories in the Mexican oral tradition. It evolved from the convergence of two tragic female heroines: one in Aztec mythology and another in Spanish history.

La Llorona originates with the Aztec goddess Cihuacoatl, who warned of the impending Spanish conquest of Montezuma's empire. The mother goddess wandered through the city of Tenochtitlán as a weeping woman draped in flowing white cloth. In the darkness, she was heard lamenting: "Oh, my sons! Now has come the time for your destruction."

The legend of La Llorona is also mixed with Spanish history. In 1519 Spanish conquistador Hernán CORTÉS landed on the shores of Mexico and eventually succeeded in overcoming the Aztec people. Cortés's triumph had been contingent on an Aztec captive, La Malinche, also known as Doña Marina. The indigenous woman served as an invaluable translator during Cortés's military efforts. She is a controversial character in Mexican history. Some portray her as a traitor to her people; others see her as an unwilling participant. Cortés eventually took Doña Marina as his mistress, and she bore him a son. When the time came for the conquistador to return to Spain, however, Cortés took the boy with him and left his Aztec mistress behind. Devastated by the loss of her son, Doña Marina died shortly after. According to legend, her restless soul searches for her lost child and she wails in endless pain.

Literary critics explain the image of a lost Aztec woman in mourning as analogous to the demise of indigenous culture after the Spanish conquest. In modern-day Mexican and Mexican-American culture, numerous adaptations of the legend of La Llorona are still told to children.

A Work about La Llorona
Kraul, Edward Garcia, and Judith Beatty. *The Weeping Woman: Encounters with La Llorona.* Santa Fe, N.M.: Word Process, 1988.

Lomonosov, Mikhail (1711–1765)
scientist, poet, grammarian
Mikhail Lomonosov was born near Kholmogory, a town in northern Russia. His mother, Elena, was the daughter of a deacon, and his father a merchant of peasant origins. When Lomonosov was 10 years old, he began accompanying his father on business, but he remained more interested in academics. In 1731 he traveled to Moscow and gained admission to the Slavo-Greco-Latin Academy by pretending to be a nobleman's son.

Lomonosov's intellectual promise rapidly became clear. In 1736 he was one of 12 students chosen to enroll in the new University of St. Petersburg. He then attended universities in Marburg and

Freiburg to study mathematics, chemistry, metallurgy, and related subjects. In 1740 he married Elizabeth Zilch in Marburg. After returning to St. Petersburg the following year, he received a post at the Russian Academy of Sciences, where he remained for the rest of his career. Lomonosov helped to found the University of Moscow in 1755. His career declined during the reign of CATHERINE THE GREAT.

Lomonosov's wide-ranging scientific activities, like those of his contemporary Benjamin FRANKLIN, typify the RATIONALISM of the ENLIGHTENMENT. His scientific works, most written in Latin, include *Reflections on the Causes of Heat and Cold* (1744), *Oration on Aerial Phenomena, proceeding from the Force of Electricity* (1753), *A Dissertation on Greater Exactitude in Navigation* (1759), and *The First Principles of Metallurgy* (1763). Lomonosov also carried out numerous experiments with porcelain and with colored glass for mosaics. In 1752 the Russian Senate gave him permission to establish a glass factory, and an imperial decree the next year provided him with land and 212 serfs to work there. The factory eventually manufactured a number of glass products, including a large mosaic for one of Catherine II's palaces, although Lomonosov struggled to make the enterprise profitable.

Lomonosov burst upon the Russian literary scene in 1739, when he sent a "Letter on the Rules of Russian Poetry" to the Academy of Sciences and accompanied it with an ode celebrating a Russian military victory over the Turks. In the "Letter," Lomonosov insists that Russian poets should consider not only the number of syllables in each line, but also the placement of accented syllables. The ode, written in iambic tetrameter, illustrates his argument. It greatly impressed academy members.

Lomonosov's output includes historical works, translations of poems by Horace and ROUSSEAU, two dramas, and a number of odes celebrating special occasions at the Russian court. His poetry is thick with imagery, often involving allusions to Roman and Greek mythology. He praises Russia, the good ruler (who usually resembles Peter I), science, and learning.

Lomonosov's rival Alexander SUMAROKOV mocked his poems as bombastic and exaggerated, but he respected his competitor's lyricism. This lyricism is evident in two of Lomonosov's most significant poems, the "Morning" and "Evening Meditations on the Majesty of God" (1743). In the "Evening Meditation," the appearance of the northern lights causes the poet to reflect on their possible causes and the vast universe God has created. In the "Morning Meditation," Lomonosov writes that the sun is "an ocean burning evermore." Yet, "This awe-inspiring enormity / Is but a mere spark" before God. A later work, "Letter on the Use of Glass" (1752), also combines Lomonosov's scientific interests with religion and poetry. The poem begins with a list of the various uses of glass, including windows, mirrors, and jewelry. Men have killed for gold, but no wars have begun over glass; instead, Lomonosov writes, the glass in telescopes has allowed scientists to confirm the theories of Nicolaus COPERNICUS about the solar system. "Through optics," the poet exclaims, "glass leads us to [God], having expelled from us the profound darkness of ignorance!"

Lomonosov's theoretical works contributed significantly to the development of the Russian language. His *Rhetoric* (1748) offers advice to would-be poets, complete with examples from ancients like Homer, Anacreon, Juvenal, Seneca, and Martial, as well as the modern LA FONTAINE. *On the Use of Church Books in the Russian Language* (1757) regulates Russian vocabulary by categorizing words as either "high," "middle," or "low." Finally, Lomonosov's *Grammar* (1757), the first in Russian, remained definitive through 1831.

Alexander Pushkin summed up Lomonosov's wide-ranging career in the following words:

Combining unusual will power with an unusual power of comprehension, Lomonosov embraced all the branches of knowledge. . . . Historian, rhetorician, mechanician, chemist, mineralogist, artist, and poet—he scrutinized and fathomed everything.

English Versions of Works by Mikhail Lomonosov

Mikhail Vasil'evich Lomonosov on the Corpuscular Theory. Translated by Henry M. Leicester. Cambridge, Mass.: Harvard University Press, 1970.

"Mikhail V. Lomonosov," in *The Literature of Eighteenth-Century Russia*, vol. 1. Translated by Harold Segel. New York: Dutton, 1967.

Works about Mikhail Lomonosov

Brown, William Edward. "Mikhail Lomonosov and the Solemn Ode," in *A History of Eighteenth-Century Russian Literature.* Ann Arbor, Mich.: Ardis, 1980.

Menshutkin, Boris N. *Russia's Lomonosov: Chemist, Courtier, Physicist, Poet.* Princeton, N.J.: Princeton University Press, 1952.

Pavolova, Galina Evgen'evna. *Mikhail Vasilievich Lomonosov: His Life and Work.* Translated by Arthur Aksenov. Moscow: Mir, 1984.

Lope de Vega Carpio, Félix (1562–1635)
dramatist, poet

Lope de Vega was born in Madrid to Félix, an embroiderer, and Francisca Fernandez Flores. At age 10, he began studies in Latin and Castilian under the poet Vicente Espinel, and the following year entered the Jesuit Imperial College, where he began to study the rudiments of the humanities. In 1577 the bishop of Avila (Jerónimo Manrique), impressed by Lope de Vega's talent, took him to the Alcalá de Henares to study for the priesthood. This did not agree with Lope de Vega's tempestuous nature, however, and he soon left the school in pursuit of a married woman. He continued his education through intensive readings in anthologies.

By 1583, Lope de Vega had begun to establish himself as a poet in Madrid and also acted as attendant to various nobles. In addition, his sensual nature led him on a course of numerous passionate entanglements. His romantic involvement with the actress Elena Osorio, which lasted five years, was marred by his intense jealousy. When she left him, he wrote poems of such a libelous nature against her and her family that a court case was brought against him. As a result, Lope de Vega was sentenced to eight years of exile from Castile. In the midst of this scandal, he abducted 16-year-old Isabel de Urbina (the "Belisa" of many of his poems) and was forced to marry her. Only a few weeks later, Lope de Vega set sail with the Spanish Armada in an excursion against the English (1588). During his time on board, he wrote *La hermosura de Angélica* and other poems in which Isabel, his wife, is addressed as "Belisa."

Upon returning from the voyage, Lope de Vega retrieved Isabel and spent the remainder of his exile in Valencia, a dramatic center where he began to write ballads plays in earnest. When his exile ended, he moved to Toledo and became secretary to the duke of Alba. Isabel died in 1594 in childbirth, after which Lope de Vega moved to Madrid. He married Juana de Guardo in 1598. During their marriage, Lope de Vega had an affair with actress Micaela de Luján, which created quite a scandal, as he wrote numerous poems to Micaela, and contributed to his reputation as a womanizer. Despite his personal intrigues and upheavals, Lope de Vega continued to read and write profusely, and while his personal life is certainly interesting, it is his literature that gained him the greatest recognition.

Critical Analysis

Lope de Vega was a prolific writer who became increasingly identified as a playwright of the *comedia*, a term applied to the new drama of Spain's Golden Age. He was influenced by Horace, PETRARCH, ARIOSTO, TASSO, and CERVANTES, among others. From 1593 to 1632, he wrote more than 1,500 plays, as well as PASTORAL romances, EPIC poems, verse biographies of Spanish saints, and various lyric compositions. Many of these works reflect Lope de Vega's thoughts and feelings concerning his loves, exile, marriage, and friends. Lyricism and originality abound in all of his works. Sadly, most of these works have not survived.

In regard to his *comedias*, the influence of Valencian playwright Cristobal de Virues was profound. It was Lope de Vega, however, who took the form to its greatest heights. Many of his plays were historic and cloak-and-sword plays (*capa y espada*), which focused on contemporary manners and intrigue. His cloak-and-sword plays are largely made up of the same basic characters and situations: ladies and gallants falling in and out of love, a "point of honor" being engaged, and servants who imitate and parody the main characters, thereby exposing the follies of their superiors.

The "point of honor" was one of Lope de Vega's favorite devices. He called it the best theme "since there are none but are strongly moved thereby." In the context of his plays and the society of his day, honor was largely equivalent to social reputation. Men were to be brave, proud, and unwilling to accept any insult to their integrity. Women were generally required to maintain their chastity and fidelity. Upholding this point of honor usually led to an accumulation of tragic events with an emphasis on misunderstandings, intrigues, and other intricate plot devices, sometimes at the expense of in-depth character portrayals.

In the play, *El perro del hortelano (The Gardener's Dog)*, the countess Diana becomes enamoured of her employee, Teodoro, but accepts the impossibility of their union until she learns of her lady-in-waiting's intent to wed him. This causes Diana to pursue him with renewed vigor until he becomes elevated to a social status suitable for her consideration. Edward H. Friedman remarks in "Sign Language: the Semiotics of Love in Lope's *El Perro del Hortelano*": "[The play] . . . is ostensibly about love, passion and caste, but the leading characters, showing signs of distress over what they fear are unattainable goals, seem to be more captivated by the psychological challenges than the human object." Other famous plays of this type include *La dama boba (The Lady Nit-Wit)*, *La moza de cántaro (The Girl with the Jug)*, and *Por la puente Juana (Across the Bridge, Juana)*.

From 1605 until his death, Lope de Vega maintained a relationship as secretary to the duke of Sessa, who paid for Lope de Vega's funeral. Their correspondence, along with Lope de Vega's written works, is the best source of critical study of Lope de Vega's personal feelings about the people and events of his life.

In 1608 Lope de Vega was promoted to a position as a familiar of the Inquisition and became widely known as "the phoenix of Spanish wits," or simply, "the Phoenix." Several years later he wrote his famous *Arte nuevo de hacer comedias en este tiempo (New Art of Writing Plays at This Time)*, which effectively served as a manual for writing *comedias*. In this work, he rejects classical and neoclassical standards of writing and proposes a distinctive style that blends TRAGEDY, comedy, and metrical variety. This new style of writing, he suggests, gives lyricism to the dramatic form.

In 1610, after having been married several times and experienced many passionate scandals, Lope de Vega moved his household from Toledo to Madrid. Following the death of his wife, Juana, in 1613 and his favorite son Carlos Felix, age seven, he experienced a religious crisis and entered the first of various religious orders. He began to write almost exclusively religious works and became a priest in 1614. Following the publication of his verse epic *La corona trágica (The Tragic Queen)*, he was awarded a doctorate in theology from the Collegium Sapientiae and the cross of the order of Malta, which allowed him the proud use of the title Fray ("brother").

Though Lope de Vega's final years were fraught with gloom, he wrote in his treatise on the *comedia* form: "Tragedy with comedy—Terence with Seneca—will cause much delight. Nature gives us the example, being through such variety beautiful." His most enduring and popular works include *La Dorotea* (1632), a semi-autobiographical novel; the lyric poems of *La vega del Parnaso* (1637); the SONNETS of *La hermosura de Angélica* (1602), which were influenced by Petrarch and included *La Dragontea*, an epic poem in which Vega criticizes Sir Francis Drake; and, of course, his numerous plays, of which *Fuente ovejuna*, *Punishment without Revenge*, and *The Knight from Olmedo* are among his most entertaining.

While Lope de Vega is most remembered for his dramatic works, he was also a remarkably skilled poet. In his later poetry, we see a different, more mature and religious Lope de Vega than the impassioned youth who penned *The Gardener's Dog*. In "The Good Shepherd," for example, the poet addresses Christ, pleading:

> *Lead me to mercy's ever-flowing fountains;*
> *For Thou my shepherd, guard, and guide*
> *shalt be;*
> *I will obey Thy voice, and wait to see*
> *Thy feet all beautiful upon the mountains.*
>   (trans. by Henry W. Longfellow)

In another vein, more attuned to the transience of life, is Lope de Vega's appreciation for the power of nature, as can be seen in "O Navis":

> *Poor bark of Life, upon the billows hoarse*
> *Assailed by storms of envy and deceit,*
> *Across what cruel seas in passage fleet*
> *My pen and sword alone direct thy course!*
> *My pen is dull; my sword of little force;*
> *Thy side lies open to the wild waves' beat*
> *As out from Favor's harbors we retreat,*
> *Pursued by hopes deceived and vain*
> *remorse.*
>   (trans. by Roderick Gill)

Lope de Vega's ability to metaphorically transcribe the challenges of life and the struggles of the soul into words can also be seen in "A Christmas Cradle," in which the poet pits the "stormy winds," "sorrows," and "cold blasts" of the world against the innocence of baby Jesus. And in "Tomorrow," the poet recognizes that he was called to his faith many times:

> *How oft my guardian angel gently cried,*
> *"Soul from thy casement look, and thou*
> *shalt see*
> *How He persists to knock and wait for*
> *thee!"*

Yet the poet's desire to experience earthly pleasures kept him ever denying the call:

> *. . . how often to that Voice of sorrow,*
> *"Tomorrow we will open," I replied,*
> *And when the morrow came I answered*
> *still "Tomorrow."*
>   (trans. by Henry W. Longfellow)

In *Ten Centuries of Spanish Poetry*, Elizabeth Turnbull comments on Lope de Vega's use of nature and his inner struggles:

> [Lope de Vega] is the precursor of modernism, a man in constant struggle with himself. There is a great deal of the romantic in him. The romantic, for his direct awareness, converts his own vital experience into poetry. . . . He was extremely natural, but he was also a man of culture who aspired to express in a certain ordered way that natural element converted into poetry.

The quality of Lope de Vega's poetic lyricism and the fluency of his language, as well as the contributions he made to Spanish drama have made him one of the most well known and appreciated writers in the history of world literature.

English Versions of Works by Félix Lope de Vega Carpio

Desire's Experience Transformed: A Representative Anthology of Lope de Vega's Lyric Poetry. Translated by Carl W. Cobb. Rock Hill, S.C.: Spanish Literature Publications, 1991.

La Dorotea. Translated by Edwin Honig and Alan S. Trueblood. Cambridge, Mass.: Harvard University Press, 1985.

Lady Nitwit/La Dama Boda. Translated by William I. Oliver. Melbourne: Bilingual Press, 1997.

Madness in Valencia and Peribanez. Translated by David Johnston. Bath, England: Absolute Classics, 1995.

The Best Boy in Spain. Translated by David M. Gitlitz. Melbourne: Bilingual Press, 1999.

Three Major Plays: Fente Ovejuna, The Knight from Olmedo, Punishment without Revenge. Translated by Gwynne Edwards. Oxford: Oxford University Press, 1999.

Works about Félix Lope de Vega Carpio

Drake, Dana, and Jose A. Madrigal. *Studies in the Spanish Golden Age: Cervantes and Lope de Vega.* Miami, Fla.: Ediciones Universal, 2001.

Love's Dialectic: Mimesis and Allegory in the Romances of Lope de Vega. University, Miss.: Romance Monographs, 2000.

McKendrick, Melveena. *Playing the King: Lope de Vega and the Limits of Conformity.* Suffolk, U.K.: Tamesis Books, 2002.

Ostlund, DeLys. *The Re-Creation of History in the Fernando and Isabel Plays of Lope de Vega.* New York: Peter Lang, 1998.

Yarbro-Bejarano, Yvonne M. *Feminism and the Honor Plays of Lope de Vega.* West Lafayette, Ind.: Purdue University Press, 1994.

López de Gómara, Francisco
(ca. 1512–ca. 1572) *historian*

Francisco López de Gómara studied at Alcalá and was later ordained as a priest. He joined the Spanish household of Hernán CORTÉS as secretary-chaplain. He accompanied Cortés on an expedition to Algiers and, after Cortés's death, continued employment in the household of Cortés's son, Martín.

Although López de Gómara reportedly never traveled to the New World, he joined the ranks of other authors of 16th-century histories who wrote about the heroic adventures of the conquistadors and their campaigns in the New World. He gathered the information secondhand from his famous employer, crafting a glowing biography of Cortés and an historical accounting of his exploits.

Published in 1552, López de Gómara's chronicle is written in two parts. In contrast to other New World chroniclers, he takes a geographic approach to his narrative, as opposed to a chronological one. Part one, *Crónica de la conquista de la Nueva España,* covers the discovery and conquest of areas of the New World other than Mexico. Part two, *La historia de las Indias y conquista de México,* relates the adventures of Cortés in Mexico.

Also, in contrast to the majority of authors of firsthand accounts of New World travels, López de Gómara was a trained man of letters and composed his narrative in a highly literary manner. He makes use of irony, puns, and allusions, and illustrates universal themes through the circumstances of Cortés's exploits.

López de Gómara portrays Cortés as a hero bordering on EPIC proportions. This drew public objection from Bernal DÍAZ DEL CASTILLO, another popular Spanish historian of the time. He published *Verdadera historia* in reply to López de Gómara's work. López de Gómara's history also criticized certain decisions of Carlos V, resulting in a ban by Philip II upon the circulation of the work in 1553. These censures contributed to the obscurity of the publication until after 1727, when the ban was finally lifted.

López de Gómara also authored *Crónica de los muy nombrados Omiche y Haradin Barbarrojas* and collected materials for a history of the reign of Charles V, which were published during the 20th century as *Annuals of the Emperor Charles V.*

English Versions of Works by Francisco López de Gómara

Conquest of the West Indies. Delmas, N.Y.: Scholars' Facsimiles and Reprints, 1940.

Cortés: The Life of the Conqueror of Mexico by His Secretary, Francisco López de Gómara. Edited by Lesley B. Simpson. Berkeley: University of California Press, 1977.

A Work about Francisco López de Gómara

Carman, Glen Edgar. *Cortes, Gomara, and the Rhetoric of Empire.* Ithaca, N.Y.: Cornell University Press, 1993.

Luo Guanzhong   (Luo Kuan-chung)
(ca. 1330–1400) *playwright, novelist*

Luo Guanzhong was a native of Taiyuan and a novelist and playwright of reserved character living at the end of the Yuan dynasty. Three plays have been attributed to him, including *Song Taizong longhu fengyan hui (Sung T'ai-tsu lung-hu feng-yun hui; The wind-cloud meeting of the Sung founder)* and *Zhongzheng xiaozi lianhuan qian (Chung-cheng hsiao-tzu lien-huan chien; The repeated admonition of an upright devoted son).*

Not much is known of Luo Guanzhong, but he has become a semi-mythical figure for having begun the tradition of full-length novels in Chinese. Six major novels are also attributed to him, the most famous of which is *Sanguozhi yanyi (San-guo zhi yan-yi; The Romance of the Three Kingdoms).* In this work, Luo creates one of the first Chinese novels and describes through his characters the power, diplomacy, and war that contributed to the disintegration of the Han dynasty.

Luo is also credited with being one of the authors, along with SHI NAIAN, of the novel *Shuihuzhuan (Shui-hu chuan; Outlaws of the Marsh),* which was compiled from the 1300s to the 1500s. His other novels include *Sui Tang Liangchao Jizhuan (Sui T'ang Liang-ch'ao chi-chuan; Romance of the Sui and Tang Dynasties)* and *Can-Tang Wudai shi yanyi (Ts'an-T'ang Wu-tai shih yen-I; Romance of the Late Tang and the Five Dynasties).*

Luo Guanzhong's works have provided fertile ground for scholarly explorations of the craft of professional storytelling, the modification of texts over time, and the processes of transmission and publication. For all the mystery surrounding his life, his name has become synonymous with popular Chinese literature.

English Versions of Works by Luo Guanzhong

Romance of the Three Kingdoms, vols. 1 and 2. Translated by C. H. Brewitt-Taylor. Princeton, N.J.: Princeton University Press, 2002.

Three Kingdoms: A Historical Novel. Translated by John S. Service and Moss Roberts. Berkeley: University of California Press, 1994.

Luther, Martin (1483–1546) *theologian*

Martin Luther, the founder of Protestant Christianity, is one of the most important figures in Western religious history. Before Luther, the Roman Catholic Church was the single religious authority over all of Western Europe; after Luther, numerous other churches arose, and Christian unity was a thing of the past. Luther's actions fundamentally altered the structure of Christianity, and his writings greatly influenced religious thought. In addition, he had a significant impact on the German language.

Martin Luther was born in the German town of Eisleben on November 10, the son of a moderately prosperous miner. After receiving an excellent education, he planned to become a lawyer. However, in 1505, while walking down a road near the town of Stotternheim, he was caught in a terrifying thunderstorm and feared he would be killed. According to the story, which has become a famous part of the Luther legend, he called out to God, offering to become a monk if his life were spared. Having survived the storm, he kept his word and was ordained as an Augustinian monk in 1507.

Luther served as a relatively ordinary and undistinguished monk for 10 years, during which time he visited Rome. He eventually became a college professor at the University of Wittenberg. However, Luther gradually became disturbed and disillusioned by what he saw as the corruption of Roman Catholic leadership. In particular, he was upset over the practice of selling indulgences, which the church claimed would allow a person to avoid damnation merely by paying money to the church.

In 1517 Martin Luther produced a list of complaints and suggestions for reform called the Ninety-five Theses. In writing this, he blasted the church's use of indulgences as well as other aspects of church corruption and, in his view, misinterpretation of theology. Following the custom of the day, he nailed this list to the door of the Castle Church at Wittenberg. Much to his surprise, this action made him famous within a few weeks, for the Ninety-five Theses were quickly translated into German and, through the use of the newly invented printing press, rapidly spread throughout Germany.

Church authorities were greatly distressed by what they saw as Luther's defiance of church dogma. Over the next few years, Luther's ideas continued to spread and became increasingly independent of the Catholic hierarchy. He believed in the doctrine of justification by faith rather than works, and he also believed that ordinary people should be allowed to interpret the Bible for themselves.

In 1521 the church summoned Luther to the town of Worms and demanded that he give up his heretical ideas. He refused, and the church excommunicated him. Luther escaped capture with the help of sympathetic German noblemen and then embarked on the daunting task of creating an entirely new church. Those who followed Luther's ideas became known as Protestants.

Now under the protection of a Protestant German prince at the castle of Wartburg, Luther began the great stage of his literary career. Working zealously for 11 weeks, he translated the entire New Testament into German, as he wanted to make it possible for ordinary people to read the Scriptures. This work was one of Luther's masterpieces and would have a substantial impact on the development of the German language. Almost immediately after completing this work, Luther embarked upon a German translation of the Old Testament, which he completed in 1532. He continued to revise and perfect these two translations until his death.

For the rest of his life, Luther produced a constant stream of religious texts, covering all manner of religious subjects. He sought to create an entirely new theology for Protestantism. His works stress his conviction that all Christian beliefs should be firmly based on the Bible itself, rather than on theological tradition. Many of his works were commentaries on the various books of the Bible, and his writings reveal a mind with an incredible grasp both of theology and language.

Luther also wrote on political matters when they affected his religious concerns. In the early 1520s, he wrote *On Secular Authority and How Far One Should Be Obedient to It*. In this work, he argued that secular rulers have authority over their subjects in all worldly matters, but that they have no authority over matters of religious faith. In other words, a king may order you to pay taxes or serve in the army, but he cannot rightfully order you to change your religious beliefs.

Luther could be a bitter and vengeful person. He constantly launched personal attacks against any person, Catholic or Protestant, who disagreed with his views. He denounced the scientific ideas of Nicolaus COPERNICUS and also wrote an anti-Semitic tract titled *Against the Jews and Their Lies*. When the peasants of Germany rose in revolt against their noble lords in 1525, Luther called for the rebellious peasants to be exterminated.

By the time of Luther's death, Protestantism was firmly established. His writings helped transform religious thought throughout Western civilization and his influence on the German language was immense.

English Versions of Works by Martin Luther

Bondage of the Will. Greenville, S.C.: Emerald House Group, 2004.

Luther: Letters of Spiritual Counsel. Library of Christian Classics Series, vol. 18. Edited by Theodore G. Tappert. Vancouver, B.C.: Regent College Publishing, 2003.

Works, 56 vols. Edited by Jaroslav Jan Pelikan, et al. St. Louis: Concordia Publishing House, 1955–86.

Works about Martin Luther

Kolb, Robert. *Martin Luther as Prophet, Teacher, and Hero: Images of the Reformer, 1520–1620*. Grand Rapids, Mich.: Baker Books, 1999.

Lohse, Bernhard. *Martin Luther: An Introduction to His Life and Work*. Translated by Robert Schultz. Philadelphia: Fortress Press, 1986.

Lohse, Bernhard. *Martin Luther's Theology: Its Historical and Systematic Development*. Translated by Roy A. Harrisville. Minneapolis, Minn.: Augsburg Fortress, 1999.

Mullett, Michael. *Martin Luther*. London: Taylor and Francis, 2004.

Lydgate, John (ca. 1370–1450) *poet*

Born in Lidgate in Suffolk, John Lydgate began his education at the abbey of Bury Saint Edmunds and later became a priest. After attending Gloucester College, Oxford, he returned to Bury Saint Edmunds and taught rhetoric to sons of noble families. Upon his return home, he began writing prolifically.

Lydgate's works are numerous and wide-ranging, and despite his varied style, he was criticized repeatedly for being too ornate and wordy. Included among his works, which exhibit both depth and breadth, are didactic poems, religious prayers, lyrics, fables, satires, and mummings, poems recited alongside performers who gesture and move but who do not speak.

Two of his most important works are *The Siege of Thebes* (1420–22) and *The Fall of Princes* (1431–38). *The Siege of Thebes* is a verse translation of an anonymous Old French poem titled *Roman de Thebes* (ca. 1150). In Lydgate's version, the author-narrator imagines himself a fellow pilgrim accompanying those featured in CHAUCER's *Canterbury Tales*. Offering to tell a tale to help pass the time on the return trip to London, the author-narrator tells a story about the siege of Thebes. This story depicts events leading up to the time when the story told by Chaucer's "Knight's Tale" begins. The narrative frame, as well as the many instances in the text where Lydgate mimics Chaucer's language, attests to Lydgate's well-known admiration of Chaucer.

Despite the readability of *The Siege of Thebes*, *The Fall of Princes* was Lydgate's most popular work during his lifetime. It is a verse translation, with creative additions by Lydgate, of a French version of BOCCACCIO's *De Casibus Virorum Illustrium*. As his longest work, *The Fall of Princes* offers innumerable biblical and classical stories detailing the rise and fall, and the ambitions and disastrous grave mistakes of aspiring individuals. The work's ultimate purpose is to show that sin results from immoral action.

During the 15th through the 17th centuries, Lydgate was considered equal to Chaucer and GOWER as a poet of estimable skill. In addition, the sheer volume of his work helped develop the East Midland dialect as part of the Modern English language.

Works by John Lydgate

Bergen, Henry, ed. *Lydgate's* Fall of Princes. London: Boydell and Brewer, 1967.
Erdmann, Axel. *Lydgate's* Siege of Thebes I. London: Boydell and Brewer, 1996.

Works about John Lydgate

Ebin, Lois A. *John Lydgate.* Boston: Twayne, 1985.
Schirmer, Walter F. *John Lydgate: A Study in the Culture of the XVth Century.* Westport, Conn.: Greenwood Press, 1979.

Machiavelli, Niccolò (1469–1527)

political philosopher, nonfiction writer

Niccolò Machiavelli is one of the most famous and influential political philosophers in Western history. His very name was used to coin the word *Machiavellian*, which describes a deceitful and ruthless person, willing to do anything to achieve his or her objectives. The ideas and principles Machiavelli introduced into political philosophy have influenced our world ever since, and continue to do so today. Many of his ideas, however, have been greatly misunderstood.

The time and place in which Machiavelli lived had a profound effect on his political views. He was born in Florence, the son of a wealthy lawyer. During his lifetime, Italy was going through a cultural revolution known as the RENAISSANCE, which produced art and literature greater than anything seen since the time of the ancient Romans. However, it was also an age of political instability. Rival city-states competed for power and influence throughout Italy and were often engaged in full-scale warfare. Within individual city-states themselves, different political factions struggled for dominance, often reporting to violence and murder to get what they wanted. Often, these factions were focused around powerful families, such as the Medicis and the Borgias. Machiavelli's own city of Florence experienced a great deal of political violence, and this eventually led to fateful consequences for him.

Machiavelli would not begin writing until rather late in life. He almost certainly received an excellent education, and throughout his life he displayed an astonishing knowledge of classical history. In 1494 he took an administrative job with a new Florentine government, which had just overthrown the Medici family in a coup d'état.

A few years later, Machiavelli was given a diplomatic position in the government. As a result, he spent several years traveling through Italy, France, and Germany. His observations and experiences during these years would greatly influence his political ideas. He met with powerful rulers and officials, including the pope, the king of France and the Holy Roman Emperor. He also met and befriended the great artist, LEONARDO DA VINCI. Most important of all, he encountered the infamous Cesare Borgia, the brilliant but ruthless warlord who then dominated much of central Italy. Later, Borgia would become the inspiration for Machiavelli's masterpiece, *The Prince*.

Machiavelli held other important positions in the Florentine government and helped reorganize the city-state's military. But in 1512, with the assistance of a foreign army, the Medici once again seized control of Florence. Because he had served the government that had earlier overthrown them, Machiavelli was arrested by the Medici. For some time, he suffered imprisonment and torture, which undoubtedly affected him for the rest of his life. In 1513 he was released from prison and banished to the country estate of San Casciano, forbidden to play any role in Florentine politics.

It was during his exile in San Casciano that Machiavelli began his literary career. It was partly an effort to gain favor with the Medici, but Machiavelli also desired some activity to lessen the dullness of his exile. In a relatively short time, he produced a body of work that completely revolutionized political philosophy and changed the way Western civilization thought about affairs of state for the next several centuries.

His first book, *The Prince,* was quite short, but it was by far his most famous and influential work. In it, Machiavelli describes the ideal ruler, one who is best able to seize and control political power. Although written in 1513, *The Prince* was not published until 1532, after Machiavelli's death.

Between 1513 and 1517, Machiavelli wrote *Discourses on the First Decade of Titus Livy,* which is usually known simply as the *Discourses.* In this work, Machiavelli analyzes the history of the Roman Republic by studying the work of the Roman historian Livy, using the information to lay out his own theories of government and political organization. While *The Prince* seems to favor an authoritarian and monarchist form of government, *Discourses* takes the opposite viewpoint, seeming to favor a republican form of government. This contradiction in Machiavelli's views has puzzled many historians and created much confusion concerning what form of government Machiavelli truly favored.

Despite its focus on a republican form of government, *Discourses* contains rather frank and cynical political views. Machiavelli argues that politics must be completely divorced from ethical and moral considerations and through repeated examples shows leaders being ruined because they allowed their ethical views to blind them to political reality. Machiavelli also presents his view that, in the end, brute force is the key element in affairs of state.

During the same time period in which Machiavelli wrote *The Prince* and *Discourses,* he also produced *The Art of War,* in which he presents his ideas concerning the interrelationship between politics and warfare. Many of his conclusions were later shown to be quite flawed; for example, he dismissed the value of artillery, which later came to dominate military tactics. His most important assertion in *The Art of War,* which he also discusses in *The Prince,* is that a city-state should rely on a military made up of its own citizens, rather than on one made up of mercenary soldiers. Citizen-soldiers, he claims, will obviously be more loyal to the state, because they will serve out of patriotic loyalty, rather than merely a desire to be paid.

In addition to his treatises on political philosophy, Machiavelli became a playwright. He wrote *Andria* in 1517 and *Mandragola* in 1518. Between 1520 and 1525, he also wrote a history of Florence. While well-written and interesting, these works are not nearly as famous as Machiavelli's work on political philosophy.

After Machiavelli's death, his political writings became extremely popular and were read throughout Europe. Much of what he wrote was banned by the Catholic Church, but this likely increased the works' reputation rather than decreased it. Over the next several centuries, Machiavelli was condemned as an evil man whose vision in *The Prince* contributed to the rise of such villains as Adolf Hitler and Joseph Stalin. Machiavelli did not advocate authoritarian government when he wrote *The Prince;* he merely stated what, to him, was the reality of his time. Machiavelli has been criticized for his cynical view of human nature and his belief that political theory should be divorced from ethics. Nevertheless, he remains perhaps the most influential political philosopher of the Western world.

Critical Analysis

Of all his writings, Machiavelli is most renowned for *The Prince,* which is one of the most famous pieces of Western literature. In this work, Machiavelli describes his view of the ideal prince, who is able to seize and maintain power in a nation or city-state. Although intended to describe the circumstances of 16th-century Italy, the author's insights into human nature and the affairs of state have a universal applicability, irrespective of time or place.

On many occasions in *The Prince,* Machiavelli states that the exercise of political power must be completely detached from any ethical or moral consideration. He believed that any prince who acted out of moral principle would inevitably be destroyed, because he would be surrounded by rival princes who would not be so constrained. However, in order to maintain appearances, Machiavelli believed a prince should always work hard to appear moral and ethical, even if it would be foolish to actually be moral and ethical.

To Machiavelli, this attitude could not be judged as morally right or wrong; it was simply reality. He was not attempting to advocate a particular way in which princes should govern, but was simply attempting to describe the actual way in which such governing was done. He did not see anything necessarily immoral in authoritarian rule, so long as it benefited the people. He recognized that a strong authoritarian government often provided order and stability, whereas a weak republican government often resulted in chaos and disorder. Through the use of his superior knowledge of classical and contemporary history, he provided many examples of such events.

Another important quality of *The Prince* is Machiavelli's sense of realism. Throughout the work, he stresses the role played by "Fortune," and warns princes to beware of sudden and unexpected shifts in the balance of power. He states that wise princes should be prepared for such unforeseen events by constantly training themselves in the methods of warfare and diplomacy and always anticipating the worst.

After its publication in 1532, *The Prince* became widely popular and influential throughout Europe and gained a reputation as a textbook for those who sought to win political power. Its influence remains with us to this day.

English Versions of Works by Niccolò Machiavelli

Art of War. Edited by Christopher Lynch. Chicago: University of Chicago Press, 2003.

Discourses on Livy. Translated by Julia C. and Peter Bondanella. Oxford: Oxford University Press, 2003.

Florentine History. Translated by W. K. Marriott. New York: Barnes and Noble, 2004.

The Prince. Translated by Luigi Ricci. New York: Penguin Group, 1980.

Works about Niccolò Machiavelli

De Grazia, Sebastian. *Machiavelli in Hell.* New York: Vintage Books, 1989.

Falco, Maria J., ed. *Feminist Interpretations of Niccolo Machiavelli.* University Park: Pennsylvania State University Press, 2004.

Skinner, Quentin. *Machiavelli: A Very Short Introduction.* Oxford: Oxford University Press, 2000.

Viroli, Maurizio. *Niccolò's Smile: A Biography of Machiavelli.* Translated by Anthony Shugaar. New York: Farrar, Straus and Giroux, 2000.

Malory, Thomas (1410?–1471) *novelist*

The enduring status of King Arthur as the most popular hero of English literature is due in large part to a man whose own origins remain mysterious. Little is known for certain about Thomas Malory aside from the facts that he was a knight, he was at some point a prisoner, and he finished *Le Morte D'Arthur (The Death of Arthur)* in the year 1469. The consensus holds that he was born in Warwickshire and knighted in 1441. After he served in the English army and in Parliament, the next records show him in prison for charges of robbery, vandalism, assault, rape, and attempted murder. He insisted on his innocence. Despite two dramatic escape attempts—once by swimming the castle moat—he spent the last years of his life in Newgate prison, where he composed his epic work.

Malory's English sources are the alliterative *Morte Arthur* and the anonymous SIR GAWAIN AND THE GREEN KNIGHT. He probably drew on Geoffrey of Monmouth's legendary history of Britain for the characters of Merlin, Guinevere, and Mordred. The rest of Malory's material—the characters of Lancelot, Tristan, the quest for the Holy Grail, and the codes of chivalry and courtly love—came from the large body of French romances that circulated on the continent. Of these, the *Lais* of Marie de France, the romances of Chrétien de Troyes, and an anonymous work called the *Prose Lancelot* all have their echoes in Malory's collection. Several Arthurian characters are also the subject of the collection of Welsh tales known as *The Mabinogion*, but it is unknown whether Malory knew the Celtic tradition.

Malory also drew extensively on the cultural climate of his own time. The upper class in 15th-century England followed a veritable cult of chivalry, engaging in tournaments, combat, and romance nearly as frequently as Malory's characters do. Knights errant traveled the countryside, and organizations such as the Order of the Garter modeled themselves after the Round Table. In a world fraught with disorder, adherence to a code of ethics and loyalty proved a stabilizing force. This is the theme Malory took up in his work.

Le Morte D'Arthur encompasses the entire life of Arthur, although its title suggests that it focuses on the elements that lead to the king's eventual demise. The colorful characters of Arthur's court form a constellation around the ideal of knighthood embodied by Arthur himself. Destiny is a driving force in the Arthurian saga, and mysterious supernatural beings intervene in the course of events. Yet all of Malory's characters possess the ability to make their own choices, and tragedy often results from the flaws in human nature, not from the caprices of the world outside.

The plot, structured as a series of individual stories, develops through a series of tests: Knights are tested for their courage, their skill at arms, and their loyalty to king and lady. Though Malory delights much more in describing battle scenes than in analyzing a character's emotion, the reader can enjoy Malory's conversational tone, his extravagant dialogue, his alternating moments of irony and pathos, and the subtle humor that surfaces throughout, as in this passage:

> "Wherefore this is my counsel: that our king and sovereign lord send unto the kings Ban and Bors by two trusty knights with letters well devised, that and they will come . . . to help him in his wars, that he would be sworn unto them to help them in their wars. . . . Now, what say ye unto this counsel?" said Merlin.
> "This is well counselled," said the King.

Thomas Caxton printed the first edition of *Le Morte D'Arthur* in 1485. Despite the French title, *Le Morte D'Arthur* was written in Middle English. In 1934 a manuscript was discovered at Winchester College that contains elements that the printed edition left out. Many scholars consider the Winchester manuscript closer to Malory's true vision for the tale.

The number of reprints, editions, and retellings of Malory's stories stand as proof of the popularity of the Arthurian legends. Malory was read and admired by such later British writers as Philip SIDNEY, Sir Walter Scott, Edmund Spenser, and Alfred Tennyson. The never-ending fascination with the myth of Arthur suggests that these narratives satisfy some deep need on the part of reading audiences—a need, perhaps, to believe in a world in which justice prevails, the mighty are committed to high ideals, the vulnerable are defended and evil defeated, and magic is a very real force.

Works by Thomas Malory

Le Morte D'Arthur: Complete, Unabridged, Illustrated Edition. Edited by John Matthews. London: Cassell, 2003.

Le Morte D'Arthur: The Winchester Manuscript. Edited by Helen Cooper. New York: Oxford University Press, 1998.

Works about Thomas Malory

Armstrong, Dorsey. *Gender and the Chivalric Community of Malory's Morte D'Arthur.* Gainesville: University Press of Florida, 2003.
Field, P. J. C. *The Life and Times of Sir Thomas Malory.* Rochester, N.Y.: Boydell and Brewer, 1999.

March, Ausiàs (ca. 1397–1459) *poet*

Ausiàs March was a Catalan poet especially concerned with the emotions of life: love, death, pain, and spirituality. Born in Gandia in the kingdom of Valencia, March wrote his poems in his native language, much to the displeasure of one of his editors. "Had March written in Spanish," argues Robert Archer, "he would by now undoubtedly be more widely recognized as the finest lyric poet in the Iberian Peninsula before the sixteenth century."

March's immense poetic talent focused on womanly beauty and love. He believed that "as a 'composite' being . . . man is pulled by body and soul towards two opposed forms" of good (Archer). This sensation of torment, the stretching of one's nature in two seemingly opposing directions, became the topic of March's poems about love. His greatest work was "Cant spiritual" ("Spiritual Song"), in which the poet confesses that his fear of God is greater than his love for God.

March was greatly interested in the works of Aristotle and Dante and was influenced by the Provençal troubadours, including Arnaut Daniel. March created courtly love poems that went far beyond the physical realm, as well as poems in which he took hold of the metaphysical to explore death and faith through poetry. He is remembered for having founded Catalan poetry, and his works are valued for their eloquent presentation of love as a moral and spiritual experience.

English Versions of Works by Ausiàs March

Ausiàs March: A Key Anthology. Edited by Robert Archer. Oxford: Anglo-Catalan Society Occasional Publications, 1992.
Ausiàs March: Selected Poems. Edited by Arthur Terry. Austin: University of Texas Press, 1976.

Works about Ausiàs March

Archer, Robert. *The Pervasive Image: The Role of Analogy in the Poetry of Ausiàs March.* Philadelphia: John Benjamins Publishing, 1985.
McNerney, Kathleen. *The Influence of Ausiàs March on Early Golden Age Castilian Poetry.* Amsterdam: Rodopi B.V., 1982.

Marguerite de Navarre (Marguerite d'Angoulême, Margeurite d'Alençon, Marguerite of Navarre) (1492–1549) *poet, dramatist, novelist*

The daughter of Charles d'Orléans, comte d'Angoulême, Marguerite was raised in Angoulême, in western France, by her widowed mother, Louise de Savoie, who ensured that her children were thoroughly educated. At age 17, Marguerite was married to the duc d'Alençon and went to live with him at Alençon, in Normandy. In 1515 her younger brother François succeeded his cousin Louis XII as king of France. François continued military campaigns in Italy that Louis XII had begun; in his absences, his mother acted as regent, and Marguerite began to spend much of her time at court. She was interested in all the arts, supported writers, and transformed the court into a brilliant literary center. She was also deeply engaged by religious thought. She had contacts among many of the leaders of the religious reform movement that was developing at the time, among them John CALVIN. In the early 1520s, she began to write religious poetry.

The duc d'Alençon died in battle in 1525, and two years later Marguerite married Henri d'Albret, king of Navarre, at the time a separate country in the Pyrenees Mountains, now part of France. She divided her time between François's court and her husband's. She and Henri had two children: a daughter, Jeanne d'Albret, who inherited the throne of Navarre, and a son who died in 1530, a few months after birth.

The death of her son, and of her mother the following year, seem to have made writing more important to Marguerite. In 1530 she published her first poem, *Miroir de l'âme pêcheresse (Mirror of the Sinful Soul)*, which was banned by theologians at the Sorbonne for what they considered to be heresy. During the 1530s she wrote both religious and secular lyrics, as well as plays that were staged at both courts. She also began this decade with a great deal of influence over François and his policies, but gradually the two became estranged as François began to feel threatened by the religious reformers close to Marguerite. By 1540 she was no longer welcome at François's court.

It was probably in the early 1540s that Marguerite wrote her two long philosophical poems, *La Coche, ou le Debat sur l'Amour (The Coach, or the Debate on Love)* and *Le Triomphe de l'Aigneau (The Triumph of the Lamb)*. In 1547 she published two collections of her works: *Les Marguerites de la Marguerite des Princesses tres Illustre Royne de Navarre (The Pearls of the Pearl of Princesses, the Illustrious Queen of Navarre)* and *Suyte des Marguerites . . . (More Pearls . . .)* Each book contained examples of all the genres she had attempted: plays, FARCE, lyrics, sacred allegories (see ALLEGORY), and longer poems.

At the time of her death, Marguerite was working on a collection of stories modeled on BOCCACCIO's *Decameron*. The plots are drawn from French folklore, and the focus is generally on the trials endured by women and their need to maintain their chastity and love of God. But they include much humor and a wealth of fascinating detail about everyday life. Marguerite completed only 72 of the 100 stories she had planned. Two themes that run throughout the stories are sorrow over the death of loved ones and, primarily, love, which is, in turn,

related to her social and religious subjects. The collection was published in 1558 under the title *Heptaméron des Nouvelles (Heptameron of Stories)*, the work for which Marguerite of Navarre is best known today.

English Versions of Works by Marguerite de Navarre

Marguerite de Navarre: The Coach and the Triumph of the Lamb. Translated by Hilda Dale. Bristol, U.K.: Intellect, 2003.

The Heptameron. Translated by P. A. Chilton. New York: Viking Penguin, 1984.

Works about Marguerite de Navarre

Cottrell, Robert D. *The Grammar of Silence: A Reading of Marguerite de Navarre's Poetry.* Washington, D.C.: Catholic University of America Press, 1986.

Lyons, John D., and Mary B. McKinley, eds. *Critical Tales: New Studies of the Heptameron and Early Modern Culture.* Philadelphia: University of Pennsylvania Press, 1993.

Stephenson, Barbara. *Power and Patronage of Marguerite de Navarre.* Aldershot, Hampshire, U.K.: Ashgate Publishing, 2004.

Thysell, Carol. *The Pleasure of Discernment: Marguerite de Navarre as Theologian.* New York: Oxford University Press, 2000.

Wertheimer, Molly Meijer, ed. *Listening to Their Voices: The Rhetorical Activities of Historical Women.* Columbia: University of South Carolina Press, 1997.

Williams, H. Noel. *The Pearl of Princesses: The Life of Marguerite D'Angouleme, Queen of Navarre.* Whitefish, Mont.: Kessinger, 2004.

Marieke van Nimwegen (Mariken van Nieumeghen, Mary of Nemmegen)

(ca. 1500) *medieval Dutch story*

The Dutch story Marieke van Nimwegen dates to the late medieval period, around 1500. At that time, belief in witchcraft was very prominent, and witches were believed to be women who had sexual relationships with the devil. *Marieke van Nimwegen* is the story of such a woman and her eventual redemption. The story is a "miracle play," a medieval drama dealing with religious subjects.

The story's main character is Marieke, a young and beautiful orphan who lives with her uncle Gijsbrecht, a pious priest, near the town of Nimwegen. After her father and mother, Gijsbrecht's sister, died, she came to live with her uncle to keep his house for him. One evening, Marieke goes to the market in Nimwegen and accidentally gets caught away from home in the dark. She begs refuge with her aunt, Gijsbrecht's other sister, but her aunt refuses her and accuses her of prostitution and drunkenness. Marieke is enraged and storms out of the town to find some bushes by the road to sleep under.

When Marieke angrily swears that she does not care whether it is God or the devil who comes to her aid, a one-eyed devil appears in the road before her. He introduces himself as Moenen, the Master of Arts. He says that if she comes to live with him in Antwerp, he can teach her seven arts: grammar, rhetoric, logic, arithmetic, geometry, music, and alchemy. Marieke badly wants to learn these things and agrees to live with him. Before they leave, Moenen makes her change her name to Emmeken (since Marieke means Mary, a name unpleasant for the devil) and swear never to make the sign of the cross.

When Marieke does not return from the market, Gijsbrecht gets worried and goes to Nimwegen to ask his sister if she has seen her. His sister first denies it but finally tells Gijsbrecht that she had turned his niece away. Gijsbrecht returns home deeply saddened and worried.

After living with Moenen for seven years and learning many things from him, Marieke becomes homesick and tired of the sinful life they live. She convinces the devil to take her back to Nimwegen, where she immediately slips away and returns to Gijsbrecht. The devil attempts to murder her but is prevented by God because Marieke is repentant. Marieke and Gijsbrecht travel to Rome, where she visits the pope to repent for betraying God and living with the devil. Three rings of iron are put around her neck and arms, and she is told that if the rings fall off, everything she has done will be forgiven. Deeply repentant, Marieke spends the next 24 years at a monastery for converted sinners with the weight of the rings upon her. Finally, an angel comes to her and removes the rings, and Marieke is at last redeemed.

The story of Marieke van Nimwegen is a famous tale in the Netherlands and was made into a movie titled *Mariken Van Nieumeghen* in 1974. Today, a statue of Marieke stands in Nimwegen, Holland.

English Versions of Marieke van Nimwegen

Raferty, Margaret M., ed. *Mary of Nemmegen. Medieval and Renaissance Texts,* vol. 5. Leiden, Netherlands: Brill Academic Publishers, 1991.

Rietbergen, P. J. A. N. *Europe: A Cultural History.* New York: Routledge, 1999.

Warner, Marina. *From the Beast to the Blonde: On Fairy Tales and their Tellers.* New York: Noonday Press, 1996.

Marivaux, Pierre Carlet de Chamblain de (1688–1763) *playwright, novelist*

Pierre Carlet was born in Paris to Nicolas Carlet, a military officer, and Marie-Anne Bullet. In 1698 the Carlet family moved to Riom, where Nicolas had taken a job as director of the royal mint. Pierre began studying law in Paris in 1710. A few years later, he settled in Paris, where he gained entrance to literary salons and began to publish under the name Marivaux. In 1717 Marivaux married Colombe Bollogne, with whom he had a daughter. Soon after, he unfortunately lost most of the family's money in land speculation. Although he eventually finished his law degree (1721), he devoted most of his time to literature. In 1742, he was honored with election to the ACADÉMIE FRANCAISE.

As a writer, Marivaux was influenced by CORNEILLE, RACINE, LA FONTAINE, and BOILEAU. His novels include a number of FARCES. In *Pharsamon* (written 1713, published 1737), which paid homage to CERVANTES's *Don Quixote,* the protagonists suffer through a series of adventures because they have read too many ROMANCES. *Telemachus, a Parody* (1714, published 1736) rewrites FÉNÉLON's *Telemachus* in a way that mocks social conditions in France. In 1716 Marivaux even attempted a mock EPIC parodying Homer's *Iliad.*

The following year, as Oscar Haac notes, Marivaux abandoned parody and "began writing in the realistic style that became his distinguishing mark and brought him success." *The Life of Marianne* (1731–41) and *The Peasant Who Gets Ahead in the World* (1734–35) feature narrators looking back on how they achieved their comfortable social positions. *Marianne* almost certainly influenced Samuel RICHARDSON. Along with Madame de LAFAYETTE's work, it set the standard for the modern novel.

Marivaux also composed some three dozen plays. Unlike MOLIÈRE, whose work Marivaux disliked, he emphasizes dialogue over plot. His plays observe the traditional UNITIES, but their style is original, and his tragedies are far less gloomy than those of his predecessors and contemporaries. He wrote his comedies in prose, rather than verse, and they contain not only noble but even tragic elements. More important, as Haac argues, for Marivaux "comedy becomes an effective technique for analysis," notable for its "realism, the comic imitation of refined manners on the part of servants who never succeed in mastering them, the ambiguity of human motives ever present even in refined speech which barely covers up greed and sensuous desire." This realism is evident in one of Marivaux's best plays, *The Game of Love and Chance,* a three-act comedy first performed in 1730. In the opening scenes, Silvia awaits the arrival of her intended husband, Dorante. She decides to switch places with her servant Lisette so that she can observe Dorante without his knowledge. Unbeknownst to her, however, Dorante has switched places with his servant Harlequin. Thus, Silvia finds herself falling in love with a "menial servant" (the disguised Dorante), as does Dorante (with the disguised Silvia). Meanwhile, Lisette and

Harlequin parade their version of noble airs, but each worries that the other is in love with who they are pretending to be. It is only after much soul-searching on the nobles' part, and comical dialogue on the servants' part, that a happy ending is reached.

At the time in which the play was written, not everyone appreciated Marivaux's works. VOLTAIRE complained that Marivaux's plots involved "weighing flies' eggs in scales of gossamer," and the term *marivaudage* came to be applied to exaggerated, overly refined speech. Over time, a larger audience has begun to agree with Haac that Marivaux's works possess both emotional and intellectual appeal. His plays are now produced more often in France than any except those of Molière.

See also ENLIGHTENMENT.

English Versions of Works by Marivaux

Le Paysan Parvenu: or, The Fortunate Peasant. New York: Garland, 1979.
Pharsamond. New York: Garland, 1974.
Plays. London: Methuen, 1988.
Seven Comedies by Marivaux. Edited by Oscar Mandel and translated by Oscar and Adrienne S. Mandel. Ithaca, N.Y.: Cornell University Press, 1968.

Works about Marivaux

Greene, E. J. H. *Marivaux.* Toronto: Toronto University Press, 1965.
Haac, Oscar A. *Marivaux.* New York: Twayne, 1973.
Jamieson, Ruth. *Marivaux, A Study in Sensibility.* New York: King's Crown Press, 1941.
Showalter, English. *The Evolution of the French Novel, 1641–1782.* Princeton, N.J.: Princeton University Press, 1972.

Marlowe, Christopher (1564–1593)
dramatist, poet, translator

Christopher Marlowe was born in Canterbury to Catherine and John Marlowe, a cobbler. He attended the King's School, Canterbury, and Corpus Christi College at the University of Cambridge on scholarship. He graduated with a B.A. in 1584 and went on to pursue a master's degree. When the university refused to grant his degree in 1587, influential members of Elizabeth I's privy council interceded on his behalf by writing a letter. From this letter, scholars deduce that Marlowe was a governmental spy. In the following years, a combination of events and evidence arose that, taken together with Marlowe's controversial writings, led critics to consider him an atheist, possibly a reason for which he was murdered.

As a writer, Marlowe began his career by writing for the Admiral's Men at the Rose Theatre, quickly becoming the city's most popular playwright. He was also the author of numerous poems and translations. Perhaps his most famous lyric poem is "The Passionate Shepherd to His Love" (ca. 1587), in which the speaker invites his mistress to join him in a PASTORAL setting, rendering physical love an innocent part of nature. Marlowe's greatest contribution to world literature, however, is his dramatic verse.

Instead of rhymed verse, Marlowe wrote his dramas in blank verse, unrhymed iambic pentameter, creating a poetic form paralleling the natural rapidity, power, and flow of spoken language: "Was this the face that launched a thousand ships, / And burnt the topless towers of Ilium?"

Marlowe's numerous plays include *The Jew of Malta* (ca. 1590) and *Doctor Faustus* (1593). In *The Jew of Malta*, he presents a Jewish villain far more charming than his Christian counterparts. Barabas is a brutal stereotype of a miser and hideous criminal whose crimes constitute revenge against Christian discrimination. T. S. Eliot called *The Jew of Malta* a "savage farce."

In *Doctor Faustus*, Faustus is a scholar who sells his soul to the devil, Mephistopheles, for years of power and knowledge. The play focuses on his vain pursuits as he confronts the pleasures and the mysteries of the world.

Other of Marlowe's works include *Dido, Queen of Carthage* (ca. 1586), which ponders the devastating effects of an empire upon women; *The Massacre at Paris* (ca. 1590), which highlights the dangerously thin line separating the Protestant monarchy in France from the Catholic one it had replaced; and *Edward II* (ca. 1592), the TRAGEDY of a homosexual king who is deposed and brutally murdered. One of Marlowe's most important works, however, is *Tamburlaine*, a tragedy in which a "Scythian shepherd"—Tamburlaine—rises to power by his martial and rhetorical brilliance.

Marlowe wrote Part I of *Tamburlaine*, which ends with Tamburlaine's marriage to an Egyptian princess, around 1587, while he wrote Part II, which traces Tamburlaine's demise and destruction, in 1588. The work was published in 1590.

Emily C. Bartels states that alienation is the tragic state for most of Marlowe's protagonists, and it is Tamburlaine's ambition that both defines him as great and ultimately alienates him. Particularly telling of Tamburlaine's character and tragic end is the failure of his sons to carry on his legacy; in essence, he has created a world no one else can sustain.

In Part II, Tamburlaine is blinded by pride from his triumph over Islamic nations: "In vain, I see, men worship Mahomet: / My sword hath sent millions of Turks to hell, / Slew all his priests, his kinsmen, and his friends, / And yet I live untouched by Mahomet." He burns copies of the Koran, but a few moments later announces, "I feel myself distempered suddenly," signaling the beginning of his downfall, which is tied to this blasphemous action. Critics argue the purpose of this scene. Some believe it implies Marlowe's approval of Tamburlaine's destruction of the enemies of the Christian world. Other critics argue that Marlowe's purpose was more orthodox, that he presents Tamburlaine's burning of the Koran as blasphemy (the Koran figures allegorically as the Bible here) and that will be punished in the end.

Marlowe's ability to make Tamburlaine a character with whom readers can identify, led critic Harry Levin to claim that "no other poet has been, so fully as Marlowe, a fellow-traveler with the subversive currents of his age." During his age, Marlowe was greatly admired, and his works influenced other, greater writers who followed, including SHAKESPEARE, JONSON, Chapman, and Drayton.

Other Works by Christopher Marlowe

Complete Plays and Poems. Rutland, Vt.: Charles E. Tuttle, 2002.

Ovid's Elegies and *Lucan's First Book*, in *Christopher Marlowe: The Complete Poems and Translations.* Edited by Stephen Orgel. Middlesex, England: Penguin, 1971.

Works about Christopher Marlowe

Bartels, Emily C. *Spectacles of Strangeness: Imperialism, Alienation, and Marlowe.* Philadelphia: University of Pennsylvania Press, 1993.

Eliot, T. S. *Elizabethan Dramatists.* London: Faber, 1963.

Kuriyama, Constance Brown. *Christopher Marlowe: A Renaissance Life.* Ithaca, N.Y.: Cornell University Press, 2002.

Marot, Clément (ca. 1496–1544) *poet*

Clément Marot was born in Cahors, France, to Jean Marot, a poet who held a post at the court of Anne de Bretagne, and later was court poet to Francis I. Marot studied law at the University of Paris and spent much of his life in court service. Upon his father's death, he took the post of *valet du chambre* to Francis I. His Protestant sympathies led to his arrest on several occasions, and he spent time in exile in both Geneva and Italy.

Marot is widely acknowledged as one of the greatest poets of the French RENAISSANCE. He used his vast knowledge of Latin classics and Italian literary forms to great effect, introducing a number of forms into French poetry, including the elegy and the epigram, a form for which he is renowned. He also translated many Latin works into French, including those of Ovid, Catullus, and Virgil. In addition, CALVIN much admired Marot's translations of the Psalms (1541–43).

Marot also invented a lyrical form called the *blason,* a type of satiric verse generally describing a part of the female body in great detail. This form achieved great popularity in France in his time, inspiring a slew of imitators. Two epigrams written in the *blason* style are "Du beau tétin" and "Du laid tétin."

Marot's first collection of poems, *L'Adolescence clémentine,* was published in 1532, and his second collection, *Suite de l'Adolescence clémentine,* in 1533. His poetry is noted for its grace, warmth, and elegance and was admired by the Elizabethan poets, most notably Edmund Spenser.

English Versions of Works by Clément Marot

Le Ton Beau de Marot: In Praise of the Music of Language. Edited by Douglas R. Hofstadter. New York: Basic Books, 1997.

Lyrics of the French Renaissance: Marot, Du Bellay, Ronsard. Edited by Norman Shapiro. New Haven: Yale University Press, 2002.

Works about Clément Marot

Screech, M. A. A. *Clément Marot: A Renaissance Poet Discovers the Gospel.* Netherlands: Brill Academic Publishers, 1993.

Williams, Annwyl. *Clément Marot: Figure, Text and Intertext.* Lewiston, N.Y.: Edwin Mellen Press, 1990.

Marulić, Marko (Marcus Larulus Spalatensis) (1450–1524) *poet, scholar*

Marko Marulić was born in the ancient Croatian city of Split, located on the coast of the Adriatic Sea. A scholar and a poet, Marulić became famous as the "Humanist from Split," one of the most notable figures of the Central European RENAISSANCE.

Until the 16th century, Croatian literary works were exclusively religious and devotional in character. In 1521, Marulić 's *The History of the Holy Widow Judith* broke the tradition. This first Croatian EPIC tells the biblical story from the book of Judith and the slaying of Holofernes.

The History of the Holy Widow Judith is an Old Testament story that was extremely popular with the population of Croatia. It was especially loved by women and girls, who were untrained in Latin, the official language of the literature of the time. The work had a social purpose, as well as literary value; it was meant to unite the Croatian nation in the spirit of Christianity in its struggle with the Turks of the Ottoman Empire.

The spirit of patriotism is also central to Marulić's other works, notably *The Prayer Against the Turks*, a poem simple in form and deep in emotion in which the speaker claims, "We suffer every moment from the evil barbarian hands!"

As was customary at the time, Marulić also wrote under his Latin name. As Marcus Larulus Spalatensis, he was the author of works covering a broad range of subjects, including religious morality, history, and archaeology. He also wrote poetry in Latin. Marulić is important as the author of the first secular work in the history of Croatian literature.

An English Version of a Work by Marko Marulić

Judita, in English and Croatian. Edited and translated by Henry R. Cooper Jr. New York: Columbia University Press, 1991.

A Work about Marko Marulić

Lansperger, Johannes. *Epistle in the Person of Christ to the Faithfvll Soule, Written First by . . . Lanspergivs, and after Translated into English by One of No Small Fame*. Microfilm. Ann Arbor, Mich.: University Microfilms, 1955.

Mather, Cotton (1663–1728) *theologian, historian, scientist*

Cotton Mather was born into one of the most eminent New England families. His father, Increase MATHER, was a renowned minister, and both of his grandfathers (Richard Mather and John Cotton) were highly regarded members of the first generation of New England Puritan divines.

Though frail and weakly as a child, Mather pursued his studies wholeheartedly. Biographer Kenneth Silverman notes that by the time he entered Harvard at age 11, he had "read in Cato, Tully, Ovid, and Virgil, gone through a great part of the New Testament in Greek . . . and begun Hebrew grammar."

College life was not easy for him. He stuttered and was often abused by other students. Yet, as Silverman observes, Mather's "stutter played into his scientific interests." The "impediment led him almost to despair of becoming a minister, and to apply himself to becoming a physician." The fruits of his early scientific research manifested themselves in his later works. His *The Christian Philosopher* (1721) was the first general scientific book to be written in America, and *The Angel of Bethesda . . . An Essay upon the Common Maladies of Mankind . . . and direction for the Preservation of Health* (1722) was an influential medical text. In 1721, during a smallpox epidemic, Mather advocated the use of inoculation and managed to institute a successful program of vaccination. Emory Elliott explains that the success of this program turned Mather into "a hero in the history of eighteenth-century American medicine.

Though his stammering caused him to worry about entering an occupation like the ministry, Mather followed in the footsteps of his forefathers. Shortly after graduating from Harvard at age 15, he began delivering sermons to his father's congregation and those once led by his illustrious grandfathers. From 1685 to 1723, Mather served under his father as teacher of the Old North Church, and when Increase died, he assumed responsibility for the flock until his own death four years later.

Life did not get much easier for Mather after leaving Harvard. Each of his three marriages ended painfully; his first two wives died, and his third wife, who was mentally ill, left him. Nine of his 13 children died. Four of his children and one of his wives died from the measles within just a few days of each other. Moreover, according to Vernon Parrington, Mather was, at times, "intensely emotional, high-strung and nervous, . . . subject to ecstatic exaltations and . . . given to seeing visions."

Nevertheless, he was remarkably prolific and composed a number of important works.

In his 65 years of life, Mather wrote more than 400 sermons, historical treatises, and scientific works. He is often remembered for the two books he published on the Salem witchcraft crisis of the 1690s. *Memorable Providences, Relating to Witchcrafts and Possessions* (1689) and *The Wonders of the Invisible World* (1693) are based both on official documents and on his firsthand experience with individuals appearing to be bewitched or possessed. However, Mather's most significant work was *Magnalia Christi Americana; Or, the Ecclesiastical History of New England, from Its First Planting in the Year 1620, unto the Year of our Lord, 1698* (1702). The 800-page book is divided into seven sections that describe the settlement of New England; contain biographies of the colony's leading ministers and governors; provide a chronicle of Harvard College and the lives of its most notable graduates; comment upon church polity; document memorable divine providences in the colony; and address problems associated with heretical activity, Indians, and the devil.

Mather declared that his goals were to "write the *Wonders of the CHRISTIAN RELIGION, flying from the Depravations of Europe, to the American Strand*" and to use this "Report" of the "*Wonderful Displays*" of God's "Infinite Power" and "Wisdom" as a means of keeping "Alive . . . the Interests of Religion in our Churches." Mather's father once lamented that no document existed that would preserve the "memory of the great things the Lord hath done for us." The *Magnalia* ensured that the history of the early decades of the New England colonies would be "transmitted to posterity," and, as Silverman points out, "lifted New England history into the realm of heroic action."

Works by Cotton Mather

A Family Well-Ordered. Edited by Don Kistler. Morgan, Pa.: Soli Deo Gloria Ministries, 2001.
Selections from Cotton Mather. New York: Harcourt, Brace, 1926.

The Christian Philosopher. Edited by Winton U. Solberg. Champaign: University of Illinois Press, 2000.

Works about Cotton Mather

Boas, Ralph, and Louise Boas. *Cotton Mather, Keeper of the Puritan Conscience.* Whitefish, Mont.: Kessinger, 2003.
Lutz, Nora Jean. *Cotton Mather: Author, Clergyman and Scholar.* Minneapolis, Minn.: Sagebrush Education Resources, 2000.
Silverman, Kenneth. *The Life and Times of Cotton Mather.* New York: Harper and Row, 1984.

Mather, Increase (1639–1723) *theologian*

Increase Mather was born in Dorchester, Massachusetts, where his father, Richard, was a minister. Mather received his early education at home, at school in Boston, and at Harvard. After graduating in 1656, he traveled to Ireland, where his older brother was a minister, and earned a master's degree at Trinity College. Shortly after his return to New England in 1661, he accepted a ministerial appointment at Boston's Old North Church and wed Maria Cotton, daughter of John Cotton, a highly respected Puritan preacher. The first child born to the couple was Cotton MATHER, who became one of the most prominent thinkers of his age.

The stern theologian spent about 16 hours each day in his study. A colleague remarked that Mather "lov'd this *Study* to a kind of excess, and in a manner *liv'd* in it from his Youth to a great Old Age." The fruits of Mather's intellectual and spiritual diligence were many: He composed and published nearly 150 treatises, histories, and sermons. *An Essay for the Recording of Illustrious Providences* (1684), one of his most popular works, describes how signs of God's presence are revealed in natural phenomena, like thunderstorms, as well as in scripture. In *Cases of Conscience Concerning Evil Spirits* (1693), which Mather wrote in response to the witchcraft hysteria that seized New England in the early 1690s, he attempted to establish a legitimate and reliable means of discerning whether or not an individual was a witch. The titles of just a few of his many sermons—"Sleeping at Sermons, is a Great and Dangerous Evil" (1682), "Wo to Drunkards" (1673), "The Renewal of the Covenant the Great Duty" (1677), and "The Divine Right of Infant-Baptisme" (1680)—point to the range of practical, moral, and theological issues Mather concentrated on when preaching to his congregation. In *The Puritans: A Sourcebook of Their Writings,* Perry Miller notes that Mather was an "exponent of the plain style" and wrote in a "solid, logical, and learned" manner.

Works by Increase Mather

An Essay for the Recording of Illustrious Providences. Delmar, N.Y.: Scholars' Facsimiles and Reprints, 1977.
Relation of the Troubles Which Have Happened in New England by Reason of the Indians There. Whitefish, Mont.: Kessinger, 2003.
Remarkable Providences. Introduction by George Offor. Whitefish, Mont.: Kessinger, 2003.

Works about Increase Mather

Hall, Michael G. *The Last American Puritan: The Life of Increase Mather, 1639–1723.* Middletown, Conn.: Wesleyan University Press, 1990.
Murdock, Kenneth B. *Increase Mather, the Foremost American Puritan.* Temecula, Calif.: Reprint Services, 1991.

Maya epics and fables (n.d.–present)

The Maya are the largest and most homogenous group of indigenous peoples to populate the American continents north of Peru. The first Maya settlements date to 4000 B.C., and during the Classic Period, between 200 and 900 A.D., several million Maya lived in present-day Guatemala, Belize, the Yucatán Peninsula, and the western portions of Honduras and El Salvador. The Maya developed soaring architecture, a sophisticated system of writing and mathematics, and the most accurate calendar to predate the modern era. Following 900, Maya culture benefited from contact with the Toltec cultures, but in the late Post-Classic period, the years 1200–1500, famine, wars, and internal strife greatly weakened the empire. At the time of the arrival of Spanish explorers in 1519, only about 2 million Maya remained.

During the Spanish conquest, from 1519 to 1546, many valuable records of Maya civilization were lost or destroyed. What present-day cultures are able to learn about Maya culture comes from three major sources: three preconquest documents that escaped destruction; two postconquest documents, the *Book of the Jaguar Priest* (1593) and the POPOL VUH; and the lively tradition of oral literature that descendants of the Maya keep alive in the form of epics, fables, and folktales.

In Maya societies, anyone can tell a story. Words and sounds play a considerable role in the way people communicate. The Maya like to play with words, and they listen to the sound of the words as they would listen to the song of birds. The spoken word carries power in the Maya world, and performance dominates their oral literature. The FABLES, EPICS, and folktales the Maya share are frequently short, and rather than depending on a detailed description of events or their context, these narratives use gestures, repetition of words and phrases, and audience behavior to create effect. One might call a Maya story a drama rather than a poem or story.

There are various types of epics and fables in Maya culture. First and foremost, there are creation myths and historical narratives. These are divided between the "True Ancient Narrative," which refers to the creation of the Earth and humans, and the "True Recent Narrative," which refers to modern history as well as contemporary events. The story of the assistants who worked with the Germans, which relates how electricity arrived in Guatemala, is a good example of the latter. There is also an important tradition of joke-telling among the Maya, which is reflected in their oral literature. Some of the narratives are called "Lies" or "Frivolous Language" because they are deliberate fabrications, intended only for amusement and wordplay. The beginning of "The Destruction of the First People," narrated by Salvador López Sethol in *Telling Maya Tales,* a collection by Gary H. Gossen, shows this. Although it is a historical narrative, it is a good illustration of the frivolous language that marks the fables:

Monkeys were still people long ago.
The people became monkeys because they were evil.
And what were the deeds of these people long ago?
They used to eat their children long ago.
What size were their children when they ate them?
They were already nearly grown up when they ate them.

Spirituality and religion figure greatly in Maya society and therefore are important themes in the fables. Maya society was organized under a king, who was considered the mediator between the gods and the common people. All strata of society practiced rituals with religious significance, meant to ensure the favor of the gods in protecting crops and guarding against war and famine. Though the king was the chief authority, and was aided by priests who helped interpret the will of the gods and led important ceremonies, all members of Maya society were expected to play their parts in religious observance. Thus, a story of a farmer making an offering in his fields has no less importance than a ritual wherein the king offers a cup of his blood to please the gods.

A widespread adoption of the Christian faith caused a change in the spiritual beliefs and religious practice of the Maya and their descendants, but many of the fables preserve beliefs that predate Spanish or even Aztec influence. These tales burst with images drawn from the ancient world: sorcerers, animals transforming into gods, and rituals so old that their meaning has been forgotten.

Maya epics and fables depict an extremely rich world, where animals play key roles in the natural world and everything that exists has a meaning. The ancient Maya believed in a series of gods and goddesses who governed human existence, but they also believed in the power of animals. The beginning of a fable called "Story of the Owl," told by Ignacio Bizarro Ujpán and translated by James D. Sexton in *Heart of Heaven, Heart of Earth and Other Mayan Folktales,* explains the significance of the owl:

As a very old story goes, our old folks of earlier times and those of present times maintain the idea that one must be careful not to kill owls, because they are guardians and policemen of the world. They only follow orders of the *duenos del mundo* [guardians of the world]. That is why when one [an owl] comes into a homesite or alights and hoots above the house of a person, the person must not bother it, because if one bothers or hurts an owl, that person can easily die within a few days.

What is most fascinating about Maya epics and fables is their amazing ability to assimilate new and old influences into one original corpus of oral literature, where the cyclical time of an ancient culture meets modern concepts. Several of the older fables preserve much of their ancient nature, while also embracing the values and ideals of Christianity. In the same way, the Maya adopted the Aztec MYTH OF QUETZALCOATL, renaming him Kukulcán in their language.

The subjects and events of Maya fables frequently echo the fables and tales of other cultures, such as African and Native American. Tales of tricksters, like the coyote tales of native North American peoples, appear often in the Maya fables. On the whole, these fables, still passed among descendants of the Maya and enjoyed in translation by readers all over the world, preserve valuable information about the beliefs, practices, and values of a culture the knowledge of which might otherwise be utterly and entirely lost.

See also BOOK OF CHILAM BALAM OF CHUMAYEL; CHILAM BALAM, THE BOOKS OF; EPIC OF KOMAM Q'ANIL; MESOAMERICAN MYTHOLOGY.

English Versions of Maya Epics and Fables

Baldwin, Neil. *Legends of the Plumed Serpent.* New York: Public Affairs, 1998.

Gossen, Gary H. *Telling Maya Tales.* New York: Routledge, 1999.

Mayan Folktales: Folklore from Lake Atitlàn, Guatemala. Edited and translated by James D. Sexton. Albuquerque: University of New Mexico Press, 1999.

Sexton, James D., and Ignacio Bizarro Ujpàn. *Heart of Heaven, Heart of Earth and Other Mayan Folktales.* Washington, D.C.: Smithsonian Institution Press, 1999.

Tedlock, Dennis. *Popol Vuh: The Definitive Edition of the Maya Book of Dawn of Life and the Glories of Gods and Kings.* New York: Simon & Schuster, 1996.

Works about Maya Epics and Fables

Bennett, Evan. *The Maya Epic.* River Falls: University of Wisconsin River Falls Press, 1974.

Bierlein, J. F. *Parallel Myths.* New York: Ballantine Books, 1994.

Burns, Allan Franck. *An Epoch of Miracles: Oral Literature of the Yucatec Maya.* Austin: University of Texas Press, 1983.

Schuman, Michael A. *Mayan and Aztec Mythology.* Berkeley Heights, N.J.: Enslow Publishers, 2001.

Medici, Lorenzo de' (il Magnifico, The Magificent) (1449–1492) *political figure, poet*

During the 15th century, the city-states of Italy experienced a dramatic flourishing of culture, with new heights being reached in art, architecture, and literature. This time period is known as the RENAISSANCE, or "rebirth." The city-state of Florence stood at the center of this cultural flowering, and Florence itself reached its height under the rule of Lorenzo de' Medici.

De' Medici came from one of the richest and most powerful families in all of Europe. The Medici family controlled the Italian banking system, which gave them tremendous political and economic influence. This made the Medicis the virtual rulers of Florence for generations, although they held no formal title.

Lorenzo de' Medici and his brother Giuliano assumed the rule of Florence when their father died in 1469. After Giuliano's assassination in 1478, Lorenzo became the sole ruler, reigning until his death. During his rule, he proved to be both tyrannical as well as artistically inclined. He made Florence greatly prosperous and became a fabulous patron of the arts, supporting artists such as Sandro Botticelli, MICHELANGELO, and LEONARDO DA VINCI. His patronage helped make Florence the cultural center of Europe.

In addition to being a patron of the arts, de' Medici was himself a gifted poet. He wrote philosophical love poems, all of them in the Tuscan vernacular language, which focused on the enjoyment of life, the pleasures of nature, and love. De' Medici wrote a collection of poems titled *Comento de' miei sonetti (Comment on My Sonnets)* and cowrote with POLIZIANO the *Raccolta aragonese,* a collection of Tuscan verse written by numerous writers, including Dante and de' Medici himself.

When de' Medici was criticized for his use of the vernacular and his choice of subject matter (love), he defended his choices by stating that even the great writers Dante and BOCCACCIO wrote in the vernacular. His poetry is a reflection of both the political power of the Medicis in Florence and the true Renaissance spirit of the time.

English Versions of Works by Lorenzo de' Medici

Lorenzo de' Medici: Selected Poems and Prose. University Park: Pennsylvania State University Press, 1992.

Political Philosophy of the Great de' Medici as Revealed by Their Correspondence. Edited by Cosimo Giovanni. Albuquerque, N.M.: Institute for Economic and Political World Strategic Studies, 1985.

Works about Lorenzo de' Medici

Greenblatt, Miriam. *Lorenzo de' Medici and Renaissance Italy.* Tarrytown, N.Y.: Marshall Cavendish, 2002.

Hook, Judith. *Lorenzo de' Medici: A Historical Biography.* London: Hamish Hamilton, 1984.

Kent, F. W. *Lorenzo de' Medici and the Art of Magnificence.* Baltimore, Md.: Johns Hopkins University Press, 2004.

Melanchthon, Philipp (1497–1540)
theologian

The man to be known as Melanchthon was born in Bretten, Germany, to an armor maker named Georg Schwartzerd, whose name meant "black earth." Philipp's tutor, Reichlin, called him by the Greek equivalent, Melanchthon, which the young man adopted. A prodigious student, he earned his B.A. from the University of Heidelberg in 1511 and his M.A. from the University of Tübingen in 1514. Martin LUTHER posted his famous theses at the University of Wittenberg in 1517; Melanchthon began teaching there in 1518. Students crowded the auditoriums to hear his commentaries on Scripture and then published his lecture notes to share with others. He earned the distinguished title of Preceptor (teacher) of Germany and was often asked by other schools to advise them on curricula. In 1520 he married Katherine Krapp, the mayor's daughter, with whom he had four children. He stayed at Wittenberg throughout his career and died of a fever early in 1540.

The practice of commentary had begun with the Greeks, with short glosses on the texts of Homer. This practice continued throughout the Middle Ages and by Melanchthon's time had become a rhetorical art. Though his *Annotations on Corinthians* (1522) are simply collected notes on the Scripture, the commentaries on Romans (1532) and Daniel (1543) show the power of his focused thought as well as his commitment to the ideals of the Reformation. Melanchthon believed wholeheartedly in the Lutheran doctrine of justification by faith, which maintained that faith alone led to salvation without the need for the rituals demanded by the Catholic Church. Melanchthon's contributions to the Lutheran Church proved to be enormous. He wrote its confession text, the Augsburg Confession, and collected its major points of dogma in the *Loci Communes* (1522). As Luther's successor, he represented the new faith at the councils of Leipzig and Worms. He continually came into conflict with radicals who proposed reform through strong action. Melanchthon, like Luther, advocated reform through moderation and the ideals of humanism as taught by ERASMUS. Melanchthon's ultimate message is a call to "love the simple truth . . . and guard it."

English Versions of Works by Philipp Melanchthon

Annotations on the First Epistle to the Corinthians. Translated and edited by John Patrick Donnelly. Milwaukee, Wis.: Marquette University Press, 1995.

Commentary on Romans by Philipp Melanchthon. Translated by Fred Kramer. St. Louis: Concordia Publishing House, 1992.

Works about Philipp Melanchthon

Maag, Karin. *Melanchthon in Europe.* Grand Rapids, Mich.: Baker Books, 1999.

Stump, Joseph. *The Life of Melanchthon.* Murrieta, Calif.: New Library Press, 2003.

Mesoamerican mythology (n.d.–present)

The term *Mesoamerican* is used to refer to the civilizations existing in Central America and Mexico at the time of the arrival of the Spanish at the beginning of the 16th century. Justification for its use rests on the fact that these peoples, despite geographical, linguistic, and ethnic differences, shared similar cultural and religious systems. These systems have four common themes: representations of the cosmos; beings of power; transformation in time; and sacrifice.

Mesoamerican cosmos were divided into layers that could vary from four to as many as 14, such as the heavens, the earth, the waters, and the underworld. In each of these worlds resided beings, whether animals, humans, or deities, who embodied powers that caused them to exist. However, both the beings and the space that they inhabited were subject to constant change. Thus the idea of transience, or the impermanent nature of life, is repeatedly expressed in the works of poets like NEZA-HUALCOYOTL:

> May your heart find its way:
> here no one will live forever.

The POPOL VUH, a narrative of the Maya, tells of a succession of five ages in which the gods attempt to perfect their creation through various transformations. These civilizations also produced elaborate calendars to commemorate these events.

Lastly, sacrificial rites were an important aspect of Mesoamerican religious life. Accounts tell of dramatic acts of human sacrifice, though these were actually rare. More common were acts of bloodletting on special occasions, such as the naming of children and state ceremonies. The more routine forms of sacrifice were of harvests and animals. Such rituals were intended to bring about renewal and were seen as a continuation of life.

In the eyes of the invading Spanish, such beliefs seemed misguided. Unwilling to tolerate a worldview different from their own, they imposed Catholicism on the natives. Despite the ensuing decline of native religions, some aspects have merged with and become indistinct from Catholic beliefs. This process is called syncretism. For example, stories of floods exist in both traditions.

Although it is tempting to view Mesoamerican religions as pagan mythologies, they were in fact sophisticated institutions that played an important role in regulating the daily lives and nurturing the morals of Mesoamerican peoples. The myths of these ancient peoples continue to be told and retold through the oral tradition, as well as through printed texts. They reflect not only old world values and customs, but also contemporary concerns, such as those relating to the destruction of the environment.

Works of Mesoamerican Mythology

Bierhorst, John. *Mythology of Mexico and Central America.* Oxford: Oxford University Press, 2002.
Spence, Lewis. *Myths of Mexico and Peru.* Whitefish, Mont.: Kessinger, 2003.

Works about Mesoamerican Mythology

Read, Kay Almere, and Jason J. Gonzalez. *Handbook of Mesoamerican Mythology.* Oxford: Oxford University Press, 2002.
Wilcox, Joan Parisi. *Masters of the Living Energy: The Mystical World of the Q'ero of Peru.* Rochester, Vt.: Inner Traditions International, 2004.
Yamase, Shinji. *History and Legend of the Colonial Maya of Guatemala.* Lewiston, N.Y.: Edwin Mellen Press, 2003.

Metastasio, Pietro (1698–1782) *poet, librettist*

Pietro Armando Dominico Trapassi was born into a butcher's family in Rome and at a young age began working as a goldsmith's apprentice. At age 10, his skill at improvising verse brought him to the attention of Vincenzo Gravina, a jurist and a man of letters. Gravina took the boy into his household, provided him with a solid education, and left him a considerable inheritance, which made the young man financially independent. Gravina also convinced Pietro to take the Greek translation of his name, Metastasio. Metastasio's early writing earned him admittance into the prestigious Academy of Arcadia in 1718.

In 1719 he moved to Naples, began practicing law, and gained access to aristocratic circles with his occasional verse. After producing several notable melodramas, he traveled to Vienna in 1730 to become poet laureate to the Austrian Empire under the patronage of Charles VI. After Maria Theresa took the throne in 1740, Metastasio kept his place and continued to write librettos, verse, and literary criticism until his death.

Metastasio wrote his first drama at age 14. *Justin,* a tragedy in the style of Seneca, was considered remarkable for its considerable quality and its highly musical verse. Metastasio published a book of verse in 1717, but his true genius lay in the *melodramma,* or romantic TRAGEDY. His first serenade, composed in 1721 to honor the birthday of the empress of Austria, was performed by the celebrated prima donna La Romanina. At her request, he gave up his law practice and turned full-time to writing opera librettos.

An extremely prolific author, Metastasio composed about 1,800 pieces, including 28 operas, more than 70 melodramas, a number of ballets, and *canzonette,* which were celebrations of festivals combining dialogue, poetry recital, music, and drama. His first lyric tragedy, *Dido Forsaken,* was performed in 1724 and followed by several others: *Siroe, Catone in Utica, Semiramis, Alexander in the Indies,* and *Artaserse. Attilio Regolo* (1750) is considered Metastasio's masterpiece. It tells the heroic story of how Attilio, sent in chains from Carthage to Rome, triumphs over his enemies in a stirring display of nobility and justice.

Metastasio's other writings include his *Letters* and a work of criticism, a response to the *Poetics* of Aristotle (1782), in which he outlined his own theories of dramatic composition. Metastasio's lyric poetry was ever popular for its rich handling of the musical repertoire of the Italian language and its universal themes: the torments of love, freedom, and infidelity. In his "Introduction to Volate," set to music by Nicola Vacca, Metastasio compares faithfulness to a white snow cover: It is destroyed by a single footprint left on it. While these themes are not particularly new, Metastasio employs them with noticeable diversity. He borrows from a rich variety of sources, spanning the mythology and history of the ancient world.

Most likely, Metastasio's success with the public rested on his careful avoidance of unhappy endings and his lively, witty dialogues, which were often interrupted by appealing musical moments. He was considered a model poet, and his work, published in several editions even during his own lifetime, was widely translated into other European languages.

One of the most influential librettists of his period, Metastasio was the first to draw a sharp dividing line between serious and comic opera. His librettos were set to music by many composers, including Gluck, Handel, Mozart, Pergolesi, and Rossini, making him the most popular librettist of his century and earning him fame as the father of serious opera.

English Versions of Works by Pietro Metastasio

Temistocle: Opera Seria in Three Acts. Edited by Ernest Warburton. New York: Garland Publishers, 1988.

Three Melodramas. Translated by Joseph G. Fucilla. Lexington: University Press of Kentucky, 1981.

Works about Pietro Metastasio

Burney, Charles. *Memoirs of the Life and Writings of the Abate Metastasio.* Cambridge, Mass.: Da Capo Press, 1971.

Stendhal, Maurice. *Lives of Haydn, Mozart and Metastasio.* Translated by Richard N. Coe. New York: Grossman Publishers, 1972.

Talbot, George, ed. *Lord Charlemont's History of Italian Poetry from Dante to Metastasio.* New York: Edwin Mellen Press, 2000.

Michelangelo Buonarroti (1475–1564)
artist, poet

During the 15th and 16th centuries, Europe experienced an incredible revival of its intellectual and artistic culture. This time period became known as the RENAISSANCE and marked the end of the Middle Ages. The Renaissance was most pronounced in Italy, and one of the greatest figures of the period was Michelangelo, whose achievements would make him one of the most legendary artists in human history.

Michelangelo was born near Florence, Italy. Throughout his life, which lasted nearly 90 years, Italy was never a unified nation-state but instead a collection of small kingdoms and city-states that were almost always in conflict with one another. Europe in general and Italy in particular experienced immense political, social, and religious convulsions as various powers and interests fought for supremacy. Michelangelo lived through the discovery of the New World, the Protestant Reformation, the Turkish invasion of Europe, and a multitude of other life-altering events.

Michelangelo came from a somewhat distinguished family that had fallen on hard times. In his youth, he received a good education, and his fascination with art and sculpture dated from his early years. When he was 13, in the face of his father's stern disapproval, Michelangelo decided to pursue an artistic career, studying both painting and sculpture.

By a stroke of luck, he soon found himself a member of the household of Lorenzo de' MEDICI. The Medici family was extremely powerful throughout Renaissance Italy and effectively controlled the political and economic institutions of Florence. During his years in the Medici household, Michelangelo intensively studied art, gradually becoming a master of both painting and sculpture. He also learned the philosophy of Neoplatonism and developed a profound love of literature during this period, inspired by those writers who visited the Medici.

The 1490s were a time of political turmoil in Florence, with various rival powers gaining and losing control of the city as the years passed. To escape the chaos, Michelangelo left Florence for Rome.

Beginning with his time in the Medici home and lasting throughout his life, Michelangelo spent time with many learned and powerful men, some of whom were his patrons. Arising from these contacts were two of Michelangelo's ambitions—his desire to be accepted and his desire not only to surpass Greek and Roman classical sculptors, whose works he studied, but also to ever improve his own skill.

In Rome, Michelangelo began producing a number of outstanding sculptures. Few had pagan themes, for he was a devout Christian and most of the subjects of his painting and sculpture were taken from the Bible. In 1500 he completed his first great masterpiece, a sculpture known as the *Pieta,* which depicts a grieving Virgin Mary holding the body of Christ. It is one of the most famous sculptures in the world.

Following the restoration of political stability in Florence, Michelangelo returned there in 1501. In 1504 his greatest work of all was unveiled, *David,* an enormous statue of the biblical king. During this time, as a result of some sort of misunderstanding, he engaged in a bitter feud with LEONARDO DA VINCI. Michelangelo always had a terrible temper and bore grudges for a very long time.

In addition to his sculpture, Michelangelo was continuing to develop as a painter. In 1508 the pope called him to Rome, asking that he paint the ceiling of the Sistine Chapel. Although reluctant to do so, Michelangelo eventually agreed and spent the next few years working on the monumental project, often spending days in the rafters without food or water. When the project was completed, it was universally hailed as a masterpiece.

Taken together, the *Pietà,* the *David,* and the ceiling of the Sistine Chapel are usually regarded as the greatest of Michelangelo's artistic achievements. But the artist still had many years to live, and although the rest of his life was often filled with disappointment and even despair, he continued to create great works of art.

Michelangelo moved back and forth between Rome and Venice for many years. In the 1540s, still productive and skillful despite his advancing age, he turned to architecture when the pope commissioned him to construct St. Peter's Basilica. The plans had already been drawn up by the architect Donato Bramante, but it fell to Michelangelo to complete the work.

In addition to being a masterly sculptor and painter, Michelangelo was also a writer of much skill. He left behind a series of letters and diary entries that illuminate the complicated and often tormented nature of his personality. He was homosexual and never married or had children.

Much of his personal writing is taken up with his inner struggles, but he expresses his feelings most forcefully in his poetry.

Michelangelo's long life came to an end on February 18 in Rome, and he was buried in Florence. During the course of his life, he had witnessed astonishing changes in the world around him and had created some of the greatest works of art the world has ever known.

Critical Analysis

Michelangelo is known to history because of his extraordinary achievements in sculpture and painting, and it is said that he preferred the physical labor involved with both. However, he wrote numerous works, including letters, diary entries, and poems. While his letters and diary entries are often overlooked, they reflect his complicated and contradictory personality, as well as his view of the world, which was shaped by the time in which he lived.

His literary abilities are most marked in his poetry, which he wrote throughout his long life. Many of his poems are addressed to both men and women, while his mystical religious poems are addressed to no one in particular. Dealing with deep emotional issues, his poetry is not so subtle as that of many other poets, which perhaps is a reflection of his artistic inclinations.

At times, Michelangelo wrote of his sculpting, giving form to the thoughts and emotions he experienced while performing his master talent. In "On the Painting of the Sistine Chapel," for example, he describes the physical demands of painting on a ceiling:

> In front my skin grows loose and long; behind,
> By bending it becomes more taut and strait;
> Crosswise I strain me like a Syrian bow. . . .
> (trans. by W. S. Merwin)

At other times, he speaks of love—either for sculpting stone or for God. He combines both passions in "'Night' in the Medici Chapel":

> Sleep's very dear to me, but being stone's
> Far more, so long as evil persevere.
> It's my good fortune not to see nor hear:
> Do not wake me; speak in the softest tones.
> (trans. by William Jay Smith)

Some of his best poetry was addressed to a woman named Vittoria Colonna, who was a cultured woman, poet, and Michelangelo's closest friend. The two of them engaged in an enduring exchange of letters and poems, celebrating their friendship and respect for each other, combining their mutual interests of Platonic philosophy and devout Catholicism. Their relationship was apparently entirely platonic in nature.

Michelangelo also wrote numerous SONNETS and other poems to various men that subtly reflect his underlying homosexuality. His style seems to have been influenced by PETRARCH and POLIZIANO.

Although Michelangelo will forever be known for his sculpture and paintings, his poetry is also an expression of his brilliant mind. The influence of his creative talents continues to change the perceptions of what art and artists are supposed to be.

English Versions of Works by Michelangelo Buonarroti

The Complete Poems and Selected Letters of Michelangelo. Translated by Creighton E. Gilbert and edited by Robert N. Linscott. Princeton, N.J.: Princeton University Press, 1990.

The Drawings of Michelangelo. Introduction by Irving Stone. Master Draughtsman Series. Los Angeles: Borden Publishing, 1999.

The Poetry of Michelangelo: An Annotated Translation. Translated by James M. Saslow. New Haven, Conn.: Yale University Press, 1993.

Works about Michelangelo Buonarroti

Bull, George. *Michelangelo: A Biography.* New York: St. Martin's Griffin, 1995.

Cagno, Gabriella di, et al. *Michelangelo.* New York: McGraw-Hill, 2000.

Symonds, John A. *Life of Michelangelo Buonarroti.* Philadelphia: University of Pennsylvania Press, 2001.

Milton, John (1608–1674) *poet, essayist, dramatist*

John Milton was born in London and educated at Christ Church College, Oxford. In the years following college graduation, he wrote several enduring poetic works, including *Comus* (1634), a masque or verse play, with musical interludes; *Lycidas* (1637), an elegy for a drowned classmate; and *L'Allegro* and *Il Penseroso* (ca. 1632), a contrasting pair of poems celebrating, respectively, convivial pleasures and the solitary, contemplative life.

A journey to France and Italy, begun in 1638, was cut short by the political situation in England. King Charles I's long-brewing conflict with Parliament was about to explode in the English Civil War, which would culminate in Charles's execution (1649) and a period of non-monarchical government called the Commonwealth, in which Milton became an important official.

Milton devoted much of his early career to writing polemical tracts. Among the more famous is *The Doctrine and Discipline of Divorce* (1642), in which he argues that the grounds for divorce should include spiritual incompatibility. The essay was probably inspired by his estrangement from his wife, Mary Powell, who returned to her parents shortly after her marriage to Milton. Mary later reunited with her husband and bore him three daughters before her death, at age 27, in 1652. Milton married twice more. His second wife died in childbirth in 1658, which led Milton, in his sorrow, to write the moving SONNET that begins, "Methought I saw my late espoused saint. . . ."

The title of the *Areopagitica* (1644) refers to a tract of the same name by Isocrates. The essay was a response to an act of Parliament that instituted prepublication censorship. Milton argues that truth can emerge through only debate:

Let her and Falsehood grapple; who ever knew Truth put to the worse in a free and open encounter?

Although it had little impact in its day, the *Areopagitica* influenced the arguments of many later proponents of freedom of the press, including the framers of the U.S. Bill of Rights.

One of Milton's most famous sonnets, "On His Blindness," was composed during this period. By 1652, Milton's eyesight, which had been failing for many years, was gone. After this, Milton wrote through dictation.

Milton's greatest works, published during the late 1660s and early 1670s, are the epic poem *Paradise Lost* (1667), which tells the story of the fall of Adam and Eve; its sequel, *Paradise Regained* (1671), which deals with the redemption of humanity through Christ; and the drama *Samson Agonistes* (1671), which portrays the revenge of the blind biblical hero Samson.

Many consider *Paradise Lost* one of the greatest poetic works in English and world literature, sublime in both subject and style. Milton summarizes the poem in his opening invocation to the muse, in which he urges her to sing:

> *Of Mans First Disobedience, and the Fruit*
> *Of that Forbidden Tree, whose mortal tast*
> *Brought Death into the World, and all our*
> *   woe. . . .*

He concludes the first section with a plea to the muse to help him "justifie the wayes of God to men."

The action opens in Hell, as Satan and his followers recover from defeat after their rebellion against God. Satan vows to continue his revenge on Earth and to tempt Adam and Eve to evil. Despite warnings by Raphael, Eve succumbs to Satan's praise of her beauty and the seeming reasonableness of his arguments. She then tries to convince Adam to do as she has done and taste the forbidden fruit. Despite his understanding of the consequences, Adam eats the fruit because he cannot bear to have eternal life while Eve is condemned to die. The central dilemma of faith at the heart of Milton's epic is that human reason is flawed, for God's truth cannot be arrived at by reason.

Many scholars and critics who have read *Paradise Lost* have been seduced by Satan fully as much as Eve was. The Romantics, in particular, found Satan to be magnificent in his defiance and admirable in his rebellion. In the 20th century, Milton's Eve has inspired almost as much controversy as his Satan. Although modern readers may be somewhat put off by many of Milton's attitudes toward women, which are indicative of his time, no one with a taste for poetry can ignore the sheer beauty of his verse.

Works by John Milton

Areopagitica and Other Prose Works. Whitefish, Mont.: Kessinger, 2004.
The Poetical Works of John Milton. IndyPublish.com, 2003.
The Riverside Milton. Edited by Roy Flannagan. New York: Houghton Mifflin, 1998.

Works about John Milton

Fish, Stanley Eugene. *How Milton Works.* Cambridge, Mass.: Harvard University Press, 2001.
Lewalski, Barbara. *The Life of John Milton: A Critical Biography.* Oxford: Blackwell, 2002.

Molière (Jean-Baptiste Poquelin)
(1622–1673) *playwright, actor*

Molière was born the oldest of six children at the so-called Monkey House, a large, centuries-old dwelling in an elegant quarter of Paris near the Louvre, to Jean Poquelin the younger, King Louis XIII's *tapissier* (master merchant upholsterer/furnisher), and Marie Cressé, the daughter of a prosperous colleague in the trade who also carried the title of *bourgeois de Paris,* an honor bestowed on those Parisians who attained a certain level of affluence and social refinement. Molière lost his mother at age 10, his stepmother Catherine Fleurette at age 14, and both his maternal grandparents at age 16.

As an adolescent, he attended the Collège de Clermont located in the Latin Quarter near the Seine River. This large, competitive Jesuit school attended by the elite was the trendiest secondary school in Paris at the time, offering a rigorous classical humanities curriculum including Latin and Greek, rhetoric, acting, debate, philosophy, science, and theology. Evidence suggests he later studied law, possibly at Orléans, and perhaps philosophy as well.

On December 14, 1637, Molière inherited his father's title and office of *tapissier du roi* and spent at least one summer on the royal military campaign trail by the Mediterranean shores. He was in charge of arranging one of two tents that served as royal field palaces and contained identical sets of King Louis's furnishings. But the lure of the stage, stimulated by his grandfather Cressé's passion for the theater, the many plays staged at the Collège de Clermont, and the numerous street performances he undoubtedly witnessed in his native Paris neighborhood, proved too intense for the young Jean-Baptiste to ignore. In 1643 he ceded his royal office to his brother Jean, equally shedding the status of a potential law career, and formed the Illustre Théâtre troupe with his mistress, Madeleine Béjart, a beautiful and talented actress four years his elder. The troupe's beginnings, however, were fraught with difficulty. Catering to the tastes of the time, the actors performed traditional tragedies featuring male heroes, with Madeleine as their star actress. They produced their plays inside a leased indoor tennis court, yet they failed to attract a sufficiently large audience. Soon they could not make ends meet. Molière was arrested and jailed until a friend posted bail, and after only two years the Illustre Théâtre was doomed.

For the next 13 years, Molière and Madeleine lived the lives of itinerant artists, mostly in the southern provinces where they obtained the patronage of the prince de Conti, under whom Molière embarked on his career as a playwright. In 1658 the actors returned to Paris to perform at court under the protection of Monsieur, King Louis XIV's brother. Molière's first successful play, *Les Précieuses ridicules (The Folly of Affection),* which ran for 34 almost-sold-out consecutive performances, testified to the author's extraordinary talent and ingenuity for comedy. King Louis XIV was enthralled by the play, and henceforth Molière was destined to become, as Judd Hubert remarks in his *Molière and the Comedy of Intellect,* "by far the greatest creator of dramatic forms in the entire history of French literature, comparable in this respect to Shakespeare."

Molière worked incessantly, completing 19 plays in quick succession, most of them commissioned, during a decade that witnessed a series of magnificent masterpieces such as *The Misanthrope, Dom Juan, Tartuffe, The School for Wives, The Would-be Gentleman,* and *The Miser.* Besides his busy role as author, he functioned as manager and accountant of his troupe, as well as producer, director, and main actor of its plays. The band performed theater in Paris but also provided often elaborate entertainments—such as the renowned *Pleasures of the Enchanted Isle*—featuring sophisticated set design, music, dance, fireworks, reflecting pools, fountain shows, and dramatic amusement. All of this entertainment was provided at the king's behest during special festivals at various châteaux when the court resided outside the capital.

When he was 40, Molière married Armande Béjart, 20 years his junior and daughter of his former mistress, Madeleine, and, some unconventional historians intimate, perhaps his very own. In his writing, he turned completely to comedy, and the public, both noblemen and bourgeois, regularly thronged the Palais-Royal Theater to see his plays. However, the plays' increasingly satirical vein and strong social criticism, which often clashed with traditional morality as well as religious and social norms, made Molière some enemies. In *Molière, A Theatrical Life,* Virginia Scott states, "Molière

argues that since the duty of comedy is to correct men while diverting them, he had thought it appropriate to render this service to the honorable people of the kingdom." He mocked the high aristocracy, the nouveaux-riches, physicians, pedants, cuckolds, *précieuses* (women espousing a style of excessive refinement), and, of course, religious hypocrites. The notable *Tartuffe* controversy pitting the author against ecclesiastical authority raged for five years until Louis XIV finally allowed a modified version of the play to be staged. Later, Molière's falling-out with composer Lully, with whom he had a very successful partnership for the production of *comédie-ballets,* caused him the loss of his rights to several of his works. But Molière also had influential courtly and literary allies at Versailles, such as LA FONTAINE, RACINE, and BOILEAU, not to mention the Sun King himself.

On February 17, 1673, an ill and weak Molière acted the role of the Hypochondriac in the fourth performance of the play by the same name. Aware of his feebleness, his wife begged him not to perform that day but he refused to let down all the theater workers who depended on him for their livelihood. He managed to get through nearly all his lines until he was seized with a convulsion, which he attempted to cover up with laughter. He died an hour later while awaiting the arrival of a priest; because he had not renounced his life as an actor, Armande had to appeal to the king to be allowed to bury her husband in consecrated ground, albeit in a nighttime ceremony. The very chair in which Molière acted during his last performance remains on display to this day at the Comédie-Française.

In his *Life of Monsieur de Molière,* Mikhail Bulgakov tells of his colleague Zotov recounting a scene that may well have taken place between Molière's friend, the prince de Condé, and King Louis XIV:

"The king is coming. He wishes to see Molière. Molière! What's happened to him?" the prince asks.

"He died," someone tells him.

The prince, running to Louis, exclaims, "Sire, Molière is dead!"

Louis removes his hat and states with confidence: "Molière is deathless!"

Seven years after his death, Molière's troupe merged with two other Parisian companies, giving birth to the illustrious Comédie-Française, to this day the premier stage in all of France and the rightful "House of Molière."

Critical Analysis

Virginia Scott recounts Molière biographer Grimarest's recording of the following exchange between Louis XIV and Molière at a court dinner: "Look, isn't that your doctor? What does he do for you?" "Sire," answered Molière, "we reason together; he orders remedies for me; I don't take them, and I get well." Discouraged by his declining health and the inability of the medical profession to cure him, Molière satirizes its inefficient and dogmatic procedures in his last *comédie-ballet* entitled *Le Malade imaginaire (The Hypochondriac; The Imaginary Invalid)*. Ever the sharp observer of society, Molière once again chose a major character flaw as his comedy's subject. Its star is Argan, played by Molière himself, who lives among his potions and drugs, and surrounds himself with a bevy of doctors and apothecaries. They rule his world, often confusing medicine with religion, as they require strict adherence to a barrage of ritual bleedings, purges, and prescriptions. When Argan misses one of his treatments, the irate doctor Purgon chastises him and condemns him to a litany of ailments and even death: "dysentery, dropsy, and deprivation of life." Against the wishes of his distraught daughter, Argan vows to provide himself with a physician son-in-law to have at his beck and call.

In step with a recurrent leitmotiv in Moliere's plays, here, too, the servant provides the voice of reason amidst the madness. Keenly aware that pretense can be cured only by make-believe, chambermaid Toinette enters her master's realm of fakery by impersonating an illustrious physician in this famous exchange from Act III, Scene 10:

TOINETTE: What on earth are you doing with this arm?
ARGAN: What?
TOINETTE: There is an arm I would cut off straight away if I were you.
ARGAN: But why?
TOINETTE: Don't you see that it is taking all of the nutrients, and that it is keeping the other side from benefiting?

The play ends in a frenzied grand finale where the hypochondriac is consecrated as a doctor during a farcical music and dance ceremony conducted in hilarious macaronic Latin. Here comedy and entertainment reign supreme, and while it is perhaps the greatest comedic irony and paradox that Molière died in the very role of an imaginary invalid—during which he actually impersonated a corpse—this very fact underscores more than anything, in Hallam Walker's words, that "his final physical efforts, like his whole existence, had been dedicated to the service of his art."

English Versions of Works by Molière

Doctor in Spite of Himself. Translated by S. H. Landes and edited by William-Alan Landes. Studio City, Calif.: Players Press, 2003.

Misanthrope. Translated by Charles H. Wall. Studio City, Calif.: Players Press, 2003.

Tartuffe. Translated by Ranjit Bolf. New York: Theatre Communications Group, 2003.

The Blunderer. Holicong, Pa.: Wildside Press, 2003.

The Imaginary Invalid (Le Malade Imaginaire). IndyPublish.com 2004.

Works about Molière

Koppisch, Michael S. *Rivalry and the Disruption of Order in Molière's Theater*. Madison, N.J.: Fairleigh Dickinson University Press, 2004.

Polsky, Zachary. *The Comic Machine, the Narrative Machine, and the Political Machine in the Works of Molière*. Lewiston, N.Y.: Edwin Mellen Press, 2003.

Scott, Virginia. *Molière, A Theatrical Life*. Cambridge: Cambridge University Press, 2000.

Walker, Hallam. *Molière*. Boston: Twayne, 1990.

Weiskel, Portia Williams, and Harold Bloom. *Molière.* Langhorne, Pa.: Chelsea House, 2003.

Montaigne, Michel de (1533–1592)
moralist, essayist

Celebrated for more than 400 years as the father of the essay form, Michel Eyquem de Montaigne was born on February 28 to an influential family in Bordeaux. The family was named to the nobility when Montaigne's great-grandfather Raymon Eyquem acquired the land and house of Montaigne in 1477, located about 30 miles from Bordeaux.

Montaigne was born to a Catholic father and a Protestant mother at a time when Catholic-Protestant tensions were mounting in many parts of Europe. The marriage between Pierre Eyquem de Montaigne and Antoinette de Louppes withstood religious friction, although family relations were not always harmonious. Catholic Montaigne spoke little about his mother, and Antoinette expressed marked bitterness toward her children and marriage after her husband's death.

Montaigne's education was thorough, marked by the singularity that he was trained to speak and write Latin by his tutors, family, and others as if it were the everyday language of the region. This is not to say, however, that Montaigne was not instructed in other languages or that he was not encouraged to learn French. His lower-class godparents taught him French and, at the same time, humility.

Montaigne was sent at age six to the Collège de Guyenne, where he acquired over a period of seven years a distaste for the structured educational system and its methods of discipline. From there, he continued his education, but exactly where and for what duration scholars are uncertain.

In the mid-1550s, Montaigne received a counselorship when his father, who had purchased a seat in the Cour des Aides of Périgueux, resigned the position. When the court was incorporated into the parliament of Bordeaux in 1557, Montaigne and fellow Pirigordians were met with political hostility. He persevered for 13 years in various positions before resigning, finding his work largely unmeaningful and unrewarding. Nonetheless, one of the greatest events of Montaigne's life occurred while he was in Bordeaux: He met Étienne de La Boétie, who became his most cherished friend and confidant.

For two years, Montaigne sought more rewarding employment in Paris, to no avail, and in 1565 he married Françoise de la Chassaigne, with whom he had six girls, only one of whom survived childhood. His relationship with his wife, which continued until his death, never matched his great friendship with La Boétie, which reveals, in part, Montaigne's tepid attitude toward marriage. Shortly after his marriage to Françoise, his father died in 1568, and Montaigne inherited the title and estate. He persisted in seeking service in Paris that he judged to be of merit, but he returned home at age 38. The adjustment to such living was not an easy one. During this period, Montaigne began to contemplate the composition of *Essays,* although it would take him several years to realize his project fully.

Critical Analysis

The death of Montaigne's dearest friend in 1563 served as a catalyst for his most well-known and superior achievement, the *Essays.* The first edition, including books one and two only, was printed on March 1, 1580, in Bordeaux. Two subsequent editions were printed thereafter, with the third edition of 1588, including books one, two, and three, published in Paris. This third edition is known as the "Bordeaux Copy."

The title of Montaigne's *Essays* derives from the Latin *exagium,* meaning "a weighing." In this sense, then, essays are explorations wherein attitudes toward a particular subject are weighed, measured, and considered. Each of the three books of *Essays* contains many essays, what Montaigne calls "chapters." Book one is composed of 57 chapters; book two has 37; and book three has 13. Although these chapters appear to be haphazardly arranged and attempts to understand the essays according to an overall philosophical pattern invariably fall short, their arrangement suggests some development. Pierre Villey, for example, argues that the work moves from the stoic to the skeptical to the natural, and Marcel Tetel observes that "[a]s the essays progress . . . , Montaigne exhibits more and more intimate details about himself," such as "[t]he wines and dishes he likes or does not like." Donald Frame's remark that "Montaigne resists simple definitions" is most compelling.

Montaigne began writing essays with the intent to keep a record of his past and present experiences as well as his thoughts and observations, but the *Essays* function additionally as mirrors to the human condition, reflecting its follies, foibles, hardships, habits, pleasures, and relationships. The chapters are rich in variation both within themselves and in juxtaposition and comparison to one another. Together, they form a mosaic that offers readers vehicles for exploring the self. As readers engage Montaigne's revolving habit-of-mind, they find themselves delving into their own minds as well.

Several essays begin with "Of" followed by some state of being, such as "Of Idleness," "Of Constancy," "Of Drunkenness," "Of Anger," "Of Conscience," and "Of Repentance." Other chapter titles take the form of a proverb, such as "That the Taste of Good and Evil Depends in Large Part on the Opinion We Have of Them," "Fortune is Often Met in the Path of Reason," and "That Our Desire Is Increased by Difficulty." These titles reflect the then-popular pastime of recording aphoristic statements in small books and memorizing and reciting such sayings and pithy statements to others as if the words spring instantly to mind.

In "Of the Inconsistency of Our Actions," Montaigne comments on the contradiction of human actions, stating, "irresolution seems to me the most common and apparent defect of our nature." He goes on to say: "In all antiquity it is hard to pick out a dozen men who set their lives to a certain and constant course, which is the principal goal of wisdom." Throughout the essay, Montaigne quotes such ancient philosophers and writers as Horace, Lucretius, Homer, and Tibullus; yet, in the end, he shows a somewhat humorous bent:

[A] sound intellect will refuse to judge men simply by their outward actions; we must probe the inside and discover what springs set men in motion. But since this is an arduous and hazardous undertaking, I wish fewer people would meddle with it.

In another essay on the theme of human inconstancy titled "Apology for Raymond Sebond," Montaigne states that "Presumption is our natural and original malady. The most vulnerable and frail of all creatures is man, and at the same time the most arrogant."

Then, in the essay, "Of Repentance," Montaigne states what perhaps can be considered his purpose for writing—to simply tell others what is on his mind:

Let me here excuse what I often say, that I rarely repent and that my conscience is content with itself—not as the conscience of an angel or a horse, but as the conscience of a man; always adding this refrain, not perfunctorily but in sincere and complete submission: that I speak as an ignorant inquirer, referring the decision purely and simply to the common and authorized beliefs. I do not teach, I tell.

Often an essay's content does not initially appear to relate to the piece's respective title. Such is the case with "Of Cannibals," which opens with an account of Roman history, then moves to discuss a person who had dwelled in Brazil, or "Antartic France" as the area was known during Montaigne's time. From there, Montaigne discusses an act of cannibalism and then behavior he deems barbarous, observing "[t]he most valiant are sometimes the most unfortunate."

Montaigne's meandering, detached, and ironical style, while awkward to most present-day readers unfamiliar with the *Essays,* was not unique to this work. His essays reflect a keen, discerning eye and a thorough understanding of history, literature, and philosophy. His displays of knowledge border on the encyclopedic, which discourages readers who regard copious examples and quotations as impediments to understanding the essay's points. But these examples are essential to grasping the context of the *Essays* and function as important keys to understanding their messages.

Montaigne influenced such writers as DIDEROT and ROUSSEAU. His ability to combine personal thoughts and beliefs with quotations, allusions, theories, and interpretations not only gives readers of later ages a glimpse into the progression of one man's intellect, but also makes his *Essays* a classic in French and world literature.

English Versions of Works by Michel de Montaigne

Apology for Raymond Sebond. Translated by Marjorie Glicksman Grene and Roger Ariew. Indianapolis, Ind.: Hackett Publishing, 2003.
Autobiography of Michel de Montainge. Edited by Marvin Lowenthal. Boston: David R. Godine, 1999.
The Complete Essays of Montaigne. Translated by Donald M. Frame. Palo Alto, Calif.: Stanford University Press, 1965.

Works about Michel de Montaigne

Hartel, Anne. *Michel de Montaigne: Accidental Philosopher.* New York: Cambridge University Press, 2003.
Hoffmann, George. *Montaigne's Career.* Oxford: Oxford University Press, 1998.
Leschemelle, Pierre. *Montaigne: The Fool of the Farce.* Translated by William J. Beck. New York: Peter Lang, 1995.
Sichel, Edith. *Michel de Montaigne.* La Vergne, Tenn.: University Press of the Pacific, 2003.
Tetel, Marcel. *Montaigne.* Boston: Twayne, 1990.

Montesquieu, Charles-Louis de Secondat, baron de (1689–1755)
novelist, philosopher

Born into an old and aristocratic French family, young Charles-Louis was schooled near Paris, where he was first exposed to ENLIGHTENMENT ideals. He studied at the University of Bordeaux, married, and in 1716 inherited the estate of Montesquieu. The estate entailed a position in parliament, and Montesquieu settled down to practice law.

He published his first important work in 1721, *Lettres Persanes (Persian Letters).* This bold and witty satire features two fictitious visitors from Persia who travel the world and write letters home, commenting on what they see. Following the success of the work, Montesquieu undertook a grand tour of Europe, and returned home convinced that his best contributions to the world of ideas could be made through literature.

In 1734 he printed *The Universal Monarchy,* later revoked, and *Reflections on the Romans,* in which he analyzes the causes for the grandeur and decline of the Roman Empire. By far his most influential work was *The Spirit of Laws* (1748), which became a classic text of political philosophy and outlines Montesquieu's theory of government. Using a historical approach to examine different forms of government, Montesquieu concludes that the animating principle of a government was either honor or fear. He advocates the separation of powers into executive, legislative, and judicial bodies, and he suggests that a country's climate influences its policy. The immense work also includes a discussion of religion and an analysis of the creation of French law.

The Spirit of Laws won Montesquieu a place among the greatest figures of the Enlightenment. Controversy led him to publish a *Defense* in 1751, but his fame was secure. He wrote his last work, *Essay on Taste,* for the ENCYCLOPEDIA of Denis DIDEROT and Jean Le Rond d'ALEMBERT.

Montesquieu's political ideals have become a permanent feature of democracy: His belief in the separation of powers influenced the French Revolution and was incorporated into the American Constitution.

English Versions of Works by Charles-Louis de Secondat, baron de Montesquieu

Considerations on the Causes of the Greatness of the Romans and Their Decline. Translated by David

Lowenthal. Indianapolis, Ind.: Hackett Publishing, 1999.

The Spirit of Laws. Edited by Anne M. Cohler. Cambridge: Cambridge University Press, 1989.

Persian Letters. Translated by C. J. Betts. New York: Penguin, 1977.

Works about Charles-Louis de Secondat, baron de Montesquieu

Carrithers, David Wallace, Michael A. Mosher, and Paul A. Rahe, eds. *Montesquieu's Science of Politics.* Lanham, Md.: Rowman and Littlefield, 2000.

Conroy, Peter V. *Montesquieu Revisited.* New York: Twayne, 1992.

Moore, Milcah Martha (1740–1829)
poet, pedagogical writer

Milcah Martha Moore's Book circulated in the 18th century but appeared in print only recently. Moore was both a contributor to and primary organizer of this handwritten "commonplace" book, which consists of poetry and prose by more than 16 different authors. The book is "a documentary testament to the significance of women's literacy for forming relationships and expressing sentiments" about politics, marriage, housework, and life during the American Revolution (Wulf).

The daughter of Richard Hill and Deborah Moore, both Quakers from Maryland, Milcah Martha Moore was born in the town of Funchal on the island of Madeira. In 1751 Moore's mother died, and her aunt escorted her and her brother back to Philadelphia, where she entered a house full of sisters and new relations. In 1767 Moore married her cousin, Dr. Charles Moore. The Quakers at the time were attempting to move away from intermarriage. Thus, Moore's marriage was not sanctioned, and she and her husband were formally removed from the Quaker Society of Friends. However, Moore remained a Quaker her entire life and rejoined the society after her husband's death in 1801.

Moore corresponded with numerous women during her day, including the other prominent contributors to the book: Susanna Wright, Hannah Griffits, and Elizabeth Graeme Ferguson. Their letters often included poems, excerpts from books they were reading, jottings from religious texts, and "trifles." These writings were used for entertainment purposes as well as spiritual instruction. Often, religious and political sentiments were expressed, either in prose or poetic form. Though shared and passed around, these books were rarely formally published.

Due to their belief in pacifism, many Quakers including Moore had mixed feelings about America's war for independence. Though they sympathized with the patriots, their religious beliefs mandated neutrality. Some of the contributors to the book were clearly loyal to the British cause, but others expressed support for the colonists. Much of the poetry found in *Milcah Martha Moore's Book* "expresses this ambivalence" (Wulf). It is interesting to note that Moore copied everything into her book during the American Revolution.

During the war, Moore and her husband moved from Philadelphia to the Montgomery township in the northern area of the county. Her husband practiced medicine while she kept at her correspondence. She also opened a school for girls, and in 1787 published an educational primer called *Miscellanies, Moral and Instructive.*

Moore's contribution to early American literature has only recently been acknowledged. Her *Book* testifies to the importance and role of education and written communication among women within the Quaker foundations of early America.

A Work by Milcah Martha Moore

Le Courreye, Blecki, and Karin A. Wulf, eds. *Milcah Martha Moore's Book: A Commonplace Book from Revolutionary America.* University Park: Pennsylvania State University Press, 1997.

Moquihuitzín (Macuilxochitzín)
(ca. 1435–unknown) *poet*

Moquihuitzín was the daughter of Tlacaélel, a powerful adviser to the leaders of Mexico-

Tenochtitlán. She was named after the goddess of art, song, and dance, so that from birth she seemed destined to be a great poet.

Moquihuitzín lived at the time when Tenochtitlán had become an important commercial center and dominated the Mexica (Aztec) Empire, then at its peak. As a woman of noble birth, she most certainly enjoyed a life of leisure and could devote herself to traditional arts and crafts, but she also took an uncommon interest in her father's political activities.

In the capacity of chief adviser to the rulers of Tenochtitlán, Tlacaélel had planned the successful series of military campaigns that helped Tenochtitlán to assert its power in the region. During one of these conquests, AXAYACATL, the leader of Tenochtitlán, was seriously wounded by an Otomi captain. It was only the sudden arrival of the Mexica army that saved him. Moquihuitzín, who followed affairs of state with great interest, composed the song "Macuilxochitzín Icuic," or "Song of Macuilxocitl," to record this event for posterity. She begins it by giving thanks to the supreme god of the Mexica people:

> I raise my songs,
> I, Macuilxochitl
> with these I gladden the Giver of Life,
> may the dance begin!

This celebratory song is also notable for telling the story of the Otomi women who pleaded with Axayacatl to spare the life of the man who wounded him:

> He was full of fear, the Otomi,
> but then his women made supplication for
>   him to
> Axayatacl.

Such details indicate that her interest in public affairs was so deep that she took trouble to be intimate with even the secondary incidents connected with important matters.

No other poems of Moquihuitzín survive. The chronicler Tezozomoc writes that "of her was born

the prince Cuauhtlaptalzén." But little else is known; though it is likely that she lived out the remaining years of the century. The survival of her song is confirmation of the claims of the Mexican chroniclers that women too were highly educated and skilled in the art of poetry.

See also NAHUATL POETRY; NEZAHUALCOYOTL; NEZAHUALPILLI.

English Versions of Works by Moquihuitzín

Bierhorst, John, trans. *Cantares Mexicanos: Songs of the Aztecs.* Palo Alto, Calif.: Stanford University Press, 1985.

León-Portilla, Miguel, ed. *Fifteen Poets of the Aztec World.* Norman: University of Oklahoma Press, 1992.

More, Sir Thomas (1478–1535) *novelist, nonfiction writer*

Thomas More was born in London, the son of John More, a prominent lawyer and later a judge. He became a page in the household of Archbishop Morton at age 13, and went to Oxford the following year. He received a B.A. in 1494, going on to study law. In 1529 he was appointed lord chancellor of England, the most powerful position in the kingdom below the king himself. He later resigned, however, was convicted of treason, and beheaded. In 1935 the Catholic Church acknowledged his loyalty by making him a saint.

More was perhaps the single most important intellectual in early-16th-century England, and was instrumental in helping introduce HUMANISM to England. As early as 1505, when it is believed he considered entering the priesthood, he was translating *The Life of Pico* (1509), about the famous 15th-century Italian humanist. Richard J. Schoeck notes that More's translation of Pico's biography is "important for being a serious effort in English, at a time when nearly any imaginative effort in English was experimental and involved a manifesto, implicitly or explicitly, on the potential of the use of the vernacular," or the native tongue. The biography also sheds light on how Italian humanism traveled to England.

Also a historian, More wrote *The History of Richard III* between 1514 and 1518, in which he innovatively forges a symbolic connection between Richard's physical and moral deformity. This history helped establish the myth that Richard III was an evil, physically deformed dictator who murdered his brothers and nephews to become king of England, a myth that continued to be taught as historical truth in British grammar schools well into the 20th century.

More's most famous work is his philosophical romance *Utopia* (1516), in which a mariner tells a story about an ideal state. The novel was written in Latin and spawned numerous imitations. *Utopia*, which means "nowhere" and is the name More gave to his fictional island, reads like a call for social reform. "When I run over in my mind," says Raphael Hythlodaeus, the character who describes Utopia, "the various commonwealths flourishing today, so help me God, I can see nothing in them but a conspiracy of the rich, who are fattening up their own interests under the name and title of the commonwealth," a word that simultaneously suggests a state and the common wealth in the 16th century. In this passage, according to the RENAISSANCE critic Jonathan Dollimore, More acknowledges not only that the laws are corrupt, but also "that law and morality have their origins in custom rather than with an eternal order of things." The argument is strengthened, Dollimore argues, because of the book's explicit comparison of Utopian society with European society.

Hythlodaeus also advances religious views that are extremely liberal, especially since throughout early 16th-century Europe people were required to accept the pope's authority. The punishment for dissent, or heresy, was death. In *Utopia*, though:

> "There are different forms of religion throughout the island," Hythlodaeus explains, "and in each particular city as well. Some worship as a god the sun, others the moon, and still others the planets. There are some who worship a man of past ages who was conspicuous either for virtue or glory; they consider him not only a god but the supreme god."

Such ideas make More seem like a forerunner of the Reformation, the religious movement that undermined the hold the Catholic Church had over Europe. Indeed, More's ideas are more radical than those of any of the reformers, since in each place where a reformed church appeared, its citizens were required to conform to the tenets of the new church. According to scholar Stephen Greenblatt, while Utopians are allowed their own religious beliefs, most Utopians "believe in a single power, unknown, eternal, infinite, inexplicable, far beyond the grasp of the human mind, and diffused throughout the universe" and everyone is required to attend the same house of worship and to believe in life after death. In *Utopia*, the people do not count one who denies this belief "as one of their citizens, since he would undoubtedly betray all the laws and customs of society." Utopia, envisioned by More is not a state of freedom, but a state in which dissent is impossible. Such ideas were considered radical at the time Utopia was published, and the kind of religious toleration proposed by More would not be achieved until the 18th century.

Works by Sir Thomas More

Saint Thomas More: Selected Writings. Edited by John F. Thornton and Susan B. Varenne. Vancouver, Wash.: Vintage Books, 2003.

Utopia. Translated by Paul Turner. New York: Penguin, 1965.

Works about Sir Thomas More

Greenblatt, Stephen. *Renaissance Self-Fashioning: From More to Shakespeare.* Chicago: University of Chicago Press, 1984.

Murphy, Anne. *Thomas More.* Liguori, Mo.: Liguori Publications, 1997.

Sargent, Daniel. *Thomas More.* Whitefish, Mont.: Kessinger, 2003.

Motolinía, Toribio de (ca. 1495–ca. 1569)
missionary, historian

"Motolinía" is the name assumed by the Spanish Franciscan Fray Toribio de Benavente. Motlinía was a lifelong student of Indian lore who wrote about the indigenous Indian civilizations of New Spain with deep insight and appreciation. As a Franciscan friar in 1524, he was one of the first clergy to receive orders to go to Mexico. Repeatedly hearing the Aztec word *motolinía*, meaning "poor," during his first visit to Mexico City, he adopted it as his own name. His change of name also was deliberately symbolic of his affection for the Indians.

As a Franciscan, Motlinía helped to establish convents, churches, and the city of Puebla. He worked to protect the Indians despite experiencing legal difficulties with authorities. In 1529 he was sent to Guatemala and Nicaragua to evangelize Indian populations. He learned Indian languages and experienced considerable success with his work. When he died in Mexico City, he was considered by many to be a saint.

Motlinía's most important work deals with the history and culture of the indigenous peoples he served. As a part of his work, he was instructed to write an account of the Indians in pre-Spanish times and a history of the work of the Franciscans among them. Completed in 1541, *Historia de los indios de Nueva España* is considered to be the first history of the Mexican Indians written by a Spaniard.

An English Version of a Work by Toribio de Motolinía

History of the Indians of New Spain, vol. 4. Translated by Elizabeth A. Foster. Oxford, U.K.: Greenwood Publishing, 1970.

Munford, Robert (ca. 1737–1783)
playwright

Robert Munford was born in Virginia to Anna Bland and Robert Munford II, both descendants of prominent if not wealthy colonial families. Mun-ford's father was a landowner, but his heavy drinking led to the ruin of the family estate and to his death in 1745. Munford's uncle, William Beverly, raised the boy until Munford was 14. He was then sent to England with Beverly's own children to be educated at Wakefield Grammar School. When Beverly died in 1756, leaving no provisions for Munford in his will, Munford returned to Virginia, where he studied law with his cousin, Peyton Randolph.

In 1760 or 1761, Munford married his cousin and childhood friend, Anna Beverly. In the next few years he extended his family's tobacco plantations and rose to prominence as a wealthy landowner. After Mecklenburg County was formed in Virginia in 1765, he held several important political offices, including county lieutenant, burgess, and member of the Virginia House of Delegates (1779–81). Politically, Munford was a moderate, but he was an early supporter of American independence and signed the anti–Stamp Act resolutions with Patrick Henry in 1774. He also helped recruit troops for the war and even served as a major in 1781.

Munford's background would figure into his literary output, which included two plays, a few poems, and an unfinished translation of Ovid's *Metamorphoses*. However, none of his works seem to have been published or produced onstage during his lifetime. Indeed, it was Munford's son, William, who helped to posthumously publish his father's work in 1798 as *A Collection of Plays and Poems, by the Late Colonel Robert Munford, of Mecklenburg County, in the State of Virginia.*

Munford's plays are regarded by some literary historians to be the first comedic works by an American dramatist. *The Candidates*, perhaps "the first real American farce" (Kemp), was a sharp-witted look at the electoral system in the Virginia colonies and, like his play *The Patriots*, was filled with sly satires and caricatures of Munford's contemporaries. *The Patriots* uses the traditional five-act plot structure that was common in much theater of the time and revolves around three romances, "the first serious, the second comic, and the third farcical" (Kemp). The play, which dealt with two men falsely accused of being Tories or British sympathizers, was a direct reflection of Munford's political views, as it argued that patriotism was a good thing to exercise, but only on reasoned moderation. Today, Munford's works are valued for the insight they provide into historical events and people of 18th-century Virginia.

Works by Robert Munford

The Plays of Robert Munford. Tucson, Ariz.: American Eagle Publications, 1992.

A Work about Robert Munford

Baine, Rodney M. *Robert Munford, America's First Comic Dramatist.* Athens: University of Georgia Press, 1967.

Muratori, Ludovico Antonio

(1672–1750)   *historian*

Ludovico Antonio Muratori was born to poor parents and became a Roman Catholic priest. Early in his career, he served as a librarian in Milan. In 1700 he became chief archivist and ducal librarian at the city of Modena, and in this post developed a reputation as one of the leading scholars in Europe. He achieved renown for his discovery of the so-called Muratorian Canon, a second-century Christian document containing the earliest known list of New Testament books. He also edited a 28-volume collection of medieval manuscripts, as well as a 12-volume history of Italy, but is best remembered today for *A Relation of the Missions of Paraguay* (1750). The only work of Muratori available in an English translation, *A Relation of the Missions of Paraguay* is a chronicle and description of the Jesuit settlements in South America.

Muratori had never been to South America, and compiled his research mainly from discussions with travelers and letters from the missionaries. As a result, in the opinion of the historian R. B. Cunninghame Graham, the books of Muratori and another, similar chronicler "contain the faults and mistakes of men . . . writing of countries of which they were personally ignorant. Both give a good account of the customs and regimen of the missions, but both seem to have believed too readily fabulous accounts of the flora and fauna of Paraguay." After his death, Muratori was remembered as one of the greatest scholars and medievalists of his time. His reputation was particularly great in his native Italy, where his ideas helped inspire the 19th-century nationalist Risorgimento.

A Work about Ludovico Antonio Muratori

Cunninghame Graham, R. B. *A Vanished Arcadia: Being Some Account of the Jesuits in Paraguay.* New York: Haskell House, 1968 [1901].

Murray, Judith Sargent   (1751–1820)

essayist, poet, playwright

Judith Sargent Murray was born in Gloucester, Massachusetts, the eldest of eight children born to Winthrop and Judith Saunders Sargent. Her father was a prosperous merchant, as well as ship owner and sea captain. Because the Sargents cared about education, they allowed Judith to receive tutoring alongside her brothers. Such schooling was rare for women at the time, and even rarer for them to be taught Greek, Latin, and math.

In 1788 she married John Murray, with whom she had two children: a daughter born in 1791, and a son who died shortly after birth. His death led to Murray's first forays into poetry, when she composed "Lines, occasioned by the Death of an Infant." Her other verse was "didactic and marked by the conventional couplet typical of the eighteenth century" (Lawton).

Murray is best known for a series of essays that she published in the *Massachusetts Magazine* in the 1790s, often under the pen name Constantia. The essays were eventually collected and published in 1798 under the title *The Gleaner.* The book contained, among other things, essays on history, women's education, and political affairs. Murray was a strong advocate for female education, arguing that women needed education as much as men to better support their families and themselves. As a strong nationalist, she also praised the excellence of American literature in both essays and poetry.

When the ban on performing plays was struck down in 1793, the same year Murray and her husband moved to Boston, Murray turned her creative energies to writing plays, making her "one of only three women to attempt play writing in New England before 1800" (Hornstein). The two plays she wrote, *The Medium* (1795), retitled *Virtue Triumphant* in 1798, and *The Traveller Returned* (1796), were both performed in Boston, though neither met with much success.

After her husband's death in 1814, Murray oversaw the publication of his memoirs and ser-

mons. Her own works are valued for the insight they give to a woman's perspective in 18th-century America.

Works by Judith Sargent Murray

Selected Writings of Judith Sargent Murray. Edited by Sharon M. Harris. Oxford: Oxford University Press, 1995.
The Gleaner: A Miscellany. Edited by Nina Baym. Syracuse, N.Y.: Syracuse University Press, 1993.

A Work about Judith Sargent Murray

Skemp, Sheila L. *Judith Sargent Murray: A Brief Biography with Documents.* New York: St. Martin's Press, 1998.

Nahuatl poetry

Nahuatl was the language of the various indigenous peoples of central Mexico, commonly known as the Aztec, at the time of the arrival of the Spanish. Although strictly speaking the word *Aztec* refers only to the ancestors of the Mexica and Tenochca of the twin cities of Tenochtitlán and Tlatelolco, it is often employed as a generic term to describe peoples who spoke dialects of a common Nahuatl language. Sharing a similar culture, they organized themselves into a powerful coalition of three, consisting of Tenochtitlán, Texcoco, and Tlacopan.

A member of the Uto-Aztecan family of languages, Nahuatl evolved as a pictographic writing system based on images. In this respect, it resembles Egyptian and Chinese writing forms. It was employed for both secular and religious purposes. Among the documents written in Nahuatl were sacred texts, genealogies, maps, and historical records. However, the *xochicuicatl* ("flower songs"), the name for poetry, represent the highest achievement of this language before the unexpected invasion of the Spanish.

The most distinctive feature of this literary form is derived from the pictorial nature of Nahuatl writing. Thus the flower songs uniquely fuse poetry and painting into a single art. The pictorial elements aside, Nahuatl poetry frequently used other literary devices. One of the most common is the repetition of grammatical patterns:

> [M]y heart has tasted it,
> my heart has been inebriated
> the flowering chocolate drink is foaming
> the flowery tobacco is passed around.

Another noticeable trait of this poetry is the merging of two metaphors, or figurative terms. An example of this is the compound word *flower song*. These words come together to produce a meaning that can be translated as poetry, art, or symbolism.

Among the famous composers of Nahuatl flower songs are NEZAHUALCOYOTL, his son NEZAHUALPILLI, and the female poet MOQUIHUITZÍN. The social rank of these poets suggests that poetry was an exclusively aristocratic art.

In the wake of the Spanish conquest, the ability to read Nahuatl was gradually lost. However, several Nahuatl manuscripts were preserved, transcribed into alphabetic script and, eventually, translated into Spanish, English, and other languages.

The most comprehensive anthologies of Nahuatl poetry are *Cantares mexicanas* and *Romances de los señores de la Nueva España*.

See also MESOAMERICAN MYTHOLOGY.

English Versions of Nahuatl Poetry

Bierhorst, John, trans. *Cantares Mexicanos: Songs of the Aztecs.* Palo Alto, Calif.: Stanford University Press, 1985.

León-Portilla, Miguel, ed. *Fifteen Poets of the Aztec World.* Norman: University of Oklahoma Press, 1992.

neoclassicism (1600s–1700s)

In a broad sense, neoclassical literature is that which embraces prescribed, formal conventions and styles of literature existing in previous eras, especially those of classical Rome and Greece. Such literature focuses upon the control of human passions and the search for order in all aspects of life, and emphasizes the importance of societal needs over individual ones. Neoclassical writing often exudes a sense of optimism, although some texts feature a strong satirical element that coincides with this sense.

In France, neoclassical literature flourished in the 17th century during the reign of the Sun King, Louis XIV (1638–1715). Three master playwrights, Pierre CORNEILLE, Jean RACINE, and MOLIÈRE (Jean Baptiste Poquelin), are most often recognized as producers of the best neoclassical drama of the period. In keeping with neoclassical tenets, these playwrights wrote with the rules of classical dramatic UNITIES in mind. These rules, as suggested by Aristotle, pertain to unities of time, place, and action. Aristotle also calls for the distinct separation of tragedy and comedy. Corneille's *Le Cid* (1636), Racine's *Andromaque* (1667), and Molière's *Amphitryon* (1668) are emblematic of this popular style in France. Other French neoclassical texts include Molière's *Tartuffe* and François-Marie Arouet VOLTAIRE's *Candide.*

In England, neoclassical literature was *en vogue* from approximately 1660 to 1798. John Dryden's *All for Love,* Jonathan SWIFT's *Gulliver's Travels,* Alexander POPE's *Essay on Criticism* and *Rape of the Lock,* and Samuel Johnson's *Rambler* essays and preface to SHAKESPEARE's dramatic works are but a few examples of neoclassical writing of the period in England.

Works about Neoclassicism

Cronk, Nicholas. *The Classical Sublime and the Language of Literature.* Charlottesville, Va.: Rookwood, 2002.

Irwin, David. *Neoclassicism.* Boston: Phaidon Press, 1997.

Simon, Irene. *Neo-Classical Criticism 1600–1800.* Columbia: University of South Carolina Press, 1971.

Nezahualcoyotl (ca. 1402–ca. 1473) *poet, philosopher-king, architect*

The name *Nezahualcoyotl* literally means "hungry coyote," and many literary historians consider his "flower songs," or *xochicuicatl,* to be the highest achievement of Ancient Mexican literature.

"Flower Song" is the name given to the poetry and art practiced by the ancient Mexicans. The lyrics were composed in a language called Nahuatl, spoken by peoples who called themselves Mexica or Tenochca, now known as the Aztec.

Nezahualcoyotl was the king of Texcoco and the most influential intellectual in a period of extraordinary cultural development. Aside from his enduring fame as a lyric poet, he also enjoyed a considerable reputation as a builder, legislator, and philosopher. Among his many works are the construction of Texcoco's library of pictographic or "painted" books, a zoological and botanical garden, and a university dedicated to scholarship and the arts. Under his rule, Texcoco also forged a political alliance with Tenochtitlán, the most powerful state of the Mexica Empire, which became the cultural center of the Nahuatl-speaking world.

The flower songs of Nezahualcoyotl are now preserved in various anthologies. The best known are the *Cantares mexicanos,* or *Mexican Songs,* and the *Romances de los señores de la Nueva España,* or *The Romances of the Sages of New Spain.* In one of his compositions, Nezahualcoyotl gives a lyrical illustration of the ideals embodied in the flower songs:

With flowers You paint,
O Giver of Life!
With songs You give color,
with songs You shade
those who will live on the earth. . . .
We live only in Your book of paintings,
here on the earth.

This poem expresses the theme of transience, or the temporary nature of life. Nezahualcoyotl's emphasis of transience, however, is not negative; it is, rather, a positive ideal that allows him to distill the lasting spiritual essence that connects society to the cosmos and the after-life.

Sadly and ironically, within a century of Nezahualcoyotl's death, Mexican civilization would be devastated as Spanish colonization abruptly ended its remarkable achievements.

See also NAHUATL POETRY.

English Versions of Works by Nezahualcoyotl

Cantares Mexicanos: Songs of the Aztecs. Translated by John Bierhorst. Palo Alto, Calif.: Stanford University Press, 1985.

Chants of Nezahualcoyotl and Obsidian Glyph. Translated by Prospero Saiz. Madison, Wis.: Ghost Pony Press, 1996.

A Work about Nezahualcoyotl

Gillmor, Frances. *Flute of the Smoking Mirror: A Portrait of Nezahualcoyotl, Poet-King of the Aztecs.* Salt Lake City: University of Utah Press, 1983.

Nezahualpilli (1464–1515) *poet, king*

Nezahualpilli, or "fasting son," succeeded his father NEZAHUALCOYOTL in 1473 as king of Texcoco, one of the kingdoms of the triple alliance of the Mexica (Aztec) Empire.

Throughout his life, Nezahualpilli exhibited a strong sense of filial piety so that he consciously modeled his life on the example of his illustrious father. Nezahualpilli thus continued the legacy of promoting learning. The chronicler Juan Torquemada writes that Nezahualpilli's enthusiasm for science led him to erect an observatory in his palace. Above all, Nezahualpilli inherited his father's humane spirit and fair-mindedness. He is thus credited with abolishing capital punishment for lesser crimes and displaying leniency toward the lower classes of society.

Nezahualpilli also emulated his father as a composer of "flower songs," the pictographic lyrics of the Nahuatl language. Unfortunately, of his work only a long fragment survives. Called *Icuic Nezahualpilli yc Tlamato Huexotzinco*, or *Song of Nezahualpilli during the War with Huexotzinco*, this poem celebrates victory in battle while lamenting the loss of life:

My heart is sad,
I am young Nezahualpilli.
I look for my captains,
the lord has gone,
the flowering quetzal,
the young and strong warrior has gone,
the blue of the sky is his house.
Perhaps Tlatohuetzin and Acapipiyol will
* come*
to drink the flowery liquor,
here where I weep?

Characteristic of flower songs, Nezahualpilli refers to death as intoxicating and expresses the theme of life's impermanence in relation to its eternal nature.

As the poem also reveals, Nezahualpilli's reign was a constant struggle to maintain the independence of Texcoco at a time of increasing centralization of power in Tenochtitlán. He was thus obliged against his own judgment to take part in such wars to maintain strategic alliance with Tenochtitlán.

Eventually, his relations with Montezuma, the ruler of Tenochtitlán, became strained, and toward the end of his life he undermined Montezuma's political ambitions with a startling prediction. He foretold the coming of a new people who would become masters of the land. Soon after Nezahualpilli's

death, Hernan CORTÉS arrived with his army, and Montezuma was stoned to death by his own people.
See also NAHUATL POETRY; MOQUIHUITZÍN.

English Versions of Works by Nezahualpilli
Cantares Mexicanos: Songs of the Aztecs. Translated by John Bierhorst. Palo Alto, Calif.: Stanford University Press, 1985.

León-Portilla, Miguel, ed. *Fifteen Poets of the Aztec World.* Norman: University of Oklahoma Press, 1992.

Nguyen Trai (1380–1442) *poet*
Nguyen Trai was born in Nhi Khe, Ha Dong province, North Vietnam. He was the son of Nguyen Phi Khanh, a scholar-official of the Vietnamese court. Nguyen Trai received his degree when he was 20, and was appointed to the position of deputy head provincial administrator soon after. When his father was taken as a prisoner of war after the Ming dynasty's successful occupation of North Vietnam, Nguyen Trai joined the liberation army of King Le Loi. Le Loi defeated the Ming Chinese in 1428 and made Nguyen Trai a high official in his bureaucracy. When the new emperor Le Thai Tong ascended the throne, Nguyen Trai retired and lived a simple life in Con Son. He married Nguyen Thi Lo, a country girl with whom the new emperor became smitten. In 1442 Le Thai Tong died mysteriously after paying a visit to Nguyen Trai and his wife. Nguyen Trai was accused of committing regicide and his whole family was executed.

As a close adviser to Le Loi during his campaign, Nguyen Trai allegedly wrote many pronouncements and letters, which were sent in Le Loi's name to the Ming generals during the war of liberation. These letters were all collected in *Quang Trung Tu Menh Tap* (Letters and commands from the time of military service, 1418–28). In these writings, Nguyen Trai showed his clever use of propaganda and verse. He wrote most of his poems in the Chu Nom script, but his best known poem, "Binh Ngo Sach" (Book on defeating the Wu), was written in classical Chinese in 1428, in the aftermath of Le Loi's victory. The poem became Vietnam's declaration of independence.

All of Nguyen Trai's Vietnamese poems were collected in *Quoc Am Thi Tap* (Volume of poems in the national tongue, 1480). His poetry expresses deep concern for filial piety, loyalty, and moral duties. His texts set the precedent for proper actions and behavior for Vietnamese leaders such as Le Loi. Nguyen Trai's honorable character and idealism mark him as a well-loved poet in Vietnamese history.

An English Version of Works by Nguyen Trai
Nguyen Trai, One of the Greatest Figures of Vietnamese History and Literature. Hanoi: Foreign Languages Publishing House, 1980.

A Work about Nguyen Trai
A Thousand Years of Vietnam Poetry. Edited and translated by Ngoc Bich Nguyen. New York: Knopf, 1974.

Nikitin, Afanasij (early 1400s–1472) *travel writer*
Afanasij Nikitin was a merchant from the Muscovite city of Tver. He composed a travelogue entitled *Journey Across Three Seas.* First published by Nikolai KARAMZIN, the *Journey* describes Nikitin's travels through the Caspian, Indian, and Black Sea regions.

In 1466 Nikitin sailed down the Volga River on a trading expedition to Persia. Pirates robbed him of everything en route. He nevertheless continued on to Persia and India, where he spent three years (1469–72). Nikitin also visited Armenia, Ethiopia, and Arabia. He died at the city of Smolensk on the way home.

The *Journey* contains some fictional material, but it also includes a great deal of factual information. Nikitin describes his activities and observations abroad; lists distances, travel times, and prices; and ruminates on religion and culture. He emphasizes practical matters. "Thank God, I reached Junnar in good health," he writes, "but the passage cost me a hundred rubles." Later, he notes that "pepper and dyes are cheap . . . [But] the duty is high and, moreover, there are many pirates at sea."

Nikitin's *Journey* is significant because it describes a commercial voyage; most European travel tales of the time depict religious pilgrimages. Nikitin was also one of the first, if not the first, Europeans to explore and write about India. His stories offer fascinating glimpses into Indian and Middle Eastern cultures as he saw them. Perhaps most notably, Nikitin shows surprising tolerance for other religions and cultures. He wrote parts of the *Journey* in a Middle Eastern trading dialect. In the words of Lowell Tillett, the *Journey* "has something of interest for the psychologist, sociologist, and theologian, as well as for the historian, geographer, and economist."

An English Version of a Work by Afanasij Nikitin

Afanasy Nikitin's Journey Across Three Seas, in *Medieval Russia's Epics, Chronicles, and Tales,* rev. ed. Edited and translated by Serge A. Zenkovsky. New York: E.P. Dutton, 1974.

Nikolev, Nikolai Petrovich (1758–1815)
poet, playwright

Nikolai Petrovich Nikolev was born in Russia and lost his parents at a young age. He was raised by the duchess Dashkova, a distant relative and one of the most respected and highly educated women of her time. Nikolev entered military service, but after an encounter than cost him his eyesight, he retired and devoted himself to literature. He became a member of the Russian Academy, and many influential figures, including Czar Paul I, patronized Nikolev and highly valued his work. After Nikolev's death, his friends established a society that met regularly and held literary readings in his honor.

Nikolev's writings included pseudo-classical odes, sentimental folk-style songs, and tragedies. He gained the most success with his dramas *Palmyra, The Self-Enamored Poet, Genuine Consistency,* and *Phoenix.* These dramas appeared in the influential journal *Russian Theater. The Self-Enamored Poet,* which appeared in 1781, parodied the tragedies of the great Russian dramatist Alexander SUMAROKOV. The play, like most of Nikolev's works, incorporated the ideals of NEOCLASSICISM, which were highly regarded by educated tastes, but mercilessly exposed Sumarokov's tendency to begrudge other playwrights their success.

Between 1795 and 1798, Nikolev published five volumes of his works under the title *Creations.* In the literary world, Nikolev was known as the Russian MILTON. Czar Paul I called Nikolev "the blind clairvoyant."

A Work about Nikolai Petrovich Nikolev

Maltseva, T. V. *Literaturnaia Polemika i Protsess Zhanroobrazovaniia v Komediografii XVIII Veka. Monografiia. (Literary Polemics and the Process of Genre Emergence in 18th Century Comediography.)* Monograph St. Petersburg: Leningradskii Gosudarstvennyi Oblastnoi Universitet Im. A.S. Pushkina, 2000.

Noh (Nō) (1300s–present) *classical Japanese form of performance*

The Noh form of performance, developed in 14th- and 15th-century Japan, includes elements of dance drama, music, and poetry, which are combined to create a subtle and aesthetic stage art. The central unifying concept of Noh is that of *yugen,* which translates as "gentle gracefulness," implying a focus on expressing beauty through simplicity, restraint, and suggestion.

Noh drama was developed largely by Kannami Kiyotsugu (1333–84) and his son ZEAMI Motokiyo (1364–43). Zeami, a prolific writer, wrote 100 of the 240 plays still in the active repertoire, enjoying the patronage of the military ruler, Shogun Ashikaga Yoshimitsu. During the Edo period (1603–1868), the military regime proclaimed Noh the government's official performance art. The Meiji period (1868–1912) brought many reforms to Japanese society, one of which was an end to the patronage of Noh drama. Private sponsors, however, kept the classical art form active.

Noh plays can be classified in five subject categories, those that feature: gods, warriors, women, supernatural creatures, and miscellaneous characters (often mad women). Action in the play is usually focused on one central character called the *shite* (pronounced "sh'tay"), who often appears as an ordinary person in the first half of a play in disguise and reappears in the second half in his true form, such as the ghost of a long-dead famous personage. An accompanying character called *tsure* often appears as well, along with the *waki,* or secondary character, who is often a traveling priest who develops the story line by questioning the main character.

Accompanying chorus and instrumentalists are important for the full expression of Noh drama. The eight-person chorus, called *jiutai,* is located to the side of the stage and narrates the background and action of the story, often explaining characters' thoughts and emotions. The instrumentalists, or *hayashi,* are located at the back of the stage and include a transverse flute and three drums of different types. The highly prescribed rhythms of the drums, called *kakegoe,* add an important texture to the sound of the performance.

The setting and accessories for Noh performances are elaborate and intended to portray exquisite beauty by creating certain moods and emotions. Almost every character wears a finely carved, expressive, and superbly beautiful mask. The costumes are similarly gorgeous and expressive, created in elaborate patterns of dyed silk meant to reveal the character's nature. The elaborate color and design of Noh costumes finds a suitable arena for display on the simple stage on which the plays are performed. The stage has no curtain and is composed of a square connected to the backstage with a bridge, whereby the characters enter and exit.

Today, Noh is still actively performed. Though not widely popular in the whole of Japanese society, its professional practitioners are well trained and enjoy devoted and enthusiastic supporters. Busy at teaching and performing their art, as many as 1,500 performers today make their living through Noh. The tradition of the Noh performance is passed down within families, especially in the cities of Tokyo, Osaka, and Kyoto. There is a thriving community of amateur practitioners, as well, who perform the chant, dance, and instrumental elements of Noh.

English Versions of Noh

Chifumi Shimazaki. *Warrior Ghost Plays from the Japanese Noh Theater: Parallel Translations with Running Commentary.* Ithaca, N.Y.: Cornell University Press, 1993.

Zeami Motokiyo. *On the Art of the No Drama: The Major Treatises of Zeami.* Translated by J. Thomas Rimer, edited by Masakazu Yamazaki. Princeton, N.J.: Princeton University Press, 1984.

Works about Noh

Fenollosa, Ernest, and Ezra Pound. *'Noh' or Accomplishment: A Study of the Classical Stage of Japan.* Gretna, La.: Pelican Publishing, 1999.

Smethurst, Mae J., and Christina Laffin, eds. *Noh Ominameshi: A Flower Viewed from Many Directions.* Ithaca, N.Y.: Cornell University Press, 2003.

Novalis (Friedrich Leopold von Hardenberg) (1772–1801) *poet, novelist*

The second of 11 children born to Heinrich, Baron von Hardenberg, Fritz, as he was called, took the penname Novalis from one of the family's ancient titles. Born into the early German romantic movement, he himself became a figure of romance. Blond, tall, handsome, with wide eyes and a gentle disposition, his biographers maintain that he was a dreamy youth who, at 22, fell in love at first sight with Sophie von Kühn, who died of consumption a year before they could be married. Novalis himself died of consumption (known today as tuberculosis) before he turned 29.

In truth, Novalis was more than a dreamy poet. He studied philosophy, history, literature, and law, and privately pursued interests in mathematics, science, and language theory. He wrote on religious and philosophical issues as well as poetry and prose. Some of his ideas were quite scandalous to contemporaries, leading to heavy editing when the first edition of his collected works was published in 1802.

Novalis's ideas about philosophy and science, influenced by SCHILLER and GOETHE, gained less attention than his theories of poetry as a combination of inspired genius and meticulous craft. Of his writings, the works most studied today are two poetic compositions, *Hymns to the Night* and *Spiritual Songs,* and two unfinished novels, *Henry of Ofterdingen* and *The Novices of Saïs,* all composed between 1799 and 1801.

Though Novalis had practical concerns in science, medicine, and mathematics, which surface in his fiction, he is best remembered for the mystical, brooding spirit captured in *Hymns to the Night* and so characteristic of the romantic age:

> *Far off lies the world*
> *With its motley of pleasures.*
> *Elsewhere doth the Light*
> *Pitch its airy encampment.*
> *What if it never returned . . . ?*

English Versions of Works by Novalis

Henry von Ofterdingen. Translated by Palmer Hilty. Long Grove, Ill.: Waveland Press, 1990.
Novalis: Hymns to the Night. Translated by Dick Higgins. New York: McPherson & Co., 1998.

Works about Novalis

O'Brien, William Arctander. *Novalis: Signs of Revolution.* Durham, N.C.: Duke University Press, 1994.
Stoljar, Margaret Mahony, trans. *Novalis: Philosophical Writings.* Albany: State University of New York Press, 1997.

novel, epistolary (1700s)

The epistolary novel, which enjoyed its greatest popularity during the late 18th century, is a genre of prose fiction that uses letters of correspondence to narrate a story. Practically more than any other fictional genre, the epistolary novel calls for the reader's participation in interpreting and understanding the letters that create the narrative.

Samuel RICHARDSON's three novels—*Pamela* (1740), *Clarissa* (1748), and *The History of Sir Charles Grandison* (1754)—opened the doors to the creative and psychological possibilities of fiction writing. Richardson created distinctively different voices for each of his characters and explored their emotional states in traumatic situations. His characters reveal as much in their unconscious emotions as their consciously stated feelings and thoughts. Richardson claimed that his epistolary novels were morally instructive, to be read as much for self-education as for entertainment.

Richardson is often referred to as the inventor of the modern novel, and his influence had far-reaching effects. In England and France, Charles de MONTESQUIEU, Françoise de GRAFFIGNY, Jean-Jacques ROUSSEAU, and Pierre-Choderlos de LACLOS all wrote epistolary novels influenced by Richardson, as did Johann Wolfgang von GOETHE, whose *The Sorrows of Young Werther* became a best-seller in Germany.

Other writers of the epistolary novel who followed or were influenced by Richardson include Henry Fielding (1707–54), whose *Joseph Andrews* (1742) is a parody of Richardson's *Pamela;* Tobias Smollett (1721–71), whose masterpiece *Humphry Clinker* (1771) is a collection of comedic letters shared among members of a traveling party; and Laurence Sterne (1713–68), whose novel *The Life and Opinions of Tristram Shandy* (1760–67) takes the epistolary form to new heights in its use of psychological time, rather than chronological, as a framework for storytelling.

By the early 19th century, the epistolary novel no longer dominated fiction, but the exploration of characters' thoughts and emotions, to which the epistolary novel gave birth, live on today in every aspect of modern fiction.

See also PRÉVOST; SÉVIGNÉ.

English Versions of Epistolary Novels

Goethe, Johann Wolfgang von. *The Sorrows of Young Werther, and Selected writings.* Translated by Catherine Hutter. New York: New American Library, 1982.

Richardson, Samuel. *Clarissa, or the History of a Young Lady.* New York: Penguin Books, 1985.

Works about Epistolary Novels

Black, F. G. *The Epistolary Novel in the Late Eighteenth Century.* Eugene: University of Oregon Press, 1940.

Jensen, Katharine Ann. *Writing Love: Letters, Women, and the Novel in France, 1605–1776.* Carbondale: Southern Illinois University Press, 1995.

Occom, Samson (1723–1792) *missionary, clergyman, schoolmaster, hymnist*

Samson Occom, a Moghegan Indian, was influenced by evangelism during the "Great Awakening" and converted to Christianity in 1739. From 1743 to 1747 he was educated by Eleazar Wheelock, who later became the first president of Dartmouth College. Through missionary work, Occom offered an alternative spiritual vision for eastern Indians in 18th-century America. He mastered Latin, dressed like a Puritan, and served as a Christian missionary to the Indians, using native languages and traditions in support of his ministry. White contemporaries referred to Occom as the "Pious Mohegan," "Indian Preacher," "Red Christian," and "Praying Indian."

In 1749 Occom became schoolmaster and minister to the Montauk tribe and later the Oneida tribe in the areas of New York and Connecticut. As a Native American, he was able to gain the trust and respect of his students. In contrast to the white missionaries, Occom did not believe that Christianity and Western culture should replace Indian culture. He used Indian culture to teach Christianity and the English language alongside native traditions. He taught a phonetic approach to learning English, using letter recognition games and flash cards fashioned of paper and cedar chips.

Although Occom did not have formal theological training, he was ordained by the Long Island Presbytery in 1759 because of his success as a missionary. In 1765 he visited England and helped to raise money that was later used to establish Dartmouth College as a college for Native-American students.

English Versions of Works by Samson Occom

An Account of the Montauk Indians, on Long Island, Massachusetts Historical Collections (ser. 1, 10 (1809): 105–111.

Samson Occom, Mohegan: Collected Writings by the Founder of Native American Literature. Edited by Joanne Brooks. Oxford: Oxford University Press, 2004.

Works about Samson Occom

De Loss Love, William. *Samson Occom and the Christian Indians of New England.* Syracuse, N.Y.: Syracuse University Press, 1999.

Peyer, Bernd. *The Tutor'd Mind: Indian Missionary-Writers in Antebellum America.* Amherst: University of Massachusetts Press, 1997.

Olivares, Miguel de (1675–1768) historian

Born at Chillán in Chile, Father Miguel de Olivares wrote *Historia militar, civil y sagrada de lo acaecido en la conquista y pacificación del Reino de Chile*. This chronicle, not published until 1864, remains the best source of information about indigenous Chilean customs during the period of Spanish colonization. His other notable work is *Breve noticia de la provincia de la Compañia de Jesús en Chile 1593–1736*, published in 1870. Unfortunately, no English translations of his work are in print.

Olivares entered the Jesuit order, became a missionary, and began his travels in 1701 to cities in Chile, including Quillota, Polpaico, Tiltil, and Limache. From 1712 to 1720, he was the director of the Calubco and Nahuelhuapi missions. Ten years later, he witnessed the earthquake that destroyed the city of Concepción. In the course of his travels, Olivares studied the Jesuit archives and, beginning in 1736, while in Santiago, began to compile his history.

From 1740 to 1758, Olivares served in the Araucania missions. Like the earlier Jesuit historian of Chile, Diego de ROSALES, he learned the language of the natives and continued writing.

When Charles III issued a decree exiling the Jesuits, Olivares, by then an old man, was obliged to leave the country. On his way through Lima, he encountered more misfortune when the viceroy had his manuscripts confiscated. After reaching Imola in Italy, he petitioned for their return. The king himself responded favorably by ordering that the histories be sent to Spain, but Olivares died before they arrived in Madrid.

Compared to Rosales, Olivares was more attentive to the details of life around him. Through careful and precise observation, he describes the beliefs and customs he encountered firsthand.

Olmedo, José Joaquín (1780–1847) poet

José Joaquín Olmedo was born in Guayaquil, in the then-Spanish colony of Ecuador, to a Spanish father and Ecuadorean mother. He studied law and became a civil servant and politician, holding several governmental posts in Spain and the newly liberated Ecuador. He was instrumental in the liberation of Ecuador and its establishment as a separate country, and when Ecuador had gained its independence from Spain in 1830, he became the country's first vice president.

Olmedo is known as a neoclassical poet, and his poems were highly praised during his lifetime. His long poem *La victoria de Junín* (*The Victory of Junín*, 1825) celebrates the famous South American liberator Simón Bolívar, a compatriot and comrade of Olmedo. The following passage illustrates its heroic tone:

> So in the centuries of courage and glory
> where the lone warrior and the poet
> were worthy of honor and memory.

Olmedo's poems were published first in *Obras poéticas* (*Poetical Works*, 1848) and again in *Poésias completas* (*Complete Poems*, 1947). His inspirational outlook remains influential. Unfortunately, English translations of his works are not in print.

A Work about José Joaquín Olmedo

Harvey, Robert. *Liberators: Latin America's Struggle for Independence 1810–1830*. New York: Overlook Press, 2000.

Orléans, Charles d' (1394–1465) poet

Charles d'Orléans was born in the midst of the Hundred Years' War. His mother, Valentina Visconti, was the daughter of the duke of Milan, and his father, Louis d'Orléans, was the brother of King Charles VI. As a youth he was exposed to the tradition of French lyrical poetry through his father's patronage of such artists as Jean FROISSART and Christine de PISAN. D'Orléans's first poetic effort was *The Retinue of Love*, an imitation of the allegorical style (see ALLEGORY) of the courtly love poetry inherited from the southern troubadours and developed by Jean de Meun.

Captured by the English king at the Battle of Agincourt in 1415, d'Orléans was held hostage at a series of English castles for 25 years. With only books, servants, and visits, as well as messages from friends in France to amuse him, d'Orléans turned to writing poetry. Though a great number of his poems draw on the formulaic images and language of the courtly love motif, the themes of solitude and imprisonment add an original and introspective touch to the poetry he composed during his exile. By the time of his release in 1440, he had written another long narrative poem called *Dream in the Form of a Complaint,* a collection of carols, more than 86 songs, and almost 100 ballads. Two manuscripts of these works exist, the English version containing elements not found in the French.

Following failed efforts to negotiate peace between England and France and to restore properties taken from him during his imprisonment, d'Orléans retired to Blois, where he led a court known for its poetic activity and lively entertainment. He continued composing poetry, largely in the form of the *rondeau,* and mentored several younger poets, among them François VILLON. The wry humor and cynicism of the aging d'Orléans mark his later poems. As a whole the body of his work demonstrates the evolution of French poetry from the highly stylized patterns of the later Middle Ages to the observations of direct experience and inward thought that signaled the HUMANISM of the RENAISSANCE.

An English Version of Works by Charles d'Orléans

Fox, John. *The Lyric Poetry of Charles d'Orléans.* Oxford: Clarendon Press, 1969.

A Work about Charles d'Orléans

McLeod, Enid. *Charles of Orleans: Prince and Poet.* New York: Viking Press, 1970.

Ozerov, Vladislav Aleksandrovich
(1769–1816) *dramatist*

Vladislav Aleksandrovich Ozerov was born and raised in Russia. He graduated at the top of his class from a military school and, once in military service, participated in several campaigns. Ozerov's literary tastes were hugely influenced by 17th- and 18th-century French literature, which he read in great quantities. As a consequence, he wrote his first poems in French.

Ozerov's first works were odes and fables, which, while they showed the extent of his familiarity with the French traditions, were not considered unduly remarkable. His first TRAGEDY, *Death of Oleg Drevlianskii,* staged in St. Petersburg in 1798, did not bring its author any considerable recognition, either. Great success, however, followed his second tragedy, *Oedipus in Athens.* Ozerov did not read Greek, so he borrowed his Oedipus not from the classical dramatist Sophocles, but from the French playwright Dussie. This altered the entire tone of tragedy, forgoing all the antique solemnity. Ozerov's Oedipus is not a severe, fate-driven king but a weak, sensitive, forgiving old man.

Ozerov's most acclaimed tragedy was *Fingal.* His interpretation of the plot, borrowed from the poems of Ossian, concentrated on the contradiction between the vicious, plotting character of Swaran and the pure, sincere love of Fingal and Moina. The tragedy was deeply touching and evoked storms of emotion among audiences.

Ozerov's fame reached its zenith in 1807, when his tragedy *Dmitrii Donskoi* was staged. The work with its patriotic themes roused the loyalties of its Russian audiences, who were feeling particularly nationalistic due to the war with Napoleon. The elements of a touching love story combined with lofty heroism never failed to produce a thunderstorm of applause.

Historically speaking, Ozerov is mainly known as the dramatist who brought the elements of sentimentality into Russian tragedy, while strictly following the formal canons of pseudo-classical drama.

Paine, Thomas (1737–1809) *journalist, essayist, pamphleteer*

Thomas Paine, one of the most influential revolutionary writers of the modern era, was born into a British family of modest means. At the Thetford Grammar School, the inquisitive young boy studied mathematics, science, and poetry. Paine was particularly fond of John MILTON and John Bunyan, authors known for their radical perspectives on politics and religion. At age 13, however, Frances and Joseph Paine, members of the working class, withdrew their only child from school so that he could become apprenticed to his father, a corset maker. Paine went along with the decision but eventually escaped his obligations by running off to sea and working as a privateer. Over the years, he found employment selling tobacco products, teaching school, and serving as an exciseman (a governmental employee who imposed taxes on domestic commodities).

At 37 years of age, Paine made a decision that was to have momentous consequences: He resolved to go to America. A letter of introduction from Benjamin FRANKLIN, whom he had met earlier, served him well. In 1774, after a difficult voyage on the *London Packet*, Paine arrived in Philadelphia, the city founded by Quaker William Penn, and was soon employed by a local printer. A year later, he was appointed editor of the *Pennsylvania Magazine*, a publication that flourished under his direction. The man who had spent years struggling just to eke out a living finally discovered a professional niche for himself.

Paine did more than edit articles submitted to the magazine; he also became a journalist and essayist. In *Thomas Paine: Firebrand of the Revolution*, Harvey J. Kaye observes that "the paradox of . . . black bondage in the midst of a prosperous, liberty-loving, and spiritual people astounded him" and inspired him to write "African Slavery in America" (1775), an article that advocated abolition.

Paine also found himself becoming increasingly critical of the ways in which Great Britain wielded its authority over the colonies. He expressed his outrage in *Common Sense* (1776), a pamphlet that Thomas Gustafson, in *Representative Words: Politics, Literature, and the American Language, 1776–1865*, argues effected a "transformation in the terms of the political debate between Britain and the Colonies."

In *American Crisis* (1776), a series of 13 pamphlets Paine composed during the American Revolution, he continued to probe issues related to the quest for liberty. In the first of these leaflets, Paine writes of how these are "times that try men's souls," and he declares that those who do not "shrink from the service of this country" deserve the "love and thanks of man and woman" for having fought against the tyrannical rule of the British. Legend has it that selections from this particular booklet were read to George Washington's troops in order to bolster their spirits as they prepared for an attack on the oppressor.

In 1787 Paine returned to England and turned his attention to writing *Rights of Man* (1791–92). In part one, he expressed his support of the French Revolution and challenged the idea of hereditary monarchy. In part two, he extended his argument to include the problem of inequalities based on social class. Paine held that "something must be wrong in the system of government" when we see, "in countries that are called civilized," the aged being sent "to the workhouse and [the] youth to the gallows." "Why is it," he asked, "that scarcely any are executed but the poor?" Kaye explains that Paine wanted the government to "provide income to the poor and special relief to families with children; pensions for the elderly; public funding of education; financial support for newly married couples and new mothers; funeral expenses for the working poor; and job centers to address unemployment."

Rights of Man met with immediate success: More than 50,000 copies of it were sold within a month of its first publication. Conservative forces, however, were quick to condemn the work, and they claimed his work was treasonous libel. Paine never attended his trial. Instead, he fled to France, where he attained citizenship and celebrity-like status for having so boldly defended the country's cause. Yet when he objected to the execution of King Louis XVI, who as Kaye points out, had "corresponded and conspired with France's enemies," he found himself imprisoned. Fortunately, an American ambassador granted him American citizenship and promised to assist him in traveling back to New York.

The last decades of Paine's life were not easy ones, and he died, impoverished, in 1809.

Critical Analysis

Common Sense, a pamphlet in which Paine called for the inhabitants of America to separate from Britain, is without a doubt Paine's most significant work. The pamphlet was extraordinarily popular. Within a year of its publication, nearly half a million copies were sold. Kaye remarks that Paine "sought no material rewards" from his booklet: He "declined all royalties, insisting that any profits due him be used to purchase mittens for Washington's troops."

In a letter Paine wrote toward the end of his life, he explained that the "motive and object in" all of his "political works" was "to rescue man from tyranny and false systems and false principles of government, and enable him to be free." Paine's genius lay in the way he recognized the extent to which language and thinking could be used to either enslave or liberate humankind. In "Reflections on Titles" (1775), for instance, he analyzes the influence that "high sounding names" have on different types of people. The "reasonable freeman," he explains, "sees through the magic of a title, and examines the man before he approves him." Paine claimed, however, that titles "overawe the superstitious vulgar, and forbid them to inquire into the character of the possessor." He went on to declare that "this sacrifice of common sense is the certain badge which distinguishes slavery from freedom: for when men yield up the privilege of thinking, the last shadow of liberty quits the horizon." In the first chapter of *Common Sense,* Paine builds on his earlier critique of titles in order to challenge the concepts of monarchical rule and the hereditary succession of power. He argues that while "male and female are the distinctions of nature, good and bad the distinctions of heaven," there exist "no truly natural or religious reason" behind the "distinction of men into KINGS AND SUBJECTS." "That difference," as Gustafson observes, has been "created by words and by words alone or by words enforced by fraud and brute force." Denouncing the British form of government was just the first step Paine took in his effort to release the linguistic and mental shackles that bound the colonies to Britain.

In the second and most important chapter, Paine engages in a revolutionary analysis of the specific terms that had been used to describe the relationship between Britain and the colonies. Britain had long been considered the parent country and the colonies her children. As Gustafson notes, debates centered on "whether it was time for Britain to fulfill its role by ending its protection and granting the colonies their independence or whether the colonies were still obliged to be obedient." Drawing upon his "common sense," Paine declares:

> Europe, and not England, is the parent country of America. This new world hath been the asylum for the persecuted lovers of civil and religious liberty from *every part* of Europe. Hither have they fled, not from the tender embraces of the mother, but from the cruelty of the monster; and it is so far true of England, that the same tyranny which drove the first emigrants from home, pursues their descendents still.

In this passage, according to Gustafson, we can see how Paine renounced as "misapplications" the "very words that had defined the relationship between the colonies and Britain." The rulers of Britain had used—or abused—language in order to perpetuate their control over the colonies. Paine, on the other hand, demonstrated to the colonists how they could employ language for other, more liberating purposes.

The reading public was ready to hear what Paine had to say. As Kaye remarks, *Common Sense* "transformed the colonial rebellion into a war for independence" by harnessing the Americans' "shared (but as yet unstated) thoughts" and communicating them in language that was "bold and clear."

Other Works by Thomas Paine

Age of Reason. Whitefish, Mont.: Kessinger Publishing, 2004.

American Crisis. Whitefish, Mont.: Kessinger Publishing, 2004.

Common Sense. Whitefish, Mont.: Kessinger Publishing, 2004.

Rights of Man. Introduction by David Taffel. New York: Barnes and Noble, 2004.

Thomas Paine: Collected Writings. New York: Library of America, 1995.

Works about Thomas Paine

Gustafson, Thomas. *Representative Words: Politics, Literature, and the American Language, 1776–1865.* New York: Cambridge University Press, 1992.

Kaye, Harvey J. *Thomas Paine: Firebrand of the Revolution.* New York: Oxford University Press, 2000.

Keane, John. *Tom Paine: A Political Life.* New York: Grove/Atlantic, 2003.

McLeese, Don. *Thomas Paine.* Vero Beach, Fla.: Rourke Publishing, 2004.

Parini, Giuseppe (1729–1799) *poet*

Giuseppe Parini was born in Bosisio, a small village near Milan, Italy. His father later moved the family to Milan so that Giuseppe could acquire a formal education. Parini began writing poetry under the anagram of Ripano Eupilino and published *Some Verses by Ripano Eupilino* in 1752, which won him a place in the selective Academy of the Transformed in Milan.

In 1754 Parini was ordained as a priest and eventually became a tutor in the Serbelloni family, a post that pleased him only in that it provided material for his *Dialogue on Nobility* (1762), in which the corpses of a nobleman and a poet converse on the true nature of nobility. The publication of "Morning" and "Midday" in 1763, his poetic satire on the aristocracy later collected as *The Day,* improved Parini's circumstances. He became a professor of literature at the Palatine School, and one of his plays, *Ascanio in Alba,* was put to music by Mozart and performed as an opera in 1771. During the French occupation, Parini reluctantly held a government post but was said to have distributed his stipend among the poor in protest of Bonaparte's rule.

Parini also published his *Odes* (1795) and several literary treatises, including a tract on aesthetics, *Principles of Literature* (1801), but *The Day* is his most accomplished work. In the form of a mock EPIC similar to Alexander POPE's *The Rape of the Lock, The Day* chronicles the daily routine of an idle fop as though his activities were heroic deeds. The poem's satire skewered the Milanese aristocracy, exposing the elaborate and superficial rituals of fashionable society by using the dandified nature of its hero.

After Parini's death, "Evening" and "Night" were found among his papers, and the first complete edition of *The Day* was published in Milan in 1801. Its elegant verse, playful tone, and sharp insights into the follies of the idle life provided a model for later poets who, following Parini's lead, hoped to use laughter to arouse shame and curb error.

An English Version of a Work by Giuseppe Parini

The Day: Morning, Midday, Evening, and Night. Translated by Herbert Morris Bower. Westport, Conn.: Hyperion Press, 1978.

Works about Giuseppe Parini

Griffiths, C. E. J., and R. Hastings, eds. *The Cultural Heritage of the Italian Renaissance.* New York: Edwin Mellen Press, 1993.

Tusiani, Joseph. "Giuseppe Parini, Poet of Education." *Paideia* 3, no. 1 (1974): 26–33.

Pascal, Blaise (1623–1662) *scientist, mathematician, theologian*

The 17th century was a time of tremendous intellectual activity in many different fields. The scientific revolution was in full swing and many of Europe's leading minds were turning their attention to the mysteries of the physical world. At the same time, scholars and philosophers were debating profound questions of religion and ethics. Among the great thinkers who emerged during this period was the French genius, Blaise Pascal.

Pascal was born in the town of Clermont. His mother died when he was only three, and he was raised almost entirely by his father, Étienne Pascal, who was a moderately prosperous civil servant.

Etienne devoted himself to the education of his son, and moved the family to Paris in 1631. Rather than rely on uncertain tutors, Etienne himself took the largest responsibility for the teaching of his son. Under the tutelage of his father, Pascal soon proved to be a mathematical prodigy. Through his father, Pascal was introduced to a group known as the Académie Mersenne, which contained some of the leading mathematical minds in Paris.

The Pascal family moved to the city of Rouen in 1639. A few years later, Pascal invented a machine that could do mathematical calculations. This invention was widely admired by many of the intellectual elite of France, although it was never manufactured on a large scale. Pascal also engaged in scientific work, conducting experiments in an attempt to discover the nature of a vacuum. In 1640, when he was still a teenager, he published an essay titled "Essai sur les coniques," which dealt with highly complicated geometrical problems. Although he was still quite young, it had become clear that he possessed great intellectual abilities.

Also during the years in Rouen, Pascal came under the influence of the religious sect known as the Jansenists. The Jansenists followed an unconventional form of Catholicism but, unlike the Protestant sects, remained nominally loyal to the Roman Catholic Church. The effect of Jansenist teachings turned Pascal's attention toward religious matters, although he also remained extremely interested in mathematical and scientific subjects.

Pascal returned to Paris in 1647, intending to devote himself to serious academic studies. On two occasions, he met the famous French scientist and philosopher, Rene DESCARTES. Pascal published a work entitled *Expériences Nouvelles,* in which he describes many of his ideas concerning physics. It was well received by the scientific thinkers of Paris. During all this time, Pascal engaged in academic debates, in which he distinguished himself, with some of the foremost intellectuals of the day.

The more time he spent in Paris, the more attracted he became to its frivolous and lighthearted lifestyle. Paris was, at this time, the most cultured and refined city in the world, with innumerable pleasurable distractions. Gradually, Pascal began spending more of his time in idle social amusements than in doing his work. His fondness for social interaction conflicted with his religious beliefs and desire to make intellectual contributions. On November 23, 1654, he apparently had an intense religious experience, during which he renounced his social lifestyle and resolved to devote himself to religion.

After his experience, Pascal moved to the Jansenist convent of Port-Royal, although he did not take holy orders to become a monk. From then on, he lived an austere life, thinking and writing on religious and mathematical subjects, until his death eight years later.

In his first literary effort after his 1654 experience, Pascal became involved in disputes between the Jansenists and the Jesuit order. A Jansenist professor, Antoine Arnauld, has been criticized by the Jesuits for his views. Pascal wrote out a spirited defense of Arnauld titled *Lettres Provinciales.* Using both logical and moral arguments, Pascal refuted the attacks of the Jesuits, while criticizing them for their biased attitude toward the Jansenists.

During this time, Pascal engaged in other literary battles in defense of Jansenism and was preparing a complete defense of the Christian religion in general. He also wrote on the subject of miracles, which was in stark contrast to the developing scientific and rational atmosphere of the age.

In the late 1650s, Pascal began writing the fragments of work that would later be put together to form his most famous and influential work, the *Pensées,* or *Thoughts.* He was, however, in extremely poor health, and the intellectual energy that had once characterized his work was beginning to fade. On August 19, 1662, at age 39, Pascal died in the home of his sister.

Critical Analysis

The most famous of Pascal's works is the *Pensées,* which were written in patchy form in the last few years of his life. Technically, it is not a book at all, but simply a collection of scattered fragments in which he jotted his thoughts on religious matters.

He had intended to unify these disconnected pieces into a comprehensive defense of the Christian religion, but this project was still incomplete when he died.

Despite its incompleteness and lack of organization, the *Pensees* remains a masterpiece of theological thought. Some of Pascal's arguments, such as the discussion of prophecies and miracles, had been used by many theologians before him. But the most innovative and influential idea presented in the work was quite original. It is known as "Pascal's Wager."

Pascal presents the idea that accepting Christianity might not appear reasonable to a rational person, but neither can it appear unreasonable. Therefore, a rational person should accept Christianity for the following reason. If a person accepts Christianity and Christianity is true, the rewards for the person are infinite, but if a person accepts Christianity and Christianity is not true, the person loses nothing. On the other hand, if a person rejects Christianity and Christianity is true, the person faces the penalties of damnation, while if a person rejects Christianity and Christianity is not true, he has gained nothing. For all these reasons, Pascal argues, a reasonable person should accept Christianity.

This argument has certain flaws. For example, it does not take into account the existence of other religions, simply presenting the choice as being between Christianity and atheism. Furthermore, the idea of choosing salvation entirely for reasons of self-interest has been criticized by many theologians. Nevertheless, Pascal's Wager became an important part of theological thought.

Although his life was comparatively short, Pascal made great contributions to a variety of fields. The clarity of his style made a significant impact on the French language. He was an excellent mathematician and significantly advanced the study of geometry. His scientific work, though overshadowed by such scientists as Isaac Newton and Galileo GALILEI, was also quite important. However, it is in the subjects of theology and religion that the true importance of Pascal's work remains. Although

Jansenism has disappeared, Pascal's work in defense of the sect caused him to devise some of the most important theological arguments of the 17th century. Furthermore, the ideas contained in the *Pensees* influence religious thought to the present day.

English Versions of Works by Blaise Pascal

Contradictions, Oppositions and Denials in the Life of the Mind. Albuquerque, N.M.: American Classical College Press, 1987.

Mind on Fire: A Faith for the Skeptical and Indifferent. Edited by James M. Houston. Vancouver, B.C.: Regent College Publishing, 2003.

Pensées. Translated by W. F. Trotter. Mineola, N.Y.: Dover, 2003.

Provincial Letters. Eugene, Ore.: Wipf and Stock Publishers, 1997.

The Gospel of the Gospels. Torino, Italy: Allemandi, Umberto & Company, 2000.

Works about Blaise Pascal

Davidson, Hugh M. *Blaise Pascal.* Boston: Twayne, 1983.

Ludwin, Dawn M. *Blaise Pascal's Quest for the Ineffable.* New York: Peter Lang, 2001.

O'Connell, Marvin R., et al. *Blaise Pascal: Reasons of the Heart.* Grand Rapids, Mich.: William B. Eerdmans, 1997.

Shea, William R. *Designing Experiments and Games of Chance: The Unconventional Science of Blaise Pascal.* Sagamore Beach, Mass.: Watson Publishing, 2003.

pastoral   (200s B.C.–A.D. 1800s)

Named after the Latin word *pastor,* meaning "shepherd," pastorals are poems that idealize rustic, country life and feature shepherds and other rural persons. Typically, the shepherds of these poems speak in elevated language and dress in a manner above their status. The first pastorals were penned by Theocritus (ca. 310–ca. 250 B.C.) in his *Idylls.*

Pastorals are organized according to three main groups: monologues, eclogues, and laments. Pastoral monologues are poems praising or complaining about a particular person; eclogues are those poems involving the notion of a singing contest; and laments mourn a dead loved one.

The pastoral style has contributed to the creation of other literary forms, including the pastoral drama, pastoral romance, and pastoral elegy. Pastoral dramas developed in RENAISSANCE Italy and emerged thereafter in England. *Aminta* by the Italian Torquato TASSO, is an example of the form, as is William SHAKESPEARE's play *As You Like It.*

Pastoral romances are stories written in prose that involve characters with pastoral names, such as Cuddie, Colin, and Meliboeus, and feature complicated plotlines interspersed with songs. Examples of pastoral romances include the Italian romance *Ameto* by Giovanni BOCCACCIO, *Arcadia* by Sir Philip SIDNEY of England, and *Diana enamorada* by the Spanish writer Jorge de Montemayor.

Pastoral elegies evolved from Virgil's models of traditional pastorals, as seen in his *Eclogues.* In a pastoral elegy, the speaker of the poem, usually a shepherd-poet, asks a muse for inspiration, mourns the loss of a fellow shepherd-poet, criticizes the dead shepherd's guardians (usually nymphs) for their neglect, introduces a procession of fellow mourners, questions divine providence, and offers a closing consolation. This formula is referred to as *Conventions* and can best be seen in John MILTON's "Lycidas."

See also Christopher MARLOWE.

English Versions of Pastorals

Pope, Alexander. *Pastoral Poetry and an Essay on Criticism.* New Haven, Conn.: Yale University Press, 1961.

Theocritus. *Idylls.* Translated by Richard Hunter and Anthony Verity. Oxford: Oxford University Press, 2003.

Virgil. *The Eclogues of Virgil.* Translated by David Ferry. New York: Farrar, Straus and Giroux, 2000.

Works about Pastorals

Empson, William. *Some Versions of Pastoral.* London: Chatto and Windus, 1935.

Greg, W. W. *Pastoral Poetry and Pastoral Drama: A Literary Inquiry.* New York: Russell and Russell, 1959.

Metzger, Lore. *One Foot in Eden: Modes of Pastoral in Romantic Poetry.* Chapel Hill: University of North Carolina Press, 1986.

Rosenmeyer, Thomas G. *Green Cabinet: Theocritus and European Pastoral Poetry.* London: Bristol Classic Press, 2003.

Pearl poet (1300s) *poet*

The identity of the *Pearl* poet remains unknown, but he is attributed with the writing of four Middle English poems: *Pearl, Patience, Purity* (or *Cleanness*), and SIR GAWAIN AND THE GREEN KNIGHT, all composed in the latter half of the 14th century and written down around 1400. The poet's work suggests that he was well read, perhaps trained as a clerk, and he was acquainted with life in the higher social classes. Though he lived at the same time as CHAUCER and LANGLAND, he seems not to have been influenced by them. The *Pearl* poet was more at home in the countryside and traditions of northern and western Britain and had little to do with the fashionable circles of London.

The *Pearl* poet was part of the Alliterative Revival, which involved a resurgence of interest in earlier English heroic themes and the style of alliterative verse, which uses frequent repetition of sound for musical effect. His use of scripture proves the poet knew the Latin Bible, and the motif of the allegorical dream-vision along with the stanza formats and rhyme schemes are inherited from French tradition.

The plot of *Pearl* is simple: The narrator, sorrowing over the grave of his two-year-old daughter, has a vision in which she appears to him. His address to her conveys his sorrow:

> "O Pearl!" said I, "in pearls arrayed,
> Are you my pearl whose loss I mourn?
> Lament alone by night I made. . . ."

As the poem proceeds, the young girl converses with the narrator about the joys of heaven and the errors of human grief. She grants him a glimpse of Paradise, which so excites him that, when he tries to join her, he is rudely awakened.

Composed in an intricate rhyme pattern, the poem uses the image of the pearl on multiple levels to represent the young girl, the delights of paradise, and the wisdom of Christian understanding. The poem is at once an elegy for the daughter, a consolation for loss, and an illumination of Christian doctrine, rendered in an artistic unity that makes it a work of singular beauty in the canon of Middle English literature.

Works by the *Pearl* Poet

The Complete Works of the Pearl *Poet.* Translated by Casey Finch and edited by Malcolm Andrew and C. Peterson. Berkeley: University of California Press, 1993.

The Pearl *Poem in Middle and Modern English.* Edited by William Vantuono. New York: University Press of America, 1987.

Works about the *Pearl* Poet

Moorman, Charles. *The* Pearl-*Poet.* New York: Twayne, 1968.

Rhodes, James Francis. *Poetry Does Theology: Chaucer, Grosseteste, and the* Pearl-*Poet.* Notre Dame, Ind.: University of Notre Dame Press, 2001.

Pepys, Samuel (1633–1703) *diarist*

Samuel Pepys (pronounced "peeps") was born in 1633, the fifth of 11 children of a tailor, John Pepys. He attended Magdalene College, Cambridge, on a scholarship, receiving his bachelor's degree in 1654. He secured a job as secretary to his relative Sir Edward Montagu, and the following year married 15-year-old Elizabeth St. Michel.

In 1660 Pepys began his *Diary.* He wrote in code, solely for his own enjoyment. He begins with the adventure of going to sea with his employer, Sir Edward Montagu, to escort Charles Stuart from

Holland for his coronation as King Charles II (since the execution of Charles I in 1649 England had been without a king). On the return journey from Holland, Pepys heard the king's stories of his flight from the army that destroyed his father:

> It made me ready to weep to hear the stories that he told. . . . As his traveling four days and three nights on foot, every step up to the knees in dirt . . . with nothing but a green coat and a pair of country breeches on and a pair of country shoes, that made him so sore all over his feet that he could scarce stir.

Soon after the royal party's arrival in London, Pepys was appointed to an administrative job in the Royal Navy Dockyards; he served the navy for the rest of his working life.

In 1661 Pepys observed the coronation of Charles II. Pepys's description of this day is so detailed that he even includes the memory of desperately needing an outhouse and of sneaking into the banquet hall to get a bit of food from the tables. Pepys admits to drinking too much that night, and vomiting as a result.

Pepys's journal is full of accounts of parties where the wine flows freely. He is something of a womanizer, and writes of his adventures with women quite freely, yet his affairs do not alienate the reader; rather, they allow Pepys to be seen as a believable, real person. His tender regard for his wife is convincing too, as well as his pride in her beauty.

Pepys loved the theater, and the diary is an important source of information about the theatrical scene in Restoration London. He was intellectually curious and was friends with many of the important thinkers of his day, whose conversations can be reconstructed through his records.

His career was another focus of the *Diary*. Pepys advanced through the ranks of the navy by being a sharp observer, both of the people he worked with and what needed to be done. Pepys's meticulous journal-keeping may have given him skills that helped him do well professionally.

In 1665 he recorded London's terrible epidemic of bubonic plague:

> This day, much against my Will, I did in Drury-lane, see two or three houses marked with a red cross upon the doors, and "Lord have mercy upon us" writ there; which was a sad sight to me. . . . It put me into an ill conception of myself and my smell, so that I was forced to buy some roll-tobacco to smell and to chaw, which took away the apprehension.

One-fourth of the population of London was killed by the plague.

The next year another tragedy struck London: the Great Fire. Strong easterly winds and a summer drought culminated in the worst destruction the city would see until the Blitz of 1940. Pepys's birthplace was destroyed, but his home and office were spared. He admits he was "much terrified in the nights . . ., with dreams of fire and falling down of houses."

In 1669 Pepys discontinued his diary because he feared that his eyesight was failing. His wife died of a fever the next year, but Pepys lived for another 34 years, achieving considerable rank in the navy and winning an enviable sociable position. In 1684 he was made president of the Royal Society. His friend John Evelyn described him as "universally beloved, hospitable, generous, learned in many things, skilled in music, a very great treasurer of learned men."

Pepys bequeathed his diary to his alma mater, Magdalene College, but it was not deciphered until the 19th century; an edited version was published in 1825, and the full diary of almost 4,000 pages in 1893. One of Pepys's most famous admirers was the novelist Robert Louis Stevenson (1850–94), who notes Pepys's sincerity:

> He was not unconscious of his errors—far from it; he was often startled into shame, often reformed, often made and broke his vows of change. But whether he did ill or well, he was still his own unequalled self; still that entrancing ego of whom alone he cared to write. . . . He

shows himself throughout a sterling humanist. Indeed, he who loves himself, not in idle vanity, but with a plenitude of knowledge, is the best equipped of all to love his neighbors.

Works by Samuel Pepys

Particular Friends: The Correspondence of Samuel Pepys and John Evelyn. Edited by Guy de la Bedoyere. Rochester, N.Y.: Boydell and Brewer, 1997.

The Diary of Samuel Pepys (Abridged). Edited by Richard Le Gallienne. New York: Random House, 2003.

Works about Samuel Pepys

Coote, Stephen. *Samuel Pepys.* New York: Palgrave, 2001.

Taylor, Ivan E. *Samuel Pepys.* Boston: Twayne, 1989.

Tomalin, Claire. *Samuel Pepys: The Unequalled Self.* New York: Vintage, 2003.

Peralta Barnuevo, Pedro de (1664–1743)

poet, dramatist, scholar

The Peruvian scholar Pedro de Peralta Barnuevo produced more than 80 works covering a diverse range of subjects, including history, religion, medicine, literature, astronomy, and military engineering.

Born in Lima, Peralta was a Criollo or Creole, the name given to persons of Spanish origin born in the colonies. After studying law at the University of San Marcos, he became professor of mathematics and later rector of that institution.

From 1718 to 1743 Peralta held the office of cosmographer, completing *Conocimientos de los Tiempos,* begun in 1680 by his predecessor, Juan Ramón Koenig. Peralta also served as chief engineer of Peru and comptroller of the *audiencia,* or tribunal, of Lima. When the ancient wall of Callao was destroyed by the earthquake of 1687, it was Peralta who devised plans for its reconstruction.

Among his literary works for the stage are a number of plays in the baroque style. They include comedies such as *Triunfo de amor y muerte (The*

Triumph of Love and Death, 1710) and *Afectos vencen finezas (Affections Conquer Finenesses,* 1720). His tragedy *La Rodoguna* (1710) shows the influence of the French playwright CORNEILLE.

Fluent in six languages, Peralta could write poetry in each of them. Perhaps the best known of his poetic works is the epic *Lima fundada o conquista del Peru (The Founding of Lima or Conquest of Peru,* 1732), which deals with the life of Pizarro. His other major work of poetry was *Pasión y triunfo de Cristo (Passion and Triumph of Christ,* 1737).

Until 1730, when he published *Historia de España vindicada,* Peralta's work reflected a European worldview. With *Lima fundada,* however, he began to target a Criollo readership. Like many Criollos, Peralta was dissatisfied with the political and cultural censorship exercised by Spain over its colonies.

In *Diálogo de los muertos: la causa académica (Dialogue of the Dead: The Academic Case),* modeled on the Roman satirist Lucian, Peralta ridiculed the institutions with which he had been associated as an official. While he did not break completely with traditional Spanish culture, he nonetheless began to articulate a Criollo viewpoint from which later radical intellectuals would develop a distinct Latin American identity.

English Versions of Works by Pedro de Peralta Barnuevo

Censorship and Art in Pre-Enlightenment Lima: Pedro de Peralta Barnuevo's Dialogo de Las Muertos: La Causa Academica. Translated by Jerry M. Williams. Madrid, Spain: Scripta Humanistica, 1994.

Peralta Barnuevo and the Discourse of Loyalty: A Critical Edition of Four Selected Texts. Translated by Jerry M. Williams. Phoenix: Arizona State University, Center for Latin American Studies, 1997.

A Work about Pedro de Peralta Barnuevo

Hill, Ruth Ann. *Sceptres and Sciences in the Spains: Four Humanists and the New Philosophy.* Liverpool, U.K.: Liverpool University Press, 2000.

Perrault, Charles (1628–1703) *poet, fiction writer*

The son of Pierre Perrault, a magistrate in the Paris Parlement, Charles Perrault received a law degree in 1651. In 1662 he became a member of the Petite Académie des Inscriptions et Belles-Lettres, and in that capacity designed and wrote inscriptions for the palaces of the Louvre and Versailles. In 1672 he married Marie Guichon and had three children.

In 1671 Perrault was elected to the ACADÉMIE FRANÇAISE. He resigned his government post in 1682, however, to dedicate his life to writing. He described his public life in his *Mémoires*, which remained unpublished until the 19th century. His other works include *Parallèle des Anciens et des Modernes* (1688–97), in which he claimed that modern writers were superior to ancient classical authors, and the poem "Le Siècle de Louis le Grand" (1687), in which he claimed the age of Louis XIV should have a Christian culture distinct from that of the ancient world.

Perrault also authored numerous fairy tales, including "Cinderella," "Sleeping Beauty" and "Puss in Boots." He originally titled his collection *Contes de ma Mère l'oye,* or *Tales of Mother Goose* (1697), a traditional French expression for folktales. They became immensely popular in France and first appeared in English in 1729.

Perrault based many of his tales on earlier stories, including works by Italian writers Basile and Straparola, contributing his own elegant and witty style to each. "Little Red Riding Hood," however, is said to be a Perrault original.

The settings of the tales are contemporary, and each comes with a stated or implied moral. The setting, for instance, in "Sleeping Beauty" is a palace with a hall of mirrors resembling the one at Versailles. And, according to Perrault, the moral of the story is that, while it is a fine thing to wait 100 years for the right husband, "we can no longer find a girl who would sleep so tranquilly."

Perrault said that he wrote the *Contes* as moral tales for children, but he also intended them to be modern works that could be appreciated by a so-phisticated, adult audience. As Jeanne Morgan Zarucchi notes, Perrault wrote "one of the handful of works whose message is accessible to later generations, and whose readership crosses barriers of time and nationality."

An English Version of Works by Charles Perrault

Cinderella, Puss in Boots, and Other Favorite Tales as told by Charles Perrault. Translated by A. E. Johnson. New York: Abrams, 2000.

A Work about Charles Perrault

Zarucchi, Morgan, Jeanne. *Perrault's Morals for Moderns.* New York: Peter Lang, 1985.

Petrarch (Francesco Petracco) (1304–1374) *poet*

Petrarch was born at Arezzo, in Tuscany. The young poet who later signed his works "Petrarca" grew up in Marseilles, France, studying Latin grammar and rhetoric. In 1316 his father sent him to the University of Montpellier to study law, but Francesco was more interested in reading Latin classics. When his father attempted to burn the books he felt were wasting his son's time, young Francesco protested so loudly that his father reached into the fire to rescue his two favorites: Virgil and the *Rhetorics* of Cicero.

After his father's death in 1326, Petrarch abandoned the legal profession and returned home to write. A pivotal moment of his life took place on April 6, 1327, when he saw and instantly fell in love with a young woman whom he called Laura. Although the two never married, the poems he wrote for her completely transformed the genre of lyrical poetry, ensuring Petrarch's fame.

Petrarch moved to Vaucluse to devote himself to a solitary life of study, correspondence with close companions, and the writing of both Latin and Italian poetry and prose. In 1341 he was crowned poet laureate at Rome, a coveted honor. He began to study the Greek language and found inspiration in the Greek ideals of philosophy and literature. In 1348 the Black Plague swept Italy, claiming the lives of thousands, including his beloved Laura, which lent a deep melancholy to Petrarch's poetry. In 1350 he received a letter from an admirer named Giovanni BOCCACCIO, and a lifelong friendship began.

A restless spirit all his life, beginning works and then putting them aside or finishing them and not sending them to their intended recipients, Petrarch traveled frequently throughout his life. He lived successively in Milan, Padua, and Verona, Italy, and in his later years turned to revising, editing, and collecting his finished works. He died at Arquà at age 70.

For Petrarch, his contentment with the quiet serenity of solitary life vied constantly with his desire to travel and be of use to others. A peaceful soul, he lived in a century characterized by famine, plague, and the advent of the Hundred Years' War. Poets tended to see it as a century of moral decline and looked with nostalgia to the Golden Age of classical times. Though he loved the voices from the past and addressed letters to some of his favorites, including Seneca and Horace, Petrarch delighted in the artists of his own time, including Dante and Boccaccio. Standing between the Middle Ages and the RENAISSANCE, and at the forefront of Italian HUMANISM, Petrarch reaches us as the voice of one man feeling the greatness within and around him and captivated by the simplest moments of life.

While most famous as the plaintive lover of the *Canzoniere* (the *Lyric Poems*, also called the *Rhymes*), Petrarch tried his hand at a variety of works, including a scholarly edition of Livy's *Decades*. In 1337 he began *On Illustrious Men*, a series of biographies he later extended to include Old Testament and Christian heroes as well as those of classical antiquity. He also wrote a series of *Triumphs*, designed as allegorical contemplations on Love, Chastity, Death, Fame, Time, and Eternity.

In 1343 Petrarch began the *Secretum* (*Secret Book*), modeled on a work he adored, the *Confessions* of Augustine. In these soul-searchings composed as a dialogue between two characters named Petrarch and Augustine, the distressed poet analyzes his sins and imagines himself bound by two golden chains: his love for Laura and his desire for glory. His other works included *On the Life of Solitude* (1346), addressed to his friend Philippe; *On Religious Leisure* (1356), addressed to his brother Gherardo; and *Remedies for Fortune Fair and Foul* (1354). In 1367 he wrote *On His Own Ignorance and That of Many Others* partly to dispel rumors that he was excessively wealthy. In 1370 he composed his last will and testament.

Throughout his life, Petrarch wrote letters in verse, collected in *Metrical Letters*, sometimes separated as the *Letters on Familiar Affairs* and *Letters of Riper Years*. One of his most read letters is his epistle addressed to Posterity. Creating work that would survive him was one of Petrarch's lifelong concerns. He could not have foreseen that his collection of *Canzoniere* would become one of the most influential books of Western literature, that the forms he used would be named after him (the Petrarchan SONNET), or that his style would so inspire future generations that later writers would not dare to call themselves poets unless they had thoroughly read and studied Petrarch's work.

Critical Analysis

The poems collected in the *Canzoniere* show an impressive range of forms: There are 317 sonnets, 29 canzoni, nine sestinas, seven ballads, and four madrigals. The metaphors and conceits that Petrarch used to create a poetic language of love have been so often imitated as to be extremely familiar to contemporary readers, but in Petrarch's time these images were refreshingly new, such as his description of love at first sight in poem 61:

> Oh blessed be the day, the month, the year,
> the season and the time, the hour, the instant,
> the gracious countryside, the place where I
> was struck by those two lovely eyes that
>   bound me.

He goes on to describe himself as a prisoner held in bondage by the force of love, calling Laura's eyes and Laura's presence the bows and arrows of love that have wounded his heart.

In his collection of poetry, Petrarch shows an impressive depth of knowledge about the Latin tradition of poetry (he had long studied authors such as Ovid and Catullus), but he also takes advantage of the new respect for Italian writing won by his predecessor, Dante. Petrarch opposes the medieval tradition of writing solely to provide moral instruction and instead, in the poetic introduction to his works, points out that they are full of literary, moral, and other defects. The author seems to write out of a sense of deep shame and awareness of his self-absorption and vanity. Even so, he vows that the extent of his passion presses him to write, and he goes on to do so with such innovative expressions of beauty that, despite the errors, he raises the experience of heartbreak to a sublime transformation.

Throughout the *Canzoniere*, Petrarch explores his inner feelings in great detail, exposing the peaks of emotional ecstasy and the depths of human sincerity, looking first at the vastness of creation and then tenderly observing a single moment of wonder. The poems contain a subtle irony, revealing an author adept at describing natural works as well as accurately portraying human nature. Some critics accused Petrarch of worshiping Laura to the point of idolatry, but some felt his ability to understand and render the intricacies of human experience inspired in others a new respect for individuality and potential, a foundation of humanistic thought.

Along with Dante and Boccaccio, the other two crowns in the "three crowns of Italy," Petrarch's writing left an enduring stamp on European writers to follow. Poets such as France's Pierre de RONSARD and England's Geoffrey CHAUCER employed and elaborated on Petrarch's language of love, as did authors of the medieval romances. Significantly, Petrarch's influence is due not to his ambitious works of epic scope but to his studies of the complex and bewildering human heart. Of Petrarch's poetry, translator Mark Musa says, "the pleasure of reading the *Canzoniere* [comes] suddenly, from its many small revelations . . . inviting us to rage, weep, or laugh." In a modern gallery of illustrious men, Petrarch would certainly claim a place.

English Versions of Works by Petrarch

My Secret Book. Translated by J. G. Nichols. London: Hesperus Press, 2002.
Selections from the Canzoniere and Other Works. Translated by Mark Musa. New York: Oxford University Press, 1999.
Shearer, Susan, S., ed. *Petrarch: On Religious Leisure*. New York: Italica Press, 2002.

Works about Petrarch

Hainsworth, Peter. *Petrarch the Poet*. New York: Routledge, 1988.
Petrie, Jennifer. *Petrarch*. Dublin: Irish Academic Press, 1983.
Reeve, Henry. *Petrarch*. La Vergne, Tenn.: University Press of the Pacific, 2002.
Robinson, James H. *Petrarch: The First Modern Scholar and Man of Letters*. La Vergne, Tenn.: University Press of the Pacific, 2003.

Pico della Mirandola, Count Giovanni
(1463–1494) *poet, nonfiction writer*

One of the greatest and most influential writers of the Italian RENAISSANCE, Giovanni Pico della Mirandola is celebrated for his contributions to the HUMANISM movement, which emphasized the importance of humankind in the universe and sought to reconcile or integrate the classical, pagan past with the Christian present.

Pico was born in Mirandola, a territory near Modena, Italy. He received a thorough education, including training in Latin, Greek, Hebrew, and Arabic. As a result of his studies, Pico ardently believed that all philosophies and theologies contained important insights and were deserving of study. A humanist and defender of scholastic philosophy,

Pico wrote several works, including *Apologia,* a defense of his *Oration; Heptaplus,* an interpretation of the Creation story in Genesis; *De Ente et Uno (On Being and Unity),* a philosophical work that attempts to reconcile Aristotelianism and Platonism; as well as poems in Italian and Latin.

Oration on the Dignity of Man is his most celebrated work. In it, Pico elaborates upon Marcilio Ficino's belief in humankind's universality and argues further that humans possess the freedom to choose to live however they desire. In the following passage, for example, God tells Adam:

> Thou . . . art the molder and maker of thyself; thou mayest sculpt thyself into whatever shape thou dost prefer. Thou canst grow downward into the lower natures which are brutes. Thou canst again grow upward from thy soul's reason into the higher natures which are divine.

In this passage and in others, Pico present humans not as entities who are forced to act within a fixed hierarchy of order, but as agents free to become whatever they choose.

In his later years, Pico became increasingly concerned with conflicts between religion and philosophy, but his interest in reconciling multiple philosophies and cultural beliefs and in the importance of individual agency did not waver. His embracing of multiple viewpoints from a variety of cultures and his interest in the nature of humankind made him a model scholar for fellow humanists and for those future humanist thinkers who followed.

An English Version of a Work by Count Giovanni Pico della Mirandola
Pico Della Mirandola: On the Dignity of Man, On Being and the One, Heptaplus. Translated by Charles Glenn Wallis. New York: Bobbs-Merrill, 1940.

A Work about Count Giovanni Pico della Mirandola
Craven, William G. *Giovanni Pico della Mirandola: Symbol of His Age: Modern Interpretations.* Geneva: Libraire Droz, 1981.

Pisan, Christine de (Pizan) (ca. 1364– ca. 1431) *poet, scholar*
Christine de Pisan is considered one of the first professional female writers. Born in Venice to Thomas of Pisan, a physician and astrologer, the young Christine moved with her family to Paris in 1368. In 1379 she married Étienne de Castel, a royal secretary. The ascension of Charles VI in 1380 and the death of her father in 1385 caused difficulties in the family's fortunes, and then the death of her husband left Christine with three small children to support. Where most women would have remarried or entered a convent, Christine, who had received more than the usual education for women, thanks to her father, began to write. She first composed love poetry and devotional texts, and then turned to longer prose works. In 1418 she fled a collapsing political scene and lived in seclusion for 11 years. In 1429 she wrote a celebration of the life of Joan of Arc and, perhaps fortunately, did not live to see her hero betrayed and executed.

Though she composed in French, Christine's writing shows a familiarity with Latin prose and traditions. Her poetry and prose demonstrate her versatility, technical mastery, and intellectual refinement. Born at court and practiced in courtesy, she was subtle rather than revolutionary in her critiques of society, particularly its attitudes toward women. She participated in the famous quarrel over Guillaume de Lorris and Jean de Meun's *The Romance of the Rose,* which she maintained was immoral and unflattering in its representations of women. In works such as the *Book of Feats of Arms and Chivalry* (1410) and *Book of the Three Virtues* (1405), the reader can see, cunningly concealed behind her words, the outrage she felt over the way women were treated in French society. This outrage achieved its best expression in her work in defense of women most familiar to readers today, *The Book of the City of Ladies* (1404–05).

In this book Christine uses a popular medieval literary convention, the author's conversation with a series of allegorical figures, to celebrate the deeds of valiant women of the past. This series of revelations has the effect of highlighting the positive contributions women have made to history and challenging current stereotypes of the nature and accepted social status of women. In the *City of Ladies* the narrator, who is female, converses with other female characters named Reason, Justice, and Rectitude, who offer instruction to the reader in the ways of right-thinking and right action. This passage from the *Book* shows Christine's style, theme, and sly humor:

> "After Lady Rectitude had told me all this, I answered her, 'Certainly, my lady, it seems to me an outstanding honor to the feminine sex to hear about so many excellent ladies. Everyone should be extremely pleased that, in addition to their other virtues, such great love could reside in a woman's heart. . . . Let Mathéolus and all the other prattlers who have spoken against women with such envy and falsehood go to sleep and stay quiet.'"
>
> (II.19.1)

Scholar Maria Warner writes "*The Book of the City of Ladies* represents a determined and clearheaded woman's attempt to take apart the structure of her contemporaries' prejudices." Warner also observes, "Christine here is at her best as a storyteller when she writes from personal truth and emotion, and her rebukes rise from within the sting of lived experience." Though her advocating for education for women was revolutionary for her time, Christine meant only to question, not overturn, social order. Critic Renate Blumenfeld-Kosinski states Christine's "dearest wishes were that women should be recognized for their true worth and be treated well," and that "people should treasure learning." Christine used her pen as a tool in a larger struggle to resist the social prejudices and pressures of her day, and her work raises questions about violence toward and treatment of women that have yet to be resolved.

English Versions of Works by Christine de Pisan

Selected Writings of Christine de Pizan. Edited by Renate Blumenfeld-Kosinski. New York: W.W. Norton, 1997.

The Book of the City of Ladies. Translated by Earl Jeffreys Richards. New York: Persea Books, 1982.

Works about Christine de Pisan

Richard, Earl Jeffreys, ed. *Christine de Pizan and Medieval French Lyric.* Gainesville: University Press of Florida, 2000.

Willard, Charity Cannon. *Christine de Pizan: Her Life and Works.* New York: Persea Books, 1984.

Pléiade (1549–1589)

The Pléiade was a 16th-century group of poets and critics who revolutionized French poetry. They named themselves after a group of seven Hellenistic tragic poets who flourished in Alexandria during the third century B.C. "Pleiad" is also the astronomer's name for a group of seven stars in the constellation Taurus, as well as the term referring to seven lovely mountain nymphs in Greek mythology. It is an appropriate term for the seven men who banded together to introduce classical forms and clarity to French poetry during the REN-AISSANCE. The group consisted of its leader Pierre de RONSARD, and Joachim du BELLAY, Rémy Belleau, Étienne Jodelle, Pontus de Tyard, Jean-Antoine Baïf, and the humanist scholar Jean Daurat.

The official manifesto of the Pléiade, *La Deffence et Illustration de la Langue Françoyse (The Defense and Illustration of the French Language),* was written by du Bellay and appeared in 1549. This work clearly demands a break from the medieval poetic traditions and forms and embraces the Renaissance rediscovery of classical models. Du Bellay demands that poets should find new themes of inspiration and create new genres based upon Greek and Latin writers. Like Dante Alighieri had argued almost 300 years before, du Bellay urges writers to use French, rather than Latin, for their serious work. However, he admits that the French language needs help in becoming as expressive as Latin or Greek and suggests that writers borrow from the two classical languages, as well as from Old French, and collect unusual words from the special vocabularies of hunting, falconry, and various handicrafts. The Pléiades introduced such important forms as the alexandrine, the sestina, and the SONNET into French poetry.

Ronsard and du Bellay were the strongest poets of the Pléiade. They not only mastered classical forms and found inspiration in classical themes, but they also used fresh, innovative language and images to capture universal human feelings that transcend cultures. Both men believed in the French language's potential for great poetic expression, and both used their knowledge of classical languages to enrich French without Latinizing it. Ronsard, especially, seemed aware of time's passage and the fleeting sweetness of love and life; this infuses his poetry with an appealing wistfulness. Du Bellay wrote two great sonnet sequences, *L'Olive* and *Antiquitez de Rome;* the former is heavily influenced by PETRARCH's love sonnets, but the latter is more personal and original as it charts du Bellay's stay in Rome and his reactions to the ruins of the great classical past and their comparison to the present.

Even though they would be repudiated by later critics and poets, the Pléiade's acknowledgment and embrace of classical forms and inspiration helped spring French poetry into the Renaissance and set it on its path as one of the most important national literatures of Europe.

An English Version of Works by the Pléiade

Leitch, Vincent B., ed. *The Norton Anthology of Theory and Criticism.* New York: Norton, 2001.

Works about the Pléiade

Bailey, John Cann. *The Claims of French Poetry: Nine Studies in the Greater French Poets.* Freeport, N.Y.: Books for Libraries Press, 1967.

Castor, Grahame. *Pléiade Poetics: A Study in Sixteenth-Century Thought and Terminology.* Cambridge: Cambridge University Press, 1964.

Clements, Robert J. *Critical Theory and Practice of The Pléiade.* New York: Octagon Books, 1970.

Satterthwaite, Alfred W. *Spenser, Ronsard, and Du Bellay: A Renaissance Comparison.* Port Washington, N.Y.: Kennikat Press, 1972.

Poliziano, Angelo Ambrogini (Politian) (1454–1494) *poet, humanist*

Poliziano is considered by many to be the most brilliant humanist of the RENAISSANCE. Born in Tuscany, he went to Florence at age 10 to further his education. He was talented and precocious, and began to translate Homer at age 16. Several of his Greek and Latin epigrams attracted the attention of the powerful Lorenzo de' MEDICI, who later assigned Poliziano the task of tutoring his son.

Poliziano's first major literary effort was his translation of books two through five of Homer's *Iliad* into Latin. Between 1473 and 1478, the years when he was part of the Medici household and had access to Lorenzo's formidable library, Poliziano produced a variety of verses that are now considered exemplars of the poetics of HUMANISM. His epigrams, elegies, and odes show the influence of the Latin and Italian masters PETRARCH, Ovid, and Dante Alighieri. In style and form, Poliziano not only adopted and improved upon the works of his predecessors but also positioned himself within a great historical tradition of Latinate poetry reaching back to the time of the Roman Empire. Far from being trapped in the past, however, Poliziano, like other Renaissance thinkers, looked to CLASSICISM as a way to renew and revitalize ancient forms of poetry in order to reflect new ways of thinking. He became something of a cultural celebrity, socializing with the most renowned scholars and artists of his time. Poliziano was a personal friend of PICO DELLA MIRANDOLA and Marsilo Ficino, and his poetry was said to have inspired the paintings of Botticelli and MICHELANGELO.

Poliziano's poetic masterpiece is his *Stanze,* written in Italian between 1475 and 1478. The poem praises the victory of Lorenzo's brother Giuliano de' Medici at a Florentine tournament in 1475. These tournaments were organized regularly by the Medici to provide a public spectacle and a demonstration of Medici power. Poliziano's poem describes the passion between Giuliano (the "Julio" of the poem) and Simonetta, the young and beautiful wife of Mario Vespucci (cousin of Amerigo VESPUCCI).

The poem has become one of the masterworks of Italian literature and expresses the themes and atmosphere of the Renaissance. It infuses the stylistic rigor of classical poetry with the lyrical spontaneity of the vernacular Italian language, giving the contemporary events of the poem a classical setting and an antique flavor (complete with animal chases, the chase of love, and the appearance of the love-god Cupid). The poem's praise of beauty reflected humanist thinking, which elevated human gifts and powers. Due to Simonetta's death in 1476, followed by Giuliano's murder in 1478 in an incident of civil unrest, Poliziano left the *Stanze* incomplete.

Poliziano also wrote nonfiction along with his poetry. Aided by Lorenzo's approval, Poliziano's *Stanze* inspired a general appreciation for the beauties of vernacular (non-Latin) literature, which Poliziano supported in his introduction to *The Aragon Collection* (1477), a collection of Tuscan verse. In the letter of dedication, Poliziano analyzes the history of vernacular poetry and defends its value as a form of poetic expression. He also wrote a dramatic report of Giuliano's death in 1478.

Following an argument with Lorenzo's wife, Poliziano left the Medici household in 1479 and traveled throughout Italy in search of a new patron. One remarkable work from this time is his dramatic *Orfeo*, which recounts the legend of Orpheus and Eurydice. In 1480 he was granted a post at the University of Florence, where between 1482 and 1486 he gave a series of lectures in verse, known collectively as the *Sylvae*, or *Trees*.

In addition to his poetic works in Italian, Latin, and Greek, Poliziano also composed a series of Latin letters addressing stylistics problems in literature. He later published his extensive commentaries on classical texts as the *Miscellany* (1489), comprising two collections of notes. This collection, along with his other works, introduced the field of classical philology, or the study of language.

Due to his extensive writings covering everything from poetry and literature to language and politics, Poliziano can truly be regarded as a form-

ative scholar of the Renaissance. His variety of interests, his talent with a pen, and his memorable poetry provided models both literary and personal for many Italian scholars and poets to follow.

English Versions of Works by Angelo Ambrogini Poliziano

Silvae. Translated by Charles Fantazzi. Cambridge, Mass.: Harvard University Press, 2004.

The Stanze of Angelo Poliziano. Translated by David Quint. University Park: Pennsylvania State University Press, 1993.

A Translation of the Orpheus of Angelo Politian and the Aminta of Torquato Tasso. Edited by Louis E. Lord. Westport, Conn.: Hyperion Press, 1979.

Works about Angelo Ambrogini Poliziano

Colilli, Paul. *Poliziano's Science of Tropes.* New York: Peter Lang, 1989.

Godman, Peter. *From Poliziano to Machiavelli.* Princeton, N.J.: Princeton University Press, 1998.

Pirrotta, Nina, and Elena Povoledo. *Music and Theatre From Poliziano to Monteverdi.* Translated by Karen Eales. New York: Cambridge University Press, 1981.

Pope, Alexander (1688–1744) *poet, satirist*

Alexander Pope was born in London, the son of a Catholic linen merchant, also named Alexander, and Edith Turner. Pope's aunt, Elizabeth Turner, taught him to read, and, as he told his friend Joseph Spence, he taught himself to write "by copying from printed books." Although he received instruction in Greek and Latin from the family priests and spent several years in private schools, Pope remained mostly self-taught.

At age 12, Pope contracted Pott's disease, tuberculosis of the vertebrae that caused the gradual collapse of his spine, pain, insomnia, depression, and deformity. (Years later, one insensitive critic called Pope "a hunch-back'd toad.")

Despite his affliction, Pope was ambitious. At age 16, he wrote his *Pastorals* (1709), which he modeled after Virgil, and at age 18, he edited William Wycherley's *Miscellany Poems.* These early PASTORAL were mainly an exercise in technique and experimentation for Pope.

As Pope read, translated, and imitated such classical writers as Homer and Horace, he began to formulate guiding rules for writers and critics based on the ancients' admonishments, techniques, and styles. In 1711 he published *An Essay on Criticism,* 744 didactic lines of rhymed heroic couplets (iambic pentameter verse), which Samuel Johnson praised as a work of distinction and comprehension. In *An Essay on Criticism,* Pope creates delightful and memorable nuggets of wisdom and advice:

> True ease in writing comes from art, not
> chance,
> As those move easiest who have learn'd to
> dance.
> 'Tis not enough no harshness gives offense,
> The sound must seem an echo to the sense.

He also provides a fitting definition of the term *wit:* "True wit is Nature to advantage dressed, / What oft was thought but ne'er so well expressed." For Pope, "Nature" means the way in which the world reflects God's grand design. The poem sums up neoclassical assertions (a revival of the literary standards of Greek and Roman writers) that literature should both instruct and delight through wit, reason, restraint, and balance (see NEOCLASSICISM.)

During the next nine years, Pope published an extraordinary number of works, including his mock-heroic masterpiece *The Rape of the Lock* (1712, 1714); the pastoral *Windsor Forest* (1713); *The Temple of Fame* (1715), which contains his plea, "Oh grant an honest fame, or grant me none"; and *Eloise to Abelard* (1717). *The Rape of the Lock,* one of his best-known poems, is a mock-epic that treats the simple event of cutting a snip of hair in the elevated style of such epics as the *Aeneid,* complete with invocation to the Muse; prophetic dreams; the use of epic similes; descrip-

tions of sacrifices, battles, feasts, supernatural beings; and transformations, all to reveal, "What mighty contests rise from trivial things." In true EPIC form, Pope also published his six-volume translation of the *Iliad* (1715–20), which made him famous and wealthy enough to buy a house at Twickenham on the Thames.

Almost 20 years later, Pope's poetry took a philosophical turn with the publication of his *Essay on Man* (1733–34), in which he aimed to "vindicate the ways of God to man." VOLTAIRE called it "the most beautiful, the most useful, and the most sublime didactic poem ever written in any language." It is perhaps most famous for the line "One truth is clear; Whatever is, is right."

If *Essay on Man* represents the upbeat, generous, positive side of Pope, then *The Dunciad* (1743), his masterpiece of satire against "dulness" or bad writing, shows us his dark, vengeful side where, "Art after art goes out, and all is Night."

Despite Pope's fervent dislike for critics and "dunces" (bad writers), at his death Lord Bolingbroke said, "I never in my life knew a man that had so tender a heart for his particular friends, or a more general friendship for mankind." Biographer Peter Quennell concludes, "His reforming influence on English language and literature was exerted primarily through the use of words, which he handled more boldly, yet more delicately and sensitively, with a finer appreciation of their lightest shades of meaning, than almost any other English poet."

Works by Alexander Pope

Alexander Pope. Edited by Douglas Brooks-Davis. London: Everyman Poetry Library, 1997.

Essay on Man and Other Poems. London: Dover Publications, 1994.

The Complete Poems of Alexander Pope. New York: Penguin, 1999.

Works about Alexander Pope

Quennell, Peter. *Alexander Pope: The Education of a Genius.* New York: Stein and Day, 1970.

Rogers, Pat. *The Alexander Pope Encyclopedia*. Oxford, U.K.: Greenwood Publishing Group, 2004.

Rosslyn, Felicity. *Alexander Pope: A Literary Life*. London: Macmillan, 1990.

Popol Vuh (1500s) *epic poem*

The *Popul Vuh* records, in 5,237 lines of poetry, the history of the ancient Quiché Maya people of Guatemala from creation to the 16th century. It relates the mythic adventures of the Maya gods, and also includes a list of all the Quiché Maya rulers up to 1550. It is considered the most important document of Maya civilization. Its title can be translated as "The Book of Council."

The book opens with a preamble in which the unknown 16th-century writer who wrote it down explains, in enigmatic terms, the purpose of recording the old traditions of the Quiché Maya, writing as he does "amid the preaching of God, in Christendom now."

The beginning tells of the creation of the world and of the first efforts of the gods to create human beings. The gods' goal is to make creatures that will be able to work, to multiply, to live in an orderly way, and to praise the gods. First they try to teach the animals they have already made to fulfill these tasks. But the animals fail to learn to speak words of praise, and are condemned to live in the forests as prey for the people who are to come. The gods' second attempt at making people, out of mud this time, also fails, as does the third attempt, when the gods use wood as the material. The wood figures look like people and talk like people. They also succeed in multiplying, but they fail to remember to praise the gods, and are ultimately destroyed, partly through a flood sent by the gods, partly through a revolt by their own cooking utensils and domestic animals. Their descendants remain on earth as monkeys.

The following extract from the first part of the poem, in Dennis Tedlock's 1985 translation, describing the state of affairs before the world's creation, gives the flavor of the work's poetic style:

Whatever might be is simply not there: only murmurs, ripples, in the dark, in the night. Only the Maker, Modeler alone, Sovereign Plumed Serpent, the Bearers, Begetters are in the water, a glittering light.

In Part Two, the narrator drops the creation story, for the time being, to tell of how the powerful and arrogant god Seven Macaw and his two sons, whose amusement is to stomp around the Earth causing earthquakes, are overthrown by the trickery of the hero twins, Hunahpú and Xbalanqué.

Part Three goes back in time to relate the miraculous birth of Hunahpú and Xbalanqué and their adventures in the gruesome kingdom of Xibalba, the underworld. Hunahpú and Xbalanqué are passionate ball-players. They make so much noise playing ball that they can be heard in Xibalba, and the lords of death, annoyed by the noise, summon them to come to Xibalba and play ball against the lords. After a complex series of reversals, in which the trickery on each side escalates, the twins conquer death both metaphorically and literally, and are lifted up into the sky as stars.

Part Four returns to the theme of the creation of human beings. Xmucané, the grandmother of Hunahpú and Xbalanqué, makes dough out of corn meal and from it forms people who are handsome, intelligent, and perceptive, and who thank the Heart of Heaven for having created them. In spite of the new people's gratitude, their perfect vision and perfect knowledge are potentially a threat to the gods. After a discussion, the gods decide to fog human eyes so that they will see only what is near to them. One result of this limited vision is that the people, as they multiply, begin to break into different groups with different languages; another is that they begin to worship idols and lesser gods instead of the true god, the Heart of Heaven. Part Four concludes with an account of the early migrations of the Quiché Maya and their domination by the god Tohil, who gives them fire.

Part Five, the last part, details how Tohil's domination and protection, and the human sacrifices he demanded, led to both the prosperity and the destruction of the Quiché Maya. The very last section is a genealogy of the tribes of the Quiché.

Modern knowledge of the *Popol Vuh* has developed over a long period of time. When Spanish conquerors invaded Guatemala in the 16th century, the Roman Catholic missionaries who accompanied them deliberately destroyed any Maya manuscripts they could find, believing them to be products of an alien and heretical religion. Great bonfires were lighted, and today only a handful of Maya hieroglyphic manuscripts survive. However, to disseminate Christian knowledge, the missionaries taught the Maya the Roman alphabet, and between 1554 and 1558, a Quiché Maya writer, or perhaps several, used Roman writing to record, in the Quiché language, the *Popol Vuh*.

Although the writers must have kept their manuscript hidden from the prying eyes of the missionaries, Don Francisco Ximénez, an 18th-century Guatemalan priest, was able to borrow the manuscript from one of his parishioners long enough to make a copy of it. Next to his copy, on the right sides of the pages, Ximénez composed a Spanish translation. His manuscript was seen in the 19th century by a French scholar, Father Charles-Étienne Brasseur, who published a French translation. This became the first introduction of Maya thought to the European public. The Ximénez manuscript vanished, and was not found again until the 1940s, when the Guatemalan diplomat Adrian Recinos found it in a library in Chicago, bound with another Ximénez manuscript and not yet cataloged.

Recinos published the Spanish text and arranged for the first English translation, which was published in 1951. Since then, many versions and studies have been published. Numerous Latin American authors, especially the 20th-century, Nobel Prize–winning novelist Miguel Angel Asturias, have been influenced by the *Popol Vuh*. As Sylvanus Morley states in the foreword to his translation, "The chance preservation of this manuscript only serves to emphasize the magnitude of the loss which the world has suffered in the almost total destruction of aboriginal American literature."

English Versions of the *Popol Vuh*

Moraga, Cherríe L., and Irma Mayorga. *The Hungry Woman: A Mexican Medea: Heart of the Earth. A Popul Vuh Story.* Victoria, Australia: West End Press, 2001.

Morley, Sylvanus G., and Delia Goetz, trans. *The Popol Vuh: The Sacred Book of the Mayas.* Norman: University of Oklahoma Press, 1991.

Tedlock, Dennis, trans. *Popol Vuh: The Mayan Book of the Dawn of Life.* New York: Simon & Schuster, 1996.

Works about the *Popol Vuh*

Preuss, Mary H. *Gods of the Popol Vuh: Xmukane', K'ucumatz, Tojil, and Jurakan.* Culver City, Calif.: Labyrinthos, 1988.

Tedlock, Dennis. "What the Popol Vuh Tells Us About Itself," in *The Book, Spiritual Instrument.* Edited by Jerome Rothenberg and David Guss. New York: Granary Books, 1996.

Prado, Diego de (de Prado y Tovar) (ca. 1570–after 1615)

Little is known of the life of Don Diego de Prado beyond what can be gathered from his surviving works, which consist of two letters to Spanish government officials, written after a voyage of exploration in the southern Pacific, and the *Relación (Relation)*, a document reporting on that voyage and addressed to the king of Spain.

Knowledge of the *Relación* was lost until the early 1920s, when a copy in Prado's own handwriting was found among some miscellaneous Spanish manuscripts. It forced historians to revise their understanding of the European discovery of Australia, which had previously been credited to Pedro Fernandez de Quirós and Luis Vaez de Torres (after whom the Torres Strait, which separates Australia from New Guinea, is named). In Prado's account we learn dramatic facts about the expedition that set out from Peru in December 1605. There were three vessels in the fleet: the *Capitana*, commanded by Prado; the *Almirante*, commanded by Torres; and a much smaller launch. Quirós was the overall commander of the expedition and berthed on the *Capitana*. He rapidly lost the confidence of the *Capitana*'s crew. A mutiny ensued, which resulted in the *Capitana* sailing back to Mexico with Quirós as a prisoner, as Prado learned many months later after arriving in the Philippines.

At the time, the people on the *Almirante* knew only that the *Capitana* had disappeared. They decided to continue their mission to find out what land there might be in the Pacific south of 20 degrees latitude. They proceeded to sail along the southern coast of what is now Papua New Guinea, stopping on islands along the way, many of which are now considered part of Australia.

Apart from the events surrounding the disappearance of the *Capitana*, Prado's account focuses primarily on the physical details most relevant to sailors and to the king's ambitions for his empire: the presence of natural harbors and drinkable water, the edible plants and animals available, and the presence of mountains that might contain valuable minerals. There is also information about the customs of the inhabitants of the islands, but the often violent encounters with them, most often settled by the Spanish use of firearms, are related in an offhand way. Prado is a devout Catholic (he became a monk after his return to Spain) who assumes that capturing people and taking them away from their homes forever is perfectly Christian so long as an effort is made to convert them to Christianity. On one occasion Prado does command that a beautiful young girl be released to the care of "a good old woman of her own people"—lest some on the ship "might fall away with her and offend God."

The *Relación* is important for the details it provides about the southern Pacific in the early days of European imperialism, Spain's initial exploration of the area, and the life and culture of Spanish sailors and the people they encountered.

An English Version of a Work by Diego de Prado

New Light on the Discovery of Australia: As Revealed by the Journal of Captain Don Diego de Prado y Tovar. Translated by George F. Barwick. London: Hakluyt Society, 1930; reprinted Millwood, N.Y.: Kraus, 1967.

Prévost, Antoine-François (Abbé Prévost) (1697–1763) *novelist, translator*

Antoine-François Prévost was born to a wealthy attorney in Artois and was educated by Jesuits at their schools in Hesdin and Paris. From 1716 to 1719, he served in the army and then joined the Benedictine order in 1720. He was ordained a priest in 1726 and became the abbot of Saint-Germain de Pres (Paris) in 1728. He left the abbey without leave in 1728 and a *lettre de cachet* (royal arrest warrant) was issued for him. Prévost fled to England and later to Holland, where he stayed until 1734, when he reconciled with the Benedictine superiors. He took positions in monasteries until he became an almoner of the prince de Conti and, in 1754, became prior at St. Georges de Gesnes. He died in Chantilly.

Prévost began writing fiction before 1728 and published his most important work, *Mémoires et aventures d'un homme de qualité qui s'est retiré du monde (Memoirs of a Man of Quality Retired from the World)* in seven volumes (1728–30). He also wrote several historical novels based in England, such as *L'Histoire de Monsieur Cleveland (The History of Mr. Cleveland*, 1731–39) and *Le Doyen de la Killerine (The Master of Killarney*, 1735–40). Prévost's fascination with English history and culture led him to translate Samuel RICHARDSON's great novels into French, thus spreading their influence throughout Europe.

Prévost's greatest contribution to world literature is the love story of the Chevalier des Grieux and Manon Lescaut, which appeared in *The Memoirs of a Man of Quality*'s last volume and was republished separately in 1731. The tale of a well-bred, naïve young man involved in a self-destructive love affair with a beautiful amoral prostitute resounded in the European imagination for more than a century. Prévost's genius lay in capturing the psychological complexities of a dysfunctional love without judgment; he lets the characters, especially des Grieux the narrator, implicate themselves with their own actions and rationalizations. *Manon Lescaut* was so popular that both Puccini (1893) and Massenet (1884) created operas based on the novel; both versions are still performed and recorded today.

An English Version of a Work by Antoine-François Prévost

Larkin, Steven, trans. *Manon Lescaut*. New York: Penguin Classics, 1992.

Works about Antoine-François Prévost

Francis, R. A. *Prévost, Manon Lescaut*. London: Grant and Cutler, 1993.

Segal, Naomi. *The Unintended Reader: Feminism and Manon Lescaut*. New York: Cambridge University Press, 1986.

Prokopovitch, Feofan (Eleazar Prokopovitch) (1681–1736) *sermonist, dramatist, political philosopher*

Feofan Prokopovitch came from a merchant family in the Ukrainian city of Kiev. He attended the Kiev Academy, then studied in several Polish and Italian cities. After completing his studies, Prokopovitch became a monk and took the name Feofan. By 1705 he held a teaching position at the Kiev Academy. In 1715 Peter I called him to St. Petersburg, where he worked as the Czar's ardent supporter. He became bishop of Pskov in 1718 and archbishop of Novgorod in 1725.

Prokopovitch wrote treatises in support of Peter I's policies. In *Justice of the Monarch's Will* (1722), he argues that the Czar has the right to choose his own successor. His *Spiritual Regulation* (1721) subjects the Russian Orthodox Church to state authority. James Cracraft notes that Prokopovitch may only have edited these works, not written them. Nevertheless, they reflect his ENLIGHTENMENT position as an innovator rather than a traditionalist.

In 1725 Prokopovitch spoke at Peter's funeral. "Oh, how certain is our misfortune!" he lamented. "In a brief sermon can we encompass his glory,

which is beyond all reckoning?" Prokopovitch's many panegyrics to Peter I later influenced Mikhail LOMONOSOV.

Prokopovitch also led the "learned band," a group of writers that included Dimitrie CANTEMIR's son Antiokh. Writing in Latin, Polish, and Russian, Prokopovitch composed discourses on theology and rhetoric as well as sermons, a play, and poems commemorating Russian military victories. According to Harold Segel, Prokopovitch's sermons are notable for their "clarity and directness of communication." His tragic-comedy *Vladimir* (1705), about Russia's conversion to Orthodoxy, was one of Russia's earliest dramas.

In the realm of poetry, Prokopovitch broke with his predecessors' reliance on rhyming couplets and introduced the rhyme scheme *abab* into Russian literature. Recognizing Prokopovitch's contributions to Russian literature, particularly in the field of oratory, Alexander SUMAROKOV called him "an adornment of the Slavic people."

English Versions of Works by Feofan Prokopovitch

"Sermon on the Interment of the Most Illustrious, Most Sovereign Peter the Great," in *The Literature of Eighteenth-Century Russia*, vol. I. Edited by Harold Segel. New York: Dutton, 1967.

The Spiritual Regulation of Peter the Great. Translated and edited by Alexander V. Muller. Seattle and London: University of Washington Press, 1972.

Works about Feofan Prokopovitch

Cracraft, James. "Did Feofan Prokopovitch Really Write *Pravda voli monarshei*?" *Slavic Review* 40, no. 2 (Summer 1981): 173–193.

Sherech, Jurij. "On Teofan Prokopovitch as Writer and Preacher in His Kiev Period." *Harvard Slavic Studies* 2 (1954): 211–223.

Pulci, Luigi (1432–1484) *poet, humanist*

Luigi Pulci has been called the first Romantic poet after Dante Alighieri. Pulci's Florentine family had given birth to several writers during the RENAISSANCE; Luigi's brothers, Luca and Bernardo, along with Bernardo's wife, were also poets. Lorenzo de' MEDICI brought Pulci into his circle of artists and scholars of HUMANISM, including Angelo POLIZIANO and PICO DELLA MIRANDOLA. For a time Pulci served Lorenzo as an emissary and diplomat, but later in life took a more quiet post with a patron in the north, Roberto Sanseverino.

Pulci wrote prodigiously, all in his native language of Italian. Critics have pointed out a certain burlesque quality of his work. Pucli's taste for parody caused him more than a few problems with the church, and though he was extremely popular among intellectual circles, many disapproved his parodies of biblical scriptures. The fact that he was never arrested or declared a heretic is probably due to the Medici family's protection.

Pulci's most famous poem is the chivalrous and romantic "Morgante," based on the classic Carolingian EPIC, the *Song of Roland*. Pulci takes this exemplary heroic tale of chivalry in the Middle Ages and turns it into a humorous parody, thanks to a character of his invention: Morgante, a giant converted to Christianity by Roland. By infusing the mock-heroic chivalric tone with a humor to be found only in the streets of Florence, Pulci created a work that blended an at-times serious and even bitterly contemplative tone with a biting comic romp. *Morgante* not only contains insight into the morals of the time but also reflects the fate of religious ideals in a world in which salvation could be won through personal achievement rather than through faith.

Later poets greatly admired Pulci, and he had a major influence on the English Romantic poets, including Lord Byron. The 28 cantos of *Morgante*, published in 1483, are often studied as an exemplary work of the Renaissance.

An English Version of a Work by Luigi Pulci

Morgante: The Epic Adventures of Orlando and His Giant Friend Morgante. Translated by Joseph Tusiani. Bloomington: Indiana University Press, 2000.

Works about Luigi Pulci

Davie, Mark. *Half-Serious Rhymes: The Narrative Poetry of Luigi Pulci.* Dublin: Irish Academic Press, 1997.

Jordan, Constance. *Pulci's Morgante: Poetry and History in Fifteenth Century Florence.* Washington, D.C.: Folger Books, 1986.

Pushkin, Vasilii L'vovich (Puskin, Vvasilii L'vovich) (1766–1830) poet

Vasilii L'vovich Pushkin is perhaps most famous for his relation to one of Russia's most noted poets, Aleksander Pushkin, who was his nephew. But Vasilii Pushkin also led a comfortable, and at times critiqued, life in the Russian public eye as a poet.

Pushkin's childhood, along with his brother Sergei's (father of Aleksander), was relaxed and lavish, with both boys tutored at home in the style of the French. This early appreciation of French language and customs influenced Vasilii throughout his life. Several poems in the language and style of French literature appear in his first poetic works, published in 1793.

In his public life, Pushkin aligned himself with the Russian literary group called the *Karamzinians,* whose goal was to elevate the respect for and reception of Russian language and literature within Western Europe. Pushkin's poem commemorating V. A. Zhuskovskomu reflected the Russian ENLIGHTENMENT and the grandeur of Peter the Great. The poem received grand praises by the Karamzinian party and harsh criticism from their opposition, the Slavic party, which read it as a major attack.

Pushkin likewise received great praise for his next work, "Opasnyi sosed" ("The Dangerous Neighbor"), a short narrative poem imitating the typical style of Russian EPICS of the time. Though written between 1810 and 1811, the poem, which included scenes that took place inside a brothel, was considered too scandalous to be published until 1901.

Pushkin published another collection of his poetry in 1822, in which most of the poems were either representations of French poetry or adaptations and imitations from other Russian poets. His collected works appeared in 1855, well after his death. Though cherished for his own merit and not solely for his patronage of his talented nephew, Vasilii Pushkin's place in Russian literature is as a poet known best for his playful verse and his spirited style of living.

Works about Vasilii L'vovich Pushkin

Rydel, Christine A. *Russian Literature in the Age of Pushkin and Gogol: Poetry and Drama*, in *Dictionary of Literary Biography*, vol. 205. Farmington Hills, Mich.: Gale Group, 1999.

Thompson, Ewa M., ed. *The Search for Self-definition in Russian Literature*. Amsterdam: J. Benjamins, 1991.

Quetzalcoatl, myth of (n.d.–1558)

The Quetzalcoatl myth is the epic creation myth of the Mesoamerican cultures of the Aztec and Toltec peoples. Although no complete version of the myth survived the Spanish Conquest of 1519, scholars have since been able to piece together much of the story, which looks to be a mixture of fact and fiction. Quetzalcoatl comes from two Nahuatl words: *quetzal,* which is a Guatemalan bird with very long, green tail feathers, and *coatl,* which means serpent. The easiest translation of *Quetzalcoatl* is therefore "feathered serpent."

In an ironic twist, the story itself is partly to blame for its being mostly lost to history. Since part of the myth entailed Quetzalcoatl coming back to save the Aztec Empire, many Aztec mistakenly assumed that Spanish conqueror Hernán CORTÉS was the returning god when his army swept through Mexico in 1519. All that remains comes from a handful of pre-Columbian sources, later Aztec accounts (which were heavily influenced by Christianity), and a fragmentary archaeological record.

One of the Aztec's principal gods, Quetzalcoatl was the creator of all life, forming humans by splashing his blood on the bones and ashes of previous generations to give birth to new life. He took on many forms, including that of high priests, and is responsible for the end of human sacrifice, substituting the sacrifice of snakes, butterflies, and birds for humans by preaching that, if human blood is to be sacrificed, it should be given directly by the person making the sacrifice.

English Versions of the Myth of Quetzalcoatl

Baldwin, Neil, trans. *Legends of the Plumed Serpent: Biography of a Mexican God.* New York: Public Affairs, 1998.

Florescano, Enrique, and Lysa Hochroth, trans. *The Myth of Quetzalcoatl.* Baltimore, Md.: Johns Hopkins University Press, 2002.

Quevedo, Francisco de (1580–1645)

poet, playwright, novelist, essayist

Francisco de Quevedo was born in Madrid to the royal administrator Pedro Gómez de Quevedo and his wife, María de Santibáñez. Quevedo studied at a Jesuit college before going on to the universities of Alcalá and Valladolid, where he received a degree in theology.

From a young age Quevedo earned a reputation as a talented and controversial writer, inspiring the animosity of the prominent poet GÓNGORA Y AR-

GOTE and a distant friendship with the playwright LOPE DE VEGA. He composed his most well known work, the picaresque novel *Historia de la vida del buscón* (*The Scavenger,* 1604), while still a student. Over the following years Quevedo also published work in an amazing variety of genres, including satires, historical essays, and lyric poetry.

In the years 1612 and 1613 Quevedo underwent a spiritual crisis that would find expression in much of his later writing. As a functionary of the viceroy of Sicily, he traveled frequently between Italy and Madrid. For his role in a political intrigue against the ruling party in Venice, he was imprisoned in 1621–22, and this began a period of intense literary activity. He finished his *Sueños (Dreams),* a series of what might be called satiric, allegorical fantasies on political and moral themes. His attacks against public figures and his outspoken political opinions continued to earn him enemies, and despite his successful career as a diplomat he became increasingly isolated. After marrying, becoming a widower, and serving again as a political prisoner, he died in Villanueva de los Infantes.

Quevedo left behind a wide variety of writings, both political and religious. The tone and style of his work varied from sober religious reflection to vulgar comedy. Yet in all his works, Quevedo demonstrated a mastery of literary forms, flexible language, and much originality. *The Scavenger* is considered the prototype of picaresque fiction, and his lyric poetry is among the most accomplished in the Spanish language.

English Versions of Works by Francisco de Quevedo

Lazarillo de Tormes and the Swindler: Two Spanish Picaresque Novels. Edited by Michael Alpert. New York: Penguin, 2003.

Six Masters of the Spanish Sonnet. Translated by Willis Barnstone. Carbondale: Southern Illinois University Press, 1997.

Works about Francisco de Quevedo

Mariscal, George. *Contradictory Subjects: Quevedo, Cervantes, and Seventeenth Century Spanish Culture.* Ithaca, N.Y.: Cornell University Press, 1991.

Walters, D. Gareth. *Francisco de Quevedo: Love Poet.* Washington, D.C.: Catholic University of America Press, 1986.

R

Rabelais, François (ca. 1494–1553) *comic novelist*

During the late 15th and early 16th centuries, the new ideas and intellectual attitudes of the RENAISSANCE were pouring out of Italy and sweeping through Europe. The spread of knowledge fostered a new humanist scholarship, which was changing the way people think. HUMANISM caused a shift away from the focus of religious ways of thinking and, aided by the rediscovery of the knowledge of ancient Greece and Rome, turned scholars toward an in-depth study of human beings. The recent invention of the printing press allowed writers to produce works more quickly and in greater numbers than ever before. One of the most profound thinkers of this stimulating period was the French writer François Rabelais.

Little is known of Rabelais's public life, and even less of his private life. Studies have revealed that his father was a lawyer in Chinon in the Loire valley and that he influenced his son's study of law. Rabelais, however, found that the law was not a profession that suited him; he decided instead to join the Franciscan monastery of Le Puy Saint-Martin in Fontenay-le-Comte in 1510. He remained there, gaining a solid education, until 1524. Evidence suggests that during this time he began translating Greek philosopher Lucian's works into Latin, but the translation is no longer extant. Because the Franciscans frowned upon Greek philosophy, Rabelais moved to the Benedictine monastery Saint-Pierre-de-Maillezais some time around 1523 or 1524.

Through his studies with the Benedictines, Rabelais became well versed in Greek and Latin and received a broad education in law, philosophy, and the classics. He abandoned his holy orders, however, to pursue a secular life. In the early 1530s, he studied medicine at the University of Montpellier, where he translated the works of Hippocrates and Galen from the original Greek and Latin. After completing his medical education, he began a career as a doctor and published several medical works no longer extant. By this time, he had come under the influence of the great humanist scholar Desiderius ERASMUS, who inspired Rabelais and perhaps turned his thoughts toward a literary life.

In 1532 Rabelais produced his first book, *Pantagruel,* which he wrote under the fictitious name of Alcofribas Nasier. The character Pantagruel was known in popular French culture as a small devil; in Rabelais's work, he is transformed into a giant who, in later books, becomes the symbol of wisdom, a foil for the character Panurge, who is foolish and self-absorbed, and who also appears in Rabelais's later work *Tiers livre. Pantagruel* is a comic story about a giant who spreads thirst. It was an immediate success, despite being criticized by at least one professor at the Sorbonne, the leading university of France.

After a trip to Rome, Rabelais produced his second book, *Gargantua*, in 1534. The character Gargantua is the father of Pantagruel, and their stories are similar in the telling of their lives, as children, warriors, and heroes. *Gargantua* was also a comic story but differed from *Pantagruel* in that Rabelais's use of language as a means to express his views on some of the controversial issues then shaking Europe became more imaginative and inventive. His comic tale, set within an ideal society (based loosely on Thomas MORE's *Utopia*), includes a battle in which Rabelais satirizes the evil emperor (often alluded to by critics as Charles V). The characters in *Gargantua* include those from Arthurian legends, and the story operates on multiple levels—contemporary, as well as classical and biblical.

Rabelais's works include numerous digressions and stilting transitions from one scene to another. These digressions, and Rabelais's narrative style as a whole, are meant to disconcert readers at critical points in the stories. Thus, what scholars and other readers have come to value in *Gargantua* and other of Rabelais's writings is his ability to invent with unparalleled language and sensibility a comic criticism of historical and social events and issues of his day. For this reason, it is important to read Rabelais's works not as "modern" novels, but as burlesque portrayals of the 16th-century way of life, and not as formal philosophical criticisms of social vice, but as comic stories of human nature.

After publishing *Pantagruel* and *Gargantua*, Rabelais wandered through France, Italy, and Germany, spending time in the late 1530s and early 1540s teaching and practicing medicine. His opinions on religious and political matters caused him trouble with the authorities of various states, and he only narrowly avoided persecution.

In 1546 he published *Tiers livre*, which means "The Third Book." It was completely unlike his two earlier works. The plot concerns the question of whether a man named Panurge should get married, but the story line is exceedingly thin. Through the events that happen to Panurge, Rabelais expresses his views not only of marriage, but also of war, money, and politics. However, because of Rabelais's subtle and ironic style, his views can be interpreted in many different ways, providing much fodder for current scholarship. *Tiers livre* was condemned by the Sorbonne and other authorities, who considered the work heretical. As a result, Rabelais fled France and moved to the German city of Metz. In 1552 he published *The Fourth Book,* which was also condemned by the Sorbonne.

Some years after Rabelais's death, *The Fifth Book* was published. Although this work was credited to Rabelais, many historians question whether he actually wrote it.

Rabelais was one of the major literary figures of the 16th century, when such writers as Thomas More and Erasmus were producing brilliant work. He influenced such writers as MONTAIGNE, Hugo, and Flaubert. In a time of political uncertainty, increased by the Protestant Reformation, Rabelais stood as a literary giant, using wit and comedy in an attempt to express reasonable views in an unreasonable age.

English Versions of Works by François Rabelais

Complete Works of François Rabelais. Translated by Donald M. Frame. Berkeley: University of California Press, 1999.

Five Books of The Lives, Heroic Deeds and Sayings of Gargantua and His Son Pantagruel. Whitefish, Mont.: Kessinger Publishing, 2004.

Gargantua and Pantagruel. Herts, U.K.: Wordsworth Editions, 2001.

Works about François Rabelais

Berry, Alice F. *Charm of Catastrophe: A Study of Rabelais's Quart Livre.* Chapel Hill: University of North Carolina Press, 2001.

Carron, Jean-Claude. *François Rabelais: Critical Assessments.* Baltimore, Md.: Johns Hopkins University Press, 1995.

Frame, Donald M. *François Rabelais: A Study.* New York: Harcourt, Brace, Jovanovich, 1977.

Plattard, Jean. *Life of François Rabelais.* Translated by L. D. Roache. London: Taylor and Francis, 1968.

Rabinal Achi (700s) *Maya play*

The *Rabinal Achi* is the only pre-Columbian Maya play known today. The residents of Rabinal, a small town in Guatemala, still perform it as they have for centuries. The play, originally written in the Maya language of K'iche (Quiche), became available outside Guatemala when Charles-Étienne Brasseur, a 19th-century French scholar also known as "l'abbe Bourbourg," published a French translation. He obtained the play from a resident of Rabinal, Bartolo Sis.

Dennis Tedlock recently translated the play into English from the original K'iche. He notes that it is a representation of both Maya history and culture and that elements in the play have roots in pre-Columbian court dramas. Tedlock compares the style of the play to Japanese NOH theatre.

The *Rabinal Achi* includes musical accompaniment and the actors perform stylized dances that reveal the relationships of characters to one another, but they do not speak while dancing. Actors wear masks specific to each character. The dialogue is a series of speeches in which characters frequently repeat and respond to another character's dialogue.

In the opening scenes, Cawek of the Forest People and the Man of Rabinal challenge each other. The Man of Rabinal takes Cawek captive, and a long exchange occurs between the two in which they describe the conflict between them. Eventually, Cawek appears before Lord Five Thunder, and there is a debate about Cawek's wrongdoing. Finally, the play ends with Cawek's ritual execution, represented by a dance sequence, during which Cawek urges his executioners to "do your duty." He ends with a prayer for them that echoes other prayers in the drama: "May Sky and Earth be with you too / little Eagle, little Jaguar."

The *Rabinal Achi* has inspired other artists. The contemporary playwright Luis Valdez told the *San Diego Union Tribune* that he translated the play from Spanish to help him create dialogue in a recent multimedia work. The play's influence rests upon its action and plot; combination of dance, dialogue, and music; and its representation of Guatemalan history.

An English Version of the *Rabinal Achi*

Tedlock, Dennis, trans. *Rabinal Achi: A Mayan Drama of War and Sacrifice.* New York: Oxford University Press, 2003.

Racine, Jean (1639–1699) *playwright*

For most of the 17th century, France was ruled by the powerful, ambitious and energetic King Louis XIV. Under his rule, France would not only become the most powerful nation in Europe, but would also develop into the intellectual and cultural center of the world, superseding both England and Italy. Among the great achievements of this golden age of French culture was an amazing flourishing of literature, and one of the most important French writers during the reign of Louis XIV was Jean Racine.

Racine was born on December 20 in La Ferté-Milon in Aisne to a middle-class family. Both of his parents died within a few years of his birth, and he was raised by his paternal grandmother. During his youth, he received an outstanding education from members of a religious group known as the Jansenists. The Jansenists were ostensibly loyal to the Roman Catholic Church but held unorthodox views about how the church should be reformed. As a result, they were regarded by the authorities with a great deal of suspicion.

Under the tutelage of Jansenist teachers, Racine gained extensive knowledge about classical literature, as well as a generally broad-based education. His teachers thought he would make an excellent lawyer and sent him to study law at a university in Paris. The city was not only the political capital of

France, but also the center of French culture and literature. Once he arrived, Racine became utterly enchanted with Paris and resolved to make his mark on society. He worked to curry favor with high French officials, including some who had been persecuting the Jansenists.

Eventually, Racine decided that the best way of becoming famous in Parisian society would be to become a playwright. This would damage his relationship with the Jansenists, to whom the theater was abhorrent, but by then Racine was focused entirely on his own social progress. He sought out Jean-Baptiste Poquelin MOLIÈRE, who was not only the leading writer of French theater, but also controller of one of France's most important theatrical production companies.

Molière agreed to produce Racine's play *La Thébaïde, (The Story of Thebes),* which was based upon the rivalry among Oedipus's sons. It appeared on the Paris stage in 1664 and was a considerable success, running for 17 consecutive nights. A year later, Molière's company produced Racine's second play, *Alexandre le Grand (Alexander the Great),* which was a heroic portrayal of King Louis XIV as a victorious conqueror. The play was an even greater success than *La Thébaïde* and confirmed Racine's place in the world of the French theater.

Racine then double-crossed Molière, both professionally and personally. Without Molière's knowledge, Racine arranged for a rival theater company, the Hotel de Bourgogne, to produce a second showing of *Alexandre le Grand.* This production was presented at the court of Louis XIV and was a striking success. On a personal level, Racine had an affair with the leading actress from Molière's troupe, Thérèse Du Parc, and he persuaded her to leave Molière's employ and join him. As in his relationship with the Jansenists, these actions demonstrate Racine's willingness to forgo honor in the pursuit of professional and social success.

With his work now being produced by the Hôtel de Bourgogne, Racine continued to write plays. In 1667, his third play, *Andromaque,* was performed both in the court of Louis XIV and to the general public. This dramatic tale of tragic love was a huge success, ensuring Racine's place among the greatest of contemporary French playwrights.

Racine, whose energy for writing and work was enormous, produced several plays in the years that followed. *Les Plaideurs,* his only comedy, which satirizes the legal profession, was produced in 1668, to great acclaim. The TRAGEDY *Brittannicus,* which was produced in 1669, did not fare as well, although the members of the king's court still appreciated it. *Bérénice* was produced in 1671, *Bajazet* in 1672, *Mithridate* in 1673, and *Iphigénie* in 1674. All of these plays were successful. Racine was elected to the ACADÉMIE FRANÇAISE in 1672, which was a great honor.

The themes Racine dealt with in his writings were not overly complex but were intensely human and thus had broad appeal. The ideas of unrequited love, sibling rivalry, sadness at the loss of loved ones, and the ruthless impartiality of fate were all subjects to which Racine's audiences could easily relate. He developed characters that were recognizably human, rather than the idealistic heroes that featured so prominently in others' plays.

Racine was appointed royal historiographer to King Louis XIV in 1677, one of the greatest honors the monarch could bestow upon a writer. In the same year, Racine produced his ultimate masterpiece, *Phèdre.* A few years later, the Hôtel de Bourgogne merged with another theater company to create the Comédie-Française, the greatest of all French theater companies. *Phèdre* was selected as the company's inaugural performance.

For the next several years, Racine devoted his energies to his duties as royal historiographer and dealt with difficult issues in his personal life. He married Catherine de Romanet, who, strangely, was said to have never read a word of Racine's writings during her lifetime. In addition, he was involved in a vicious scandal when he was accused of poisoning his mistress, Marquise Du Parc, but no formal charges were ever brought against him.

Toward the end of his life, Racine produced two religious plays. *Esther* premiered in 1689, and

Athalie in 1691. Both plays were performed by the female students at the school of Saint-Cyr. Some of his historical works were also published during this time, but they were little more than royalist propaganda designed to ingratiate him with King Louis XIV. Racine died of cancer on April 21, and was buried in the church of Saint-Etienne du Mont in Paris.

Critical Analysis

Of all the many plays Racine produced, none has greater fame or reputation than his masterpiece, *Phèdre*. It is upon this play that Racine's own fame as a tragic playwright chiefly rests.

In writing the story of *Phèdre*, Racine was following in the footsteps of the Greek tragedian Euripides, who composed the story in his play *Hippolytus*. In subsequent ages, other writers returned to the story and continually adapted it, but Racine's effort has become the most famous.

The plot of *Phèdre* is recognizably classical in origin. *Phèdre* is the wife of Thésée, the strong and heroic king of Athens. However, she has a secret, burning passion for her stepson, Hippolyte. Thus, the stage is set for tragic love. After *Phèdre* is incorrectly told that her husband is dead, she declares her love for Hippolyte. He does not return her affection, because he loves another, named Aricie; thus, *Phèdre*'s emotional anguish is futile.

King Thésée, who is very much alive, returns to Athens and is given a false report of what has happened. Told by the queen's treacherous confidant, Oenone, that Hippolyte has seduced his wife, he executes his own son. When informed of these events, Phèdre holds herself responsible for Hippolyte's death and commits suicide.

Phèdre contains many classical themes of drama. Unreciprocated love leads to despair; the father and the son regard each other with jealousy and suspicion; and trust in a confidant is betrayed. These are not only aspects of life that most people can easily relate to, but also classical examples of tragic fate; thus, it is not surprising that Racine's portrayal of human nature—in all its virtue and vice—made him greatly popular with French audiences and monarchs alike.

Racine was perhaps the greatest French dramatist of his age. Although he engaged in fierce and bitter competition with Molière and Pierre CORNEILLE, he both influenced and was influenced by them. During the century after Racine's death, the style and content of the great French playwright VOLTAIRE would be heavily affected by Racine's work, although Voltaire often criticized Racine for the similarity of his characters. Despite his personal shortcomings, Racine stands as a shining example of the literature of one of the golden ages of European culture.

English Versions of Works by Jean Racine

Bajazet. Translated by Alan Hollinghurst. New York: Random House, 1992.

Berenice. St. Paul, Minn.: Consortium Book Sales, 1991.

Racine: Mithridate. Edited by Gustave Rudler. London: Bristol Classic Press, 1979.

Three Plays of Racine: Andromache, Brittanicus, Phaedra. Translated by George Dillon. Chicago: University of Chicago Press, 1961.

Works about Jean Racine

Caldicott, Edric E., and Derval Conroy, eds. *Racine: The Power and the Pleasure.* Dublin: University College of Dublin Press, 2001.

Goodkin, Richard E. *Birth Marks: The Tragedy of Primogeniture in Pierre Corneille, Thomas Corneille, and Jean Racine.* Philadelphia: University of Pennsylvania Press, 2000.

Hawcroft, Michael. *Word as Action: Racine, Rhetoric, and Theatrical Language.* Oxford: Oxford University Press, 1992.

Knapp, Bettina L. *Jean Racine: Mythos and Renewal in Modern Theater.* Tuscaloosa: University of Alabama Press, 1971.

Lemaitre, Jules. *Jean Racine.* Murrieta, Calif.: Classic Books, 2001.

Tobin, Ronald W. *Jean Racine Revisited.* New York: Twayne, 1999.

Radishchev, Aleksander Nikolayevich
(1749–1802) political polemicist

Aleksander Radishchev was born into a wealthy Russian family. His obvious intelligence earned him the opportunity to study at Leipzig University at the state's expense; after five years there, he returned to Russia and entered government service. Radishchev resigned from service upon his marriage in 1775, but he soon found the income from his 300 serfs to be inadequate. In 1777 he assumed a post in the College of Commerce, where he spent the next 13 years rising through the ranks.

Radishchev's minor publications include "Diary of a Week" (1770s), a sentimental chronicle of seven days spent apart from friends, and a historical translation and a biography in which he condemns absolutism and injustice.

His most significant work, however, is *A Journey from St. Petersburg to Moscow* (1790), a travelogue modeled on Laurence Sterne's *Sentimental Journey*. Radishchev's *Journey* became famous not for its stilted, archaic prose (which Nikolai KARAMZIN's fluid style would soon supersede), but for its content. Within the *Journey*, Radishchev denounces the many evils he sees in society, especially serfdom. The work also includes an ALLEGORY in which a self-satisfied ruler suddenly sees that his "glittering garments" are "stained with blood and drenched with tears." R. P. Thaler notes that Radishchev "condemned equally the sovereign's despotism, the gentry's tyranny, and the peasants' violence. He did not want a revolution. . . . He wanted reforms."

CATHERINE THE GREAT saw the *Journey* as a criminal attack on authority. She deduced that the anonymous author was Radishchev and had him arrested and sentenced to death, a sentence she eventually commuted to ten years' exile in Siberia. Educated Russians, meanwhile, read illicit copies of the book, and Catherine's son Paul pardoned Radishchev in 1796. In 1801 Radishchev completed a poem (including praise of Catherine) about the 18th century. He also joined a commission studying legal reform. After the commission's chair threatened him with another exile, he committed suicide.

See also TRAVEL NARRATIVE.

An English Version of a Work by Aleksander Nikolayevich Radishchev

A Journey from St. Petersburg to Moscow. Translated by Leo Wiener and edited by R. P. Thaler. Cambridge, Mass.: Harvard University Press, 1958.

Works about Aleksander Nikolayevich Radishchev

Clardy, Jesse. *The Philosophical Ideas of Aleksander Radishchev.* New York: Astra Books, 1964.

Lang, David Marshall. *The First Russian Radical: Aleksander Radishchev, 1749–1802.* Westport, Conn.: Greenwood Press, 1977.

McConnell, Alan. *A Russian Philosophe: Aleksander Radishchev, 1749–1802.* Westport, Conn.: Hyperion Press, 1981.

rationalism

During the 18th century, an intellectual movement known as the ENLIGHTENMENT swept across Europe. For several generations, it dominated the literary, artistic, musical, and philosophical worlds of much of Europe, as well as the European colonies in the New World. The idea that formed the basis of the Enlightenment was called rationalism.

In the 18th century, French writers and thinkers known as philosophes applied the scientific method, developed the century before, to philosophical, religious, and social questions. They believed that all questions about life must be approached rationally and that truth must be discovered through reason.

The most famous of these writers was unquestionably VOLTAIRE, whose works represent perhaps the clearest statement of Enlightenment ideals. Other important philosophes included MONTESQUIEU, Denis DIDEROT, Jean d'ALEMBERT, and Jean-Jacques ROUSSEAU.

Rationalist thinkers were skeptical of ideas that had been accepted in Europe for centuries. Many questioned the absolute right of monarchs to rule their countries, while others discarded traditional religion to become deists or atheists. Because their religious and political opinions challenged established authority, rationalists were often persecuted for their beliefs.

During the Enlightenment, rationalism led to the production of several important works. The novel *Candide,* Voltaire's most famous work, explores the nature of good and evil, and the question of fate versus free will. The ENCYCLOPEDIA, a joint effort by both Diderot and d'Alembert, represents an effort on the part of the philosophes to systematize all human knowledge using the principles of rationalism.

During the 19th century, rationalism, and the Enlightenment as a whole, was superseded by the emergence of romanticism, and the cultural focus of Europe shifted from France to England and Germany. The influence of rationalism on world literatures and cultures, however, continues to the present day.

Works of Rationalism

Descartes, René, and Gottfried Wilhelm Leibniz. *Rationalists: Five Basic Works on Rationalism.* New York: Doubleday, 1989.

Diderot, Denis. *Thoughts on the Interpretation of Nature and Other Philosophical Works.* Translated by Lorna Sandler and David Adams. Manchester, U.K.: Clinamen Press, 2000.

Works about Rationalism

Cottingham, John. *Rationalism.* Bristol, U.K.: Thoemmes Press, 1998.

Hartpole-Lecky, William E. *History of the Rise and Influence of the Spirit of Rationalism in Europe.* La Vergne, Tenn.: University Press of the Pacific, 2001.

Parkinson, G. H. R. *The Renaissance and 17th-Century Rationalism.* Routledge History of Philosophy Series, vol. 4. London: Routledge, 2003.

Rej, Mikkolaj (1505–1569) *poet, fiction writer, translator*

Mikkolaj Rej was a Polish country squire. He received no formal education, but his literary talent, humanistic views, and patriotic sentiment helped him become one of the central figures of the Polish Renaissance.

Rej is traditionally called the Father of Polish national literature. He wrote all his works in Polish, although at the time it was traditional to write in Latin, and he wrote his philosophical works in the form of dialogue. His main works include *A Short Conversation between Three Persons: Pan, Voit, and Pleban* (1543); a didactic poem aimed at explaining and instructing, titled *A Real Account of the Life of a Respectable Person* (1558); and a prosaic version of *David's Psalms* (1545).

Rej was especially popular for his secular satirical works, such as *The Zoo* (1562) and *Trifles* (1562). His short witty epigrams were known and widely quoted. A distinguishing feature of Rej's satirical writing is his vast use of colloquial language, which was a novelty for the literature of the corresponding epoch. The persistent use of dialectal language was deliberate: It was a tool to awaken Polish national identity, to introduce folk language into the official sphere of literature and education. Mikkolaj Rej is a distinguished humanist, whose input into the development of Polish literature and culture is hard to overestimate. Sadly, English translations of his works are not currently in print.

Renaissance (1300s–1500s)

The term *Renaissance,* a French word meaning "rebirth," describes a period of time in Western Europe marked by significant changes in politics, art, and scholarship. Though the term may refer to any period characterized by artistic vitality or advanced thought, it traditionally refers to the 14th-, 15th-, and 16th-century cultures of Italy, France, Spain, England, Germany, and the Low Countries.

The "rebirth" of the Renaissance departed from the modes of thought that had dominated the

Middle Ages in Europe. The decline of feudalism, the increase in trade and commerce, and the growth of cities all changed the fabric of society. The bubonic plague, or Black Death, swept through Europe several times, killing up to one-third of the population. The Protestant Reformation led by Martin LUTHER and John CALVIN splintered the Catholic Church. Scholars and artists of the 14th century felt they lived in a world being reborn from the ignorance, darkness, and superstition of the medieval period. Political, social, and scientific changes followed, but the greatest achievements of the Renaissance were in literature and the arts.

Italy during the 1300s witnessed the beginning of two movements that characterized the Renaissance. The first was a renewed interest in the literature of ancient Greece and Rome, a movement known as CLASSICISM, largely begun by the scholar and poet PETRARCH. The second was the influence of HUMANISM, which began as a reform of the traditional humanistic education in rhetoric and evolved into a mode of thought focused on the human instead of on God. Scholars and artists gathering in Florence under the patronage of the powerful Medici family, which included Lorenzo de' MEDICI, reflected this interest in their art, most famously in the work of MICHELANGELO. Popes and monarchs began collecting their own personal libraries, and universities flourished.

In addition, authors wrote less frequently in Latin and more frequently in the vernacular or native languages, while Johannes Gutenberg's invention of moveable type around 1440 made printing possible. These changes made education, scholarship, and literature more widely available than ever before. Some landmark authors of the Italian Renaissance were Giovanni BOCCACCIO, Pietro BEMBO, Baldessare CASTIGLIONE, Niccolò MACHIAVELLI, and Ludovico ARIOSTO. LEONARDO DA VINCI—painter, architect, engineer, and musician—exemplified the Renaissance ideal of the "universal man" who was highly-educated, accomplished in the arts as well as the sciences, and unfailingly pleasant in all company.

From Italy, the values of the Renaissance spread to France, where they were best modeled in the poetry of Pierre de RONSARD, the fiction of François RABELAIS, and the essays of Michel de MONTAIGNE. In Germany, Desiderius ERASMUS was the most renowned Renaissance scholar, famed for his refinement of humanistic ideals and his influence on many other thinkers and poets, particularly the English Sir Thomas MORE, whose *Utopia* (1516), which described the values of a perfect society, was modeled after Plato's *Republic*. English arts and literature in the Renaissance flourished in the poetry of Philip SIDNEY and Edmund Spenser, but the highest achievement was in drama, in the works of William SHAKESPEARE, Christopher MARLOWE, Ben JONSON, and their contemporaries.

In Spain, the most celebrated authors of the Renaissance were LOPE DE VEGA, who wrote hundreds of plays, and Miguel de CERVANTES, whose *Don Quixote* (1605) is still considered by many to be the greatest modern novel. Spanish explorers led the Europe of the Renaissance in world exploration, stretching the boundaries of the known world. In addition, developments in science significantly changed established doctrines. In 1543 COPERNICUS dared to suggest that the Earth orbited the Sun, and around 1600 Galileo GALILEI began his experiments in physics.

Though a span of time marked by war, plague, and resistance to new ideas, the Renaissance in Europe profoundly and irrevocably changed the social structure. The renewed interest in the human form and the human mind, the advances in knowledge, the spread of learning, and the zeal for discovery that took place during the Renaissance led to the ENLIGHTENMENT and still underlie European and European-influenced cultures to this day.

English Versions of Works from the Renaissance

Bocaccio, Giovanni. *The Decameron.* Translated by Mark Musa. New York: Signet, 2002.

Cervantes, Miguel de. *Don Quixote.* Translated by Tobias Smollett. London: Modern Library, 2004.

Erasmus, Desiderius. *The Praise of Folly and Other Writings.* Edited by Robert M. Adams. New York: W.W. Norton, 1989.

Montaigne, Michel de. *The Complete Essays.* Translated by M. A. Screech. New York: Penguin, 1993.

Shakespeare, William. *The Complete Works.* Edited by Stanley Wells and Gary Taylor. Oxford: Oxford University Press, 1999.

Works about the Renaissance

Grendler, Paul, et al., eds. *Renaissance Encyclopedia for Students.* New York: Charles Scribner's Sons, 2003.

Manchester, William. *A World Lit Only by Fire.* Boston: Back Bay Books, 1993.

Rabb, Theodore. *Renaissance Lives: Portraits of an Age.* New York: Basic Books, 2001.

Tuchman, Barbara W. *A Distant Mirror.* New York: Ballantine Books, 1987.

Richardson, Samuel (1689–1761) *novelist*

Samuel Richardson was born in Mackworth, Derbyshire, to Samuel Richardson, a joiner or woodworker, and his wife, Elizabeth. Richardson attended Merchant Taylor's school for some years and at age 17 became apprenticed to a printer. When his apprenticeship ended in 1715, he became a compositor for a printer in London. Six years later he set up his own printing shop and married Martha Wilde, daughter of the man under whom he had apprenticed. Richardson initially printed political material and in 1733 became the House of Commons' official printer.

Richardson's first complete work, *The Apprentice's Vade Mecum* (*Young Man's Pocket Companion,* 1733), was written for apprentices. In 1739 he was commissioned to write a collection of letters for rural readers to copy for their own use. Eventually published as *Familiar Letters* (1741), it inspired Richardson's better-known work, *Pamela* (1740), an epistolary NOVEL (a novel written in letters) about a virtuous servant girl fending off the advances of Mr. B, her master. Richardson packaged the work as nonfiction, but its success forced him

to admit the disguise. While *Pamela* drew the admiration of the masses, one of its detractors was Henry Fielding, who parodied the work in *Shamela* (1741).

Richardson published a sequel, commonly referred to as *Pamela II,* following the heroine's fate after she marries Mr. B. In another novel, *Clarissa* (1748), Richardson retained the epistolary structure; the focus on a young, virtuous woman; and the sentimentality of his Pamela novels. He altered the formula, making the heroine an heiress, rewriting romance as tragedy, and increasing the novel's length and number of letter-writers. Richardson continued to revise *Clarissa* throughout his life.

Even more successful than *Pamela, Clarissa* sparked a fashion for sentimental and epistolary novels, including GOETHE's *The Sorrows of Young Werther* and ROUSSEAU's *Julie.* Richardson also completed *The History of Sir Charles Grandison* (1753–54), an epistolary novel about a man torn between two women.

Richardson's novels have provided fruitful ground for critics. Marxist critic Terry Eagleton claims: "These novels are an agent, rather than a mere account, of the English bourgeoisie's attempt to wrest a degree of ideological hegemony from the aristocracy in the decades which follow the political settlement of 1688." And critic Ira Konigsberg writes: "Richardson analyzed more deeply the characters of the novel and displayed in them a larger number of mental and emotional states. He was able to accomplish this in large part by his skillful writing of letters in which the fictitious correspondent explicitly recreates his or her inward being."

Elizabeth Brophy has commented on his first novel's psychological vividness: "By 'writing to the moment' he enabled readers to follow the inward struggles of Pamela, to participate in her uncertainties, and to undergo her trials."

Recent critical debates about *Clarissa* concern the heroine's degree of power. Michael Suarez contends that Clarissa's power is her ability to refuse: "Clarissa's 'No' is an attempt to assert her own autonomy, to secure her right to a will of her own";

and Donnalee Frega regards Clarissa's self-imposed starvation as a form of power.

The title character of Richardson's *Sir Charles Grandison* is an idealized man: "In his aspect there is something great and noble, that shews him to be of rank. Were kings to be chosen for beauty and majesty of person, Sir Charles Grandison would have few competitors." Richardson explains:

> The Example of a Man acting uniformly well thro' a Variety of trying Scenes, because all his Actions are regulated by one steady Principle: A Man of Religion and Virtue; of Liveliness and Spirit; accomplished and agreeable; happy in himself, and a Blessing to others.

Critic Jocelyn Harris holds that "*Grandison* as an individual work is often an advance on *Clarissa.* The variety, the gaiety smoothly integrated with seriousness, the deft handling of a large group of characters . . . such matters frequently outclass anything that Richardson had done before."

Finally, in *The Rise of the Novel,* Ian Watt remarks:

> Richardson's deep imaginative commitment to all the problems of the new sexual ideology and his personal devotion to the exploration of the private and subjective aspects of human experience produced a novel where the relationship between the protagonists embodies a universe of moral and social conflicts of a scale and complexity beyond anything in previous fiction.

Other Works by Samuel Richardson

The Clarissa Project. Edited by Florian Stuber. New York: AMS Press, 1990.
Selected Letters. Edited by John Carroll. Oxford: Clarendon Press, 1964.

Works about Samuel Richardson

Blewett, David, ed. *Passion and Virtue: Essays on the Novels of Samuel Richardson.* Toronto: University of Toronto Press, 2001.

Eaves, T. C. Duncan, and Ben D. Kimpel. *Samuel Richardson: A Biography.* Oxford: Clarendon Press, 1971.
Warner, William Beatty. *Reading Clarissa: The Struggles of Interpretation.* New Haven, Conn.: Yale University Press, 1979.

Riebeeck, Jan van (1618–1677) *diarist*

Jan Anthoniszoon van Riebeeck was born in Culemborg in the Netherlands. At age 20, he joined the mighty Dutch East India Company as an assistant surgeon and was posted to Batavia (modern Jakarta, Indonesia). In 1645 the company gave the ambitious Riebeeck command of a trading station in present-day Vietnam. He was soon dismissed from this post for engaging in his own trading ventures, a practice strictly discouraged by the East India Company.

Riebeeck remained in their black books until 1652, when the company ordered him to establish a station to provision the company's ships at the Cape of Good Hope, midway on their long journey around Africa to the East Indies. Riebeeck arrived at the site of modern-day Cape Town in April of that year. He landed with 100 men and built a fort and infirmary as well as a primitive port. Food shortages bedeviled the settlement, however, and in 1655 Riebeeck advocated sending "free burghers" from Holland to work their own farms (as opposed to slaves or indentured servants). He thus paved the way for the settlement of South Africa and the origins of the Boer people, descendants of the first settlers who began arriving in 1657. Under his leadership, the colonists fought a bloody war with the nearby Hottentot people in 1659–60.

Riebeeck had long believed his talents were being wasted, and in 1662 he was delighted to be appointed governor of Malacca in the East Indies. Three years later, he became secretary to the Council of India, one of the most prestigious offices in the company's Asian empire. He died in Batavia, and occupies a hallowed place in Boer memory, the "Father of South Africa" after whom many streets, towns, and landmarks are named. His voluminous

Journals, though rather ponderous reading by modern standards, are detailed accounts of the founding of Cape Town.

A Work by Jan van Riebeeck

Journal, 3 vols. Cape Town: Van Riebeeck Society, 1952–58.

A Work about Jan van Riebeeck

Spilhaus, Margaret Whiting. *Company's Men.* Cape Town: J. Malherbe, 1973.

romance

In literature, the term *romance* encompasses several types of writing. To modern readers, a romance is simply a love story where plot and event are secondary to the emotions of the characters. The first important romance was *Daphnis and Chloe,* written by Longus in ancient Greek. The romance genre began to evolve in the Middle Ages and initially referred to any narrative written in the vernacular or native language. The medieval romance differed from the EPIC in that it featured lighter subject matter; though they might borrow epic events and involve issues of heroism, strength, or greatness, the romances typically featured knights and ladies and described their adventures in terms of chivalry and courtly love. The romance possessed qualities of lightness and mystery, and tended to be looser in construction than the weighty epic.

During the RENAISSANCE, the romance transformed into a new genre, the romantic epic. The style gained popularity and achieved credibility as a lengthy narrative poem combining aspects of medieval romance with features of the classical epic. The traditional elements of the romance, such as a loose structure and an emphasis on love, incorporated such epic conventions as elaborate similes, long speeches, and an invocation to a muse to turn love into the greatest and most lofty pursuit available to the human soul.

Italian Renaissance poets Matteo Maria Boiardo and Ludovico ARIOSTO used the romantic epic form in their lengthy verse narratives on Roland, which elaborate on the medieval *Song of Roland.* Torquato TASSO added a stronger moral element to the form with his *Jerusalem Delivered* (1581). English poet Edmund Spenser used the form for a religious, moral, and nationalistic purpose in his dense poem *The Faerie Queene* (1596, unfinished).

Don Quixote (1605) by Miguel de CERVANTES was and still is lauded as the greatest prose romance, as well as the precursor to the modern novel, which often incorporates a romantic storyline. The domestic fiction, which took form in 18th-century England, often involved a romance between characters, as seen in the works of Samuel RICHARDSON and Henry Fielding. The Gothic tales of Matthew Lewis, Horace Walpole, and Ann Radcliffe introduced a supernatural element into the romance, and the Romantic movements in England, Germany, France, and Spain spread to the Americas and left an enduring imprint on literature to come. Today, the romance is a popular genre of the mass media market and comprises a significant segment of book sales around the world.

Works of Romance

Lewis, Matthew Gregory. *The Monk: A Romance.* Edited by Christopher Maclachlan. New York: Penguin, 1999.

Middle English Romances. Edited by Stephen Shepherd. New York: W.W. Norton, 1995.

Seven Viking Romances. Edited by Hermann Palsson. New York: Penguin, 1986.

Works about Romance

Brackett, Virginia. *Classic Love and Romance Literature: An Encyclopedia of Works, Characters, Authors, and Themes.* Santa Barbara, Calif.: ABC-CLIO, 1999.

Gwara, Joseph, and E. Michael Gerli. *Studies on the Spanish Sentimental Romance (1440–1550).* London: Tamesis Books, 1997.

Keller, Hans-Erich. *Romance Epic.* Kalamazoo: Western Michigan University, 1987.

Mussell, Kay, ed. *Where's Love Gone: Transformations in the Romance Genre.* Los Angeles: Delta Productions, 1997.

Sommer, Doris. *Foundational Fictions: The National Romances of Latin America.* Berkeley: University of California Press, 1993.

Ronsard, Pierre de (1524–1585) *poet*

The day after his birth to Louis de Ronsard and Jeanne de Chaudrier in the Vendômois of France, the infant Pierre was dropped while being carried to the church for christening. The story goes that the flowers caught him gently, and that moment established his affinity with the natural world that would emerge so skillfully in his poetry. Son to a knight of the king, Pierre de Ronsard became a page to the French court in 1536 and, in 1539, entered the Royal Riding School in Paris for the sons of noblemen. At college in Paris he studied Greek and Latin, which exposed him to the myths and characters of classical antiquity. While recovering from bouts of fever that left him partially deaf, the adolescent Ronsard began composing poetry. Several successful early publications brought him to court, where he had various important patrons but was most dear to Charles IX, for whom he became court poet. After the death of the king, he retired to the priories or church domains that had been granted to him and continued to compose, revise, and publish successive editions of his work. Following prolonged bouts of illness, Ronsard died in 1585, having earned an enduring reputation as "the prince of poets."

Ronsard's combined poetic endeavors constitute nearly 20 volumes of work. His first *Odes*, published in 1550, marked a turning point in the history of French poetry. Ronsard scorned the traditions that treated poetry as a mere craft and instead advocated a return to the ideals of the Greco-Roman age in which poetry was inspired by the muses and poets were considered prophets, seers, and interpreters of the divine mystery of the universe. Ronsard, who modeled his *Odes* on Pindar and Horace, was often criticized for using this artificial and ancient form to capture and describe contemporary events. But the *Odes* exhibit the familiarity with metaphor and myth as well as the control of poetic feeling and technique that established his fame.

In 1552 Ronsard published his first collection of SONNETS, a form he borrowed from PETRARCH. The abundance of classical allusions in these poems can strike readers as being excessive or even tedious, but the topics and language show the Ronsard who is best remembered as a sensitive lover of nature, mourning for beauty that inevitably fades. He frequently incorporated the theme of carpe diem, to seize the delights of life before they pass, and skillfully refreshed conventional images of nature, adding a poignant touch, as in these lines translated by Nicholas Kilmer:

> Fall chases summer,
> And the harsh raging of wind
> Falls after storm.
> But the pain
> Of love's grieving
> Stays constant in me
> And will not falter.

Though best remembered for his lyric poetry, much of which was set to music during his lifetime, Ronsard tried his hand at a variety of forms, among them elegies and occasional verse. Two books of *Hymns* were published in 1555 and 1556. His poems from the period 1559–74 show the consequences of being court poet in a climate of civil-religious wars, in which Ronsard took the side of the Catholics against the Protestants. These poems have a patriotic tone and contain pleas for peace, moderation, and loyalty to king and church.

After he withdrew from court following Charles's death in 1574, Ronsard wrote poems that often contain a personal touch and a mature consciousness, best reflected in the *Sonnets to Helene* (1578). Here the conventional themes and restrained form of the sonnet clash with the poet's disillusionment with love and convey, in some cases, a note of irony or, as in these lines, hopelessness:

> The wound is to the bone. I am no longer
> the man I was.

I see my death abandoned to despair.
Patience is cast off. . . .

As he aged, Ronsard turned more and more to the great themes of the ancients: the changeability of fortune and the vanity of human wishes. His last poems, published the year of his death, are elegiac in tone, full of philosophical speculation.

Despite popularity in his lifetime, fashions in French poetry changed, and Ronsard was forgotten until the 1830s. While critical opinion still varies on Ronsard's depth and complexity as a poet, he represents the humanist spirit of the French Renaissance and is remembered as one of the greatest and most influential lyric poets ever to compose in that language.

English Versions of Works by Pierre de Ronsard

Poems of Pierre de Ronsard. Translated and edited by Nicholas Kilmer. Los Angeles: University of California Press, 1979.

Pierre de Ronsard: Selected Poems. Translated by Malcolm Quainton and Elizabeth Vinestock. New York: Penguin Books, 2002.

A Work about Pierre de Ronsard

Jones, K. R. W. *Pierre de Ronsard.* New York: Twayne Publishers, 1970.

Rosales, Diego de (1601–1677) *chronicler*

Father Diego de Rosales was one of the first chroniclers and writers of Chile in the era of Spanish colonization. His most important work, *Historia general del Reino de Chile (General History of the Kingdom of Chile),* is one of the first eyewitness accounts written in Spanish about the region.

Rosales was born in Madrid, where he entered the order of Jesuits. In 1629 he went to Chile to serve as army chaplain. While there he took keen interest in the customs of the Mapuche tribes. His knowledge of the Araucan language of the natives made him especially valuable to successive Spanish governors of Chile. Thus, Rosales was asked in 1641 and again in 1647 to accompany officials on missions to assist in negotiations with the native inhabitants of Chile.

In 1650 he received a commission to make a systematic study of the tribes and went on two journeys for this purpose. However, due to Spanish exploitation of the natives for slave labor in the mines, a revolt ensued in 1655, leading to the evacuation of Baroa by the Spanish.

Thereafter, Rosales was transferred to Concepción, where he was appointed director of the Jesuit school. He continued his steady climb up the ranks of the Jesuit order and in 1662 moved to the capital at Santiago, where he assumed leadership of the Jesuit order in Chile. In 1666 he also took charge of the Jesuit college there.

Rosales's history of Chile contains some of the earliest descriptions of the geographical features, flora, fauna, and indigenous peoples of the region, as well as events occurring there up to the 1655 revolt.

Among other works by Diego Rosales worthy of note is a history of the Jesuits in Chile. It is a series of biographical portraits, typical of the writing of this time, of the major missionaries with numerous accounts of miracles. Unfortunately, only parts of the work have survived.

Despite the flaws that make them unreliable for historical study, Rosales's books are still of immense importance for the insight they provide into Spanish colonization and the spread of Christianity in Chile. Unfortunately, English translations of his works are no longer in print.

Rousseau, Jean-Jacques (1712–1778) *philosopher*

During the 18th century, a wave of intellectual activity known as the ENLIGHTENMENT swept over Europe, affecting such fields as philosophy, religion, science, and politics. The writers and thinkers of the age, many of whom were known as philosophes, challenged long-accepted beliefs and traditions, arguing that RATIONALISM should be the primary tool through which people discovered the truth. Toward the end of the Enlightenment, however, the views of the philosophes would be challenged by the powerful ideas of Jean-Jacques Rousseau, who turned the intellectual currents of European thought away from pure reason and toward human emotion and intuition, setting the stage for the rise of romanticism. Furthermore, the political ideas espoused by Rousseau helped spark the French Revolution and would subsequently contribute to the many revolutions that would shake Europe throughout the 19th century.

Rousseau was born in the independent Swiss city of Geneva, then an independent republic. Ten days after his birth, his mother died from complications of childbirth. He was raised by his father, a watchmaker, and other relatives. Geneva was then a Calvinist state, adhering to a strict form of Protestantism, and it was in this religious environment that Rousseau grew up. Irritated with life in Geneva, he moved to Savoy, a Catholic region, where he was taken in by Madame de Warens, an agent of the king of Savoy. Under her influence, he rejected Protestantism and converted to Catholicism.

Rousseau lived with Madame de Warens for eight years as both a friend and a lover, during which time he undertook an intense program of self-study. He studied Latin, literature, science, philosophy, and music. Surrounded by the beautiful countryside, he also developed a strong love of nature.

Rousseau worked briefly as the secretary to the French ambassador to Venice. When Madame de Warens took another lover in 1742, he moved to Paris, where he was determined to become respected and famous. He earned his wages as a copier of music, while writing his own musical compositions. Although his musical works were not particularly successful, music remained one of Rousseau's great loves. During this time, he also became acquainted with a number of philosophes, including Denis DIDEROT and wrote several articles on music and economics for the famous ENCYCLOPEDIA.

In 1749 Rousseau learned that the Academy of Dijon was sponsoring an essay competition, the question being whether or not the revival of the arts and sciences had helped or hurt the human race. He pondered this question as he walked along a country road on his way to visit Diderot, who was in prison in Vincennes at the time. During this walk, Rousseau experienced a sudden "awakening," or awareness, which he later described in terms resembling a religious experience. He resolved to enter the contest and wrote an essay setting out his belief that the arts and sciences had, in fact, hurt the human race.

His essay, *Discourse on the Arts and Sciences*, won the Académie de Dijon prize after its publication in 1751 and made him famous virtually overnight. In this work, Rousseau explains his belief that the development of science—in the form of agriculture, which necessitated the need for private property and the division of labor—made humanity lose sight of its true nature and thus helped destroy individual liberty. Such loss and destruction, he reasoned, created political power based on and serving the wealthy. As for the arts, Rousseau believed that they merely distracted people from the fact that their liberty had been lost.

Rousseau argued that people should turn their backs on civilization and return to a more natural state of existence, for this was where he believed true nobility of spirit could be found. Thus, the idea of the "noble savage" was born. This idea became very fashionable among the French upper class, but it proved to be little more than a fad, as it did not allow for the luxuries to which the nobility was accustomed.

Rather than enjoying his fame, Rousseau became uncomfortable with the attention he received. He decided to practice what he preached and abandoned his life in Paris for a cottage in the countryside, where he lived with his barely literate mistress, Thérèse Levasseur, whom he did not marry until late in life. He later gained the patronage of the marshal-duke of Luxembourg, and during the years from 1756 to 1762 produced his three greatest and most well-known works (*The Social Contract*, *Émile*, and *Julie, or the New Heloise*), as well as *Moral Letters* (which he addressed to Sophie d'Houdetor, a former lover) and *Letter to d'Alembert* (in response to d'ALEMBERT's *Encyclopedia* articles on Geneva).

In 1761 Rousseau published *La Nouvelle Héloïse,* a love story told in the form of letters between a young woman named Julie and her tutor, St. Preux, who develop a passionate affair. Although the book was said to be based upon Rousseau's dreams and fantasies of love, Rousseau used the tale he created in reality as a means to express his own views of morality to his European audience. The book met with great success.

A year after the publication of *La Nouvelle Héloïse,* Rousseau published two works: *Émile* and *The Social Contract.* In *Émile,* Rousseau uses the tale of a young man as a device to convey his views on education, which were revolutionary at the time. Rousseau believed that natural judgment and intuition, rather than intellect, should be nurtured. Furthermore, he believed that teachers should endeavor to discover what the natural inclinations and interests of a child were and then labor to develop them within the child, rather than try to steer the child in directions society expected the child to go. *The Social Contract* presents Rousseau's ideas in the field of political theory. Both *Émile* and *The Social Contract* would prove to be powerful contributions to Western intellectual thought.

In the last years of his life, Rousseau seemed to become increasingly unstable. He broke with his friend Diderot and engaged in a long-running dispute with VOLTAIRE, who held Rousseau in contempt after he dared to criticize the theater. He also wrote *Letter to Christophe de Beaumont* (1763), in which he criticizes the archbishop of Paris, and *Letters Written on the Mountain* (1764), in which he describes his distaste for the power of the elite. Due to the unorthodox ideas presented in *Émile,* the French authorities ordered the book confiscated and the author arrested. Rousseau fled to Great Britain, where he received the generous help of the Scottish philosopher, David Hume. However, Rousseau proved ungrateful to Hume, accusing the

Scot of plotting against him. Rousseau became increasingly paranoid, convinced that everyone was seeking to undermine or persecute him. To some extent, this was true.

During these years, Rousseau wrote the *Confessions,* which is perhaps the first modern autobiography. He also composed *Letter on French Music* (1753), *Essay on the Origin of Languages* (1753), *Dictionary of Music* (1767), two works on politics, several works on botany, and enough correspondence with friends and enemies alike to fill more than 50 volumes (which where collected and edited by R. A. Leigh in 1965). In his last years, Rousseau returned to France, finally married his longtime mistress, with whom he had five children, and later died at Ermenonville, in the home of a sympathetic friend, the marquis de Girardin. As a hero of the French Revolution, which began approximately eight years after Rousseau's death, the author's remains were later moved to the Pantheon in Paris, where he would lay beside such other notables as Voltaire and Mirabeau.

Critical Analysis

The Social Contract, published in 1762, is perhaps Rousseau's most influential work. The ideas contained in the work were not wholly original, however; English philosopher John LOCKE had discussed similar ideas a century before. But by systematizing the concept of the social contract and presenting it so that it was accessible to the public, Rousseau made a powerful contribution to the spread of the new political ideas of the 18th century.

The general concept of a social contract is fairly easy to illustrate. Rousseau, like Locke, believed that human beings once lived in a natural state, each person trying to survive on his or her own. However, for mutual benefit, people gradually united together to take advantage of the strengths of a group. This was the origin of society and civilization that allowed people to enjoy certain advantages, such as mutual protection from common enemies, and that required people to agree to follow the rules society imposed. For example, in the state of nature, there is no protection against being murdered, but in a society, rules and safeguards are put into place to try and prevent murder. The price a person pays for accepting such protection is to agree not to commit murder; thus, a social contract is formed.

In *The Social Contract,* Rousseau presents the idea of the General Will, the collective desire of all the members of a society. This is similar to the idea of the *Volksgeist* articulated by Johann HERDER. The idea of the General Will formed the basis for the nationalist movements that transformed Europe after Rousseau's death. In particular, *The Social Contract* was regarded almost as a textbook by the activists of the French Revolution, who used it to justify their destruction of the old order.

Rousseau's influence is difficult to overstate. He is certainly one of the most influential writers in all of Western thought. His renunciation of rationalism in favor of pure nature and the power of human emotion set the stage for the advent of Romanticism, which dominated European intellectual and cultural life throughout the 19th century. The political ideas expressed in *The Social Contract* set the stage for both the French Revolution and many nationalistic revolutions that followed. While some, such as Leo Tolstoy, viewed Rousseau in a positive light, others claimed the author was responsible for the destruction of society as they knew it. Throughout the 19th and 20th centuries, it is fair to say that there was not a single important thinker or writer who was not, directly or indirectly, influenced by the ideas of Rousseau.

English Versions of Works by Jean-Jacques Rousseau

The Collected Writings of Jean-Jacques Rousseau. Edited by Roger D. Masters and Christopher Kelly. Hanover, N.H.: University Press of New England, 1989.

Confessions. Translated by Patrick Coleman and edited by Angela Scholar. Oxford: Oxford University Press, 2000.

Emile, or Treatise on Education. Translated by William H. Payne. Buffalo, N.Y.: Prometheus Books, 2003.

The Social Contract and The First and Second Discourses. Edited by Gita May and Susan Dunn. New Haven, Conn.: Yale University Press, 2002.

Works about Jean-Jacques Rousseau

Compayre, Gabriel. *Jean Jacques Rousseau and Education from Nature.* La Vergne, Tenn.: University Press of the Pacific, 2002.

Friedlander, Eli. *J. J. Rousseau: An Afterlife of Words.* Cambridge, Mass.: Harvard University Press, 2004.

Lange, Lynda, ed. *Feminist Interpretations of Jean-Jacques Rousseau.* Preface by Nancy Tuana. University Park: Pennsylvania University Press, 2002.

O'Hagan, Timothy. *Rousseau.* London: Routledge, 2003.

Qvortrup, Mads. *The Political Philosophy of Jean-Jacques Rousseau: The Impossibility of Reason.* Manchester, U.K.: Manchester University Press, 2004.

Reisert, Joseph R. *Jean-Jeacques Rousseau: A Friend of Virtue.* Ithaca, N.Y.: Cornell University Press, 2003.

Rowlandson, Mary (ca. 1635–ca. 1711)
memoirist

Mary White was born in England to John and Joane White and immigrated to Massachusetts with her family in 1639. In 1656, when in her early 20s, she wed Joseph Rowlandson, a minister of the town of Lancaster, and in the following years gave birth to four children.

In 1682 Rowlandson published *A Narrative of the Captivity and Restoration of Mrs. Mary Rowlandson,* an autobiographical account of her capture by Native Americans at the height of King Philip's War. The war began in 1675, when Metacomet (called King Philip) formed an alliance to fight the colonists' usurpation of Native American lands. Rowlandson's narrative opens with a description of the extremely bloody attack on Lancaster. Several members of her family were murdered, while both Rowlandson and her youngest daughter were taken captive. Rowlandson's account, divided into sections called "Removes," details the physical, spiritual, and psychological challenges she faced during her 11 weeks and five days of captivity.

Rowlandson's captivity narrative was enormously popular: It was reprinted three times in 1682 and more than a dozen editions of it appeared in the following centuries. Like the many captivity narratives that followed in its wake, Rowlandson's text is highly religious in its tone and incorporates a moral theme in its conclusions that her "punishment" was brought about by failure in her Christian duties. Rowlandson's narrative is important to scholars because it allows readers to witness one woman's private struggle to make sense of a painful experience in terms of her Puritan belief. In addition, the autobiography documents the transformation of a colonist's perceptions of Native Americans. At first Rowlandson considers them inhumane and devilish creatures, but over time she comes to recognize their humanity and to experience their compassion.

After her husband ransomed her, Rowlandson returned home. She remarried after her husband's death in 1678 and lived in Connecticut until her death in 1711.

A Work by Mary Rowlandson

Sovereignty and Goodness of God, Together With the Faithfulness of His Promises Displayed: Being a Narrative of the Captivity and Restoration of Mrs. Mary Rowlandson. New York: Bedford/St. Martin's, 1997.

Works about Mary Rowlandson

Breitwieser, Mitchell R. *American Puritanism and the Defense of Mourning: Religion, Grief, and Ethnology in Mary White Rowlandson's Captivity Narrative.* Madison: University of Wisconsin Press, 1992.

Casiglia, Christopher. *Bound and Determined: Captivity, Culture-Crossing, and White Womanhood from Mary Rowlandson to Patty Hearst.* Chicago: University of Chicago Press, 1996.

Rowson, Susanna (1762–1824) *fiction writer*

Susanna Haswell Rowson was born in Portsmouth, England, the daughter of a lieutenant in the British navy. When Rowson was a baby, her father moved to Massachusetts to pursue a career as a royal customs officer. As a young adult, Rowson became a governess in the household of the duchess of Devonshire. She also began writing and publishing stories and poems. The duchess encouraged Rowson's literary aspirations and subsidized the publication of her first novel, *Victoria* (1786). She married William Rowson in 1786 and continue to write assiduously, publishing four more novels in quick succession in the 1790s, the most famous of which is *Charlotte: A Tale of Truth* (1791), later titled *Charlotte Temple.* In 1797, Rowson opened a girls' school in Boston. She ran the school for the next 25 years, becoming highly respected as an educator.

An American edition of *Charlotte: A Tale of Truth* appeared in Philadelphia in 1794. Written as a cautionary tale "for the perusal of the young and thoughtless of the fair sex," it captivated its mostly female readers. A seductive British officer, John Montraville, persuades the attractive and innocent Charlotte to accompany him to colonial New York, where he abandons her for another woman. Charlotte dies after bearing Montraville's child and after he has turned her away when she seeks refuge with him during a snowstorm. The novel's prose, often overwrought, carries a powerful moral message, and *Charlotte: A Tale of Truth* became one of the most celebrated novels in the new republic.

One of the reasons for the popularity of Rowson's novels was their subtext that pitted democratic values against aristocratic corruption and immorality. *Charlotte Temple* continues to interest critics and scholars of the present day.

Works by Susanna Rowson

Charlotte Temple. Introduction by Jane Smiley. New York: Random House, 2004.

Mary: Or the Test of Honour. Temecula, Calif.: Reprint Services Corp., 1999.

Miscellaneous Poems. Murieta, Calif.: Classic Books, 2004.

Slaves in Algiers: A Struggle for Freedom. Edited by Jennifer Margulis and Karen M. Poremski. Acton, Mass.: Copley Publishing, 2000.

Victoria, 1786: The Inquisitor: Or, Invisible Rambler. Temecula, Calif.: Reprint Services Corp., 1999.

Works about Susanna Rowson

Bontatibus, Donna. *The Seduction Novel of the Early Nation*. East Lansing: Michigan State University Press, 1999.

Parker, Patricia L. *Susanna Rowson*. Boston: Twayne, 1986.

Ruiz de Alarcón, Juan (de Alarcón y Mendoza) (1580–1639) *playwright*

Juan Ruiz de Alarcón is one of the four greatest dramatists of the Spanish Siglo de Oro, or Golden Age. He was born in Mexico to Spanish parents and was deformed from birth with a hunchback. At age 33, Ruiz de Alarcón established himself in Spain for the longer and more productive part of his life. Although he is remembered primarily as a playwright, he was by profession a lawyer. By self-admission, he wrote his plays primarily for income, yet it is apparent that he took pride and care in crafting his 24 plays.

It is thought that a combination of Ruiz de Alarcón's deformity, his personality, and persecution from other writers of the age created the moral resentment that he expresses in his plays. He wrote comedies of manners in which he illustrates particular moral truths. As a keen observer of social abuses and follies, he attacks vices such as lying, slander, and inconstancy through his characters. Surprisingly, however, his plays display very little bitterness; rather, they convey concern with human values, conduct, and relationships.

His best-known work is *La verdad sospechosa (The Truth Suspect)*. It is considered to be Alarcón's best drama and has firmly established him among the great playwrights of Spain and the world. Both Pierre CORNEILLE and Carlo GOLDONI used this play as a source for some of their works.

Other works by Ruiz de Alarcón include *La prueba de las promesas (The Test of Promises)*, another structural and thematic masterpiece and a study of ingratitude; *Las paredes oyen (The Walls Have Ears)*, a COMEDY OF MANNERS that illustrates the ill effects of slander; and *No hay mal que por bien no venga (It Is an Ill Wind That Blows No Good)*, in which Ruiz de Alarcón creates a psychological picture, rather than a moral lesson, through characterization.

Ruiz de Alarcón's contributions to the *comedia*, the Spanish stage, and to world theater include carefully crafted plots, a minimum of extraneous activity, a direct and staightforward style, and masterful psychological development.

An English Version of a Work by Juan Ruiz de Alarcón

Truth Can't Be Trusted or the Liar. Translated by Daikin Matthews. New Orleans, La.: University Press of the South, 1998.

A Work about Juan Ruiz de Alarcón

Poesse, Walter. *Juan Ruiz De Alarcón*. New York: Twayne Publishers, 1972.

Ruusbroec, Jan van (1293–1381) *theologian*

Jan van Ruusbroec was born in the small town of Ruusbroec (or Ruisbroek), just south of Brussels in what was then the province of Brabant. At age 11 he left his mother and moved to Brussels, where his uncle, Jan Hinckaert, took charge of his education in Latin, grammar and rhetoric, and the arts. In 1317 he was ordained and made a chaplain at St. Gudula. In 1343 he withdrew with his uncle and his friend Vrank van Coudenberg to the forest of Soignes to lead a more secluded and contemplative life. The community, Groenendaal, adopted the Rule of St. Augustine in 1350 and thus became an official monastery, of which Ruusbroec was made prior. He spent the remainder of his life there pursuing what he considered his calling: a life of prayer and of helping others discover their own spiritual mission.

Ruusbroec's writings about his spiritual experiences have earned him recognition as one of the finest theologians of the late medieval period and an important contributor to trinitarian thinking. Ruusbroec lived during times troubled by plague, the Hundred Years' War, political revolts, and radical social changes. In addition, the church was troubled by movements outside of the accepted religious orders, including the Beguines and the Brethern of the Free Spirit who did not recognize official church authority. Himself an orthodox Catholic, Russbroec saw a widespread need for spiritual instruction, and by writing in Dutch hoped to make his teachings accessible to a broader audience.

Ruusbroec's first book, *The Kingdom of Lovers,* written between 1330 and 1340, was not intended for publication, and Ruusbroec expressed dismay when he realized his clerk had circulated it. The book described the spiritual life as a progress toward God through a series of seven holy gifts. The text proved difficult for some readers, and Ruusbroec strove to organize his thoughts on the development of the spiritual life in his second and major work, *The Spiritual Espousals* (ca. 1335). In three parts, the text addresses human growth toward a personal encounter with God through three levels: the active life or the life of virtue, the life of yearning, and the contemplative life.

The next treatise Ruusbroec wrote, *The Sparkling Stone,* summarizes the main points of the *Spiritual Espousals* and transcribes a conversation he reportedly had with a hermit on how to achieve the contemplative life. *The Four Temptations* describes the dangers that can lead one away from the spiritual life, including pursuit of bodily pleasures, hypocrisy, arrogance, and laziness. *The Christian Faith* was a simple explanation of the 12 articles of the creed. *The Spiritual Tabernacle,* the last of the works written in Brussels, proved to be his longest work and the most popular during his own time, judging from the number of existing manuscripts. The text provided a detailed and elaborate allegorical narrative from the Old Testament about the building of the Ark of the Covenant.

Ruusbroec composed his next works, which have a female audience in mind, after 1350. The Beguines were women who decided to live a religious life but did not take vows in a convent. Some contemporaries reviled the practice and considered the Beguines heretics, but Ruusbroec did not appear to share this opinion. *The Seven Enclosures* (1350), *The Mirror of Eternal Blessedness* (1359), and the later *Seven Rungs* were addressed to Margareta van Meerbeke, a nun of Clare whom Ruusbroec often visited. *The Little Book of Clarification,* probably composed after 1360, provided commentary on Ruusbroec's first book. His last work is *The Twelve Beguines.* He also left behind a set of letters.

During his life, translations of his works in German and Latin appeared, and after his death in English, Italian, French, and Spanish. The breadth of circulation affirms the number of people interested in Ruusbroec's recommendations for leading the spiritual and contemplative life. Based largely on his personal experience but also borrowing from orthodox sources and deeply respectful to church authority, Ruusbroec's writings exemplify the joyful faith and loving relationship with the divine that have proved inspirational for later generations seeking a spiritual path. Among other Middle Dutch or Flemish exponents of theories of love-mysticism such as Beatrice of Nazareth and Hadewijch of Antwerp, Ruusbroec remains, in the words of scholar Paul Verdeyen, "the brightest star in a constellation of spiritual writers."

An English Version of Works by Jan van Ruusbroec

John Ruusbroec: The Spiritual Espousals and Other Works. Translated by James A. Wiseman. Mahwah, N.J.: Paulist Press, 1986.

A Work about Jan van Ruusbroec

Verdeyen, Paul. *Ruusbroec and His Mysticism.* Translated by André Lefevere. Collegeville, Minn.: Liturgical Press, 1994.

Ryokan (Yamamoto Eizo) (1758–1831)
poet, Zen Buddhist priest

The Zen poet Ryokan was born Yamamoto Eizo in Izumozaki on the northwest coast of the big island of Japan. His father was a HAIKU poet, village leader, and custodian of the local Shinto shrine. At age 17, Yamamoto began religious training at a local Zen Buddhist temple, shaved his head, became a monk, and took the religious name Ryokan.

Ryokan spent from 1779 to 1789 as a disciple of the Zen master Kokusen. After achieving full enlightenment, he became a Zen master and spent five years wandering about the country. Little is known of his whereabouts or what he did during this period.

After his father committed suicide in 1795, Ryokan came back to his native region, where he stayed in a number of temples before settling into a small hut on Mount Kugami in 1804. He remained there for 13 years. While many Zen masters had a temple of their own, Ryokan spent his time alone, meditating and writing poetry, dubbing himself the "Great Fool" because of his hermetic existence. Despite his self-disparaging nickname, he lived a long, productive life.

Ryokan primarily wrote *tanka*—31-syllable poems divided among five lines. His subjects ranged from daily chores, to the seasons, to talks with friends. Though he achieved renown as a poet and calligrapher, he did not collect his work in volumes. Instead, he gave occasional pieces to friends or acquaintances who shared his great talents with others. Scholars have accumulated more than 1,800 of his poems written in both Japanese and Chinese, many of which have been collected in English translations.

English Versions of Works by Ryokan

Between the Floating Mist Poems of Ryokan. Translated by Dennis Maloney and Hide Oshiro. Buffalo, N.Y.: Springhouse Editions, 1992.

Great Fool: Zen Master Ryokan—Poems, Letters, and Other Writings. Translated by Ryuichi Abe and Peter Haskel. Honolulu: University of Hawaii Press, 1996.

The Zen Poems of Ryokan. Translated by Nobuyuki Yuasa. Princeton, N.J.: Princeton University Press, 1981.

Works about Ryokan

Kownacki, Mary Lou. *Between Two Should: Conversations with Ryokan.* Grand Rapids, Mich.: William B. Eerdmans, 2004.

Stevens, John. *Three Zen Masters: Ikkyu, Hakuin, Ryokan.* New York: Kodansha America, 1993.

Sachs, Hans (1494–1576) *poet, dramatist, essayist, Meistersinger*

Hans Sachs was born in the city of Nuremberg to a tailor family. As a youth he attended a Latin school, which allowed him to become familiar with the classical literary tradition. After finishing school, he was trained to be a shoemaker, the trade he would practice, along with singing and writing, for the rest of his life. At age 16, Sachs set out on foot on a journey through the cultural centers of southwestern Germany. It was on this trip that he was exposed to the art of *Meistergesang,* a German tradition of popular song and performance that dates to the Middle Ages. Upon his return to Nuremberg, he established his own shoemaking shop, married, began writing carnival plays, and studied to become a Meistersinger.

As the Reformation spread through Germany and Europe, Sachs immersed himself in Martin LUTHER's writings. Sachs was very much moved by the reformist's message and in 1523 wrote a pamphlet in defense of Luther's principles and beliefs. The so-called *Wittembergisch Nachtigall (Wittembergischer Nightingale)* was popular, but also sparked fierce controversy, and Sachs soon found himself in the middle of a fierce dialectical battle. At the same time the shoemaker's poems and versions of the psalms had also become popular, and

he was thus a well-known figure not just in Nuremberg but also throughout Germany. His bitter verbal attacks on the pope and clergy were, however, frowned upon by Nuremberg authorities, and in 1527 he was prohibited from publishing there.

Sachs's *Ode to the City of Nuremberg* (1530), in which he characterizes the city as a kind of paradise where citizens and the city council work together in blissful harmony, may very well have motivated the lifting of the publication ban against him. Thereafter he once again began writing and publishing essays on religious and political themes, though his writing seemed to be less controversial. From this time on he lived comfortably with his family, practicing the trade of shoemaking and continuing his literary and artistic activities, which included directing a singing school and producing his own theatrical works. He died at age 82 in his native city of Nuremberg.

It is not any single work by Sachs, but the incredible extent of his writing and the influence it had on his own and future generations that distinguishes him as a major figure in German literature. His work can be divided into various genres, though there is some crossover between styles and forms. His extensive works of *Meistergesang* were and are less well known, as they were typically performed only by private societies and rarely published. Yet it was precisely the nonpublic nature of these compositions that allowed Sachs to experiment with themes and language that would otherwise have been censored. His poetry offers a stark contrast to the *Meistergesang* in that it had a much broader audience and conformed for the most part to the established lyrical tradition of the age. His prose dialogues, though a less important facet of his literary work, were revolutionary both for their form and content. In these he took on themes related to Christian faith and the role of the common man in religious and governmental institutions. His dramatic writings included both carnival plays and classical drama, and were often based on biblical scenes or works of medieval and ancient literature.

In more ways than one Sachs represented a new kind of author for his time. For one, he combined his artistic activities with his profession as a tradesman. This trade afforded him financial independence from aristocratic or religious patrons and, as a result, afforded him a unique freedom in choosing subject, style, and genre. For the breadth of his writings, as well as for his humanistic perspective and intense political engagement, the Nuremberg shoemaker stands out as an enigmatic but crucial figure in the development of German thought and literature.

An English Version of Works by Hans Sachs
Nine Carnival Plays. Translated by Randall Listerman. Ottawa: Dovehouse Editions, 1990.

Sade, marquis de (Donatien-Alphonse-François de Sade) (1740–1814) *novelist*
The word *sadist* describes a person who enjoys inflicting cruel pain on others. The word comes from the name of the French novelist, the marquis de Sade, who lived and worked in France during the 18th and early 19th centuries. His writings contain flashes of literary skill mixed with foul and disgusting descriptions of excessive vice. He is famous today for his graphic descriptions of sexual exploitation, as well as for the bizarre events of his life.

The marquis de Sade was born in Paris. His parents were nobles associated with the court of Louis XV, king of France. During the mid-18th century, the upper class of France was enjoying an age of pleasure-seeking and luxurious overindulgence. It was also the Age of ENLIGHTENMENT, when philosophically minded writers such as VOLTAIRE and Denis DIDEROT were challenging conventional traditions regarding politics, science, and religion.

After receiving an education at a Jesuit school, Sade joined the French army and served as a cavalry officer during the Seven Years' War. He began the life of a libertine after the fighting ended. He had affairs with actresses in Paris and constantly solicited the services of prostitutes. These activities shocked the people of Paris, and the police kept Sade under observation. Despite his marriage in 1763 to Renée-Pélagie de Montreuil, his immoral way of life continued, and many people who came into contact with him accused him of assault.

The French authorities became increasingly disturbed at Sade's behavior, and he was arrested in 1777. In 1784 he was transferred to the Bastille, the most notorious of all French prisons. It was during his imprisonment in the Bastille that he wrote *120 Days of Sodom*, his first major work and the one for which he is best known.

120 Days of Sodom is the story of four men who have achieved sudden wealth through corruption and the murder of their own relatives. The characters are utter scoundrels whose only goals in life are to satisfy their own perverted desires and to cause pain and suffering to other human beings. The plot is simple, with the four characters spending 120 days together at the chateau of Silling. They go to considerable trouble to bring in the most alluring young men and women to serve as subjects for their perverse experiments. In addition to being sexually exploitive, the activities of the four characters often feature bizarre insults to religious symbols. The entire story is, in essence, a collection of the foulest and most disturbing thoughts that emanated from the marquis de Sade's mind.

Sade was released from prison when the Bastille was destroyed at the beginning of the French

Revolution. However, after some involvement in revolutionary politics, he was once again thrown in jail and only narrowly escaped being executed.

During this time period, he continued to write novels and plays. His novel *Justine* is the story of two sisters, one of whom is moral while the other is wicked. In keeping with Sade's view of the world, the virtuous sister experiences a life of sadness and horrible misfortune, while the unscrupulous sister lives in ease and comfort, wealthy after having murdered her husband and receiving a large inheritance.

In 1801, with France now under the rule of Napoleon, Sade was once again arrested for scandalous writings. A few years later, he was transferred to the insane asylum of Charenton. He lived out the rest of his life there, continuing to secretly write despite the efforts of authorities to deny him writing materials. He died in 1814. Much of the material Sade produced during this time was burned by his son after his death.

Sade is best remembered as a perverse and rather sickening author whose works were written chiefly to shock the public. He seemed to delight in everything that was foul and disturbing, and his writings reflect a belief that behaving with decency was a useless exercise and a waste of time. Nevertheless, despite his well-deserved reputation for vulgarity, many see his repeated imprisonments as symbolic of the struggle for literary freedom, saying that the marquis de Sade should have been free to write whatever he chose.

An English Version of a Work by the Marquis de Sade

120 Days of Sodom and Other Writings. Translated by Austryn Wainhouse and Richard Seaver. New York: Grove Press, 1987.

Works about the Marquis de Sade

Lever, Maurice. *Sade: A Biography.* Translated by Arthur Goldhammer. New York: Farrar, Straus and Giroux, 1993.
Schaeffer, Neil. *The Marquis de Sade: A Life.* New York: Alfred A. Knopf, 1999.

Santa Cruz y Espejo, Francisco Javier Eugenio de (ca. 1747–1795) *nonfiction writer*

One of the first intellectuals of Latin America to call for political independence from Spain, Francisco Javier Eugenio de Santa Cruz y Espejo was an Ecuadorian writer, doctor, and social activist. He was born in Quito, and was a meztizo, a person of mixed Indian, African, and Spanish ancestry.

It is said that Santa Cruz y Espejo wrote his first lessons in the sand, because the small school that he attended lacked the most basic resources. In spite of conditions, he excelled at his studies, attending the Dominican Seminary and later the University of Santo Tomás, where he took a doctoral degree. However, it was his father, an assistant to the doctors in the hospital at Quito, who inspired him to study further for a medical degree.

His scientific spirit and his compassion attracted Santa Cruz y Espejo to the ideals expressed by the leading thinkers of the ENLIGHTENMENT. Following their example, he set about exposing the deficiencies of Spanish culture in *El nuevo Luciano de Quito,* (The New Lucian of Quito, 1779), a harsh critique of Jesuit education and a defense of the practice of vaccination.

In 1781 he wrote a controversial piece titled *Retrato de golilla* (Portrait of a ruffled collar), in which he criticized the Spanish king. His political enemies used it as a pretext to exile him to Colombia some years later. While there, he forged a political alliance with Antonio de Nariño, another kindred spirit.

He later returned home and became a member of the Society of Patriots of Chile, which was set up with the king's consent. As secretary of this organization, Santa Cruz y Espejo was responsible for the publication of a bi-monthly newspaper called *Primicias de la cultura de Quito,* through which he planted the seeds that would later lead to political independence.

In 1792 he became the first director of the Public Library of Ecuador, which now bears his name. Despite these appointments, he continued to be harassed by the local authorities who felt threatened by his radical views. Unwavering in his commitment to justice, Santa Cruz y Espejo met his end in prison in 1795. English translations of his works are no longer in print.

Schiller, Friedrich von (1759–1805)
playwright, essayist, poet

Born in Marbach, Württemberg (present day Germany), to Johannes Kaspar Schiller, an army officer and surgeon, and Elizabeth Schiller, Friedrich von Schiller was raised in a pious Lutheran home. His father disapproved of his interests in literature and theater and forbade him to write poetry. When he was 14, Schiller went to an academy to study law and later medicine. He was expelled from medical school in 1780 for writing On *The Relation Between Man's Animal and Spiritual Nature,* an essay that questioned LUTHER's official theology. Schiller returned to Marbach and joined his father's army regiment, but he hated army life and avoided his duties so often that he was almost arrested for neglecting them.

Schiller did not abandon writing, and his first play, *The Robbers,* appeared in 1781. Depicting a noble outlaw, Karl Moor, who violently and passionately rejects his father's conservative ideology in his quest for justice, *The Robbers* simultaneously reflects Schiller's conflict with his father and the ideological struggle between conservative and liberal political forces in Germany. The play was warmly greeted in Germany and was admired by the English Romantics. The theme of liberty that appears in *The Robbers* permeates virtually everything Schiller wrote. The play *Don Carlos* (1787), for instance, is about the conflict between Philip II of Spain and his son, who is torn between passionate love and the political intrigues of his father's ministers.

Between 1783 and 1784, Schiller worked as a playwright and stage manager for the theater in Mannheim. Five years later, in 1789, he became professor of history at the University of Jena and worked on a history of the Thirty Years' War for the next three years. Declining health obliged Schiller to abandon his professorship, and he became an assistant to Johann Wolfgang von GOETHE, then director of the Weimar court theater.

Schiller also distinguished himself as a poet. "Ode to Joy" (1785), which was set to music by Ludwig van Beethoven, is the anthem of the European Union. More significant, in poems like *Wilhelm Tell* (1804), which describes the close relationship that the Swiss hero had with nature, Schiller helped to forge a Romantic aesthetic. The attention to nature, human emotions, and the ideals of liberty and political freedom found in his works are in fact the primary ingredients in most Romantic art.

Schiller's interest in history resulted in several historical plays. *Mary Stuart* (1800) describes the turbulent relationship between Elizabeth I and Mary Queen of Scots in the final days before Mary's execution. The captive, wild environment of the castle of Fotheringay provides a dark, melancholy background that amplifies Mary as a tragic figure in the play. The dramatic trilogy *Wallenstein* (1796–99) depicts Germany during the Thirty Years' War and captures the deep fragmentation of society along the lines of religion. German national identity and the idea of nationhood are juxtaposed with the ruinous conflict created by the religious strife and the political scheming of the rulers.

Many of Schiller's ideas were influenced by the works of 18th-century German philosopher Immanuel KANT. In *On the Aesthetic Education of Man* (1795), Schiller deals with the bloody aftermath of the French Revolution and how it changed the way humans thought about freedom. The key to freedom, he argues, is the fundamental aesthetic development of the individual and society, and a true sense of freedom and liberty is connected to one's experience of the sublime and the beautiful—two important philosophical categories in Kant's works.

In *On the Naïve and Sentimental in Literature* (1795), Schiller creates a series of dialectical dichotomies, such as feeling and thought, nature and culture, finitude and infinity, and finally sentimental and naïve modes of writing. Although describing himself as a sentimental or "reflective" writer, Schiller paid homage to his close friend Goethe, whom he described as the ultimate archetype of the naïve genius. Here, *naïve* is not used in the conventional sense of the word, but rather as a philosophical term that describes something that is utterly pure and good and closely connected with nature.

Today, Schiller is considered one of the foremost German writers. His drama and poetry contributed significantly to the literature of the Romantic movement, and his magnificent control and elegant use of the German language have inspired generations of readers, writers, and poets.

English Versions of Works by Friedrich von Schiller

Essays. Edited by Walter Hinderer and Daniel Dahlstrom. New York: Continuum, 1993.

Schiller's Five Plays: The Robbers, Passion and Politics, Don Carlos, Mary Stuart, and Joan of Arc. Translated by Robert McDonald. New York: Consortium Books, 1998.

Works about Friedrich von Schiller

Carlyle, Thomas. *The Life of Friedrich Schiller.* Edited by Jeffrey Sammons. Columbia, S.C.: Camden House, 1992.

Sharpe, Lesley. *Friedrich Schiller: Drama, Thought, and Politics.* Cambridge: Cambridge University Press, 1991.

Thomas, Calvin. *The Life and Works of Friedrich Schiller.* McLean, Va.: Indypublish.com, 2004.

Schlegel, Friedrich (1772–1829) *critic, novelist, philosopher, scholar*

Friedrich Schlegel was born in the city of Hanover in northern Germany to the family of a Protestant minister. After completing school in his native city, he went on to study law and linguistics, first in Göttingen and then in Leipzig. As a student he developed close intellectual friendships with his brother August Wilhelm as well as NOVALIS, the great German Romantic poet.

The History of Greek and Roman Poetry (1798) was the first fruit of Schlegel's lifelong engagement with classic literature and philosophy. In this work he examines the relation between ancient and contemporary poetry and argues that, rather than turning away from the classics, artists should strive to incorporate into their work the balance and harmony of classical poetry and drama. Between 1798 and 1800, Schlegel and his brother edited the influential literary journal *Athenaeum,* in which works by virtually all of the most important writers of the age appeared.

In 1802 Schlegel moved to Paris and began a new intellectual phase. After reading extensively in French and Portuguese literature and studying European fine art and architecture, he began to learn Sanskrit and to study Indian philosophy. These studies greatly influenced his *On the Language and Wisdom of India* (1808), a book that would have a profound influence on his generation. Also in 1808, Schlegel converted to Catholicism and moved to Vienna, where he spent the rest of his life.

In Vienna Schlegel became active in the movement to overthrow Napoleon's regime, worked as an editor of another literary journal, and published his collected works. In 1827 he began work on what was to be a series of lectures on the history of Western literature and philosophy, in which he hoped to summarize the evolution of his intellectual development, a project he never completed.

Though Schlegel left behind no single work of overwhelming importance, the influence of his creative, critical, and scholarly work on his own and later ages is not to be underestimated. He defined many of the principles of poetry and philosophy that would become characteristic of German Romanticism, and his ideas continue to be influential among German artists and intellectuals.

An English Version of a Work by Friedrich Schlegel

Philosophical Fragments. Translated by Peter Firchow. Minneapolis: University of Minnesota Press, 1991.

A Work about Friedrich Schlegel

Eichner, Hans. *Friedrich Schlegel.* New York: Twayne, 1970.

Schopenhauer, Arthur (1788–1860)
philosopher

Arthur Schopenhauer was born into a wealthy family in the city of Danzig. He spent much of his youth traveling from one country to another, during which time he mastered many languages and received a good education. He earned a doctorate in philosophy from the University of Jena. After his father's death, Schopenhauer received a large inheritance, which freed him from having to work for a living. Ensured of financial independence, he devoted the rest of his life to scholarship and philosophy.

The main ideas of Schopenhauer's philosophy were presented in his work *The World as Will and Representation* (1818), in which he argues that the world can exist only as an idea in the mind of a person trying to perceive the world. Schopenhauer saw human will as the primary agent of existence and believed that it controlled every human action, no matter how insignificant.

Schopenhauer was heavily influenced by Plato, Immanuel KANT, and Johann Wolfgang von GOETHE. In addition, he was the first major Western philosopher who undertook a serious study of Buddhism and Hinduism, which also had a great effect on him. On the other hand, he was very hostile to the thinking of his contemporary, philosopher Georg Wilhelm Friedrich Hegel.

Schopenhauer was not seen as being an important philosopher during his own lifetime, but after his death, his influence on others, particularly German philosopher Friedrich Nietzsche, would be profound. By the mid-20th century, Schopenhauer had been recognized as being a major figure in the development of Western thought.

English Versions of Works by Arthur Schopenhauer

The Art of Controversy. La Vergne, Tenn.: University Press of the Pacific, 2004.

The Art of Literature. La Vergne, Tenn.: University Press of the Pacific, 2004.

The Wisdom of Life. Mineola, N.Y.: Dover, 2004.

The World as Will and Representation. Translated by E. F. J. Payne. Mineola, N.Y.: Dover, 1966.

Works about Arthur Schopenhauer

Janaway, Christopher. *Schopenhauer: A Very Short Introduction*. New York: Oxford University Press, 2002.

Safranski, Rudiger. *Schopenhauer and the Wild Years of Philosophy*. Cambridge, Mass.: Harvard University Press, 1990.

Wallace, W. *Life of Arthur Schopenhauer*. La Vergne, Tenn.: University Press of the Pacific, 2003.

Scottish poets of the fifteenth century
(1400s)

Fostered by the presence of a refined court society, the literature of Scotland in the 15th century experienced a concentrated period of poetic achievement. During this time King James I of Scotland, Robert Henryson, Gavin Douglas, and William Dunbar all produced works that imitated the poetry of Geoffrey CHAUCER in form, rhetorical style, subject matter, and technique. Some of the works follow Chaucer's model of parody and the form of his allegorical dream visions (see ALLEGORY). For this reason, the poets of this group are often referred to as the "Scottish Chaucerians." The group is part of a larger tradition sometimes called the "Middle Scots Poets," a label that often extends back to the 14th century to include John Barbour (1320–95) and the poet known as "Blind Harry," author of *Schir William Wallace* (ca. 1450). William Dunbar himself called his contemporaries the "Makars" (makers) in the poem "Lament for the Makars."

The first remarkable work of the period is the poem *The Kingis Quair* (sometimes *Quhair*, 1423), an allegorical dream vision usually attributed to King James I of Scotland. Scholars have interpreted this poem as an autobiographical work in which James I describes his courtship of Jane Beaufort, the daughter of the English earl of Somerset, in 1424. This poem is a prototype of Chaucerian imitation, borrowing both the dream-vision narrative frame and rhyme royal meter from Chaucer. It also makes reference to Palamon and Arcite, two of the central characters in "The Knight's Tale" from Chaucer's *Canterbury Tales*.

Perhaps the most famous of the Scottish Chaucerians, Robert Henryson (ca. 1425–1506) was master of the Benedictine Abbey Grammar School at Dunfermline and a member of the newly founded University of Glasgow. He was the author of a number of fables and several allegorical poems offering moral instruction. His most famous poem, the *Testament of Cresseid,* often appears in anthologies and offers a type of sequel to Chaucer's famous *Troilus and Creseyde.* This poem is harsh and graphic, but not unsympathetic, in its portrayal of Chaucer's heroine. In it, Henryson paints Cresseid as a faithless lover punished with leprosy and disease but shows her later redemption as she enters a nunnery in repentance for her sins. It is a work grim and serious in tone. However, Henryson displays an ability to produce more cheerful work with poems such as "Robene and Makyne," a lighthearted parody of the courtly love tradition. This poem reverses the traditional gender roles assigned in courtly love lyrics; here the rustic girl Makyne tries to instruct the shepherd boy Robene in matters of love. He resists her advice, but later he realizes his mistake and returns to seek her counsel, only to have Makyne say that he has waited too long to act. The poem's theme of carpe diem ("seize the day") anticipates some of the poetry of the 16th century.

In addition to being influenced by Chaucer, William Dunbar also possessed a fascination with the language of alliterative poetry, a form still popular in Scotland in the 15th century though its popularity had waned in England. Dunbar wrote many occasional poems inspired by events associated with the court of King James IV of Scotland, as well as a number of divine poems and parodies like "The Flyting of Dunbar and Kennedie," a humorous address to one of his rivals. By contrast, the "Lament for the Makars" is a more serious devotion that contemplates the mortality of the poet and gives tribute to the "brother" poets whom death has claimed: "In Dunfermline he [death] hes done roune / With maister Robert Henrisoun." Because he offers commentary on both the court and his contemporaries, Dunbar contributes greatly to our knowledge of this period of Scottish literature.

As a member of a prominent Scottish clan, Gavin Douglas (1474–1522) was very well educated, having attended schools at St. Andrews and perhaps Paris. Like his contemporaries, he wrote some works in imitation of Chaucer, such as his early work *The Palice of Honour,* a long allegorical dream vision based loosely on Chaucer's *House of Fame,* but also bearing the influence of Ovid and BOCCACIO. However, Douglas's translation of Virgil's *Aeneid* into Middle Scots, the *Aeneis,* arguably displays his best work. He divides his translation into 13 books, each with a prologue in which he often discusses subject matter, style, or circumstances of composition. His translation, regarded by many to be one of the best translations of the EPIC, strikes a balance between Virgil's classic language and Douglas's own lively Scots verse. After the passing of Douglas, the power of Scottish poetry would decline until the career of Robert Burns in the late 18th century.

Works by Scottish Poets of the Fifteenth Century

Dunbar, William. *William Dunbar: Selected Poems.* Edited by Harriet H. Wood. London: Routledge, 2003.
Henryson, Robert. *Poems and Fables.* Edinburgh: Oliver and Boyd, 1958.

A Work about the Scottish Poets

Henderson, T. F. *Scottish Vernacular Literature: A Succinct History.* Edinburgh: Scotpress, 1988.

Scudéry, Madeleine de (1607–1701)
novelist

Madeleine de Scudéry was born in Provence, France, to impoverished lower nobility. Orphaned at an early age, she was educated by her uncle and joined her brother Georges, a minor playwright and critic, in Paris in 1637. Intelligent, charming, and kind, she became involved in the intellectual gatherings known as salons, where noble and upper-class women, male scholars, writers, and artists met to discuss a variety of topics. Madeleine never married, but served as a hostess and collaborator with her brother.

Scudéry wrote several long historical romances that made her one of the best-selling and most influential writers in western European prose fiction. Her novels include *Ibrahim, ou le basse illustre* (*Ibrahim, or the Illustrious Basha,* 1641); *Artamene, ou le grande Cyrus* (*Artamene or the Great Cyrus,* 1649–53); and *Clélie* (1654–60). These novels used historical characters and exotic settings to explore contemporary concerns, such as politics and proper relationships between men and women. Scudéry based many of her characters on friends and contemporaries, so people read the novels eagerly for gossip about one another. The novels were translated into English and other languages and spread French ideas about platonic love, elegant speech, and social behavior throughout Europe.

Scudéry was not just a popular novelist, but also an influential theorist about fiction. In her preface to *Ibrahim,* she claimed prose fiction could be just as instructive and serious as EPIC poetry, and she proposed a theory of literary realism based on realistic characters and probable incidents: "As for me, I hold, that the more natural adventures are, the more satisfaction they give; and the ordinary course of the Sun seems more mervailous to me, than the Strange and deadly rayes of Comets."

When the vogue for long, multivolume romances faded in the 1670s, Scudéry wrote and published shorter essays on polite behavior and conversation, which influenced other essayists. She herself rose above the common stereotype, which depicted women as ignorant and frivolous, to gain respect for her learning and intellectual curiosity. She was recognized by the ACADÉMIE FRANÇAISE, awarded a pension by King Louis XIV, and elected to the *Academia dei Ricovrati* of Padua (1684). Scudéry's works are not widely available today, but scholars of world literature study them for what they reveal about the intellectual and cultural changes in early modern France, and especially the change in the status of women.

English Versions of Works by Madeleine de Scudéry

Selected Letters, Orations, and Rhetorical Dialogues. Edited by Jane Donawerth. Chicago: University of Chicago Press, 2004.

The Story of Sapho. Translated by Karen Newman. Chicago: University of Chicago Press, 2003.

Works about Madeleine de Scudéry

Aronson, Nicole. *Madeleine de Scudéry.* New York: Twayne, 1978.

DeJean, Joan. *Tender Geographies: Women and the Origins of the Novel in France.* New York: Columbia University Press, 1991.

Se-jong (1397–1450) *nonfiction writer, king*

Se-jong was one of the greatest rulers of Korea. He was the fourth king of the Joseon or Choson dynasty (1392–1910), coming to the throne in 1418 at age 22, when his father T'aejong abdicated to allow his son to rule. King Se-jong was a devout Confucian and a humanist who enacted policies to help the poorest of his subjects. His policies included establishing relief programs to help people in the wake of natural disasters and providing government loans to help farmers who lost their crops.

King Se-jong's literary achievements were many, including the invention of a system to write the Korean language, called *Hunmin jeongeum* ("correct sounds to teach the people"), that was simple enough for everyone to learn. Until Se-jong's time, Korean had been written using Chinese characters, which were so numerous that few ordinary people could master them. His alphabet, now called Hangeul, contains 11 vowels and 17 consonants and can be learned in a very short period of time, even by people with little education.

Se-jong himself wrote *Dongguk jeong-un* (*Dictionary of Proper Sino-Korean Pronunciation,* 1447), and he used his new alphabet to write *Yongbi eocheon ga* (*Songs of Flying Dragons,* 1445), a series of 125 cantos celebrating the accomplishments of the Choson dynasty. Among the most beautiful of lines in this work are these from the second canto, celebrating the strength and endurance of Se-jong's ancestors:

Trees with deep roots do not sway in the wind,
But bear fine flowers and bountiful fruit,
Water welling from deep springs never dries up,
But becomes rivers and flow to the seas.

King Se-jong was a man of many talents. In addition to his literary and social accomplishments, he was also a scientist and inventor. He gathered the best scientists in the country to his court and supported their work in medicine and astronomy. He himself invented a water clock and a rain gauge.

King Se-jong died at age 52 and was succeeded by his son Munjong. A performing arts center in Seoul and Korea's base in Antarctica are both named for this great ruler.

A Work about Se-jong

Kim-Renaud, Young-Key. *King Se-jong the Great: The Light of Fifteenth-Century Korea.* Seoul, Korea: International Circle of Korean Linguistics, 1997.

Sévigné, Madame de (Marie de Rabutin-Chantal, marquise de Sévigné)
(1626–1696) *correspondent*

Marie de Rabutin-Chantal was born into a long-standing aristocratic family; her father, Celse Bénigne de Rabutin, was the baron de Chantal, and her mother, Marie de Coulanges, possessed an equally distinguished lineage. Wealth did not ensure health, however, and upon being orphaned at age seven, Marie was raised by her maternal grandparents and then, upon their deaths, by her uncle Christophe. Her uncle provided her with generous financial support, advice, and an excellent education; one of her tutors was Ménage, whose instruction she shared with her lifelong friend Madame de LAFAYETTE. Marie knew both Italian and Spanish, read widely, and had a charming personality; one admirer described her as vivacious and animated, musical and neat, a woman altogether pleasing in manner and pretty in looks, from which her square

nose and different-colored eyes did nothing to detract. At age 18 she married Henri, marquis de Sévigné, and had two children: Françoise was born in 1646 and Charles in 1648. After her unfaithful, irresponsible husband was killed in a duel in 1651, Madame de Sévigné maintained a happy and comfortable widowhood, devoting herself to her family and friends. She traveled, entertained, took an active interest in political and social events, and managed to satisfactorily arrange the marriages of her children and grandchildren. She died of smallpox in 1696.

Madame de Sévigné earned her fame through her prodigious correspondence, which she kept throughout her life and which spans 10 volumes. She lived in the reign of both Louis XIII and Louis XIV, in a France that was increasingly becoming the center of the civilized world, and a Paris that was the cultural center of France. The high society of Madame de Sévigné's day revolved around the drawing room, the salon, where people met to exchange news, politics, and gossip, and the leisured wealthy fostered the creative work of artists and writers. Madame de Sévigné is one of the best examples of these inhabitants of the salon, the fashionable, cultivated woman combining intellect with charm. Her letters reveal the habits and ideals of her culture as well as the advantages and prejudices of her class. Though the effusive praise of her admirers can be as excessive as the unflattering accusations of her enemies, the native voice of her letters reveals a lively personality, a quick wit, and a warm heart. An early epistle to her beloved daughter, to whom she addressed the bulk of her correspondence, displays all the devotion of an adoring mother:

Even if you could succeed in loving me as much as I love you, which is not possible or even in God's order of things, my little girl would have to have the advantage; it is the overspill of the love I feel for you. . . . I shall be so grateful if for love of me you take a great deal of care of yourself. Ah, my dear, how easy it will always be to pay your debt to me! Could treasures and all the wealth in the word give me as much joy as your affection?

She adds in this letter a teasing, meddling note to her daughter's husband:

> . . . although you are of all men the most fortunate in being loved, you have never been loved, nor can be, by anybody more sincerely than by me. I wish you were here in my mall every day, but you are proud, and I see quite well that you want me to come and see you first. You are very fortunate that I am not an old granny.

A typical letter to her friend Madame de Lafayette is full of the most ordinary details as well as salacious gossip, told in a voice that makes everything interesting:

> I don't know of any news to send you today, for I have not seen the *Gazette* for three days. But you must know that Mme de N—is dead, and that Trévigny, her lover, nearly died of grief. For my part I would have preferred him really to die of it for the honour of the ladies.

Madame de Sévigné was aware that her letters had a wide audience; she knew the recipient would circulate them among her acquaintances. But she could not know that, even centuries later, readers would enjoy her zest for gossip and her accounts of the important events of her day. She was, without knowing it, a journalist, a social historian, and a great writer whose legacy clearly evokes the spirit of her age.

An English Version of Madame de Sévigné's Letters
Madame de Sévigné: Selected Letters. Translated by Leonard Tancock. New York: Penguin Books, 1982.

A Work about Madame de Sévigné
Mossiker, Frances. *Madame de Sévigné.* New York: Columbia University Press, 1983.

Shakespeare, William   (1564–1616)
dramatist, poet
William Shakespeare was born in Stratford-on-Avon, England, to middle-class parents. He was probably educated at a local grammar school, where he would have learned Latin, rhetoric (how to be persuasive and argue a case), and classical literature. He married young and had a twin son and daughter, Hamnet and Judith, by the time he was 21. Not long after their birth, he went to London, alone, to seek his fortune.

He found work as an actor first, in the lively theatrical scene that was burgeoning in late 16th-century London, encouraged by Queen Elizabeth I's enthusiasm. Before long he was writing plays. All told, he wrote or cowrote at least 35 dramas, not to mention a remarkable SONNET sequence and other short poems. The first collection of Shakespeare's plays was published in 1622–23, several years after his death. By the end of his career, Shakespeare was already considered by his peers to be one of the greatest writers in England.

Critical Analysis
Shakespeare's earliest known plays are comedies, typically focusing on romantic relationships and ending in marriage. The early comedies *The Taming of the Shrew* and *The Comedy of Errors,* both of which are on record as first being staged in 1594, are less complex than the later masterpieces *As You Like It* (ca. 1599) and *Twelfth Night* (ca. 1600–01), but they contain evidence of Shakespeare's genius—complex language, unique characters, and interesting plots.

The first two plays are sometimes referred to as citizen comedies, or urban comedies, because they portray nonroyal figures in public settings, such as marketplaces and town squares. The *Comedy of Errors* is a story of mistaken identity (a popular theme in English comedy), while the *Taming of the Shrew* explores issues of romance and female identity. The latter two plays are considered PASTORAL, because, like the Italian plays in whose tradition they follow, the story shifts from the city to the country. In *As You Like It,* the participants in the drama retreat to the forest of Arden (a real place near Stratford, where Shakespeare grew up) before returning home to the city, a bit older and wiser as a result of their adventures.

The tragedies *King Lear* (ca. 1605) and *Macbeth* (ca. 1606) are mature examples of Shakespeare's turn toward the darker themes of murder and madness and how they relate to politics (both title characters are national leaders who lose their minds and lives). *Othello* (ca. 1604), *Antony and Cleopatra* (ca. 1606–07), and, of course, *Hamlet* (ca. 1600) are considered to be among the greatest achievements in world literature. All of these plays depict the demise of military or royal figures, honorable men who are fatally flawed or self-destructive.

The final works of Shakespeare's career are best described as "problem plays" or tragicomedies—dramatic stories that combine elements of both tragedy and comedy while exploring the complexities of human existence. *The Winter's Tale* (ca. 1610–11) and *The Tempest* (ca. 1611) address a variety of issues, ranging from the personal (parenthood, friendship, and ambition) to the social (politics, sexuality, and slavery).

In his plays, Shakespeare developed what today has become recognized as a modern understanding of human character. The critic Joel Fineman credits Shakespeare with inventing the psychological view of the self that is assumed in modern thought. Harold Bloom, in a similar vein, has argued that Shakespeare is responsible for "the invention of the human."

One of the themes that Shakespeare develops in depth is the complicated relationship between the outer self and the inward self. In *Hamlet,* Queen Gertrude, Hamlet's mother, attempts to convince her son that it is time to stop mourning for his dead father. When she asks Hamlet why he seems to mourn so deeply, he replies:

'Tis not alone my inky cloak, good mother,
Nor customary suits of solemn black, . . .
That can denote me truly. These indeed seem,
For they are actions that a man might play;
But I have that within which passes show,
These but the trappings and the suits of woe.

Hamlet begins this speech assuring his mother of the authenticity of his behavior. He does not seem to mourn; he truly mourns. His exterior, the way he dresses in mourning for his dead father,

cannot reveal his true inner self, just as outward signs—sighs, tears, and dejected behavior—cannot truly represent that which is within: the human spirit, or individual identity.

While much criticism has been and continues to be written about Hamlet's character, one might assume that Shakespeare intended Hamlet to represent his opinion that the "outward" person can never be anything more than an inauthentic representation of the "inward." This, in turn, reflects the disappearance of the traditional social order taking place in England at the time.

Perhaps the play that best represents Shakespeare's understanding of social change is *King Lear,* in which an elderly king, who is foolishly taken in by his daughters' flattery, relinquishes his power and ultimately loses not only his throne but also his sense of self. The playwright reflects how the medieval monarchical system, in which power passed in an orderly way from father to son and position was essentially fixed at birth, was being called into question by ambitious individuals seeking to reinvent themselves—and sometimes succeeding. Lear's tragedy is, thus, an English TRAGEDY, a national problem.

Although Shakespeare was not the only playwright to write about this problem, his drama is unique because he is able to address social issues through stories about individual people, like Lear and Macbeth. A theme that runs through both is that thirst for power corrupts. While Elizabeth in the final years of the 16th century was relatively secure, members of the aristocracy were in constant fear of losing their power, money, and lives. Shakespeare suggests that these threats are more than just individual problems. Rather, they are at the heart of social unrest and damage the nation as a whole. When Lear loses his sense of reality, we are meant to question what happens when non-kings can gain power through evil deeds.

What differentiates Shakespeare's most memorable and lifelike characters from those of other Elizabethan dramatists is their self-awareness. Renowned scholar Harold Bloom considers Sir John Falstaff—of the history plays *Henry IV,* parts one and two, *Henry V, Henry VI* part one, and *The Merry Wives of Windsor*—to be, along with Hamlet, the most psychologically realistic of Shakespeare's characters. He is a larger-than-life figure, an overweight, over-the-hill knight whose main interests are alcohol, food, money, and bragging. What is so interesting about his character is that he is the childhood friend of Prince Hal (the boy who becomes King Henry V) and has a sensitive side that is occasionally visible. Falstaff understands that his existence is meaningless compared to that of his young friend; he recognizes that he is not a noble being. There is something pathetic and even touching in his sense of humor, which makes him someone who simultaneously laughs at others and is laughed at:

> Men of all sorts take a pride to gird at me. The brain of this foolish-compounded clay, man, is not able to invent any thing that intends to laughter more than I invent or is invented on me: I am not only witty in myself, but the cause that wit is in other men.

The word *invention* is important because it refers to the ability to create oneself, or to play a role. This concept echoes Jaques's famous line about how life is a drama from *As You Like It:* "All the world's a stage, / And all the men and women merely players." For modern audiences, the outlook that society is composed of actors is not as pessimistic as it might seem. For Shakespeare, the theater is a place of possibility and wonder.

What Shakespeare ultimately suggests about human character is that there is always a difference between what people consider to be their authentic selves and how people reveal themselves to others. One is always obliged, in a sense, to act like, rather than to be, one's self. This idea is the same message that 20th-century novelists package as selfhood. Shakespeare's greatest achievement, Bloom thus argues, is that he was able to demonstrate "how new modes of consciousness come into being."

Works by William Shakespeare

Complete Works. Edited by Richard Proudfoot, et al. New York: Arden, 2001.

The Portable Shakespeare. New York: Penguin Classics, 2004.

Works about William Shakespeare

Bloom, Allan. *Shakespeare on Love and Friendship.* Chicago: University of Chicago Press, 1993.

Bloom, Harold. *Shakespeare: The Invention of the Human.* New York: Riverhead, 1998.

Boyce, Charles. *Critical Companion to William Shakespeare.* New York: Facts On File, 2005.

De Sousa, Geraldo U. *Shakespeare's Cross-Cultural Encounters.* New York: St. Martin's Press, 1999.

Foakes, R. A. *Hamlet Versus Lear: Cultural Politics and Shakespeare's Art.* New York: Cambridge University Press, 2004.

Greenblatt, Stephen. *Will in the World: How Shakespeare Became Shakespeare.* New York: W.W. Norton, 2004.

Honan, Park. *Shakespeare: A Life.* Oxford: Oxford University Press, 1998.

Knapp, Jeffrey. *Shakespeare's Tribe: Church, Nation, and Theater in Renaissance England.* Chicago: University of Chicago Press, 2004.

Shen Fu (1763–after 1809) *nonfiction writer*

Shen Fu is remembered for one work, *Six Records of a Floating Life,* a memoir of his life and especially of his relationship with his beloved wife, Chen Yun (Ch'en Yün). Shen Fu arranged his memories thematically, not chronologically. The first section, "The Joys of the Wedding Chamber," tells how he first met Yün and about their life together, including, surprisingly for modern Western readers, the story of Yün's attempt to secure a concubine for her husband. "The Pleasures of Leisure" gives details of the couple's daily life; it tells how they achieved beautiful effects in their home for not much money and about the ingenious entertainments they devised for each other and their friends. "The Sorrows of Misfortune" relates the underside of the beauty described in the first two sections, revealing how the couple became alienated from Shen Fu's family and went ever more deeply into debt, while Yün's health became progressively worse. In this section we first hear of the existence of their two children, when Shen Fu describes the wrenching parting from them that ensued when they decided to stay with a friend in the country for the sake of Yun's health. It also includes the tragic scene of Yun's death at age 40, but it ends with Shen Fu's accepting from a friend the gift of a concubine, whom he describes as "a young woman who renewed in me the spring dreams of life." The fourth section, "The Delights of Roaming Afar," is a travelogue, evoking the beauties of temples, gardens, and landscapes all over eastern China that Shen Fu visited in the course of his work as a secretary for government officials, and showing something of his relationships with friends and courtesans.

Nothing is known of Shen Fu's life after 1809, when according to *Six Records* he was working on the book. The manuscript, containing only four sections, was discovered and published in the 1870s. An allegedly complete version was published in Shanghai in the 1930s, but scholars agree that the fifth and sixth sections given there are forgeries.

Incomplete as it is, the book provides readers with a uniquely intimate view of life in late imperial China and gives access to a world view that, with its combination of romanticism and frankness, has great appeal. As Leonard Pratt and Chiang Su-Hui remark in the introduction to their translation, "Shen Fu has left us a lively portrait of his era that in places strikes chords that are remarkably resonant with those of our own times."

An English Version of a Work by Shen Fu

Six Records of a Floating Life. Translated by Leonard Pratt and Chiang Su-hui. New York: Penguin, 1983.

Shi Naian (Shih Nai-an) (fl.? 1400s) *novelist*

Shi Naian is considered by most critics to be the principal author of the influential novel *Shuihu zhuan* (*Shui-hu chuan*, 1300s–1500s). The other author is believed to be LUO GUANZHONG (ca. 1330–1400), although, in truth, more authors could have contributed to the story. Perhaps the problem of determining exact authorship is related to how early modern Chinese novels were written; authors of Chinese vernacular literature often borrowed parts of other works—whether fiction, poetry, songs, drama, or stories from the oral tradition—and developed them into their own stories. Given this form of "borrowing," it is speculated that Shi Naian took part of one of Luo Guanzhong's works and either added to it or adapted it. *Shuihu zhuan* has been given several English titles, depending on its translator, including *Wild Boar Forest, Water Margin, Outlaws of the Marsh,* and *The Men of the Marshes.*

In its most complete, printed form, *Shuihu zhuan* has 120 chapters. John and Alex Dent Young's recent translation is titled *Marshes of Mount Liang* and divides the lengthy story into four parts. The story is about 108 bandits who try to help the Chinese emperor overthrow the prime minister, whom Shi Naian depicts as cruel and despotic. These bandits and their struggle against unfair or uncivil authority have often been compared to the tales of Robin Hood and his band of men.

Pearl S. Buck translated the novel as *All Men Are Brothers.* She discussed the novel in her Nobel speech in 1938, stating that Shi Naian's novel is considered a great work of fiction because "it portrays so distinctly one hundred and eight characters that each is to be seen separate from the others."

The outlaw protagonists of the work continue to have a hold on the popular imagination. The Japanese name of the tale, "Suikoden," is also the name of a video game. More significant, an anonymous author in the early 17th century developed an event described in *Shuihu zhuan* into one of the greatest Chinese novels ever written, JIN PING MEI (*Golden Lotus,* 1617).

English Versions of Works by Shi Naian

All Men Are Brothers. Translated by Pearl S. Buck. Kingston, R.I.: Asphodel Press, 2001.

Outlaws of the Marsh. Translated by Sidney Shapiro. Beijing: Foreign Languages Press, 1998.

The Broken Seals: Part One of the Marshes of Liang. Translated by John and Alex Dent-Young. Hong Kong: Chinese University Press, 1994.

Wild Boar Forest. Translated by Li Shau Chwun and edited by John D. Mitchell. Midland, Mich.: Northwood University Press, 1995.

Sidney, Sir Philip (1554–1586) *fiction writer, critic, poet*

Philip Sidney was born at Penshurst, Kent, the son of Sir Henry Sidney and Lady Mary Dudley. The Sidneys were a prominent family with close ties to the court of Queen Elizabeth I. Sidney was educated at the Shrewsbury School and at Christ Church, Oxford, after which he traveled in Europe for three years under the tutelage of Hubert Languet, a humanist scholar.

Returning to England in 1576, Sidney was appointed to the honorary position of cupbearer to the queen and spent some time in Ireland assisting his father. His first published work, a treatise called *Discourse on Irish Affairs* (1577), supported his father's harsh anti-Irish policies. When Sidney went back to England the following year, he wrote *The Lady of May,* a PASTORAL entertainment in the queen's honor.

Sidney began to take an active interest in diplomatic affairs, and to write about the issues of the day. Serving in parliament in 1581 and again in 1584–85, he became an avid supporter of the New World explorations of Sir Martin Frobisher and others, and helped promote plans to settle an English colony in Virginia. Sidney maintained a rich correspondence with artists and intellectuals, many of whom sought his patronage or dedicated works to him.

In 1586 Sidney volunteered in a campaign to thwart Spanish military maneuvers in Zutphen, Holland, and was mortally wounded there. The courage with which he faced death became legendary, and his death occasioned deep mourning throughout Europe.

Like most aristocratic writers of the time, Sidney considered it beneath him to attempt to gain financially from his writings by publishing them. It was not until 1598, some 11 years after his death, that his sister published his significant works in a collection called *The Countess of Pembroke's Arcadia.*

Sidney's most prolific period as a writer spanned the nine years from 1577, when he started writing his most acclaimed work, *The Arcadia,* until his death. Probably completed in 1580, the earliest version of *Arcadia* was a ROMANCE in five books, whose muse was undoubtedly his sister, Mary, of whom he wrote: "You desired me to do it, and your desire to my heart is an absolute commandment." In crafting this masterwork, Sidney drew on his considerable knowledge of chivalric romances in French and Italian as well as the Arthurian legends in English. Critics have also pointed out the influence of classical works, including Apuleius's *Golden Ass* and Heliodorus's *Æthopian Historie.* Replete with damsels in distress, knights in shining armor, gender reversals, and sexual license, *Arcadia* in many ways epitomizes the cult of courtly love. *Arcadia* also draws heavily on the forms of pastoral poetry, making it reminiscent of Virgil's *Eclogues.*

Sidney's SONNET sequence, *Astrophel and Stella* (ca. 1582; published 1591), tracks the unhappy love of Astrophel for Stella, who can be identified with a real (married) lady of Sidney's circle. The 108 sonnets are written in variations of the sonnet form invented by PETRARCH. The collection was a success and sparked a craze for sonnet sequences.

Sidney's other most important work, *The Defence of Poesie,* was written in 1579 or 1580 and published in 1595 (another edition, published in the same year, was titled *An Apologie for Poetry*). In this essay Sidney demonstrates the power of poetry to persuade and teach, laments the decline in poetry since classical times, and expresses confidence in the English language as a medium for the finest poetry in every genre, which he prophetically declares is yet to come. Sidney's eloquence and his wide-ranging examples made the work popular, and the boost he gave to the confidence of writers working in English may be credited with contributing to the great flowering of English literature that took place over the next two decades.

Sidney also undertook a new English rendition of the Old Testament Psalms of David. He completed only 43 of the 150 psalms, each of which he wrote in a different metrical form; his sister, Mary, continued the project after his death. Some of the psalms are still sung as hymns today.

According to biographer Allen Stewart, "Among the gilded youth of Elizabethan England, no one was more golden than Philip Sidney. Courtier, poet, soldier, diplomat—he was one of the most promising young men of his time."

Works by Sir Philip Sidney

Sidney's Defence of Poesy and Selected Renaissance Literary Criticism. Edited and with an introduction by Gavin Alexander. New York: Penguin Classics, 2004.

Sir Philip Sidney: Selected Prose and Poetry. Edited by Robert Kimbrough. Madison: University of Wisconsin Press, 1994.

Sir Philip Sidney: The Major Works. Edited by Katherine Duncan-Jones. New York: Oxford University Press, 2002.

Works about Sir Philip Sidney

Berry, Edward I. *The Making of Sir Philip Sidney.* Toronto: University of Toronto Press, 1998.

Stewart, Alan. *Philip Sidney: A Double Life.* New York: Thomas Dunne Books/St. Martin's Press, 2001.

Sir Gawain and the Green Knight

(late 1300s) *poem*

Sir Gawain and the Green Knight survives in a single medieval manuscript along with the poems *Patience, Purity* (also called *Cleanness*), and PEARL. Though it is clear that the same person composed these poems in the latter half of the 14th century, the author's identity has been a subject of long debate. Well-educated and highly literate, which suggests training by or for the church, the poet also reveals through his detailed descriptions of hunting and etiquette that he was familiar with life in the higher social classes. He may have been attached to a noble household; we might imagine the poem read or sung aloud in the hall of a castle by a skilled minstrel who would need to employ every trick he knew to keep his listeners enthralled and thus earn his dinner.

Though he little knew it, the *Gawain* poet lived in a time when the social order was changing: The feudal system in England was slowly turning into a constitutional monarchy; a new way of life and a new middle class were emerging in the growing towns; and the long-accepted authority of the Catholic Church was being questioned. The Hundred Years' War introduced a climate of constant violence and devastation, but the close contact with France also exposed the literate class to a rich tradition of poetry. The subject matter of the troubadours' songs and tales such as Jean de Meun's *Romance of the Rose* had a powerful effect on English literature, as shown in the works of Geoffrey CHAUCER and others.

But in telling the story of the Green Knight, the *Gawain* poet called on an already-ancient native legend. King Arthur and his warriors had been a subject of popular literature for centuries, for instance in the pseudo-chronicle of Geoffrey of Monmouth and the romances of Marie de France and Chrétien de Troyes. The figures of Merlin, Gawain, Guinevere, and the fairy princess Morgan had their roots in Celtic myth but took on new forms in the Arthurian romances of the 14th century and later in the works of Thomas MALORY and Edward Spenser. Just as there is a real man behind the legendary Arthur, the motifs of the green knight and his chapel, the beheading ceremony, and the plot device of the tested hero contain echoes of a distant past with its rituals of death and regeneration.

The poem reflects the paradox of knighthood: The demands of courtly love created a conflict of loyalties, and the chivalric code romanticized the real-life violence. The poem embodies this conflict in the spectacle of the Green Knight, who barges in on Arthur's feast and challenges the best knight to a beheading contest. When Gawain responds with ease, the knight picks up his head and issues another challenge: A year hence, Gawain must let the Green Knight behead him in turn. Thus Gawain, the most exemplary of knights, takes up the quest to find the Green Knight's chapel and stand good on his oath. During the course of the poem his integrity is repeatedly tested, most famously by the seductive wife of his host. Gawain's nobility is perhaps best shown in the lines where he takes leave of Arthur, feeling himself bound to uphold the terms of his dreadful promise. In a stanzaic form peculiar to this poem alone, he conveys his resolution to face his fate, no matter what:

> *"The knight ever made good cheer,*
> *saying, 'Why should I be dismayed?*
> *Of doom the fair or drear*
> *by a man must be assayed.'"*

The poem continually returns to the themes of fidelity to promise, upright behavior, honesty, and bravery even in the face of certain doom, while the active language and vivid detail create a textured world full of suspense, magic, and mystery.

Sir Gawain and the Green Knight is a favorite in the canon of English literature for its gripping narrative and fascinating language and detail. Readers find themselves, like Gawain, undertaking a dangerous and perplexing task, and though new discoveries lie in wait with each return, part of the poem's appeal is that it is continually baffling. Critic W. S. Merwin says: "In the figure of the Green Knight the poet has summoned up an original spirit with the unsounded depth of a primal myth, a presence more vital and commanding than any analysis of it could be." *Gawain* reminds readers of the sheer power—and pleasure—of a good story.

English Versions of *Sir Gawain and the Green Knight*

Harrison, Keith, trans. *Sir Gawain and the Green Knight.* New York: Oxford University Press, 1998.
Merwin, W. S. *Sir Gawain and the Green Knight.* New York: Alfred A. Knopf, 2002.

Works about *Sir Gawain and the Green Knight*

Brewer, Derek, and Jonathan Gibson, eds. *A Companion to the Gawain-Poet.* New York: Boydell and Brewer, 1999.
Morgan, Gerald. *Sir Gawain and the Green Knight and the Idea of Righteousness.* Dublin: Irish Academic Press, 1992.

Putter, Ad. *Sir Gawain and the Green Knight and the French Arthurian Romance.* Oxford: Oxford University Press, 1995.

Skelton, John (ca. 1460–1529) *poet, dramatist, translator*

John Skelton was educated at both Cambridge, Oxford, and the university at Louvain in Belgium. He was already well known as a translator and rhetorician when he became tutor (1496–1501) to the future king, Henry VIII. ERASMUS, in a 1500 ode entitled "De Laudibus Britanniae" ("In Praise of Britain"), congratulated the prince on having Skelton, "a light of British letters," as his teacher.

In 1498 Skelton was ordained a priest. That year he wrote a satirical poem, "The Bowge of Court," about life at the king's court ("bowge" means "reward"). In a dream in the poem, the narrator meets characters who represent the qualities of royalty's hangers-on; Favell represents flattery and Hervy Hafter represents deceit.

"Philip Sparrow," which Skelton wrote before retiring from court life in 1508, reflects elements of PASTORAL life. The poem is addressed to a young lady whose pet sparrow was killed by a cat. The bird and his mistress's grief are described at length, and all the birds are called to the funeral. The poem shows Skelton's lively awareness of the natural world.

In 1512, when Henry VII died, Skelton wrote an elegy for him. Henry VIII soon brought Skelton back to court as an official poet, and Skelton wrote several poems celebrating English military victories. He also wrote a play, *Magnyfycence* (1515–16), a morality play with characters named Felicity, Counterfeit Countenance, Fancy, Liberty, Despair, and Magnificence (the word *magnificence* in Skelton's time meant the ostentatious display of wealth). The play's message is that no mortal happiness can be relied upon: "Today it is well; tomorrow it is all amiss. . . ."

Skelton also wrote several poems attacking the powerful Cardinal Wolsey for his worldly ways, and spent some time in prison at Wolsey's behest. While Skelton died before the great upheavals of Henry VIII's court, he is remembered for his lively verse and form, for which Skeltonics (poetry written in short lines of two or three stresses and with a variable, rough rhythm) were named.

Works by John Skelton

John Skelton, the Complete English Poems. Edited by John Scattergood. New Haven, Conn.: Yale University Press, 1983.

Magnyfycence. Edited by Robert Lee Ramsay. Oxford: Oxford University Press, 2000.

Works about John Skelton

Kinney, Arthur F. *John Skelton, Priest as Poet: Seasons of Discovery.* Chapel Hill: University of North Carolina Press, 1987.

Walker, Greg, et al. *John Skelton and the Politics of the 1520s.* New York: Cambridge University Press, 2002.

Smith, John (1580–1631) *essayist*

John Smith was born in Lincolnshire, England, to Alice and George Smith, a farmer. Little is known about his early life other than that he attended grammar school, where he learned to write and was introduced to Latin.

From his teenage years onward, Smith led the life of an enterprising adventurer: He was an apprentice to a merchant; traveled to the Netherlands to help free the Dutch from Spanish rule; fought against the Turks, was captured, and escaped enslavement with the help of a woman to whom he was given as a gift. In addition, he was selected to become a member of the governing body of the Virginia colony; embarked for America in 1606; returned to England a few years later, after suffering injury from a gunpowder explosion; and later managed to find a backer for an expedition to New England in 1614.

Smith wrote about his experiences and the first 13 months of the Jamestown Colony in *A True Relation of Such Occurrences and Accidents of Note as Happened in Virginia* (1608). *A Map of Virginia and The Proceedings of the English Colony in Virginia* (1612) continues the story of the colony up until 1610. In *A Description of New England* (1616), Smith coins the phrase "New England." He also wrote *New England's Trials* (1620–22) and later revised and collected all of these works, with other books on America, in *The General History of Virginia, New England and the Summer Isles* (1624).

Smith's writings describe the profits that could be made by turning the country's resources into commodities, and they contain an early expression of the American Dream. Smith came to see that America was a place where commoners could, through their own merit, rise above the social class into which they were born. J. A. Leo Lemay points out that Smith is "our primary source for Virginia's earliest years. He gave more detailed and exact information than any other early writer; his writings are more exiting than others . . . and his plain style is more readable."

Works by John Smith

Captain John Smith: A Select Edition of His Writings. Edited by Karen Ordahl Kupperman. Chapel Hill: University of North Carolina Press, 1988.

A Work about John Smith

Vaughan, Alden T., and Oscar Handlin. *American Genesis: Captain John Smith and the Founding of Virginia.* New York: Harper Collins, 1995.

sonnet

The sonnet, a name derived from the Italian *sonnetto,* meaning song, is a 14-line poetic form that developed near the close of the Middle Ages. Italian Giacomo da Lentino (1188–1240) and other members of the court of Frederick II (1194–1250) are known as the inventors of the form, and Provençal courtly love poetry was an important influence. The sonnet increased in popularity throughout Europe during the RENAISSANCE. Many writers sought to model their verses upon those of another Italian, Francesco PETRARCH (1304–74), who created what is known as the Petrarchan sonnet.

A sonnet is typified by three distinct forms, the Italian form being the most common. Developed from the Sicilian *strambotto* (meaning a Sicilian peasant song), this verse form consists of two quatrains and two tercets. In the Italian sonnet, the octave develops one thought, and the sestet grows out of the octave's thought, varying and completing it as if the sestet were a response to the octave, with a possible change in point of view. The usual rhyme scheme is *abba abba* (the octave) and *cde cde* (the sestet). The octave may be known as two quatrains if printed in quatrains, and the sestet may be known as two tercets.

Following the introduction of the Italian sonnet into English poetry by Henry Howard, Earl of Surrey (1517–47), and its further development by Sir Thomas Wyatt (1503–42), two other major forms developed. They are the Shakespearean sonnet (named after William SHAKESPEARE) and the Spenserian sonnet (named after Edmund Spenser). These English sonnet forms were conceived during the reign (1509–47) of Henry VIII and came into their own during the reign (1558–1603) of Elizabeth I.

The Shakespearean sonnet is written in iambic pentameter and consists of three quatrains concluded by a rhyming couplet. The rhyme scheme is *abab cdcd efef gg*. Different from the Shakespearean sonnet in its rhyme scheme is the Spenserian sonnet, which rhymes *abab bcbc cdcd ee*. The key distinguishing feature of this form is interlocking quatrains, or enveloped quatrains, with the repetition of the rhyme from one quatrain's last line to the next quatrain's first line.

Both sonnet forms typically function as miniature essays, whose main points are arranged according to their respective rhyme scheme. In Shakespearean sonnets, for example, each quatrain has a rhetorical function and a poetic function. The first quatrain presents the argument and premise that lead to the theme expressed in the second quatrain. The third quatrain presents a paradox (the dialectic) that furthers the argument and theme. The rhyming couplet acts as the conclusion to the argument and binds together the preceding three quatrains, making sense of them. Thus, the Shakespearean sonnet resembles a poetic essay in three paragraphs with a two-line conclusion.

Although the sonnets' rhyme schemes vary according to the tastes of the particular poet and the limitations of the language the poem is written in, the verses generally follow the established forms and argumentative patterns.

Many poets wrote sonnets not as stand-alone pieces but as parts of a larger whole. Such collections, which are arranged according to a central theme, are called sonnet sequences. Three famous sequences are Petrarch's *Canzoniere (Rime)*, du Bellay's *L'Olive*, and Shakespeare's *Sonnets*. Many more sequences were written during the Renaissance, and many have been written since. As with most sequences, these collections revolve around love and the delights, trials, joys, and sadness of the poem's speaker.

Numerous poets from the Middle Ages and the Renaissance continue to be celebrated as masters of the sonnet form. Well-known sonneteers include Shakespeare and Petrarch, as mentioned, as well as Pierre de RONSARD and Joachim du BELLAY of France; Gottfried August Burger and Johann Wolfgang von GOETHE of Germany; Luis de GÓNGORA Y ARGOTE and Juan Boscán of Spain; and Luíz Vaz de CAMÕES of Portugal.

Works of Sonnets and Sonnet Sequences

Bellay, Joachim du. *Ordered Text: The Sonnet Sequences of Du Bellay.* Edited by Richard A. Katz. New York: Peter Lang, 1985.

Hollander, John, ed. *Sonnets: From Dante to the Present.* New York: Knopf, 2001.

Ronsard, Pierre De. *Songs and Sonnets of Pierre de Ronsard.* New York: Hyperion Books, 1985.

Wordsworth, William. *Sonnet Series and Itinerary Poems, 1820–1845.* Ithaca, N.Y.: Cornell University Press, 2004.

Works about Sonnets and Sonnet Sequences

Bermann, Sandra L. *The Sonnet Over Time: A Study in the Sonnets of Petrarch, Shakespeare, and Baudelaire.* Chapel Hill: University of North Carolina Press, 1988.

Oppenheimer, Paul. *The Birth of the Modern Mind: Self, Consciousness, and the Invention of the Sonnet.* New York: Oxford University Press, 1989.

Sonsan of Kaarta, Epic of (after 1650)
African epic

The state of Kaarta was located on the upper Niger River in what is now Mali. Founded by the Bambara, who occupied the region beginning in 1650, the state of Kaarta was consistently overshadowed by its neighbor Segu in a northwest region now known as Beledugu (north of Bamako). Kaarta was not as prosperous or powerful as Segu, and there are various records of attacks from Segu on Kaarta, the former being almost always the winner. However, the founders of Segu and Kaarta are said to descend from the same ancestors, which is described in the *Epic of Sonsan of Kaarta*. Both peoples belonged to the Kulubali clan and thus are related to Sonsan's ancestor, the hunter Kalajan, who is said to have come from the east. The descendants of the son of Sonsan became the rulers of Kaarta.

The *Epic of Sonsan of Kaarta* is the story of the rivalry between two brothers who share the same father but have different mothers. Sonsan's charisma provokes jealousy among his stepbrothers. This EPIC also illustrates the resistance of the Bamana Empire to the influence of Islam. Unlike most people in West Africa, the people of Bamana converted to Islam fairly late.

As in the EPIC OF BAMANA SEGU, the storyteller performing the *Epic of Sonsan of Kaarta* is accompanied by the *ngoni*, a small string instrument resembling the lute, which punctuates the narrative with musical interludes. Like other epics of old Mali, for instance the *Epic of Son-Jara*, the *Epic of Sonsan of Kaarta* remains a valuable cultural record for describing the rituals and culture of this ancient state and its people.

An English Version of the *Epic of Sonsan of Kaarta*

Johnson, John-William, Thomas A. Hale, and Stephen Belchers, eds. *Oral Epics from Africa.* Bloomington: Indiana University Press, 1997.

Works about the *Epic of Sonsan of Kaarta*

Belcher, Stephen. *Epic Traditions of Africa.* Bloomington: Indiana University Press, 1999.

Courlander, Harold, and Ousmane Sako. *The Heart of the Ngoni, Heroes of the African Kingdom of Segu.* New York: Crown, 1982.

Spinoza, Benedictus (Baruch) de
(1632–1677) *philosopher*

During the 17th century, the country of the Netherlands was unique in Europe for possessing an open tolerance of new and unorthodox ideas. Because of this, it became a center of science, art, and philosophy. This time period is known as the Dutch Golden Age, during which many brilliant artists, writers, and thinkers made extraordinary achievements. One of the greatest philosophers who worked in the Netherlands during the Dutch Golden Age was Benedictus de Spinoza.

Spinoza was the son of Jewish parents who fled the anti-Semitic persecutions of Portugal and settled in the city of Amsterdam. Unlike other nations, the Netherlands permitted Jews to practice their religion freely. As a young man, Spinoza was educated according to Jewish tradition and intended to become a businessman, but he was also fascinated by science and philosophy. In 1656 the Jewish leaders of Amsterdam angrily excommunicated Spinoza for criticizing biblical scriptures, casting him out of the Dutch Jewish community forever. Most likely, his unusual philosophical and religious ideas upset the tradition-minded Jewish leaders.

Spinoza spent the rest of his life studying philosophy and producing his own philosophical works. Although he was given an inheritance by his father, Spinoza gave it away and supported himself financially by working as a lens grinder. After his excommunication, he became a loner, concentrating exclusively on his philosophy and his writings. Only one of his works, *A Theologico-Political Treatise* (1670), was published during his lifetime.

In terms of his philosophy, Spinoza was heavily influenced by medieval Jewish thought, as well as the more contemporary philosophy of René DESCARTES, which is especially evident in Spinoza's belief that the philosophical foundations of the universe might be understandable in the same precise manner as geometry. In other words, Spinoza believed that if one started with a few basic and self-evident truths, all other truths about the universe could be deduced; in geometry, all geometric facts can be deduced from a few basic geometric axioms.

Much of Spinoza's philosophy deals with his ideas concerning God, which were very different from most theological concepts. Rather than perceiving God as a separate being, Spinoza saw God as being an all-encompassing entity. In other words, everything that existed was part of or caused by God. This theological idea is known as pantheism. Spinoza's ideas about pantheism would greatly influence many thinkers in later centuries. However, the unusual nature of the idea at the time led to charges that Spinoza was an atheist.

Spinoza's most famous and lasting work is undoubtedly *Ethics*, which he finished around 1665 (published 1677). It essentially sums up all of Spinoza's thoughts concerning religion, philosophy, and morality, and is considered to be one of the most original philosophical works in Western history.

Ethics is divided into five books, each dealing with a particular aspect of Spinoza's philosophy. Throughout the work, the author organizes his writing in the manner of a complicated geometry problem, laying out a number of axioms and propositions that lead to logical conclusions.

The first book of *Ethics* is titled *On God* and expresses the pantheism that marked Spinoza as a truly unique philosopher. The other books discuss his views on metaphysics and human morality. He denied the existence of free will, believing that everything that occurred must come from logical necessity.

Spinoza was highly regarded by Albert Einstein, and his work influenced the development of German philosophy, as well as such writers and philosophers as LESSING, HERDER, and GOETHE.

English Versions of Works by Benedictus de Spinoza

Correspondence of Spinoza. Translated by A. Wolf. Whitefish, Mont.: Kessinger Publishing, 2003.

Ethics: Treatise on the Emendation of the Intellect and Selected Letters. Translated by Samuel Shirley. Indianapolis, Ind.: Hackett Publishing, 1998.
The Collected Works of Spinoza. Translated by Edwin Curley. Princeton, N.J.: Princeton University Press, 1985.

Works about Benedictus de Spinoza

Gullan-Whur, Margaret. *Within Reason: A Life of Spinoza.* New York: St. Martin's Press, 1998.
Nadler, Steven. *Spinoza: A Life.* Cambridge: Cambridge University Press, 1999.

Staden, Hans (1520–ca. 1565) *travel writer, biographer*

Hans Staden was a Hessian soldier who traveled to Brazil on Portuguese ships. While serving in a coastal Portuguese fort in 1552, he was captured by Tupinamba Indian warriors. After months in captivity, he escaped and subsequently wrote a two-part narrative on his confinement and Tupinamba captors.

Published in 1557, *Hans Staden: The True History of His Captivity,* became an immediate bestseller. It contains important ethnographic descriptions of many aspects of the now extinct Tupinamba culture, including descriptions of villages, subsistence, crafts, customs, political practices, and cannibalism. The work is an absorbing account of an incredible experience.

The first part of the work contains a narration of Staden's first two voyages to Brazil up to the time of his capture. The second part focuses on descriptions of Tupinamba culture and practices. Significantly, graphic woodcuts depicting cannibalism and other elements of Tupinamba life are included with the narrative. These represent the earliest published images of Native Americans and served to present to European audiences an authentic, graphic view of Native American life.

Through his narratives and images, Staden brought the world closer to understanding Native American culture by placing cannibalism and other practices within their proper cultural context.

Instead of sensationalizing the pagan practices as demonic, Staden illustrates the practices as part of a complex tribal social system in which retribution is taken against the cruelties of Spanish and Portuguese enemies as acts of war.

English Versions of Works by Hans Staden

The Adventures of Hans Staden. Washington, D.C.: Alhambra, 1998.

The Captivity of Hans Staden of Hesse, in A.D. *1547–1555: Among the Wild Tribes of Eastern Brazil.* Translated by A. Tootal and edited by R. F. Burton. New York: Burt Franklin, 1964.

Works about Hans Staden

Goodman, Edward J. *The Explorers of South America.* Norman: University of Oklahoma Press, 1992.

Moffit, John F., and Sebastiân Santiago. *O Brave New People: The European Adventure of the American Indian.* Albuquerque: University of New Mexico, 1998.

Sumarokov, Alexander Petrovich

(1718–1777) *poet, dramatist*

Alexander Sumarokov was born into the nobility in St. Petersburg. When he was 14, he entered the Corps of Cadets. After graduating in 1740, he held positions at court and eventually served as the director of the Russian Imperial Theater. His ego and quarrelsome nature made his work difficult, however, and in 1761 he was forced to retire.

Sumarokov's writings include a literary journal, *The Industrious Bee,* nine tragedies, 12 comedies, approximately 150 love songs, 374 verse Fables, satirical verses, SONNETs, elegies, odes, and more. These works reflect Sumarokov's ENLIGHTENMENT belief that literature should instruct as well as entertain.

Sumarokov admired French CLASSICISM but used a simpler, more direct style than that of Mikhail LOMONOSOV and Feofan PROKOPOVITCH, whose poetry he disdained. He also observes the UNITIES in plays such as *Hamlet* (1748), a loose adaptation of SHAKESPEARE's work; and *Dimitrii the*

Impostor (1771), a well-received work set in Russia's Time of Troubles.

Two of Sumarokov's most significant works appeared in 1747: "Epistle on the Russian Language" and "Epistle on the Art of Poetry." Both are composed of rhyming couplets in iambic hexameter. In the first, Sumarokov asserts that Russian is an excellent literary language awaiting only competent writers. In the second, which includes references to Greek mythology, he explains the style and subject matter appropriate to each type of poetry. Sumarokov holds up as models modern poets such as MOLIÈRE, LA FONTAINE, MILTON, POPE, and BOILEAU-DESPRÉAUX, as well as ancients such as Homer, Sophocles, Ovid, and Virgil.

Sumarokov's poems, dramas, and theoretical works influenced Russian writers for decades. He was, in William Brown's words, an "astonishingly versatile innovator."

See also NEOCLASSICISM; TRAGEDY.

English Versions of Works by Alexander Petrovich Sumarokov

Selected Aesthetic Works of Sumarokov and Karamzin. Translated by Henry M. Nebel Jr. Washington, D.C.: University Press of America, 1981.

Selected Tragedies of A. P. Sumarokov. Translated by Richard and Raymond Fortune. Evanston, Ill.: Northwestern University Press, 1970.

A Work about Alexander Petrovich Sumarokov

Brown, William Edward. "Alexander Sumarokov and Russian Classicism," in *A History of Eighteenth-Century Russian Literature.* Ann Arbor, Mich.: Ardis, 1980.

Swedenborg, Emanual (Emanual Swedborg) (1688–1772) *scientist, mystic*

Emanual Swedenborg was born to Sara Behm and her husband Jesper Swedberg, a Lutheran bishop, in the city of Stockholm. Little is known about Swedenborg's childhood, but he graduated from the University of Uppsala before traveling to England to study physics under Isaac Newton.

Over the next several years, in Holland, France, Germany, and his native Sweden, Swedenborg devoted himself to the study of science, publishing important papers, and working on various inventions. *Principia* (1734) would have important implications for Western philosophy, as it was in this work that the idea of the nebulae was first expounded, a theory later appropriated by the German philosopher Immanuel KANT.

The years 1743 through 1745 signaled a dramatic transition for Swedenborg, as the focus of his thought and writing shifted from science and philosophy to religion and mysticism. Swedenborg professed that around 1743 his intelligence was miraculously opened, and that he was able to see into the next world and speak with spirits and angels. From this time until his death, he documented his spiritual visions and beliefs in books and essays on various spiritual themes. Among his most important works is *On Heaven and Its Wonders and on Hell* (1758), in which he recounts his mystical experiences and communications with angels.

For the incredible variety and extent of his writings, Swedenborg is a remarkable figure in the intellectual history of Europe. His philosophical and religious works have influenced successive generations of writers and philosophers in Europe and throughout the world.

English Versions of Works by Emanual Swedenborg

Apocalypse Explained, Vol. 3. Translated by John Whitehead. West Chester, Pa.: Swedenborg Foundation, 1995.
Essential Readings. Edited by Michael Stanley. Berkeley, Calif.: North Atlantic Books, 2003.

Works about Emanual Swedenborg

Benz, Ernst. *Emanual Swedenborg: Visionary Savant in the Age of Reason.* Translated by Nicholas Goodrick-Clarke. West Chester, Pa.: Swedenborg Foundation, 2002.

Dusen, Wilson Van. *The Presence of Other Worlds.* West Chester, Pa.: Swedenborg Foundation, 2004.
Swainson, W. P. *Emanual Swedenborg: The Swedish Seer.* Whitefish, Mont.: Kessinger, 2003.

Swift, Jonathan (1667–1745) *poet, satirist*

Jonathan Swift was born in Dublin to Abigail Erick Swift and Jonathan Swift, an English couple who immigrated to Ireland in 1660. Swift had an unusual early life: His father died before Swift was born, and Swift was kidnapped as a baby for several years by a former nurse. After he was returned to his mother, he was sent to grammar school in Kilkenny. He later earned a B.A. from Trinity College, Dublin, and then traveled to England to work as a secretary for Sir William Temple. Swift received an M.A. from Oxford in 1692, and in 1695 became a priest of the Church of Ireland. He took a doctor of divinity degree from Trinity in 1702.

Swift suffered throughout his life from Ménière's syndrome, an inner ear disorder that causes vertigo, deafness, and giddiness. Because of this condition, he was rumored to have gone mad in the last years of his life. He aided this impression by leaving his money to a madhouse.

Critical Analysis

During his frequent visits to London, Swift joined the literary circle surrounding Joseph Addison and Richard Steele and contributed essays to Steele's *Tatler.* Swift created a memorable narrative persona in the *Bickerstaff Papers* (1708–09), in which the character Bickerstaff is a parody of the astrologer John Partridge.

By 1710, Swift had become associated with the ruling Tory party. He shifted his allegiance from the Whiggish Addison and Steele to a new group that included Alexander POPE, John Gay, and Dr. John Arbuthnot, who formed the Scriblerus club. The Scriblerians met weekly in 1714 collaborating on satirical works. A decade later, Swift wrote *Drapier's Letters* (1724), in which an Irish drapier protests against the corruption of a scheme of the

Walpole administration to flood Ireland with worthless currency. Because Swift called attention to this scheme, it was withdrawn, and he became a national hero.

Swift was also a poet. Two of his most notable poems are "The Lady's Dressing Room" (1730) and "A Beautiful Young Nymph Going to Bed" (1731), which display an apparent misogyny. Feminist critic Margaret Doody, however, argues that Swift was actually more respectful toward women than many 18th-century writers: "When Swift deals with the dirty or disagreeable in females, or when his tone is scolding, he is still urging self-respect, and he never imposes the injunctions to docility, obedience, and mental lethargy so commonly repeated to women throughout the century."

Swift's first major work was *A Tale of a Tub* (1704), a wildly experimental satire accompanied by *The Battle of the Books,* a more straightforward, comic piece in which he dramatizes the "ancients vs. moderns" debate (the hotly contested debate over whether modern learning had surpassed that of the Greek and Roman classics) as a literal battle between ancient and modern books.

Critic Nigel Wood comments that *A Tale of a Tub* is "one of the most self-conscious pieces of writing. The Teller's desperate desire to please his readers by incessantly putting them in the picture so determines the mood of the writing that it usurps what would seem to be its main function: to tell a tale." Before the tale even begins, readers encounter a parody in the form of a list of other works by the author, including "A Panegyrical Essay upon the Number THREE" and "A general History of *Ears.*" The text then goes through dozens of pages of prefatory material before beginning its ostensible subject, an allegorical story of three brothers, Peter, Martin, and Jack, who represent Catholicism, the Church of England, and Protestant Dissenters, respectively. The narrator continually strays from his subject, even including "A Digression in Praise of Digressions." Swift scholar Ricardo Quintana has attempted to summarize the text's main themes: "The two themes of

zeal in religion and of enthusiasm in learning and knowledge have been inextricably woven into one."

Norman O. Brown, critic of psychoanalysis, has analyzed what he terms Swift's "excremental vision": "Any reader of Jonathan Swift knows . . . his analysis of human nature . . . becomes the decisive weapon in his assault on the pretentions, the pride, even the self-respect of mankind." Examples of this can be found in almost all of Swift's writings, but is perhaps most pronounced in his poetry. His early poem "Description of a City Shower" (1710) vividly portrays the filth of urban living: "Sweepings from Butchers Stalls, Dung, Guts, and Blood, / Drown'd Puppies, stinking Sprats, all drench'd in Mud, / Dead Cats and Turnip-Tops come tumbling down the Flood." In "The Lady's Dressing Room" Swift humanizes a poetic nymph by revealing what goes on behind the scenes of a lady's boudoir. Strephon is disgusted to learn that "*Celia, Celia, Celia* shits!" but the moral of the poem seems to be that this is only natural: "Such Order from Confusion sprung, / Such gaudy Tulips rais'd from Dung."

In his later writings, Swift became concerned about the condition of the Irish people, most famously in "A Modest Proposal" (1729), which is also a masterpiece of irony. Taking on the persona of a "projector," he proposes a novel and strikingly satirical solution to Irish poverty and famine:

> I have been assured by a very knowing *American* of my Acquaintance in *London;* that a young healthy Child, well nursed, is, at a Year old, a most delicious, nourishing, and wholesome Food; whether *Stewed, Roasted, Baked,* or *Boiled;* and, I make no doubt, that it will equally serve in a *Fricasie,* or a *Ragoust.*

His ironic intentions reveal themselves by the end of the essay. The projector lists a series of other solutions, including taxing absentee landlords and buying Irish rather than imported goods, but dismisses them: "let no Man talk to me of these and the like Expedients; till he hath, at least, a Glimpse of Hope, that there will ever be some hearty and sincere Attempt to put them in Practice."

In his masterpiece, *Gulliver's Travels* (1726), Swift touches on all his major themes: disgust with the human body, misanthropy, the satire of modern learning, human nature, and a criticism of English policies toward Ireland. Attempting to conceal his authorship of the work, Swift brought the manuscript with him on a trip to London, sent it anonymously to a publisher, and returned to Ireland before it was printed. Despite these precautions, the reading public recognized Swift's hand. It became his greatest success and inspired an array of "Gulliveriana," including verses by Pope and a poem that Henry Fielding attributed to Gulliver.

The deceptively simple text purports to be a travel tale by Lemuel Gulliver, who undertakes four fantastic voyages to Lilliput, inhabited by a miniature race of people; Brobdingnag, a land of giants; the floating island of Laputa; and the country of the Houyhnhnms, talking horses who rule over the Yahoos, a degenerate form of humanity. Critics remain divided about Swift's ultimate object of satire. Critic James Clifford identified two interpretations, which he terms "hard" and "soft." "Hard" interpreters see Swift as a misanthrope who condemns humanity, while the "soft" believe that "Swift's basic attack is not upon man but upon the various false ideals which have misled him—rationalism, inevitable progress, and the essential goodness of human nature."

Swift is perhaps the most gifted and complex satirist in the English language. His rampant misanthropy, misogyny, and revulsion with the human body make much of his work difficult for more sensitive readers, but the complexity of his irony, his use of narrative personae, and his philosophical ruminations on human nature are superb. His work is often compared to those of his contemporaries Pope and Gay, and his influences include RABELAIS, CERVANTES, and Lucian. Critic Robert Mahony remarks, "Toward the end of the twentieth century, Swift remains a presence in Irish culture more vivid than that of any other from eighteenth-century Ireland—more vivid, indeed, than most from any historical period."

Works by Jonathan Swift

The Basic Writings of Jonathan Swift. Edited by Claude Rawson. New York: Modern Library, 2002.

The Correspondence of Jonathan Swift. Edited by Harold Williams. Oxford: Clarendon Press, 1963.

The Writings of Jonathan Swift. Edited by Robert A. Greenberg and William B. Piper. New York: W.W. Norton, 1973.

Works about Jonathan Swift

Kelly, Ann Cline. *Jonathan Swift and Popular Culture: Myth, Media, and the Man.* New York: Palgrave, 2002.

Mahony, Robert. *Jonathan Swift: The Irish Identity.* New Haven, Conn.: Yale University Press, 1995.

Palmeri, Frank, ed. *Critical Essays on Jonathan Swift.* New York: G.K. Hall, 1993.

T

Takeda Izumo (1691–1756) *dramatist*

This master of BUNRAKU or *ninyo joruri* (puppet plays) was originally a theater promoter, which was also his father's profession. A prolific author, Takeda wrote many plays, including the well-known *Chushingura,* sometimes called 47 Ronin. Variations of this piece, written for the stock puppets of Bunraku, are also performed in KABUKI theater. Izumo's contributions to Japanese literature are enduring, and his tomb in Osaka is a modern-day tourist attraction.

Translator Donald Keene explains that the story of *Chushingura,* attributed to Izumo and two other authors, Miyoshi Shoraku and Namiki Senryu, is based on a true-crime story from the early 18th century. Using a trick typical of writers at the time, the authors set the play in the distant past to skirt government restrictions on writing about real events.

The lengthy play begins with tension between samurai over etiquette, but more serious matters quickly arise. Moranao, a samurai lord, attempts to instigate an affair with another lord's wife. The virtuous woman turns him down in a note. Her husband, Enya Hangen, is present when the rejected man receives the note. Moranao turns his anger against Hangen, who, offended, attacks him. Hangen must commit ritual suicide (*seppuku*) for this crime, but he tells his samurai: "Yuranosuke, I leave you this dagger as a memento of me! Avenge me!" Hangen's loyal warriors, the 47 Ronin, eventually decapitate Moranao.

Chushingura still attracts audiences, and story variations continue to appear in Japanese drama, film, and television. Scholar Alan Atkinson comments in a gallery guide to Japanese prints that the play "has proved as inspirational to Japanese artists over the years as it has to Japanese theater goers."

An English Version of a Work by Takeda Izumo

Chushingura: The Treasury of Loyal Retainers. A Puppet Play by Takeda Izumo, Miyoshi Shoraku and Namiki Senryu. Translated by Donald Keene. New York: Columbia University Press, 1971.

A Work about Takeda Izumo

Brandon, James R., ed. *Chushingura: Studies in Kabuki and the Puppet Theatre.* Honolulu: University of Hawaii Press, 1982.

Tang Xianzu (T'ang Hsien-tsu, T'ang Hsien-Tzu) (1550–1616) *dramatist*

Tang Xianzu was a minor government official in the Ming dynasty, but he was also a revered Chinese playwright. His most famous work is *The*

Peony Pavilion, part of a set of pieces called *The Four Dreams of Linchuan.* This drama uses the conventions of *zhuanji* (*chuan-chi;* "grand music drama" or "kun music drama," also known as *kunju* opera), a style typical of the Ming dynasty. The plays of this era featured music and very complicated plots.

The Peony Pavilion tells the story of a well-to-do young girl who dies while waiting for the lover who has appeared to her in dreams. She leaves behind a painting of herself. The lover, a young scholar, finds the painting and in turn falls in love with her ghost. After many difficulties and trials, the young scholar and the girl, who turns out to be alive after all, are reunited and live happily ever after.

Tang Xianzu drew on earlier works for his plots and used known music for his melodies, but he is recognized as an innovative, original playwright. Today, certain portions of *The Peony Pavilion* are still performed.

An English Version of a Work by Tang Xianzu

The Peony Pavilion by Tang Xianzu (Tang Hsien-Tzu). Translated by Cyril Birch. Bloomington: Indiana University Press, 1980.

Tasso, Torquato (1544–1595) *poet, dramatist*

Torquato Tasso was born near Sorrento, south of Naples, the second child of Bernardo Tasso, a courtier and poet. At age 10, the younger Tasso joined his father in Rome, leaving behind his mother, who died in 1556. In 1560 Tasso enrolled in the University of Padua to study law but instead concentrated on poetry. In 1565 he went to Ferrara to join the service of Cardinal Luigi d'Este and later of Duke Alfonso de'Este. In 1579, after making a scene at the duke's marriage festivities, Tasso was confined at the Hospital of St. Anna under suspicion of madness. He was kept there, comfortably housed and supplied with books and writing materials, until 1586. He spent the last years of his life traveling in search of a patron, and died in Rome.

Tasso published his first work, a ROMANCE narrative named *Rinaldo* (1562), when he was only 18. Rinaldo was a figure from the popular legends of Charlemagne, which provided the subject matter for many a song and story. Tasso had studied the classic EPICS—Homer's *Odyssey* and Virgil's *Aeneid*—and he knew ARIOSTO's *Orlando Furioso.* These masters, Tasso felt, had already covered the traditional ground of battles, heroics, and damsels in distress; for his own epic, therefore, he turned to the Christian wars and chose the setting of the First Crusade.

In response to the Reformation taking place in the north of Europe, begun by Martin LUTHER, the Catholic Church launched the Counter-Reformation. Fearing the Inquisition and the Council of Trent, which had banned books by many, including CASTIGLIONE and ERASMUS, Tasso circulated the manuscript of his epic among friends and asked their advice. Tasso's anxieties over the work are probably what led to his nervous collapse. *Jerusalem Revisited* appeared in print in 1581 to widespread acclaim. The Council of Trent found nothing unorthodox in the book, but Tasso was never completely satisfied with it. A new version, *Jerusalem Conquered,* appeared in 1593.

Tasso also wrote a tragicomedy called *Aminta,* first performed in 1573, and the TRAGEDY *King Torrismondo* (1587), as well as a collection of 28 dialogues, most while residing at St. Anna.

Tasso's *Dialogues* borrows a great deal from Plato and reveals his interest in philosophy, which he studied while at Padua. *Aminta,* which shows the influence of the *Poetics* of Aristotle, contributes to the genre of the PASTORAL play that developed in the courts of Italy during the 16th century. The pastoral drama used rustic settings and drew a simple, romantic picture of country life. In Tasso's play, Sybil is a pretty nymph and Aminta, the shepherd, falls madly in love with her. The play ends happily, unlike *King Torrismondo,* a classic tragedy. Tasso's later long poem *On the Creation of the World* (1592) has been considered artistically arid and is an example used by critics when they suggest that the quality of Tasso's poetic output is uneven.

Composed in 20 chapters or cantos and arranged in rhymed stanzas, *Jerusalem Revisited* is an epic romance in the tradition of Ariosto but calls itself a true history. Though in the heroic style, its tone is one of lyric melancholy. The story focuses on the knightly crusader Godfrey and the hero Rinaldo, who comes to help Godfrey besiege Jerusalem. The subplots follow three heroines, Clorinda, Armida, and Ermina, and their adventures in love. Scholar Ralph Nash praises the poem for its "genuine zest for the sheer drama of history in the making," as in this passage where the Christian hosts make ready their final assault on the city:

> The one and the other army seems to be a lofty forest thick with trees, with so many spears each one abounds. The bows are drawn, the lances are set in rest, the darts are waving and every sling is whirling; every war-horse too is ready for battle . . . he stamps, he paws, he curvets and neighs, he flares his nostrils and breathes forth smoke and flame.

Like the cousins in the legends of Charlemagne, Tasso, who championed Rinaldo, felt a lifelong rivalry with Ariosto's *Orlando*. Alexander POPE, VOLTAIRE, ROUSSEAU, and Lord Byron would all count themselves among Tasso's admirers. He inspired Edmund Spenser and MILTON to take up the tradition of the epic romance, and several other poems, operas, and the drama *Tasso* by GOETHE are based on his work.

English Versions of Works by Torquato Tasso

Jerusalem Delivered. Edited by Anthony M. Esolen. Baltimore, Md.: Johns Hopkins University Press, 2000.

King Torrismondo by Torquato Tasso. Translated by Maria Pastore Passaro. New York: Fordham University Press, 1997.

A Work about Torquato Tasso

Finucci, Valeria. *Renaissance Transactions: Ariosto and Tasso.* Durham, N.C.: Duke University Press, 1999.

Taylor, Edward (1642–1729) *theologian, poet*

Edward Taylor was born into a farming family in rural England. He received his early education in England and for a time worked as a teacher. However, as Donald E. Stanford points out, his Puritan convictions ultimately made it impossible for him to obtain the license needed to "preach, teach, or attend the universities of Cambridge or Oxford." In 1688 he sailed to New England, where, at age 29, he entered Harvard College. Thereafter, he served as a minister in Westfield, Connecticut (now a part of Massachusetts), married twice, and had 14 children.

Taylor wrote thousands of lines of poetry, only a few of which were published during his lifetime. It was not until the 1930s, when a manuscript containing almost 400 pages of verse was discovered, that the minister's significance to American literature became clear. Samuel Eliot Morison notes that in poems like "Huswifery," Taylor draws "similes from the humble occupations" of "spinning and weaving" as a way of imaginatively exploring the relationship between God and humans. His most sophisticated poems are contained in a collection titled *Preparatory Meditations*. Taylor used these poetic meditations (at least 217 of which have survived) to prepare his heart and soul for the sacred act of administering the Lord's Supper. These devotional poems grant insight into the way in which the early American literary imagination emerged out of Puritan theological beliefs and practices. Norman Grabo notes that the recovery of Taylor's poetry challenged the earlier tendency to "ignore the artistic side of colonial literature for its more attractive intellectual sister" and revealed the "influence of a vital emotional tradition on the thought and expression of American Puritans."

Works by Edward Taylor

The Poems of Edward Taylor. Edited by Donald E. Stanford. Chapel Hill: University of North Carolina Press, 1994.

Works about Edward Taylor

Gatta, John. *Gracious Laughter: The Meditative Wit of Edward Taylor*. Columbia: University of Missouri Press, 1989.

Hammond, Jeffrey A. *Edward Taylor: Fifty Years of Scholarship and Criticism*. Rochester, N.Y.: Boydell and Brewer, 1993.

Schuldiner, Michael. *Studies in Puritan American Spirituality: Essays on Anne Bradstreet, Edward Taylor, Nathaniel Hawthorne and Catharine Maria Sedgwick,* vol. 7. Lewiston, N.Y.: Edwin Mellen Press, 2001.

Tench, Watkin (ca. 1758–1833) *travel writer, historiographer*

Watkin Tench was born in England, but spent part of his childhood in France. In 1778 he was commissioned a lieutenant in the Royal Marines and fought against the rebels in the American War of Independence until taken prisoner in Maryland. A captain by 1786, he volunteered for guard duties on the first ships transporting convicts to Australia. The "First Fleet" arrived at Botany Bay on January 20, 1788. Tench remained behind to guard the convict settlers. One year later, he published in London *A Narrative of the Expedition to Botany Bay,* an account of the arduous sea voyage.

In 1791 Tench led an expedition into the unexplored areas north and west of present-day Sydney, accompanied by Governor Philip, of the principal settlement at Port Jackson. He returned to England later that same year, and in 1793 published *A Complete Account of the Settlement at Port Jackson*. This work describes the physical environment of the new colony, the struggles of the convict settlers, and relations with the local aborigines. The *Complete Account* proved a popular sourcebook on Australia and was translated into several European languages during Tench's lifetime.

Serving again in the Royal Marines, Tench was taken prisoner by French forces in 1794, and remained in captivity for six months. In 1796 he published an account of this experience, *Letters Written in France to a Friend in London*. He retired from the marines in 1821 with the rank of lieutenant-general and died in Devonshire.

Tench's writings are noteworthy for their convivial tone and humility. According to the historian Tim Flannery, "Tench was a great wit, always ready to enjoy a joke at his own expense." He was also a thoughtful and humane man who was fascinated by the customs and language of the aborigines and treated them as equals, as illustrated by this passage from the *Complete Account:* "Soon after they [aborigine guides] bade us adieu, in unabated friendship and good humour . . . and we shook them by the hand, which they returned lustily." In a sense, it is appropriate that the birth of Australia became, in Tench's writings, the occasion for the birth of Australian literature.

Works by Watkin Tench

1788: Comprising 'A Narrative of the Expedition to Botany Bay' and 'A Complete Account of the Settlement at Port Jackson'. Melbourne: Text Publishing, 1996.

Letters from Revolutionary France. Edited by Gavin Edwards. Cardiff: University of Wales Press, 2001.

The Explorers: Stories of Discovery and Adventure from the Australian Frontier. Edited by Tim Flannery. New York: Grove Press, 2000.

Teresa of Avila, St. (1515–1582) *autobiographer, theologian*

Teresa de Cepeda y Ahumada was born in the Spanish city of Ávila, the third child of Alonso Sánchez de Cepeda and his second wife, Beatriz de Ahumada y Tapia. Both were of the nobility. As a child, Teresa loved novels of chivalry. Teresa's mother died in 1528, and in 1531 Teresa's father sent her to stay in a convent, where she fell ill. She was sent to stay with her uncle to speed her recovery.

At the time, Spaniards such as Ignatius of LOYOLA were beginning to launch a Counter-Reformation against the activities of Martin LUTHER and

John CALVIN, while Spanish missionaries labored to convert Native Americans to Christianity. Religious fervor was in the air. Reading St. Jerome's letters, Teresa began to fear purgatory and hell. Against her father's wishes, she reentered convent life and in 1536 became a Carmelite nun under the name Teresa de Jesús.

Her illness, however, returned. She suffered severe pain, vomiting, and even partial paralysis. During her slow recovery, she became more spiritual. She began to have visions and noticed the ways in which the convent, with its relaxed rules, had become worldly. In 1562 Teresa received permission to found the first Discalced Carmelite convent, which would observe a stricter rule. She went on to travel across Spain, founding more than a dozen convents and contributing to the establishment of two dozen more. She mentored younger individuals, including St. JOHN OF THE CROSS, and impressed almost everyone with her piety and inner drive. She died while visiting the duchess of Alba.

Teresa's literary works include the *Book of Her Life,* an autobiography begun in 1562 and finished in 1565; *The Way of Perfection* (1562), which taught nuns the best way to pray; *Spiritual Relations* (1563–79), a continuation of the *Life*'s description of her mystic experiences; *Book of the Foundations* (1573–82), descriptions of her work establishing convents; and *The Interior Castle* (1577), which describes the soul as a castle with seven concentric mansions or levels of spirituality. She also composed 31 poems and more than 450 letters.

Writing in the Castilian literary language that King Alfonso X had established centuries before, she impressed readers with vivid images that helped them to understand religious experiences. Helmut Hatzfeld notes that her works display not only "originality [and] spontaneity" but also "pedagogical skill in the expression of concepts usually considered ineffable."

Along with *The Interior Castle,* Teresa's most admired work is her *Life.* In a famous passage, she describes a vision she had in 1559 of a cherubim:

. . . not tall, but short, and very beautiful, his face so aflame that he appeared to be one of the highest types of angel. . . . In his hands I saw a long golden spear and at the end of the iron tip I seemed to see a point of fire. With this he seemed to pierce my heart several times so that it penetrated to my entrails. When he drew it out, I thought he was drawing them out with it and he left me completely afire with a great love for God.

In another well-known section of the *Life,* Teresa compares four kinds of prayer to the four ways in which one can water a garden: pulling the water up by hand, turning a waterwheel, using a flowing stream or river, and receiving rain. Each successive stage involves less labor on the part of the gardener. If one achieves the final stage, in which prayer comes as easily as rain sent to water the dry soul, "there is no feeling, but only rejoicing, unaccompanied by any understanding of the thing in which the soul is rejoicing."

The Catholic Church made Teresa a saint in 1622. Luis de GÓNGORA Y ARGOTE paid her literary tribute, and LOPE DE VEGA wrote two plays about her. She eventually became co-patron saint of Spain. Francisco de QUEVEDO later argued that she was too feminine to hold this honor. The Catholic Church and most of its members disagreed with him, however. In 1970 St. Teresa became the first woman honored as a Doctor of the Church. Her works remain widely read.

English Versions of Works by St. Teresa of Avila

The Complete Poetry of St. Teresa de Avila: A Bilingual Edition. Translated by Eric W. Vogt. New Orleans: University Press of the South, 1996.

The Complete Works of Saint Teresa of Jesus, 3 vols. London: Sheed and Ward, 1944–46.

The Letters of St. Teresa of Jesús, 2 vols. Translated and edited by E. Allison Peers. London: Burns, Oates and Washbourne, 1951.

The Life of Saint Teresa of Avila by Herself. Translated by J. M. Cohen. London: Penguin, 1987.

Works about St. Teresa of Avila

Hoornaert, R. *Saint Teresa in Writings*. London: Trend and Co., 1931.

Lincoln, Victoria. *Teresa: A Woman, A Biography of Teresa of Avila*. Albany: State University of New York Press, 1984.

Medwick, Cathleen. *Teresa of Avila: The Progress of a Soul*. New York: Knopf, 2000.

Peers, E. Allison. *Handbook to the Life and Times of St. Teresa and St. John of the Cross*. Westminster, Md.: Newman Press, 1954.

Thomas à Kempis (1380–1471) *theologian*

Thomas Hammerken was born in Kempin, near Cologne, Germany, which accounts for the surname by which he is known (*à Kempis* is Latin for "from Kempis"). At age 12 he was sent to Deventer, in the Netherlands, to join the Brethren of the Common Life. Co-founded by Gerard Groote (1340–84) and Florentius Radewyn (1350–1400), this community strove to live simply and in harmony under the rule set up by Augustine. Later Thomas went to Mount St. Agnes to join his brother John. He was ordained a priest at age 33 and remained at St. Agnes for the rest of his life.

Kempis trained as a copyist of manuscripts, which exposed him to the works of the greatest thinkers of pagan and Christian antiquity, not just Augustine, Bernard of Clairvaux, Francis of Assisi, Thomas Aquinas, and Gregory the Great, but also Aristotle, Ovid, and Seneca. The Brethren habitually kept notes on what they read, and Thomas used these records to inform and arrange *The Imitation of Christ*, now considered a devotional masterpiece for the Christian faith.

Begun in 1420 and first circulated in 1429, *The Imitation of Christ* has four parts. The first examines the spiritual life, the second contemplates the interior life, the third looks at finding consolation within, and the fourth reflects on the sacrament of the altar. Kempis's themes stress the humanity of Christ, knowledge of self, the practice of virtue, and the reading of scripture as a form of meditation.

The Imitation of Christ is often considered a companion piece to the Christian Bible. Since its first translation into English in 1503, it has never been out of print. Perhaps it appeals because its ideals are so modest. Humility and simplicity are its foundation, and the author, feeling no need for fame or fortune, celebrates the simple life. Kempis speaks to the human need to know God, and in the tradition of the medieval mystics, he seeks guidance from the soul within, suggesting that the spark of the divine is contained within us all.

An English Version of a Work by Thomas à Kempis

The Imitation of Christ in Four Books: A Translation from the Latin. Translated by Joseph N. Tylenda. New York: Vintage Books, 1998.

A Work about Thomas à Kempis

Montmorency, J. E. G. de. *Thomas à Kempis: His Age and Book*. New York: Kennikat Press, 1970.

Till Eulenspiegel (1519)

Till Eulenspiegel is a collection of folktales about a German peasant named Till Eulenspiegel who lived around 1300. "Eulenspiegel" was a German surname at the time, but the literal translation of the word is "owl-mirror." As owls are often a symbol of wisdom, it has been suggested that the character and tales in *Till Eulenspiegel* acted as a kind of "wise mirror" held up to society to point out foolishness. However, in medieval times, the owl also was viewed as the "devil's bird," representing stupidity or evil, which makes it an appropriate symbol for the character Till's nasty antics. Till is a typical trickster, one whose pranks poke fun at or teach lessons to the rich, mean, or pompous. Tricksters in other world literatures include Anansi the

Spider from Africa, Loki from Norse mythology, and Reynard the Fox from France.

Through an anonymous narrator named "N," the tales of *Till Eulenspiegel* relate Till's life and how he uses his tricks to get by in medieval Germany. In many of these tales, Till points out the silliness of people's words by following directions literally. In the 11th tale, for example, he is hired by a rich merchant who tells him to cook a roast "coolly and slowly" so as not to burn it. Instead, Till puts the roast on a spit over two barrels of beer to keep it cool. When the merchant fires Till and tells him to "clear out," Till obediently takes all the furniture out of the house and puts it in the street. Typical of Till, these incidents "hold a mirror" back at the speaker, reflecting their words.

Till Eulenspiegel supposedly died in 1350, but there is no evidence that proves he ever truly existed. According to legend, he was buried beneath a gravestone marked by a carving of an owl holding a mirror. Nevertheless, the legend of Till Eulenspiegel and his antics lives on. The first publication of the tales appeared in 1519, and was followed by William Copland's translation, titled *A merye jest of a man that was called Howleglas,* in 1555 or 1560. In Germany, there are statues, restaurants, and a museum honoring Till Eulenspiegel. There also has been a Till Eulenspiegel ballet and an EPIC poem based on his life. The most famous Eulenspiegel-inspired work of art is composer Richard Strauss's 1895 tone poem, *Till Eulenspiegel's Merry Pranks.*

An English Version of *Till Eulenspiegel*
Till Eulenspiegel. Introduction by Paul Oppenheimer. London: Routledge, 2001.

Tirso de Molina   (Gabriel Téllez)
(ca. 1580–1648) *dramatist*
Tirso de Molina was the pseudonym of Gabriel Téllez, who was born in Madrid and educated at the University of Alcalá. He joined the Order of

Mercy in 1601 and was made the superior of the monasteries in Trujillo in 1626 and Soria in 1645.

Despite his religious profession, Tirso de Molina was very active in the literary circles that flourished during the Spanish Golden Age. He wrote between 300 and 400 plays during the course of his life, of which about 86 survive. The plays range from historical and religious dramas to palace comedies and romantic tragedies. Tirso de Molina was greatly influenced by the Golden Age dramatist LOPE DE VEGA, particularly in his principles of dramatic composition. However, Tirso de Molina's plays are individualized by his own theological interests, which often surface in themes of the human will in conflict with the divine, and by his geographical and historical knowledge, gathered from the trips he took throughout Spain, Portugal, and even the West Indies.

Tirso de Molina also tried his hand at short prose, releasing a collection of stories called *The Gardens of Toledo* in 1621 and in 1635 *Pleasure with Profit,* a collection of stories, plays, and verse. Tirso de Molina's real skill, however, emerged in his plays, which were made remarkable by the vivid characters he created, whose psychological torments he portrayed with accuracy and depth. Some of his more memorable dramas were *Prudence in Woman* (1634) and *The Rape of Tamar* (1634), which were both chillingly realistic in their portrayal of human agony. In contrast, in *The Bashful Man in the Palace* (1621) and *Don Gil of the Green Stockings* (1635), events unfold with a merry and light-hearted rapidity.

Tirso de Molina is most celebrated for his two most sophisticated and mature plays, *El condenado por desconfiado* (*The Doubted Damned,* 1635) and *El burlador de Sevilla* (*The Seducer of Seville,* also translated as *Don Juan and the Stone Guest,* 1634). In the second of these, the infamous character Don Juan makes his first appearance in dramatic literature. Drawing on popular legends of the wily seducer, Tirso de Molina created a literary figure that would inspire several later writers and dramatists, including MOLIÈRE, Byron, and George Bernard Shaw, as well as move Mozart to compose *Don Giovanni*.

The Don Juan of Tirso's play is very different from later versions of the character. He is not the middle-aged Casanova but rather a very young and inexperienced man. In *The Seducer of Seville*, he searches for his own limits and explores the limits of the society in which he lives in order to transgress them. His character, in essence, is a reflection of the aristocratic young Spaniards of Tirso de Molina's day. In her introduction to *Don Juan of Seville,* Lynne Alvarez writes:

> It is the blind thoughtlessness, the youthful arrogance of this famous character that ultimately destroys him. Because it never occurs to Don Juan he will encounter a situation which he cannot somehow talk his way out of. Aristocratic Spaniards could talk their way out of just about anything. . . . Just as one could travel from wealth to rags at the snap of an imperial finger, so one could transform oneself from great sinner to great saint via a well-spoken confession.

Tirso de Molina's portrayal of Don Juan did not meet with absolute approval; the council of Castile denounced him as a "corrupter of public morals" in 1625. Later, however, Tirso de Molina's *General History of the Order of Mercy* (1637), a work he undertook as part of his role as the order's official historian, established him as a respectable theologian. As a playwright, he was for a long time eclipsed by the popularity of CALDERÓN DE LA BARCA, but Tirso de Molina is now considered an outstanding figure of 17th-century Spanish literature. His ability to scale the heights and depths of human experience has caused some critics to compare him to William SHAKESPEARE, and his mastery of a number of genres ranging from prose and poetry to drama and fiction has established him permanently in the history of Spanish letters.

English Versions of Works by Tirso de Molina

Damned for Despair. Translated by Lawrence Boswell. Hygiene, Colo.: Eridanos Press, 1992.

Don Juan of Seville. Translated by Lynne Alvarez. New York: Playwright's Press, 1989.

Don Juan: The Beguiler of Seville and The Stone Guest. Translated by Max Oppenheimer. Lawrence, Kans.: Coronado Press, 1976.

The Rape of Tamar. Translated by Paul Whitworth. New York: Theatre Communications Group, 1999.

Works about Tirso de Molina

Albrecht, Jane White. *Playgoing Public of Madrid in the Time of Tirso de Molina*. New Orleans: University Press of the South, 2001.

Galoppe, Raul. *Tirso de Molina: His Originality Then and Now*. Edited by Henry Sullivan. Toronto: Dovehouse Editions, 1996.

Sola-Sole, Josep M. *Tirso's Don Juan: The Metamorphosis of a Theme*. Edited by Georges E. Gingras. Washington, D.C.: Catholic University of America Press, 1989.

tragedy

The word *tragedy* derives from the Greek word *tragoida,* meaning "goat song." Originally, it referred to the ancient act of sacrificing a goat to the Greek god, Dionysus, and later came to be associated with the dramas performed as festivals honoring the god. In his *Poetics*, Aristotle defined the critical components of a tragedy as "Plot, Character, Language, Thought, Spectacle, and Melody," of which character and plot are the most important. According to Aristotle, tragedies depict "an action that is serious, complete, and possessing magnitude" and arouses emotions of "pity and fear."

The "tragic hero" is typically of high stature and encounters a reversal of fortune through a fault of character or an uncontrollable accident. Happy at the outset, a tragic hero experiences a succession of hardships resulting from his or her *hamartia* or "tragic flaw." The narrative movement plunges from an elevated state of happiness to one of sadness and misery, and the impact on the audience is a *catharsis,* a purgation that releases individuals from the grip of a powerful emotion. Tragedies of the present day more or less still meet Aristotle's criteria, though the term may be loosely applied to any story that ends unhappily.

The revenge tragedy developed in England in the mid-to-late 1500s and was heavily influenced by the works of the Roman playwright Seneca. Besides the revenge theme, these tragedies contain lurid, ritualistic action and have ornate and bombastic dialogue, multiple plotlines (both serious and comic), and vengeful ghosts. Unlike conventional tragic heroes, the hero of the revenge tragedy begins as, rather than developing into, a malcontent. Thomas Kyd's *The Spanish Tragedy* functioned as a model for subsequent revenge tragedies.

Tragedies have always worked best on the stage, and some of the greatest examples are Aeschylus's *Oresteia,* Christopher MARLOWE's *Dr. Faustus,* William SHAKESPEARE's *Macbeth,* Jean RACINE's *Andromaque,* Pedro CALDERÓN DE LA BARCA's *The Painter of His Own Dishonour,* TIRSO DE MOLINA's *The Seducer of Seville,* and LOPE DE VEGA's *The Knight from Olmeda.*

Works of Tragedy

Classical Tragedy. Edited by Robert Corrigan. New York: Applause Books, 1991.
Four Revenge Tragedies. Edited by Katharine Maus. Oxford: Oxford University Press, 2000.
Shakespeare, William. *The Tragedies.* New York: Modern Library, 1994.
Sophocles. *The Complete Greek Tragedies.* Edited by David Grene and Richmond Lattimore. Chicago: University of Chicago Press, 1992.

Works about Tragedy

Frye, Prosser H. *Romance and Tragedy.* Norman: University of Oklahoma Press, 1980.

Kitto, H. D. F. *Greek Tragedy: A Literary Study.* New York: Routledge, 2002.
Spencer, Theodore. *Death and Elizabethan Tragedy.* St. Clair Shores, Mich.: Scholarly Press, 1985.

travel narrative   (travel log)

Travel, due to military, merchant, religious, or personal reasons, has always been a part of human activity, and the retelling of adventures experienced during traveling is one of the earliest forms of oral literature. Travelers' diaries, letters home, and memoirs of exploration are all examples of travel narratives, from the *Tosa Diary* of Ki no Tsurayuki to the journals kept by world explorer Amerigo VESPUCCI. Travel as part of the human quest emerges at the very beginnings of literature, in the journey of Gilgamesh in the *Epic of Gilgamesh* and in the adventures of Odysseus in Homer's *Odyssey.* Even the rituals described in the Egyptian Book of the Dead entail travel from this world to the next.

As a literary genre, the travel narrative began to grow in popularity in the West during the 15th-century Age of Exploration. The spirit of the RENAISSANCE and its accompanying belief of HUMANISM, which valued the power and inventiveness of human abilities, inspired the desire for discovery and a readiness to explore the wide world and make it familiar. Travel literature provided people with a chance to learn about the world without actually having to undertake a risky journey. In the 18th-century, travel narratives abounded as Europeans became more curious about cultures beyond their own borders. Women as well as men kept diaries, travel logs, and correspondence; two popular examples are *The Journeys of Celia Fiennes* (1697) and Lady Mary Wortley Montagu's *Turkish Embassy Letters* (1717).

Travel narratives might be accounts of actual travel, such as adventures inside colonial America or travels taken to the Old World from the New, for instance, the autobiographical account of Olaudah EQUIANO. Some popular narratives were descriptions of imaginary journeys, like *Gulliver's Travels* by Jonathan SWIFT. Travel narratives also varied in their function. They could be purely entertaining, like the later adventure fiction of Jules Verne, or they could recount a spiritual journey or pilgrimage. These narratives were as frequently written by disappointed high society dandies as they were by devoted missionaries.

Travel narratives could also be highly political: *A Journey from St. Petersburg to Moscow* by Aleksandr RADISHCHEV was considered so dangerous from a political point of view that czarist censorship prohibited its publication. The lead character of the *Journey,* a young, conscientious nobleman, travels between two major Russian cities. He makes subtle and revealing observations of the common people's life, which boil down to harsh criticism of czarist Russia.

The popularity of the travel narrative as a genre has endured over the last several centuries. The works belonging to this vast field provide not only entertaining reading full of adventure, exoticism, and the spirit of discovery, allowing readers to explore the distant places and peoples of the world, but also a comparative perspective, helping readers to better understand their own culture and identity.

English Versions of Travel Narratives

Fish, Cheryl J. *Black and White Women's Travel Narratives: Antebellum Explorations.* Gainesville: University Press of Florida, 2004.

Homer. *The Odyssey.* Translated by Rodney Merrill. Ann Arbor: University of Michigan Press, 2002.

Maiden Voyages and Infant Colonies: Two Women's Travel Narratives of the 1790s. London: Cassell Academic, 1999.

Martin, Wendy, ed. *Colonial American Travel Narratives.* New York: Penguin, 1994.

Vivies, Jean, ed. *English Travel Narratives in the Eighteenth Century.* Translated by Claire Davison. Aldershot, Hampshire, U.K.: Ashgate Publishing, 2002.

Works about Travel Narratives

Brown, Christopher. *Encyclopedia of Travel Literature.* Santa Barbara, Calif.: ABC-CLIO, 2000.

Brown, Sharon Rogers. *American Travel Narratives as a Literary Genre from 1542 to 1832.* Lewiston, N.Y.: Edwin Mellen Press, 1993.

Gilroy, Amanda, ed. *Romantic Geographies: Discourses of Travel, 1775–1844.* New York: St. Martin's Press, 2000.

Westrem, Scott D. *Broader Horizons: A Study of Johannes Witte de Hese's Itinerarius and Medieval Travel Narratives.* Cambridge, Mass.: Medieval Academy of America, 2001.

typology

Typology is a form of interpretation. It originated as a branch of hermeneutics, which originally referred to principles for interpreting the Bible and has since become the term used for the general interpretation of texts. Typology established relationships between the people and events in the Old and New Testaments and was originally aimed at making both Testaments into one cohesive work. St. Augustine, an early medieval theologian, explained in a letter that "In the Old Testament the New Testament is concealed; in the New Testament the Old Testament is revealed."

Typology supports the idea that the events of the New Testament fulfilled the prophecies of the Old Testament. Often, Old Testament figures are called types, and the New Testament characters they prefigure are called anti-types. One example is reading Adam as a prefigure of Christ. Another example is the idea that the manna provided to the children of Israel wandering in the wilderness prefigures the bread used in the sacrament of Communion. St. Paul and the early church founders were the first to use this sort of biblical interpretation in order to give their new religion a sense of tradition. Typology became a literary device used in much of the Christian literature that followed, including John MILTON's *Paradise lost.*

See also ALLEGORY.

Works about Typology

Keenan, Hugh T., ed. *Typology and Medieval English Literature.* Stoughton, Mass.: AMS Press, 1992.

Lodge, David. *The Modes of Modern Writing: Metaphor, Metonymy, and the Typology of Modern Literature.* Ithaca, N.Y.: Cornell University Press, 1977.

Lupton, Julia Reinhard. *Afterlives of the Saints: Hagiography, Typology, and Renaissance Literature.* Palo Alto, Calif.: Stanford University Press, 1996.

Miner, Earl, ed. *Literary Uses of Typology: From the Late Middle Ages to the Present.* Princeton, N.J.: Princeton University Press, 1977.

unities

The term *unities* is used in drama criticism to refer to the use of action, time, and place. In his *Poetics,* Aristotle emphasizes that unity of action was the most important factor in TRAGEDY, which he calls "an imitation of an action that is complete and whole and of a certain magnitude." Completion means having a beginning, middle, and end. Aristotle also states that unity cannot be achieved simply by making one character the focus of tragedy; instead it comes from structural unity of smaller actions that constitute one larger, complete action. Aristotle does not explicitly comment on unity of time and place, but it can be inferred from *Poetics* and such examples as Sophocles' *Oedipus Rex* and Euripides' *Medea* that unity of action assumes a limited time span and location.

Aristotle's descriptions of tragedies and unities have been molded over time into a series of rules for judging contemporary drama. These rules were most strongly influenced, especially during the 16th century and the development of NEOCLASSICISM, by Italian critic Ludovico Castelvetro, in his commentary on Aristotle's *Poetics.*

During the 17th century, the great French dramatist Pierre CORNEILLE relied on Aristotle's definition of unity in discussing plot, but he narrowed the definition by arguing that a play's action should cover no more than a day because such restraint would support the imitation of reality and probability that audiences expect. Since he was a working playwright, Corneille admitted that dramatists might have to bend these rules to satisfy their audiences.

Another playwright, John Dryden, showed the advantages and disadvantages of strictly following the unities, which he did not fully support, in his *Essay of Dramatic Poesy* (1668). While the unities make for neat, symmetrical drama in which nothing is wasted, they also can make a play claustrophobic and lifeless if too literally obeyed. Dryden upholds the English tradition of multiple plots and variety in actions as more lively and appealing.

The unities continued to be an important factor, though less rigidly observed, in the 19th century, especially with the rise of Henrik Ibsen and realism in drama.

See also CLASSICISM.

Works about the Unities

Aristotle. *Aristotle's Theory of Poetry and Fine Art.* Translated by S. H. Butcher. New York: Dover, 1955.

Corneille, Pierre. "Of the Three Unities," in *The Continental Model: Selected French Critical Essays of the Seventeenth Century.* Edited by Scott Elledge and Donald Schier. Minneapolis: University of Minnesota Press, 1960.

Dryden, John. "An Essay of Dramatic Poesy," in *Critical Theory Since Plato*. Edited by Hazard Adams. New York: Harcourt Brace Jovanovich College Publishers, 1992.

utopia

Utopia, meaning an imaginary ideal world, comes from the Greek words for "no place." The term was first used by Thomas MORE in his satirical *Utopia* (1516), in which a man named Raphael Hythloday, who had sailed with Amerigo VESPUCCI, gives a detailed description of the island of Utopia, where there is no private property.

More was not the first to come up with a plan for an ideal society. Plato described his ideal of the state in his *Republic*, but More was the first to give a detailed narrative about a society that was supposed to exist in the present or future. Such narratives have been called "Utopias" ever since. According to Krishna Kumar in *Utopianism*, "Utopia was born with modernity." During the RENAISSANCE, the period when the New World was discovered, curiosity began to grow about unknown societies. At the same time, people began to believe that humankind could be perfected by use of reason, and that an ideal society might be established. Many people began to write about such societies.

In Francis BACON's *The New Atlantis* (1627), the most important institution of the island of Ben-salem is Salomon's House, or the College of the Six Days' Works, made up of scientists who seek to "enlarge the bounds of Human Empire, to the effecting of all things possible." In Tommaso CAMPANELLA's, *The City of the Sun* (1623), the perfect society is devoted to the life of the mind, especially the arts and sciences. Other utopias were political. The ideal government in James Harrington's *Oceana* (1656) has a series of checks and balances to prevent too much power being invested in any one body. His work may have influenced John Adams, one of the framers of the U.S. Constitution (1787). In 1770 Louis-Sébastien Mercier wrote the first utopia to be set in the definitive future: *The Year 2440*, in which government is based on science and reason.

Early 19th-century utopianism was largely devoted not to literary works, but to social theory and experiments in utopian communal living, such as those of Robert Owen and Charles Fourier. Literary utopias revived again in the late 19th and 20th centuries.

Works of Utopia

Bruce, Susan, ed. *Three Early Modern Utopias: Utopia, New Atlantis, the Isle of Pines*. New York: Oxford University Press, 1999.

A Work about Utopia

Kumar, Krishna. *Utopianism*. Minneapolis: University of Minnesota Press, 1991.

Vesalius, Andreas (1514–1564) *nonfiction writer*

Vesalius's voluminous medical text, *De Humanis Corporis Fabrica Libri Septem (Seven Books on the Construction of the Human Body, 1543)*, challenged long-held concepts about the anatomy of the human body that were based largely upon the writings of Galen, who was the recognized authority on the human body until the time of Vesalius.

Born in Brussels, Vesalius was the son of Andreas Vesalius, the court apothecary to Holy Roman Emperor Charles IV. Vesalius attended the University of Louvain and later studied at Padua, where he received a doctor of medicine degree and taught as professor of anatomy and surgery. Following the publication of *De Humanis Corporis Fabrica*, Vesalius was appointed court physician to Emperor Charles V. Not long after he became physician to Philip II, Vesalius died while on a pilgrimage to Jerusalem and Mount Sinai.

Composed in Latin, the language of scholarly discourse during the period, *De Humanis Corporis Fabrica* is a lengthy prose work detailing human anatomy. Vesalius modeled his writing upon classical Latin rhetoric, most notably that of Marcus Tullius Cicero. Such an antiquated style was unusual for medical texts of the period, but Vesalius wished to model his sentences upon the great stylists of antiquity; he considered his work to fit within the context of the spirit of great texts written by anatomists and physicians from the classical past.

De Humanis Corporis Fabrica's seven books are divided according to major components of the body, each of which is discussed at length: bones, muscles, blood vessels, nerves, abdominal organs, chest and neck, and brain. Each section contains many intelligent, detailed, and graphic renderings of the human body that are keyed to textual descriptions. These illustrations were executed by skilled artisans, one of whom is believed to be artist Jan Stephan van Calcar, a pupil of Titian. Vesalius's work was deemed superior to earlier works by scholars of his day, in part because his book resulted from firsthand experience dissecting the body.

De Humanis Corporis, while strikingly innovative and highly valuable to physicians and students of anatomy and surgery, was believed controversial and remained under constant scrutiny. Nevertheless, the publication marked the birth of modern medicine.

A Work about Andreas Vesalius

O'Malley, Charles Donald. *Andreas Vesalius: 1514–1564*. Berkeley: University of California Press, 1964.

Vespucci, Amerigo (ca. 1451–1512)
cosmographer, navigator, explorer

Amerigo Vespucci was a clerk in the commercial office of the rich and powerful rulers of Florence, the House of Medici, when word of Colombus's successful crossing of the ocean reached Italy. Although Vespucci had a successful career as a Florentine merchant, in his student days he acquired an interest in the natural sciences, cosmography, and navigation. The news about Columbus's crossing aroused his curiosity of the newly found lands and inspired him to immediately set off for Spain in search of a contract to furnish supplies for Columbus's next voyage.

Little reliable information exists on the number of voyages Vespucci made to the New World. Traditional accounts place the number at four, but later scholarship suggests that there may have been as few as two voyages. This information is largely based on cartographic information and three handwritten letters by Vespucci discovered in Florentine archives during the last half of the 18th century. In one account of doubtful authenticity, Vespucci was purported to have sailed between 1497 and 1498 on his first voyage to Paria. This information is based on a "Letter to Soderini," first printed in 1505, and attributed to Vespucci.

By 1499 Vespucci was reported to have interested the court in his own expedition to the lands across the Atlantic. He sailed from southern Spain to South America under the command of Alonzo de Ojeda as the representative of the financial interests backing the voyage. The report of this voyage is believed to be authentic.

In 1502 his second or third voyage landed on the coast of Brazil. A short account of this 1501–02 voyage down the coast of South America was detailed by Vespucci in a 1503 letter he sent to former Florentine employer, Lorenzo di Pier Francesco de' Medici. The account was later popularized in a pamphlet as *Mundus novas.* The manuscript experienced a large circulation in Italian before being published in Latin in 1504. The work was widely popular and may have been the most influential of all the early New World travel writings.

Mundus novas and a second pamphlet, *Lettera . . . quattri . . . viaggi,* circulating between 1504 and 1506, are characterized by vivid and fantastic descriptions of the New World and its inhabitants. The prose style of both works is very readable. Detailed descriptions of exotic places as well as lurid accounts of cannibalism, naked savages, and sexual practices made the pamphlets a popular success.

A copy of *Mundus novas* was acquired by the German geographer Martin WALDSEEMÜLLER. In a 1507 treatise entitled *Cosmographiae Introductio,* Waldseemüller comments: "A fourth part of the earth has been discovered by Amerigo Vespucci. . . . I see no reason why anyone could justly object to naming this part Amerige, that is, the land of Amerigo, or America, after its discoverer." Waldseemüller's comment is credited, in large part, to the naming of the American continents.

Vespucci may have taken two subsequent voyages (1501–02 and 1503–04) under the service of Portugal. The authenticity of reports of these voyages, however, remains unsubstantiated. In 1506 Vespucci was appointed first *piloto mayor* of Spain by Queen Juana, a position he retained until his death. He provided instruction for individuals headed for the Indies, as well as elaborated and updated the official nautical chart.

An English Version of Works by Amerigo Vespucci

Letters of Amerigo Vespucci and Other Documents Illustrative of His Career. Edited by Clements R. Markham. New York: Burt Franklin, 1994.

Works about Amerigo Vespucci

Fitzpatrick, Ann. *Forgotten Voyager: The Story of Amerigo Vespucci.* Minneapolis, Minn.: Lerner Publishing Group, 1991.

Marsh, David. "Letters from a New World: Amerigo Vespucci's Discovery of America," *Renaissance Quarterly* 27, no. 2 (Summer 1994): 398(3).

Ray, Kurt. *Amerigo Vespucci: Italian Explorer of the Americas.* New York: Rosen Publishing, 2003.

Vico, Giambattista (1668–1744)
philosopher

Giambattista Vico was born into a world transitioning from the RENAISSANCE to the ENLIGHTENMENT. The son of a Neapolitan bookseller, Vico's passion for learning led him from a career in law to a position as tutor to the nephews of his mentor, the bishop of Ischia. Later he returned to Naples and in 1695 married Teresa Destito. In 1699 he became a professor of rhetoric at the University of Naples. Before his death, he briefly served as royal historiographer for Charles III.

Vico's lifework, *New Science,* was first published in 1725. In it he introduced new theories about the nature of human knowledge and the formation of history. Though Peter Burke calls it "a book stuffed so full of ideas that it almost bursts at the seams," Vico's "new critical art" was so little understood by his peers that he found it necessary to print a second and fuller edition in 1730. He continued revising throughout his life.

Among many original ideas in *New Science* was Vico's pattern of the history of nations, where the age of gods led to the age of heroes, and then to the age of humans. He believed that mythology is the first science. Imagination, the power by which humans understand and order the world, eventually gives way to logic and reason. To Vico, knowledge was "made" or invented, and fields like mathematics or history were simply human inventions. Since the physical sciences required experimentation with nature, they could not be fully understood. Truth, Vico claimed, was knowable only to whoever created the truth.

In addition, he believed the purpose of education was to cultivate the divine within the human mind through self-knowledge and the pursuit of wisdom. Vico's disagreements with the theories of René DESCARTES, which he regarded as too narrow and misinformed about the nature of scientific knowledge, led to unpopularity in his own lifetime and the neglect of his works after his death.

Many modern scholars think that Vico was simply ahead of his time. His ideas influenced such later writers as Samuel Taylor Coleridge and James Joyce.

An English Version of a Work by Giambattista Vico
The New Science of Giambattista Vico, 2nd ed. Translated by Thomas Bergin and Max Harold Fisch. Ithaca, N.Y.: Cornell University Press, 1983.

Works about Giambattista Vico
Burke, Peter. *Vico.* New York: Oxford University Press, 1985.
Pompa, Leon. *Vico: A Study of the 'New Science'.* Cambridge: Cambridge University Press, 1990.

Villon, François (1431–after 1463) *poet*

François de Montcorbier was born in Paris and later took his name from the guardian who raised and educated him, Guillaume de Villon. Aside from the existence of certain scholastic and criminal records, what is known of Villon's biography comes from his poetry. He received his B.A. in 1449 and his M.A. in 1452 from the University of Paris. He had a restless mind, was often in trouble for brawling, and was a notorious prankster. While at university he angered officials by being part of a squad of reckless youths who stole street signs and performed mock marriages with them. As he matured, however, his crimes grew serious; in 1455 Villon was charged with killing a priest but was pardoned because the death was proved accidental. A year later he and four conspirators robbed the College of Navarre, and to avoid capture Villon left Paris. Records from 1461 list him as a prisoner in Orléans, but he was freed with the other city prisoners, as was custom, when the newly crowned Louis XI passed through the town. In 1462 an arrest for petty theft in Paris brought him to the attention of authorities from the College of Navarre who begrudged the earlier loss and had him imprisoned, tortured, and sentenced to death. Through eloquent pleading he managed to get the sentence commuted to banishment for 10 years.

After Villon left Paris in 1463, he was never heard from again.

Villon's poetic inventions are closely tied to his personal trials and experiences and reflect the opinions of an outsider and rebel. The social world into which he was born had two authorities, the church and the law, both of which Villon managed to offend. The literary culture that he entered had two authorities, sacred scripture and the authors of classical antiquity, both of which Villon used in his poetry. Villon had studied the Bible as well as Greek and Roman philosophers, and he was well-versed in the tradition of French literature, especially the works of Guillaume de Machaut and Eustace Deschamps.

The mock will was a popular genre, and Villon employed this form in composing *The Legacy* in 1456 as he prepared to leave Paris. These 300 verses about disillusioned love, lovers going astray, or lovers in distress are full of wry counterpoints, irony, and dark humor, as in these lines in which a lover speaks of leave-taking with no assurance of return:

> *I'm not without my faults, nor made*
> *of tougher stuff than other men;*
> *human life is an uncertain thing*
> *and there's no respite from death;*
> *also, I have far to go. . . .*

The work that does Villon the most credit is *The Testament*, which he composed in 1461. This work also is structured like a will, wherein he addresses friends, enemies, and his own alter ego using dialogue, self-examination, and jokes. This long poem, somewhat more elevated in tone, contains dark insights, as in these lines:

> *So, have your fill of love,*
> *go to parties and to banquets,*
> *in the end you'll be no better off*
> *and the only thing you'll break will be your*
>   *head.*
> *Foolish love makes beasts of men . . .*
> *That man is lucky who has nothing.*

Villon also wrote many shorter pieces, many of them addressed to people who aided him, among them Charles d'Orléans, the parliamentarian who ultimately pardoned him, and his jailer in prison. He has been accused of being a poet insensitive to beauty, but the scarcity of pleasant moments in his poetry may reflect the scarcity of pleasurable moments in his life. Many of the so-called slang poems, those written in the jargon of the criminal underworld, are manipulative, sarcastic, and even vitriolic. Throughout his work his outlook is pessimistic but honest, and his poems emerge from his attempts to come to terms with his experiences. Criticism of Villon's criminal activities has traditionally colored criticism of his work, but virtually all students of literature have heard the echo, in some form, of Villon's most melancholy line: "Where are the snows of yesteryear?" Though his morals are questionable, his influence is a fact. As biographer Anthony Bonner states, in a mere six years Villon "turned out a body of poetry great enough to leave him with few rivals in the literature of his own country or in that of any other."

English Versions of Works by François Villon

Book of François Villon: The Little Testament and Ballads. Translated by Algernon C. Swinburne. New York: Branden Publishing, 1997.

Poems of François Villon. Translated by Peter Dale. London: Anvil Press Poetry, 2001.

Works about François Villon

Burl, Aubrey. *Danse Macabre: François Villon.* New York: Sutton, 2000.

Fein, David A. *François Villon Revisited.* New York: Twayne, 1997.

Voltaire (François–Marie Arouet)
(1694–1778) *novelist, playwright, poet, historian*

François-Marie Arouet, universally known as Voltaire (an assumed name), is perhaps the best-known literary figure of the European

ENLIGHTENMENT. During his long and eventful life, he experimented with virtually every genre of literature—EPIC poetry, history, philosophy, fiction, and drama—and produced a prodigious amount of work. Although he was best known in his own time for his plays, his most widely read work today is his novel *Candide.*

Voltaire was born in Paris and was provided with a classical education by the religious order of the Jesuits at Louis-le-Grand. Although his father, a successful notary and member of the bourgeoisie, wanted him to become a lawyer, Voltaire disliked the legal profession and preferred to pursue a life of literature. His first great success was his play *Œdipe* (1718), a story based upon the tragic Greek legend of Oedipus. He spent some time in jail for writing scandalous poetry and was later exiled to England. While in England, he met famous literary figures and became interested in philosophy and science. He also wrote *La Henriade* (originally titled *La Ligue;* published in 1723), an epic poem in 10 cantos based upon Henry III's siege of Paris in 1589, and *Histoire de Charles XII* (1731), a history of the reign of King Charles XII of Sweden.

Upon his return from England, Voltaire wrote his first masterpiece, *Letters Concerning the English Nation.* In this collection of essays, he contrasts the general freedom and tolerance of England with the oppressive religious and political climate of France. This made him very unpopular with the French government.

From the early 1730s to the mid-1740s, Voltaire mostly lived in his château of Cirey with his mistress, Madame du Châtelet. During his time there, he wrote a number of plays and historical works, including *Brutus* (1730), in which the character Titus is torn between his love for a tyrant's daughter and his responsibility to help liberate his country; *La Mort de César* (1731), on the death of the Roman general and statesman Julius Caesar; and *Zaïre* (1732), the story of a Christian child, who is kidnapped by a Turkish army, and her father, whose attempt to save her instead results in her murder. Voltaire also translated the scientific works

of Sir Isaac Newton in *Éléments de la Philosophie de Newton* (1736), which did much to make science more popular in France; and began a famous correspondence with Frederick the Great, king of Prussia. He was also appointed court poet despite his enemies (who favored neither his literary attacks on established social, political, and religious issues nor his success and wealth), and wrote *La Princesse de Navarre* (1744) and *Poème de Fontenoy* (1745). In the late 1740s, he began writing short stories in prose, including *Zadig, ou la Destinée* (1748), a story about a young man who loses his fortune and then experiences a series of "fateful" incidents that only Providence (or destiny) can understand. Voltaire was also appointed to the ACADÉMIE FRANÇAISE in 1746, and completed three more tragedies: *Sémiramis* (1746), *Oreste* (1749), and *Rome sauvée* (1749).

After Madame du Châtelet's death in 1749, Voltaire spent a few years living in Berlin at the court of Frederick the Great. During this time, he continued to add to a collection of essays that he had begun during his time at Cirey with Madame du Châtelet. The essays were eventually published as *Essay on the Manners and the Spirit of Nations* (1756). In this historical and highly philosophical work, Voltaire states that people are responsible for their own destinies, that they have the will and the means to overcome all obstacles, including those that are religious, political, cultural, and economical. Voltaire also began to develop, in concept, what would become *The Philosophical Dictionary* (1764), a series of 73 critical social essays that was repeatedly banned by authorities for Voltaire's portrayal of the social ills and unrest caused not only by the government, but also by the established church. In addition to this work, Voltaire finished writing *Le Siècle de Louis XIV* and *Poème sur la loi naturelle.*

At age 60, Voltaire moved to the small town of Ferney, where he bought an estate in 1758, and lived there almost the rest of his life. Once he had settled down, he produced a massive amount of literature in almost every genre. He continued writing plays, produced historical works concerning King Louis XIV of France and Czar Peter the Great of Russia, wrote the dramatic poem *The Lisbon Earthquake* and the novel *Candide,* as well as completed *The Philosophical Dictionary.* It is for these works and the place in which they were written that Voltaire is often referred to as the "Sage of Ferney."

Throughout his life, Voltaire was bitterly hostile toward organized religion. He viewed the ignorance of those who unethically and immorally used faith and church law to further their own causes as both the cause itself of much human suffering and the enemy of "enlightened" thought. He even went so far as to sign many of his letters with the phrase *"Ecrasez L'infame,"* or "Crush the Infamous," which stood for his position that people should fight the oppression and bigotry caused by organized religion. In keeping with his penchant for ever-changing styles and topics, however, Voltaire also published *A Treatise on Tolerance,* in which he begs people to overlook their religious differences and treat one another with respect. From his home at Ferney, Voltaire used his writing abilities and his immense network of personal connections to fight campaigns against injustice throughout Europe, particularly in cases of religious persecution or unfair criminal justice systems.

In 1778, with only a few months left to live, Voltaire returned to Paris, not having visited the city for nearly a quarter of a century. He was welcomed home by the Parisian people as a hero, and the premiere of his final play, *Irène,* was a smashing success. Voltaire died in Paris on May 30. In the "Introduction" to *Voltaire: Candide, Zadig, and Selected Stories,* Donald M. Frame states that "for much of his life Voltaire's greatest fame was as the leading successor to Corneille and Racine in classical French verse tragedy, which he spiced with themes from Shakespeare and the East, colorful and violent visual effects, and thinly veiled social and religious criticism."

Critical Analysis

In nearly all of his writing, Voltaire employed a brilliant sarcastic wit and a highly developed sense of irony; in *Candide,* these gifts reached their full expression.

Candide is the fanciful story of a young man who wanders around the world, experiencing horrible disasters and witnessing terrifying events. Voltaire uses the story to present his views on the nature of good and evil, the absurdity of life, and the futility of hope. The entire work is, in effect, an attack on the views of other writers and philosophers such as Alexander POPE and Gottfried Wilhelm LEIBNIZ who believed that the human race lived in "the best of all possible worlds." Voltaire's message in *Candide* is that the world could be better, that it is not yet what it could be.

In the story, the character of Candide falls in love with the beautiful Cunegonde, the daughter of the castle's baron. As a result, he is kicked out of the castle where he grew up. For the rest of the story, Candide wanders, sometimes searching for Cunegonde but often simply trying to escape from various disasters that continually befall him.

Candide is forcibly recruited into the Bulgar army (which is really a thinly disguised Prussian army, led by a thinly disguised Frederick the Great). He is caught in the Lisbon earthquake, persecuted by the Inquisition, finds and loses a fabulous treasure in El Dorado, and sees many friends die horrible deaths. Until the very end, Candide believes everything that happens is for the best, for that is what he has been taught by his teacher, Doctor Pangloss (who may simply be a caricature of Leibniz).

In addition to directly experiencing great hardships, Candide also bears witness to others' hardships. At one point, he encounters six men at a dinner. It is soon revealed that these men were once powerful monarchs who had been overthrown. Through part of his adventure, Candide is accompanied by a character known simply as "the old woman," the pope's illegitimate daughter, who was enslaved by North African pirates and who had half of her buttock cut off by Turkish soldiers during the siege of Azov.

In addition, Candide witnesses the execution of an English captain whose only crime was not engaging the enemy closely enough. This particular part of the story provides one of Voltaire's celebrated quotes: "[I]n this country it is considered a good thing to kill an admiral from time to time so as to encourage the others." The episode was inspired by the actual execution of Admiral Sir John Byng on March 14, 1757, and is an excellent example of how Voltaire uses his writing as commentary about social and political events.

In his adventures, Candide is accompanied by various unusual characters, many of whom seemingly die only to puzzlingly reappear later in the story. There is Doctor Pangloss, who stubbornly continues to believe, despite all the evidence, that everything in the world happens for the best. There are Martin, a cynic and realist who seems to be the only voice of true reason in the story; Cacambo, a faithful servant to Candide despite the fact that his connection to Candide brings him nothing but misfortune; and finally, Cunegonde, a rather simple-minded young woman who remains the object of Candide's affections.

The story ends in the city of Constantinople, where Candide and his friends settle down to a simple life of gardening. At the conclusion, Pangloss still believes that they live in the best of all possible worlds, but Candide has become disillusioned. Having seen and suffered so much, the young man decides that the only way to achieve any happiness in life is, as Voltaire puts it, to "cultivate our garden."

Among his many other works, *Candide* helped make Voltaire one of the most famous writers of the European Enlightenment and, in the opinion of many, the greatest. Certainly he was the most prolific, leaving behind more than 10,000 letters on every subject imaginable, hundreds of pamphlets, plays, short stories, poems, and novels. The central theme running through all of his work is the power of human reason to overcome prejudice and to improve life for all humanity.

English Versions of Works by Voltaire

Candide. Holicong, Pa.: Wildside Press, 2003.
Complete Romances of Voltaire. Whitefish, Mont.: Kessinger Publishing, 2003.
Voltaire and His Letters. Translated by S. G. Tallentyre. Miami: International Law and Taxation, 2004.
Voltaire: Candide, Zadig, and Selected Stories. Translated by Donald M. Frame. New York: New American Library, 1961.
Voltaire: Treatise on Tolerance. Edited by Simon Harvey. New York: Cambridge University Press, 2000.
Voltaire's Correspondence: An Epistolary Novel, vol. 5. Edited by Deidre Dawson and Gita May. New York: Peter Lang, 1994.

Works about Voltaire

Bonhome, Denise. *What Voltaire Tries to Tell Us*. Lincoln, Neb.: iUniverse, 2000.
Hugo, Victor. *Oration on Voltaire*. La Vergne, Tenn.: University Press of the Pacific, 2003.
Knapp, Bettina Liebowitz. *Voltaire Revisited*. New York: Macmillan Library Reference, 2000.
Tallentyre, S. G. *Life of Voltaire*. Miami: International Law and Taxation, 2004.
Thaddeus, Victor. *Voltaire, Genius of Mockery*. Whitefish, Mont.: Kessinger Publishing, 2003.
Walsh, Thomas. *Readings on Candide*. Farmington Hills, Mich.: Gale Group, 2000.

Vondel, Joost van den (1587–1679)
dramatist

Joost van den Vondel, known as Holland's national playwright and "Prince of Poets," was originally born in Cologne but moved to the Netherlands as a child and settled with his family in Amsterdam. His father hoped he would take up the family trade of being a hatter, but the younger Vondel married the daughter of a Flemish clothier who looked after the family business while Vondel wrote. His long life was marked by personal tragedy, including the early deaths of his wife and two children and near-bankruptcy caused by a son who was then banished to the East Indies and died at sea. At age 70, Vondel was obliged to find a job in a bank but was eventually allowed to retire.

Over the course of his life Vondel produced a huge body of work, including 30 full-length dramas, beginning with *Het Pascha (The Passover)* in

1612. He also wrote lyrical and religious poetry and printed translations of Greek and Latin classics. His plays frequently feature biblical themes, adhere to classical forms, and show impressive cadences of thought and language. The 10 volumes of Vondel's work, collected after his death, illustrate in words the Dutch and Flemish Golden Age that Rembrandt, Van Dyck, and Rubens rendered in their paintings.

In addition to being a dramatist and poet, Vondel was also a patriot and a campaigner for political and religious freedom. *Lucifer* (1654) probably inspired John MILTON with its portrayal of the fallen archangel torn by personal ambition and perceived injustice. The portrayal of heavenly beings as capable of all-too-human frailty caused such outrage that the play was banned after its second performance. *Lucifer* was followed by *Exile* (1664) and *Noah* (1667), creating a trio of tales from the Bible. *Lucifer* and *Gijsbrecht van Aemstel* (1637) are considered the best works of an author remembered as one of the greatest poets and certainly the greatest dramatist of the Netherlands.

English Versions of a Work by Joost van den Vondel

Lucifer: Joost Van den Vondel. Translated by Noel Clark. Bath, U.K.: Absolute Classics, 1990.
Lucifer. New York: Theatre Communications Group, 1991.

A Work about Joost van den Vondel

Mody, Jehangir R. P. *Vondel and Milton.* Norwood, Pa.: Norwood Editions, 1977.

Waldseemüller, Martin (1470–ca. 1521)
cartographer

Martin Waldseemüller was born near Lake Constance in the southern reaches of the Black Forest in what is now Germany. He studied theology at the University of Freiburg and served as a cleric in his native diocese of Constance. He also spent time at Strasburg and Basel studying geography, particularly the ancient maps of Ptolemy. By 1507 he came to the monastery at St. Die in the mountains of Lorraine, where he was made a canon in 1514. In typical humanistic fashion he often used a Grecianized form of his name, Martinus Ilacomilus.

In Waldseemüller's lifetime, the voyages of COLUMBUS, Amerigo VESPUCCI, and other explorers significantly revised the scope of the known world. After his third voyage, Vespucci published an account of his survey of the coastline of South America. He named the accounts, and the lands he had explored, *Mundus Novus (The New World)*. Up to this point, Columbus and his contemporary Europeans insisted that the lands they had reached were islands, but Vespucci was aware he had reached a new continent, inhabited he said, "by more numerous peoples and animals than in our Europe or Asia or Africa." When Vespucci's *Mundus Novus* reached the small community of scholars, geographers, and

cartographers at St. Die, Waldseemüller immediately began working on a new map of the world.

In 1507 Waldseemüller published the *Introduction to Cosmography, With Certain Necessary Principles of Geometry and Astronomy, To Which Are Added The Four Voyages of Amerigo Vespucci*. In addition to the core treatise on cosmography, the work includes two maps, one a globe and one a plane projection map, as well as the already-famous letter written by Amerigo Vespucci to the duke of Lorraine, describing the voyages he conducted between 1497 and 1503. Recognizing the debt that modern cartography owed to the ancients, Waldseemüller included a figure of Ptolemy on the map, overlooking the world as Waldseemüller imagined it.

The 1507 map is unique in many respects. It is the first published map to represent all 360 degrees of the known world. It is the first to label the new continent "America," since, as Waldseemüller declared, "I see no reason why anyone should justly object to calling this part Amerige, *i.e.*, the land of Amerigo, or America, after Amerigo, its discoverer." In addition, Waldseemüller speculated that if the new lands were indeed a continent, then another ocean must lie between them and the Orient. Thus his map depicts the Pacific Ocean a full six years before its sighting was recorded by Vasco Nuñez de Balboa, who crossed the Isthmus of Panama in 1513.

In comparison to the 12 different woodcuts of the map, which hold a more immediate interest, particularly for students of American history, the *Cosmography* often has been overlooked. It contains a detailed analysis of the sciences of astronomy and geometry, which Waldseemüller considered crucial to the study of geography. The nine chapters cover Waldseemüller's knowledge on geometrical and astronomical terms, the circles of the heavens and the five celestial zones, the climates of the Earth as well as the winds, and various seas and islands, including their distances from one another. In his account he drew not only on Ptolemy but also on the voyages of Marco Polo. All four parts of the *Cosmography* were immediately popular. Though the 1516 reprint of the map left out the name America, Waldseemüller's suggestion had already come into common usage. His 1507 map is considered "the birth certificate of America."

An English Version of a Work by Martin Waldseemüller

Cosmographiae Introductio of Martin Waldseemüller in Facsimile. Translated by Joseph Fischer and Franz von Wieser. Manchester, N.H.: Ayer Co., 1977.

A Work about Martin Waldseemüller

Arcinieges, Germán. *Why America? 500 Years of a Name: The Life and Times of Amerigo Vespucci.* Translated by Harriet de Onís. Washington, D.C.: Villegas Editores, 2002.

Warren, Mercy Otis (1728–1814)
playwright, poet, historian

Throughout her life, Mercy Otis Warren excelled at many literary forms, including poetry and drama, but her legacy rests largely on her three-volume history of the American Revolutionary War, written in the later years of her life. She was also a prodigious letter writer, and her correspondents included John and Abigail Adams and George and Martha Washington.

Born in Barnstable, Massachusetts, Warren was the daughter of James and Mary Allyne Otis, who also had 12 other children. Warren received no formal education, but she was able to study with her brother's tutor, Reverend Jonathan Russell, who encouraged her early literary interests.

In 1754 Mercy Otis married James Warren, a prominent local farmer and merchant who would later become a Revolutionary War general. The Warrens settled in Plymouth, where Warren raised her five sons and explored her literary pursuits.

Her earliest works, satirical plays, targeted the British colonial government. She was spurred to write such works after an incident in which her brother James was beaten violently in a Boston coffeehouse by a British Tory. Her first published play—*The Adulateur, A Tragedy, As it is now acted in Upper Servia*—was written in verse and published anonymously in 1772 in the *Massachusetts Spy*. It was "the first play published by a woman born and residing in English America" (Richards). Though couched in neoclassical names and techniques, the play is an obvious attack on Governor Thomas Hutchinson, who in this play is named "Rapatio." Her other plays—including *The Group* (1775) and *The Blockheads* (1776)—were also politically satirical, though none of them was ever staged. Though written in "a refined, academic style," Warren's "primary purpose [was] to create strong political satire" (Gartner). Two additional satiric plays appeared in her *Poems, Dramatic and Miscellaneous* in 1790.

Mercy Otis Warren is best remembered for her three-volume account of the war, *History of the Rise, Progress and Termination of the American Revolution, Interspersed with Biographical, Political and Moral Observations* (1805). Her account provides personal and political views of an army wife who corresponded with many of the great figures of the time.

The history was Warren's last published work. After her husband died in 1808, she continued writing her letters, which, though often overdramatic and florid, remain important documents of female thought and life during the Revolutionary era.

A Work about Mercy Otis Warren

Zagarri, Rosemarie. *A Woman's Dilemma: Mercy Otis Warren and the American Revolution.* Wheeling, Ill.: Harlan Davidson, 1995.

Watling, Thomas (1762–ca. 1815)
correspondent, painter

Thomas Watling was born in Dumfries, Scotland, the son of a soldier. He showed talent as an artist and briefly worked as a drawing teacher and coach painter. In 1788 he was arrested for counterfeiting and only narrowly escaped hanging. In 1791, still in prison, he volunteered for transportation to the new penal colony in Australia. After an abortive escape attempt at the Cape of Good Hope, he reached Port Jackson, New South Wales, late in 1792. The first professional artist in the colony, Watling became an assistant to a surgeon, an amateur naturalist who was compiling a record of the settlement's flora and fauna and who needed Watling to draw the illustrations.

In 1794 Watling wrote *Letters from an Exile at Botany Bay to His Aunt in Dumfries,* an irreverent, informal account of life in the Australian colony. Published in England, the book was a collection of actual letters Watling wrote to his elderly Aunt Marion. In some of the letters, he describes the aborigines:

> Irascibility, ferocity, cunning, treachery, revenge, filth and immodesty are strikingly their dark characteristics, their virtues are so far from conspicuous that I have not, as yet, been able to discern them. One thing I may adduce to their credit, that they are not cannibals.

In addition to writing letters, Watling also painted many portraits of the land and its people. Before his pardon and return to England in 1797, he made more than 500 drawings of animals, land-scapes, and other scenes of the new land, almost all of them remarkable for their draftsmanship and detail. His drawings of birds proved of considerable value to later naturalists, and his portraits of local aboriginal life are an invaluable early depiction of aboriginal and colonial culture. His most famous work of art is "Sydney Cove in 1794," apparently the first oil painting ever made on Australian soil.

In 1805 Watling was again charged with forgery but was later acquitted. There is no record of him after 1814, and some historians believe he died soon afterward. His works, both in prose and paint, are unique in Australian colonial art. Watling's letters are valued not only as a classic of Australian settlement, but also as literature written from the perspective of a convict.

A Work about Thomas Watling

Thomas Watling: Dumfries' Convict Artist. Dumfries, Scotland: Dumfries Museum, 1988.

Wheatley, Phillis (ca. 1753–1784) *poet*

Phillis Wheatley was brought to Boston from Africa after having been purchased by John Wheatley, an affluent tailor, as a companion for his wife, Susannah. She was named for the slave ship, the *Phillis,* which transported her to America, and she assumed the surname of her master. Susannah Wheatley taught her slave to read and write, and within 16 months the gifted young girl mastered the English language. She was particularly fond of the writings of Alexander POPE, Thomas Gray, and John MILTON.

In her teen years, Wheatley composed a series of 39 poems, which were published in London (1773) as *Poems on Various Subjects, Religious and Moral* (1773). Her style was not particularly original, for she relied heavily on established poetic conventions, especially on the heroic couplets and elegies favored by Pope.

Many of Wheatley's poems are conciliatory in nature. For instance, in "On Being Brought from

Africa to America" (1773) and "To the University of Cambridge, in New England" (1767), she expresses gratitude for having been taken from her "*Pagan* land" to a place where her soul could come to recognize "That there's a God, that there's a *Saviour* too." Moreover, she sought to revive people's yearning to turn their souls toward God.

In other poems, Wheatley was not so conciliatory, speaking out against slavery and hypocrisy. For example, in "On the Death of General Wooster" (1778), she questions the "disgrace" of holding "in bondage Africa's blameless race."

After Wheatley was emancipated, she became active in promoting her works. As a result, her reputation as an important African-American poet grew. Even though her poetry collection was reissued a number of times, she received no financial remuneration and died in poverty at age 31.

Phillis Wheatley is remembered for having been one of the rare African-American slaves to receive an education and for having written some of the best and most poignant poetry of early American literature.

Works by Phillis Wheatley

Phillis Wheatley: Complete Writings. Edited by Vincent Carretta. New York: Penguin Classics, 2001.
The Collected Works of Phillis Wheatley. New York: Oxford University Press, 1988.

Works about Phillis Wheatley

Bloom, Harold, ed. *African-American Poets: Phillis Wheatley through Countee Cullen.* Langhorne, Pa.: Chelsea House, 2001.
Gates, Henry Louis. *The Trials of Phillis Wheatley: America's First Black Poet and Encounters with the Founding Fathers.* New York: Basic Books, 2003.

Wigglesworth, Michael (1631–1705) *poet*

Born in England, Michael Wigglesworth immigrated to America in 1638 with his Puritan parents, Edward and Esther Wigglesworth. The family eventually settled in New Haven, Connecticut.

Wigglesworth entered Harvard College at age 17, eventually earning both bachelor and master degrees. He stayed at Harvard to teach, but he also occasionally preached during this time. In 1654 he became minister at the Puritan church in Malden, married the first of three wives the next year, and was officially ordained in 1656. He also maintained a medical practice over the years.

Wigglesworth's most famous work was the poem *The Day of Doom,* published in 1662. To modern readers, the work reads more like a sermon than a poem, with its "Puritan plain style and a conviction of the rightness of New [England's] brand of Calvinism" (Bosco). Wigglesworth states his purpose for writing the poem in these lines:

> Oh! guide me by thy sacred Sprite
> So to indite, and so to write,
> That I thine holy Name may praise,
> And teach the Sons of men thy wayes.

The Day of Doom was written in ballad meter, and is filled with biblical references. It was quite popular in its time, with more than 1,800 copies sold in 1662.

His next poem, *God's Controversy with New England,* was perhaps a response to a great drought that occurred in 1661 and 1662, which Wigglesworth believed was brought on by God due to the sinful and lapsed ways of New Englanders.

In 1670 he published *Meat Out of the Eater,* a 2,000-line rhyming poem written in various meters. It is perhaps Wigglesworth's most personal poem, consisting of "a series of song . . . written as much to console as to edify 'enduring' Christians" (Bosco).

In 1670 Wigglesworth turned most of his energy to preaching in Malden. Indeed, it appears that he made very few poetic efforts during these later years. When he died, he left behind his third wife and eight children.

Works by Michael Wigglesworth

The Day of Doom or a Description of the Great and Last Judgment. Whitefish, Mont.: Kessinger, 2003.

The Diary of Michael Wigglesworth, 1653–1657: The Conscience of a Puritan. Edited by Edmund S. Morgan. Magnolia, Mass.: Smith Peter, 1990.

The Poems of Michael Wigglesworth. Edited by Ronald A. Bosco. Lanham, Md.: University Press of America, 1989.

Works about Michael Wigglesworth

Crowder, Richard. *No Featherbed to Heaven: A Biography of Michael Wigglesworth, 1631.* Textbook Publishers, 2003.

Dean, John W. *Memoir of the Revised. Michael Wigglesworth, Author of the Day of Doom.* Murieta, Calif.: New Library Press, 2003.

Williams, Roger (1603–1683) *nonfiction writer, poet, grammarian*

Roger Williams was born to a wealthy merchant, who sent him to Cambridge University, where he graduated in 1627. He later became a clergyman with Puritan sympathies and sailed to the Massachusetts colony in 1630. The colonists originally welcomed Williams, but his questioning of the validity of taking Native American lands proved too radical. Upon hearing from the colony's governor, John WINTHROP, that a warrant had been issued for his arrest, Williams fled with a handful of followers into the southern territory of sympathetic Indians. In 1636 he founded Providence Plantations, which became the colony and later the state of Rhode Island. Native Americans trusted Williams, even as their relationships with other colonists deteriorated. Williams acted unsuccessfully as peacemaker between the two warring sides in the 1660s and 1670s. He died in Providence.

In 1643 he wrote the *Key Into the Languages of America,* the first Indian grammar in English, which included rhymes depicting Native Americans as more tolerant, peaceful, and fair than contemporary European peoples. His most influential work at the time was *The Bloudy Tenent* (1644), in which he criticizes religious wars and the union of church and state. Williams wrote *The Bloudy Tenent* as a dialog between Truth and Peace in

which he states that "enforced uniformity (sooner or later) is the greatest occasion of civil war, ravishing of conscience, persecution of Christ Jesus in his servants, and of the hypocrisy and destruction of millions of souls." He argued that civil governments should confine themselves to secular affairs and allow freedom of religion to their citizens. Williams's belief in religious tolerance was considered so dangerous that *The Bloudy Tenent* was burned in England in 1645.

While Williams's initial followers were English religious and political radicals of the 1640s and 1650s, his most lasting legacy is the influence he had on later American writers and political thinkers, such as Benjamin FRANKLIN and Thomas JEFFERSON.

Works by Roger Williams

A Key into the Language of America. Bedford, Mass.: Applewood Books, 1997.

The Complete Writings of Roger Williams. New York: Russell and Russell, 1963.

A Work about Roger Williams

Gaustad, Edwin S. *Roger Williams: Prophet of Liberty.* Oxford: Oxford University Press, 2001.

Winthrop, John (1588–1649) *historian, essayist*

John Winthrop was born into a family of wealthy clothiers and lawyers in Suffolk, England. He entered Trinity College of Cambridge University in 1602, but left in 1604. He became a magistrate in 1609, studied law, and in 1626 became an attorney in the Court of Wards and Liveries. Winthrop was elected governor of the Massachusetts colony in 1629, and the following year arrived in Charlestown, Massachusetts. The colonists elected Winthrop governor annually until 1634, and then again from 1637 to 1640, 1642 to 1644, and 1646 to 1649, when he died in Boston. As the first governor of Massachusetts, he dealt with such issues as religious freedom, interactions with Native Americans, and the basic survival of the new settlements.

Like his fellow colonist Roger WILLIAMS, he wrote about government and religion. Two of his most important essays are "Arbitrary Government Described" (1644), concerning the legislative and judicial powers of the colonial government, and "Model of Christian Charity" (1629–30), a description of the type of human decency and charity Winthrop expected citizens of the Massachusetts colony to exhibit.

Winthrop also diligently kept a journal, titled *The History of New England 1630–1649*. It was not published until 1825–26, almost two centuries after his death, yet it stands as one of the most complete firsthand accounts of the early years of New England.

Works by John Winthrop

Journal of John Winthrop: 1630–1649. Edited by Richard S. Dunn, et al. Cambridge, Mass.: Belknap/Harvard University Press, 1996.
Short Story of the Rise, Reign and Ruin of the Antinomians, Familists and Libertines that Infected the Churches of New England (1644). Whitefish, Mont.: Kessinger, 2003.

Works about John Winthrop

Aronson, Marc. *John Winthrop, Oliver Cromwell, and the Land of Promise.* Boston: Houghton, Mifflin, 2004.
Bremer, Francis J. *John Winthrop: America's Forgotten Founding Father.* New York: University Press, 2003.
Connelly, Elizabeth R. *John Winthrop: Politician and Statesman.* Langhorne, Pa.: Chelsea House, 2000.
Morgan, Edmund S. *The Puritan Dilemma: The Story of John Winthrop.* Lebanon, Ind.: Pearson, 1998.

Woolman, John (1720–1772)
humanitarian, journal writer

John Woolman is best known for writing a journal that is considered to be one of the finest statements of Quaker life. *Journal and Major Essays,* published in 1774, is a classic of American spiritual experience. Woolman was also a powerful early voice in opposition to slavery, poverty, and war.

A New Jersey Quaker, Woolman was raised in Quaker schools and meetings and began his public ministry at age 22. He carried Quaker ideals of peace and Christian brotherhood across the Atlantic, ranging from the south to Pennsylvania. He worked as a storekeeper, tailor, orchard keeper, teacher, surveyor, and conveyer of deeds, leases, and bills of sale, including bills of sale for human property. Woolman died of smallpox in England while traveling for an antislavery cause.

In his *Journal and Major Essays,* Woolman relates how these transactions troubled him so much that he gave up his job rather than prepare another indenture for servitude or slave transaction. He focuses on his internal process of reasoning leading to his change of vocation. He also gives the reader a view of his private, intimate moment of conversion in this record of personal spiritual experience. The work is historically valuable in Woolman's treatment of the human drama and the injustice of the slave trade in the early United States.

Works by John Woolman

Journal of John Woolman and Plea for the Poor. Eugene, Ore.: Wipf and Stock, 1998.
Walking Humbly with God: Selected Writings of John Woolman. Nashville, Tenn.: Upper Room Books, 2000.

Works about John Woolman

Birkel, Michael Lawrence. *A Near Sympathy: The Timeless Quaker Wisdom of John Woolman.* Richmond, Ind.: Friends United Press, 2003.
Sox, David. *John Woolman: Quintessential Quaker, 1720–1772.* Richmond, Ind.: Friends United Press, 1999.

Wu Chengen (Wu Ch'eng-en) (ca. 1500– ca. 1582) *novelist, poet*

Wu Chengen was born in Kiangsu province in eastern China. His father was a merchant who loved literature, and Wu was noted for his own literary accomplishments at a very young age. Nevertheless, he repeatedly failed the arduous examinations for the imperial civil service. Finally, at the advanced age of 63, he became a provincial magistrate, only to be imprisoned two years later on groundless charges of corruption. After clearing Wu's name, the imperial court offered him another post, which he refused, preferring to devote the remainder of his life to writing.

Wu Chengen composed many works of verse that convey strong emotions. Two volumes of his poems survive, most of them discovered in imperial palaces in Kiangsu many years after his death. He is best known as the presumed author of *The Journey to the West [Hsi Yu Chi]*, an EPIC prose novel that appeared anonymously in 1592, 10 years after his death. Since then, *The Journey to the West* has appeared in many different forms and been the inspiration if not the source for various works. A picture book of the story was published in 1806. In 2000 the movie *Lost Empire*, based upon Wu's book, was released. It tells the story of journalist Nick Orton's search for the lost manuscript of *Hsi Yu Chi*. The book also served as the basis of the Japanese television series *Saiyuki* (*Monkey*, also known as *Monkey Magic*), which ran from 1978 to 1990. Finally, the computer-animated video *Monkey* (1996) by Miles Inada and Evan Carroll is also based upon *The Journey to the West*, as is the popular anime *Dragonball* series.

Critical Analysis

Like all Chinese novels of the Ming dynasty period, *The Journey to the West* was written in the vernacular rather than the formal, officially accepted classical style, and was probably published anonymously to protect its author's reputation. The theory that Wu was the novel's true author appears to have originated in his home province during the 16th century. Not all modern scholars are convinced of Wu's authorship, as there were similar published tales that existed before Wu's version. However, most scholars believe the poet's lifelong "love of strange stories [and] popular novels" (as he wrote in a preface to a collection of classical short stories) is significant evidence in his favor.

Wu was inspired to write *Journey to the West* by the epic pilgrimage of the 7th-century Buddhist monk Hsuan-Tsang (596?–664), who traveled on foot to India, today known as the birthplace of Buddhism. Hsuan-Tsang walked for many years along the fabled Silk Road in search of his faith's sacred texts, called the Sutra. After finding them, he returned to China and began translating the scriptures into Chinese. By Wu's time, Hsuan-Tsang's pilgrimage had become the subject of many fantastic legends, which had already inspired a short verse novel and a six-part drama titled *Monkey*. Wu thus had much source material for his 100-chapter novel.

In "The Story of the Monkey," comprising the first seven chapters of *Journey to the West*, the novel's protagonist Monkey is born from a magical stone egg, learns the supernatural abilities of shape-shifting and flight, and makes himself king of all the monkeys on Earth. Throughout the tale, we see Monkey transform himself into a bird, a beast of prey, and a bug. We also see him dive into the mouth of a dragon to retrieve a horse. Monkey gets into trouble on a visit to heaven, however, as his hunger for knowledge and his abuse of his powers lead to chaos. The god Erhlang subdues him, and Buddha sentences him to live under a mountain for 500 years.

The next five chapters, "The Story of Hsuan-Tsang and the Origin of the Mission to India," recount the life of Hsuan-Tsang (here called Tripitaka), whom the emperor dispatches on a journey to the "Western Paradise," where good Buddhists go after they die. Monkey is given a chance to prove himself by becoming Tripitaka's disciple and protector, and accompanying him on his pilgrimage. Monkey proves his worth by killing beasts, such as a tiger who tries to kill them, and human ruffians who try to steal Tripitaka's horse. Such events continue in the remaining chapters, called "The Pilgrimage to India," in which Wu Chengen recounts 81 separate, supernatural adventures of the monk, Monkey, and two other magical animals. The slow-witted Pigsy and the fish Sandy serve as additional protectors for Tripitaka as they journey to the Western Paradise.

While Monkey is an allegorical character with many complexities and discrepancies, Pigsy is a clear-cut representation of human desire and often sloth. In the "Editor's Notes" to the journal *Figure in the Carpet*, Jian Leng summarizes the characters and what they represent in this way:

> Readers of *Journey to the West* soon realize that the bizarre main characters are, in many ways, archetypical figures representing universal qualities of human nature. [Tripitaka], the monk sent by the king to gather the scriptures, represents "everyman" searching for meaning. The disciple Piggy embodies sensuality and appetite as well as the vitality and energy necessary to undertake a demanding journey. The disciple Sandy represents sincerity. And then, there is Monkey, who symbolizes the undisciplined intellect that must be tamed before the journey—the spiritual transformation—can be undertaken and successfully completed.

During their journey, the four friends, led by the trickster-warrior Monkey, encounter and often do battle with demons, dragons, and gods from Chinese mythology, all of which Wu Chengen vividly describes. Monkey thwarts many of these enemies with a cudgel he can reduce to the size of a needle, which he carries behind his ear. He also visits hell and reads the book of death, in which he notices his own name. He erases it, thus ensuring himself everlasting life. Perhaps most famous, however, is the novel's biting satire of the hidebound, inefficient, and inescapable Chinese bureaucracy. When Monkey visits heaven early in the novel, he meets the Jade Emperor, who is less a mighty divinity than prosaic administrator, presiding over a bloated civil service composed of numerous useless officials with pompous titles who attempt to control every aspect of life on Earth:

> Heavenly carpenters were ordered to build the office of the Great Sage to the right of the Peach Garden. It had two departments, one called Peace and Quiet and the other Calm Spirit. In each were Immortal Officers who attended Monkey wherever he went. A Star Spirit was detailed to escort Monkey to his new quarters, and he was allowed a ration of two jars of Imperial wine and ten sprays of gold-leaf flowers.

Wu's readers immediately would have recognized the analogy between the hierarchy of Wu's heaven and that of China. The scene also points out that Monkey, rather than Tripitaka, is the protagonist in the book. In her article "Getting a Jump on Dragon Ball," Alysson Wyatt states:

> The reason for this, most critics agree, is that Monkey embodies the theme that the original author tried to convey to his readers: a rebellious spirit can defy even the most untouchable of feudal rulers. This idea of defying authority was highly frowned upon in China, as the ideas of Confucianism again took hold over the newer religions in the region, Buddhism and Taoism. Confucianism was returned to its original place as the official orthodoxy of the state of China during the Tang dynasty (c.e. 618) by an iron-fisted ruling body of high-level bureaucrats. Unlike Confucianism, which teaches conformity and proper behavior within an ideal social system, Taoism and Buddhism advocate an approach to life more receptive to new ideas and change. The monk's character was necessary because it masked the importance of Monkey's rebellious nature.

Despite Tripitaka's despairing that he will ever succeed, the novel ends with the band's discovery of the sacred scrolls. For his efforts in defense of his friend the monk, the formerly disreputable Monkey is made a saint, with the new name Buddha Victorious in Strife.

In the words of its translator Arthur Waley, *Journey to the West* is "unique in its combination of beauty with absurdity, of profundity with nonsense. Folk-lore, allegory, religion, history, anti-bureaucratic satire and pure poetry—such are the singularly diverse elements of which the book is compounded."

Journey to the West is widely read in many Asian countries, Europe, and North America. In China, it proved very influential during the Cultural Revolution of the 1960s, when its satirical passages inspired the radical youth cadres who opposed bureaucracy and tradition. Today, the story is seen as both a rejoining of individual spirit and an odyssey in which the characters travel toward Buddhist enlightenment. Monkey's playful humor and Tripitaka's Buddhist-like detachment continue to enthrall readers of all ages and cultures.

Works by Wu Chengen

Monkey: Selections from Hsi Yu Chi. Translated by Arthur Waley. New York: Grove, 1984.

The Journey to the West, 4 vols. Translated by Anthony C. Yu. Chicago: University of Chicago Press, 1977.

Works about Wu Chengen

Dudbridge, Glen. *The Hsi-yu Chi: A Study of Antecedents to the Sixteenth-Century Chinese Novel.* Cambridge: Cambridge University Press, 1970.

Liu Ts'un-jen. *Wu Ch'eng-en, His Life and Career.* Leiden: E.J. Brill, 1967.

Wu Jingzi (Wu Ching-tzu) (1701–1754)
novelist

Wu Jingzi came from a well-educated family in southeastern China. Like others in his family, he was a member of the civil service. His father died when he was a young man, and Wu Jingzi wasted the considerable inheritance he received. His financial problems persisted throughout his life, and he had difficulties at work. In his later life, he chose to withdraw from society.

Wu Jingzi wrote in many genres, including poetry, but he is best known for his novel, *The Scholars (Bulin Waishi [Ju-lin wai-shih]),* sometimes called *Unofficial History of the Literati.* The book was the first satirical novel written in Chinese, and many scholars consider it to be the best of the genre.

The Scholars has an unusual structure; it is more like a collection of short stories with common links than a conventional linear novel. The number of chapters is in dispute, but the earliest known manuscript (1803) includes 55 chapters.

In *The Scholars,* Wu Jingzi attacks the corruption he sees in the government and society of his time. Because of his subject, he purposely avoids using elevated language. In his book *Wu Ching-Tzu,* Timothy Wong points out that "Wu Chingtzu chose to render his novel in a nonliterary language, and thus to place it also into the tradition of vernacular Chinese fiction," thus making it more accessible to the common people.

In contrast to earlier authors such as TANG Xianzu, who drew upon earlier stories or legends, Wu Jingzi took a more personal approach to his writing by basing his characters on people he knew, including himself.

André Levy asserts that the "episodic structure" of *The Scholars* had "a decisive influence on this subgenre at the end of the nineteenth and the start of the twentieth centuries" (*Chinese Literature, Ancient and Classical*). With its modern structure and universal themes, *The Scholars* continues to have worldwide appeal and is considered a classic of Chinese literature.

An English Version of a Work by Wu Jingzi

The Scholars. Translated by Gladys Yang and Yang Hsien-Yi. La Vergne, Tenn.: University Press of the Pacific, 2001.

A Work about Wu Jingzi

Wong, Timothy C. *Wu Ching-Tzu.* Boston: G.K. Hall, 1978.

Wycliffe, John (John Wyclif) (1324–1387)
essayist, translator

John Wycliffe was born in a small town in the county of York, England. Little is known about his childhood or family, but he received a traditional education before studying at the University of Oxford. As a university student, he established a great reputation for his talents and went on to receive a doctorate in theology before being ordained and assuming pastorates in Lutterworth and Lincoln.

Having become a well-known public figure throughout England for his writings and outspoken opinions, Wycliffe was entrusted by the royal family with important diplomatic missions. Though one of these missions was to resolve various conflicts between the pope and the English government, Wyclif was himself first censored and then condemned by the Catholic Church for his unorthodox beliefs and criticism of the clergy.

Wycliffe questioned fundamental teachings of the church in his pamphlets and essays, for the most part written in Latin and devoted to a single theological or philosophical theme. In *The Truth of the Sacred Scriptures* (1378), he argues that Christian faith should be derived directly from the Bible without the mediation of a corrupt church or clergy. Though excommunicated in 1380, he continued to receive support from the English royal family and continued to produce theological works until his death in Lutterworth.

Wycliffe's writings were extremely influential in Protestant theology, but his most important work was his translation of the Bible into English. Working from the Latin Vulgate, he sought to make a text comprehensible for all readers. The result was a text that not only would have important religious implications, but also would, at least indirectly, have a decisive impact on English prose and poetry for centuries to come. His work served as part of the basis of the King James Bible (1611), one of the most important texts in the history of English-language literature.

A Work by John Wycliffe
Select English Writings. Edited by Herbert E. Winn. New York: AMS Press, 1976.

A Work about John Wycliffe
Kenny, Anthony, ed. *Wyclif in His Times.* New York: Clarendon Press, 1986.

Yuan Hungdao (Yüan Hung-tao)

(1568–1610) *poet, nonfiction writer*

Yuan Hungdao was a government official during the last years of the Ming dynasty. He and his brothers, Yuan Zongdao (Yüan Tsung-tao) and Yuan Zhongdao (Yüan Chung-tao), were all writers from a small town, and their group became known by the town's name, the Kung-an School. They wrote at a time noted in Chinese history for its increased intellectual activity. Like their contemporary, dramatist TANG XIANZU, they were innovative in their poetry, rejecting traditional, formal styles for more individual and personal ones.

Yuan Hungdao's poems often address simple moments in life, with titles such as "Writing Down What I See" or "Improvised on the Road." In this excerpt from "Things Experienced," he blends the ordinary elements of the day with the daily news:

> People gossip of invasions in the east;
> rumors fly: "We've sent ships from the
>   north!"

> I buy some Ch'ü-chou oranges, spotted with
>   frost:
> listen all day to famous women singers.
>   (trans. by Jonathan Chaves,
>   Pilgrim of the Clouds)

In addition to writing poetry, Yuan Hungdao wrote many prose pieces, all of which are noted for their expressive language and detail. Yuan Hungdao's poetry and his prose, as well as that of his brothers, laid the early foundations for the modern period of Chinese literature.

An English Version of Works by Yuan Hungdao

Pilgrim of the Clouds: Poems and Essays from Ming China. Translated by Jonathan Chaves. New York: Weatherhill, 1992.

A Work about Yuan Hungdao

Chih-P'ing Chou. *Yuan Hung-tao and the Kung-an School.* New York: Cambridge University Press, 1988.

Zeami (Zeami Motokiyo, Motokiyo Kanze) (1363–1443) *actor, playwright, critic*

Zeami was born in Nagaoka, Japan. His mother was the daughter of a priest, and his father was the great NOH actor and playwright Kannami, also known by his stage name Kanze.

Zeami appeared in plays with his father's acting troupe, the Kanze-za, from a very early age. When he was 12, he and his father performed in front of the third shogun, Yoshimitsu. The young Zeami quickly became a favorite of the 17-year-old shogun and thus procured his first patron.

Yoshimitsu's patronage gave Zeami, a commoner, access to people in the court. One of these was Yoshimitsu's cultural adviser and poet, Nijō Yoshimoto. Whether to gain favor with the shogun or because he was actually fond of the young man, Yoshimoto took Zeami under his wing and taught him appreciation for the finer, more refined pastimes of the aristocrat, such as *renga*, or linked verse.

In 1384 Kannami died, passing on to Zeami, then 22, the direction of his theater troupe, his stage name, and the Noh knowledge and tradition. This was an auspicious time for the young artist, as he enjoyed the threefold advantage of having the shogun for a patron, Nijō Yoshimoto for a friend, and the reputation and theater troupe of his father at his disposal.

This was not to last, however. In 1408 Yoshimitsu died and his son Yoshimochi became the fourth shogun. Yoshimochi had little interest in the Noh drama that Zeami was developing and refining, preferring the more boisterous Dengaku style. Up to this time, Zeami had been revising his father's plays and writing new ones for the Kanze-za, creating more than 90 plays that are still in the Noh repertoire today. His masterpieces include such works as *Takasago* and *Matsukaze*. Under Yoshimochi's rule, however, Zeami was unable to perform his plays and so turned to writing treatises on Noh, critical and philosophical works on the aesthetics of the form. Along with his plays, these critical essays were crucial in refining Noh as a dramatic form. As Hare states in *Zeami's Style: The Noh Plays of Zeami Motokiyo*, "His treatises on performance represent the first pragmatically centered work on aesthetics in Japanese intellectual history."

Zeami's first such treatise, and undoubtedly his most famous, was completed when he was near 40. Entitled *Fūshi Kaden*, it was largely based on his father's experiences and achievements. He also presented several concepts on the aesthetics of Noh. Three of these deserve special note: *yūgen*, a visual sense of beauty that is both mysterious and ineffable; *monomane*, dramatic mimicry; and *hana*, or flower, a metaphor for those qualities that make a

Noh performance successful. These concepts appear again and again in Zeami's work and have defined the art of Noh theater in literary form.

In 1424 Zeami's life was interrupted again when the sixth shogun, Yoshinori, came to power. Yoshinori had no taste for Zeami's Noh aesthetics and revoked all the privileges that Zeami had enjoyed. Still, Zeami continued to write treatises. One of his major works of this time was *Kakyo* (*The Mirror of the Flower,* 1424), a summary of his own experience in the theater, meant to be passed on in confidence to his son Motomasa.

In 1432 Motomasa died. When told to accept his nephew Onnami as his successor, Zeami refused. As a result, he was exiled to Sado Island in 1434. He was 74 years old. When Zeami died, it was unclear whether he was still in exile or had been allowed to return home.

In the *Fūshi Kade,* Zeami said of Noh, "Everything in Noh has its own style, based upon the meaning of the words, for it is language by which the profound meaning is conveyed." Zeami's works of instruction for actors and his thoughtful, detailed theories about the writing and production of Noh plays elevated Noh theater to an art form rivaling the dignity of court poetry. His works, with their dense imagery and textured allusions to myths, legend, and literature, still captivate audiences to this day, earning Zeami his reputation as the greatest playwright in the history of Noh theater.

An English Version of Works by Zeami

On the Art of the No Drama: Major Treatises by Zeami. Translated by J. Thomas Rimer, Yamazaki Masakazu, and Wallace Chappell. Princeton, N.J.: Princeton University Press, 1984.

Works about Zeami

Nogami, Toyochiro. *Zeami and His Theories on Noh.* Tokyo: Hinoki, 1973

Zeami and the No Theatre in the World. Edited by Samuel L. Leiter, et al. New York: Martin E. Segal Theatre Center, 1998.

Selected Bibliography

Abdallah, Sayyid. *Al-Inkishafi: The Soul's Awakening.* Translated by William Hichens. Nairobi: Oxford University Press, 1972.

Acosta, José de. *Natural and Moral History of the East and West Indies.* Whitefish, Mont.: Kessinger Publishing, 2003.

———. *Natural and Moral History of the Indies.* Translated by Frances M. Lopez-Morillas. Raleigh, N.C.: Duke University Press, 2002.

Adachi, Barbara C. *Backstage at Bunraku: A Behind-the-Scenes Look at Traditional Japanese Theater.* New York: Weatherhill, 1985.

Addington, John. *Giovanni Boccaccio as Man and Author.* New York: AMS Press, 1968.

Ainsworth, Peter. *Jean Froissart and the Fabric of History.* Oxford: Clarendon Press, 1997.

Alarcón, Juan Ruiz de. *Truth Can't Be Trusted or the Liar.* Translated by Daikin Matthews. New Orleans, La.: University Press of the South, 1998.

Al-Azmeh, Aziz. *Ibn Khaldun: An Essay in Reinterpretation.* New York and Budapest: Central European University Press, 2003.

Alberti, Leon Battista. *On the Art of Building in Ten Books.* Translated by Joseph Rykwert, Neil Leach, and Robert Tavenor. Cambridge, Mass.: MIT Press, 1991.

Albrecht, Jane White. *Playgoing Public of Madrid in the Time of Tirso de Molina.* New Orleans: University Press of the South, 2001.

d'Alembert, Jean le Rond. *Preliminary Discourse to the Encyclopedia of Diderot.* Translated by Richard N. Schwab. Indianapolis, Ind.: Bobbs-Merrill, 1963.

———. *Preliminary Discourse to the Encyclopedia of Diderot.* Translated by Richard N. Schwab. Chicago: University of Chicago Press, 1995.

Alexander, John T. *Catherine the Great: Life and Legend.* Oxford: Oxford University Press, 1989.

Alfieri, Vittorio. *Of Tyranny.* Edited and translated by Julius A. Molinaro and Beatrice Corrigan. Toronto: University of Toronto Press, 1961.

———. *The Tragedies of Vittorio Alfieri.* Edited by Edgar Alfred Bowrin. Westport, Conn.: Greenwood Press, 1970.

Allan, Sian. *The Plays of Heinrich von Kleist: Ideals and Illusions.* New York: Cambridge University Press, 1996.

Allen, Gay Wilson, and Roger Asselineau. *American Farmer: The Life of St. John de Crèvecoeur.* New York: Penguin, 1990.

Allison, Henry E. *Kant's Transcendental Idealism: An Interpretation and Defense.* New Haven, Conn.: Yale University Press, 2004.

Amaral, Ricardo C. *Jose Bonifacio de Andrada e Silva.* Brazil: Brazilian Communications Group, 1999.

Anderson, Douglas. *William Bradford's Books: Of Plimmoth Plantation and the Printed Word.* Baltimore, Md.: Johns Hopkins University Press, 2003.

Anderson-Gold, Sharon. *Unnecessary Evil: History and Moral Progress in the Philosophy of Immanuel Kant.* Albany: State University of New York Press, 2001.

Appiah, Peggy. *The Pineapple Child and Other Tales from Ashanti.* London: Carlton Books, 1995.

Archer, Robert. *The Pervasive Image: The Role of Analogy in the Poetry of Ausiàs March.* Philadelphia: John Benjamins Publishing Company, 1985.

Arciniegas, Germán. *Knight of El Dorado: The Tale of Don Gonzalo Jiménez de Quesada and His Conquest of New Granada.* Translated by Mildred Adams. Oxford, U.K.: Greenwood, 1968.

———. *Why America? 500 Years of a Name: The Life and Times of Amerigo Vespucci.* Translated by Harriet de Onís. Washington, D.C.: Villegas Editores, 2002.

Aretino, Pietro. *Aretino's Dialogues.* Translated by Raymond Rosenthal and edited by Margaret Rosenthal. New York: Marsilio, 1999.

———. *The Marescalco.* Edited and translated by Leonard G. Sbrocchi and J. Douglas Campbell. New York: Italica, 2003.

Ariew, Roger, and Marjorie Grene, eds. *Descartes and His Contemporaries: Meditations, Objections, and Replies.* Chicago: University of Chicago Press, 1995.

Ariosto, Ludovico. *Orlando Furioso.* Translated by Guido Waldman. New York: Oxford University Press, 1998.

———. *Orlando Furioso: Part One.* Translated by Barbara Reynolds. New York: Viking Press, 1975.

Aristotle. *Aristotle's Theory of Poetry and Fine Art.* Translated by S. H. Butcher. Mineola, N.Y.: Dover, 1955.

Armitage, Angus. *Copernicus: The Founder of Modern Astronomy.* New York and London: Thomas Yoseloff, 1957.

Armstrong, Dorsey. *Gender and the Chivalric Community of Malory's Morte D'Arthur.* Gainesville: University Press of Florida, 2003.

Aronson, Marc. *John Winthrop, Oliver Cromwell, and the Land of Promise.* Boston: Houghton Mifflin, 2004.

Aronson, Nicole. *Madeleine de Scudéry.* New York: Twayne, 1978.

Atalay, Bulent. *Math and the Mona Lisa: The Art and Science of Leonardo da Vinci.* Washington, D.C.: Smithsonian Institution Press, 2004.

Aubigné, Agrippa d'. *His Life, to His Children.* Edited and translated by John Nothnagle. Lincoln: University of Nebraska Press, 1989.

Augustijn, Cornelis. *Erasmus: His Life, Works and Influence.* Translated by J. C. Grayson. Toronto: University of Toronto Press, 1991.

Austin, Mary. *Philip Freneau: The Poet of the Revolution.* Temecula, Calif.: Reprint Services Corporation, 1993.

Avvakum. *The Life of Archpriest Avvakum by Himself.* Translated by Kenneth N. Brostrom. Ann Arbor: Michigan Slavic Publications, University of Michigan, 1979.

Axayacatl of Tenochtitlan. *Flower and Song: Poems of the Aztec Peoples.* Translated by Edward Kissam and Michael Schmidt. Ypsilanti, Mich.: Bilingual Press, 1983.

Aylett, Robert, ed. *Hans Sachs and Folk Theatre in the Late Middle Ages.* Lewiston, N.Y.: Edwin Mellen, 1995.

Baali, Fuad. *Social Institutions: Ibn Khaldun's Social Thought.* Lanham, Md.: University Press of America, 1992.

Bacon, Francis. *Francis Bacon: The Major Works.* Edited by Brian Vickers. New York: Oxford University Press, 2002.

———. *The Advancement of Learning.* Edited by Michael Kiernan. New York: Oxford University Press, 2000.

Bailey, John Cann. *The Claims of French Poetry: Nine Studies in the Greater French Poets.* Freeport, N.Y.: Books for Libraries Press, 1967.

Baine, Rodney M. *Robert Munford, America's First Comic Dramatist.* Athens: University of Georgia Press, 1967.

Baker, Deborah Lesko. *The Subject of Desire: Petrarchan Poetics and the Female Voice in Louise Labé.* West Lafayette, Ind.: Purdue University Press, 1996.

Baker, Denise Nowakowski. *Julian of Norwich's Showings: From Vision to Book.* Princeton, N.J.: Princeton University Press, 1994.

Baker, Mona, ed. *Routledge Encyclopedia of Translation Studies.* New York: Routledge, 2001.

Balbuena, Bernardo de. *The Heroic Poem of the Spanish Golden Age.* Edited by Frank Pierce. New York: Oxford University Press, 1947.

Baldwin, Neil, trans. *Legends of the Plumed Serpent: Biography of a Mexican God.* New York: Public Affairs, 1998.

Banbera, Tayiru. *A State of Intrigue, The Epic of Bamana Segu.* Edited by David C. Conrad. London: Oxford University Press, 1990.

Banks, Joseph. *The Letters of Joseph Banks: A Selection, 1768–1820.* Edited by Neil Chambers. London: Imperial College Press, 2000.

Bartels, Emily C. *Spectacles of Strangeness: Imperialism, Alienation, and Marlowe.* Philadelphia: University of Pennsylvania Press, 1993.

Bartram, William. *William Bartram: Travels and Other Writings.* New York: Library of America, 1996.

Barzun, Jacques, and Ralph H. Bowen, trans. *Rameau's Nephew and Other Works.* Indianapolis, Ind.: Hackett, 2001.

Baskins, Wade, trans. *The Wisdom of Leonardo da Vinci.* New York: Barnes and Noble, 2004.

Beadle, Richard, ed. *The Cambridge Companion to Medieval English Theatre.* Cambridge: Cambridge University Press, 1994.

Beccaria, Cesare. *On Crimes and Punishments.* Translated by David Young. Indianapolis, Ind.: Hackett, 1997.

Bellay, Joachim du. *Ordered Text: The Sonnet Sequences of Du Bellay.* Edited by Richard A. Katz. New York: Peter Lang, 1985.

———. *The Regrets.* Translated by David R. Slavitt. Boston: Northwestern University Press, 2003.

Bembo, Pietro. *Gli Asolani.* Translated by Rudolf B. Gottfried. Bloomington: Indiana University Press, 1954.

———. *The Prettiest Love Letters in the World: Letters between Lucrezia Borgia and Pietro Bembo.* Translated by Hugh Shankland. London: Collins Harvill, 1987.

Bennett, Benjamin. *Modern Drama and German Classicism: Renaissance from Lessing to Brecht.* Ithaca, N.Y.: Cornell University Press, 1986.

Bennett, Evan. *The Maya Epic.* River Falls: University of Wisconsin River Falls Press, 1974.

Benson, Larry D., and Theodore M. Andersson. *The Literary Content of Chaucer's Fabliaux: Texts and Translations.* Indianapolis, Ind.: Bobbs-Merrill, 1971.

Benz, Ernst. *Emanuel Swedenborg: Visionary Savant in the Age of Reason.* Translated by Nicholas Goodrick-Clarke. West Chester, Pa.: Swedenborg Foundation, 2002.

Bergen, Henry, ed. *Lydgate's Fall of Princes.* London: Boydell and Brewer, 1967.

Berger, Harry. *The Absence of Grace: Sprezzatura and Suspicion in Two Renaissance Courtesy Books.* Palo Alto, Calif.: Stanford University Press, 2000.

Bergerac, Cyrano de. *Other Worlds: The Comical History of the States and Empires of the Moon and Sun.* Translated by Geoffrey Strachan. London: New English Library, 1976.

Bermann, Sandra L. *The Sonnet over Time: A Study in the Sonnets of Petrarch, Shakespeare, and Baudelaire.* Chapel Hill: University of North Carolina Press, 1988.

Bermel, Albert. *Farce: A History from Aristophanes to Woody Allen.* New York: Simon & Schuster, 1982.

Bermel, Albert, ed. and trans. *A Dozen French Farces: Medieval to Modern.* New York: Limelight Editions, 1997.

Berry, Alice F. *Charm of Catastrophe: A Study of Rabelais's Quart Livre.* Chapel Hill: University of North Carolina Press, 2001.

Berry, Edward I. *The Making of Sir Philip Sidney.* Toronto: University of Toronto Press, 1998.

Betti, Franco. *Vittorio Alfieri.* Boston: Twayne, 1984.

Beverley, John. *Aspects of Gongora's "Soledades."* Amsterdam: Benjamins, 1980.

Biagioli, Mario. *Galileo Courtier: The Practice of Science in the Culture of Absolutism.* Chicago: University of Chicago Press, 1994.

Bierlein, J. F. *Parallel Myths.* New York: Ballantine Books, 1994.

Birkel, Michael Lawrence. *A Near Sympathy: The Timeless Quaker Wisdom of John Woolman.* Richmond, Ind.: Friends United Press, 2003.

Bishop, Morris. *The Life and Adventures of La Rochefoucauld.* Ithaca, N.Y.: Cornell University Press, 1951.

Bisson, Lillian M. *Chaucer and the Late Medieval World.* New York: Palgrave Macmillan, 2000.

Black, F. G. *The Epistolary Novel in the Late Eighteenth Century.* Eugene: University of Oregon Press, 1940.

Blackburn, Carole. *Harvest of Souls: The Jesuit Missions and Colonialism in North America, 1632–1650.* Montreal: McGill-Queen's University Press, 2004.

Blackie, John Stuart. *The Wisdom of Goethe.* Whitefish, Mont.: Kessinger Publishing, 2004.

Blewett, David, ed. *Passion and Virtue: Essays on the Novels of Samuel Richardson.* Toronto: University of Toronto Press, 2001.

Bloch, Howard R. *The Scandal of the Fabliaux.* Chicago: University of Chicago Press, 1986.

Bloom, Allan. *Shakespeare on Love and Friendship.* Chicago: University of Chicago Press, 1993.

Bloom, Harold. *Geoffrey Chaucer.* Bloom's Modern Critical Views Series. Langhorne, Pa.: Chelsea House Publishers, 2003.

———. *Shakespeare: The Invention of the Human.* New York: Riverhead, 1998.

———. ed. *African-American Poets: Phillis Wheatley through Countee Cullen.* Langhorne, Pa.: Chelsea House, 2001.

Boas, Ralph, and Louise Boas. *Cotton Mather, Keeper of the Puritan Conscience.* Whitefish, Mont.: Kessinger, 2003.

Boccaccio, Giovanni. *Famous Women.* Edited and translated by Virginia Brown. Cambridge, Mass.: Harvard University Press, 2001.

———. *Life of Dante.* Translated by F. G. Nichols. London: Hesperus Press, 2002.

———. *Nymphs of Fiesole.* Translated by Joseph Tusiani. Cranbury, N.J.: Fairleigh Dickinson University Press, 1971.

———. *The Decameron.* Translated by Mark Musa. New York: Signet, 2002.

Boileau-Despréaux, Nicolas. *Nicholas Boileau-Despréaux: Selected Criticism.* Translated by Ernest Dilworth. New York: Bobbs-Merrill, 1965.

Bonansea, Bernardino M. *Tommaso Campanella: Renaissance Pioneer of Modern Thought.* Washington, D.C.: Catholic University of America Press, 1969.

Bondanella, Peter E. *Francesco Guicciardini.* Boston: G. K. Hall, 1976.

Bonhomme, Denise. *What Voltaire Tries to Tell Us.* Lincoln, Neb.: iUniverse, Inc., 2000.

Bontatibus, Donna. *The Seduction Novel of the Early Nation.* East Lansing: Michigan State University Press, 1999.

Bossuet, Jacques-Benigne. *Discourse on Universal History.* Translated by Elborg Forster and edited by Orest Ranum. Chicago: University of Chicago Press, 1976.

———. *Politics Drawn from the Very Words of Holy Scripture.* Translated by Patrick Riley. New York: Cambridge University Press, 1999.

Boswell, James. *Journal of a Tour to Corsica and Memoirs of Pascal Paoli.* New York: Turtle Point Press, 2002.

———. *Life of Johnson.* IndyPublish.com, 2002.

Boulay, F. R. H. *The England of Piers Plowman: William Langland and His Vision of the Fourteenth Century.* Rochester, N.Y.: Boydell and Brewer, 1991.

Bourbon, Anne-Marie, trans. *Debate of Folly and Love: A New English Translation with the Original French Text.* New York: Peter Lang, 2000.

Bowring, John, ed. *Specimens of the Russian Poets,* 2 vols. Boston: Cummings and Hilliard, 1822.

Boyce, Charles. *Critical Companion to William Shakespeare.* New York: Facts On File, 2005.

Brackett, Virginia. *Classic Love and Romance Literature: An Encyclopedia of Works, Characters, Authors, and Themes.* Santa Barbara, Calif.: ABC-CLIO, 1999.

Bradford, M. E. *A Better Guide than Reason: Federalists and Anti-Federalists.* Introduction by Russell Kirk. Somerset, N.J.: Transaction Publishers, 1994.

Bradford, William. *Of Plymouth Plantation.* Introduction by Samuel Eliot Morison. New York: Knopf, 2001.

Bradstreet, Anne Dudley. *The Works of Anne Bradstreet.* Edited by Jeannie Hensley. Cambridge, Mass.: Harvard University Press, 1981.

Bramly, Serge. *Leonardo: The Artist and the Man.* Translated by Sian Reynolds. New York: Penguin Books, 1994.

Branca, Vittore. *Boccaccio: The Man and His Works.* Translated by Richard Monges. New York: New York University Press, 1976.

Brand, Peter, and Lino Pertile. *The Cambridge History of Italian Literature.* New York: Cambridge University Press, 1999; 193–196.

Brandon, James R., ed. *Chushingura: Studies in Kabuki and the Puppet Theatre.* Honolulu: University of Hawaii Press, 1982.

Brandon, James R., trans. *Kabuki: Five Classic Plays.* Honolulu: University of Hawaii Press, 1992.

Brands, H. W. *The First American: The Life and Times of Benjamin Franklin.* New York: Doubleday, 2000.

Brandt, Sebastian. *The Ship of Fools.* Translated by Edwin H. Zeydel. Mineola, N.Y.: Dover, 1988.

Bredero, Gerbrand. *The Spanish Brabanter.* Translated by David H. Brumble III. Binghamton, N.Y.: Medieval and Renaissance Texts and Studies, 1982.

Breitwieser, Mitchell R. *American Puritanism and the Defense of Mourning: Religion, Grief, and Ethnology in Mary White Rowlandson's Captivity Narrative.* Madison: University of Wisconsin Press, 1992.

Bremer, Francis J. *John Winthrop: America's Forgotten Founding Father.* New York: New York University Press, 2003.

Brett, Michael. *Ibn Khaldun and the Medieval Maghrib.* Brookfield, Vt.: Ashgate Variorum, 1999.

Brewer, Derek, and Jonathan Gibson, eds. *A Companion to the Gawain-Poet.* New York: Boydell and Brewer, 1999.

Brown, Charles Brockden. *Three Gothic Novels.* New York: Library of America, 1998.

Brown, Charles Henry. *William Cullen Bryant.* New York: Scribner, 1971.

Brown, Christopher. *Encyclopedia of Travel Literature.* Santa Barbara, Calif.: ABC-CLIO, 2000.

Brown, F. Andrew. *Gotthold Ephraim Lessing.* New York: Twayne, 1971.

Brown, Hilda Meldrum. *Heinrich von Kleist: The Ambiguity of Art and the Necessity of Form.* Oxford: Oxford University Press, 1998.

Brown, Sharon Rogers. *American Travel Narratives as a Literary Genre from 1542 to 1832.* Lewiston, N.Y.: Edwin Mellen Press, 1993.

Bruce, Susan, ed. *Three Early Modern Utopias: Utopia, New Atlantis, the Isle of Pines.* New York: Oxford University Press, 1999.

Bruno, Giordano. *Cause, Principle and Unity and Essays on Magic.* Translated by Robert D. Lucca and Richard J. Blackwell. New York: Cambridge University Press, 1998.

———. *The Expulsion of the Triumphant Beast.* Translated by Arthur D. Imerti. Lincoln: University of Nebraska Press, 1992.

Buffon, Georges-Louis Leclerc. *Natural History, General and Particular.* Translated by William Smellie. Bristol, England: Thoemmes Press, 2001.

Bull, George. *Michelangelo: A Biography.* New York: St. Martin's Griffin, 1995.

Bunyan, John. *The Pilgrim's Progress.* Mineola, N.Y.: Dover, 2003.

Burgaleta, Claudio M. *Jose De Acosta, S.J. (1540–1600): His Life and Thought.* Chicago: Loyola Press, 1999.

Burke, Peter. *Vico.* New York: Oxford University Press, 1985.

Burl, Aubrey. *Danse Macabre: François Villon.* New York: Sutton, 2000.

Burney, Charles. *Memoirs of the Life and Writings of the Abate Metastasio.* Cambridge, Mass.: Da Capo Press, 1971.

Burns, Allan Franck. *An Epoch of Miracles: Oral Literature of the Yucatec Maya.* Austin: University of Texas Press, 1983.

Burns, E. Bradford. *A History of Brazil,* 3rd ed. New York: Columbia University Press, 1993.

Burrows, Ruth. *Ascent to Love: The Spiritual Teaching of St. John of the Cross.* Starrucca, Pa.: Dimension Books, 2000.

Bush, Sargent. *"Introduction." The Journal of Madam Knight, Journeys in New Worlds, Early American Women's Narratives.* Edited by William L. Andrews, 1990: 69–83.

Busoni, Rafaello. *The Man Who Was Don Quixote: The Story of Miguel Cervantes.* New York: Prentice Hall, 1982.

Cabeza de Vaca, Álvar Núñez. *Narrative of Cabeza de Vaca*. Edited and translated by Rolena Adorno and Patrick C. Pautz. Lincoln: University of Nebraska Press, 2003.

———. *The Journey and Ordeal of Cabeza de Vaca: His Account of the Disastrous First European Exploration of the American Southwest*. Translated by Cyclone Covey. Mineola, N.Y.: Dover, 2004.

Cagno, Gabriella di, et al. *Michelangelo*. New York: McGraw-Hill, 2000.

Calder, Martin. *Encounters with the Other: A Journey to the Limits of Language through Words by Rousseau, Defoe, Prevost and Graffigny*. New York: Rodopi, 2003.

Calderón de la Barca, Pedro. *Six Plays*. Translated by Edwin Honig. New York: Iasta, 1995.

Caldicott, Edric E., and Derval Conroy, eds. *Racine: The Power and the Pleasure*. Dublin: University College Dublin Press, 2001.

Cameron, Ann. *The Kidnapped Prince: The Life of Olaudah Equiano*. New York: Random House, 2000.

Cameron, Keith. *Agrippa d'Aubigné*. Boston: Twayne, 1977.

———. *Louise Labé: Renaissance Poet and Feminist*. Oxford, England: Berg Publishers, 1991.

Camões, Luíz Vaz de. *"Dear Gentle Soul,"* in *World Poetry: An Anthology of Verse from Antiquity to Our Time*. Translated by Roy Campbell and edited by Katharine Washburn and John S. Major. New York: Quality Paperback Book Club, 1998; 568.

———. *The Lusiads of Luiz de Camões*. Translated by Leonard Bacon. New York: Hispanic Society of America, 1950.

———. *The Lusiads*. Translated by Sir Richard Fanshawe. Carbondale: Southern Illinois University Press, 1963.

Campanella, Tommaso. *The City of the Sun: A Poetical Dialogue*. Translated by Daniel John Donno. Berkeley: University of California Press, 1982.

———. *The Defense of Galileo*. Edited and translated by Grant McColley. New York: Arno Press, 1975.

Cantemir, Dimitrie. *Dimitrie Cantemir. Historian of South East European and Oriental Civilizations. Extracts from* The History of The Ottoman Empire. Edited by Alexandru Dutu and Paul Cernovodeanu. Bucharest: Association internationale d'études du sud-est européen, 1973.

Carlyle, Thomas. *The Life of Friedrich Schiller*. Edited by Jeffrey Sammons. Columbia, S.C.: Camden House, 1992.

Carman, Glen Edgar. *Cortes, Gomara, and the Rhetoric of Empire*. Ithaca, N.Y.: Cornell University Press, 1993.

Carrió de la Vandera, Alonso. *El Lazarillo: A Guide for Inexperienced Travelers between Buenos Aires and Lima, 1773*. Translated by Walter D. Kline. Bloomington: Indiana University Press, 1965.

Carrithers, David Wallace, Michael A. Mosher, and Paul A. Rahe, eds. *Montesquieu's Science of Politics*. Lanham, Md.: Rowman and Littlefield, 2000.

Carron, Jean-Claude. *François Rabelais: Critical Assessments*. Baltimore, Md.: Johns Hopkins University Press, 1995.

Carver, Jonathan. *A Treatise on the Culture of the Tobacco Plant*. London: Printed by the author, 1779.

———. *The Journals of Jonathan Carver and Related Documents, 1766–1770*. Edited by John Parker. St. Paul: Minnesota Historical Society Press, 1976.

———. *Travels through the Interior Parts of North America in the Years 1766, 1767, and 1768*. London: Printed by J. Walter, 1778.

Cashier, Edward J. *William Bartram and the American Revolution on the Southern Frontier*. Columbia: University of South Carolina Press, 2000.

Casiglia, Christopher. *Bound and Determined: Captivity, Culture-Crossing, and White Womanhood from Mary Rowlandson to Patty Hearst*. Chicago: University of Chicago Press, 1996.

Caso, Adolph. *Alfieri's Ode to America's Independence*. Boston: Branden Press, 1976.

Castanien, Donald Gardner. *El Inca, Garcilaso de la Vega*. Boston: Twayne, 1970.

Castellanos, Juan de. *The Narrative of the Expedition of Sir Francis Drake to the Indies and the Taking by Him of Carthagena*. Translated by Walter Owen. Buenos Aires: n.p., 1952.

Castiglione, Baldessare. *The Book of the Courtier*. Translated by Leonard Eckstein Opdycke. Mineola, N.Y.: Dover, 2003.

Castillo, Bernal Díaz del. *Conquest of New Spain.* Translated by J. M. Cohen. New York: Viking Press, 1963.

———. *The Discovery and Conquest of Mexico: 1517–1521.* Translated by A. P. Maudslay and edited by Genaro Garcia. New York: DaCapo Press, 2004.

Castor, Grahame. *Pléiade Poetics: A Study in Sixteenth-Century Thought and Terminology.* Cambridge: Cambridge University Press, 1964.

Catherine the Great. *Documents of Catherine the Great; The Correspondence with Voltaire and the Instruction of 1767 in the English Text of 1768.* Edited by W. F. Reddaway. New York: Russell and Russell, 1971.

———. *Memoirs of Catherine the Great.* Edited and translated by Lowell Bair. New York: Bantam, 1957.

———. *Two Comedies by Catherine the Great.* Edited and translated by Lurana Donnels O'Malley. Amsterdam: Harwood Academic Publishers, 1998.

Cause-Steindle, Mariangela, and Thomas Mauch, trans. and eds. *The Elegy of Lady Fiammetta.* Chicago: University of Chicago Press, 1990.

Cawley, A. C., ed. *Everyman and Medieval Miracle Plays.* London: J.M. Dent, 1974.

———. *Everyman and Medieval Miracle Plays.* New York: Everyman's Library, 1965.

Çelebi, Evliya. *Evliya Çelebi in Albania and Adjacent Regions: Kosovo, Montenegro, Ohrid.* Edited and translated by Robert Dankoff and Robert Elsie. Boston: Brill, 2000.

———. *Evliya Çelebi in Diyarbekir: The Relevant Section of the Seyahatname.* Edited and translated by Martin van Bruinessen and Hendrik Boeschoten. Leiden, N.Y.: Brill, 1988.

Cervantes Saavedra, Miguel de. *Don Quixote.* Translated by Tobias Smollett. London: Modern Library, 2004.

———. *Don Quixote: The Ingenious Hidalgo de la Mancha.* Translated by John Rutherford. New York: Penguin Books, 2003.

———. *Exemplary Stories.* Edited by Lesley Lipson. Oxford: Oxford University Press, 1998.

———. *The Portable Cervantes.* Translated by Samuel Putnam. New York: Viking Press, 1976.

Cerwin, Herbert. *Bernal Díaz, Historian of the Conquest.* Norman: University of Oklahoma Press, 1963.

Chadwick, Owen. *From Bossuet to Newman.* New York: Cambridge University Press, 1987.

Chaucer, Geoffrey. *The Complete Poetry and Prose of Geoffrey Chaucer.* Edited by John H. Fisher. Boston: Heinle and Heinle, 1990.

———. *Chaucer's Dream Poetry.* Edited by Helen Phillips and Nick Havely. Longman Annotated Text Series. Upper Saddle River, N.J.: Pearson Education, 1997.

———. *The Canterbury Tales.* Translated by Nevill Coghill. New York: Penguin Books, 2003.

Chi Sun Rhee, ed. *The Love of Choon Hyang.* Chapel Hill, N.C.: Professional Press, 2000.

Chih-P'ing Chou. *Yuan Hung-tao and the Kung-an School.* New York: Cambridge University Press, 1988.

Chikamatsu Monzaemon. *Five Late Plays.* Translated by C. Andrew Gerstle. New York: Columbia University Press, 2001.

———. *Four Major Plays of Chikamatsu.* Translated by Donald Keene. New York: Columbia University Press, 1961.

Child, Francis James. *English and Scottish Popular Ballads.* Mineola, N.Y.: Dover, 1965.

Chin In-sook, trans. *A Classical Novel: Ch'un-hyang.* Seoul, Korea: Korean International Center, 1970.

Chocolate, Deborah M. Newton. *Talk, Talk: An Ashanti Legend.* Mahwah, N.J.: Troll Associates, 1993.

Christian Science Monitor. *The Last American Puritan: The Life of Increase Mather, 1639–1723.* Middletown, Conn.: Wesleyan University Press, 1990.

Chweh, Crystal R. *Readings on Cyrano de Bergerac.* San Diego, Calif.: Greenhaven Press, 2001.

Clardy, Jesse. *The Philosophical Ideas of Alexander Radishchev.* New York: Astra Books, 1964.

Clark, David Lee. *Charles Brockden Brown: Pioneer Voice of America.* New York: AMS Press, 1966.

Clark, Margaret Goff. *Their Eyes on the Stars: Four Black Writers.* New York: Garland Publishing, 1973.

Clarke, Samuel, and Roger Ariew, eds. *Correspondence.* Indianapolis, Ind.: Hackett Publishing, 2000.

Clements, Robert J. *Critical Theory and Practice of the Pléiade.* New York: Octagon Books, 1970.

Cleugh, James. *The Divine Aretino.* New York: Stein and Day, 1966.

Cloutier, David. *Hafiz of Shiraz.* Translated by Muriel Rukeyser. Greensburg, Pa.: Unicorn Press, 1988.

Coers, Donald Vernon. *A Review of the Scholarship on Ebenezer Cook and a Critical Assessment of His Works.* College Station: Texas A&M University, University Microfilms, 1974.

Cohen, Edward H. *Ebenezer Cooke: The Sot-Weed Canon.* Athens: University of Georgia Press, 1975.

Coldewey, John C., ed. *Early English Drama: An Anthology.* New York: Garland Publishing, 1993.

Colilli, Paul. *Poliziano's Science of Tropes.* New York: Peter Lang, 1989.

Collis, Maurice. *Cortes and Montezuma.* New York: New Directions Publishing, 1999.

Colton, Robert E. *Juvenal and Boileau: A Study of Literary Influence.* Port Jervis, N.Y.: Lubrecht and Cramer, 1987.

———. *Studies of Classical Influence on Boileau and la Fontaine.* Hildesheim, Germany: Georg Olms, 1996.

Columbus, Christopher. *Across the Ocean Sea: A Journal of Columbus's Voyage.* Edited by George Sanderlin. New York: Harper and Row, 1966.

———. *The Four Voyages.* Translated by J. M. Cohen. New York: Penguin Classics, 1992.

Comenius, Johann Amos. *Selections.* Translated by Iris Urwin. Introduction by Jean Piaget. Paris: UNESCO, 1957.

———. *The Great Didactic of John Amos Comenius.* Translated by M. W. Keatinge. London: A. and C. Black, 1921.

Compayre, Gabriel. *Jean Jacques Rousseau and Education from Nature.* La Vergne, Tenn.: University Press of the Pacific, 2002.

Conley, John, et al., ed. *The Mirror of Everyman's Salvation.* Amsterdam: Rodopi Editions, 1985.

Connelly, Elizabeth R. *John Winthrop: Politician and Statesman.* Langhorne, Pa.: Chelsea House, 2000.

Conroy, Peter V. *Montesquieu Revisited.* New York: Twayne, 1992.

Cook, Ebenezer. *Early Maryland Poetry: The Works of Ebenezer Cook.* Edited by Bernard C. Steiner. Baltimore, Md.: Printed by John Murphy Company, 1900.

Coote, Stephen. *Samuel Pepys.* New York: Palgrave, 2001.

Copernicus, Nicolaus. *Complete Works,* 4 vols. Edited by Pawel Czartoryski. London: Palgrave Macmillan, 1972–1992.

———. *On the Revolutions: Nicholas Copernicus' Complete Works.* Translated by Edward Rosen and edited by Jerzy Dobrzycki. Baltimore, Md.: Johns Hopkins University Press, 1992.

———. *Three Copernican Treatises.* Translated by Edward Rosen. Mineola, N.Y.: Dover, 2004.

Corneille, Pierre. *"Of the Three Unities." The Continental Model: Selected French Critical Essays of the Seventeenth Century.* Edited by Scott Elledge and Donald Schier. Minneapolis: University of Minnesota Press, 1960.

Cornwell, Neil, ed. *The Routledge Companion to Russian Literature.* New York: Routledge, 2003.

Corrigan, Robert, ed. *Classical Tragedy.* New York: Applause Books, 1991.

Cortés, Hernán. *Letters from Mexico.* Translated by Anthony Pagden. New Haven, Conn.: Yale University Press, 2001.

Corthell, Ronald. *Ideology and Desire in Renaissance Poetry: The Subject of Donne.* Detroit: Wayne State University Press, 1997.

Corum, Robert T. *Reading Boileau: An Integrative Study of the Early Satires, vol. 15.* West Lafayette, Ind.: Purdue University Press, 1997.

Cottingham, John. *Rationalism.* Bristol, England: Thoemmes Press, 1998.

Cottingham, John, ed. *The Cambridge Companion to Descartes.* New York: Cambridge University Press, 1992.

Cottrell, Robert D. *The Grammar of Silence: A Reading of Marguerite de Navarre's Poetry.* Washington, D.C.: Catholic University of America Press, 1986.

Courlander, Harold, and Ousmane Sako. *The Heart of the Ngoni, Heroes of the African Kingdom of Segu.* New York: Crown, 1982.

Courlander, Harold. *A Treasury of African Folklore.* New York: Marlowe and Company, 2002.

Coward, David, trans. *The Figaro Trilogy.* New York: Oxford University Press, 2003.

Craven, William G. *Giovanni Pico della Mirandola: Symbol of His Age: Modern Interpretations.* Geneva: Librairie Droz, 1981.

Crèvecoeur, Hector St. John de. *Letters from an American Farmer.* Edited by Susan Manning. Oxford: Oxford University Press, 1998.

———. *More Letters from an American Farmer: An Edition of the Essays in English Left Unpublished by Crèvecoeur.* Edited by Dennis D. Moore. Athens: University of Georgia Press, 1995.

Crompton, Samuel Willard. *Desiderius Erasmus.* Langhorne, Pa.: Chelsea House, 2004.

Crone, Anna Lisa. *Daring of Derzhavin: The Moral and Aesthetic Independence of the Poet in Russia.* Columbus, Ohio: Slavica Publishers, 2001.

Cronk, Nicholas. *The Classical Sublime and the Language of Literature.* Charlottesville, Va.: Rookwood, 2002.

Crowder, Richard. *No Featherbed to Heaven: A Biography of Michael Wigglesworth, 1631–1705.* East Lansing: Michigan State University Press, 1961.

Crowe, Ivan. *Copernicus.* Gloucestershire, England: Tempus Publishing, 2004.

Crumey, Andrew. *D'Alemebert's Principle.* New York: St. Martin's Press, 1998.

Cruz, Sor Juana Inés de la. *Sor Juana's Love Poems.* Translated by Joan Larkin and Jaime Manrique. New York: Painted Leaf Press, 1997.

Cunningham, Charles E. *Timothy Dwight.* New York: Macmillan, 1942.

Cunninghame, Graham, R. B. *A Vanished Arcadia: Being Some Account of the Jesuits in Paraguay.* New York: Haskell House, 1968 [1901].

Darnton, Robert. *The Business of Enlightenment: A Publishing History of the Encyclopedia, 1775–1800.* Cambridge, Mass.: Harvard University Press, 1979.

Davidson, Cathy N. *Revolution and the Word: The Rise of the Novel in America.* New York: Oxford University Press, 1986.

Davidson, Hugh M. *Blaise Pascal.* Boston: Twayne, 1983.

Davie, Mark. *Half-Serious Rhymes: The Narrative Poetry of Luigi Pulci.* Dublin: Irish Academic Press, 1997.

Davis, James Herbert, Jr. *Fénelon.* Boston: Twayne, 1979.

Davis, Jessica Milner. *Farce.* New Brunswick, N.J.: Transaction, 2003.

Dean, John W. *Memoir of the Revised. Michael Wigglesworth, Author of the Day of Doom.* Murrieta, Calif.: New Library Press, 2003.

Defoe, Daniel. *A General History of Pyrates.* Edited by Manuel Schonhorn. New York: Dover, 1999.

———. *Memoirs of an English Officer and Two Other Short Novels.* London: Victor Gollancz, 1970.

———. *The Shortest Way with the Dissenters and Other Pamphlets.* Oxford: Basil Blackwell, 1927.

———. *The Travel and Historical Writings of Daniel Defoe.* Edited by W. R. Owens and P. N. Furbank. London: Pickering and Chatto, 2002.

DeGrazia, Sebastian. *Machiavelli in Hell.* New York: Vintage Books, 1989.

DeGroot, Jack. *Intertextuality through Obscurity: The Poetry of Federico Garcia Lorca and Luis de Gongora.* New Orleans: University Press of the South, 2003.

DeJean, Joan. *Tender Geographies: Women and the Origins of the Novel in France.* New York: Columbia University Press, 1991.

Della Casa, Giovanni. *Galateo.* Translated by Konrad Eisenbichler and Kenneth R. Bartlett. Toronto: Centre for Reformation and Renaissance Studies, 1986.

———. *Giovanni della Casa's Poem Book.* Edited by John Van Sickle. Binghamton, N.Y.: Medieval and Renaissance Texts and Studies, 1999.

DeLoss Love, William. *Samson Occom and the Christian Indians of New England.* Syracuse, N.Y.: Syracuse University Press, 1999.

Derzhavin, Gavriil Romanovich. *Poetic Works.* Translated by Alexander Levitsky and Martha T. Kitchen. Providence, R.I.: Brown University, 2001.

Descartes, René. *Discourse on Method and Meditations on First Philosophy,* 4th ed. Translated by Donald Cress. Indianapolis, Ind.: Hackett Publishing, 1999.

———. *Discourse on Method and The Meditations.* Translated by F. E. Sutcliffe. New York: Penguin Books, 1998.

———. *Philosophical Essays and Correspondence.* Edited by Roger Ariew. Indianapolis, Ind.: Hackett Publishing, 2000.

———. *The Philosophical Writings of Descartes,* vol. 1. Edited by John Cottingham, et al. New York: Cambridge University Press, 1985.

———. *Treatise of Man.* Translated by Thomas Steele Hall. New York: Prometheus Books, 2003.

Descartes, René, and Gottfried Wilhelm Leibniz. *Rationalists: Five Basic Works on Rationalism.* New York: Doubleday, 1989.

DeSousa, Geraldo U. *Shakespeare's Cross-Cultural Encounters.* New York: St. Martin's Press, 1999.

Dickinson, John. *Letters from a Farmer in Pennsylvania to the Inhabitants of the British Colonies.* Murrieta, Calif.: Classic Textbooks, 2003.

———. *The Political Writings of John Dickinson.* Edited by Paul Leicester Ford. New York: DaCapo Press, 1970.

Diderot, Denis. *A Diderot Pictorial Encyclopedia of Trades and Industry.* Edited by Charles C. Gillispie. Mineola, N.Y.: Dover, 1994.

———. *Denis Diderot's The Encyclopedia; Selections.* Edited and translated by Stephen J. Gendzier. New York: Harper and Row, 1967.

———. *Jacques the Fatalist and His Master.* Translated by David Coward. Oxford: Oxford University Press, 1999.

———. *Rameau's Nephew and d'Alembert's Dream.* Translated by Leonard Tancock. New York: Penguin Classics, 1976.

———. *Selected Philosophical Writings.* Cambridge: Cambridge University Press, 1953.

———. *Thoughts on the Interpretation of Nature and Other Philosophical Works.* Translated by Lorna Sandler and David Adams. Manchester, England: Clinamen Press, 2000.

Dominian, Helen G. *Apostle of Brazil: The Biography of Padre José de Anchieta.* New York: Exposition Press, 1958.

Donne, John. *John Donne's Sermons on the Psalms and Gospels: With a Selection of Prayers and Meditations.* Edited by Evelyn M. Simpson. Berkeley: University of California Press, 2003.

———. *The Complete English Poems.* New York: Penguin, 1971.

———. *The Sermons of John Donne.* Edited by George R. Potter and Evelyn Simpson. Berkeley: University of California Press, 1984.

Downer, Lesley. *On the Narrow Road: Journey into a Lost Japan.* New York: Summit Books, 1989.

Drake, Dana, and Jose A. Madrigal. *Studies in the Spanish Golden Age: Cervantes and Lope de Vega.* Miami: Ediciones Universal, 2001.

Dryden, John. "Absalom and Achitophel," in *Selected Poetry and Prose of John Dryden.* Edited by Earl Miner. Los Angeles: Random House, 1969.

———. "An Essay of Dramatic Poesy," in *Critical Theory Since Plato.* Edited by Hazard Adams. New York: Harcourt Brace Jovanovich, 1992.

Dudbridge, Glen. *The Hsi-yu Chi: A Study of Antecedents to the Sixteenth-Century Chinese Novel.* Cambridge: Cambridge University Press, 1970.

Dunbar, William. *William Dunbar: Selected Poems.* Edited by Harriet H. Wood. London: Routledge, 2003.

Dusen, Wilson Van. *The Presence of Other Worlds.* West Chester, Pa.: Swedenborg Foundation, 2004.

Duval, John, trans. *Cuckolds, Clerics, and Countrymen: Medieval French Fabliaux.* Fayetteville: University of Arkansas Press, 1982.

Dwight, Timothy. *America; or, A Poem on the Settlement of the British Colonies.* New Haven, Conn.: T.&S. Green, 1780.

———. *Greenfield Hill.* New York: AMS Press, 1970.

———. *The Conquest of Canaan; A Poem in Eleven Books.* Westport, Conn.: Greenwood Press, 1970.

Earle, T. F. *The Muse Reborn, The Poetry of António Ferreira.* New York: Oxford University Press, 1988.

Eaves, T. C. Duncan, and Ben D. Kimpel. *Samuel Richardson: A Biography.* Oxford: Clarendon Press, 1971.

Ebin, Lois A. *John Lydgate.* Boston: Twayne, 1985.

Eckermann, Johann. *Conversations of Goethe.* Translated by John Oxenford. New York: DaCapo Press, 1998.

Edmonson, Munro S., trans. *The Ancient Future of the Itza: The Book of Chilam Balam of Tizimin.* Austin: University of Texas Press, 1982.

———. *Heaven Born Merida and Its Destiny, The Book of Chilam Balam of Chumayel.* Austin: University of Texas Press, 1986.

Edwards, David L. *John Donne: Man of Flesh and Spirit.* Grand Rapids, Mich.: Eerdmans, 2002.

Edwards, Jonathan. *A Jonathan Edwards Reader.* Edited by Harry S. Stout and Kenneth P. Minkema. New Haven, Conn.: Yale University Press, 1995.

———. *The Sermons of Jonathan Edwards: A Reader.* Edited by Wilson H. Kimnach, Kenneth P. Minkema, and Douglas A. Sweeney. New Haven, Conn.: Yale University Press, 1999.

Eichner, Hans. *Friedrich Schlegel.* New York: Twayne, 1970.

Eliot, John. *John Eliot's Indian Dialogues.* Edited by Henry W. Bowden and James P. Ronda. Westport, Conn.: Greenwood Press, 1980.

———. *The Bay Psalm Book, a facsimile reprint of the first edition of 1640.* Chicago: University of Chicago Press, 1956.

———. *The Eliot Tracts.* Edited by Michael P. Clark. Westport, Conn.: Praeger, 2003.

Eliot, T. S. *Elizabethan Dramatists.* London: Faber, 1963.

Empson, William. *Some Versions of Pastoral.* London: Chatto and Windus, 1935.

Equiano, Olaudah. *The Interesting Narrative of the Life of Olaudah Equiano, or Gustavus Vassa, the African.* New York: Random House, 2004.

Erasmus, Desiderius. *Adages of Erasmus.* Translated by Margaret Mann Phillips. Cambridge: Cambridge University Press, 1964.

———. *Erasmus on Women.* Edited by Erika Rummel. Ontario: University of Toronto Press, 1996.

———. *In Praise of Folly.* Translated by Clarence Miller. New Haven, Conn.: Yale University Press, 1979.

———. *Selections from Erasmus.* IndyPublish.com, 2004.

———. *The Praise of Folly and Other Writings.* Edited by Robert M. Adams. New York: W.W. Norton, 1989.

Erdmann, Axel. *Lydgate's Siege of Thebes I.* London: Boydell and Brewer, 1996.

Ewan, Joseph. *William Bartram: Botanical and Zoological Drawings, 1756–1788. Reproduced from the Fothergill Album in the British Museum (Natural History).* Philadelphia: American Philosophical Society, 1958.

Falco, Maria J., ed. *Feminist Interpretations of Niccolo Machiavelli.* University Park: Pennsylvania State University Press, 2004.

Falvo, Joseph D. *The Economy of Human Relations: Castiglione's Libro del Cortegiano.* New York: Peter Lang, 1992.

Faulkner, John Alfred. *Erasmus: The Scholar.* Miami, Fla.: International Law and Taxation, 2003.

Fein, David A. *François Villon Revisited.* New York: Twayne, 1997.

Fellows, Otis. *Diderot.* Boston: Twayne, 1989.

Fénelon, François de. *Meditations on the Heart of God.* Edited by Hal M. Helms. Orleans, Mass.: Paraclete Press, 1997.

———. *Telemachus.* Edited by Patrick Riley. New York: Cambridge University Press, 1994.

Fenollosa, Ernest, and Ezra Pound. *'Noh' or Accomplishment: A Study of the Classical Stage of Japan.* Gretna, La.: Pelican Publishing, 1999.

Fernandez de Lizardi, Jose. *The Itching Parrot.* Translated by Eugene Pressley and Katherine Anne Porter. Garden City, N.Y.: Doubleday, 1942.

———. *The Mangy Parrot.* Translated by David Frye. Indianapolis, Ind.: Hackett Publishing, 2004.

Ferreira, António. *The Comedy of Bristo, or, The Pimp (Comédia do Fanchono ou de Bristo).* Translated by John R. C. Martyn. Ottawa, Canada: Dovehouse Editions, 1990.

———. *The Tragedy of Ines de Castra.* Translated by John R. C. Martyn. Coimbra, Portugal: Universidad de Coimbra, 1987.

Ficino, Marsilio. *Three Books on Life.* Edited by Carol V. Kaske and John R. Clark. Binghamton, N.Y.: Medieval and Renaissance Texts and Studies, 1989.

Field, P. J. C. *The Life and Times of Sir Thomas Malory.* Rochester, N.Y.: Boydell and Brewer, 1999.

Finucci, Valeria. *Renaissance Transactions: Ariosto and Tasso.* Raleigh, N.C.: Duke University Press, 1999.

Fish, Cheryl J. *Black and White Women's Travel Narratives: Antebellum Explorations.* Gainesville: University Press of Florida, 2004.

Fish, Stanley Eugene. *How Milton Works.* Cambridge, Mass.: Harvard University Press, 2001.

Fisher, John H. *John Gower: Moral Philosopher and Friend of Chaucer.* New York: New York University Press, 1964.

Fitzpatrick, Ann. *Forgotten Voyager: The Story of Amerigo Vespucci.* Minneapolis, Minn.: Lerner Publishing Group, 1991.

Florescano, Enrique, and Lysa Hochroth, trans. *The Myth of Quetzalcoatl.* Baltimore, Md.: Johns Hopkins University Press, 2002.

Flower, Milton E. *John Dickinson: Conservative Revolutionary.* Charlottesville: University Press of Virginia, 1983.

Flynn, Gerard. *Sor Juana Inés de la Cruz.* New York: Twayne 1971.

Foakes, R. A. *Hamlet versus Lear: Cultural Politics and Shakespeare's Art.* New York: Cambridge University Press, 2004.

Foster, David William. *Luis de Góngora.* New York: Twayne, 1973.

Fox, John. *The Lyric Poetry of Charles d' Orléans.* Oxford: Clarendon Press, 1969.

Fox, Robert, ed. *Thomas Harriot: An Elizabethan Man of Science.* Burlington, Vt.: Ashgate, 2000.

Frame, Donald M. *François Rabelais: A Study.* New York: Harcourt Brace Jovanovich, 1977.

Francis, R. A. *Prévost, Manon Lescaut.* London: Grant and Cutler, 1993.

Franco, Jean. *An Introduction to Spanish-American Literature.* Cambridge: Cambridge University Press, 1995.

Franklin, Benjamin. *A Benjamin Franklin Reader.* Edited by Walter Isaacson. New York: Simon & Schuster, 2003.

———. *Autobiography and Other Writings.* Oxford: Oxford University Press, 1993.

———. *Wit and Wisdom from Poor Richard's Almanack.* Edited by Steve Martin. Introduction by Dave Barry. New York: Random House, 2000.

Freneau, Philip Morin. *Poems, 1786 and Miscellaneous Works (1778) of Philip Freneau.* Delmar, N.Y.: Scholars Facsimiles & Reprints, 1975.

———. *The Last Poems of Philip Freneau.* Temecula, Calif.: Reprint Services Corporation, 1993.

Friedlander, Eli. *J. J. Rousseau: An Afterlife of Words.* Cambridge, Mass.: Harvard University Press, 2004.

Froissart, Jean. *Chronicles.* Translated by John Joliffe. New York: Penguin Books, 2001.

———. *Jean Froissart: An Anthology of Narrative and Lyric Poetry.* Edited by K. M. Figg and R. B. Palmer. New York: Routledge, 2001.

Frye, Prosser H. *Romance and Tragedy.* Norman: University of Oklahoma Press, 1980.

Fubini, Riccardo. *Humanism and Secularization: From Petrarch to Valla.* Translated by Martha King. Raleigh, N.C.: Duke University Press, 2003.

Fumaroli, Marc, and Jean Marie Todd, trans. *The Poet and the King: Jean de la Fontain and His Century.* South Bend, Ind.: University of Notre Dame Press, 2002.

Galilei, Galileo. *Achievements of Galileo.* Edited and translated by James D. Brophy and Henry Paolucci. Toronto: Griffon House, 2003.

———. *Dialogue Concerning the Two Chief Systems of the World.* Translated by Stillman Drake. New York: Modern Library, 2001.

———. *Discoveries and Opinions of Galileo.* Translated by Drake Stillman. New York: Doubleday, 1989.

Gallyon, Margaret. *Margery Kempe of Lynne and Medieval England.* Norwich: Canterbury Press, 1995.

Galoppe, Raul. *Tirso de Molina: His Originality Then and Now.* Edited by Henry Sullivan. Toronto: Dovehouse Editions, 1996.

Gama, José Basilio da. *The Uruguay: A Historical Romance of South America.* Berkeley: University of California Press, 1982.

Ganss, George E. *Ignatius of Loyola: Spiritual Exercises and Selected Works.* Mahwah, N.J.: Paulist Press, 1991.

Gascoine, John. *Science in the Service of Empire: Joseph Banks, the British State, and the Uses of Science in the Age of Revolution.* New York: Cambridge University Press, 1998.

Gates, Henry Louis. *The Trials of Phillis Wheatley: America's First Black Poet and Encounters with the Founding Fathers.* New York: Basic Books, 2003.

Gatta, John. *Gracious Laughter: The Meditative Wit of Edward Taylor.* Columbia: University of Missouri Press, 1989.

Gatti, Hilary. *The Renaissance Drama of Knowledge: Giordano Bruno in England.* New York: Routledge, 1989.

Gaukroger, Stephen. *Francis Bacon and the Transformation of Early-Modern Philosophy.* New York: Cambridge University Press, 2001.

Gaustad, Edwin S. *Roger Williams: Prophet of Liberty.* Oxford: Oxford University Press, 2001.

Gay, Peter. *The Enlightenment: The Science of Freedom.* New York: W.W. Norton, 1996.

Genesis: Captain John Smith and the Founding of Virginia. New York: HarperCollins, 1995.

George, Monteiro. *The Presence of Camões: Influences on the Literature of England, America and Southern Africa.* Lexington: University of Kentucky Press: 1996.

Gerould, Gordon Hall. *The Ballad of Tradition.* Oxford: Clarendon Press, 1932.

Gerstle, Andrew C. "Heroic Honor: Chikamatsu and the Samurai Ideal," *Harvard Journal of Asiatic Studies* (December 1977): 307–382.

———. *Circles of Fantasy: Convention in the Plays of Chikamatsu.* Cambridge, Mass.: Harvard University Press, 1986.

Gerstle, Andrew C., Kiyoshi Inobe, and William Malm. *Theater as Music: The Bunraku Play "Mt. Imo and Mt. Se."* Ann Arbor: University of Michigan, 1990.

Gillmor, Frances. *Flute of the Smoking Mirror: A Portrait of Nezahualcoyotl, Poet-King of the Aztecs.* Salt Lake City: University of Utah Press, 1983.

Gilman, Donald, ed. *Everyman and Company.* New York: AMS Press, 1989.

Gilroy, Amanda, ed. *Romantic Geographies: Discourses of Travel, 1775–1844.* New York: St. Martin's Press, 2000.

Gingerich, Owen. *The Book Nobody Read: Chasing the Revolutions of Nicolaus Copernicus.* New York: Walker, 2004.

Godman, Peter. *From Poliziano to Machiavelli.* Princeton, N.J.: Princeton University Press, 1998.

Goethe, Johann Wolfgang von. *Erotic Poems.* Edited by Hans R. Vaget and translated by David Luke. New York: Oxford University Press, 1999.

———. *Faust.* Edited by Cyrus Hamlin and translated by Walter W. Arndt. New York: W.W. Norton, 2000.

———. *Italian Journey.* Translated by Elizabeth Mayer. New York: Penguin, 1992.

———. *The Sorrows of Young Werther and Selected Writings.* Translated by Catherine Hutter. New York: New American Library, 1987.

———. *The Works of Johann Wolfgang Von Goethe,* vol. 1. IndyPublish.com, 2004.

Goldoni, Carlo. *Carlo Goldoni's Villeggiatura Trilogy.* Translated by Robert Cornthwaite. Lyme, N.H.: Smith and Kraus, 1995.

———. *The Comedies of Carlo Goldoni.* Westport, Conn.: Hyperion Press, 1978.

———. *The Servant of Two Masters.* Adapted by Dorothy Louise. Chicago: Ivan R. Dee, 2003.

Gollub, Matthew. *Cool Melons—Turn to Frogs! The Life and Poems of Issa.* New York: Lee and Low Books, 1998.

Góngora y Argote, Luis de. *Las Soledades.* Translated by Philip Polack. London: Bristol Classical Press, 1997.

———. *Selected Shorter Poems.* London: Anvil Press Poetry, 1995.

———. *The Fable of Polythemus and Galatea.* Translated by Miroslav John Hanak. New York: Peter Lang, 1988.

———. *The Sonnets of Luis de Gongora.* Translated by R. P. Calcraft. Durham: University of North Carolina Press, 1980.

Goodkin, Richard E. *Birth Marks: The Tragedy of Primogeniture in Pierre Corneille, Thomas Corneille, and Jean Racine.* Philadelphia: University of Pennsylvania Press, 2000.

Goodman, Edward J. *The Explorers of South America.* Norman: University of Oklahoma Press, 1992.

Gordon, Helen Heightsman. *Voice of the Vanquished: The Story of the Slave Marina and Hernan Cortes.* New York: New York University Editions, 1995.

Gossen, Gary H. *Telling Maya Tales.* New York: Routledge, 1999.

Graffigny, Madame Françoise de. *Letters from a Peruvian Woman.* Translated by David Kornacker. New York: Modern Language Association of America, 1993.

Grafton, Anthony. *Leon Battista Alberti: Master Builder of the Italian Renaissance.* New York: Hill and Wang, 2000.

Grauer, Ben. *How Bernal Díaz's "True History" Was Reborn.* New York: B. Grauer, 1955.

Greenblatt, Miriam. *Lorenzo de' Medici and Renaissance Italy.* Tarrytown, N.Y.: Marshall Cavendish, 2002.

Greenblatt, Stephen. *Hamlet in Purgatory.* Princeton, N.J.: Princeton University Press, 2001.

———. *Renaissance Self-Fashioning: From More to Shakespeare.* Chicago: University of Chicago Press, 1984.

Greene, E. J. H. *Marivaux.* Toronto: Toronto University Press, 1965.

Greer, Allan, ed. *The Jesuit Relations: Natives and Missionaries in Seventeenth-Century North America.* Boston: Bedford/St. Martin's, 2000.

Grendel, Frederic. *Beaumarchais: The Man Who Was Figaro.* New York: HarperCollins, 1977.

Grendler, Paul, et al., eds. *Renaissance Encyclopedia for Students.* New York: Charles Scribner's Sons, 2003.

Griffin, Nigel, trans. *Short Account of the Destruction of the Indies.* New York: Penguin, 1999.

Griffin, Robert. *Ludovico Ariosto.* New York: Twayne, 1974.

Griffiths, C. E. J., and R. Hastings, eds. *The Cultural Heritage of the Italian Renaissance.* New York: Edwin Mellen Press, 1993.

Grosholz, Emily. *Cartesian Method and the Problem of Reduction.* New York: Oxford University Press, 1991.

Gudzy, N. K. *"Archpriest Avvakum and His Works,"* in *History of Early Russian Literature.* Translated by Susan Wilbur Jones. New York: Octagon Books, 1970; 378–396.

Guicciardini, Francesco. *Sweetness of Power: Machiavelli's Discourses and Guicciardini's Considerations.* Translated by James B. Atkinson and David Sices. DeKalb: Northern Illinois University Press, 2002.

———. *The History of Italy.* Edited by Sidney Alexander. Princeton, N.J.: Princeton University Press, 1984.

Gullan-Whur, Margaret. *Within Reason: A Life of Spinoza.* New York: St. Martin's Press, 1998.

Gustafson, Thomas. *Representative Words: Politics, Literature, and the American Language, 1776–1865.* New York: Cambridge University Press, 1992.

Gwara, Joseph, and E. Michael Gerli. *Studies on the Spanish Sentimental Romance (1440–1550).* London: Tamesis Books, 1997.

Haac, Oscar A. *Marivaux.* New York: Twayne, 1973.

Háfiz. *Drunk on the Wine of the Beloved: Poems of Hafiz.* Translated by Thomas Rain Crowe. Halifax, Nova Scotia: Shambhala, 2001.

———. *Gift: The Poems by Hafiz, the Great Sufi Master.* Translated by Daniel Ladinsky. New York: Penguin, 1999.

———. *Hafiz of Shiraz: Thirty Poems.* Translated by John Heath-Stubbs. Kincardine, Scotland: Handsel Books, 2003.

———. *New Nightingale, New Rose.* Translated by Richard le Gallienne. Oregon House, Calif.: Bardic Press, 2003.

Haig, Stirling. *Madame de Lafayette.* New York: Twayne, 1970.

Hainsworth, Peter. *Petrarch the Poet.* New York: Routledge, 1988.

Hale, Edward Everett. *Life of Christopher Columbus from His Own Letters and Journals.* IndyPublish.com, 2002.

Halford, Aubrey S. *The Kabuki Handbook.* Rutland, Vt.: C.E. Tuttle, 1956.

Halliday, F. E. *Chaucer and His World.* London: House of Stratus, 2001.

Hamburger, Henri. *The Function of the Predicate in the Fables of Krylov.* Amsterdam: Rodopi, 1981.

Hammon, Jupiter. *America's First Negro Poet: The Complete Works.* Edited by Stanley Austin Ransom. New York: Associated Faculty Press, 1983.

Hammond, Jeffrey A. *Edward Taylor: Fifty Years of Scholarship and Criticism.* Rochester, N.Y.: Boydell and Brewer, 1993.

Hanke, Lewis. *All Mankind Is One: A Study.* DeKalb: Northern Illinois University Press, 1994.

Hankins, Thomas L. *Jean d'Alembert: Science and the Enlightenment.* Oxford: Clarendon Press, 1970.

Hanning, Robert W. *Castiglione: The Ideal and the Real in Renaissance Culture.* New Haven, Conn.: Yale University Press, 1983.

Happe, Peter. *Four Morality Plays.* New York: Viking Press, 1988.

Hariot, Thomas. *A Briefe and True Report of the New Found Land of Virginia.* Edited by Paul Hulton. Mineola, N.Y.: Dover, 1972.

———. *The Greate Invention of Algebra: Thomas Harriot's Treatise on Equations.* Edited by Jacqueline Stedall. New York: Oxford University Press, 2003.

Harrison, Keith, trans. *Sir Gawain and the Green Knight.* New York: Oxford University Press, 1998.

Harrison, Robert L. *Gallic Salt: Eighteen Fabliaux Translated from the Old French.* Berkeley: University of California Press, 1974.

Hart, Pierre R. *G. R. Derzhavin: A Poet's Progress.* Columbus, Ohio: Slavica Publishers, 1979.

Hartel, Anne. *Michel de Montaigne: Accidental Philosopher.* New York: Cambridge University Press, 2003.

Hartley, David. *Patriotism in the Work of Joachim du Bellay: Study of the Relationship between the Poet and France.* Lewiston, N.Y.: Edwin Mellen Press, 1993.

Hartpole-Lecky, William E. *History of the Rise and Influence of the Spirit of Rationalism in Europe.* La Vergne, Tenn.: University Press of the Pacific, 2001.

Harty, Kevin J. *Chester Mystery Cycle: A Casebook.* London: Taylor and Francis, 1992.

Hawcroft, Michael. *Word as Action: Racine, Rhetoric, and Theatrical Language.* Oxford: Oxford University Press, 1992.

Headley, John. *Tommaso Campanella and the Transformation of the World.* Princeton, N.J.: Princeton University Press, 1997.

Heck, Thomas F. *Commedia Dell' Arte: A Guide to the Primary and Secondary Literature.* Lincoln, Neb.: iUniverse, Inc., 2000.

Heine, Stephen. "Tragedy and Salvation in the Floating World: Chikamatsu's Double Suicide Drama as Millenarian Discourse," *Journal of Asian Studies* (May 1944): 367–394.

Helvetius, Claude-Adrien. *Claude-Adrien Helvetius: Philosophical Works.* Bristol, England: Thoemmes Press, 2000.

Henderson, T. F. *Scottish Vernacular Literature: A Succinct History.* Edinburgh, Scotland: Scotpress, 1988.

Henryson, Robert. *Selected Poems of Robert Henryson and William Dunbar.* Edited by Douglas Gray. New York: Penguin, 1998.

Herder, Johann Gottfried. *Philosophical Writings.* Edited and translated by Michael N. Forster. Cambridge: Cambridge University Press, 2002.

Herrera, Robert A. *Silent Music: The Life, Work, and Thought of St. John of the Cross.* Grand Rapids, Mich.: Eerdmans, 2004.

Hesse, Everett Wesley. *Calderón de la Barca.* New York: Twayne, 1967.

Hewett-Smith, Kathleen M. *William Langland's Piers Plowman: A Book of Essays.* New York: Routledge, 2001.

Hilliard, Kevin. *Philosophy, Letters, and the Fine Arts in Klopstock's Thought.* London: Institute of Germanic Studies, 1987.

Hodgson, Richard G. *Falsehood Disguised: Unmasking the Truth in La Rochefoucauld.* West Lafayette, Ind.: Purdue University Press, 1995.

Hoffmann, George. *Montaigne's Career.* Oxford: Oxford University Press, 1998.

Holbach, Paul Henri Thiery. *System of Nature,* vol. 1. Translated by H. D. Robinson and edited by Denis Diderot. Manchester, England: Clinamen Press, 2000.

Hollander, John, ed. *Sonnets: From Dante to the Present.* New York: Knopf, 2001.

Hollander, Robert. *Boccaccio's Dante and the Shaping Force of Satire.* Ann Arbor: University of Michigan Press, 1997.

Holme, Timothy. *A Servant of Many Masters: The Life and Times of Carlo Goldoni.* London: Jupiter Books, 1976.

Homer. *The Odyssey.* Translated by Rodney Merrill. Ann Arbor: University of Michigan Press, 2002.

Honan, Park. *Shakespeare: A Life.* Oxford: Oxford University Press, 1998.

Honour, Hugh. *Neo-Classicism.* New York: Penguin Books, 1996.

Hook, Judith. *Lorenzo de' Medici: A Historical Biography.* London: Hamish Hamilton, 1984.

Hoornaert, R. *Saint Teresa in Writings.* London: Trend and Co., 1931.

Horowitz, Louise K. *Love and Language: A Study of the Classical French Moralist Writers.* Columbus: Ohio State University Press, 1977.

Hsia, C. T. "Love and Compassion in 'Dream of the Red Chamber,'" *Criticism* 5 (Summer 1963): 261–271.

Hugo, Victor. *Oration on Voltaire.* La Vergne, Tenn.: University Press of the Pacific, 2003.

Huizinga, Johan. *Erasmus and the Age of Reformation.* London: Phoenix Press, 2002.

Hume, David. *Essays: Moral, Political, and Literary.* Edited by Eugene F. Miller. Indianapolis, Ind.: Liberty Fund, 1991.

Hus, Jan. *The Church.* Translated by David S. Schaff. Westport, Conn.: Greenwood, 1974.

———. *The Letters of Jan Hus.* Translated by Matthew Spinka. Manchester, England: Manchester University Press, 1972.

Ibn Khaldūn, Abu Zayd 'Abd al-Rahman ibn Muhammad. *An Arab Philosophy of History: Selections from the Prolegomena of Ibn Khaldun of Tunis (1332–1406).* Translated by Charles Philip Issawi. Princeton, N.J.: Darwin Press, 1987.

———. *The Muqaddemah: An Introduction to History.* Translated by Franz Rosenthal. Princeton, N.J.: Princeton University Press, 1969.

Idigoras, J. Ignacio Tellechea. *Ignatius of Loyola: The Pilgrim Saint.* Translated by Cornelius Michael Buckley. Chicago: Loyola Press, 1994.

Irwin, David. *Neoclassicism.* Boston: Phaidon Press, 1997.

Irwin, Robert. *Night and Horses and the Desert: An Anthology of Classical Arabic Literature.* New York, Anchor Books, 1999.

Jacob, Margaret C. *Living the Enlightenment: Freemasonry and Politics in Eighteenth-Century Europe.* Oxford: Oxford University Press, 1994.

Jamieson, Ruth. *Marivaux, A Study in Sensibility.* New York: King's Crown Press, 1941.

Janaway, Christopher. *Schopenhauer: A Very Short Introduction.* New York: Oxford University Press, 2002.

Jardine, Lisa, and Alan Stewart. *Hostage to Fortune: The Troubled Life of Francis Bacon, 1561–1626.* New York: Hill and Wang, 1999.

Jefferson, Thomas. *Light and Liberty: Reflections on the Pursuit of Happiness.* Edited by Eric Petersen. New York: Random House, 2004.

———. *State of the Union Addresses of Thomas Jefferson.* IndyPublish.com, 2004.

———. *The Life and Selected Writings of Thomas Jefferson.* Edited by Adrienne Koch and William Peden. New York: Random House, 2004.

Jensen, Katharine Ann. *Writing Love: Letters, Women, and the Novel in France, 1605–1776.* Carbondale: Southern Illinois University Press, 1995.

Jippensha Ikku. *Shank's Mare or Hizakurige: Japan's Great Comic Novel.* Translated by Thomas Satchell. Rutland, Vt.: Charles E. Tuttle, 1990.

John of the Cross, Saint. *The Collected Works of Saint John of the Cross.* Translated by Kieran Kavanaugh and Otilio Rodriguez. Washington, D.C.: ICS Publications, 1991.

———. *The Poems of Saint John of the Cross.* Translated by Roy Campbell. London: Harvill Press, 2000.

Johnston, William. *The Mysticism of the Cloud of Unknowing.* New York: Fordham University Press, 2000.

Jones, K. R. W. *Pierre de Ronsard.* New York: Twayne, 1970.

Jonson, Ben. *The Alchemist and Other Plays.* Edited by Gordon Campbell. New York: Oxford University Press, 1998.

———. *The Complete Poems.* Edited by George Parfitt. New York: Penguin, 1988.

———. *Volpone.* Edited by Robert Watson. New York: W.W. Norton, 2003.

Jordan, Constance. *Pulci's Morgante: Poetry and History in Fifteenth Century Florence.* Washington, D.C.: Folger Books, 1986.

Julian of Norwich. *A Lesson of Love: The Revelations of Julian of Norwich,* unabridged. Lincoln, Neb.: iUniverse, 2003.

———. *The Revelations of Divine Love of Julian of Norwich.* Translated by James Walsh. St. Meinrad, Ind.: Abbey Press, 1961.

Kant, Immanuel. *A Critique of Judgment.* New York: Barnes and Noble, 2004.

———. *A Critique of Pure Reason.* Edited and translated by Paul Guyer and Allen Wood. Cambridge: Cambridge University Press, 1998.

———. *Groundwork for the Metaphysics of Morals.* New Haven, Conn.: Yale University Press, 2002.

———. *Kant—Metaphysical Foundations of Natural Science.* Edited by Michael Friedman. New York: Cambridge University Press, 2004.

———. *Observations on the Feeling of the Beautiful and Sublime.* Translated by John T. Goldthwait. Berkeley: University of California Press, 2004.

———. *On Education.* Mineola, N.Y.: Dover, 2003.

Kaye, Harvey J. *Thomas Paine: Firebrand of the Revolution.* New York: Oxford University Press, 2000.

Keane, John. *Tom Paine: A Political Life.* New York: Grove/Atlantic, 2003.

Keating, Clark L. *Joachim du Bellay.* New York: Twayne, 1971.

Keenan, Hugh T., ed. *Typology and Medieval English Literature.* New York: AMS Press, 1992.

Keene, Donald. *Seeds in the Heart: Japanese Literature from Earliest Times to the Late Sixteenth Century.* New York: Henry Holt, 1993.

Keene, Donald, trans. *Major Plays of Chikamatsu.* New York: Columbia University Press, 1990.

Keller, Hans-Erich. *Romance Epic.* Kalamazoo: Western Michigan University, 1987.

Kellogg, Frederick. *A History of Romanian Historical Writing.* Bakersfield, Calif.: Charles Schlacks, 1990.

Kelly, Ann Cline. *Jonathan Swift and Popular Culture: Myth, Media, and the Man.* New York: Palgrave, 2002.

Kempe, Margery. *The Book of Margery Kempe.* Edited and translated by Lynn Staley. New York: W.W. Norton, 2001.

Kempis, Thomas à. *The Imitation of Christ in Four Books: A Translation from the Latin.* Translated by Joseph N. Tylenda. New York: Vintage Books, 1998.

Kenny, Anthony, ed. *Wyclif in His Times.* New York: Clarendon Press, 1986.

Kent, F. W. *Lorenzo de' Medici and the Art of Magnificence.* Baltimore, Md.: Johns Hopkins University Press, 2004.

Kenton, Edna, ed. *The Jesuit Relations and Allied Documents: Travels and Explorations of the Jesuit Missionaries in North America (1610–1791).* Introduction by Reuben Gold Thwaites. Toronto: McLelland & Stewart, 1998.

Khatib, Lisan al-Din Ibn al-. *The Jaysh al-tawshih of Lisan al-Din Ibn al-Khatib.* Edited by Alan Jones. Cambridge, England: Trustees of the "E.J.W. Gibb Memorial," 1997.

Kindrick, Robert L. *Robert Henryson.* Boston: Twayne, 1979.

Kinney, Arthur F. *John Skelton, Priest as Poet: Seasons of Discovery.* Chapel Hill: University of North Carolina Press, 1987.

Kirkham, Victoria. *Fabulous Vernacular: Boccaccio's Filocolo and the Art of Medieval Fiction.* Ann Arbor: University of Michigan Press, 2001.

Kitto, H. D. F. *Greek Tragedy: A Literary Study.* New York: Routledge, 2002.

Kleist, Heinrich von. *Heinrich von Kleist: Three Major Plays.* Translated by Carl R. Mueller. Lyme, N.H.: Smith and Kraus, 2001.

———. *The Marquise of O—and Other Stories.* Translated by Martin Greenberg. New York: Ungar, 1973.

Knapp, Bettina L. *Jean Racine: Mythos and Renewal in Modern Theater.* Tuscaloosa: University of Alabama Press, 1971.

Knapp, Bettina Liebowitz. *Voltaire Revisited.* New York: Macmillan Library Reference, 2000.

Knapp, Jeffrey. *Shakespeare's Tribe: Church, Nation, and Theater in Renaissance England.* Chicago: University of Chicago Press, 2004.

Kneib, Martha. *Christopher Columbus: Master Italian Navigator in the Court of Spain.* New York: Rosen, 2003.

Knight, Sarah, trans. *Momus.* Edited by Virginia Brown. Cambridge, Mass.: Harvard University Press, 2003.

Knight, Sarah Kemble. *The Journal of Madame Knight.* Boston: D.R. Godine, 1972.

Knoerle, Jeanne. *The Dream of the Red Chamber: A Critical Study.* Bloomington: Indiana University Press, 1972.

Knox, Edward C. *Jean de la Bruyère.* New York: Twayne, 1974.

Knutson, Harold C. *The Triumph of Wit: Moliere and Restoration Comedy.* Columbus: Ohio State University Press, 1968.

Kobayashi Issa. *Spring of My Life.* Translated by Sam Hamill. Boston: Shambhala, 1997.

———. *The Year of My Life.* Translated by Nobuyuki Yuasa. Berkeley: University of California Press, 1972.

Kochanowski, Jan. *Poems of Jan Kochanowski.* Edited by George R. Noyes, et al. Berkeley: University of California Press, 1928.

———. *Treny: The Laments of Kochanowski.* Translated by Adam Czeriawski and edited by Piotr Wilczek. Oxford: Legenda, 2001.

Koepke, Wulf. *Johann Gottfried Herder: Language, History and the Enlightenment.* Columbia, S.C.: Camden House, 1990.

Kohl, Karin M. *Rhetoric, the Bible, and the Origins of Free Verse: The Early Hymns of Friedrich Gottlieb Klopstock.* New York: W. de Gruyter, 1990.

Kolb, Robert. *Martin Luther as Prophet, Teacher, and Hero: Images of the Reformer, 1520–1620.* Grand Rapids, Mich.: Baker Books, 1999.

Kolve, V. A. *The Play Called Corpus Christi.* Palo Alto, Calif: Stanford University Press, 1966.

Koppisch, Michael S. *Rivalry and the Disruption of Order in Moliere's Theater.* Cranbury, N.J.: Fairleigh Dickinson University Press, 2004.

Kownacki, Mary Lou. *Between Two Should: Conversations with Ryokan.* Grand Rapids, Mich.: Eerdmans, 2004.

Kraul, Edward Garcia, and Judith Beatty. *The Weeping Woman: Encounters with La Llorona.* Santa Fe, N.M.: Word Process, 1988.

Kristeller, Paul Oskar. *Renaissance Thought and Its Sources.* Edited by Michael Mooney. New York: Columbia University Press, 1979.

Krylov, Ivan. *Fifteen Fables of Krylov.* Translated by Guy Daniels. New York: Macmillan, 1965.

———. *Krylov's Fables.* Westport, Conn.: Hyperion Press, 1977.

———. *Russian Satiric Comedy: Six Plays.* Edited and translated by Laurence Senelick. New York: Performing Arts Journal Publications, 1983.

Kuehn, Manfried. *Kant: A Biography.* New York: Cambridge University Press, 2001.

Kuhn, Thomas S. *The Copernican Revolution: Planetary Astronomy in the Development of Western Thought.* Cambridge, Mass.: Harvard University Press, 1957.

Kumar, Krishna. *Utopianism.* Minneapolis: University of Minnesota Press, 1991.

Kuriyama, Constance Brown. *Christopher Marlowe: A Renaissance Life.* Ithaca, N.Y.: Cornell University Press, 2002.

Kynell, Kurt von S. *Mind of Leibniz: A Study in Genius.* Lewiston, N.Y.: Edwin Mellen Press, 2003.

Labé, Louise. *Louise Labé: Sonnets.* Translated by Graham D. Martin. Austin: University of Texas Press, 1972.

———. *Louise Labe's Complete Works.* Edited and translated by Edith R. Farrell. Troy, N.Y.: Whitson Publishing, 1986.

Laclos, Pierre Choderlos de. *Les Liaisons Dangereuses.* Translated by Douglas Parmée. New York: Oxford University Press, 1995.

Lacy, Norris J. *Reading Fabliaux.* Birmingham, Ala.: Summa Publications, 1999.

Lafayette, Madame de. *Madame de Lafayette: The Princesse de Clèves.* Translated by Terence Cave. New York: Oxford University Press, 1999.

———. *The Secret History of Henrietta, Princess of England.* Translated by J. M. Shelmerdine. New York: Howard Fertig, 1993.

La Fontaine, Jean de. *Complete Tales in Verse.* Translated by Guido Waldman. London: Routledge: 2001.

———. *La Fontaine: Selected Fables.* Translated by James Michie. New York: Viking Press, 1979.

Lang, David Marshall. *The First Russian Radical: Alexander Radishchev, 1749–1802.* Westport, Conn.: Greenwood Press, 1977.

Lange, Lynda, ed. *Feminist Interpretations of Jean-Jacques Rousseau.* Preface by Nancy Tuana. University Park: Pennsylvania University Press, 2002.

Lange, Victor. *The Classical Age of German Literature, 1740–1815.* New York: Holmes and Meier, 1982.

Langland, William. *Piers Plowman.* Edited and translated by A. V. C. Schmidt. New York: Oxford University Press, 1992.

Lansperger, Johannes. *Epistle in the Person of Christ to the Faithfvll Soule, Written First by . . . Lanspergivs, and after Translated into English by One of No Small Fame.* Microfilm. Ann Arbor, Mich.: University Microfilms, 1955.

La Rochefoucauld, François, duc de. *Moral Maxims.* Edited by Irwin Primer. Newark: University of Delaware Press, 2002.

———. *The Maxims of La Rouchefoucauld.* Translated by Louis Kronenberger. New York: Random House, 1959.

Larungu, Rute. *Myths and Legends from Ghana for African-American Cultures.* Akron, Ohio: Telcraft Books, 1992.

Le Courreye, Blecki, and Karin A. Wulf, eds. *Milcah Martha Moore's Book: A Commonplace Book from Revolutionary America.* University Park: Pennsylvania State University Press, 1997.

Lee, Meredith. *Displacing Authority: Goethe's Poetic Reception of Klopstock.* Heidelberg, Germany: Universitätsverlag C. Winter, 1999.

Lefevre, Wolfgang. *Between Leibniz, Newton, and Kant: Philosophy and Science in the Eighteenth Century.* Hingham, Mass.: Kluwer Academic Publishers, 2001.

Leitch, Alexander, ed. *Companion.* Princeton, N.J.: Princeton University Press, 1978.

Leitch, Vincent B., ed. *The Norton Anthology of Theory and Criticism.* New York: W.W. Norton, 2001.

Leiter, Samuel L., ed. *The Kabuki Reader: History and Performance.* Armonk, N.Y.: M.E. Sharpe, 2002.

Lemaitre, Jules. *Jean Racine.* Murrieta, Calif.: Classic Books, 2001.

Leonardo da Vinci. *Leonardo on Art and the Artist.* Mineola, N.Y.: Dover, 2002.

———. *The Notebooks of Leonardo da Vinci.* IndyPublish.com, 2003.

———. *The Wisdom of Leonardo da Vinci.* Translated by Wade Baskins. New York: Barnes and Noble, 2004.

Leon-Portilla, Miguel, and Earl Shorris, et al. *In the Language of Kings: An Anthology of Mesoamerican Literature—Pre-Columbian to the Present.* New York: W.W. Norton, 2001.

Leon-Portilla, Miguel. *Aztec Thought and Culture: A Study of the Ancient Nahuatl Mind.* Translated by Jack Emory Davis. Norman: University of Oklahoma Press, 1990.

———. *Fifteen Poets of the Aztec World.* Norman: University of Oklahoma Press, 1992.

Leschemelle, Pierre. *Montaigne: The Fool of the Farce.* Translated by William J. Beck. New York: Peter Lang, 1995.

Lesker, G. A. *Three Late Medieval Morality Plays.* New York: W.W. Norton, 1984.

Lessing, Gotthold. *Laocoon: An Essay on the Limits of Painting and Poetry.* Translated by Edward A. McCormick. Baltimore, Md.: Johns Hopkins University Press, 1990.

———. *Lessing's Theological Writings: Selections in Translation.* Translated by Henry Chadwick. Palo Alto, Calif.: Stanford University Press, 1994.

———. *Nathan the Wise, Minna von Barnhelm, and Other Plays and Writings.* Edited by Peter Demetz. New York: Continuum, 1991.

Lestringant, Frank. "The Philosopher's Breviary: Jean de Léry in the Enlightenment," in *New World Encounters.* Edited by Stephen Greenblatt. Berkeley: University of California Press, 1993.

Lever, Maurice. *Sade: A Biography.* Translated by Arthur Goldhammer. New York: Farrar, Straus & Giroux, 1993.

Levi, Anthony. *Richelieu and the Making of France.* New York: Carroll and Graf, 2000.

Lewalski, Barbara. *The Life of John Milton: A Critical Biography.* Oxford: Blackwell, 2002.

Lewis, C. S. *The Allegory of Love: A Study in Medieval Tradition.* New York: Oxford University Press, 1990.

Lewis, Geoffrey L., trans. *The Book of the Dede Korkut.* New York: Penguin, 1998.

Lewis, Matthew Gregory. *The Monk: A Romance.* Edited by Christopher Maclachlan. New York: Penguin, 1999.

Lincoln, Victoria. *Teresa: A Woman, A Biography of Teresa of Avila.* Albany: State University of New York Press, 1984.

Lincoln, W. Bruce. *Sunlight at Midnight: St. Petersburg and the Rise of Modern Russia.* New York: Basic Books, 2002.

Little, Katharine Day. *François de Fenelon: Study of a Personality.* New York: Harper and Brothers, 1951.

Liu Ts'un-jen. *Wu Ch'eng-en, His Life and Career.* Leiden: Brill, 1967.

Lodge, David. *The Modes of Modern Writing: Metaphor, Metonymy, and the Typology of Modern Literature.* Ithaca, N.Y.: Cornell University Press, 1977.

Loewenstein, Joseph. *Ben Jonson and Possessive Authorship.* New York: Cambridge University Press, 2002.

Lohse, Bernhard. *Martin Luther: An Introduction to His Life and Work.* Translated by Robert Schultz. Philadelphia: Fortress Press, 1986.

———. *Martin Luther's Theology: Its Historical and Systematic Development.* Translated by Roy A. Harrisville. Minneapolis, Minn.: Augsburg Fortress, 1999.

Loloi, Parvin. *Hafiz, Master of Persian Poetry: A Critical Bibliography.* London: I.B. Tauris, 2004.

Lomonosov, Mikhail. *Mikhail Vasil'evich Lomonosov on the Corpuscular Theory.* Translated by Henry M. Leicester. Cambridge, Mass.: Harvard University Press, 1970.

Lope de Vega Carpio. *Desire's Experience Transformed: A Representative Anthology of Lope de Vega's Lyric Poetry.* Translated by Carl W. Cobb. Rock Hill, S.C.: Spanish Literature Publications, 1991.

———. *La Dorotea.* Translated by Edwin Honig and Alan S. Trueblood. Cambridge, Mass.: Harvard University Press, 1985.

———. *Lady Nitwit/La Dama Boda.* Translated by William I. Oliver. Melbourne: Bilingual Press, 1997.

———. *Love's Dialectic: Mimesis and Allegory in the Romances of Lope de Vega.* University, Miss.: Romance Monographs, 2000.

———. *Madness in Valencia and Peribanez.* Translated by David Johnston. Bath, England: Absolute Classics, 1995.

———. *The Best Boy in Spain.* Translated by David M. Gitlitz. Melbourne: Bilingual Press, 1999.

———. *Three Major Plays: Fente Ovejuna, The Knight from Olmedo, Punishment without Revenge.* Translated by Gwynne Edwards. Oxford: Oxford University Press, 1999.

López de Gómara, Francisco. *Conquest of the West India.* Delmas, N.Y.: Scholars' Facsimiles and Reprints, 1940.

———. *Cortés: The Life of the Conqueror of Mexico by His Secretary, Francisco López de Gómara.* Edited by Lesley B. Simpson. Berkeley: University of California Press, 1977.

Lough, John. *Essays on the Encyclopedie of Diderot and D'Alembert.* London: Oxford University Press, 1968.

Ludwin, Dawn M. *Blaise Pascal's Quest for the Ineffable.* New York: Peter Lang, 2001.

Lumiansky, R. M., and D. Mills, eds. *The Chester Mystery Cycle,* vol. 1. Rochester, N.Y.: Boydell and Brewer, 1974.

Lund, Roger, ed. *Critical Essays on Daniel Defoe.* New York: G.K. Hall, 1997.

Lupton, Julia Reinhard. *Afterlives of the Saints: Hagiography, Typology, and Renaissance Literature.* Palo Alto, Calif.: Stanford University Press, 1996.

Luther, Martin. *Bondage of the Will.* Greenville, S.C.: Emerald House Group, 2004.

———. *Luther: Letters of Spiritual Counsel.* Library of Christian Classics Series, vol. 18. Edited by Theodore G. Tappert. Vancouver: Regent College Publishing, 2003.

———. *Works,* 56 vols. Edited by Jaroslav Jan Pelikan, et al. St. Louis: Concordia Publishing House, 1955–86.

Lutz, Nora Jean. *Cotton Mather: Author, Clergyman and Scholar.* Minneapolis, Minn.: Sagebrush Education Resources, 2000.

Lyons, John D., and Mary B. McKinley, eds. *Critical Tales: New Studies of the Heptameron and Early Modern Culture.* Philadelphia: University of Pennsylvania Press, 1993.

Maag, Karin. *Melanchthon in Europe.* Grand Rapids, Mich.: Baker Books, 1999.

Machiavelli, Niccolò. *The Prince.* Translated by Luigi Ricci. New York: Penguin Group, 1980.

———. *Art of War.* Edited by Christopher Lynch. Chicago: University of Chicago Press, 2003.

———. *Discourses on Livy.* Translated by Julia C. Bondanella and Peter Bondanella. Oxford: Oxford University Press, 2003.

———. *Florentine History.* Translated by W. K. Marriott. New York: Barnes and Noble, 2004.

Madariaga, Isabel de. *Catherine the Great: A Short History.* New Haven, Conn. and London: Yale University Press, 2002.

Maddox, Donald, and Sara Sturm-Maddox. *Froissart across the Genres.* Gainesville: University Press of Florida, 1998.

Mahony, Robert. *Jonathan Swift: The Irish Identity.* New Haven, Conn.: Yale University Press, 1995.

Maiden Voyages and Infant Colonies: Two Women's Travel Narratives of the 1790s. Herndon, Va.: Cassell Academic, 1999.

Makemson, Maud Worcester, trans. *The Book of the Jaguar Priest: A Translation of the Book of Chilam Balam of Tizimin.* New York: Henry Schuman, 1951.

Makoto Ueda, trans. *Dew on the Grass: The Life and Poetry of Kobayashi Issa.* The Netherlands: Brill Academic Publishers, 2004.

Makoto Ueda. *Basho and His Interpreters.* Palo Alto, Calif.: Stanford University Press, 1995.

———. *Matsuo Bashō.* New York: Kodansha International, 1983.

Malory, Thomas. *Le Morte D'Arthur: Complete, Unabridged, Illustrated Edition.* Edited by John Matthews. London: Cassell, 2003.

———. *Le Morte D'Arthur: The Winchester Manuscript.* Edited by Helen Cooper. New York: Oxford University Press, 1998.

Manchester, William. *A World Lit Only by Fire.* Boston: Back Bay Books, 1993.

March, Ausiàs. *Ausiàs March: A Key Anthology.* Edited by Robert Archer. Oxford: Anglo-Catalan Society Occasional Publications, 1992.

———. *Ausiàs March: Selected Poems.* Edited by Arthur Terry. Austin: University of Texas Press, 1976.

Mariscal, George. *Contradictory Subjects: Quevedo, Cervantes, and Seventeenth Century Spanish Culture.* Ithaca, N.Y.: Cornell University Press, 1991.

Marivaux, Pierre Carlet de Chamblain de. *Le Paysan Parvenu: or, The Fortunate Peasant.* New York: Garland, 1979.

———. *Pharsamond.* New York: Garland, 1974.

———. *Plays.* London: Methuen, 1988.

———. *Seven Comedies by Marivaux.* Edited by Oscar Mandel and translated by Oscar and Adrienne S. Mandel. Ithaca, N.Y.: Cornell University Press, 1968.

Marlowe, Christopher. *Complete Plays and Poems.* Rutland, Vt.: Charles E. Tuttle, 2002.

———. *Ovid's Elegies* and *Lucan's First Book,* in *Christopher Marlowe: The Complete Poems and Translations.* Edited by Stephen Orgel. Middlesex, England: Penguin, 1971.

Marlowe, Stephen. *The Death and Life of Miguel de Cervantes.* New York: Arcade Books, 1997.

Marot, Clément. *Le Ton Beau de Marot: In Praise of the Music of Language.* Edited by Douglas R. Hofstadter. New York: Basic Books, 1997.

Martin, Peter. *A Life of James Boswell.* New Haven: Yale University Press, 2000.

Martin, Wendy. *An American Triptych: Anne Bradstreet, Emily Dickinson, Adrienne Rich.* Chapel Hill: University of North Carolina Press, 1984.

Martin, Wendy, ed. *Colonial American Travel Narratives.* New York: Penguin, 1994.

Maruli, Marko. *Judita.* English and Croatian. Edited and translated by Henry R. Cooper, Jr. New York: Columbia University Press, 1991.

Mather, Cotton. *Selections from Cotton Mather.* New York: Harcourt Brace, 1926.

———. *A Family Well-Ordered.* Edited by Don Kistler. Morgan, Pa.: Soli Deo Gloria Ministries, 2001.

———. *The Christian Philosopher.* Edited by Winton U. Solberg. Champaign: University of Illinois Press, 2000.

Mather, Increase. *An Essay for the Recording of Illustrious Providences.* Delmar, N.Y.: Scholars' Facsimiles and Reprints, 1977.

———. *Relation of the Troubles Which Have Happened in New England by Reason of the Indians There.* Whitefish, Mont.: Kessinger, 2003.

———. *Remarkable Providences.* Introduction by George Offor. Whitefish, Mont.: Kessinger, 2003.

Matsuo Bashō. *A Haiku Journey: Bashō's "Narrow Road to a Far Province."* Translated by Dorothy Britton. New York: Kodansha America, 2002.

———. *Narrow Road to the Interior, and Other Writings.* Translated by Sam Humill. Boston: Shambhala Publications, 2000.

———. *The Complete Basho Poems.* Edited by Keith Harrison. Northfield, Minn.: Black Willow Press, 2002.

———. *The Narrow Road to Oku.* Translated by Donald Keene. New York: Kodansha America, 1997.

Maus, Katharine, ed. *Four Revenge Tragedies.* Oxford: Oxford University Press, 2000.

McAvoy, Liz Herbert. *Authority and the Female Body in the Writings of Julian of Norwich and Margery Kempe.* London: Boydell and Brewer, 2004.

McCaskie, T. C. *State and Society in Pre-Colonial Asante.* Cambridge: Cambridge University Press, 1995.

McCaw, R. John. *The Transforming Text: A Study of Luis de Gongora's Soledades.* Potomac, Md.: Scripta Humanistica, 2000.

McConnell, Alan. *A Russian Philosophe: Alexander Radishchev, 1749–1802.* Westport, Conn.: Hyperion Press, 1981.

McEntire, Sandra J., ed. *Margery Kempe: A Book of Essays.* New York: Garland, 1992.

McKendrick, Melveena. *Playing the King: Lope de Vega and the Limits of Conformity.* Suffolk, U.K.: Tamesis Books, 2002.

McLeese, Don. *Thomas Paine.* Vero Beach, Fla.: Rourke, 2004.

McLeod, Enid. *Charles of Orleans: Prince and Poet.* New York: Viking Press, 1970.

McNerney, Kathleen. *The Influence of Ausiàs March on Early Golden Age Castilian Poetry.* Amsterdam: Rodopi B.V., 1982.

McWilliam, G. H., trans. *The Decameron.* New York: Penguin, 2003.

Medici, Lorenzo de'. *Lorenzo de' Medici: Selected Poems and Prose.* University Park: Pennsylvania State University Press, 1992.

———. *Political Philosophy of the Great de' Medici as Revealed by Their Correspondence.* Edited by Cosimo Giovanni. Albuquerque, N.M.: Institute for Economic and Political World Strategic Studies, 1985.

Medwick, Cathleen. *Teresa of Avila: The Progress of a Soul.* New York: Knopf, 2000.

Mee, Charles L. *Erasmus: The Eye of the Hurricane.* New York: Coward, McCann and Geoghegan, 1973.

Melanchthon, Phillip. *Annotations on the First Epistle to the Corinthians.* Edited and translated by John Patrick Donnelly. Milwaukee, Wis.: Marquette University Press, 1995.

———. *Commentary on Romans by Philip Melanchthon.* Translated by Fred Kramer. St. Louis: Concordia Publishing House, 1992.

Melnick, Arthur. *Themes in Kant's Metaphysics and Ethics.* Washington, D.C.: Catholic University of America Press, 2004.

Menard, Valerie. *Alvar Núñez Cabeza de Vaca.* Hockessin, Del.: Mitchell Lane Publishers, 2002.

Menshutkin, Boris N. *Russia's Lomonosov: Chemist, Courtier, Physicist, Poet.* Princeton, N.J.: Princeton University Press, 1952.

Merchant, Paul. *The Epic.* London: Methuen, 1971.

Merwin, W. S. *Sir Gawain and the Green Knight.* New York: Alfred A. Knopf, 2002.

Metastasio, Pietro. *Temistocle: Opera Seria in Three Acts.* Edited by Ernest Warburton. New York: Garland, 1988.

———. *Three Melodramas.* Translated by Joseph G. Fucilla. Lexington: University Press of Kentucky, 1981.

Meyer, Michael C., and William H. Beezley, eds. *The Oxford History of Mexico.* Oxford: Oxford University Press, 2000.

Michelangelo Buonarroti. *The Complete Poems and Selected Letters of Michelangelo.* Translated by Creighton E. Gilbert and edited by Robert N. Linscott. Princeton, N.J.: Princeton University Press, 1990.

———. *The Drawings of Michelangelo.* Introduction by Irving Stone. Master Draughtsman Series. Los Angeles: Borden Publishing, 1999.

———. *The Poetry of Michelangelo: An Annotated Translation.* Translated by James M. Saslow. New Haven, Conn.: Yale University Press, 1993.

Michels, Georg. *At War with the Church: Religious Dissent in Seventeenth-Century Russia.* Palo Alto, Calif.: Stanford University Press, 1999.

Mickel, Leslie. *Ben Jonson's Antimasques: A History of Growth and Decline.* Brookfield, Vt.: Ashgate, 1999.

Miller, Perry. *Errand into the Wilderness.* Cambridge, Mass.: Harvard University Press, 1956.

———. *Jonathan Edwards.* New York: Meridian Books, 1959.

Mills, David. *Recycling the Cycle: The City of Chester and Its Whitsun Plays,* vol. 4. Toronto: University of Toronto Press, 1998.

Milton, John. *Areopagitica and Other Prose Works.* Whitefish, Mont.: Kessinger, 2004.

———. *The Poetical Works of John Milton.* IndyPublish.com, 2003.

———. *The Riverside Milton.* Edited by Roy Flannagan. New York: Houghton Mifflin, 1998.

Miner, Earl, ed. *Literary Uses of Typology: From the Late Middle Ages to the Present.* Princeton, N.J.: Princeton University Press, 1977.

Mody, Jehangir R. P. *Vondel and Milton.* Norwood, Pa.: Norwood Editions, 1977.

Moffit, John F., and Sebastiân Santiago. *O Brave New People: The European Adventure of the American Indian.* Albuquerque: University of New Mexico, 1998.

Molière. *Doctor in Spite of Himself.* Translated by S. H. Landes and edited by William-Alan Landes. Studio City, Calif.: Players Press, 2003.

———. *Misanthrope.* Translated by Charles H. Wall. Studio City, Calif.: Players Press, 2003.

———. *Tartuffe.* Translated by Ranjit Bolf. New York: Theatre Communications Group, 2003.

———. *The Blunderer.* Holicong, Pa.: Wildside Press, 2003.

———. *The Imaginary Invalid (Le Malade Imaginaire).* IndyPublish.com, 2004.

Molina, Tirso de. *Damned for Despair.* Translated by Lawrence Boswell. Hygiene, Colo.: Eridanos Press, 1992.

———. *Don Juan of Seville.* Translated by Lynne Alvarez. New York: Playwright's Press, 1989.

———. *Don Juan: The Beguiler of Seville and The Stone Guest.* Translated by Max Oppenheimer. Lawrence, Kans.: Coronado Press, 1976.

———. *The Rape of Tamar.* Translated by Paul Whitworth. New York: Theatre Communications Group, 1999.

Montaigne, Michel de. *Apology for Raymond Sebond.* Translated by Marjorie Glicksman Grene and Roger Ariew. Indianapolis, Ind.: Hackett Publishing, 2003.

———. *Autobiography of Michel de Montaigne.* Edited by Marvin Lowenthal. Boston: David R. Godine, 1999.

———. *The Complete Essays of Montaigne.* Translated by Donald M. Frame. Palo Alto, Calif.: Stanford University Press, 1965.

———. *The Complete Essays.* Translated by M. A. Screech. New York: Penguin, 1993.

Montejo, Victor. *El Q'Anil, Man of Lightning: A Legend of Jacaltenango.* Translated by Wallace Kaufman and Susan G. Rascon. Tucson: University of Arizona Press, 2001.

Montesquieu, Charles-Louis de Secondat, baron de. *Considerations on the Causes of the Greatness of the Romans and Their Decline.* Translated by David Lowenthal. Indianapolis, Ind.: Hackett Publishing, 1999.

———. *Persian Letters.* Translated by C. J. Betts. New York: Penguin, 1977.

———. *The Spirit of Laws.* Edited by Anne M. Cohler. Cambridge: Cambridge University Press, 1989,

Montmorency, J. E. G. de. *Thomas à Kempis: His Age and Book.* New York: Kennikat Press, 1970.

Moore, Mary B. *Desiring Voices: Women Sonneteers and Petrarchism.* Carbondale: Southern Illinois University Press, 2000.

Moorman, Charles. *The* Pearl-*Poet.* New York: Twayne, 1968.

More, Thomas. *Saint Thomas More: Selected Writings.* Edited by John F. Thornton and Susan B. Varenne. Vancouver, Wash.: Vintage Books, 2003.

———. *Utopia.* London: Everyman's Library, 1992.

———. *Utopia.* Translated by Paul Turner. New York: Penguin, 1965.

Morgan, Edmund S. *Benjamin Franklin.* New Haven, Conn.: Yale University Press, 2002.

———. *The Puritan Dilemma: The Story of John Winthrop.* Lebanon, Ind.: Pearson, 1998.

Morgan, Gerald. *Sir Gawain and the Green Knight and the Idea of Righteousness.* Dublin, Ireland: Irish Academic Press, 1992.

Morgan, Jeanne. *Perrault's Morals for Moderns.* New York: Peter Lang, 1985.

Morison, Samuel Eliot. *Admiral of the Ocean Sea: A Life of Christopher Columbus.* New York: MJF Books, 1942.

Morley, Carolyn Anne. *Transformation, Miracles, and Mischief: The Mountain Priest Plays of Kyogen.* Ithaca, N.Y.: Cornell University East Asia Program, 1993.

Morley, Sylvanus G., and Delia Goetz, trans. *The Popol Vuh: The Sacred Book of the Mayas.* Norman: University of Oklahoma Press, 1991.

Mossiker, Frances. *Madame de Sévigné.* New York: Columbia University Press, 1983.

Motokiyo Zeami. *On the Art of the No Drama: Major Treatises by Zeami.* Translated by J. Thomas Rimer, Yamazaki Masakazu, and Wallace Chappell. Princeton, N.J.: Princeton University Press, 1984.

———. *Zeami and the No Theatre in the World.* Edited by Samuel L. Leiter, et al. New York: Martin E. Segal Theatre Center, 1998.

Motolinía, Toribio de. *History of the Indians of New Spain,* vol. 4. Translated by Elizabeth A. Foster. Oxford, England: Greenwood Publishing, 1970.

Mourgues, Odette de. *Two French Moralists: La Rochefoucauld & La Bruyère.* Cambridge: Cambridge University Press, 1978.

Mullan, Elder Father, S.J., trans. *The Spiritual Exercises of Saint Ignatius of Loyola.* New York: P. J. Kennedy and Sons, 1914.

Mullett, Michael. *Martin Luther.* London: Taylor and Francis, 2004.

Munford, Robert. *The Plays of Robert Munford.* Tucson, Ariz.: American Eagle Publications, 1992.

Murdock, Kenneth B. *Increase Mather, the Foremost American Puritan.* Temecula, Calif.: Reprint Services Corp., 1991.

Murphy, Anne. *Thomas More.* Liguori, Mo.: Liguori Publications, 1997.

Murphy, Daniel. *Comenius: A Critical Reassessment of His Life and Work.* Dublin, Ireland: Irish Academic Press, 1995.

Murphy, James J., and Izora Scott. *Controversies over the Imitation of Cicero in the Renaissance: With Translations of Letters between Pietro Bembo and Gianfrancesco Pico.* Mahwah, N.J.: Erlbaum, 1995.

Murray, Judith Sargent. *Selected Writings of Judith Sargent Murray.* Edited by Sharon M. Harris. Oxford: Oxford University Press, 1995.

———. *The Gleaner: A Miscellany.* Edited by Nina Baym. Syracuse, N.Y.: Syracuse University Press, 1993.

Musa, Mark, trans. *Selections from the Canzoniere and Other Works.* New York: Oxford University Press, 1999.

Musgrove, Margaret W. *Ashanti to Zulu: African Traditions.* New York: Puffin, 1992.

Mussell, Kay, ed. *Where's Love Gone: Transformations in the Romance Genre.* Los Angeles: Delta Productions, 1997.

Nadler, Steven. *Spinoza: A Life.* Cambridge: Cambridge University Press, 1999.

Nauert, Charles G., Jr. *Humanism and the Culture of Renaissance Europe.* Cambridge: Cambridge University Press, 1995.

Navarre, Marguerite de. *The Coach and the Triumph of the Lamb.* Translated by Hilda Dale. Bristol, U.K.: Intellect, 2003.

———. *The Heptameron.* Translated by P. A. Chilton. New York: Viking Penguin, 1984.

Nebel, Henry M., Jr., trans. *Selected Aesthetic Works of Sumarokov and Karamzin.* Washington, D.C.: University Press of America, 1981.

Nerimanoglu, Kamil Veli. *The Poetics of "The Book of Dede Korkut."* Ankara, Turkey: Ataturk Culture Center Publications, 1999.

Newman, John Kevin. *The Classical Epic Tradition.* Madison: University of Wisconsin Press, 1986.

Nezahualcoyotl. *Cantares Mexicanos: Songs of the Aztecs.* Translated by John Bierhorst. Palo Alto, Calif.: Stanford University Press, 1985.

———. *Chants of Nezahualcoyotl and Obsidian Glyph.* Translated by Prospero Saiz. Madison, Wis.: Ghost Pony Press, 1996.

Nguyen Trai. *A Thousand Years of Vietnam Poetry.* Edited and translated by Ngoc Bich Nguyen. New York: Knopf, 1974.

———. *Nguyen Trai, One of the Greatest Figures of Vietnamese History and Literature.* Hanoi: Foreign Languages Publishing House, 1980.

Nicholl, Charles. *Leonardo da Vinci: Flights of the Mind.* New York: Viking, 2004.

Nikitin, Afanasij. "Afanasy Nikitin's Journey across Three Seas," in *Medieval Russia's Epics, Chronicles, and Tales,* rev. ed. Edited and translated by Serge A. Zenkovsky. New York: E.P. Dutton, 1974; 333–353.

Novak, Maximilian E. *Daniel Defoe: Master of Fictions: His Life and Ideas.* Oxford: Oxford University Press, 2001.

Novalis. *Henry von Ofterdingen.* Translated by Palmer Hilty. Prospect Heights, Ill.: Waveland Press, 1990.

———. *Novalis: Hymns to the Night.* Translated by Dick Higgins. New York: McPherson, 1998.

O'Brian, Patrick. *Joseph Banks: A Life.* Chicago: University of Chicago Press, 1997.

O'Brien, William Arctander. *Novalis: Signs of Revolution.* Durham, N.C.: Duke University Press, 1994.

O'Connell, Marvin R., et al. *Blaise Pascal: Reasons of the Heart.* Grand Rapids, Mich.: Eerdmans, 1997.

O'Hagan, Timothy. *Rousseau.* London: Routledge, 2003.

O'Malley, Charles Donald. *Andreas Vesalius: 1514–1564.* Berkeley: University of California Press, 1964.

O'Neale, Sondra A. *Jupiter Hammon and the Biblical Beginnings of African-American Literature.* Metuchen, N.J.: Scarecrow, 1993.

Occom, Samson. "An Account of the Montauk Indians, on Long Island," *Massachusetts Historical Collections* (ser. 1) 10 (1809): 105–111.

———. *Samson Occom, Mohegan: Collected Writings by the Founder of Native American Literature.* Edited by Joanne Brooks. Oxford: Oxford University Press, 2004.

Oppenheimer, Paul. *The Birth of the Modern Mind: Self, Consciousness, and the Invention of the Sonnet.* New York: Oxford University Press, 1989.

Ostlund, DeLys. *The Re-Creation of History in the Fernando and Isabel Plays of Lope de Vega.* New York: Peter Lang, 1998.

Paine, Thomas. *American Crisis.* Whitefish, Mont.: Kessinger Publishing, 2004.

———. *Age of Reason.* Whitefish, Mont.: Kessinger Publishing, 2004.

———. *Common Sense.* Whitefish, Mont.: Kessinger Publishing, 2004.

———. *Rights of Man.* Introduction by David Taffel. New York: Barnes and Noble, 2004.

———. *Thomas Paine: Collected Writings.* New York: Library of America, 1995.

Palmer, John. *The Comedy of Manners.* New York: Russell and Russell, 1962.

Palmeri, Frank, ed. *Critical Essays on Jonathan Swift.* New York: G.K. Hall, 1993.

Palsson, Hermann Palsson, ed. *Seven Viking Romances.* New York: Penguin, 1986.

Papazia, Mary Arshagouni, and Ronald Corthell, eds. *John Donne and the Protestant Reformation: New Perspectives.* Detroit, Mich.: Wayne State University Press, 2003.

Parini, Giuseppe. *The Day: Midday, Evening, and Night.* Translated by Herbert Morris Bower. Westport, Conn.: Hyperion Press, 1978.

Parker, Patricia L. *Susanna Rowson.* Boston: Twayne, 1986.

Parkinson, G. H. R. *The Renaissance and Seventeenth-Century Rationalism.* The Routledge History of Philosophy Series, vol. 4. London: Routledge, 2003.

Pascal, Blaise. *Contradictions, Oppositions and Denials in the Life of the Mind.* Albuquerque, N.M.: American Classical College Press, 1987.

———. *Mind on Fire: A Faith for the Skeptical and Indifferent.* Edited by James M. Houston. Vancouver: Regent College Publishing, 2003.

———. *Pensées.* Translated by W. F. Trotter. Mineola, N.Y.: Dover, 2003.

———. *Provincial Letters.* Eugene, Ore.: Wipf and Stock Publishers, 1997.

———. *The Gospel of the Gospels.* London: Allemandi, Umberto and Company, 2000.

Pasternack, Lawrence R. *Immanuel Kant: Groundwork of the Metaphysics of Morals in Focus.* London: Taylor and Francis, 2002.

Pavolova, Galina Evgen'evna. *Mikhail Vasilievich Lomonosov: His Life and Work.* Translated by Arthur Aksenov. Moscow: Mir, 1984.

Pearl Poet. *The Complete Works of the* Pearl *Poet.* Translated by Casey Finch. Edited by Malcolm Andrew and C. Peterson. Berkeley: University of California Press, 1993.

Peers, E. Allison. *Handbook to the Life and Times of St. Teresa and St. John of the Cross.* Westminster, Md.: Newman Press, 1954.

Pepys, Samuel. *Particular Friends: The Correspondence of Samuel Pepys and John Evelyn.* Edited by Guy de la Bedoyere. Rochester, N.Y.: Boydell and Brewer, 1997.

———. *The Diary of Samuel Pepys (Abridged).* Edited by Richard Le Gallienne. New York: Random House, 2003.

Percy, Thomas. *Reliques of Ancient English Poetry,* 3 vols. London: Routledge, 1996.

Perrault, Charles. *Cinderella, Puss in Boots, and Other Favorite Tales as told by Charles Perrault.* Translated by A. E. Johnson. New York: Abrams, 2000.

Petrarch. *My Secret Book.* Translated by J. G. Nichols. London: Hesperus Press, 2002.

———. *Selections from the Canzoniere and Other Works.* Translated by Mark Musa. Oxford: Oxford University Press, 1999.

Petrie, Jennifer. *Petrarch.* Dublin: Irish Academic Press, 1983.

Peyer, Bernd. *The Tutor'd Mind: Indian Missionary-Writers in Antebellum America.* Amherst: University of Massachusetts Press, 1997.

Pflueger, Lynda. *Thomas Jefferson: Creating a Nation.* Berkeley Heights, N.J.: Enslow Publishers, 2004.

Philbrick, Thomas. *St. John de Crèvecoeur.* Farmington Hills, Mich.: Gale Group, 1970.

Philipps, Mark. *Francesco Guicciardini: The Historian's Craft.* Toronto: University of Toronto Press, 1977.

Pico della Mirandola, Count Giovanni. *Pico Della Mirandola: On The Dignity of Man, On Being and the One, Heptaplus.* Translated by Charles Glenn Wallis. New York: Bobbs-Merrill, 1940.

Pirrotta, Nina, and Elena Povoledo. *Music and Theatre from Poliziano to Moteverdi.* Translated by Karen Eales. New York: Cambridge University Press, 1981.

Pizan, Christine de. *Selected Writings of Christine de Pizan.* Edited by Renate Blumenfeld-Kosinski. New York: W.W. Norton, 1997.

———. *The Book of the City of Ladies.* Translated by Earl Jeffreys Richards. New York: Persea Books, 1982.

Plattard, Jean. *Life of François Rabelais.* Translated by L. D. Roache. London: Taylor and Francis, 1968.

Poesse, Walter. *Juan Ruiz De Alarcón.* New York: Twayne, 1972.

Poliziano, Angelo Ambrogini. *A Translation of the Orpheus of Angelo Politian and the Aminta of Torquato Tasso.* Edited by Louis E. Lord. Westport, Conn.: Hyperion Press, 1979.

———. *Silvae.* Translated by Charles Fantazzi. Cambridge, Mass.: Harvard University Press, 2004.

———. *The Stanze of Angelo Poliziano.* Translated by David Quint. University Park: Pennsylvania State University Press, 1993.

Pollard, Alfred W., ed. *English Miracle Plays, Moralities and Interludes: Specimens of the Pre-Elizabethan Drama.* Oxford: Oxford University Press, 1978.

Polsky, Zachary. *The Comic Machine, the Narrative Machine, and the Political Machine in the Works of Moliere.* Lewiston, N.Y.: Edwin Mellen Press, 2003.

Pompa, Leon. *Vico: A Study of the "New Science."* Cambridge: Cambridge University Press, 1990.

Poole, Stafford, trans. *In Defense of the Indians.* DeKalb: Northern Illinois University Press, 1992.

Pope, Alexander. *Alexander Pope.* Edited by Douglas Brooks-Davis. London: Everyman Poetry Library, 1997.

———. *Essay on Man and Other Poems.* London: Dover, 1994.

———. *The Complete Poems of Alexander Pope.* New York: Penguin, 1999.

Porter, Roy. *The Enlightenment.* New York: Palgrave Macmillan, 2001.

Pourafzal, Haleh, and Roger Montgomery. *The Spiritual Wisdom of Hafez: Teachings of the Philosopher of Love.* Rochester, Vt.: Inner Traditions International, 1998.

Prado, Diego de. *New Light on the Discovery of Australia: As Revealed by the Journal of Captain Don Diego de Prado y Tovar.* Translated by George F. Barwick. London: Hakluyt Society, 1930. Reprinted Millwood, N.Y.: Kraus, 1967.

Preuss, Mary H. *Gods of the Popol Vuh: Xmukane', K'ucumatz, Tojil, and Jurakan.* Culver City, Calif.: Labyrinthos, 1988.

Prévost, Antoine-François. *Manon Lescaut.* Translated by Steven Larkin. New York: Penguin Classics, 1992.

Prokopovitch, Feofan. "Sermon on the Interment of the Most Illustrious, Most Sovereign Peter the Great," in *The Literature of Eighteenth-Century Russia,* vol. 1. Edited by Harold Segel. New York: Dutton, 1967; 141–148.

———. *The Spiritual Regulation of Peter the Great.* Edited and translated by Alexander V. Muller. Seattle and London: University of Washington Press, 1972.

Pulci, Luigi. *Morgante: The Epic Adventures of Orlando and His Giant Friend Morgante.* Translated by Joseph Tusiani. Bloomington: Indiana University Press, 2000.

Putter, Ad. *Sir Gawain and the Green Knight and the French Arthurian Romance.* Oxford: Oxford University Press, 1995.

Quennell, Peter. *Alexander Pope: The Education of a Genius.* New York: Stein and Day, 1970.

Quevedo, Francisco de. *Lazarillo de Tormes and the Swindler: Two Spanish Picaresque Novels.* Edited by Michael Alpert. New York: Penguin, 2003.

———. *Six Masters of the Spanish Sonnet.* Translated by Willis Barnstone. Carbondale: Southern Illinois University Press, 1997.

Qvortrup, Mads. *The Political Philosophy of Jean-Jacques Rousseau: The Impossibility of Reason.* Manchester, England: Manchester University Press, 2004.

Rabb, Theodore. *Renaissance Lives: Portraits of an Age.* New York: Basic Books, 2001.

Rabelais, François. *Complete Works of François Rabelais.* Translated by Donald M. Frame. Berkeley: University of California Press, 1999.

———. *Five Books of the Lives, Heroic Deeds and Sayings of Gargantua and His Son Pantagruel.* Whitefish, Mont.: Kessinger Publishing, 2004.

———. *Gargantua and Pantagruel.* Herts, England: Wordsworth Editions, 2001.

Racevskis, Karlis. *Voltaire and the French Academy.* Chapel Hill: University of North Carolina, Department of Romance Languages, 1975.

Racine, Jean. *Bajazet.* Translated by Alan Hollinghurst. New York: Random House, 1992.

———. *Bérénice.* St. Paul, Minn.: Consortium Book Sales and Distribution, 1991.

———. *Racine: Mithridate.* Edited by Gustave Rudler. London: Bristol Classic Press, 1979.

———. *Three Plays of Racine: Andromache, Brittanicus, Phaedra.* Translated by George Dillon. Chicago: University of Chicago Press, 1961.

Radishchev, Alexander Nikoláevich. *A Journey from St. Petersburg to Moscow.* Translated by Leo Wiener and edited by R. P. Thaler. Cambridge, Mass.: Harvard University Press, 1958.

Raeff, Marc, ed. *Catherine the Great: A Profile.* New York: Hill and Wang, 1972.

Raffini, Christine. *Marsillo Ficino, Pietro Bembo, Baldassare Castiglione: Philosophical, Aesthetic, and Political Approaches in Renaissance Platonism.* New York: Peter Lang, 1998.

Raitt, Janet. *Madame de Lafayette and "La Princesse de Clèves."* London: George G. Harrap, 1971.

Ramazani, Rouhollah K. *Future of Liberal Democracy: Thomas Jefferson and the Contemporary World.* New York: Palgrave Macmillan, 2004.

Ramen, Fred. *Hernan Cortes: The Conquest of Mexico and the Aztec Empire.* New York: Rosen, 2003.

Rattray, Robert. *Akan-Ashanti Folk Tales.* New York: AMS Press, 1983.

Ray, Kurt. *Amerigo Vespucci: Italian Explorer of the Americas.* New York: Rosen, 2003.

Reeve, Henry. *Petrarch.* La Vergne, Tenn.: University Press of the Pacific, 2002.

Regosin, Richard L. *The Poetry of Inspiration: Agrippa d'Aubigne's Les tragiques.* Chapel Hill: University of North Carolina Press, 1970.

Reidt, Heinz. *Carlo Goldoni.* Translated by Ursule Molinaro. New York: Ungar, 1980.

Reisert, Joseph R. *Jean-Jeacques Rousseau: A Friend of Virtue.* Ithaca, N.Y.: Cornell University Press, 2003.

Remesal, Antonio de. *Bartolome De Las Casas, 1474–1566.* Translated by Felix Jay. New York: Edwin Mellen Press, 2002.

Rescher, Nicholas. *On Leibniz.* Pittsburgh: University of Pittsburgh Press, 2003.

Reston, James. *Galileo: A Life.* New York: Harper-Collins, 1994.

Reynolds, Ernest Edwin. *Bossuet.* Garden City, N.Y.: Doubleday, 1963.

Rhodes, James Francis. *Poetry Does Theology: Chaucer, Grosseteste, and the* Pearl-*Poet.* Notre Dame, Ind.: University of Notre Dame Press, 2001.

Richard, Earl Jeffreys, ed. *Christine de Pizan and Medieval French Lyric.* Gainesville: University Press of Florida, 2000.

Richards, Kenneth, and Laura Richards. *The Commedia dell'Arte: A Documentary History.* Cambridge, Mass.: Blackwell for the Shakespeare Head Press, 1990.

Richardson, Samuel. *Selected Letters.* Edited by John Carroll. Oxford: Clarendon Press, 1964.

———. *Clarissa, or the History of a Young Lady.* New York: Penguin Books, 1985.

———. *The Clarissa Project.* Edited by Florian Stuber. New York: AMS Press, 1990.

Riebeeck, Jan van. *Journal,* 3 vols. Cape Town: Van Reibeeck Society, 1952–58.

Rietbergen, P. J. A. N. *Europe: A Cultural History.* New York: Routledge, 1999.

Robinson, James H. *Petrarch: The First Modern Scholar and Man of Letters.* La Vergne, Tenn.: University Press of the Pacific, 2003.

Rodriguez, Alfred. *Plus Ultra: Life and Times of Alvar Núñez Cabeza de Vaca.* Lincoln, Neb.: iUniverse, 2001.

Rogers, Pat. *The Alexander Pope Encyclopedia.* Westport, Conn.: Greenwood Publishing Group, 2004.

Ronsard, Pierre de. *Pierre de Ronsard: Selected Poems.* Translated by Malcom Quainton and Elizabeth Vinestock. New York: Penguin Books, 2002.

———. *Poems of Pierre de Ronsard.* Edited and translated by Nicholas Kilmer. Los Angeles: University of California Press, 1979.

———. *Songs and Sonnets of Pierre de Ronsard.* New York: Hyperion Books, 1985.

Rosbottom, Ron. *Choderlos de Laclos.* Boston: Twayne, 1978.

Rose, Martial, ed. *The Wakefield Mystery Plays: The Complete Cycle of Thirty-Two Plays.* New York: W.W. Norton, 1994.

Rosenmeier, Rosamund. *Anne Bradstreet Revisited.* Boston: Twayne, 1981.

Rosslyn, Felicity. *Alexander Pope: A Literary Life.* London: Macmillan, 1990.

Rosslyn, Wendy. *Anna Bunina (1774–1829) and the Origins of Women's Poetry in Russia.* Studies in Slavic Language and Literature, vol. 10. New York: Edwin Mellen Press, 1997.

Rostand, Edmond. *Cyrano de Bergerac.* Translated by Christopher Fry. New York: Oxford University Press, 1998.

Rousseau, Jean-Jacques. *Confessions.* Translated by Patrick Coleman and edited by Angela Scholar. Oxford: Oxford University Press, 2000.

———. *Emile, or Treatise on Education.* Translated by William H. Payne. Buffalo, N.Y.: Prometheus Books, 2003.

———. *The Collected Writings of Jean-Jacques Rousseau.* Edited by Roger D. Masters and Christopher Kelly. Hanover, N.H.: University Press of New England, 1989.

———. *The Social Contract and the First and Second Discourses.* Edited by Gita May and Susan Dunn. New Haven, Conn.: Yale University Press, 2002.

Rowlandson, Mary. *Sovereignty and Goodness of God, Together With the Faithfulness of His Promises Displayed: Being a Narrative of the Captivity and Restoration of Mrs. Mary Rowlandson.* New York: Bedford/St. Martin's, 1997.

Rowson, Susanna. *Charlotte Temple.* Introduction by Jane Smiley. New York: Random House, 2004.

———. *Mary: Or the Test of Honour.* Temecula, Calif.: Reprint Services Corp., 1999.

———. *Miscellaneous Poems.* Murrieta, Calif.: Classic Books, 2004.

———. *Slaves in Algiers: A Struggle for Freedom.* Edited by Jennifer Margulis and Karen M. Poremski. Acton, Mass.: Copley, 2000.

———. *Victoria, 1786: The Inquisitor: Or, Invisible Rambler.* Temecula, Calif.: Reprint Services Corp., 1999.

Roys, Ralph L., trans. *The Book of Chilam Balam of Chumayel.* Norman: University of Oklahoma Press, 1967.

Rubin, David Lee. *A Pact with Silence: Art and Thought in The Fables of Jean de La Fontaine.* Columbus: Ohio State University Press, 1991.

Russell, Terence M., and Ann-Marie Thornton, eds. *Gardens and Landscapes in the Encyclopedie of Diderot and d'Alembert: The Letterpress Articles and Selected Engravings.* Aldershot, Hampshire, U.K.: Ashgate Publishing, 1999.

Rutt, Richard, and Kim Chong-un, trans. *Virtuous Women: Three Classic Korean Novels.* Korea: Kwang Myong, 1974.

Ruusbroec, Jan van. *John Ruusbroec: The Spiritual Espousals and Other Works.* Translated by James A. Wiseman. Mahwah, N.J.: Paulist Press, 1986.

Ryokan. *Between the Floating Mist—Poems of Ryokan.* Translated by Dennis Maloney and Hide Oshiro. Buffalo, N.Y.: Springhouse Editions, 1992.

———. *Great Fool: Zen Master Ryokan—Poems, Letters, and Other Writings.* Translated by Ryuichi Abe and Peter Haskel. Honolulu: University of Hawaii Press, 1996.

———. *The Zen Poems of Ryokan.* Translated by Nobyuki Yuasa. Princeton, N.J.: Princeton University Press, 1981.

Sachs, Hans. *Nine Carnival Plays.* Translated by Randall Listerman. Ottawa: Dovehouse Editions, 1990.

Sade, Marquis de. *120 Days of Sodom and Other Writings.* Translated by Austryn Wainhouse and Richard Seaver. New York: Grove Press, 1987.

Sadler, John Edward. *J. A. Comenius and the Concept of Universal Education.* London: Allen and Unwin, 1966.

Saffar, Ruth El., ed. *Critical Essays on Cervantes.* Boston: G.K. Hall, 1986.

Safranski, Rudiger. *Schopenhauer and the Wild Years of Philosophy.* Cambridge, Mass.: Harvard University Press, 1990.

Salvucci, Claudio R., ed. *Women in New France: Extracts from the Jesuit Relations.* Bristol, Pa.: Arx Publishing, 2004.

Santosuosso, Antonio. *Bibliography of Giovanni Della Casa: Books, Readers, and Critics.* Florence: L.S. Olschki, 1979.

Sargent, Daniel. *Thomas More.* Whitefish, Mont.: Kessinger, 2003.

Satterthwaite, Alfred W. *Spenser, Ronsard, and Du Bellay: A Renaissance Comparison.* Port Washington, N.Y.: Kennikat Press, 1972.

Scala, Flamminio. *Scenarios of the Commedia dell'arte: Flamminio Scala's Teatro delle favole rappresentive.* Translated by Henry F. Salerno. New York: New York University Press, 1967.

Schaeffer, Neil. *The Marquis de Sade: A Life.* New York: Alfred A. Knopf, 1999.

Schama, Simon. *The Embarrassment of Riches: An Interpretation of Dutch Culture in the Golden Age.* New York: Vintage, 1997.

Schiller, Friedrich von. *Essays.* Edited by Walter Hinderer and Daniel Dahlstrom. New York: Continuum, 1993.

———. *Schiller's Five Plays: The Robbers, Passion and Politics, Don Carlos, Mary Stuart, and Joan of Arc.* Translated by Robert McDonald. New York: Consortium Books, 1998.

Schirmer, Walter F. *John Lydgate: A Study in the Culture of the Seventeenth Century.* Westport, Conn.: Greenwood Press, 1979.

Schlegel, Friedrich. *Philosophical Fragments.* Translated by Peter Firchow. Minneapolis: University of Minnesota Press, 1991.

Schonle, Andreas. *Authenticity and Fiction in the Russian Literary Journey, 1790–1840.* Cambridge, Mass.: Harvard University Press, 2000.

Schopenhauer, Arthur. *The Art of Controversy.* La Vergne, Tenn.: University Press of the Pacific, 2004.

———. *The Wisdom of Life.* Mineola, N.Y.: Dover Publications, 2004.

———. *The World as Will and Representation.* Translated by E. F. J. Payne. Mineola, N.Y.: Dover, 1966.

Schrecker, Paul, and Anne Martin Schrecker, trans. *Monadology and Other Philosophical Essays.* Indianapolis, Ind.: Bobbs-Merrill, 1965.

Schuldiner, Michael. *Studies in Puritan American Spirituality: Essays on Anne Bradstreet, Edward Taylor, Nathaniel Hawthorne and Chatharine Maria Sedgwick,* vol. 7. Lewiston, N.Y.: Edwin Mellen Press, 2001.

Schuman, Michael A. *Mayan and Aztec Mythology.* Berkeley Heights, N.J.: Enslow Publishers, 2001.

Scott, Virginia. *Molière, A Theatrical Life.* Cambridge: Cambridge University Press, 2000.

Screech, M. A. A. *Clément Marot: A Renaissance Poet Discovers the Gospel.* The Netherlands: Brill Academic Publishers, 1993.

Scudéry, Madeleine de. *Selected Letters, Orations, and Rhetorical Dialogues.* Edited by Jane Donawerth. Chicago: University of Chicago Press, 2004.

———. *The Story of Sapho.* Translated by Karen Newman. Chicago: University of Chicago Press, 2003.

Segal, Naomi. *The Unintended Reader: Feminism and Manon Lescaut.* New York: Cambridge University Press, 1986.

Sévigné, Madame de. *Madame de Sévigné: Selected Letters.* Translated by Leonard Tancock. New York: Penguin Books, 1982.

Sexton, James D., ed. and trans. *Mayan Folktales: Folklore from Lake Atitlàn, Guatemala.* Albuquerque: University of New Mexico Press, 1999.

Sexton, James D., and Ignacio Bizarro Ujpàn. *Heart of Heaven, Heart of Earth and Other Mayan Folktales.* Washington, D.C.: Smithsonian Institution Press, 1999.

Shakespeare, William. *Complete Works.* Edited by Richard Proudfoot, et al. New York: Arden, 2001.

———. *The Complete Works.* Edited by Stanley Wells and Gary Taylor. Oxford: Oxford University Press, 1999.

———. *The Portable Shakespeare.* New York: Penguin Classics, 2004.

———. *The Tragedies.* New York: Modern Library, 1994.

Shapiro, Norman R., ed. *Lyrics of the French Renaissance: Marot, Du Bellay, Ronsard.* New Haven, Conn.: Yale University Press, 2002.

Sharma, Ram Chandra. *Themes and Conventions in the Comedy of Manners.* Folcroft, Pa.: Folcroft Library Editions, 1977.

Sharpe, Lesley. *Friedrich Schiller: Drama, Thought, and Politics.* Cambridge: Cambridge University Press, 1991.

Sharratt, Michael. *Galileo: Decisive Innovator.* New York: Cambridge University Press, 1996.

Shea, William R. *Designing Experiments and Games of Chance: The Unconventional Science of Blaise Pascal.* Sagamore Beach, Mass.: Watson Publishing, 2003.

Shearer, Susan, S., ed. *Petrarch: On Religious Leisure.* New York: Italica Press, 2002.

Shen Fu. *Six Records of a Floating Life.* Translated by Leonard Pratt and Chiang Su-hui. New York: Penguin, 1983.

Shepherd, Gregory J. *An Exposition of Jose De Acosta's "Historia Y Moral de Las Indias," 1590.* New York: Edwin Mellen Press, 2002.

Shepherd, Stephen, ed. *Middle English Romances.* New York: W.W. Norton, 1995.

Shio Sakanishi. *Japanese Folk Plays: The Ink-smeared Lady and Other Kyogen.* Tokyo: C.E. Tuttle, 1960.

Shirley, John William. *Thomas Harriot: A Biography.* Oxford: Clarendon Press, 1983.

Showalter, Elaine. *Madame de Graffigny and Rousseau: Between the Two Discours.* Oxford: Voltaire Foundation, 1978.

———. *The Evolution of the French Novel, 1641–1782.* Princeton, N.J.: Princeton University Press, 1972.

Shuzaburo Hironaga. *Bunraku Handbook: A Comprehensive Guide to Japan's Unique Puppet Theater, with Synopses of All Popular Plays.* Tokyo: Maison des Arts, 1976.

Sichel, Edith. *Michel de Montaigne.* La Vergne, Tenn.: University Press of the Pacific, 2003.

Sidney, Sir Philip. *Selected Prose and Poetry.* Edited by Robert Kimbrough. Madison: University of Wisconsin Press, 1994.

———. *Sidney's Defence of Poesy and Selected Renaissance Literary Criticism.* Edited and with introduction by Gavin Alexander. New York: Penguin Classics, 2004.

———. *The Major Works.* Edited by Katherine Duncan-Jones. New York: Oxford University Press, 2002.

Silverman, Kenneth. *The Life and Times of Cotton Mather.* New York: Harper and Row, 1984.

———. *Timothy Dwight.* New York: Twayne, 1969.

Sime, James. *Life of Johann Wolfgang Goethe.* La Vergne, Tenn.: University Press of the Pacific, 2003.

Simon, Irene. *Neo-Classical Criticism 1600–1800.* Columbia: University of South Carolina Press, 1971.

Sisman, Adam. *Boswell's Presumptuous Task: The Making of the Life of Dr. Johnson.* New York: Farrar, Straus & Giroux, 2000.

Skelton, John. *John Skelton, The Complete English Poems.* Edited by John Scattergood. New Haven, Conn.: Yale University Press, 1983.

———. *Magnyfycence.* Edited by Robert Lee Ramsay. Oxford: Oxford University Press, 2000.

Skemp, Sheila L. *Judith Sargent Murray: A Brief Biography with Documents.* New York: St. Martin's Press, 1998.

Skinner, Quentin. *Machiavelli: A Very Short Introduction.* Oxford: Oxford University Press, 2000.

Smethurst, Mae J., and Christina Laffin, eds. *Noh Ominameshi: A Flower Viewed from Many Directions.* Ithaca, N.Y.: Cornell University Press, 2003.

Smith, John. *Captain John Smith: A Select Edition of His Writings.* Edited by Karen Ordahl Kupperman. Chapel Hill: University of North Carolina Press, 1988.

Sobel, Dava. *Galileo's Daughter: A Historical Memoir of Science, Faith, and Love.* New York: Walker, 1999.

Sola-Sole, Josep M. *Tirso's Don Juan: The Metamorphosis of a Theme.* Edited by Georges E. Gingras. Washington, D.C.: Catholic University of America Press, 1989.

Sommer, Doris. *Foundational Fictions: The National Romances of Latin America.* Berkeley: University of California Press, 1993.

Sophocles. *The Complete Greek Tragedies.* Edited by David Grene and Richmond Lattimore. Chicago: University of Chicago Press, 1992.

Sorell, Tom. *Descartes: A Very Short Introduction.* New York: Oxford University Press, 2000.

Sox, David. *John Woolman: Quintessential Quaker, 1720—1772.* Richmond, Ind.: Friends United Press, 1999.

Spencer, Theodore. *Death and Elizabethan Tragedy.* St. Clair Shores, Mich.: Scholarly Press, 1985.

Spiegel, Harriet. *Marie de France: Fables.* Toronto: University of Toronto Press, 1987.

Spilhaus, Margaret Whiting. *Company's Men.* Cape Town: J. Malherbe, 1973.

Spinka, Matthew. *John Amos Comenius: That Incomparable Moravian.* Chicago: University of Chicago Press, 1943.

———. *John Hus: A Biography.* Princeton, N.J.: Princeton University Press, 1968.

Spinoza, Benedictus. *Correspondence of Spinoza.* Translated by A. Wolf. Whitefish, Mont.: Kessinger Publishing, 2003.

———. *Ethics: Treatise on the Emendation of the Intellect and Selected Letters.* Translated by Samuel Shirley. Indianapolis, Ind.: Hackett Publishing, 1998.

———. *The Collected Works of Spinoza.* Translated by Edwin Curley. Princeton, N.J.: Princeton University Press, 1985.

St. Cyres, Viscount. *François de Fenelon.* New York: Kennikat, 1970.

Staden, Hans. *The Adventures of Hans Staden.* Washington, D.C.: Alhambra, 1998.

———. *The Captivity of Hans Staden of Hesse, in A.D. 1547–1555: Among the Wild Tribes of Eastern Brazil.* Translated by A. Tootal and edited by R. F. Burton. New York: Burt Franklin, 1964.

Stendhal, Maurice. *Lives of Haydn, Mozart and Metastasio.* Translated by Richard N. Coe. New York: Grossman, 1972.

Stepanov, Nikolay. *Ivan Krylov.* New York: Twayne, 1973.

Stephenson, Barbara. *Power and Patronage of Marguerite de Navarre.* Aldershot, Hampshire, England: Ashgate, 2004.

Stevens, John. *Three Zen Masters: Ikkyu, Hakuin, Ryokan.* New York: Kodansha America, 1993.

Stewart, Alan. *Philip Sidney: A Double Life.* New York: Thomas Dunne Books/St. Martin's Press, 2001.

Stoljar, Margaret Mahony, trans. *Novalis: Philosophical Writings.* Albany: State University of New York Press, 1997.

Stone, P. W. K., trans. *Les Liaisons Dangereuses.* New York: Penguin Classics, 1961.

Stump, Joseph. *The Life of Melanchthon.* Murrieta, Calif.: New Library Press, 2003.

Subtelny, Orest. *Domination of Eastern Europe: Native Nobilities and Foreign Absolutism, 1500–1715.* Kingston and Montreal: McGill-Queen's University Press, 1986.

Sumarokov, Alexander Petrovich. *Selected Tragedies of A. P. Sumarokov.* Translated by Richard and Raymond Fortune. Evanston, Ill.: Northwestern University Press, 1970.

Sümer, Faruk, Ahmet E. Uysal, and Warren S. Walker, eds. and trans. *The Book of Dede Korkut: A Turkish Epic.* Austin: University of Texas Press, 1991.

Summers, Claude J., and Ted-Larry Pebworth. *Ben Jonson Revised.* New York: Twayne, 1999.

Swainson, W. P. *Emanuel Swedenborg: The Swedish Seer.* Whitefish, Mont.: Kessinger, 2003.

Swedenborg, Emanual. *Apocalypse Explained,* vol. 3. Translated by John Whitehead. West Chester, Pa.: Swedenborg Foundation, 1995.

———. *Essential Readings.* Edited by Michael Stanley. Berkeley, Calif.: North Atlantic Books, 2003.

Sweetser, Marie-Odile. *La Fontaine.* Boston: Twayne, 1987.

Swift, Jonathan. *The Basic Writings of Jonathan Swift.* Edited by Claude Rawson. New York: Modern Library, 2002.

———. *The Correspondence of Jonathan Swift.* Edited by Harold Williams. Oxford: Clarendon Press, 1963.

———. *The Writings of Jonathan Swift.* Edited by Robert A. Greenberg and William B. Piper. New York: W.W. Norton, 1973.

Symonds, John A. *Life of Michelangelo Buonarroti.* Philadelphia: University of Pennsylvania Press, 2001.

Takeda Izumo. *Chushingura: The Treasury of Loyal Retainers. A Puppet Play by Takeda Izumo, Miyoshi Shoraku and Namiki Senryu.* Translated by Donald Keene. New York: Columbia University Press, 1971.

Takeda, Sharon Sadako. *Miracles and Mischief: Noh and Kyogen Theater in Japan.* Los Angeles: Los Angeles County Museum of Art, Agency for Cultural Affairs, 2002.

Talbot, George, ed. *Lord Charlemont's History of Italian Poetry from Dante to Metastasio.* New York: Edwin Mellen Press, 2000.

Tallentyre, S. G. *Life of Voltaire.* Miami, Fla.: International Law and Taxation, 2004.

Tang Hsien-tsu. *The Peony Pavilion by Tang Xianzu (Tang Hsien-Tzu).* Translated by Cyril Birch. Bloomington: Indiana University Press, 1980.

Tasso, Torquato. *Jerusalem Delivered.* Edited by Anthony M. Esolen. Baltimore, Md.: Johns Hopkins University Press, 2000.

———. *King Torrismondo by Torquato Tasso.* Translated by Maria Pastore Passaro. New York: Fordham University Press, 1997.

Tavernor, Robert. *On Alberti and the Art of Building.* New Haven, Conn.: Yale University Press, 1999.

Taylor, Edward. *The Poems of Edward Taylor.* Edited by Donald E. Stanford. Chapel Hill: University of North Carolina Press, 1994.

Taylor, Ivan E. *Samuel Pepys.* Boston: Twayne, 1989.

Tedlock, Dennis. "What the Popol Vuh Tells Us about Itself," in *The Book, Spiritual Instrument.* Edited by Jerome Rothenberg and David Guss. New York: Granary Books, 1996.

———. *Popol Vuh: The Definitive Edition of the Maya Book of Dawn of Life and the Glories of Gods and Kings.* New York: Simon & Schuster, 1996.

Tedlock, Dennis, trans. *Popol Vuh: The Mayan Book of the Dawn of Life.* New York: Simon & Schuster, 1996.

———. *Rabinal Achi: A Mayan Drama of War and Sacrifice.* New York: Oxford University Press, 2003.

Tench, Watkin. *1788: Comprising "A Narrative of the Expedition to Botany Bay" and "A Complete Account of the Settlement at Port Jackson."* Melbourne, Australia: Text Publishing, 1996.

———. *Letters from Revolutionary France.* Edited by Gavin Edwards. Cardiff: University of Wales Press, 2001.

Teresa of Avila, Saint. *The Life of Saint Teresa of Avila by Herself.* Translated by J. M. Cohen. London: Penguin, 1987.

———. *The Complete Works of Saint Teresa of Jesus,* 3 vols. London: Sheed and Ward, 1944–46.

———. *The Letters of St. Teresa of Jesús,* 2 vols. Edited and translated by E. Allison Peers. London: Burns, Oates and Washbourne, 1951.

———. *The Complete Poetry of St. Teresa de Avila: A Bilingual Edition.* Translated by Eric W. Vogt. New Orleans: University Press of the South, 1996.

Tetel, Marcel. *Montaigne*. Boston: Twayne, 1990.

Thaddeus, Victor. *Voltaire, Genius of Mockery*. Whitefish, Mont.: Kessinger Publishing, 2003.

Thelander, Dorothy R. *Laclos and the Epistolary Novel*. Geneva: Librairie Droz, 1963.

Thomas, Calvin. *The Life and Works of Friedrich Schiller*. McLean, Va.: Indypublish.com, 2004.

Thompson, Carol. *The Asante Kingdom*. New York: Franklin Watts, 1999.

Thompson, Ewa M., ed. *The Search for Self-Definition in Russian Literature*. Amsterdam: J. Benjamins, 1991.

Thorlby, Anthony, ed. *The Penguin Companion to Literature 2, European*. Middlesex, England: Penguin Books, 1969; 154–155.

Thysell, Carol. *The Pleasure of Discernment: Marguerite de Navarre as Theologian*. New York: Oxford University Press, 2000.

Till Eulenspiegel. Introduction by Paul Oppenheimer. London: Routledge, 2001.

Tiller, Terence, trans. *Confessio Amantis [The Lover's Shrift]*. Baltimore, Md.: Penguin, 1963.

Tobin, Ronald W. *Jean Racine Revisited*. New York: Twayne, 1999.

Tomalin, Claire. *Samuel Pepys: The Unequalled Self*. New York: Vintage, 2003.

Tomei, Christine D., ed. *Russian Women Writers*, vols. 1 and 2. New York: Garland, 1999.

Toshimasa Yasukata. *Lessing's Philosophy of Religion and the German Enlightenment*. Oxford: Oxford University Press, 2002.

Toyochiro Nogami. *Zeami and His Theories on Noh*. Tokyo: Hinoki, 1973.

Tsao Hsueh-Chin. *The Dream of the Red Chamber*. Translated by Chi-Chen Wang. New York: Twayne, 1958.

———. The *Dream of the Red Chamber*. Translated by Florence and Isabel McHugh. New York: Pantheon Books, 1958.

Tuchman, Barbara W. *A Distant Mirror*. New York: Ballantine Books, 1987.

Tucker, Georges Hugo. *The Poet's Odyssey: Joachim Du Bellay and Les Antiquitez de Rome*. Oxford: Oxford University Press, 1991.

Turner, Frederick. *Natural Classicism: Essays on Literature and Science*. New York: Paragon House, 1985.

Underhill, Evelyn, ed. *The Cloud of Unknowing: The Classic of Medieval Mysticism*. Mineola, N.Y.: Dover, 2003.

Vance, John, ed. *Boswell's Life of Johnson: New Questions, New Answers*. Athens: University of Georgia Press, 1985.

Van Cleve, John. *Sebastian Brant's* The Ship of Fools *in Critical Perspective, 1800–1991*. New York: Camden House, 1993.

Van Horne, John. *El Bernardo of Bernardo de Balbuena: A Study of the Poem*. Urbana: University of Illinois, 1927.

Van Laun, Henri, trans. *Characters*. London: Oxford University Press, 1963.

Vantuono, William, ed. *The Pearl Poem in Middle and Modern English*. New York: University Press of America, 1987.

Varner, John Grier. *El Inca: The Life and Times of Garcilaso de la Vega*. Austin: University of Texas Press, 1968.

Vega, Garcilaso de la. *Poems*. Translated by Elias L. Rivers. London: Grant and Cutler, 1981.

———. *Royal Commentaries of the Incas and General History of Peru*. Austin: University of Texas Press, 1966.

Verdeyen, Paul. *Ruusbroec and His Mysticism*. Translated by André Lefevere. Collegeville, Minn.: Liturgical Press, 1994.

Vespucci, Amerigo. *Letters of Amerigo Vespucci and Other Documents Illustrative of His Career*. Edited by Clements R. Markham. New York: Burt Franklin, 1994.

Vico, Giambattista. *The New Science of Giambattista Vico*, 2nd ed. Translated by Thomas Bergin and Max Harold Fisch. Ithaca, N.Y.: Cornell University Press, 1983.

Villon, François. *Book of François Villon: The Little Testament and Ballads*. Translated by Algernon C. Swinburne. New York: Branden, 1997.

———. *Poems of François Villon*. Translated by Peter Dale. London: Anvil Press Poetry, 2001.

Viroli, Maurizio. *Niccoli's Smile: A Biography of Machiavelli*. Translated by Anthony Shugaar. New York: Farrar, Straus & Giroux, 2000.

Vivies, Jean, ed. *English Travel Narratives in the Eighteenth Century.* Translated by Claire Davison. Brookfield, Vt.: Ashgate, 2002.

Vogeley, Nancy J. *Lizardi and the Birth of the Novel in Spanish America.* Gainesville: University Press of Florida, 2001.

Volkov, Solomon. *Conversations with Joseph Brodsky: A Poet's Journey through the Twentieth Century.* New York: Free Press, 2002.

Voltaire. *Complete Romances of Voltaire.* Whitefish, Mont.: Kessinger Publishing, 2003.

———. *Candide.* Holicong, Pa.: Wildside Press, 2003.

———. *Voltaire and His Letters.* Translated by S. G. Tallentyre. Miami, Fla.: International Law and Taxation, 2004.

———. *Voltaire: Candide, Zadig, and Selected Stories.* Translated by Donald M. Frame. New York: New American Library, 1961.

———. *Voltaire: Treatise on Tolerance.* Edited by Simon Harvey. New York: Cambridge University Press, 2000.

———. *Voltaire's Correspondence: An Epistolary Novel,* vol. 5. Edited by Deidre Dawson and Gita May. New York: Peter Lang, 1994.

Vondel, Joost van den. *Lucifer: Joost Van den Vondel.* Translated by Noel Clark. Bath, England: Absolute Classics, 1990.

Vroon, Ronald, and John E. Malmstad, eds. "Fet and the Poetic Tradition: Anapestic Tetrameter in the Work of Polonsky, Golenishchev-Kutuzov, and Lokhvitskaya," in *Russian Modernism. To Honor Vladimir Fedorovich Markov.* Moscow: Nauka, 1993; 173–188.

Waddington, Raymond B. *Aretino's Satyr: Sexuality, Satire, and Self-Projection in Sixteenth-Century Literature and Art.* Toronto: University of Toronto Press, 2003.

Wagner, Irmgard. *Goethe.* Boston: Twayne, 1999.

Waldseemüller, Martin. *Cosmographiae Introductio of Martin Waldseemüller in Facsimile.* Translated by Joseph Fischer and Franz von Wieser. Manchester, N.H.: Ayer Co., 1977.

Walker, Greg, et al. *John Skelton and the Politics of the 1520s.* New York: Cambridge University Press, 2002.

Walker, Hillam. *Molière.* Boston: Twayne, 1990.

Wallace, W. *Life of Arthur Schopenhauer.* La Vergne, Tenn.: University Press of the Pacific, 2003.

Walsh, Thomas. *Readings on Candide.* Farmington Hills, Mich.: Gale Group, 2000.

Walters, D. Gareth. *Francisco de Quevedo: Love Poet.* Washington, D.C.: Catholic University of America Press, 1986.

Ward, Adolphus William. *Geoffrey Chaucer.* La Vergne, Tenn.: International Law and Taxation Publishers, 2003.

Warner, Marina. *From the Beast to the Blonde: On Fairy Tales and Their Tellers.* New York: Noonday Press, 1996.

Warner, William Beatty. *Reading Clarissa: The Struggles of Interpretation.* New Haven, Conn.: Yale University Press, 1979.

Watkins, Renee N., trans. *The Family in Renaissance Florence.* Long Grove, Ill.: Waveland Press, 1994.

Watling, Thomas. *Thomas Watling: Dumfries' Convict Artist.* Dumfries, Scotland: Dumfries Museum, 1988.

Wegelin, Oscar. *Jupiter Hammon.* Miami, Fla.: Mnemosyne Publishing, 1969.

Weiger, John G. *The Substance of Cervantes.* Cambridge: Cambridge University Press, 1985.

Weiner, Leo, ed. *Anthology of Russian Literature: From the Tenth Century to the Close of the Eighteenth Century.* Honolulu: University Press of the Pacific, 2001.

Weiskel, Portia Williams, and Harold Bloom. *Molière.* Langhorne, Pa.: Chelsea House, 2003.

Welsh, David. *Jan Kochanowski.* New York: Twayne, 1974.

Werner, Stephen. *Blueprint: A Study of Diderot and the "Encyclopedie" Plates.* Birmingham, Ala.: Summa Publications, 1993.

Wertheimer, Molly Meijer, ed. *Listening to Their Voices: The Rhetorical Activities of Historical*

Women. Columbia: University of South Carolina Press, 1997.

West, Richard. *Daniel Defoe: The Life and Strange, Surprising Adventures.* New York: Carroll and Graf, 1998.

Westbrook, Perry D. *William Bradford.* Boston: Twayne, 1978.

Westrem, Scott D. *Broader Horizons: A Study of Johannes Witte de Hese's Itinerarius and Medieval Travel Narratives.* Cambridge, Mass.: Medieval Academy of America, 2001.

Whatley, Janet, trans. *History of a Voyage to the Land of Brazil.* Berkeley: University of California Press, 1990.

Wheatley, Phillis. *Phillis Wheatley: Complete Writings.* Edited by Vincent Carretta. New York: Penguin Classics, 2001.

———. *The Collected Works of Phillis Wheatley.* New York: Oxford University Press, 1988.

White, Michael. *Leonardo: The First Scientist.* New York: St. Martin's Griffin, 2000.

———. *The Pope and the Heretic: The True Story of Giordano Bruno, the Man Who Dared to Defy the Roman Inquisition.* New York: HarperCollins, 2003.

Whitman, Jon. *Allegory: The Dynamics of an Ancient and Medieval Technique.* Cambridge, Mass.: Harvard University Press, 1987.

Wickham, Glynne. *The Medieval Theatre.* Cambridge: Cambridge University Press, 1987.

Wigglesworth, Michael. *The Day of Doom or a Description of the Great and Last Judgment.* Whitefish, Mont.: Kessinger, 2003.

———. *The Diary of Michael Wigglesworth, 1653–1657: The Conscience of a Puritan.* Edited by Edmund S. Morgan. Magnolia, Mass.: Smith Peter, 1990.

———. *The Poems of Michael Wigglesworth.* Edited by Ronald A. Bosco. Lanham, Mass.: University Press of America, 1989.

Willard, Charity Cannon. *Christine de Pizan: Her Life and Works.* New York: Persea Books, 1984.

Williams, Annwyl. *Clément Marot: Figure, Text and Intertext.* Lewiston, N.Y.: Edwin Mellen Press, 1990.

Williams, H. Noel. *The Pearl of Princesses: The Life of Marguerite D'Angouleme, Queen of Navarre.* Whitefish, Mont.: Kessinger, 2004.

Williams, John. *The Life of Goethe: A Critical Biography.* Malden, Mass.: Blackwell Publishers, 2001.

Williams, Roger. *A Key into the Language of America.* Bedford, Mass.: Applewood Books, 1997.

———. *The Complete Writings of Roger Williams.* New York: Russell and Russell, 1963.

Wilson, Arthur M. *Diderot.* New York: Oxford University Press, 1972.

Winslow, Ola Elizabeth. *John Eliot, "Apostle to the Indians."* Boston: Houghton Mifflin. 1968.

Winthrop, John. *Journal of John Winthrop: 1630–1649.* Edited by Richard S. Dunn, et al. Cambridge, Mass.: Belknap/Harvard University Press, 1996.

———. *Short Story of the Rise, Reign and Ruin of the Antinomians, Familists and Libertines That Infected the Churches of New England (1644).* Whitefish, Mont.: Kessinger, 2003.

Wong, Timothy C. *Wu Ching-Tzu.* Boston: G.K. Hall, 1978.

Woolhouse, R. S., and Richard Francks, eds. *Philosophical Texts.* Oxford: Oxford University Press, 1998.

Woolman, John. *Journal of John Woolman and Plea for the Poor.* Eugene, Ore.: Wipf and Stock, 1998.

———. *Walking Humbly with God: Selected Writings of John Woolman.* Nashville, Tenn.: Upper Room Books, 2000.

Wordsworth, William. *Sonnet Series and Itinerary Poems, 1820–1845.* Ithaca, N.Y.: Cornell University Press, 2004.

Wu Ch'eng-en. *Monkey: Selections from Hsi Yu Chi.* Translated by Arthur Waley. New York: Grove, 1984.

———. *The Journey to the West,* 4 vols. Translated by Anthony C. Yu. Chicago: University of Chicago Press, 1977.

Wu Ching-tzu. *The Scholars.* Translated by Gladys Yang and Yang Hsien-Yi. La Vergne, Tenn.: University Press of the Pacific, 2001.

Wu Shi-Chang. *On the Red Chamber Dream.* Oxford: Clarendon Press, 1961.

Wyclif, John. *Select English Writings.* Edited by Herbert E. Winn. New York: AMS Press, 1976.

Yarbro-Bejarano, Yvonne M. *Feminism and the Honor Plays of Lope de Vega.* West Lafayette, Ind.: Purdue University Press, 1994.

Yuan Hung-tao, and Hongdao Yuan. *Pilgrim of the Clouds: Poems and Essays from Ming China.* Translated by Jonathan Chaves. New York: Weatherhill, 1992.

Zagarri, Rosemarie. *A Woman's Dilemma: Mercy Otis Warren and the American Revolution.* Wheeling, Ill.: Harlan Davidson, 1995.

Zerner, Henri. *Renaissance Art in France: The Invention of Classicism.* Paris: Flammarion, 2004.

INDEX

Boldface page references refer to main entries.

A

Aardema, Verna 10
Abdallah, Sayyid **1**
Abenaljatib. *See* Ibn al-Khatīb
Abraham and Isaac 66
The Abridgement of the Public Laws of Virginia
    (Beverly) 22
Academia dei Ricovrati 264
Academia de los Ociosos 8
Academia Imitatoria 8
Académie française **1–2**, 25, 64, 145, 149, 174,
    221, 240, 264, 298
Academy of Arcadia 184
Academy of Dijon 250
Academy of Idlers 8
Academy of Imitators 8
Academy of Sciences (France) 4
Academy of Sciences (Russia) 160
Academy of the Transformed 214
An Account of Corsica (Boswell) 28
"An Account of the Montauk Indians on Long
    Island" (Occom) 209
"Account of the Vine of North America"
    (Bartram) 17
"A Córdoba" ("To Córdoba"; Góngora y Argote)
    105
Acosta, José de **2–3**
Across the Bridge, Juana (Lope de Vega). *See Por la
    puente Juana*
Adages (Erasmus) 88
Adams, Abigail 303
Adams, John 122, 293, 303
Addison, Joseph 278
An Address to the Negroes in the State of New-York
    (Hammon) 111
Admiral's Men 176
Adoration of the Magi (Leonardo da Vinci) 155
The Adulateur, A Tragedy (Warren) 303
The Advancement of Learning (Bacon) 14
Adventures in the unknown interior of America
    (Cabeza de Vaca) 35
The Adventures of Hans Staden (Staden) 276–277
Adventures of Huckleberry Finn (Twain) 50
The Aeneid (Virgil) 86, 87, 263, 282
Aeneis (Douglas, trans.) 263
Aeschylus 289

Aesop 10, 91, 142, 149
Aethopian Historie (Heliodorus) 270
Afectos vencen finezas (*Affections Conquer
    Finenesses;* Peralta) 220
The Affected Young Ladies (Molière) 58
Affections Conquer Finenesses (Peralta). *See Afectos
    vencen finezas*
African-American literature 87, 111–112,
    304–305
African literature 10–11, 16
"African Slavery in America" (Paine) 212
Against the Jews and Their Lies (Luther) 166
Aglaia (periodical) 77
Alba, Duchess of 285
Alba, Duke of 161
Alberti, Leon Battista **3–4**
Albrecht (prince of Königsberg) 140
Albret, Henri d' (king of Navarre) 172–173
Albret, Jeanne d' (queen of Navarre) 173
The Alchemist (Jonson) 127
Alcuin: A Dialogue (Brown) 31
Alejandra (Aregensola) 8
Alembert, Jean Le Rond d' 2, **4–5**
    Académie française and 2
    Encyclopédia and 76, 82, 85, 194, 243, 251
    Enlightenment and 85, 242, 243
Alembert's principle 4
Alençon, duc d' 172
Alexander in the Indies (Metastasio) 185
Alexander the Great (Racine). *See Alexandre le
    Grand*
Alexandre le Grand (*Alexander the Great;* Racine)
    240
Alfieri, Vittorio 5
Alfonso X (king of Spain) 285
Algonquian Bible 81–82
Algonquin tribe 124
Alien Talk (Dmitriev) **77–78**
allegory **5–6**, 23, 59, 66, 150, 173, 210, 242, 263
All for Love (Dryden) 202
Allison, Robert J. 87
Alliterative Revival 218
All Men Are Brothers (Shi Naian and Luo
    Guanzhong). *See Shuihuzhuan*
Almirante (ship) 230–231
Alvarez, Lynne 288

America (Dwight) 79
"America Independent" (Freneau) 97
American Crisis (Paine) 212–213
American Philosophical Society 121
American Revolution
        figures in 79, 95–96, 133, 198, 212–214, 284
        works on 5, 65, 74–75, 97, 303
American writers 28–30, 31–32, 60–61, 65,
    74–75, 79, 80–82, 87, 94–97, 111–112,
    121–123, 178–180, 195, 198–199, 199–200,
    212–214, 253–254, 273, 283–284, 303–304,
    304–307
Ameto (Boccaccio) 217
Aminta (Tasso) 217, 282
Amphitriões (Camões) 38
Amphitryon (Kleist, trans.) 137
Amphitryon (Molière) 202
Anacreon 72, 160
Anacreontic Songs (Derzhavin) 72
Anchieta, José de **6–7**
anchorites 128
ancients v. moderns debate 279
And My Little Things (Dmitriev) 77
Andrada e Silva, José Bonifácio de 7
Andrea del Verrocchio 154–155
Andria (Machiavelli) 169
Andromaque (Racine) 202, 240, 289
"Anecdote of an American Crow" (Bartram) 17
The Angel of Bethesda (Mather) 178
Anne de Bretagne 177
Anniversaries (Donne) 78
Annotations on Corinthians (Melanchthon) 183
Annuals of the Emperor Charles V (López de
    Gómara) 164
The Antidote (Catherine the Great) 46
Antiquitez de Rome (*The Antiquities of Rome;*
    Bellay) 20, 226
The Antiquities of Rome (Bellay). *See Antiquitez de
    Rome*
Antoinette de Louppes 192
Antony and Cleopatra (Shakespeare) 267
Aonid (periodical) 77
Apocalypse Explained (Swedenborg) 278
Apologia (Pico della Mirandola) 224
An Apologie for Poetry (Sidney) 270
Apologues (Dmitriev) 77

"Apology for Raymond Sebond" (Montaigne) 193
The Apprentice's Vade Mecum (*Young Man's Pocket Companion;* Richardson) 245
Apuleius 270
Aquinas, St. Thomas 39, 286
The Aragon Collection (Poliziano) 227
Aragonese School 8
"Arbitrary Government Described" (Winthrop) 307
Arbuthnot, John 278
Arcadia (Sidney) 217, 270
Archer, Robert 172
Areopagitica (Milton) 188
Aretino, Pietro **7–8**
Argensola, Bartolomé Leonardo de **8–9**
Argensola, Gabriel 8
Argensola, Lupercio Leonardo de **8–9**
Ariosto, Ludovico **9–10**, 283
   influences of/on 15, 21, 48, 161, 282, 283
   literary criticism on 6, 244, 247
Aristarchus of Samos 62
Aristophanes 92
Aristotle 33, 39, 292
   influence of 4, 25, 61, 62, 63, 115, 128, 157, 172, 185, 202, 282, 286
Armitage, Angus 62
Arnauld, Antonie 216
Arouet, François-Marie. *See* Voltaire
Artamene, ou le grande Cyrus (*Artamene or the Great Cyrus;* Scudéry) 264
Artaserse (Metastasio) 185
art critics 4, 157
Arte de grammatica da lingoa . . . do Brasil (Anchieta) 6
Arte nuevo de hacer comedias en este tiempo (*New Art of Writing Plays at This Time;* Lope de Vega) 162
Arthurian legend 97, 170–172, 270, 271
Arthur Mervyn (Brown) 31
Artis analyticae praxis ad aequationes algebraicas resolvendas (Hariot) 112
The Art of Controversy (Schopenhauer) 262
The Art of Literature (Schopenhauer) 262
The Art of Poetry (Boileau-Despréaux) 25
The Art of War (Machiavelli) 169
`asabbiyah 118
Ascanio in Alba (Parini) 214
Ascent of Mount Carmel (St. John of the Cross) 126
Ascham, Roger 115
Asgharzadeh, Alireza 26
Ashanti tales **10–11**
The Ash Wednesday Supper (Bruno) 32
Ashikaga Yoshimitsu 205
Astrophel and Stella (Sidney) 270
Asturias, Miguel Angel 230
As You Like It (Shakespeare) 60, 217, 266, 268
Athalie (Racine) 240–241
Athenaeum (periodical) 261
Atkinson, Alan 281
Attilio Regolo (Metastasio) 185
Aubigné, Agrippa d' **11**
Augsburg Confession 183
Augustine, Saint 6, 115, 222, 286, 290
Australia, settlement of 230–231, 284, 304
Australian literature 304
autobiography 5, 11, 12, 95–96, 119, 121, 135, 194, 251, 252–253, 262, 285
The Autobiography of Benjamin Franklin (Franklin) 95–96
Autobiography of Michel de Montaigne (Montaigne) 194

Aventures du baron de Fæneste (d'Aubigné) 11
Averroës 39
Avicenna 61
Avvakum **12**
Axayacatl of Tenochtitlán **12–13**, 196
Axelard, Jacob 97
Ayamonte, marques de 106
Aztec Empire 64, 159
Aztec literature 12–13, 36, 159, 195–196, 201–202, 202–204, 235

B

Bacon, Francis **14–15**, 56, 59, 73, 293
Bacon, Nathaniel 61
Baïf, Jean-Antoine 225
Bajazet (Racine) 240
Balboa, Vasco Nuñez de 303
Balbuena, Bernardo de **15–16**
ballads, English **84**
Bamana Segu, Epic of **16**, 275
Bambara people 275
Banks, Joseph **16–17**
Barbé-Marbois, François, marquis de 122
The Barber of Seville (Beaumarchais) 19
The Barber of Seville (Rossini) 19
Barbour, John 262
Barlaam and Josaphat 90
Bartels, Emily C. 176
Barth, John 61
Bartram, John 17
Bartram, William **17**
The Bashful Man in the Palace (Tirso de Molina) 287
Bashō **17–19**, 111
Basile, Giovanni Battista 221
Bastidion, Eketerina 72
The Baths of Algiers (Cervantes) 48
The Battle of the Books (Swift) 279
Battle of the Teutoburger Wald (Kleist) 137
Battle of Valmy 102
Battles of Coxinga (Chikamatsu) 52
Baudelaire, Charles-Pierre 19
The Bay Psalm Book 82
Beatrice of Nazareth 255
Beatus ille (Horace) 8
Beaufort, Jane 262
Beaumarchais, Pierre-Augustin Caron de **19**
"A Beautiful Young Nymph Going to Bed" (Swift) 279
Beccaria, Giambattista 46
Becket, Thomas á 51
Beeckman, Isaac 72–74
Beethoven, Ludwig von 56, 260
Beguines 255
Béjart, Armande 190
Béjart, Madeleine 189–190
Bellay, Jean du 20, 274
Bellay, Joachim du **20**, 225–226, 274
Belleau, Rémy 225
Bembo, Pietro 8, **20–21**, 71, 244
Ben al-Hatib. *See* Ibn al-Khatīb
Benoît de Saint-Maure 51, 107
Benucci, Alessandra 9
Beowulf 86
Bérénice (Racine) 240
Bergerac, Cyrano de **21**
Bergin, Thomas 24
"El Bernardo" (Balbuena) 15
Bernard of Clairvaux 286
The Best Boy in Spain (Lope de Vega) 163
bestiary 91
Beverly, Anna 198

Beverly, Robert **22**
Beverly, William 198
Biathanatos (Donne) 78
Bible
   influence of 177–178, 218, 305
   interpretation of 290
   King James, precursors of 311
   Martin Luther on 166
   translations of 81–82, 89, 243, 270–271, 311
   works on 222, 233, 311
Bickerstaff Papers (Swift) 278
Bierhorst, John 201–202
Bill of Rights, U.S., influences on 188
"Binh Ngo Sach" (Book on defeating the Wu; Nguyen Trai) 204
biographies 28, 117, 222
blason 177
Blind Harry 262
The Blockheads (Warren) 303
Bloom, Harold 267–268
The Bloudy Tenent (Williams) 306
Blumenfeld-Kosinski, Renate 225
The Blunderer (Molière) 191
Boccaccio, Giovanni **22–24**
   friends and colleagues of 22, 50, 222
   influence of 20, 48, 71, 173, 263
   literary criticism by/on 23–24, 56, 115, 182, 217, 222, 223, 244
   works by 51, 167
Boiardo, Matteo Maria 9, 48, 247
Boileau-Despréaux, Nicolas 2, **24–25**, 174, 190, 277
Bolingbroke, Lord 228
Bolívar, Simón 210
Bondage of the Will (Luther) 166
Bonner, Anthony 297
The Book of Chilam Balam of Chumayel. See Chilam Balam of Chumayel, Book of
The Book of Chilam Balam of Tizimin. See Chilam Balam of Tizimin, Book of
The Book of Dede Korkut **26**
The Book of Examples (Ibn Khaldūn). *See Kitab al-'Ibar*
Book of Feats of Arms and Chivalry (Christine de Pisan) 224
Book of Her Life (Teresa of Avila) 285
The Book of Margery Kempe (Kempe) 135
A Book of Showings (Julian of Norwich). *See Revelations of Divine Love*
The Book of the Chilam Balam of Mani. See Chilam Balam of Mani, Book of
Book of the City of Ladies (Christine de Pisan) 224–225
The Book of the Courtier. See The Courtier (Castiglione)
Book of the Dead 289
The Book of the Duchess (Chaucer) 50–51
Book of the First Navigation and Discovery of the Indies (Columbus) 57
Book of the Foundations (Teresa of Avila) 285
Book of the Jaguar Priest 180
Book of the Three Virtues (Christine de Pisan) 224
The Book of Travels (Çelebi) 46–47
Book on defeating the Wu (Nguyen Trai). *See* "Binh Ngo Sach"
The Books of Chilam Balam. See Chilam Balam, Books of
Borgia, Cesare 155, 168
Borgia, Lucrezia 20
Borgia family 168
Boscán, Juan 274

Bossuet, Jacques-Bénigne 26–27
Boswell, Alexander 27
Boswell, Euphemia 27
Boswell, James 27–28
Botticelli, Sandro 182, 226
HMS *Bounty* (ship) 16
Bourbourg, l'abbé. *See* Brasseur, Charles-Étienne
Bourges, Clemence de 145
"The Bowge of Court" (Skelton) 272
Bradford, William 28–29
Bradley, Thomas 61
Bradstreet, Anne Dudley 29–30
Bradstreet, Simon 29
Bramante, Donato 186
Brandt, Sebastian 30
Brasseur, Charles-Étienne 230, 239
Brazilian literature 6–7, 100–101
Brébeuf, Jean de, Saint 124
Brecht, Bertolt 132
Bredero, Gerbrand 30–31
Breton, André Le 76
Breve noticia de la provincia de la Campañia de Jesús en Chile 1593–1736 (Olivares) 210
"The Bride" (Derzhavin) 72
A Brief and True Report of the New Found Land of Virginia (Hariot) 112
Brief Report of the Destruction of the Indians (Las Casas) 151–152
Bristo (Ferreira) 94
British empiricism 73
Brittannicus (Racine) 240
The Broken Jug (Kleist) 137
Brophy, Elizabeth 245
Brown, Charles Brockden 31–32
Brown, Norman O. 279
Brown, William 277
Brumble, H. David 31
Brunelleschi, Filippo 4
Brunham, John 135
Bruni, Leonardo 115
Bruno, Giordano 32–33, 62
Brutus (Voltaire) 298
Buck, Pearl S. 269
Buddhism 43, 152, 262. *See also* Zen Buddhism
Budé, Guillaume 115
Bulgakov, Mikhail 190
Bulin Waishi (*Ju-lin wai-shih, The Scholars, Unofficial History of the Literati,* Wu Jingzi) 41, 310
Bunina, Anna 33
Bunraku 33–34, 52–54, 131, 281
Bunyan, John 212
Burger, Gottfried August 274
Burke, Peter 190
El burlador de Sevilla (*The Seducer of Seville; Don Juan and the Stone Guest;* Tirso de Molina) 287–288, 289
Burns, Robert 263
Bustamante Carlos Inca, Calixto 43
Butler, Samuel 60
Byng, Sir John 300
Byron, Lord 233, 283, 288

C

The Cabal of the Horse Pegasus (Bruno) 32
Cabeza de Vaca, Álvar Núñez 35–36
"Cacamatzín Icuic" ("Song by Cacamatzín"; Cacamatzín) 36
Cacamatzín of Texcoco 36
Caesar, Julius 298
Calcar, Jan Stephan van 294
calculus, invention of 153

Calderón de la Barca, Pedro 36–37, 288, 289
calligraphers 136
Callot, Jacques 107
Calvert, Benedict Leonard 61
Calvin, John 37–38, 177, 244, 284–285
Camões, Luíz Vaz de 38–39, 39, 94, 274
Campagne in Frankreich —1792 (*The Campaign in France in 1792;* Goethe) 102
Campanella, Tommaso 39, 293
Canavaggio, Jean 48
The Candidates (Munford) 198
Candide (Voltaire) 85, 154, 202, 243, 298, 299–300
Cantares mexicanas (*Mexican Songs;* Bierhorst, trans.) 201–202
Cantemir, Antiokh 232
Cantemir, Dimitrie 40, 232
The Canterbury Tales (Chaucer) 51–52, 91, 150, 167, 262
Canto a Caliope (Cervantes) 105
"Cant spiritual" ("Spiritual Song"; March) 172
canzonette 185
Canzoniere (*Lyric Poems, Rhymes;* Petrarch) 222–223, 274
Cao Xueqin (Ts`ao Hsüeh-ch'in) 40–43
Cao Yin 40
capa y espada. See cloak-and-sword plays
Capitana (ship) 230–231
Captain Singleton (Defoe) 70
captivity narratives 252–253, 276–277
The Captivity of Hans Staden of Hesse (Staden) 277
Les Caractères de Théophraste (*The Characters of Theophrastes;* La Bruyère) 145–146
Caramurú (*Sea Dragon;* Santa Ritta Durão) 100–101
Carew, Thomas 78
Carlyle, Thomas 17
carpe diem 248, 263
Carrió de la Vandera, Alonso 43–44
Carroll, Evan 308
Carroll, Jonathan 44
Cartas de relación (Cortés) 64
cartharsis 289
Carver, John 29
Carver, Jonathan 44
Cases of Conscience Concerning Evil Spirits (Mather) 179
Castel, Etienne de 224
Castellanos, Juan de 45
Castelvetro, Ludovico 292
Castiglione, Baldessare 21, 45–46, 71, 244, 282
The Castle of Perseverance 67
Catalan literature 172
Catherine II (empress of Russia). *See* Catherine the Great
Catherine the Great 46, 71, 72, 77, 105, 160, 242
Cato 178
Catone in Utica (Metastasio) 185
Catullus 71, 177, 223
Cause, Principle, and the One (Bruno) 32
Cawley, A. C. 90
Caxton, Thomas 171
Çelebi, Evliya 46–47
Cénie (Graffigny) 107
"The Century of Louis the Great" (Perrault) 2
Cepeda y Ahumada, Teresa de 284
Cervantes Saavedra, Miguel de 47–50
    influences of/on 8, 49–50, 125, 161, 174–175
    literary criticism by/on 48–50, 105, 125, 244, 247, 280
Chagall, Mark 149

Chambers *Cyclopedia* 76
Champion, Anne-Toinette 76
Chaplin, Charlie 60, 92
Chapman, George 177
The Characters of Theophrastes (La Bruyère). *See Les Caractères de Théophraste*
Charlemagne 9, 282
Charles I (king of England) 27, 188, 219
Charles I (king of Spain) 64. *See also* Charles V (Holy Roman Emperor)
Charles II (king of England) 218–219
Charles III (king of Spain) 210, 296
Charles IV (Holy Roman Emperor) 294
Charles IX (king of France) 248
Charles V (Holy Roman Emperor) 64, 164, 238, 294. *See also* Charles I (king of England)
Charles VI (Holy Roman Emperor) 184, 210, 224
Charles XII (king of Sweden) 298
Charlotte: A Tale of Truth (Rowson) 253
Charlotte Temple (Rowson) 253
Chassaigne, Françoise de la 192
Chateaubriand, François-Auguste-René de 17, 44
Châtelet, Madame du 298
Chaucer, Geoffrey 50–52
    contemporaries of 106, 150, 218
    influences of/on 91, 97, 113, 167, 223, 262, 263, 271
    literary criticism by/on 51–52, 106, 150, 167
Chaves, Jonathan 312
Cheke, John 115
Cheng, Vincent 64
Chen Yun (Ch'en Yün) 268–269
Chester cycle 66
Chesterton, G. K. 52
The Chest of Gold (Ariosto) 9
Chiang Su-Hui 269
Chibcha tribe 124
Chi-Chen Wang 41
Chichi No Shuen Nikki (*Diary of My Father's Last Days;* Kobayashi Issa) 139
Chikamatsu Hanji 34
Chikamatsu Monzaemon 34, 52–54, 131–132
Chilam Balam, Books of 25–26, 54–55
Chilam Balam of Chumayel, Book of 25–26
Chilam Balam of Mani, Book of 54–55
Chilam Balam of Tizimin, Book of 54
Chilean literature 210
Chinese literature 40–43, 125–126, 158–159, 164–165, 268–269, 269–270, 281–282, 307–310, 310, 312
Chinsa 152
chivalry 45, 171, 270, 271, 284
Chong Hasang 130
Chongjo (king of Korea) 130
Chong Zhen (Ch'ung-chen; emperor of China) 141
chonin 126
Choon Huang Jun 55
Chrétien de Troyes 171, 271
The Christian Faith (Ruusbroec) 255
The Christian Philosopher (Mather) 178, 179
Christina (queen of Sweden) 72
Christine de Pisan. *See* Pisan, Christine de
"A Christmas Cradle" (Lope de Vega) 163
Chronicle of the Battle of Ichinotani 132
Chronicle of the Romanians, Moldavians, and Vlachs (Cantemir) 40
Chronicles (Froissart) 97
chuan-chi. *See* zhuanji
ch'uan-ch'I. *See* chuanqi
chuanqi (tales of wonder) 136

Chung-cheng hsiao-tzu lien-huan chien (*The Repeated Admonition of an Upright Devoted Son;* Luo Guanzhong) 164–165
Chun Hyang (film) 55
Ch`usa. *See* Kim Jung Hee
ch'usach'e 136
Chushingura (*The 47 Ronin;* Takeda, Miyoshi, and Namiki) 131, 281
Ch'ü Yu. *See* Qu You
Cicero, Marcus Tullius 20, 56, 62, 97, 115, 221, 294
Le Cid (Corneille) 2, 63–64, 202
"Cinderella" (Perrault) 221
Cinna (Corneille) 64
Cioso (Ferreira) 94
Circulo (Ibn al-Khatīb) 117
The City of the Sun (Campanella) 39, 293
Clarissa (Richardson) 207, 245–246
classicism 55–56, 56, 115, 226, 244, 277. *See also* neoclassicism
Claudius 50
Cleanness. See Purity (*Pearl* poet)
Clélie (Scudéry) 264
Clement VII (pope) 7
Clifford, James 280
cloak-and-sword plays (*capa y espada*) 162
The Cloud of Unknowing 56–57, 129
The Coach, or the Debate on Love (Marguerite de Navarre). *See La Coche, ou le Debat sur l'Amour*
La Coche, ou le Debat sur l'Amour (*The Coach, or the Debate on Love;* Marguerite de Navarre) 173
Coffee Mill (Krylov) 142
Cognitive Space and Patterns of Deceit in La Fontaine's Contes (Grisé) 148
Coleridge, Samuel Taylor 17, 44, 84, 296
Collection of Best Secular and Folk Songs (Dmitriev) 77
A Collection of Plays and Poems, by the Late Colonel Robert Munford (Munford) 198
Colombo, Christoforo. *See* Columbus, Christopher
Colón, Cristóbal. *See* Columbus, Christopher
Colonel Jack (Defoe) 70
Colonna, Vittoria 187
"Columbia, Columbia, to Glory Arise" (Dwight) 79
Columbus, Christopher 57–58, 152, 295, 302
comedia 161–162
Comédie-Française 190, 191, 240
The Comedy of Bristo (Ferreira) 94
The Comedy of Errors (Shakespeare) 266
comedy of manners 58–59, 254
Comedy of the Florentine Nuns (Boccaccio) 23
Comenius, Johann Amos 59–60
Comento de'miei sonetti (*Comment on My Sonnets;* Medici) 182
commedia dell'arte 60, 127
commedia erudita 60
Commentary on Lucius Anneas Seneca's Two Books on Clemency (Calvin) 37
Commentary on Romans by Philipp Melanchthon (Melanchthon) 183
Comment on My Sonnets (Medici). *See Comento de'miei sonetti*
Common Sense (Paine) 212–214
Companion to Education (periodical) 105
A Complete Account of the Settlement at Port Jackson (Tench) 284
Complete Poems (Olmedo). *See Poésias completas*
The Complete Works of Louise Labé of Lyon (Labé) 144–145

Comus (Milton) 188
Concerning the System of the Mohammedan Religion (Cantemir) 40
Concolorcorvo 43
Concord (Kochanowski) 140
Condé, duc de 145
Condé, prince de 190
El condenado por desconfiado (*The Doubted Damned;* Tirso de Molina) 287
Condillac 76
Condorcet, Antoine-Nicolas de 83
Confesionario (*Regulations for the Confessors of Spaniards;* Las Casas) 152
Confessio Amantis (*Lover's Confession;* Gower) 106–107
Confessions (Augustine) 222
Confessions (Rousseau) 251
Confessions of Amant (Gower) 51
Confucius and Confucianism 43, 141, 152, 264
Congreve, William 59
Conjuração Mineira 100
conocimientos de los Tiempos (Koenig and Peralta) 220
The Conquest of Canaan (Dwight) 79
The Conquest of New Granada (Jiménez de Quesada) 124–125
Conquest of the West Indies (López de Gómara) 164
Considerations on the Causes of the Greatness of the Romans and Their Decline (Montesquieu) 194
Considerations on the Discourses of Machiavelli (Guicciardini) 108
The Consolations of Philosophy (Boethius) 51
Constantia. *See* Murray, Judith Sargent
conte moral 120
"Contemplations" (Bradstreet) 30
Contes de ma Mere l'Oye (*Tales of Mother Goose;* Perrault) 221
Contes et nouvelles en vers (*Tales and Novels in Verse;* La Fontaine) 148
Conti, prince de 190
Contradictions, Oppositions and Denials in the Life of the Mind (Pascal) 217
Conventions 217
Conversation for the Freemasons (Lessing) 158
The Conversion of St. Paul 67
conversion plays 67
Cook, Ebenezer 60–61
Cook, James 16
Cooke, E. *See* Cook, Ebenezer
Cooper, Anthony Ashley. *See* Shaftsbury, Anthony Ashley Cooper, third earl of
Cop, Nicolas 37
Copernican Theory 62, 99
Copernicus (Armitage) 62
Copernicus, Nicolaus 32, 33, 61–63, 99, 160, 166, 244
Copland, William 287
Corbaccio (*Old Crow;* Boccaccio) 23
Corneille, Pierre 63–64
friends and colleagues of 25, 241
influences of/on 174, 220, 254
literary criticism on 2, 56, 202, 292, 299
Corneille, Thomas 64
La corona trágica (*The Tragic Queen;* Lope de Vega) 162
Cortés, Hernán 36, 64–65, 74, 159, 164, 203–204, 235
Cortés, Martín 164
Cortigiana (*The Courtesan;* Aretino) 8
Cosmographiae Introductio (Waldseemüller) 295

Costa, Cláudio Manuel de 100
Coster, Simon 31
Cotton, John 178, 179
Cotton, Maria 179
Coudenberg, Vrank van 254
Coulanges, Marie de 265
Council of Trent 282
Counter-Reformation 71, 282, 284–285
The Countess of Pembroke's Arcadia (Sidney) 270
The Countess of Tende (Lafayette) 147
The Country Wife (Wycherley) 59
The Courtesan (Aretino). *See Cortigiana*
The Courtier (Castiglione) 45–46, 71
courtly love 210, 270, 271
Covey, C. 35
Cracraft, James 232
creation myths, Mayan 180, 229
Creation of Adam and Eve 66
Creations (Nikolev) 205
Crèvecoeur, J. Hector St. John de 65
Crèvecoeur, Michel-Guillaume-Jean de. *See* Crèvecoeur, J. Hector St. John de
critics. *See* Art critics; literary criticism
A Critique of Judgment (Kant) 134
A Critique of Practical Reason (Kant) 133
A Critique of Pure Reason (Kant) 132–134
Croatian literature 177–178
"Crónica de Chac-Xulub-Chen" 54
Crónica de la conquista de la Nueva España (López de Gómara) 164
Crónica de los muy nombrados Omiche y Haradin Barbarrojas (López de Gómara) 164
A Crow and a Fox (Krylov) 142
Cruz, Sor Juana Inés de la 65–66
Cuauhtlaptalzén 196
Cutter, John 82
cycle plays 66–68
Cyclopedia 76
Cyrano de Bergerac (Rostand) 21
Czech literature 59, 116

D

La dama boba (*The Lady Nit-Wit;* Lope de Vega) 162
Damned for Despair (Tirso de Molina) 288
Damon (Lessing) 157
Dangerous Liaisons (Laclos). *See Les Liasons dangereuses*
"The Dangerous Neighbor" (Pushkin). *See* "Opasnyi sosed"
Daniel, Arnaut 172
Dante Alighieri
influence of 22–23, 50, 172, 223, 226
literary criticism on/by 6, 22, 56, 87, 182, 222, 223, 225
works by 20, 182
Daoism (Taoism) 43
Daphnis and Chloe (Longus) 247
Dark Night of the Soul (St. John of the Cross) 126
Daurat, Jean 225
David (Michelangelo) 186
Davidson, Cathy N. 31
David's Psalms (Rej) 243
Davies, Rosalind 15
The Day (Parini) 214–215
The Day of Doom (Wigglesworth) 305
The Death of Agrippina (de Bergerac) 21
"The Death of Cuauhtemoc" 54
Death of Oleg Drevlianskii (Ozerov) 211
Death's Duel (Donne) 78
The Debate Between Folly and Love (Labé) 144
De beata virgine dei matre Maria (Anchieta) 6

Decades (Livy) 222
The Decameron (Boccaccio) 23–24, 48
De Casibus Virorum Illustrium (Boccaccio) 167
De Ecclesia (*The Church*; Hus) 116
De Ente e Uno (*On Being and Unity*;Pico della
    Mirandola) 224
The Defence of Poesie (Sidney) 270
Defense (Montesquieu) 194
*The Defense and Illustration of the French
    Language* (Bellay). See *La Deffence et
    Illustration de la Langue Françoyse*
The Defence of Galileo (Campanella) 39
La Deffence et Illustration de la Langue Françoyse
    (*The Defense and Illustration of the French
    Language*; Bellay) 20, 225–226
Defoe, Daniel **69–70**, 87
De Humanis Corporis Fabrica Libri Septem (*Seven
    Books on the Construction of the Human Body*;
    Vesalius) 294
De-Ka-Nah-Wi-Da **70–71**
"De Laudibus Britanniae" ("In Praise of Britain";
    Skelton) 272
"The Delights of Roaming Afar" (Shen Fu) 269
Della Casa, Giovanni 71
Della famiglia (Alberti) 3–4
De natura novi orbis (Acosta) 2
Dengaku 143, 313
De procuranda indorum salute (Acosta) 3
De Revolutionibus Orbium Coelestium (*On the
    Revolutions of the Heavenly Spheres*;
    Copernicus) 62
Derzhavin, Gavriil Romanovich **71–72**
Descartes, René 33, 56, **72–74**, 215, 275–276, 296
Deschamps, Eustace 50, 297
"Description of a City Shower" (Swift) 279
"Description of an American Species of Certhia,
    or Creeper" (Bartram) 17
Description of Moldavia (Cantemir) 40
A Description of New England (Smith) 273
Design for Good Government (Jung Yak Yong). See
    Kyongse yp'yo
Destito, Teresa 296
"The Destruction of the First People" (Sethol)
    181
Devonshire, duchess of 253–254
Devotions (Donne) 78
Dialogh: d'amore (*Philosophy of Love*; Hebreo)
    101
Diálogo de los muertos: La causa académica
    (*Dialogue of the Dead: The Academic Case*;
    Peralta) 220
*Dialogue Concerning the Two Chief Systems of the
    World* (Galileo Galilei) 99–100
Dialogue of the Dead: The Academic Case
    (Peralta). See *Diálogo de los muertos: La causa
    académica*
Dialogue on Nobility (Parini) 214
Dialogues (Tasso) 282
Diana enamorada (Montemayor) 217
Diana's Hunt (Boccaccio) 23
"Diary of a Week" (Radishchev) 242
The Diary of Michael Wigglesworth, 1653–1657
    (Wigglesworth) 306
Diary of My Father's Last Days (Kobayashi Issa).
    See *Chichi No Shuen Nikki*
Díaz del Castillo, Bernal 65, 74, 164
Diaz de Vivar, Rodrigo 63
Dickinson, Emily 39
Dickinson, John **74–75**
Dictionary of Music (Rousseau) 251
Dictionary of Proper Sino-Korean Pronunciation
    (Se-jong). See *Dongguk jeong-un*

Diderot, Denis **75–77**
    Encyclopedia and 82, 85, 194, 243, 250
    Enlightenment and 85, 242, 243, 258
    friends and colleagues of 4, 46, 250, 251
    influences of/on 157, 194
    literary criticism by/on 76–77, 107
Dido, Queen of Carthage (Marlowe) 176
Dido Forsaken (Metastasio) 185
Die Leiden des jungen Werther (*The Sorrows of
    Young Werther*; Goethe) 102–103, 207, 245
Different Works (de Bergerac) 21
Dimitrii the Impostor (Sumarokov) 277
Din, Lisan al-. See Ibn al-Khatīb
Dionysius 56
Discourse of Irish Affairs (Sidney) 270
Discourse on Metaphysics (Leibniz) 153
Discourse on Method (Descartes) 73
Discourse on Ordering the Popular Government
    (Guicciardini) 108
Discourse on the Arts and Sciences (Rousseau) 250
Discourse on Two New Sciences (Galileo Galilei)
    100
Discourses on the First Decade of Titus Livy
    (Machiavelli) 169
Dismissal of the Grecian Envoys (Kochanowski)
    140
A Dissertation on Greater Exactitude in Navigation
    (Lomonosov) 160
The Divan or the Wise Man's Parley with the World
    (Cantemir) 40
"A Divine and Supernatural Light" (Edwards) 80
The Divine Comedy (Dante) 6, 23, 87
"The Divine Right of Infant-Baptism" (Mather)
    180
Diwan (Hāfiz) 109
Dmitriev, Ivan Ivanovich **77–78**, 105
Dmitrii Donskoi (Ozerov) 211
Dr. Faustus (Marlowe) 176, 289
Doctor in Spite of Himself (Molière) 191
The Doctrine and Discipline of Divorce (Milton)
    188
Dogood, Silence 94
Dollimore, Jonathan 197
Domenico, Giovan. See Campanella, Tommaso
Dom Juan (Molière) 190
Don Carlos (Schiller) 260
Don Catrin de Fachenda (Fernández de Lizardi)
    93
Dongguk jeong-un (*Dictionary of Proper Sino-
    Korean Pronunciation*; Se-jong) 264
Don Gil of the Green Stockings (Tirso de Molina)
    287
Don Giovanni (Mozart) 288
Don Juan 287–288
Don Juan and the Stone Guest (Tirso de Molina).
    See *El burlador de Sevilla*
Donne, John 30, 50, **78–79**
Donno, Daniel 24
Don Quixote (Cervantes) 47–50, 125, 174–175,
    244, 247
Doody, Margaret 279
Dorat, Jean 20
Doré, Gustave 149
La Dorotea (Lope de Vega) 162
Double Suicide at Amijima (Chikamatsu) 52
The Doubted Damned (Tirso de Molina). See *El
    condenado por desconfiado*
Douglas, Gavin 262, 263
Douglass, Frederick 87
Le Doyen de la Killerine (*The Master of Killarney*;
    Prévost) 231
La Dragontea (Lope de Vega) 162

Drake, Sir Francis 162
Drapier's Letters (Swift) 278–279
Drayton, Michael 177
Dream in the Form of a Complaint (Orléans)
    211
Dream of Red Mansions. See *The Dream of the Red
    Chamber*
The Dream of the Red Chamber (Cao Xueqin)
    41–43
Dreams (Quevedo). See *Sueños*
"Drunkard" (Izmailov) 120
Drury, Anne 78
Dryden, John 202, 292
"Du beau tétin" (Marot) 177
"Du laid tétin" (Marot) 177
Dumas, Alexander (Fils) 52
Dunbar, William 262, 263
The Dunciad (Pope) 228
Du Parc, Thérèse 240
Dutch Academy 31
Dutch literature 30–31, 87–89, 115, 173–174,
    246–247, 254–255, 275–276, 300–301
Dwight, Timothy 79
*Dying Speeches & Counsels of such Indians as dyed
    in the Lord* (Eliot) 82

E

Eagleton, Terry 245
Eastward Ho! (Jonson) 127
Ecclesiastical Ordinances (Calvin) 37–38
eclogues 217
Eclogues (Boccaccio) 23
Eclogues (Virgil) 48, 217, 270
L'École des Femmes (Molière) 58
Ecuadorian writers 259–260
Edgar Huntly (Brown) 31
Edgerton, Sir Thomas 78
The Education of the Human Race (Lessing)
    158
Edward II (Marlowe) 176
Edward III (king of England) 50
Edwards, Jonathan 79, **80–81**
Edwards, Timothy 80
Egyptian Book of the Dead. See Book of the Dead
Eight Comedies and Eight New Interludes
    (Cervantes) 48
Einstein, Albert 276
Elegías de varones ilustres de Indias (*Elegies of
    Illustrious Men of the Indies*; Castellanos) 45
Elegies (Labé) 144
Elegies of Illustrious Men of the Indies
    (Castellanos). See *Elegías de varones ilustres de
    Indias*
Elegy of the Lady Fiammetta (Boccaccio) 23
Eléments de la Philosophie de Newton (Voltaire,
    trans.) 298
Eliot, John **81–82**
Eliot, T. S. 79, 176
Elizabeth I (queen of England) 260, 266, 267,
    270, 274
Elliott, Emory B., Jr. 97, 139, 178
Eloise to Abelard (Pope) 228
El perro del hortelano (*The Gardener's Dog*; Lope
    de Vega) 162
Emerson, Ralph Waldo 17
Émile (Rousseau) 250–251, 251
Emilia Galotti (Lessing) 157
empiricism 132, 133, 141
The Enchiridion (Erasmus) 88
Encyclopedia (Diderot, ed.) 4–5, 76, 77, **82–84**,
    85, 194, 243, 250, 251
Endeavour (ship) 16

English literature 14–15, 16–17, 22, 27–29, 50–52, 56–57, 60–61, 69–70, 78–79, **84**, 90, 106–107, 112, 115, 135–136, 138–139, 149–151, 166–167, 170–172, 175–177, 188–189, 202, 218–220, 227–229, 245–246, 252–254, 266–268, 270–271, 271–272, 272–273, 274, 278–280, 283–284, 304, 305–306, 306–307, 310–311
Enlightenment **84–86**
    characteristics of 82
    Christianity in 138
    critics of 249–250
    figures in 2, 4, 75–76, 82, 85, 102, 151, 153–154, 158, 194–195, 232, 233, 258, 259, 277, 297–300, 300
    influence of 93
    prominent works in 82–84, 85
    rationalism and 85, 101, 160, 242–243, 249–250
    reaction against 102
    Renaissance and 244
    romanticism and 132
    in Russia 46
    and U.S. Declaration of Independence 122–123
Enomoto Kikaku 110
epic(s) **86–87**
Epicoene, or the Silent Woman (Jonson) 127
Epic of Bamana Segu. *See* Bamana Segu, Epic of
Epic of Gilgamesh 289
*Epic of Komam Q`Anil. See* Komam Q`Anil, Epic of
Epic of Sundiata 16
Epigrams (Kochanowski) 140
The Epistle of Discretion in the Stirrings of the Soul 56
The Epistle of Prayer 56
The Epistle of Privy Counsel 56
"Epistle on the Art of Poetry" (Sumarokov) 277
"Epistle on the Russian Language" (Sumarokov) 277
epistolary novels. *See* novels, epistolary
Equiano, Olaudah **87**, 289
Erasmus, Desiderius 30, 47, **87–89**, 115, 183, 237, 238, 244, 272, 282
Espinel 161
"Essai sur les coniques" (Pascal) 215
An Essay for the Recording of Illustrious Providences (Mather) 179
Essay of Dramatic Poesy (Dryden) 292
Essay on Criticism (Pope) 202, 228
Essay on Man (Pope) 228
Essay on Merit and Virtue (Shaftsbury) 76
An Essay on Projects (Defoe) 69
Essay on Taste (Montesquieu) 194
Essay on the Manners and the Spirit of Nations (Voltaire) 298
Essay on the Origin of Languages (Rousseau) 251
Essays (Bacon) 14
Essays (Montaigne) 115, 192–194
Este, Alfonso d' 9, 282
Este, Luigi d' 282
Esther (Racine) 240–241
Étaples, Jacques Lefèvre d' 115
Etherege, Sir George 59
Ethics (Spinoza) 276
Eugene, or Fatal Consequences of a Poor Upbringing (Izmailov) 120
Eugénie (Beaumarchais) 19
Eupilino, Ripano. *See* Parini, Giuseppe
Euripides 241, 292
Evelyn, John 219
"Evening" (Parini) 215

"Evening Meditations on the Majesty of God" (Lomonosov) 160
An Evening Thought, Salvation by Christ, with Penetential Cries (Hammon) 111
Everyman 67, **90**
Every Man in His Humor (Jonson) 127
Every Man out of His Humor (Jonson) 127
An Examination of the Nature of Monarchy (Cantemir) 40
Exemplar of Korean Medicine (Huh Joon). See Tongui pogam
Exemplary Novels (Cervantes) 48
Exile (Vondel) 301
Expériences Nouvelles (Pascal) 215
Exposition of the Faith, of the Ten Commandments and of the Lord's Prayer (Hus) 116
The Expulsion of the Triumphant Beast (Bruno) 32
Eyquem, Raymon 192

F

fable 5, 120, 180–182
    writers of 77, 92, 106, 142–143, 149, 157, 211, 263
Fable of Polyphemus and Galatea (Góngora y Argote). *See Fábula de Polifemo y Galatea*
Fable of Pyramus and Thisbe (Góngora y Argote). *See Fábula de Piramo y Tisbe*
Fables (Dmitriev) 77
Fables (Krylov) 142
Fables and Dialogues of the Dead (Fénelon) 92
Fables choisies, mises en vers (Selected Fables, Put into Verse; La Fontaine) 149
fabliaux **91–92**
Fábula de Piramo y Tisbe (Fable of Pyramus and Thisbe; Góngora y Argote) 106
Fábula de Polifemo y Galatea (Fable of Polyphemus and Galatea; Góngora y Argote) 106
The Faerie Queene (Spenser) 6, 9, 247
Fairy Tales (Dmitriev) 77
Fall of Lucifer 66
The Fall of Princes (Lydgate, trans.) 167
Familiar Letters (Richardson) 245
The Family in Renaissance Florence (Alberti) 4
The Family Schroffenstien (Kleist) 137
A Family Well-Ordered (Mather) 179
Famous Women (Boccaccio) 23
farce 60, **92**
    writers of 31, 48, 173, 174, 198–199
The Farce of Simon without Sweetness (Bredero) 31
The Farce of the Cow (Bredero) 31
The Farce of the Miller (Bredero) 31
Farmer's Letters (Dickinson) 75
Farrell, Edith 144
Fashionable Wife (Dmitriev) 77
Fate of Illustrious Men (Boccaccio) 23
Father of a Family (Diderot). *See Père de famille*
Faulkner, William 50
Faust (Goethe) 102–103
Fénelon, François de Salignac de la Mothe **92–93**, 175
Ferdinand (king of Aragon) 57
Ferguson, Elizabeth Graeme 195
Fernández de Lizardi, José Joaquín 93
Fernandez de Quirós, Pedro 230–231
Ferreira, António **93–94**
Ficino, Marcilio 224, 226
Fielding, Henry 157, 207, 245, 247, 280
The Fifth Book (Rabelais) 238
Figure in the Carpet (periodical) 309
Filis (Aregensola) 8

La Fille d'Aristide (Graffigny) 107
Filocolo (Boccaccio) 23
Filodemo (Camões) 38
Filostrato (Boccaccio) 23
Finegal (Ozerov) 211
Fineman, Joel 267
The First Principles of Metallurgy (Lomonosov) 160
The "Five Authors" 63
Five Cantos (Ariosto) 9
Flannery, Tim 284
Flaubert, Gustave 238
Flemish literature 301
Fleurette, Catherine 189
Florentine Histories (Guicciardini) 108
Flores de poetas ilustres (Flowers of Illustrious Poets; 1603) 106
Florida del Inca (The Florida of the Incas; Garcilaso de la Vega) 101
The Florida of the Incas (Garcilaso de la Vega). *See Florida del Inca*
Flowers of Illustrious Poets (1603). *See Flores de poetas ilustres*
flower songs. *See xochicuicatl*
"The Flying of Dunbar and Kennedie" (Dunbar) 263
folk epics 86
The Folly of Affection (Molière). *See Les Précieuses Ridicules*
"Fortune is Often Met in the Path of Reason" (Montaigne) 193
The Founding of Lima or *Conquest of Peru* (Peralta). *See Lima fundada o conquista del Peru*
Fouquet, Nicolas 148
The Four Dreams of Linchuan (Tang) 282
Fourier, Charles 293
Four-Seven Debate 152
The Four Temptations (Ruusbroec) 255
The Fourth Book (Rabelais) 238
The 47 Ronin (Takeda, Miyoshi, and Namiki). *See Chushingura*
A Fox and Grapes (Krylov) 142–143
"The Fox and the Grapes" (La Fontaine) 149
Fragonard, Jean-Honoré 149
Frame, Donald 193, 299
Francis I (king of France) 172, 177
Francis of Assisi, Saint 127, 286
Franklin, Benjamin **94–96**
    contemporaries of 160
    friends and colleagues of 17, 75, 139, 212
    influences of/on 87, 121, 306
Franklin, James 94
Frears, Stephen 146
Frederick II (Holy Roman Emperor) 273
Frederick the Great (king of Prussia) 298, 299
Frederick William II (king of Prussia) 133
The Freeman's Journal (periodical) 97
free speech, origins of 85–86
The Freethinker (Lessing) 157
Frega, Donnalee 246
French literature
    neoclassicism in 202
    sonnets in 274
    works 82–84, 91, 92
    writers 4–5, 11, 19, 20, 21, 24–25, 26–27, 63–64, 72–74, 75–77, 92–93, 97–98, 107, 144–149, 151, 156–157, 172–173, 174–175, 177, 189–195, 215–217, 221, 225–226, 231–232, 237–239, 239–241, 248–249, 249–252, 258, 263–264, 265–266, 296–300

French Revolution 2, 5, 46, 85, 103, 133, 194, 250, 251, 252, 258–259
Freneau, Philip Morin 96–97
Friedman, Edward H. 162
Frobisher, Sir Martin 270
Froissart, Jean 50, 97–98, 210
Fuente ovejuna (Lope de Vega) 162
Fūshi Kaden (Zeami) 313–314

G

Galatea (Cervantes) 48
Galateo (Della Casa) 71
Galen 39, 61, 115, 237, 294
Galilei, Galileo 33, 62, 73, 99–100, 112, 216, 244
Galileo. *See* Galilei, Galileo
Gama, José Basilio da 100–101
A Game of Chess (Kochanowski) 140
The Game of Love and Chance (Marivaux) 175
Garcilaso de la Vega 48, 101
The Gardener's Dog (Lope de Vega). *See* El perro del hortelano
The Gardens of Toledo (Tirso de Molina) 287
Gargantua (Rabelais) 238
The Gates of Language Unlocked (Comenius) 59
Gay, John 278, 280
Genealogies of the Pagan Gods (Boccaccio) 23
The General History of Peru (Garcilaso de la Vega) 101
General History of the Indies (Las Casas) 152
General History of the Kingdom of Chile (Rosales). *See Historia general del Reino de Chile*
General History of the Order of Mercy (Tirso de Molina) 288
The General History of Virginia, New England, and the Summer Isles (Smith) 273
General Natural History and Theory of the Heavens (Kant) 133
Gent, E. C. *See* Cook, Ebenezer
Genuine Consistency (Nikolev) 205
Geoffrey of Monmouth 171, 271
George III (king of Great Britain) 75, 123
German literature
        classical period of 56
        sonnets and 274
        works 286–287
        writers 101–104, 113–114, 132–134, 137–138, 153–154, 157–158, 165–166, 183, 206–207, 257–258, 260–261, 261, 286, 302–303
German romanticism. *See* romanticism
Gerould, Gordon Hall 84
Gerusalemme Liberata (Tasso) 6
"Getting a Jump on Dragon Ball" (Wyatt) 309
Geziod 105
ghazal 109
Gijsbrecht van Aemstel (Vondel) 301
Gill, Roderick 163
Gilmore, Michael T. 31
Giradin, marquis de 251
The Girl with the Jug (Lope de Vega). *See* La moza de cántaro
Glass, Andrew 10
The Gleaner (Murray) 199
Gli Asolani (Bembo) 20
Gluck, Christoph W. von 185
"God" (Derzhavin) 72
God's Controversy with New England (Wigglesworth) 305
Goethe, Johann Wolfgang von 56, 62–63, 101–104, 207
        friends and colleagues of 102, 260–261

influences of/on 103, 114, 133, 138, 207, 245, 262, 276
literary criticism by/on 103, 138, 274
works by 283
Golden Ass (Apuleius) 270
Golden Lotus (Xiao Xiaosheng). *See Jin Ping Mei*
"Goldfinch-Astronomer" (Izmailov) 120
Goldoni, Carlo 104, 254
Goldsmith, Oliver 59
Golenishchev-Kutozov, Pavel Ivanovich 104–105
Gonçalves de Magalhães, José 101
Gonçalves Dias, António 101
Góngora y Argote, Luis de 8, 105–106, 235–236, 274, 285
Gonzaga, Tomás Antônio 100
"The Good Shepherd" (Lope de Vega) 163
The Gospel of the Gospels (Pascal) 217
Gossen, Gary H. 181
Gower, John 50, 51, 106–107, 167
Grabo, Norman S. 65, 283
Graffigny, Madame Françoise de 107, 207
Graham, R. B. Cunninghame 199
Grammar (Lomonosov) 160
"La grandeza mejicana" (Balbuena) 15
Gravina, Vincenzo 184
Gray, Elizabeth 110
Gray, Thomas 105, 304
Great Awakening 81, 111, 209
The Great Didactic (Comenius) 59
The Greate Invention of Algebra (Hariot) 112
The Greater Morgante (Pulci) 9
Great Fire of London (1666) 219
Great Instauration (Bacon) 14–15
Greece, classical
        farce in 92
        humanism and 115
        influence of 2, 88, 102–103, 160, 186, 225, 248–249, 270, 297, 301. *See also* classicism; neoclassicism
        rediscovery of 87, 237, 244
        works on 261, 279
Greenblatt, Stephen 197
Greenfield Hill (Dwight) 79
Gregory the Great 286
Grenville, Richard 112
Griane (Bredero) 31
Griffin, Robert 9
Griffits, Hannah 195
Grimarest, Jean Leonor 191
Grisé, Catherine 148
Groote, Gerard 286
Grosholz, Emily 73
Groundwork for the Metaphysics of Morals (Kant) 134
The Group (Warren) 303
Guardo, Juana de 161–162
Gudzy, N. K. 12
Guicciardini, Francesco 108
Guichon, Marie 221
Guillaume de Lorris 97, 224
Guillaume de Machaut 51, 97
Guillet, Pernette du 145
The Guilty Mother (Beaumarchais) 19
Gukovskii, G. A. 46
Gulliver's Travels (Swift) 202, 280, 290
Gustafson, Thomas 122, 212, 213, 214
Gustavus Vassa. *See* Equiano, Olaudah
Gutenberg, Johannes 244
Guy of Blois 97
Guyon, Madame 92

H

Haac, Oscar 175
Hadewijch of Antwerp 255
Hâfez. *See* Hâfiz
Hâfiz 109–110
haiku 18, 110–111, 139–140, 256
Hakluyt, Richard 112
Hamlet (Shakespeare) 27, 267, 277
Hamlet (Sumarokov) 277
Hammerken, Thomas. *See* Thomas à Kempis
Hammon, Jupiter 111–112
Hammond, J. R. 70
Hampton, Christopher 146
Handel, George F. 185
Hanning, Robert 45–46
Hans Staden: The True History of His Captivity (Staden) 276–277
Hardenberg, Friedrich Leopold von. *See* Novalis
Hargeul 264
Harington, John 9
Hariot, Thomas 112
Harlequin 60
Harley, Robert 69
The Harmony of the Three (Synoptic) Gospels (Calvin) 38
Harrington, James 121, 293
Harriot, Thomas. *See* Hariot, Thomas
Harris, Jocelyn 246
Hatzfeld, Helmut 285
Haydn, Franz Joseph 56, 104
Heart of Heaven, Hearth of Earth, and Other Mayan Folktales 181
Hebreo, Leo 101
Hegel, Wilhelm Friedrich 133, 262
Heliodorus 270
Helvetius 121
La Henriade (Voltaire) 298
Henrietta Maria (queen of England) 27
Henri III (king of France) 298
Henry, Patrick 198
Henry IV (king of England) 50
Henry IV (king of France) 11
Henry IV (Shakespeare) 267–268
Henry of Ofterdingen (Novalis) 207
Henryson, Robert 112–113, 262, 263
Henry the Navigator 57
Henry V (Shakespeare) 267–268
Henry VI (Shakespeare) 267–268
Henry VIII (king of England) 78, 88, 115, 272, 274
Heptaméron des Nouvelles (*Heptameron of Stories*; Marguerite de Navarre) 173
Heptaplus (Pico della Mirandola) 224
Herder, Johann Gottfried 102–103, 113–114, 252, 276
Héricart, Marie 148
hermeneutics 290
La hermosura de Angélica (Lope de Vega) 161, 162
Hernandez Cruz, Victor 140
The Heroic Frenzies (Bruno) 32
Het Pascha (*The Passover;* Vondel) 300–301
"Heuhueh Cuicatl" (Axayacatl) 12–13
Hiawatha 70–71
Hieroglyphic History (Cantemir) 40
Hinckaert, Jan 254–255
Hinduism 262
Hippocrates 39, 61, 237
Hippolytus (Euripides) 241
Hippolytus, Cardinal 9
Histoire de Charles XII (Voltaire) 298

Histoire d'un voyage faict en la terre de Brésil
    (*History of a Voyage to the Land of Brazil*; Léry)
    156–157
Histoire memorable de la ville de Sancerre (*A Memorable History of the City of Sancerre*; Léry) 157
L'Histoire universelle (d'Aubigné) 11
Historia de España vindicada (Peralta) 220
La historia de las Indias y conquista de México (López de Gómara) 164
Historia de la vida del buscón (*The Scavenger*; Quevedo) 236
Historia de los indios de Nueva España (*History of the Indians of New Spain*; Motolinía) 198
Historia general del Reino de Chile (*General History of the Kingdom of Chile*; Rosales) 249
Historia militar, civil y sagrada de lo acaecido en la conquista y pacificación del Reino de Chile (Olivares) 210
Historia natural y moral de las Indias (Acosta) 2–3
Historia verdadera de la conquista de la Nueva España (*The True History of the Conquest of New Spain*; Díaz del Castillo) 74
The History and Present State of Virginia (Beverly) 22
History of a Voyage to the Land of Brazil (Léry). See *Histoire d'un voyage faict en la terre de Brésil*
The History of Greek and Roman Poetry (Schlegel) 261
The History of Italy (Guicciardini) 108
The History of Mr. Cleveland (Prévost). See *L'Histoire de Monsieur Cleveland*
The History of New England 1630–1649 (Winthrop) 307
The History of Richard III (More) 197
The History of Sir Charles Grandison (Richardson) 207, 245
The History of the Growth and Decay of the Ottoman Empire (Cantemir) 40
The History of the Holy Widow Judith (Marulić) 177–178
History of the Indians of New Spain (Motolinía). See *Historia de los indios de Nueva España*
The History of the Ingenious Gentleman Don Quixote of La Mancha. See *Don Quixote* (Cervantes)
History of the Rise, Progress and Termination of the American Revolution (Warren) 303
Hitler, Adolf 169
Hoby, Thomas 45
Ho Chun. See Huh Joon
Hoil, Don Juan Josef 25
Homer
    epic genre and 86
    influence of 160, 175, 193, 228, 282
    literary criticism on 277
    works by/on 92, 226, 228, 289
Hongjong (king of Korea) 136
Hooker, Thomas 81
Horace
    influence of 8, 20, 25, 71, 72, 97, 148, 161, 193, 222, 228, 248
    translations of 160
Horace (Corneille) 64
Hôtel de Bourgogne (Théâtre de l'Hôtel de Bourgogne) 240
Houdetot, Sophie d' 250–251
The House of Fame (Chaucer) 51, 263
Howarth, William 19
Hozumi Ikan 53

Hsuan-Tsang (Triptaka) 308
Hubert, Judd 190
Hudibras (Butler) 60
Hugo, Victor 238
Hu hai ji (*Hu-hai chi; Poems from the Lakes and Seas*; Kong Shangren) 141
Huh Joon 114
humanism 114–116
    characteristics of 47, 56, 61, 87, 115, 291
    figures associated with 20–21, 30, 87–88, 177, 222, 223–224, 226, 233, 237, 249
    history of 22, 87, 183, 196
    Renaissance and 22, 114–115, 211, 244
    works on 20
Hume, David 133, 251
Humphry Clinker (Smollett) 207
Hundred Years War 97, 210, 222, 255, 271
Hunmin jeongeum 264
Huron tribe 124
Hus, Jan 116
Huss, John. See Hus, Jan
"Huswifery" (Taylor) 283
Hutcheson, Francis 122–123
Hutchinson, Thomas 303
Huygens, Christian 153
Hymns (Ronsard) 248
Hymns to the Night (Novalis) 207
Hyperaspistes (Erasmus) 89
The Hypochondriac (Molière). See *Le Malade imaginaire*

I

Ibn al-Khatīb 117, 118
Ibn Khaldūn 117–119, 118
Ibn Zamraq 117
Ibrahim, or the Illustrious Basha (Scudéry). See *Ibrahim, ou le basse illustre*
Ibrahim, ou le basse illustre (*Ibrahim, or the Illustrious Basha*; Scudéry) 264
Ibsen, Henrik 292
Icuic Nezahualpilli yc Tlamato Huexotzinco (*Song of Nezahualpilli during the War with Huexotzinco*; Nezahualpilli) 203
I diloghi (Aretino) 7
Idylls (Theocritus) 217
Ignatius his Conclave (Donne) 78
Ignatius of Loyola, Saint 119–120, 124, 284–285
Ilacomilus, Martinus. See Waldseemüller, Martin
Iliad (Homer) 86, 175, 226, 228
Illustre Théâtre troup 189–190
Images of Divine Things (Edwards) 80
The Imaginary Invalid (Molière). See *Le Malade imaginaire*
The Imitation of Christ (Thomas à Kempis) 64, 286
"Improvised on the Road" (Yuan Hungdao) 312
Inada, Miles 308
El Inca. See Garcilaso de la Vega
Index of Prohibited Books 62, 71, 77
The Industrious Bee (Sumarokov) 277
Inês de Castro (Ferreira) 94
The Infinite Universe and Worlds (Bruno) 32
Al-Inkishafi (Abdallah) 1
in medias res 86
"In Praise of Britain" (Skelton). See "De Laudibus Britanniae"
In Praise of Folly (Erasmus) 88–89
Inquisition 32–33, 71, 99, 162, 282, 299
Institutio Christianae Religionis (*Institutes of the Christian Religion*; Calvin) 37
Institut National (France) 2

"Instructions for My Wife, the Vice-Governor's First Lady" (Izmailov) 120
Intercenales (Alberti) 4
The Interesting Narrative of the Life of Olaudah Equiano, Or Gustavus Vassa (Equiano) 87
The Interior Castle (Teresa of Avila) 285
Introduction to Cosmology, With Certain Necessary Principles of Geometry and Astronomy (Waldseemüller) 302
"Introduction to Volate" (Metastasio) 185
Iphigénie (Racine) 240
Irène (Voltaire) 299
Iroquois literature 70–71
Iroquois tribe 124
Irwin, Robert 118
Isabel de Urbina 161
Isabella (Aregensola) 8
Isabella (queen of Spain) 57
Ischia, bishop of 296
Islam, influence of 275
Isocrates 188
Italian Journey (Goethe) 104
Italian literature
    genres 60
    humanism in 115
    three crowns of 22, 223
    writers 3–4, 5, 7–8, 8–9, 9–10, 20–21, 32–33, 39, 45–46, 57–58, 71, 104, 108, 154–156, 168–170, 182, 184–188, 199, 214–215, 221–225, 226–227, 232–233, 282–283, 295, 296
The Itching Parrot (Fernández de Lizardi). See *El periquillo sarniento*
It Is an Ill Wind That Blows No Good (Ruiz de Alarcón). See *No hay mal que por bien no venga*
Ixlilxochitl of Texcoco 36
Izmailov, Aleksandr 120
Izumi school 143

J

Jacques le fataliste et son maître (*Jacques the Fatalist and his master*; Diderot) 77
Jakaltek Mayan literature 141
James I (king of England) 14, 78, 127, 128
James I (king of Scotland) 262
James II (king of England) 69
James IV (king of Scotland) 263
Jansenists 215–216, 239–240
Japanese literature
    Bunraku. See Bunraku
    haiku. See haiku
    Kabuki. See Kabuki
    Kyogen 126, 143
    Noh (Nō). See Noh
    writers 17–19, 52–54, 126, 139–140, 256, 281, 313–314
Jara, Faama Da 16
Jara, Monzon 16
Jara, Ngolo 16
Jatib, al-. See Ibn al-Khatīb
Jean de Meun 51, 210, 224, 271–272
Jefferson, Thomas 95, 121–123, 122–123, 133, 306
Jerusalem Conquered (Tasso) 282
Jerusalem Delivered (Tasso) 247
Jerusalem Revisited (Tasso) 282–283
Jesuit Relations (periodical) 123–124
The Jew of Malta (Marlowe) 176
The Jews (Lessing) 157
Jiandeng xinhua (*New tales written while cutting the wick*; Qu You) 136–137
Jian Leng 309

Jiménez de Quesada, Gonzalo **124–125**
Jin Ping Mei (Chin P`ing Mei; The Plum in the Golden Vase; Golden Lotus; Xiao Xiaosheng) 41, **125–126**, 269
Jippensha Ikku **126**
Joan of Arc 224
Jodelle, Étienne 225
Jogues, Isaac 124
John of Gaunt 50–51
John of the Cross, Saint **126–127**, 285
Johnson, Samuel 27–28, 28, 202, 228
Jonathan Edwards (Miller) 81
Jonson, Ben 56, 58, 78, **127–128**, 177, 244
jōruri 34
Joseph Andrews (Fielding) 207
Jou pu tuan (The Carnal Prayer Mat; Li Yu) 159
Journal and Major Essays (Woolman) 307
Journal of a Tour to the Hebrides (Boswell) 28
The Journal of Madame Knight (Knight) 139
Journal of the First Voyage (Columbus) 57
Journal of the Plague Year (Defoe) 69–70
Journals (Riebeeck) 246–247
Journey Across Three Seas (Nikitin) 204–205
A Journey from St. Petersburg to Moscow (Radishchev) 242, 290
The Journeys of Celia Fiennes (Fiennes) 289
The Journey to the West (Wu Chengen) 41, 308–310
A Journey to the Western Isles (Johnson) 28
Joyce, James 296
"The Joys of the Wedding Chamber" (Shen Fu) 268
Juana (queen of Spain) 295
Juan de Yepes. *See* John of the Cross, Saint
Julian of Norwich 56, **128–129**, 135
Julie, or the New Heloise (Rousseau) 245, 250–251
Jung Mong Joo (Chöng Mong-ju) **129**
Jung Yak Yong (Chong Yagyong) **129–130**
Junto Club 94
Justice of the Monarch's Will (Prokopovitch) 232
Justin (Metastasio) 185
Justine (Sade) 259
Juvenal 160

K

Kabuki 34, 52–53, **131–132**, 281
Kagekiyo Victorious (Chikamatsu) 52
Kakyo (The Mirror of the Flower; Zeami) 314
Kangxi (Kang-hsi; emperor of China) 40–41
El Kanil. *See Komam Q`Anil, Epic of*
Kannami Kiyotsugu 205, 313
Kant, Immanuel 102–103, **132–134**, 137, 154, 260, 262, 278
Kantemir, Antiokh 40
Kantemiroglu. *See* Cantemir, Dimitrie
Kanze. *See* Kannami Kiyotsugu
Kaozhengxue (*Kao-cheng hsueh;* "empirical studies") 141
Karamzin, Nikolai 72, 77, 105, 120, 204, 242
Karamzinians 233
Karl August (duke of Saxe-Weimar) 102
Kate of Heilbronn (Kleist) 137
Kaye, Harvey J. 212, 214
Keene, Donald 54, 281
Kempe, John 135
Kempe, Margery 129, **135–136**
Kerouac, Jack 19
Key Into the Languages of America (Williams) 306
A Key to Annihilating Ignorance (Lee Yul Kok). *See Kyongmong Yogyol*
Kilmer, Nicholas 248
Kim Jung Hee (Kim Chung-hui) **136**

Kim Shi-sup (Kim Sisup) **136–137**
The Kingdom of Lovers (Ruusbroec) 255
The Kingis Quair (or *Quhair;* James I of Scotland) 262
King Lear (Shakespeare) 267
King Philip's War 82, 252
King Se-Jong 114
King Torrismondo (Tasso) 282
Ki no Tsurayuki 289
Kinsakin, Matsuo. *See* Bashō
Kitab al-`Ibar (The Book of Examples; Ibn Khaldūn) 118–119
Kleist, Heinrich von **137–138**
Kleist, Ulrike 137
Klinger, F. M. 113
Klopstock, Friedrich Gottlieb **138**
Knight, Sarah Kemble **138–139**
The Knight from Olmedo (Lope de Vega) 162, 289
"The Knight's Tale" (Chaucer) 167, 262
Knoerle, Jeanne 43
Kobayashi Issa 111, **139–140**
"Kobayashi Issa" (Hernandez Cruz) 140
Kobayashi Yatarô. *See* Kobayashi Issa
Kochanowski, Jan **140–141**
Koenig, Eva 157
Koenig, Juan Ramón 220
Kokusen 256
Komam Q`Anil, Epic of **141**
Komensk_, Jan Ámos. *See* Comenius, Johann Amos
Kong Shangren (Kung Shang-jen) **141–142**
Konigsberg, Ira 245
Kopernik, Mikotaj. *See* Copernicus, Nicolaus
Korean literature 55, 114, 129–130, 136–137, 152–153, 264–265
Kosan Kugok (Nine Songs of Kosan; Lee Yul Kok) 153
Krapp, Katherine 183
Krylov, Ivan **142–143**
Kubla Khan (Coleridge) 17
Kühn, Sophie von 198
Kulubaly, Mamani Biton 16
Kumar, Krishna 293
Kumo Sinhwa (New Stories from Golden Turtle Mountain; Kim Shi-sup) 136
Kundera, Milan 50
Kung-an School 312
kunju opera 282
Kutuzov, Mikhail 105
Kwanami Kiyotsugu 143
Kyd, Thomas 289
Kyogen 126, **143**
kyoka 126
Kyongmong Yogyol (A Key to Annihilating Ignorance; Lee Yul Kok) 152
Kyongse yp'yo (Design for Good Government; Jung Yak Yong) 130

L

Labé, Louise **144–145**
La Boétie, Étienne de 192
La Bruyère, Jean de **145–146**
The Labyrinth of the World and the Paradise of the Heart (Comenius) 59
Laclos, Pierre Choderlos de **146–147**, 207
The Lady Nit-Wit (Lope de Vega). *See La dama boba*
The Lady of May (Sidney) 270
Lady of the Camellias (Dumas Fils) 52
"The Lady's Dressing Room" (Swift) 279
Lafayette, Madame de (comptesse de Lafayette) **147–148**, 148, 151, 175, 265, 266

La Fontaine, Jean de 2, 142, 147, **148–149**, 160, 174, 190, 277
La Fontaine: Selected Fables (Michie) 149
L'Allegro (Milton) 188
"Lament for the Makars" (Dunbar) 262, 263
laments 217
Laments (Kochanowski) 140
Langland, William 6, 50, **149–151**, 218
Languet, Hubert 270
Laocoon (Lessing) 157
Laozi (Lao-tsu) 152
La Rochefoucauld, François, duc de 56, 147, 148, **151**
Las Casas, Bartolomé de **151–152**
"The Last Flight of the Quetzal Prince" 54
The Last Judgment 66
The Last Supper (Leonardo da Vinci) 155
El lazarillo de ciegos caminantes (Carrió de la Vandera) 43–44
lazzi 60
The learned band 232
Lee, Richard Henry 122
Lee Yul Kok (Yi Yulgok) **152–153**
The Legacy (Villon) 297
The Legend of Chun Hyang (film) 55
The Legend of Good Women (Chaucer) 51
Leibniz, Friedrich 153
Leibniz, Gottfried Wilhelm 137, **153–154**, 299
Leigh, R. A. 251
Leite, Maria 94
LeJeune, Paul 124
Le Loi (king of Vietnam) 204
Lemay, J. A. Leo 273
"Lembranas e Apontamentos do Governo Provisorio de São Paulo" (Andrada e Silva) 7
Lena (Ariosto) 9
Lentino, Giacomo David 273
Leonardo da Vinci 4, **154–156**, 168, 182, 186, 244
Leon-Portilla, Miguel 54
Leo X (pope) 7, 20
Léry, Jean de **156–157**
Lessing, Gotthold **157–158**, 276
Le Thai Tong (emperor of Vietnam) 204
letrilla 105
Lettera . . . quattri . . . viaggi (Vespucci) 295
Letter on French Music (Rousseau) 251
Letter on the Blind (Diderot). *See Lettre sur les aveugles*
Letter on the Deaf and Dumb (Diderot). *See Lettre sur les sourds et muets*
"Letter on the Rules of Russian Poetry" (Lomonosov) 160
Letters (Metastasio) 185
Letters, Science, and Arts Lovers Free Society 120
Letters and commands from the time of military service (Nguyen Trai). *See Quang Trung Tu Menh Tap*
Letters Concerning the English Nation (Voltaire) 298
Letters from a Farmer in Pennsylvania (Dickinson) 75
Letters from an American Farmer (Crèvecoeur) 65
Letters from an Exile at Botany Bay to His Aunt in Dumfries (Watling) 304
Letters from a Peruvian Woman (Graffigny) 107
Letters of Report (Cortés) 64
Letters on Familiar Affairs and Letters of Riper Years (Petrarch) 222
Letters Written in France to a Friend in London (Tench) 284
Letters Written on the Mountain (Rousseau) 251
Letter to Christophe de Beaumont (Rousseau) 251

Letter to d'Alembert (Rousseau) 251
"Letter to Soderini" (Vespucci) 295
Lettres d'une Péruvienne (Graffigny) 107
Lettres Persanes (*Persian Letters;* Montesquieu) 194
Lettres Provinciales (Pascal) 216
Lettre sur les aveugles (*Letter on the Blind;* Diderot) 76
Lettre sur les sourds et muets (*Letter on the Deaf and Dumb;* Diderot) 76
Levasseur, Thérèse 250, 251
Levin, Harry 176
Levy, André 310
Lewis, J. 92
Lewis, Matthew 247
L'Histoire de Monsieur Cleveland (*The History of Mr. Cleveland;* Prévost) 231
Les Liasons dangereuses (*Dangerous Liaisons;* Laclos) 146
librettists 184–185
Life (Alfieri). *See Vita*
Life (Avvakum). *See Zhitie*
The Life and Opinions of Tristam Shandy (Sterne) 207
Life in Angiers (Cervantes) 48
Life Is a Dream (Calderón de la Barca) 36–37
The Life of Archpriest Avvakum by Himself (Avvakum) 12
The Life of Dante (Boccaccio) 23
Life of Johnson (Boswell) 27–28
The Life of Marianne (Marivaux) 175
Life of Monsieur de Molière (Bulgakov) 190
The Life of Pico 196
La Ligue (Voltaire) 298
Lima fundada o conquista del Peru (*The Founding of Lima* or *Conquest of Peru;* Peralta) 220
Lincoln, Abraham 123
"Lines, occasioned by the Death of an Infant" (Murray) 199
The Lion King (musical) 34
The Lisbon Earthquake (Voltaire) 298–299
literary criticism 128, 157, 158, 160, 214, 227, 228, 264, 313
The Little Book of Clarification (Ruusbroec) 255
Little Commentary (Copernicus) 62
"Little Dove" (Dmitriev) 77
The Little Moor (Bredero) 31
"Little Red Riding Hood" (Perrault) 221
Liu Wuchi 43
The Living Flame of Love (St. John of the Cross) 126–127
Livy 8, 169, 222
Li Yu (Li Yü) **158–159**
La Llorona **159**
Lloyd, Henry 111
Loci Communes (Melanchthon) 183
Lock, William 61
Locke, John 4, 73, 83, 121, 122, 133, 251
Lomonosov, Mikhail 71–72, **159–161**, 232, 277
London Packet (ship) 212
Longfellow, Henry W. 163
Longus 247
Lope de Vega Carpio, Félix **161–164**
    contemporaries of 36, 235–236
    influences of/on 8, 287
    literary criticism on 48, 244
    works by 106, 285, 289
López de Gómara, Francisco **164**
"Lord Rendal" 84
Lost Empire (film) 308
Louis XI (king of France) 296
Louis XII (king of France) 172, 189, 265

Louis XIII (king of France) 1, 63
Louis XIV (king of France)
    court and associates of 25, 27, 92, 147, 148, 149, 240, 241
    literary interests of 2, 190–191, 264
    neoclassicism and 202
    reign of 151, 239, 265
    works on 221, 240, 298–299
Louis XV (king of France) 258
Louis XVI (king of France) 213
Lover's Confession (Gower). *See Confessio Amantis*
The Love-Suicides at Sonezaki (Chikamatsu) 52
Love Vision (Boccaccio) 23
Lowe, Nicholas 61
Lowell, Amy 19
Lucelle (Bredero) 31
Lucian 4, 50, 97, 220, 237, 280
Lucifer (Vondel) 301
Lucretius 193
Luis de Escatrón. *See* Argensola, Bartolomé Leonardo de
Luján, Micaela de 161
Lully, Jean Baptiste 190
Luo Guanzhong (Lo Kuan-chung) 125, **164–165**, 269
Os Lusíadas (*The Lusiads;* Camões) 38–39
Luther, Martin 165–166
    contemporaries of 88–89, 183
    Counter-Reformation and 282, 284–285
    influence of 257, 260
    literary criticism on 38
    Reformation and 47, 89, 244
    and science 62
Lycidas (Milton) 188, 217
Lyngate, John **166–167**
Lyons, Israel 16
Lyric Poems (Petrarch). *See Canzoniere*

M

The Mabinogion 171
Macbeth (Shakespeare) 267, 289
Machaut, Guillaume de 297
Machiavelli, Niccolò 108, 155, 168, **168–170**, 244
Macuilxochitzín. *See* Moquihuitzín
"Macuilxochitzin Icuic" ("Song of Macuilxochitl"; Moquihuitzín) 196
Maddox, Donald 98
Magnalia Christi Americana (Mather) 179
Il Magnifico. *See* Medici, Lorenzo de'
Magnyfycence (Skelton) 272
Mahabharata 86
Mahony, Robert 280
Maistre Pierre Pathelin 92
Makars 262
Le Malade imaginaire (*The Hypochondriac, The Imaginary Invalid;* Molière) 191
Malcolm X 87
Malebranche, Nicolas de 153
Malherbe, François de 148
La Malinche 159
Mallarmé, Stéphane 19
Malone, Edmond 28
Malory, Thomas **170–172**, 271
Mandragola (Machiavelli) 169
Mankind 67
Man of Lightning. *See Komam Q`Anil, Epic of*
The Man of Mode (Etherege) 59
Manon Lescaut (Prévost) 232
Manrique, Jerónimo (bishop of Avila) 161
A Map of Virginia and The Proceedings of the English Colony in Virginia (Smith) 273
Mapuche tribes 249

March, Ausiàs **172**
Il Marescalo (*The Marescalco;* Aretino) 8
Marguerite de Navarre **172–173**
Les Marguerites de la Marguerite des Princesses (*The Pearls of the Pearl of Princesses;* Marguerite de Navarre) 173
Maria Theresa (archduchess of Austria) 184
Marie de France 91, 142, 171, 271
Marieke van Nimwegen **173–174**
Mariken van Nieumeghen. See Marieke van Nimwegen
Mariken van Nieumeghen (film) 174
Marília de Dirceu (Gonzaga) 100
Marina, Doña 159
Marivaux, Pierre Carlet de Chamblain de 60, **174–175**
Marlowe, Christopher 103, **175–177**, 244, 289
Marot, Clément 115, 148, **177**
Marot, Jean 177
Marquês de Pombal 100
Marquette, Jacques 124
The Marriage of Figaro (Beaumarchais) 19
The Marriage of Figaro (Mozart) 19
Martial, influence of 160
Marulic´, Marko **177–178**
Marx, Karl 133
Marx Brothers 60, 92
Mary: Or a Test of Honour (Rowson) 253
The Maryland Muse (Cook) 61
Mary Magdalene 67
Mary of Burgundy 115
Mary Queen of Scots 260
Mary Stuart (Schiller) 260
The Masque of Beauty (Jonson) 127–128
The Masque of Blackness (Jonson) 127–128
The Masque of Queens (Jonson) 127–128
Massachusetts Magazine (Murray) 199
Massachusetts Spy (Warren) 303
The Massacre at Paris (Marlowe) 176
Massenet, Jules 232
The Master of Killarney (Prévost). *See Le Doyen de la Killerine*
Materials for the Philosophy of the History of Mankind (Herder) 114
Mather, Cotton 94, **178–179**, 179
Mather, Increase 178, **179–180**
Mather, Richard 82, 178, 179
Matsukaze (Zeami) 313
Matsuo, Bashō. *See* Bashō
Matsuo Munefusa. *See* Bashō
Maximilian (Holy Roman Emperor) 30, 115
The Maxims of Rochefoucauld (La Rochefoucauld). *See Réflexions ou sentences et maxims morales*
Mayan literature 25–26, 141, **180–182**, 184, 229–230, 258
Mayflower Compact 29
May Fourth Movement 159
Meat out of the Eater (Wigglesworth) 305
Medea (Euripides) 292
Medici, Cosimo de' 56
Medici, Giuliano de' 182, 226
Medici, Giulio de' 7
Medici, Lorenzo de' **182–183**, 186, 226, 227, 233, 244
Medici, Lorenzo di Pier Francesco de' 295
Medici family 168–169, 182, 186, 244, 295
medieval literature 6, 48, 60, 90, 91–92, 247, 274
Meditations on First Philosophy (Descartes) 73
The Medium (Murray) 200
Meerbeke, Margareta van 255
Meistergesang tradition 257

Melanchthon, Philipp **183**
Meliador (Froissart) 97
Mélite (Corneille) 63
melodramma 185
Melville, Herman 39
Memoires (Perrault) 221
Memoires et aventures d'un homme de qualité qui s'est retiré de monde (*Memoirs of a Man of Quality Retired from the World;* Prévost) 231
Memoirs (Beaumarchais) 19
Memoirs of a Cavalier (Defoe) 69
Memoirs of a Man of Quality Retired from the World (Prévost). *See Memoires et aventures d'un homme de qualité qui s'est retiré de monde*
Memoirs on the Court of France 1688–1689 (Lafayette) 147
A Memorable History of the City of Sancerre (Léry). *See Histoire memorable de la ville de Sancerre*
Memorable Providences, Relating to Witchcrafts and Possessions (Mather) 179
Ménage 265
Menander 58
Menéndez y Pelayo 15
The Men of the Marshes (Shi Naian and Luo Guanzhong). *See Shuihuzhuan*
Mercier, Louis-Sébastien 293
Mercure Galant (periodical) 147
The Merry Wives of Windsor (Shakespeare) 267–268
Merwin, W. S. 187, 272
A merye jest of a man that was called Howleglas (Copland, trans.) 287
Mesoamerican mythology **183–184**. *See also* Aztec literature; Mayan literature; Toltec culture
Messiah (Klopstock) 138
Metacomet (King Philip) 252
Metamorphoses (Ovid) 6, 107, 198
Metaphysics of Ethics (Kant) 133
Metastasio, Pietro **184–185**
Metrical Letters (Petrarch) 222
Mexican literature 93
Mexican Songs (Bierhorst, trans.). *See Cantares mexicanas*
The Mexican Thinker (periodical) 93
Michelangelo Buonarroti 56, 115, 182, **185–188**, 226, 244
Michie, James 149
"Midday" (Parini) 214
Middle Ages 23, 33, 87, 243–244. *See also* medieval literature
Middle Scots Poets 262–263
Milan, duke of 210
Milcah Martha Moore's Book (Moore, ed.) 195
Miller, Perry 81, 180
"The Miller's Tale" (Chaucer) 91
Milton, John **188–189**
influences of/on 39, 121, 212, 283, 290, 301, 304
literary criticism on 205, 217, 277
Minas Conspiracy 100
Minna von Barnhelm (Lessing) 157
Mirabeau, Honoré Gabriel Riqueti, comte de 251
miracle plays **66–68**
Le Miroir de l'âme pêcheresse (*Mirror of the Sinful Soul;* Marguerite de Navarre) 173
The Mirror of Eternal Blessedness (Ruusbroec) 255
Mirror of Man (Gower). *See Speculum Meditantis*
The Mirror of the Flower (Zeami). *See Kakyo*
Mirror of the Sinful Soul (Marguerite de Navarre). *See Miroir de l'ame pêcheresse*

The Misanthrope (Molière) 190
Miscellanies, Moral and Instructive (Moore) 195
Miscellany (Poliziano) 227
Mischief-Makers (Krylov) 142
The Miser (Molière) 190
The Misogynist (Lessing) 157
missionaries, to Native Americans 2–3, 6, 81–82, 123–124, 151–152, 198, 209, 210, 230, 231, 249, 285
Miss Quixote and Her Cousin (Fernández de Lizardi) 93
Miss Sara Sampson (Lessing) 157
Mithridate (Racine) 240
Miyoshi Shoraku 281
mock wills 297
"A Modest Proposal" (Swift) 279–280
Mohammad, Shams ud-Dīn. *See* Hāfiz
Mohammed (prophet) 47
Molière 2, 64, 137, **189–192**
friends and colleagues of 21, 240, 241
influences of/on 21, 60, 157, 288
literary criticism on 58, 63, 175, 191, 202, 277
Molière, A Theatrical Life (Scott) 190
Molière and the Comedy of Intellect (Hubert) 190
Mollel, Tololwa 10
Moll Flanders (Defoe) 69, 70
Momus (Alberti) 3
Monadology (Leibniz) 153–154
Monkey (Inada and Carroll) [anime] 308
Monkey (*Saiyuki;* television show) 308
Monkey Magic (*Saiyuki;* television show) 308
Monmouth, duke of 69
Montagu, Sir Edward 218
Montagu, Lady Mary Wortley 289
Montaigne, Michel de **192–194**
friends and colleagues of 147
influences of/on 14, 238
literary criticism by/on 48, 115, 192–194, 244
Montauk tribe 209
Montcorbier, François de. *See* Villon, François
Montdory (French actor) 63
Montemayor, Jorge de 217
Montesquieu, Charles-Louis de Secondat, baron de la Brède et de **194–195**
Encyclopedia and 76, 83
Enlightenment and 4, 85, 242
influence of 46, 121
literary criticism on 75–76, 207
Montezuma II (Aztec emperor) 13, 36, 64
Montreuil, Renée-Pélagie de 258
Moore, Charles 195
Moore, Milcah Martha **195**
Moquihuitzín **195–196**, 201
Moral, Pastoral, and Amorous Letters (Simocatta) 61
moral fable 120
morality plays **66–68**, 90
Moral Letters (Rousseau) 250–251
The Morall Fabillis of Esope the Phrygian (Henryson) 113
Moral Maxims (La Rochefoucauld). *See Réflexions ou sentences et maxims morales*
More, Anne 78
More, John 196
More, Sir Thomas 78, 115, **196–197**, 293
contemporaries of 88, 89, 238
influences of/on 238, 244
"Morgante" (Pulci) 233
Morison, Samuel Eliot 283
"Morning" (Parini) 214

"Morning Meditations on the Majesty of God" (Lomonosov) 160
La Mort de César (Voltaire) 298
Morte Arthur (anon.) 171
Le Morte D'Arthur (Malory) 170–172
Morton, Archbishop 196
Moscow Journal (periodical) 77
Motier, Jean-François 147
Motokiyo Kanze. *See* Zeami Motokiyo
Motolinía, Toribio de 198
La moza de cántaro (*The Girl with the Jug;* Lope de Vega) 162
Mozart, Wolfgang Amadeus 19, 56, 104, 185, 214, 288
Muhammad, Abu `Abdallah. *See* Ibn al-Khati$$b
Muhammad, Abu Zayd `Abd al-Rahman ibn Muhammad. *See* Ibn Khaldūn
Mundas novas (*The New World;* Vespucci) 295, 302
Munford, Robert **198–199**
Munford, William 198
Munjong (king of Korea) 265
Muqaddimah (*The Prolegomena;* Ibn Khaldūn) 117–118
Muratori, Ludovico Antonio **199**
Muratorian Canon 199
Murray, Judith Sargent **199–200**
Musa, Mark 223
muwashshah 118
My Secret Book (Petrarch) 223
mystery plays 66–68
myth of Quetzalcoatl. *See* Quetzalcoatl, myth of
mythology, Mesoamerican. *See* Mesoamerican mythology

N

Nahuatl poetry **201–202**, 202–204
Namiki Senryu 281
Naniwa Miyage (Hozumi) 53
Napoleon I (Napoleon Bonaparte) 19, 102, 146, 214, 259, 261
The Narrative of Cabeza de Vaca (Cabeza de Vaca) 35
A Narrative of the Captivity and Restoration of Mrs. Mary Rowlandson (Rowlandson) 35
A Narrative of the Expedition to Botany Bay (Tench) 284
"The Narrow Road to the Deep North" (Bashō) 18–19
Narváez, Pánfilo de 35
Nash, Ralph 283
Nasier, Alcofribas. *See* Rabelais
Nathan the Wise (Lessing) 157–158
National Gazette (periodical) 97
National Theater (Germany) 157
National Theater (Japan) 132
Native Americans
Aztec literature 12–13, 36, 159, 195–196, 201–202, 202–204, 235
education and 82
Iroquois oral literature 70–71
Mayan literature 25–26, 141, 180–182, 184, 229–230, 239
Mesoamerican mythology **183–184**
missionaries to 2–3, 6, 81–82, 123–124, 151–152, 198, 209, 210, 230, 231, 249, 285
Nahuatl poetry **201–202**, 202–204
Toltec culture 180, 181, 235
works on 22, 35, 156, 198, 249, 252–253, 276–277, 306
Natural and Moral History of the East and West Indies (Acosta) 3

Naufragios y relación de la jornada que hizo a la Florida con el adelantado Pánfilo de Narváez (Cabeza de Vaca) 35
The Necromancer (Ariosto) 9
Nelson, Lord Horatio 17
neoclassicism **202,** 228
Neo-Confucianism 129, 152–153
Neoplatonism 101, 186
The Neveu de Rameau (*Rameau's Nephew;* Diderot) 77
New Art of Writing Plays at This Time (Lope de Vega). *See Arte nuevo de hacer comedias en este tiempo*
The New Atlantis (Bacon) 15, 293
The New England Courant (periodical) 94
New England Trials (Smith) 273
New Life (Dante) 23
The New Lucian of Quito (Santa Cruz y Espejo). *See El nuevo luciano de Quito*
New Science (Vico) 296
New Stories from Golden Turtle Mountain (Kim Shi-sup). *See Kumo Sinhwa*
Newton, Sir Isaac 4, 83, 85, 133, 153, 216, 278, 298
New Tool (Bacon). *See Novum Organum*
The New Universal Geography (Carver) 44
The New World (Vespucci). *See Mundas novas*
Nezahualcoyotl 184, 201, **202–203,** 203
Nezahualpilli 36, 201, **203–204**
Nguyen Thi Lo 204
Nguyen Trai **204**
Nibelungenlied 86
Nietzsche, Friedrich 262
"Night" (Parini) 215
Night & Horses & The Desert (Irwin) 118
"Night in the Medici Chapel"(Michelangelo) 187
Nijō Yoshimoto 313
Nikitin, Afanasij **204–205**
Nikolev, Nikolai Petrovich **205**
Nine Songs of Kosan (Lee Yul Kok). *See Kosan Kugok*
Ninety-five Theses (Luther) 165–166
ninyo joruri. See Bunraku
Nirokuan Chikua 139
Noah (Vondel) 301
noble savages 250
Nogarola, Isotta 115
Noh (Nō) 131, **205–206,** 239, 313–314
No hay mal que por bien no venga (*It Is an Ill Wind That Blows No Good;* Ruiz de Alarcón) 254
Nomura school 143
Northern Group 136
Notes on the State of Virginia (Jefferson) 122, 123
La Nouvelle Héloise (Rousseau) 251
Novalis **206–207,** 261
Nova Methodus Pro Maximus et Minimus ("New Method for the Greatest and the Least"; Leibniz) 153
novels
    development of
        in China 41, 125, 165, 269, 308
        in England 69–70
        in France 147
        in Latin-America 43–44
    epistolary 107, **207–208,** 245, 251
    Korean 55
    realism in 70
The Novices of Sais (Novalis) 207
Novum Organum (*New Tool;* Bacon) 14–15
N-Town cycle 66
El nuevo luciano de Quito (*The New Lucian of Quito;* Santa Cruz y Espejo) 259
The Nun (Diderot) 77

"The Nun's Priest's Tale" (Chaucer) 91
The Nymphs of Fiesole (Boccaccio) 23

O

Obras poéticas (*Poetical Works;* Olmedo) 210
Observations on the Feeling of the Beautiful and Sublime (Kant) 134
Occom, Samson **209**
Oceana (Harrington) 293
Ocllo, Isabel Chimpu 101
La oda a la toma de Larache (*Ode on the Taking of Larache;* Góngora y Argote) 106
"Ode on the Death of Bibikov" (Derzhavin) 72
Ode on the Taking of Larache (Góngora y Argote). *See La oda a la toma de Larache*
Odes (Parini) 214
Odes (Ronsard) 248
Odes Translated and Composed Near Chitalagai Mountain (Derzhavin) 72
Ode to America's Independence (Alfieri) 5
"Ode to Felitsa" (Derzhavin) 72
"Ode to Joy" (Schiller) 260
Ode to the City of Nuremberg (Sachs) 257
Œdipe (Voltaire) 298
Odyssey (Homer) 86, 92, 282, 289
Oedipus in Athens (Ozerov) 211
Oedipus Rex (Sophocles) 292
"Of Anger" (Montaigne) 193
"Of Cannibals" (Montaigne) 193
"Of Conscience" (Montaigne) 193
"Of Constancy" (Montaigne) 193
"Of Drunkenness" (Montaigne) 193
"Of Idleness" (Montaigne) 193
"Of Insects" (Edwards) 80
Of Plymouth Plantation (Bradford) 29
"Of Repentance" (Montaigne) 193
"Of the Inconsistency of Our Action" (Montaigne) 193
Of Tyranny (Alfieri) 5
Ojeda, Alonzo de 295
Okuni 131
Okura school 143
Old Crow (Boccaccio). *See Corbaccio*
The Old Maid (Lessing) 157
"The Old Pond" (Bashō) 104
Olivares, duke of (Gaspar de Guzmán, count-duke of Olivares) 105
Olivares, Miguel de **210**
L'Olive (*The Olive;* Bellay) 20, 226, 274
Olmedo, José Joaquín **210**
"O Navis" (Lope de Vega) 163
On Being and Unity (Pico della Mirandola). *See De Ente et Uno*
"On Being Brought from Africa to America" (Wheatley) 304–305
O'Neale, Sondra A. 111
On Education (Kant) 134
120 Days of Sodom (Sade) 258
On German Architecture (Goethe) 102
On German Character and Art (Herder). *See Von deutscher Art und Kunst*
On God (Spinoza) 276
On Heaven and Its Wonders and Hell (Swedenborg) 278
"On His Blindness" (Milton) 188
On His Own Ignorance and That of Many Others (Petrarch) 115, 222
On Illustrious Men (Petrarch) 222
The Only Way (Las Casas) 151
On Noble Customs and Liberal Studies of Adolescents (Vergerio) 115
On Painting (Alberti) 4

On Religious Leisure (Petrarch) 222
On Secular Authority and How Far One Should Be Obedient to It (Luther) 166
On the Aesthetic Education of Man (Schiller) 260
On the Art of Building (Alberti) 4
On the Creation of the World (Tasso) 282
"On the Death of General Wooster" (Wheatley) 305
On the Language and Wisdom of India (periodical) 261
On the Life of Solitude (Petrarch) 222
On the Naïve and Sentimental in Literature (Schiller) 260
"On the Painting of the Sistine Chapel"(Michelangelo) 187
On the Relation Between Man's Animal and Spiritual Nature (Schiller) 260
On the Revolutions of the Heavenly Spheres (Copernicus). *See De Revolutionibus Orbium Coelestium*
On the Use of Church Books in the Russian Language (Lomonosov) 160
"Opasnyi sosed" ("The Dangerous Neighbor"; Pushkin) 233
Oragu Haru (*The Year of My Life;* Kobayashi Issa) 139
oral literature 10–11, 26, 54–55, 70–71, 159, 180–182, 289
Oration on Aerial Phenomena, proceeding from the Force of Electricity (Lomonosov) 160
Oration on the Dignity of Man (Pico della Mirandola) 224
Orazia (The horatii; Aretino) 8
Oreste (Voltaire) 298
Oresteia (Aeschylus) 289
Orfeo (Poliziano) 227
Orlando Furioso (Ariosto) 6, 9–10, 282, 283
Orlando Innamorato (Boiardo) 9
Orléans, Charles, duc d' **210–211,** 297
Orléans, duchess of 148
Orléans, Louis d' 210
Ormond (Brown) 31
Orpheus and Euridice (Henryson) 113
Orton, Nick 308
Osiander, Andreas 32
Osorio, Elena 161
Ossian 211
Othello (Shakespeare) 267
The Other World (de Bergerac) 21
Ottoman literature 46–47
Oudry, Jean-Baptiste 149
O Uraguai (Gama) 100
Outlaws of the Marsh (Shi Naian and Luo Guanzhong). *See Shuihuzhuan*
Ovid
    influence of 20, 50, 106, 107, 148, 178, 223, 226, 263, 286
    literary criticism on 6, 277
    translations of 177, 198
Owen, Robert 293
Ozerov, Vladislav Aleksandrovich **211**

P

A Pact with Silence (Rubin) 149
Paine, Thomas **212–214**
The Painter of His Own Dishonour (Calderón de la Barca) 289
Pak Che-ga 136
The Palice of Honour (Douglas) 263
Palmyra (Nikolev) 205
Pamela (Richardson) 207, 245

Pamela II (Richardson) 245
Panchatantra 10, 142
Panegyric to the Duke of Lerma (Góngora y Argote) 106
pansori 55
Pantagruel (Rabelais) 237–238
"Pantophile" 76
"Papillon du Parnasse" ("Poetic Butterfly"; La Fontaine) 148
parable, v. allegory 5
Paradise Lost (Milton) 188–189, 290
Paradise Regained (Milton) 188
Parallèle des Anciens et des Modernes (Perrault) 221
Las paredes oyen (*The Walls Have Ears*; Ruiz de Alarcón) 254
Parini, Giuseppe **214–215**
The Parliament of Fowls (Chaucer) 51
Parrington, Vernon 178
Partridge, John 278
Pascal, Blaise 56, **215–217**
Pascal, Étienne 215
Pascal, Michael Henry 87
Pascal's Wager 216
Passion and Triumph of Christ (Peralta). See *Passión y triunfo de Cristo*
"The Passionate Shepherd to His Love" (Marlowe) 176
"Passion for Poem-Making" (Izmailov) 120
Passión y triunfo de Cristo (*Passion and Triumph of Christ*; Peralta) 220
The Passover (Vondel). See *Het Pascha*
pastorals 161, 176, **217–218**, 228, 266, 270, 272, 282
Pastorals (Pope) 227–228
Patience (*Pearl* poet) 218, 271
The Patriots (Munford) 198
Paul I (czar of Russia) 205
Paul III (pope) 20, 62, 71, 119
Pavel I (czar of Russia) 105
The Paysan Parvenu: or, The Fortunate Peasant (Marivaux) 175
Peach Blossom Fan (Kong Shangren). See *Taohuashan*
Pearl 50, 150, 218, 271
Pearl poet **218**
The Pearls of the Pearl of Princesses (Marguerite de Navarre). See *Les Marguerites de la Marguerite des Princesses*
The Peasant Who Gets Ahead in the World (Marivaux) 175
The Pedant Outwitted (de Bergerac) 21
Pedro II (emperor of Brazil) 7
Penn, William 212
The Pennsylvania Gazette (periodical) 95
Pennsylvania Magazine (periodical) 212
Pensées (*Thoughts*; Pascal) 216
Il Penseroso (Milton) 188
Penthesilea (Kleist) 137
The Peony Pavilion (Tang) 282
Pepys, Samuel **218–220**
Peralta Barnuevo, Pedro de **220**
Percy, Thomas 84
Père de famille (*Father of a Family*; Diderot) 76–77
Pergolesi, Giovanni B. 185
El periquillo sarniento (*The Itching Parrot*; Fernández de Lizardi) 93
Perrault, Charles 148, **221**
Persian Letters (Montesquieu). See *Lettres Persanes*
Persian literature 109
Peruvian literature 101, 220

Peter I. See Peter the Great
Peter III (czar of Russia) 46
Peter the Great (czar of Russia) 40, 154, 232, 233, 298–299
Petite Academie de Inscriptions et Belles-Lettres 221
Petrarch (Francesco Petracco) **221–223**
    friends and colleagues of 20, 22, 50, 97, 222
    influences of/on 9, 11, 20, 23, 48, 71, 94, 144, 161, 162, 187, 222, 226, 248, 270
    literary criticism on 22, 56, 115, 222–223, 244
    works by 273, 274
Petrovich, Avvakum. See Avvakum
Phaedrus 142, 149
Pharmacopedia (Bartram) 17
Pharsamon (Marivaux) 174–175
Phèdre (Racine) 240, 241
Philip, Governor 284
Philip, King. See Metacomet
Philip II (king of Spain) 38, 47, 164, 260, 294
Philip IV (king of Spain) 105
"Philip Sparrow" (Skelton) 272
Phillipa (queen of England) 97
philosophes 85, 242–243, 249–250
The Philosophical Dictionary (Voltaire) 298, 299
Philosophical Fragments (Schlegel) 261
Philosophy of Love (Hebreo). See *Dialogi: d'amore*
Philostratus 128
Philotas (Lessing) 157
Phoenix (Nikolev) 205
The Phoenix 162
Piccinni, Niccolò 104
Pico della Mirandola, Count Giovanni **223–224**, 226, 233
Pidoux, Françoise 148
Pierrepont, Sarah 80
Piers Plowman (Langland) 6
Pietà (Michelangelo) 186
"The Pilgrimage to India" (Wu Chengen) 308
Pilgrims 28–29
Pilpay 149
Pimentel, Maria 94
Pindar 105, 248
Pisan, Christine de 145, 210, **224–225**
Pisan, Thomas of 224
Les Plaideurs (Racine) 240
Plato 6, 115, 293
    influence of 39, 56, 244, 262, 282
Plautus 9, 38, 58, 60, 92, 157
The Play of the Sacrament 67
"The Pleasures of Leisure" (Shen Fu) 268
Pleasures of the Enchanted Isle (Molière) 190
Pleasure with Profit (Tirso de Molina) 287
Pléiade **225–226**
The Plum in the Golden Vase (Xiao Xiaosheng). See *Jin Ping Mei*
Plutarch 46, 62, 115
Pocket Songbook (Dmitriev) 77
Poemas Lusitanos (Ferreira) 94
Poème de Fontenoy (Voltaire) 298
Poème sur la loi naturelle (Voltaire) 298
Poems, Dramatic and Miscellaneous (Warren) 303
Poems from the Lakes and Seas (Kong Shangren). See *Hu hai ji*
Poems on Various Subjects, Religious and Moral (Wheatley) 304
"Poesias Avulsas" (Andrada e Silva) 7
Poésias completas (*Complete Poems*; Olmedo) 210
Poetical Works (Olmedo). See *Obras poéticas*
"Poetic Butterfly" (La Fontaine). See "Papillon du Parnasse"

Poetics (Aristotle) 128, 185, 282, 288, 292
Poet's Corner 50
Polish literature 140–141, 243
Polish Renaissance 243
Political Discourses (Della Casa) 71
Poliziano, Angelo Ambrogini 187, **226–227**, 233
Pollard, Alfred W. 67
Polo, Marco 303
Polyeucte (Corneille) 64
Poor Richard's Almanac 95
Pope, Alexander **227–229**
    contemporaries of 278, 283, 299
    influences of/on 280, 304
    literary criticism on 202, 215, 277, 280
Popol Vuh 180, 184, **229–230**
Poquelin, Jean-Baptiste. See Molière
Por la puente Juana (*Across the Bridge, Juana*; Lope de Vega) 162
Portrait of a Ruffled Collar (Santa Cruz y Espejo). See *Retrato de golilla*
Portugese literature 38–39, 93–94, 274
Potemin, Grigorii 72
P'oun. See Jung Mong Joo
Powell, Mary 188
Practical Learning philosophy. See Shirhak
Prado, Diego de **230–231**
Prado y Tovar, de. See Prado, Diego de
Praise to the Science of Killing Time (Krylov) 142
Pratt, Leonard 269
The Prayer Against the Turks (Marulic´) 178
Praying Indians 82
Les Précieuses Ridicules (*The Folly of Affection*; Molière) 58, 190
Preparatory Meditations (Taylor) 283
Prévost, Antoine-François (Abbé Prévost) **231–232**
Primeiras letras (Anchieta) 6
"Primer sueño" (Cruz) 66
"Primer sueño" (Quevedo) 66
Primicias de la cultura de Quito (periodical) 259
The Prince (Machiavelli) 168–170
Prince Friedrich of Homburg (Kleist) 137
La Princesse de Navarre (Voltaire) 298
The Princess of Cleves (Lafayette) 147
The Princess of Montpensier (Lafayette) 147
Principal Navigations (Hakluyt) 112
Principia (Swedenborg) 278
Principles of Literature (Parini) 214
Printemps (Aubigné) 11
Prokopovitch, Eleazar. See Prokopovitch, Feofan
Prokopovitch, Feofan **232**, 277
The Prolegomena (*Muqaddimah*; Ibn Khaldūn) 117–118
Proof of the Spirit and of Power (Lessing) 158
Propertius 71
"The Prophesy and Advice of the Priest Xupan Nauat" 54
"The Prophesy of Oxlahun-Ti-Ku-for Katun 13 Ahau" 54
"The Prophetic Words of the Great Prophets, the Principal Gods of the Underworld, and the Great Priests" 54
Prose della Volgar Lingua (*Prose in the Vernacular*; Bembo) 20
Prose in the Vernacular (Bembo). See *Prose della Volgar Lingua*
Prose Lancelot 171
Protestant Reformation. See Reformation
Provincial Letters (Pascal) 217
Prudence in Women (Tirso de Molina) 287
La prueba de las promesas (*The Test of Promises*; Ruiz de Alarcón) 254

Pseudo-martyr (Donne) 78
Ptolemy 33, 62, 302, 303
Puccini, Giacomo 232
Pugachev Revolt 46, 72
Pulci, Bernardo 233
Pulci, Luca 233
Pulci, Luigi 9, **232–233**
Punishment without Revenge (Lope de Vega) 162
Puppet theater, Japanese. *See* Bunraku
Puritans 28–30, 69, 81–82, 178–180, 283, 305, 306
The Puritans (Miller, ed.) 180
Purity (*Cleanness*; Pearl poet) 218, 271
Pushkin, Alexander 160, 233
Pushkin, Sergei 233
Pushkin, V[v]asilii L`vovich **233–234**
"Puss in Boots" (Perrault) 221

Q

El Q`Anil. *See Komam Q`Anil, Epic of*
Qianlung (Ch'ien-lung, Qian Long; emperor of China) 41, 159
Quakers 75, 195, 307
Quang Trung Tu Menh Tap (*Letters and commands from the time of military service*; Nguyen Trai) 204
Quarrel of the Ancients and Moderns 2
Quartet (Krylov) 142
Quennell, Peter 228
Quetzalcoatl, myth of 181, **235**
Quevedo, Francisco de 66, 105–106, **235–236**, 285
Quiché Mayan literature 229–230
Quietism 92
Quintana, Ricardo 279
Quintilian 115
Quoc Am Thi Tap (*Volume of poems in the national tongue*; Nguyen Trai) 204
Qu You (Ch'ü Yu) 136–137

R

Rabelais, François 115, 148, **237–239**, 244, 280
Rabinal Achi 239
Rabutin, Celse Bénigne de, baron de Chantal 265
Rabutin-Chantal, Marie de. *See* Sévigné, Madame de
Raccolta aragonese (Medici and Poliziano, eds.) 182
Racine, Jean 2, 64, **239–241**, 289
    friends and colleagues of 24–25, 190
    influence of 174
    literary criticism on 56, 63, 202, 241, 299
Radcliffe, Ann 247
Radewyn, Florentius 286
Radishchev, Aleksander Nikolayevich **242**, 290
Ragionamenti (Aretino) 7
Raleigh, Sir Walter 30, 112
Rambler essays 28, 202
Rameau's Nephew (Diderot). *See The Neveu de Rameau*
Randolph, Peyton 198
Random Ventures in Idleness (Li Yu). *See Xian-qing ou-ji*
The Rape of Tamar (Tirso de Molina) 287
The Rape of the Lock (Pope) 202, 215, 228
rationalism **242–243**
    Enlightenment and 85, 101, 160, 242–243, 249–250
    reaction against 101
A Real Account of the Life of a Respectable Person (Rej) 243
Real Commentaries (Garcilaso de la Vega) 101

realism 70, 175, 264, 292
Recinos, Adrian 230
"The Reeve's Tale" (Chaucer) 91
Reflections of moral sentences and maxims (La Rochefoucauld). *See Réflexions ou sentences et maxims morales*
Reflections of the Causes of Heat and Cold (Lomonosov) 160
Reflections on the Romans (Montesquieu) 194
"Reflections on Titles" (Paine) 213
Réflexions ou sentences et maxims morales (*Reflections of moral sentences and maxims*; La Rochefoucauld) 151
Reformation 47, 71, 88–89, 197, 244, 282
The Regrets (Bellay) 20
Regulations for the Confessors of Spaniards (Las Casas). *See Confesionario*
The Rehabilitations of Horace (Lessing) 157
Reichlin 183
Rej, Mikkolaj **243**
Relación (*Relation*; Prado) 230–231
Relation (Prado). *See Relación*
A Relation of the Mission of Paraguay (Muratori) 199
La Religieuse (Diderot) 77
The Religion of Christ (Lessing) 158
Rembrandt 301
Remedies for Fortune Fair and Foul (Petrarch) 222
Renaissance **243–245**
    characteristics of 45, 56, 71, 244
    Enlightenment and 244
    figures in 3, 9, 57, 87, 119, 154–156, 168, 177–178, 182, 185–188, 223–224, 226, 233, 237–239, 244, 249
    and humanism 22, 114–115, 211, 244
    ideals in 45, 61, 101, 155, 244
    literature in 6, 45, 66, 94, 217, 225–226, 227, 273, 274, 289, 293
    women in 145
Renaissance men 45, 61, 155, 244
"The Renewal of the Covenant the Great Duty" (Mather) 180
renga 313
The Repeated Admonition of an Upright Devoted Son (Luo Guanzhong). *See Chung-cheng hsiao-tzu lien-huan chien*
Representative Words (Gustafson) 212
The Republic (Plato) 6, 244, 293
Restoration drama 58–59, 219
The Retinue of Love (Orléans) 210
Retrato de golilla (*Portrait of a Ruffled Collar*; Santa Cruz y Espejo) 259
Revelations of Divine Love (*A Book of Showings*; Julian of Norwich) 56, 128–129
revenge tragedies 289
The Review (periodical) 69
Reynard the Fox 91
Rheticus, Georg Joachim 62
Rhetoric (Lomonosov) 160
Rhetorics (Cicero) 221
Rhode Island, founding of 306
The Rhyme of the Ancient Mariner (Coleridge) 17
Rhymes (Boccaccio). *See Rime*
Rhymes (Petrarch). *See Canzoniere*
Richard II (king of England) 50, 97
Richard of St. Victor 56
Richardson, Samuel **245–246**
    influences of/on 31, 146, 157, 175, 207
    literary criticism on 207, 245–246, 247
    translations of 231
Richelieu, Cardinal Amand-Jean du Plessis 1–2, 63, 64

Ricordi (Guicciardini) 108
Riebeeck, Jan van **246–247**
Rights of Man (Paine) 213
Rimas (Aregensola and Aregensola) 9
Rimas (Camões) 38
Rime (*Rhymes*; Boccaccio) 23
Rinaldo (Tasso) 282
The Rise of the Novel (Watt) 70, 246
"The Rising Glory of America" (Freneau) 97
Risorgimento 199
The Robbers (Schiller) 260
"Robene and Makyne" (Henryson) 263
Robert Guiscard (Kleist) 137
"Robin Hood and Allen-a-Dale" 84
Robinson Crusoe (Defoe) 69
Rodderick and Alphonsus (Bredero) 31
La Rodoguna (Peralta) 220
romance 52, 97, 217, 247, **247–248**, 270
Romance of the Late Tang and the Five Dynasties (Luo Guanzhong) 165
The Romance of the Rose (Lorris and de Meun) 50, 224, 271
Romance of the Sui and Tang Dynasties (Luo Guanzhong) 165
The Romance of the Three Kingdoms (Luo Guanzhong). *See San-gouzhi yan-yi*
Romances de los señores de la Nueva España (*The Romances of the Sages of New Spain*) 201, 202
Roman de Thebes 167
Roman de Troie (Benoit de Sainte-Maure) 107
La Romanina 185
romantic epic 247
romanticism
    critics of 138
    Enlightenment and 132
    figures in 102, 113
    German 101, 206–207, 261
    impact of 247
    influences on 84, 138
    origins of 113, 250, 252
    roots of 260
Rome, classical
    farce in 92
    humanism and 115
    influence of 2, 88, 102–103, 160, 186, 223, 226, 248–249, 270, 297, 301. *See also* classicism; neoclassicism
    rediscovery of 87, 237, 244
    works on 169, 261, 279
Rome sauvée (Voltaire) 298
ronin 52
Ronsard, Pierre de 20, 223, 225–226, 244, **248–249**, 274
Rosales, Diego de 210, **249**
Rosand, David 45–46
Rosenthal, Franz 118
Rose Theatre 176
Rossini, Gioacchino Antonio 19
Rostand, Edmond 21
Rousseau, Jean-Jacques **249–252**
    contemporaries of 28, 76, 251, 283
    Encyclopedia and 76, 82–83
    Enlightenment and 4, 85, 242
    influences of/on 31, 114, 133, 137, 146, 194, 245, 251–252
    literary criticism on 75–76, 77, 82, 207, 251–252
    translations of 160
Rowlandson, Joseph 252–253
Rowlandson, Mary 87, **252–253**
Rowson, Susanna **253–254**
Roxana (Defoe) 69–70

Royal Society of London 16, 153, 219
Rubens, Peter Paul 301
Rubin, David 149
Ruiz de Alarcón, Juan 254
Russell, Jonathan 303
Russian Academy 205
Russian Imperial Theater 277
Russian Literature Lover's Interlocutor (periodical) 105
Russian Theater (periodical) 205
Russian writers 12, 33, 46, 71–72, 77–78, 104–105, 120, 142–143, 159–161, 205, 211, 232, 233–234, 242, 277
Ruusbroec, Jan van 254–255
Ryokan (Yamamoto Eizo) **256**

S

Sachs, Hans 257–258
Sade, Donatien-Alphonse-François de. *See* Sade, marquis de
Sade, marquis de 146, **258–259**
Sad Nights and Happy Days (Fernández de Lizardi) 93
Sagi school 143
St. Bartholomew's Day massacre 11
St. Michel, Elizabeth 218
saints' plays 67
Saiyuki (*Monkey, Monkey Magic;* television show) 308
Salem witchcraft trials 179–180
salons 263, 265
Salutati, Coluccio 115
Salviati, Diane 11
Samson Agonistes (Milton) 188
San Diego Union Tribune (periodical) 239
San-gouzhi yan-yi (*San-kuo chih t'ung-su yen-I; Romance of the Three Kingdoms;* Luo Guanzhong) 125, 165
Sansenverino, Roberto 233
Santa Cruz y Espejo, Francisco Javier Eugenio de **259–260**
Santa Ritta Durão, José de 100
Sappho 105, 144
Sarugaku 143
Satires (Ariosto) 9
The Satyr (Kochanowski) 140
Sa vie à ses enfants (Aubigné) 11
Scala, Alessandra 115
Scala, Flaminio 60
The Scavenger (Quevedo). *See Historia de la vida del buscón*
Schiller, Friedrich von 44, 56, 102, 138, 207, **260–261**
Schir William Wallace (Blind Harry) 262
Schlegel, August Wilhelm 261
Schlegel, Friedrich **261**
Schmidt, A.V.C. 150
Schoeck, Richard J. 196
The Scholars (Wu Jingzi). *See Bulin Waishi*
The School for Scandal (Sheridan) 59
The School for Wives (Molière) 58, 190
Schopenhauer, Arthur **262**
scientific method 242
Scientific Revolution 61, 215
Scott, Tom 113
Scott, Virginia 190, 191
Scott, Sir Walter 9, 84, 171
Scottish Chaucerians 262–263
Scottish poets of 15th century **262–263**
Scriblerus Club 278
Scrooby Separatists 28

Scudéry, Georges 263
Scudéry, Madeleine de 25, 148, **263–264**
Sea Dragon (Santa Ritta Durão). *See Caramurú*
Sebastian (king of Portugal) 38
Secret Book (Petrarch). *See Secretum*
The Secret History of Henrietta of England (Lafayette) 147
Secretum (*Secret Book;* Petrarch) 222
The Seducer of Seville (Tirso de Molina). *See El burlador de Sevilla*
Segel, Harold 232
Segrais, Jean Renaud de 147
Segu cycle. *See Bamana Segu, Epic of*
Se Jo (king of Korea) 136
Selected Fables, Put into Verse (La Fontaine). *See Fables choisies, mises en vers*
The Self-Enamored Poet (Nikolev) 205
Semiramis (Metastasio) 185
Sémiramis (Voltaire) 298
Seneca, influence of 8, 115, 160, 185, 222, 286, 289
Sentimental Journey (Sterne) 242
"Sermon on the Interment of the Most Illustrious, Most Sovereign Peter the Great" (Prokopovitch) 232
Sermons of Job (Calvin) 38
Servetus, Michael 37–38
Sessa, duke of 162
Sethol, Salvador López 181
The Seven Enclosures (Ruusbroec) 255
Seventh Diary (Kobayashi Issa). *See Shichiban-Nikki*
Sévigné, Henri, marquis de 265
Sévigné, Madame de (marquise de Sévigné) 147, 148, **265–266**
Sexton, James D. 181
Sforza, Duke Lodovico 155
Shaftsbury, Anthony Ashley Cooper, third earl of 76
Shakespeare, Hamnet 266
Shakespeare, Judith 266
Shakespeare, William **266–268**
    adaptations of 277
    influences of/on 27, 45, 60, 102–103, 157, 177, 299
    life of 48, 50, 127, 266
    literary criticism on 48, 54, 128, 190, 217, 244, 266–268, 288
    works by 202, 274, 289
Shamela (Fielding) 245
Shank's Mare (Jippensha). *See Tokai dochu hizakurige*
Shank's Pony along the Tokaido (Jippensha). *See Tokai dochu hizakurige*
Shaw, George Bernard 288
Shelmerdine, J. M. 148
Shen Fu **268–269**
Sheridan, Richard Brinsley 59
She Stoops to Conquer (Goldsmith) 59
Shichiban-Nikki (*Seventh Diary;* Kobayashi Issa) 139
Shi-er Lou (*Shih-erh lou; Twelve Towers;* Li Yu) 158
Shi Naian (Shih Nai-an) 125, 165, **269–270**
The Ship of Fools (Brandt) 30
Shirhak (Practical Learning philosophy) 129–130
Shorris, Earl 54
A Short Conversation between Three Persons: Pan, Voit, and Pleban (Rej) 243
The Shortest Way with Dissenters (Defoe) 69
Short Story of the Rise, Reign and Ruin of the Antinomians, Familists and Libertines that Infected the Churches of New England (Winthrop) 307

Shuihuzhuan (*Shui-hu-zhuan, Shui-hu chuan, Outlaws of the Marsh, Wild Boar Forest, Water Margin, The Men of the Marshes, Marshes of Mount Liang, All Men Are Brothers;* Shi Naian and Luo Guanzhong) 125, 165, 269
Sidney, Mary 271
Sidney, Sir Philip 30, 171, 217, 244, **270–271**
"Le Siècle de Louis le Grand" (Perrault) 221
Le Siècle de Louis XIV (Voltaire) 298
The Siege of Thebes (Lydgate, trans.) 167
"Siglo de oro en las selvas de Eriphile" (Balbuena) 15
"Sign Language: The Semiotics of Love in Lope's *El Perro del Hortelano*" (Friedman) 162
sijo 129
Silent Operas (Li Yu). *See Wu-sheng xi*
Silverman, Kenneth 178, 179
Simocatta, Theophylactus 61
"Sinners in the Hands of an Angry God" (Edwards) 81
Sir Charles Grandison (Richardson) 246
Sir Gawain and the Green Knight (*Pearl* poet) 6, 50, 150, 171, 218, **271–272**
Siroe (Metastasio) 185
Sis, Bartolo 239
Sistine Chapel 186
Six Records of a Floating Life (Shen Fu) 268–269
Skelton, John **272–273**
Skelton, Martha Wayles 121
Slaves in Algiers (Rowson) 254
"Sleeping at Sermons, is a Great and Dangerous Evil" (Mather) 180
"Sleeping Beauty" (Perrault) 221
smallpox, victims of 265, 307
Smith, John 22, **273**
Smith, William Jay 187
Smollett, Tobias 207
social comedy 58
The Social Contract (Rousseau) 250–251, 251–252
Society of Lovers of the Russian Word 72
Society of Patriots of Chile 259
The Soga Heir (Chikamatsu) 52
Las Soledades (*Solitudes;* Góngora y Argote) 106
Solitudes (Góngora y Argote). *See Las Soledades*
Some Verses by Ripano Eupilino (Parini) 214
Sondheim, Steven 132
Soneti lussuriosi (Aretino) 7
"Song: to Celia" (Jonson) 128
"Song by Cacamatzín" (Cacamatzín). *See* "Cacamatzín Icuic"
"Song of Axayacatl, Lord of Mexico" (Axayacatl) 13
"Song of Macuilxocitl" (Moquihuitzín). *See* "Macuilxochitzin Icuic"
Song of Nezahualpilli during the War with Huexotzinco (Nezahualpilli). *See Icuic Nezahualpilli yc Tlamato Huexotzinco*
The Song of Roland 9, 233, 247
"Song of the Elders" (Axayacatl) 12–13
Songs (Kochanowski) 140
Songs of Flying Dragons (Se-jong). *See Yongbi eocheon ga*
Songs of Liongo (Abdallah) 1
Song Taizong longhu fengyun hui (*The Wind-Cloud Meeting of the Sung Founder;* Luo Guanzhong) 164–165
Son-Jara, Epic of 275
sonnets 273–274
Sonnets to Helene (Ronsard) 248–249
Sonsan of Kaarta, Epic of 275
"Sons of Ben" 128

Son tradition 136
Sophocles 157, 277, 292
Sor Juana. *See* Cruz, Sor Juana Inés de la
"The Sorrows of Misfortune" (Shen Fu) 268
The Sorrows of Young Werther (Goethe). *See Die Leiden des jungen Werther*
Soto, Hernando de 101
The Sot-Weed Factor (Barth) 61
The Sot-weed Factor (Cook) 60–61
Sotweed Redivivus (Cook) 61
Souhami, Jessica 10
The Soul's Awakening (Abdallah) 1
Sovereignty and Goodness of God, Together With the Faithfulness of His Promises Displayed (Rowlandson) 252–253
Spanish-American writers 15–16, 43–44, 45, 65–66, 93, 101, 210, 220, 249, 259–260
The Spanish Brabanter (Bredero) 31
Spanish literature
    Golden Age of 36–37, 48, 161, 254, 287
    humanism in 115
    sonnets in 274
    writers 2–3, 35–36, 36–37, 47–50, 64–65, 74, 105–106, 117, 119–120, 126–127, 151–152, 161–164, 164, 198, 230–231, 235–236, 254, 284–285, 287–288
The Spanish Tragedy (Kyd) 289
The Sparkling Stone (Ruusbroec) 255
Spectator (periodical) 142
Speculum Meditantis (*Mirror of Man;* Gower) 106
"Speech Made by a Scapegrace in a Gathering of Fools" (Krylov) 142
Spence, Joseph 227
Spenser, Edmund
    influences of/on 9, 30, 45, 171, 177, 271, 283
    literary criticism on 6, 244, 247, 274
Spinoza, Benedictus (Baruch) de 33, 275–276
The Spirit of Laws (Montesquieu) 85, 194
The Spiritual Canticle (St. John of the Cross) 126–127
The Spiritual Espousals (Ruusbroec) 255
Spiritual Exercises (Ignatius of Loyola) 119–120
The Spiritual Regulation of Peter the Great (Prokopovitch) 232
Spiritual Relations (Teresa of Avila) 285
Spiritual Songs (Novalis) 207
The Spiritual Tabernacle (Ruusbroec) 255
Squanto 29
Staden, Hans 276–277
Stalin, Joseph 169
Stamp Act (1765) 75, 95
Stanford, Donald E. 283
"Stanzas of the Soul" (St. John of the Cross) 126
Stanze (Poliziano) 226–227
The Starry Messenger (Galileo Galilei) 99
Statecraft Drawn from the Very Words of the Holy Scriptures (Bossuet) 27
States and Empires of the Sun and Moon (de Bergerac) 21
Statius 50
Steele, Richard 278
Sterne, Laurence 207, 242
Stevenson, Robert Louis 219–220
Stewart, Allen 271
Stoddard, Esther 80
Stoddard, Solomon 80
"The story of Hsuan-Tsang and the origin of the Mission to India" (Wu Chengen) 308
The Story of Sapho (Scudéry) 264
The Story of Thebes (Racine). *See La Thébaïde*
"Story of the Owl" (Uípán) 181

The Story of the Stone. See The Dream of the Red Chamber
Straparola, Giovanni Francesco 221
Strauss, Richard 287
The Students (Ariosto) 9
Sturm and Drang (Klinger) 113
Sturm and Drang movement 102, 113–114
Suarez, Michael 245
Subtelny, Orest 40
Sueños (*Dreams;* Quevedo) 236
Sufism 109–110, 117
Sugimori Nobumori. *See* Chikamatsu Monzaemon
Sukeroku, Flower of Edo (Tsuchi Jihei) 131–132
Sumarokov, Alexander 71–72, 160, 205, 232, 277
A Summary View of the Rights of British America (Jefferson) 122
"The Summoner's Tale" (Chaucer) 91
Sun Jo (king of Korea) 114
Supernatural Mail (periodical) 142
Supposes (Ariosto) 9
Surrey, Henry Howard, Earl of 274
Susanna (Kochanowski) 140
Sutra 308
Suyte des Marguerites (*More Pearls;* Marguerite de Navarre) 173
Swedberg, Jesper 277
Swedborg, Emanual. *See* Swedenborg, Emanual
Swedenborg, Emanual 277–278
Swedish writers 277–278
Sweetness of Power (Guicciardini) 108
Swift, Jonathan 6, 40, 202, 278–280, 278–280, 290
"Sydney Cove in 1794" (Watling) 304
Sylvae (*Trees;* Poliziano) 227
Sylva Sylvarum (Bacon) 15

T

Tabishui (*Travel Gleanings;* Kobayashi Issa) 139
Tacitus 46
T'aejong 264
Takasago (Zeami) 313
Takeda Izumo **281**
Takemoto Gidayu 34, 53
Takemotoza theater 53
Takhmisa (Abdallah) 1
A Tale of a Tub (Swift) 6, 279
The Tale of Genji 125
Tales and Novels in Verse (La Fontaine). *See Contes et nouvelles en vers*
Tamburlaine (Marlowe) 176
The Taming of the Shrew (Shakespeare) 266
Tamurlane. *See* Timur Lang
Tang Xianzu (T'ang Hsien-tsu) **281–282**, 310, 312
Tanjong (king of Korea) 136
tanka 110, 256
Taohuashan (*T'ao-hua shan; Peach Blossom Fan;* Kong Shangren) 141–142
Ta'rif (Ibn Khaldūn) 119
The Tartar (Beaumarchais) 19
Tartuffe (Molière) 190, 202
Tasan. *See* Jung Mong Joo
Tasso (Goethe) 283
Tasso, Torquato 6, 21, 48, 161, 217, 247, **282–283**
Tatler (periodical) 278
Taylor, Edward **283–284**
Taymor, Julie 34
Tedlock, Dennis 229, 239
Telemachus (Fénelon) 92, 175
Telemachus, a Parody (Marivaux) 175
Téllez, Gabriel. *See* Tirso de Molina
Telling Maya Tales (Gossen, ed.) 181

Temistocle (Metastasio) 185
The Tempest (Shakespeare) 267
Temple, Sir William 278
The Temple of Fame (Pope) 228
Ten Centuries of Spanish Poetry (Turnbull) 163
Tench, Watkin **284**
Tencin, Madame de 4
Tennyson, Alfred, Lord 171
The Tenth Muse Lately Sprung Up in America (Bradstreet) 29–30
Terence 9, 60
Teresa of Avila, Saint 126, **284–286**
Teseida (Boccaccio) 23
The Testament (Villon) 297
The Testament of Cresseid (Henryson) 113, 263
The Testament of John (Lessing) 158
The Test of Promises (Ruiz de Alarcón). *See La prueba de las promesas*
Tetel, Marcel 193
Tezozomoc 196
Thaler, R. P. 242
"That Our Desire Is Increased by Difficulty" (Montaigne) 193
"That the Taste of Good and Evil Depends in Large Part on the Opinion We Have of Them" (Montaigne) 193
La Thébaïde (*The Story of Thebes;* Racine) 240
The Carnal Prayer Mat (Li Yu). *See Jou pu tuan*
The Church (Hus). *See De Ecclesia*
The Journey to the West (Wu Chengen). *See Xiyouji*
The Little Thunderclap (Kong Shangren). *See Xiao hu lei*
Theocritus 217
Théodicée (Leibniz) 154
A Theologico-Political Treatise (Spinoza) 275
"Things Experienced" (Yuan Hungdao) 312
Thirty Years War 59, 260
Thomas à Kempis 64, **286**
Thomas Paine (Kaye) 212
Thoughts (Pascal). *See Pensées*
"Thoughts of a Fashionable Philosopher" (Krylov) 142
The Thousand and One Nights 51
"The Three Ravens" 84
Thwaites, Reuben Gold 124
Tibullus 193
Tiers livre ("The Third Book"; Rabelais) 237, 238
Tiller, Terence 107
Tillett, Lowell 205
Till Eulenspiegel **286–287**
Till Eulenspiegel's Merry Pranks (Strauss) 287
Timur Lang (Tamurlane) 109, 119
Tirso de Molina **287–288**, 289
Titio. *See* Brandt, Sebastian
Tlacaélel 12, 195–196
"To Córdoba" (Góngora y Argote). *See* "A Córdoba"
Tōdō Yoshikiyo 18
Tōdō Yoshitada 18
T'oegye 152
"To His Mistress Going to Bed" (Donne) 78
Tokai dochu hizakurige (*Shank's Pony along the Tokaido, Shank's Mare;* Jippensha) 126
Tolstoy, Leo 252
Toltec culture 180, 181, 235
"Tomorrow" (Lope de Vega) 163
Tongui pogam (*Exemplar of Korean Medicine;* Huh Joon) 114
Toribio de Benavente. *See* Motolinía, Toribio de
Torquemada, Juan 203
Tosa Diary (Ki no Tsurayuki) 289

"To the Memory of Brave Americans" (Freneau) 97
"To the University of Cambridge, in New England" (Wheatley) 304–305
Tour thro' the Whole Island of Great Britain (Defoe) 70
tragedy **288–289**. *See also melodramma*
The Tragedy of Inês de Castro (Ferreira) 94
The Tragic Queen (*La corona trágica*; Lope de Vega) 162
Les Tragiques (d'Aubigné) 11
Travel Gleanings (Kobayashi Issa). *See Tabishui*
The Traveller Returned (Murray) 200
travel narratives 17, 18–19, 43–44, 46–47, 57–58, 156, 204–205, 242, 273, 284, **289–290**, 295
Travels Through North and South Carolina . . . and the Country of the Chactaws (Bartram) 17
Travels through the Interior Parts of North America in the Years 1766, 1767, 1768 (Carver) 44
The Treatise (Lessing) 157
The Treatise of Discerning of Spirits 56
Treatise of the Culture of the Tobacco Plant (Carver) 44
A Treatise on Tolerance (Voltaire) 299
Treatises of Civil Government (Locke) 122
Trees (Poliziano). *See Sylvae*
Treny: The Laments of Kochanowski (Kochanowski) 140
The Trials of Persiles and Segismunda (Cervantes) 48
Trifles (Rej) 243
Le Triomphe de l'Aigneau (*The Triumph of the Lamb*; Marguerite de Navarre) 173
Triptaka. *See Hsuan-Tsang*
The Triumph of Love and Death (Peralta). *See Triunfo de amor y muerte*
Triumphs (Petrarch) 222
Triunfo de amor y muerte (*The Triumph of Love and Death*; Peralta) 220
Troilus and Criseyde (Chaucer) 51, 106, 113, 263
The True-Born Englishman (Defoe) 69
The True History of the Conquest of New Spain (Díaz del Castillo). *See Historia verdadera de la conquista de la Nueva España*
A True Relation of Such Occurrences and Accidents of Note as Happened in Virginia (Smith) 273
Truth Can't Be Trusted or the Liar (Ruiz de Alarcón) 254
The Truth of the Sacred Scriptures (Wycliffe) 311
The Truth Suspect (Ruiz de Alarcón). *See La verdad sospechosa*
Tsuchi Jihei 131–132
Tully 178
Turgot, Anne-Robert-Jacques 83
Turkish Embassy Letters (Montagu) 289
Turley, Hans 70
Turnbull, Elizabeth 163
Turner, Elizabeth 227
Twain, Mark 50
Twelfth Night (Shakespeare) 266
The Twelve Beguines (Ruusbroec) 255
Twelve Towers (Li Yu). *See Shi-er Lou*
The Two Friends (Beaumarchais) 19
Tyard, Pontus de 225
typology **290–291**

U

Uemura Bunrakuken 34
Ujpán, Ignacio Bizarro 181
unities **292–293**
The Universal Monarchy (Montesquieu) 194

Unofficial History of the Literati (Wu Jingzi). *See Bulin Waishi*
Urban VIII (pope) 100
Usk, Thomas 50
Utopia (More) 197, 238, 244, 293
Utopianism (Kumar) 293
utopias **293**

V

Vacca, Nicola 185
Vaez de Torres, Luis 230
Valdez, Luis 239
Van Dyck, Sir Anthony 301
Various Songs (Brandt) 30
Vassa, Gustavus. *See Equiano, Olaudah*
La vega del Parnaso (Lope de Vega) 162
Veláquez, Diego 64
Verdadera historia (Díaz del Catillo) 164
La verdad sospechosa (*The Truth Suspect*; Ruiz de Alarcón) 254
Verdeyen, Paul 255
Vergerio, Pier Paolo 115
Vergne, Marie-Madeleine Pioche de la. *See Lafayette, Madame de*
Verne, Jules 290
Vesalius, Andreas 62, **294**
Vespucci, Amerigo 226, 289, 293, **295**, 302
Vespucci, Mario 226
Vespucci, Simonetta 226–227
Vico, Giambattista **296**
Victoria (Rowson) 253
La victoria de Junín (*The Victory of Junín*; Olmedo) 210
La vida es sueño (Calderón de la Barca) 36–37
Vie privée de Voltaire et de Mme du Châtelet (Graffigny) 107
Vietnamese literature 204
villancicos 66
Villey, Pierre 193
Villon, François 211, **296–297**, 297
Villon, Guillaume de 296
Virgil
    influence of 23, 48, 50, 71, 148, 178, 217, 221, 227–228, 270, 282
    literary criticism on 86, 87, 277
    translations of 177, 263
Virtue Triumphant (Murray) 200
Virues, Cristobal de 161
Visconti, Valentina 210
The Vision of Piers Plowman (Langland) 149–150
Vita (*Life*; Alfieri) 5
Vivaldi, Antonio 104
Vladimir (Prokopovitch) 232
Vogel, Henriette 137
Voice of One Crying (Gower). *See Vox Clamantis*
Volk 114
Volksgeist 252
Volpone, or the Fox (Jonson) 127
Voltaire **297–300**
    contemporaries of 28, 46, 107, 251, 283
    Encyclopedia and 76, 82, 85
    Enlightenment and 4, 85, 102, 242, 243, 258
    influences of/on 39, 40, 121, 154, 241
    life of 2, 251
    literary criticism by/on 75–76, 77, 82, 104, 175, 202, 228, 299–300
Voltaire (Frame) 299
Volume of poems in the national tongue (Nguyen Trai). *See Quoc Am Thi Tap*
Vondel, Joost van den 31, **300–301**

Von deutscher Art und Kunst (*On German Character and Art*; Herder) 113–114
Von deutscher Baukunst (Goethe) 102
Vox Clamantis (*Voice of One Crying*; Gower) 106
Voyage to Parnassus (Cervantes) 48

W

Waingrow, Marshall 28
Wakefield cycle 66
Wakefield Master 66
Waldman, Bryna 10
Waldseemüller, Martin 295, **302–303**
Waley, Arthur 309
Walker, Hallam 191
Wallenstein (Schiller) 260
The Walls Have Ears (Ruiz de Alarcón). *See Las paredes oyen*
Walpole, Horace 247
Wandang. *See Kim Jung Hee*
Wang Fanggang 136
Warens, Madame de 250
Warner, Maria 225
Warren, James 303
Warren, Mercy Otis **303–304**
Wars of Religion (1562-1598) 11
Washington, George 213, 303
Washington, Martha 303
"The Waterfall" (Derzhavin) 72
Water Margin (Shi Naian and Luo Guanzhong). *See Shuihuzhuan*
Watling, Thomas **304**
Watt, Ian 70, 246
Watzenrode, Lucas 61
The Way of Perfection (Teresa of Avila) 285
The Way of the World (Congreve) 59
The Way to Wealth (Franklin) 95
A Weighty Consideration (Erasmus) 89
Weimar court theater 260
Welde, Thomas 82
Welker, Glen 70
Wenscelas (duke of Brabant) 97
Wheatley, Phillis **304–305**
Wheelock, Eleazar 209
"Whither Dede Korkut?" (Asgharzadeh) 26
The Whole Booke of Psalmes Faithfully Translated into English Metre (Eliot) 82
Wieland; or, The Transformation (Brown) 31
Wife of Bath's Tale (Chaucer) 51–52
Wigglesworth, Michael **305–306**
Wild Boar Forest (Shi Naian and Luo Guanzhong). *See Shuihuzhuan*
Wilde, Martha 245
Wilde, Oscar 59
"The Wild Honeysuckle" (Freneau) 97
Wilhelm Meister's Apprenticeship (Goethe) 103
Wilhelm Tell (Schiller) 260
Williams, Roger **306**, 307
Wilson, John 82
The Wind-Cloud Meeting of the Sung Founder (Luo Guanzhong). *See Song Taizong longhu fengyun hui*
Windsor Forest (Pope) 228
A Winter Piece (Hammon) 111
The Winter's Tale (Shakespeare) 267
Winthrop, John 306, **306–307**
The Wisdom of Life (Schopenhauer) 262
Wittembergischer Nightingale (Sachs). *See Wittembergisch Nachtigall*
Wittembergisch Nachtigall (*Wittembergischer Nightingale*; Sachs) 257
Wolsey, Cardinal 272

women
　　in Aztec culture 196
　　in Colonial America 195
　　education of 199–200
　　in England 135, 139
　　in France 144–145, 224–225, 264
　　in Japan 131
　　in literature, pre-14th century 23–24
　　in Renaissance 145
　　in Russia 33
　　in Spanish America 66
　　in United States 199–200
Women Will be Women (Lessing) 157
The Wonders of the Invisible World (Mather) 179
Wong, Timothy 310
Wood, Nigel 279
The Wood of the Woods (Bacon) 15
Woolman, John 307
Wordsworth, William 17, 44, 84
The World, or Treatise on Light (Descartes) 72–73
The World as Will and Representation
　　(Schopenhauer) 262
"Wo to Drunkards" (Mather) 180
The Would-be Gentleman (*Le Bourgeois
　　Gentilhomme;* Molière) 190
Wright, Susanna 195
"Writing Down What I See" (Yuan Hungdao)
　　312
Wu Chengen (Wu Ch`eng-en; Wu Chen-en) 41,
　　125, **307–310**, 308–310
Wu Ching-Tzu (Wong) 310
Wu Jingzi (Wu Ching-tzu) 41, **310**
Wulf, Karin A. 195
Wu school 136
Wu-sheng xi (*Wu-sheng hsi; Silent Operas;* Li Yu)
　　158

Wyatt, Alysson 309
Wyatt, Thomas 274
Wycherley, William 58, 59, 228
Wyclif, John. *See* Wycliffe, John
Wycliffe, John 116, **310–311**

X

Xenophon 4, 97, 115
Xhuwan Q`Anil. *See Komam Q`Anil, Epic of*
Xian-qing ou-ji (*Hsien ch'ing ou-chi; Random
　　Ventures in Idleness;* Li Yu) 158–159
Xiao hu lei (*Hsiao-hu lei; The Little Thunderclap;*
　　Kong Shangren) 141
Xiao Xiaosheng (Hsiao-hsiaosheng) 41
Ximénez, Don Francisco 230
Xiyouji (*Hsi Yu Chi; The Journey to the West;* Wu
　　Chengen) 125
xochicuicatl ("flower songs") 201–202, 202–204

Y

Yamaguchi Sodō 110
Yamamoto Eizo. *See* Ryokan
"Ycuic Axayacatzin, Mexico Tlatohuani"
　　(Axayacatl) 13
The Year of My Life (Kobayashi Issa). *See Oragu
　　Haru*
The Year 2440 (Mercier) 293
Yedang. *See* Kim Jung Hee
"Yisaeng kyujang chŏn" (Student Yi Peers Over
　　the Wall; Kim Shi-sup) 136
Yi Song-gye 129
Yi Sunghun 130
Yi Yi. *See* Lee Yul Kok
Yongbi eocheon ga (*Songs of Flying Dragons;* Se-
　　jong) 264–265
York cycle 66

Yoshimitsu (shogun) 313
Yoshimochi (shogun) 313
Yoshinori (shogun) 314
Young, John and Alex Dent 269
Young Man's Pocket Companion (Richardson). *See
　　The Apprentice's Vade Mecum*
The Young Scholar (Lessing) 157
Yuan Hungdao (Yüan Hung-tao) **312**
Yuan Zhongdao (Yüan Chung-tao) 312
Yuan Zongdao (Yüan Tsung-tao) 312
yugen 205
Yulgok Chip (Lee Yul Kok) 152

Z

Zadig, ou la Destinée (Voltaire) 298
Zaïde (Lafayette *et al.*) 147
Zaïre (Voltaire) 298
Zarucchi, Jeanne Morgan 221
Zeami Motokiyo (Motokiyo Kanze) 143, **313–314**
Zeami Motomasa 314
Zeami's Style (Hare) 313
Zen Buddhism 18, 256
Zenge, Wilhelmine von 137
Zeydel, Edwin 30
Zhitie (*Life;* Avvakum) 12
Zhuangzi 152
zhuanji 282
Zhuskovskomu, V. A. 233
Zhu Xi (Chu Hsi) 129
Zilch, Elizabeth 160
Zipa (Chibcha ruler) 124
The Zoo (Rej) 243
Zygmunt August (king of Poland) 140